TACTICAL GunDigest

Get the serious shooters' take on high-tech firearms & gear!

EDITED BY COREY GRAFF

Published by

Gun Digest® Books, an imprint of Caribou Media Group, LLC
Gun Digest Media, 5600 W. Grande Market Drive, Suite 100
Appleton, WI 54913
www.gundigest.com

To order books or other products call 920.471.4522 ext. 104
or visit us online at **www.gundigeststore.com**

CAUTION: Technical data presented here, particularly technical data on handloading and on firearms adjustment and alteration, inevitably reflects individual experience with particular equipment and components under specific circumstances the reader cannot duplicate exactly. Such data presentations therefore should be used for guidance only and with caution. Caribou Media accepts no responsibility for results obtained using these data.

ISBN 13: 978-1-946267-52-8

Cover Design by Jeromy Boutwell & Jordan Matuszak
Interior Design by Dave Hauser, Jeromy Boutwell, & Ian Jackson

Edited by Corey Graff

Printed in the United States of America

10 9 8 7 6 5 4 3 2 1

TABLE OF CONTENTS

TACTICAL FIREARMS CATALOG

WELCOME

To the *Tactical Gun Digest*, the World's Greatest Tactical Gun Book!
By Corey Graff

It's always exciting being involved in the ground floor of a new venture, and what you hold in your hands is just that: the first all-tactical edition of the annual *Gun Digest* book — a first in its long and storied history.

Why a special edition dedicated to just tactical guns? Perhaps a better question is, What *is* a tactical gun? It's a difficult term to define objectively, for sure, but everyone seems to know what it is. It's like jazz music — hard to describe, but you know it when you hear it.

Thankfully, our sharp-eyed experts have already answered this thorny question. According to author Bob Campbell in his story, "Tactical Revolvers Today," "The term *tactical* is defined as gaining an advantage over an adversary or situation." Campbell shoots a bullseye with that one. In the context of personal

Rifles (MSRs). According to the National Shooting Sports Foundation's (NSSF) *Industry Intelligence Report, 2017 Edition,* annual production of ARs in 1990 was 74,000, while in 2015 it exceeded 1.5 million (2013 was a banner year at nearly 2.3 million produced). That's a lot of ARs. According to the NSSF, the law enforcement area of the annual Shooting, Hunting and Outdoor Trade (SHOT) show now covers some 22 percent of floor space in Las Vegas each year.

HIGHLIGHTS OF THIS EDITION

To kick things off, read Massad Ayoob's tale of tactical shotguns and their use in the defense of the home. Mas provides insights like only he can about shotshells, wound cavities and other warm fuzzies to consider should you need to sort things out with intruders. Robert Sadowski takes a look at the U.S. Army's new service pistol, which is based on the SIG P320, information that's sure to be of interest to concealed carriers. (It's a good example, by the way, of the military benefitting from trends rooted in advancements inspired by civilian armed citizens.)

But Sadowski doesn't stop there. He reveals what you need to know if you're considering Jeff Cooper's scout rifle concept. Scout rifles are as popular as ever, and we provide a look at some of the best, with special in-the-field testing of the Ruger Scout. In other news, ballistics expert Phil Massaro reveals his top 5 picks for long-range cartridges (including the

There's no doubt about it. This H&H Precision TACLT-2 Carbon Fiber Tactical isn't your grandpappy's deer rifle. It sports the finest components and machining to ensure 1/4 MOA accuracy and is available in just about any long-range caliber you can imagine. Read more page 112. Photo: H&H Precision

protection guns — whether they be post-SHTF survival or home defense guns, or concealed carry handguns — his definition is cogent and hits the mark. Scott Wagner, in his writeup on tactical shotguns, asks, "... what exactly is a 'tactical shotgun?' Simply put, it's a shotgun modified to be more effective for defensive or combat use."

You get the idea. Tactical firearms are designed for serious work — saving innocent lives from predatory people. These cutting-edge tools save lives.

It seems self-evident that tactical firearms and gear — including the concealed carry market — are among the most popular of segments today. But that can actually be quantified. Just take a gander at AR-style gun production, aka Modern Sporting

very interesting .338 Norma Magnum. Wow, check that one out). Massaro has a way of distilling complex ballistics concepts into terms that even I can understand. But coverage of long-range cartridges wouldn't be complete without a look at today's precision bolt guns, and Todd Woodard delivers detailed coverage on the present trend in affordable accuracy.

What's that? Yep, we got ARs! Jorge Amselle gives a *tour de force* of battle rifles — from AR-15s to big-bore AR-10s and numerous other handy survival guns no good citizen should be without. Tiger McKee teaches how to properly zero and practice with your AR-15, and of course there are enough ARs in the catalog section of the book to leave a permanent smile plastered on Patrick Sweeney's face. Speaking of Sweeney, the Master Blaster himself gives a Report from the Field, revealing his favorite new ARs. You'll definitely want to check them out.

But it wouldn't be any fun if we stopped at guns. Nope, you'll find an entire feature article on tactical flashlights, weapon lights and lasers by Scott Wagner. Patrick Covert and Joe Kertzman cover tactical knives in depth, and Todd Woodward emerges from his bunker yet again to lay out the best ammo and optics for any task you may need to overcome. And we stepped outside the box with a photo essay by photographer Yamil Sued that gives you an insider's look at an International Defensive Pistol Association (IDPA) match. Pictures really are worth a thousand words.

Of course, no edition of the *Gun Digest* would pass muster without the popular TEST-FIRE section. In it, we've included reviews on Ruger's Officer-Style .45 1911, Glock 40 MOS 10mm, .224 Valkryie AR, SIG Emporer Scorpion knife and the FBI's new 9mm handgun load from Hornady.

Lastly, this book contains all of the regular features for which the *Gun Digest Annual* is famous, only with a tactical twist. Those include extensive ballistics tables, catalog section of handguns, rifles, and shotguns, Reports from the Field on semi-auto handguns, revolvers, semi-auto rifles, sniper rifles, tactical shotguns, ammo and optics. Especially exciting and new for this edition is a tactical reticle section by scope manufacturer. With so many reticle options out there in today's scopes, we hope this compendium of reticle patterns helps you sort out all the options before you buy.

Finally, thank you for taking the time to pick up this book and giving it a read. With so many things competing for your attention in this busy world, I truly believe tactical guns and their use needs to be a priority. May this book aid you in your search for better tactical guns — no matter how you define them.

ACKNOWLEDGMENTS

Thank you to the many friendly "tactical" people in the gun industry too numerous to mention, who contributed stories, images, information and advice for this first edition of the *Tactical Gun Digest*. Thanks also to Jerry Lee, editor of the annual *Gun Digest* book, a true gentleman who has taught me much about editing. And a tip of the khaki-colored tactical hat to publisher Jim Schlender, for taking a giant leap of faith entrusting me with this enormous project and opportunity.

In "My 5 Favorite Long-Range Cartridges," ballistics guru Phil Massaro discusses the awesome .338 Norma Magnum, which is an improvement over the already impressive .338 Lapua Magnum. See story page 94.

ABOUT THE COVER

The Savage Model 10 GRS featured on the cover is an affordable long-range tack-driver ideally suited to sniper competitions, duty use or just plain practice out past ten football fields and beyond. Its Savage Model 10 action and heavy barrel are mated to the fully adjustable and rock-solid GRS stock. When combined with the excellent AccuTrigger, surgical accuracy from chamberings including 6mm and 6.5 Creedmoor, or 6.5 PRC and .308 Win. are well within reach. The scope is a Bushnell Elite model, popularized in the Precision Rifle Series.

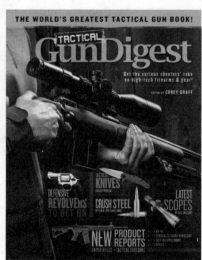

Jim Schlender | **Group Publisher**
Corey Graff | **Editor**

CONTRIBUTING EDITORS

Patrick Sweeney: ARs & Semi-Auto Handguns
Scott Wagner: Tactical Shotguns
Todd Woodard: Revolvers, Rifles, Ammo & Optics
Joe Kertzman: Tactical Knives

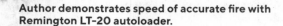

Author demonstrates speed of accurate fire with Remington LT-20 autoloader.

PERSPECTIVES ON HOME-DEFENSE SHOTGUNS

The Mossberg 930 JM Pro Series is an affordable 12-gauge autoloader — this one the Jerry Miculek signature model — ready for competition or home defense right from the box.

The Shotgun is a Classic Home-Defense Weapon, But Warrants Some Careful Thinking BY **MASSAD AYOOB**

The shoulder-fired smoothbore shotgun firing multiple projectiles per shot has been a staple of American home defense ("HD") since the Pilgrims landed. Today in our country, pistol caliber carbines and even more, AR-15 .223 rifles, have taken over a big part of that market, but the shotgun is still hugely popular for HD.

One reason is that so many homes contain at least one shotgun for sport, hunting, or clay bird shooting. Another is the comfort factor that comes from the shotgun's raw power and its long-standing reputation as a "man-stopper." When selecting a "scattergun" expressly for home defense, there are many considerations that can be easily overlooked. Let's examine some of those.

CRITICAL FACTORS

First, the home defense shotgun is a "pool weapon." By that I mean that in most households it stands ready to be grabbed up in an emergency by any member of the household authorized to do so. Just like a shotgun in a police patrol car, it may at any moment have to be employed by a petite female or a big male power-lifter or any body shape in between.

During three work shifts, the patrol car shotgun may have to be deployed by three to six different officers of different sizes. If nothing else, all of them will have been trained and qualified to use it. In the home, it's more likely that the life-threatening home invasion might require response from a family member who doesn't particularly care to practice and may not remember the last time he or she even fired that weapon. This must be taken into account during the one-gun-for-everyone selection process.

Most shotguns do not come with the telescoping stocks that are now all but standard on AR-15 rifles and carbines. Instead, shotgun stocks tend to be configured for the "average adult male." A person with shorter arms, particularly one with limited upper body strength, will have to cantilever their shoulder back to fire such a long-stocked shotgun, and the recoil can take them completely off balance. They may even join the ranks of the many of us who shot Daddy's 12 gauge when we were little kids, and got knocked flat on our butts by the "kick."

Solution: Choose a shotgun with a short "youth stock." It is a lot easier for a larger person to shoot well with a gun built for a smaller person, than vice versa.

(left) Spare 20-gauge shells ride alongside receiver on this Benelli auto set up for students by ace instructor Wes Lagomarsino. (right) Shells can also ride on the outside of shoulder stock, or both locations. Photos: Wes Lagomarsino

more than a handgun. Since longer distances or shooting into vehicles were predictable occupational hazards, that level of power was seen as essential.

In home defense, there isn't likely to be any shooting through cars, and distances are likely to be close. It is therefore likely that the homeowner can do all that needs to be done to defend the household with a shotgun less powerful than a police officer's traditional 12 gauge. Let's consider relative power levels.

muzzle at a velocity of 1,620 fps, generating 2,488 ft-lbs of energy. The 273.5-grain 20-gauge slug starts off at 1,600 fps, creating 1,865 ft-lbs of energy. By contrast, the 230-grain "GI hardball" load for the .45 ACP pistol that became known as a "legendary man-stopper" launches at 830 fps and delivers 352 ft-lbs of energy. Do the math: a 20-gauge hit is delivering the same energy as five of those .45 slugs, and change. Should be enough to solve most anti-personnel problems at home defense distances, yes?

Second, we have to ask ourselves how much power we really need. The powerful 12-gauge shotgun evolved as standard choice among law enforcement because until the late 20th century it was the only "heavy artillery" most patrol officers and detectives could reach for if they needed

A 12-gauge shotgun's standard full power ("Express") load contains an ounce of lead, which translates to 437.5 grains. A 20-gauge shotgun's standard "throw weight" is 5/8 of an ounce, or 273.5 grains. Comparing Winchester Super-X brand rifled shotgun slugs, the 437.5-grain 12-gauge slug leaves the

UNDERSTANDING SHOTGUN EFFECTIVENESS

A shotgun's massive close-range wounding effect comes from two distinct mechanisms. In close, when all the pellets strike en masse, they create what some forensic pathologists colloquially

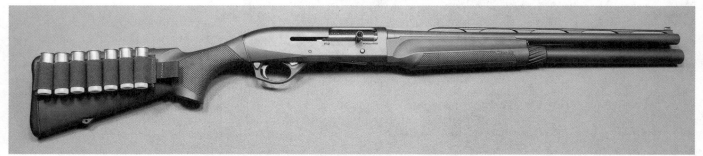

Longer magazine, spare shell attachments, vent rib and beads for fast close-range buckshot dispensing highlight this Benelli 20-gauge auto, customized for students by Wes Lagomarsino. Photo: Wes Lagomarsino

call "rat-hole wound effect." This is because the cohesive shot cluster tears a wound path of massive width. At greater distances — when the shot pellets have had time to spread — the widely dispersed swarm of pellets each create their own separate wound channel, resulting in saturation effect. Multiple organs, blood vessels, nerves and bones are violated simultaneously. Each of these wound mechanisms tend to be profoundly debilitating.

Now, let's look at the three primary loading options we have in a shotgun: the solid slug, buckshot, and birdshot. The sweet spot, as happens so often in human affairs, is in the middle in this case. Most single slug loads in a 12-gauge shotgun will go through a human body with enough power to kill whatever they strike next: not optimum in an occupied home. The slug comes into its own at a

remote home where large, dangerous animals and encounters at longer distances outside the four walls may occur.

A whole hive of tiny birdshot pellets flying together can tear a savage rat hole at very close range, but by the time you get to across-a-room distances, the itty-bitty spheres have started to spread, and they don't individually have the mass to drive deeply enough to reliably disable a homicidal adult male human.

Buckshot got its name for killing deer-size (read: man-size) mammals at short ranges. The pellets are large enough to achieve adequate penetration. Historically, police have mostly used 00 ("double-ought") buckshot, and it accordingly became the default choice of armed citizens. However, once again, there are choices to be made in buckshot size, and we'll get to that momentarily.

CHOOSING SHOTGUN TYPE

All manner of shotguns have served armed citizens well over the years, but some platforms are much more amenable to home defense than others. Let's go over those quickly.

Single shot. Whether break-open or bolt action in design, these are the cheapest to make and buy, and therefore became popular as farmers' utility guns or new shooters' first hunting shotguns, chosen in the latter case to encourage careful aim and discourage "spray and pray" shooting. A home defense situation often involves multiple offenders. Two or more lethally dangerous intruders … one shot … the math tells us that the single-shot weapon is a poor choice for home defense, right out of the starting gate.

Double barrel. Yes, when Joe Biden was Vice President he recommended that you defend your home and family with one of these. He also recommended that you empty it into the air to scare off intruders, and that you fire it through the front door at unidentified human beings. Don't listen to Joe Biden. Many years ago, at a debriefing by the LAPD Officer Involved Shooting Investigation Team, I was told that their officers — among the most highly trained with firearms on Earth, qualifying at the range monthly at that time — had a hit potential of 58 percent on the street with their shotguns. Let's see: two homicidal opponents, two shots, 58 percent likelihood of a hit. Does that math sound as bad to you as it does to me? And if we have a two-shot weapon and three opponents, the math speaks for itself.

(Yes, I realize that the great combat shooting authority Col. Jeff Cooper liked the idea of a double barrel "coach gun" for home defense. I knew Col. Cooper and visited him at his home more than once. He was never without a large caliber pistol on his hip or within reach on his desk to back up that double barrel. Most folks won't have that fallback.)

This leaves us with magazine-fed shotguns, of which there are three types:

Bolt-action shotguns were cheap to make and sell. Every one I ever fired had vicious recoil because their stock angles were not designed with shooter comfort and rapid-fire in mind. For each shot, you must take your firing hand away from the trigger, lift the bolt, rack it back, drive it forward again, lock it back down, and get your hand back to the trigger. Do the math, and once again, we do not have a satisfactory equation.

This shooter is fast with his Mossberg 590 12-gauge pump; spent shell is barely airborne and slide is already closed for next shot.

Big guy, small gal share short-stocked Remington LT-20 autoloader. Bill and Jenny Van Tuyl are both expert with it. All photos: Gail Pepin unless otherwise noted.

Slide-action or pump shotguns are probably the most popular home defense shotguns in America, and were long the standard in law enforcement. Cops used pumps instead of autoloaders for three reasons: (1) They were cheaper, and police agencies bought on bid. (2) They weren't dependent on recoil to operate, so they'd run fine with cheap training birdshot, low recoil tear gas projectiles like the Ferret, less-lethal impact munitions ("beanbag rounds"), etc. (3) Because the user could clear some "jams" with main physical force on the slide handle, they withstood the abuse and neglect they received in police service better than semi-automatic shotguns.

However, as noted before, the cops using them were (hopefully) trained and qualified with them. In the home defense environment, the desperate user may be the good person who hated guns and rarely practiced with the pump gun. Inexperienced pump-gunners can easily jam the shotgun by "short-stroking" its slide action, and after the first shot they tend to pull the trigger again, futilely, until they remember that they need to rack the action for the next shot, and they may not remember in time. If that is your situation at home, please have everyone authorized to reach for the gun at least practice racking and dry firing it every now and then, so they'll remember where the slide release lever is and habituate to the necessary feeding stroke by the forward hand.

Semi-automatic shotguns, once the round is chambered and the safety is off, need only another pull of the trigger to fire. That makes them more shootable in the hands of good guys and gals who aren't regularly "gun people." In four and a half decades of teaching firearms, I've never seen anyone short-stroke a semi-automatic shotgun once the shooting was underway. A gas-operated shotgun will also recoil significantly less than a fixed-breech gun (all the other types described above). Semi-autos cost more, but as a rule of thumb, careful shopping at the gun store can yield a good second-hand autoloader for about the same price as a new pump gun of similar quality.

The autoloading shotgun offers two more home defense advantages: One is that if the forward arm is wounded, the auto shotgun can be held to the shoulder and fired effectively at close range one-handed. The other is, quite simply, speed of fire. One drill we do in our long gun classes is the "Speed Race," in which

Jenny Van Tuyl splashes a starburst of buckshot on a steel silhouette and is still on target with her customized Remington LT-20 at Firearms Academy of Seattle.

The Mesa Tactical SureShell Aluminum Carrier and Rail holds an extra six shells at the ready and gives you a Picatinny rail atop your shotgun's receiver on which you can install a reflex- or red-dot sight.

WITH SEMI-AUTO-MATIC SHOTGUNS, THE FASTEST ELECTRONICALLY TIMED RUN FROM FIRST HIT TO FIFTH IS GENERALLY UNDER ONE SECOND. WITH PUMP GUNS, THE WINNING TIME IS GENERALLY A BIT UNDER TWO SECONDS – TWICE AS LONG.

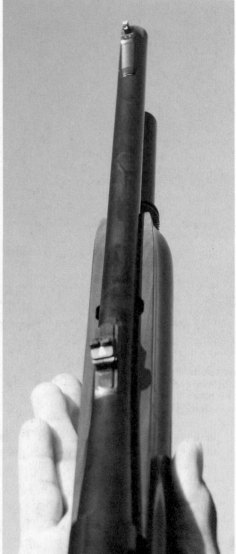

the shooter stands with gun on target at 7 yards and then fires five shots as fast as possible. If any of the shots miss the target, that shooter is disqualified from winning. With semi-automatic shotguns, the fastest electronically timed run from first hit to fifth is generally under one second. With pump guns, the winning time is generally a bit under two seconds — twice as long.

TACTICAL SHOTGUN MODIFICATIONS

Yes, Grandpa's "long Tom" duck gun with 30-inch barrel can save you from a homicidal intruder. When shop-owners successfully guarded their stores during inner-city riots with long barreled shotguns, the rioters were never heard to say "Aw, he's just got a bird gun, let's get 'im!" Still, for home defense a shorter barreled weapon will be easier and faster to manipulate, and with less weight forward will allow the householder to hold the intruder at gunpoint longer without fatigue until the police arrive. An 18-inch barrel is the minimum length allowed without going through the laborious ATF licensing procedure for a "short-barrel shotgun." However, 20 inches seems to be the sweet spot. There's room under the barrel for an extended magazine tube that will hold one more shell than you'll usually find in an 18-inch-barreled shotgun's magazine.

An extended magazine, if it's not forbidden as an "evil assault weapon feature" under the laws of the state where you live, is always a good thing. More

(above) This shooter manages his Remington 870 12-gauge pump's recoil with aggressive forward shooting stance.

(left) Rifle sights aren't quite the fastest at home defense distance, but are versatile, providing more accuracy with slugs at longer distances.

(below) Telescoping stocks are uncommon but very useful on home-defense shotguns like this pump, ditto the SureFire white light fore-end. Red-dot sight adds versatility.

ammo on board. The extended magazine also lets you rest the front of the gun on the top of your cover, without the muzzle itself being so close to the cover that it will deflect part of the buckshot charge.

Red-dot optics make sense for a police shotgun that may have to be deployed at a distance, but at in-the-house range a simple front bead is fast, and all you'll need. Rifle sights are good for versatility if you're going to be shooting single, solid slugs at significant distances.

Pistol-grip-only shotguns, and the new format of "legal to buy right now" 14-inch barrel pump guns with "not-really-pistol-grip" stocks such as the Mossberg Shockwave and Remington TAC-14 are handy to maneuver but difficult to aim and shoot effectively.

It doesn't hurt to have an attachment on the stock or the side of the shotgun (think SideSaddle) holding extra rounds. When the alarm sounds and the door comes crashing down, it's unlikely

and it may embolden him.

Don't believe that a shotgun blast will let you stand in the door, pull the trigger once, and sweep away anything in front of you in a lead storm. Police have been taught for decades that the spread of the shot pattern will be about one inch per yard of distance. While that is not perfectly true, it's close enough to be a rule of thumb at home defense distance. You'll have to aim your shotgun to get a hit, as you would a rifle or pistol.

Don't believe the old "use birdshot for home defense; it will destroy your opponent but won't go through sheetrock walls and endanger your children." Listen: you can put your fist through a sheetrock wall, but you can't put your fist through your opponent's body, something I know from having tried both. If it won't go through sheetrock, it won't go deeply enough into your opponent to stop him. Ergo, buckshot, and a

> **DON'T BELIEVE THE OLD CANARD THAT "RACKING A PUMP GUN WILL FREEZE ANY CRIMINAL IN FEAR." IF IT'S A STREET-SMART CRIMINAL, THAT SOUND ONLY TELLS HIM THAT YOU'RE SO FAR BEHIND THE CURVE YOU JUST NOW REALIZED YOU NEEDED A LOADED GUN, AND IT MAY EMBOLDEN HIM.**

in a 12 gauge has historically put four or five of its nine .33-caliber pellets through and through facing human beings at close range. Likewise, 000 "triple ought" will drive eight .36-caliber pellets even deeper. The old "urban load" of #4 buck, 27 pellets of .23-caliber diameter, is pretty good in close but didn't always penetrate deep enough at the longer ranges where police sometimes had to employ it.

I would strongly recommend the little-known #1 buckshot, and said so decades ago in my book *StressFire II: Advanced Combat Shotgun*. We had discovered by then that the 16 .30-caliber projectiles in a standard #1 buck load would generally stop just under the skin on the opposite side of the offender who was shot, and incapacitation was swift because the evenly distributed pattern of the 16 pellets pretty much took out everything in their path. My friend and mentor Ray Chapman, the first world champion of the combat pistol, had dissected and weighed buckshot shells and determined that a #1 load had about a hundred grains more lead in it than 00 or #4: it simply utilized the space inside the shell more efficiently and left less wasted air space.

The late Dr. Martin Fackler, a noted

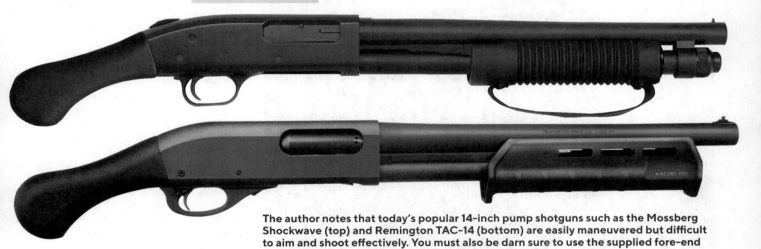

The author notes that today's popular 14-inch pump shotguns such as the Mossberg Shockwave (top) and Remington TAC-14 (bottom) are easily maneuvered but difficult to aim and shoot effectively. You must also be darn sure to use the supplied fore-end strap — it's not just for control but to ensure your hand stays behind the muzzle!

that you'll have time to strap on a belt or bandolier of extra shotgun shells.

DISPELLING MYTHS

Don't believe the old canard that "racking a pump gun will freeze any criminal in fear." If it's a street-smart criminal, that sound only tells him that you're so far behind the curve you just now realized you needed a loaded gun,

plan to interdict an intruder at a location in the home where a shot that misses or over-penetrates won't endanger innocent parties. For more explanation and proof, download my video "Ayoob on Home Defense" from panteoproductions.com.

RECOMMENDED BUCKSHOT LOADS

12 gauge: Standard power 00 buckshot

authority on terminal ballistics, subsequently came to the same conclusion. So did his protégé, the highly respected Dr. Gary Roberts. The best #1 buckshot load today, at least for police work, is Federal's Flite Control load, product code LE132-1B. It is downloaded to a "low recoil" velocity of 1,100 fps with 15 pellets, giving optimum control for 12 gauge and optimum penetration. Note: it has been my experi-

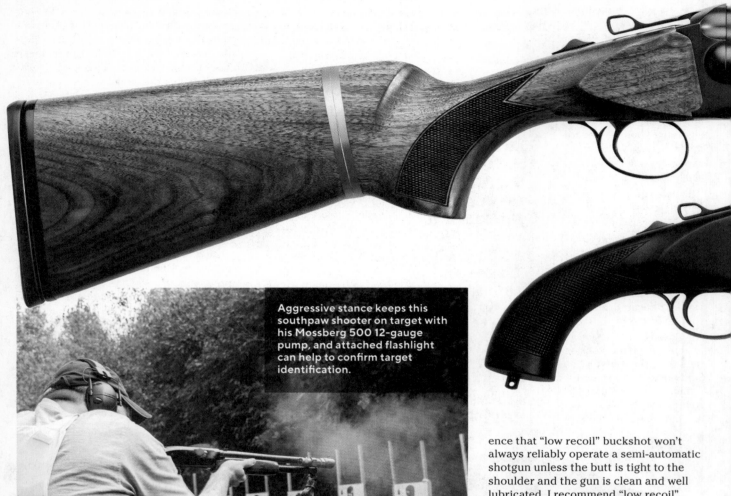

Aggressive stance keeps this southpaw shooter on target with his Mossberg 500 12-gauge pump, and attached flashlight can help to confirm target identification.

ence that "low recoil" buckshot won't always reliably operate a semi-automatic shotgun unless the butt is tight to the shoulder and the gun is clean and well lubricated. I recommend "low recoil" buck in pump guns but recommend "standard power," or Express 16-pellet #1 loads in an autoloading 12 gauge.

20 gauge: The standard buckshot load for the "Twenty" is #3 buck: 20 pellets, each .25 inch in diameter. While this might not be optimum at longer ranges or through intermediate barricades, it does not seem to have been found lacking in face to face defensive shootings. Assuming the same weight shotgun, this 20-gauge load will have only about 55 percent as much recoil as an Express 12-gauge load — less flinch, fewer misses, faster and much more accurate follow-up shots.

16 gauge: The 16 gauge is nowhere near as popular in the U.S. as it is in Europe. Consequently, no manufacturer seems to produce "tactical" shotguns in this gauge, and it usually only comes into play when a 16-gauge hunting gun is the only shotgun in the home, or the owner got a helluva good deal on it. The best home defense load for it is #1 buckshot, which throws a dozen .30-caliber projectiles.

This shooter exhibits superb control of his custom-stocked Remington 870 12-gauge pump.

The Chiappa Triple Threat is a triple-barrel break-action shotgun available in 12 and 20 gauges and .410 bore. Pictured here is the handy, light-recoiling 20-gauge model. It has three 18.5-inch barrels and a removeable buttstock for optimum storage at home, in your backpack or in a vehicle. Photo: Chiappa Firearms

At just 27 inches and only 6 pounds, the Charles Daly Honcho Triple 12 gauge is another three-barrel blaster for easy maneuverability within a home. Tip: Stoke it with Aguila MiniShells to tame the beast's recoil. Photo: Charles Daly/Chiappa Firearms

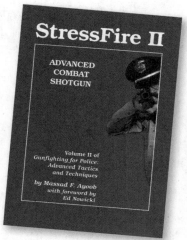

Ayoob is the author of *StressFire II: Advanced Combat Shotgun*, available from Amazon.com.

.410 bore: The little .410 is considered by most experts to be underpowered for a home defense shotgun. If a .410 was all I had, I would load it with 1/4 oz. (109-grain) slugs, rated at 1,830 fps, and treat it as a pistol-caliber carbine.

IN SUMMARY

While no longer the near-universal home defense choice in long guns, the shotgun is still very much in evidence for that purpose. Careful planning and selection — and, of course, training and practice — will maximize its formidable family protection potential. **TGD**

At only 26 inches in overall length, the KSG Bullpup tactical shotgun is a downward-ejecting design that uses dual extended magazine tubes for a whopping capacity of 14+1 2 ¾-inch shotshells.

U.S. MILITARY OPTS FOR SIG P320

Why the U.S. Army and Air Force XM17/XM18 Modular Handgun Competition Went to SIG

BY **ROBERT SADOWSKI**

The U.S. military doesn't make decisions quickly. There are equal parts administrative, evaluative and politics at work — with the attendant delays. No wonder it took about 74 years to change from the 1911A1 chambered in .45 ACP to the M9 in 9mm. Considering the quest for a handgun to replace the M9 was launched in 2011, six years to come to a decision is lightning fast.

A Soldier with C Company, 1st Battalion, 506th Infantry Regiment, 1st Brigade Combat Team, 101st Airborne Division fires the new M17. Photo: U.S. Army, Sgt. Samantha Stoffregen

In January 2017, the U.S. Army and Air Force announced that the SIG SAUER P320 had won the competition for the new XM17 full-size and XM18 compact-size pistols. By November 2017, the 101st Airborne Division began fielding the M17. Changing to a new handgun involves many factors, including logistics, training, equipment changes, and the obvious — that the new pistol is accurate, reliable and modular. After all, the investment in the new XM17 and XM18 pistols ultimately cost the Government and us taxpayers a $580 million contract for guns, accessories and ammunition to be delivered over a period of 10 years.

(above) The M18 is a compact variant that uses the same frame as the M17 only with a medium-size grip, 3.9-inch barrel and shorter slide. Photo: SIG SAUER USA

(left) The M17 is the full-size pistol that replaced the M9.

As warfare evolves so do tactics and equipment. There were multiple reasons Uncle Sam officially changed to a 9mm pistol in 1985. The .45 ACP cartridge is a potent caliber, but hard to master, and has a relatively limited magazine capacity, while the 9mm is more user-friendly with mild recoil and a higher magazine capacity. There was also political pressure from NATO countries for the U.S. to match equipment in use with NATO forces. The move to drop the .45 ACP was not without its detractors, but with over 30 years of service the M9 and later variants like the M9A1 proved to be battleworthy weapons. Is the M9 perfect? No. In fact, the Beretta 92 platform on which the M9 is built was introduced in 1976. The military made specific changes to it prior to adoption, but it was and is an old design. And now that the M9 is at the end of its effective life cycle, a replacement sidearm was warranted. With the search on for a new pistol, the military addressed some complaints from the field about the M9, including grip ergonomics, placement of the safety selector, lack of an accessory rail, no ability to add a suppressor and heavy trigger pull among others. The compact SIG SAUER M11 was in the same situation. It's based on the P226 design that was introduced in 1983 and it, too, was at the end of its useful service life. Of course, the less expensive route might have been to rebuild the M9 and M11 pistols, but that would not have addressed the dated design features of these handguns.

The U.S. Air Force and Army took the

(above) When the XM17 handgun was received by the Army, the "X," which designates the pistol as experimental, was dropped and the handgun was called the M17. Photo: U.S. Army, Sgt. Samantha Stoffregen

Weapons instructor demonstrates to Soldiers of 1st Security Force Assistance Brigade Headquarters how to properly shoot the M17 in the prone position. Photo: U.S. Army, Sgt. Ryan Tatum

XM17 MHS Program Specs

The 101st ABN DIV (AASLT), the world's only air assault division, is the first unit in the U.S. Army to field the M17 receiving more than 2,000 M17s and M18s. It began fielding the pistols on November 28, 2017. Photo: U.S. Army, Sgt. Samantha Stoffregen

According to the original MHS RFP, pistols submitted to the competition were to be commercial off-the-shelf models. Each firearm manufacturer was required to submit "handgun(s), associated ammunition and supporting accessories to include spare parts. Interested vendors will be required to supply all of the items as described under the resulting contract." The RFP did not indicate a caliber specification. Each pistol submitted was to consist of either a two-handgun solution, meaning a full-sized and compact pistol, or a pistol that could meet the requirements for both a full-sized and compact pistol. It also needed to be capable of hits on a 4-inch target at 50 meters at least 90 percent of the time throughout the gun's lifespan. The new pistol was required to be capable of 2,000 rounds between stoppages, 10,000 rounds between failures and a 35,000-round service life. Some of the specified key features included:

- Modifiable grips
- Ambidextrous controls
- Magazine options
- Accessory rail
- Manual safety

lead in finding a replacement sidearm and, in 2011, formed the XM17 Modular Handgun System (MHS) competition. Due to delays, the MHS competition actually gained traction in 2015. The military created a list of requirements for the new MHS pistol that were addressed in an RFP (Request For Proposal) in August 2015. The new handgun was to be a commercial off-the-shelf model, but it had to outperform the M9. In short, it had to surpass the M9 in ergonomics, accuracy, reliability, durability and maintainability.

and the serialized part of the pistol. It can be easily and quickly removed and inserted into three different sized grips that range from subcompact, compact and full size. The grip modules are made of lightweight glass-filled polymer. Slide assemblies correspond to the grip size with barrel lengths that include 4.7 inches (full-size grip module), 3.9 inches (carry- and compact-size module), and 3.6-inch barrel (subcompact). A competition X-Five model has a 5-inch barrel and recontoured grip. The X-Series compact was adopted by Denmark's Danish De-

SPECIFICATIONS

MODEL: M17

ACTION: Short recoil-operated, locked breech, striker-fire

CALIBER: 9mm

BARREL LENGTH: 4.7 in.

OVERALL LENGTH: 8.0 in.

WEIGHT: 28.8 oz.

GRIPS: Synthetic, modular

SIGHTS: Night sights, optics ready

FINISH: FDE

CAPACITY: 21+1

The XM17 and XM18 are based on the SIG P320 — a polymer frame, striker-fire semi-auto handgun that was introduced in 2014. Photo: **SIG SAUER USA**

The SIG P320 was one of many pistols submitted for the trials. The P320 was introduced in 2014 and was decidedly new and modular. It was not just another polymer frame, striker-fire pistol. Modular is the buzzword that has been batted around by weapons manufacturers since the early 2000s and the term wormed its way into the MHS program. But what does modular mean? In short, multi-caliber capability and multiple grip choices. The P320 easily qualifies on both counts. The ability of P320 users to change frame sizes and caliber is in the DNA of the modular system. No longer do operators need to adapt to the weapon — the weapon adapts to them. Just to put it into perspective, the commercial P320 is configurable into some 41 variants including features like a threaded barrel, red-dot optic and state compliant magazine capacity models.

The P320 uses the FCU (Fire Control Unit) chassis, which houses the trigger, striker, disconnector, slide stop, ejector, slide rails and optional external thumb safety. The FCU is the heart of the P320

The serialized part, and the heart of the M17 and M18, is the FCU chassis. Photo: **SIG SAUER USA**

SPECIFICATIONS

MODEL: M18

ACTION: Short recoil-operated, locked breech, striker-fire

CALIBER: 9mm

BARREL LENGTH: 3.9 in.

OVERALL LENGTH: 7.2 in.

WEIGHT: 26 oz.

GRIPS: Synthetic, modular

SIGHTS: Night sights, optics ready

FINISH: FDE

CAPACITY: 17+1

fense, the P320 by the Royal Thai Police in Thailand. Law Enforcement agencies in the U.S. such as the Oklahoma Highway Patrol, Pasco County Sheriff's Office in Florida, and the Alameda County Sheriff's Office in California also adopted it.

To change grip modules, you first remove the slide assembly and takedown lever from the frame and pull the FCU out of the frame. It is as easy as field-stripping the pistol. There is no need to involve an armorer if a duty-size pistol needs to be downsized to a subcompact for concealed carry, or vice versa. All caliber conversions and grip modules can be serviced at the user level.

Making the P320 user-friendly meant the pistol needed to be completely ambidextrous with grip choices to fit small- to large-hand operators. The slide release is ambidextrous and the magazine release can be reversed for user preference. If there is anything old-school about the P320 it is the short recoil-operated, locked breech mechanism and the SIG cam-operated barrel. The P320 fieldstrips without the use of tools with a rotating takedown lever

like other classic SIG pistols such as the P220 through P239 models. The trigger has a pull weight that averages about 5.5 pounds and employs a pre-tensioned double-action striker-fire trigger. The trigger is a smooth double-action pull and very consistent on the models I've tried.

The striker safety lock and disconnect are two safety features that allow the P320 to be carried safely. An optional ambidextrous manual safety that blocks the movement of the trigger bar is available.

Differences between the P320 and XM17 include modifications to prohibit operator-level access to the FCU chassis assembly. Spanner screws are added to the M17 and M18 at the takedown lever, rear of the slide and near the striker. The rear sight assembly on the M17/M18 differs from commercial P320 models. The M17/M18 features a removable rear-sight plate with an adjustable SIGLite tritium night sight. The steel plate covers and protects the mounting area for a red-dot sight. Uncle Sam also wanted a lightweight trigger with the same curvature as the one found in the P320. The M17 and M18 are both outfitted with manual safeties. RFID and unique serial number were added to Uncle Sam's gun.

The contract specified some 280,000 M17 pistols to be ordered, as well as 7,000 compact M18 versions. Other military services participating in the program may order an additional 212,000 systems. The 101st Airborne Division at Fort Campbell, Kentucky received the first 2,000 XM17s in November, 2017. The 3rd Cavalry Regiment at Fort Hood, Texas, as well as one of the Army's new security force assistance brigades received XM17s in 2017. **TGD**

Pistols Do Battle to Become Top Gun

There were nine firearm manufacturers from across the globe that submitted pistols into the MHS competition. Of note, Ruger designed its American series based on MHS specifications but did not enter it into the competition. STI and Detonics Defense collaborated on the STX pistol. Here's the list of competing handguns in alphabetical order that vied for top gun:

- Beretta APX (9mm)
- CZ P-07 MHS (9mm)
- CZ P-09 MHS (.40 S&W)
- FN Herstal FN-FNS (9mm)
- Glock G17 MHS (9mm)
- Glock G22 MHS (.40 S&W)
- Kriss Sphinx SDP (9mm)
- SIG SAUER P320 MHS (9mm)
- Smith & Wesson M&P M2.0 (9mm)
- STI/Detonics Defense STX (9mm)

Epilog: Failed Drop Test?

After the military declared the SIG P320 the winning entry in the MHS program and a production order was placed, the Dallas Police Department encountered an accidental discharge from a dropped P320. All Dallas Police personnel were instructed to stop carrying the P320 until an investigation could be conducted. The issue occurred when the back of the P320 slide hit a hard surface at a specific 33-degree angle. Although the P320 had successfully passed the drop test protocol performed by the military, it could discharge when subjected to this specific drop. SIG got in front of the issue — or non-issue, depending who you ask — and offered a free upgrade, which virtually eliminated any accidental discharges due to drops. As a bonus, that free upgrade improved the trigger, made it lighter.

THE PRICE OF $LICE

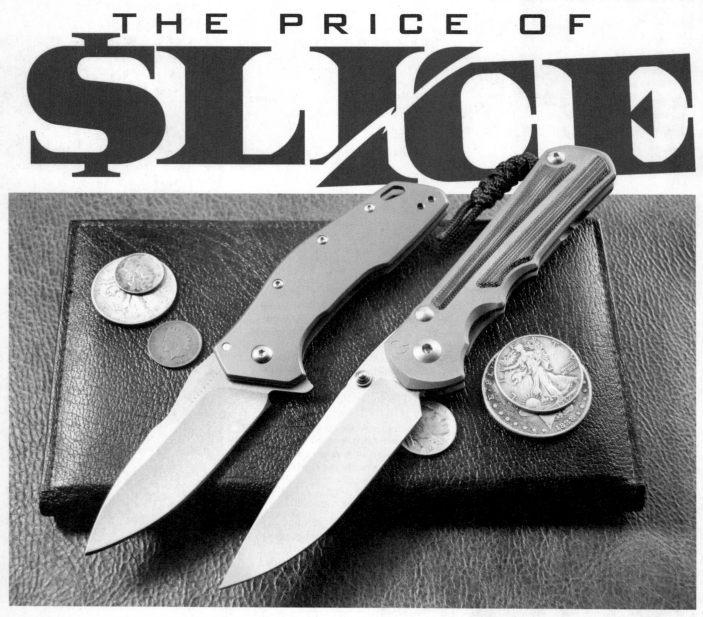

Two attractive folders, but an ocean apart in price. The Kershaw Eris (left) is for the budget-minded buyer, while the Chris Reeve Inkosi (right) is a high-end buyer's dream.

$50 vs. $500
Tactical Knives BY **PAT COVERT**

The gulf between expensive high-end knives and affordable ones is a wide one. Some knife users are aghast that anyone would pay $500 for a knife, while others stand in line to get them. Others are perfectly happy with a $50 blade to meet their everyday needs, and the market for these is voluminous. Here we explore the differences between a $500 tactical knife and a $50 one.

I chose to compare two very successful folding knives, one in each cost category. On the top end is Chris Reeve Knives' newest folder, the Inkosi, which (with black Micarta inserts) retails for $515.00. Reeve's Blade Show awards for Quality in Manufacturing over the past two decades are unparalleled. We'll compare the Inkosi to one of Kershaw's hottest sellers, the Eris, which checks in at $49.99 MSRP. Both folders are of Inte-

gral Lock (also referred to as frame-lock) design and represent their price group well. There is no winner or loser here.

Larry Connelley is the founder of Knifeart.com, one of the premier Internet sites for selling high-end knives — both custom and production. Connelley started Knifeart.com over 20 years ago and is very knowledgeable about what goes into the production of a knife. I asked Connelley his basic thoughts on

along with not cutting corners on manufacturing, provides a superior product."

MATERIAL MATTERS

Before a knife goes into production the manufacturer must choose the materials that will go into making the blade, handle and component parts. As Connelley noted, on a folding knife the choice of blade steel and frame alloy are the two most important factors in determining the cost and retail price of a knife. Most high-end folding knives have frames made of Titanium while their low-budget counterparts utilize aluminum or stainless steel for cost savings. Compared to the latter two less expensive metals, Titanium can easily cost a manufacturer 20–25 times the price per pound depending on the alloy, so it's easy to see how these choices can affect the price of a knife.

"In general, the material chosen to construct a knife's handle is indicative of its overall quality," Connelley notes. "The

(above) Handle materials make a huge difference when it comes to price. The stainless steel frame of the Eris (left) is far less expensive than the Titanium slabs found on the Reeve Inkosi (right), which also has attractive Micarta inlays.

(left) Note the difference between the frame thickness of the Eris at left versus the Inkosi at right. Not only do the thicker slabs on the Inkosi cost more, they provide a better grip.

(right) High-end knives tend to have much crisper machining and are held to tighter tolerances. At left is the Kershaw Eris, at right the Chris Reeve Inkosi.

(below) Like handle materials, blade steels are determining factors in the cost of a knife. The Inkosi (top) employs top-shelf U.S.-made S35VN Crucible steel while the Eris (bottom) uses 8Cr13MoV manufactured in China.

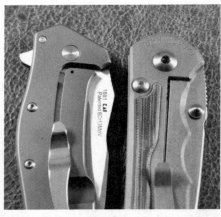

why some knives cost more than others. "The price of a knife is determined by two key factors: labor costs and price of materials," he said. "The price of higher-end knives is directly related to these factors. The importance of precision in the design of a knife cannot be overstated. High-quality American-made knives are usually produced by skilled manufacturers with a high attention to detail. The knife can be serviced domestically and provides the owner with a lifetime of service.

"The cost and quality of materials is a major factor in the final price to the consumer," Connelley added. "While the steel used for the blade and handle are major considerations, all of the other parts — such as the pivot, bushings and spacers — are just as important. All of the enhancements to materials used,

materials selected to construct a knife handle helps to determine the weight and the strength of the knife itself. While the use of high-quality base materials raises the cost to the consumer, the use of high-quality handle materials will prolong the life of a knife.

Titanium or carbon fiber are frequently used in the construction of high-quality knives — they are very strong yet much lighter. If I can choose a stronger yet lighter knife, I will make that selection every time. Heavy doesn't equal quality."

Titanium, as Connelley explained, has greater strength and withstands wear and tear better than less costly materials like stainless steel, polymers or aluminum. The increased cost of Titanium comes from longer machining times, thus greater machine shop costs.

The same goes for blade steels, which can easily drive the price of a knife higher. The modern tactical knife boom of the 1990s, spurred on by our country's involvement in the Gulf Wars, created a demand for higher-grade steels (such as ATS-34 and BG-42 stainless). The blade steel equation got kicked up several notches with the development of S30V stainless, a proprietary powdered knife steel developed by Crucible Industries, LLC and Chris Reeve. The two entities

collaborated again and released a revised version, S35VN, which remains a top-shelf blade steel to this day. Once Crucible's proprietary steels became popular, other manufacturers, such as domestic-based Carpenter Steel and Bohler-Uddeholm of Germany, jumped in. All of these manufacturer's steels add expense to a knife — especially in their early small batch stages.

Connelley gives insight into why high-end steels are so much better. "You simply cannot compare a high-alloy particle metallurgy steel blade to a low-grade steel one that is made offshore. You can't see the difference with your eyes, but a high-quality blade is the cornerstone of a dependable knife. Specialty steel manufacturers in the U.S., such as Crucible Industries, tend to employ CPM (Crucible Particle Metallurgy) performance steel that requires costly additionally steps to produce. The result is a high-performance blade with more even distribution of carbides and a higher content of alloying elements. The end product is a tougher steel that retains its edge longer."

The Kershaw Eris' modified drop point blade is made of 8Cr13MoV stainless steel, the Chinese-made version of Japanese AUS-8 steel — a popular low-budget choice by manufacturers. While both are

very adequate EDC budget steels, they don't hold a candle to the high-end proprietary metals such as the S35VN found on the Reeve Inkosi, and price-wise it isn't even close. In summary, all of the component materials that go into a knife, from frames to blades to pivot bearings and the cost of screws, add up when you consider the overall price of the knife.

COST OF LABOR

Custom knifemaker Jim Hammond has been making knives for 41 years and has been involved in dozens of design collaborations with Columbia River Knife & Tool (CRKT) dating back to CRKT's inception in 1994. Hammond is very knowledgeable about the manufacturing end of cutlery production.

"From a manufacturing standpoint, two aspects loom large — ease of fabrication and final product cost," Hammond notes. "Premium steels can degrade tooling and blanking processes much sooner than lower-quality steels. Too, the factor of seven would often be applied with component costs, such as the steel pricing for each blade. For example, a company's steel cost per blade would commonly be multiplied by seven to determine its valuation in the final retail pricing of the knife. With a targeted price point often predetermined going in, the steel selection is often made — not just with the best steel in mind, but the best steel that be used to achieve the targeted retail price point for the knife."

As Connelley noted earlier, the cost of a knife is largely determined by the wages in the country in which the manufacturer is based. A recent article by Forbes magazine suggested factory wages in China have increased drastically in the past few years to an average of approximately $3.60 per hour. It would be only a guess where workers at cutlery factories fall in the entire job market since much of this type of information is protected, but we can assume they are less than, say, a worker at an automotive plant. Computerized machining technologies and robotics are a big factor in production in both low- to high-budget knives, but manufacturers still must warm bodies running the equipment, inspecting the processes, and exercising quality control — not to mention some assembly. The average wage of the American factory worker is just north of $21.00 per hour at the time of this writing, so it's easy to see the grossly disproportionate amount of labor cost that goes into making a knife in the

Components also factor into the price of a knife. The Reeve Inkosi at left has an inset Titanium pocket clip that matches the frame, the Eris a stainless steel clip that doesn't.

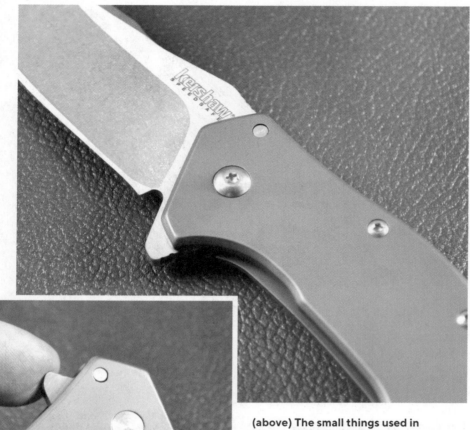

because more surface area blocks the blade tang.

The quality of manufacture shows up in the crispness of the design and added elements to the whole package. Less expensive knives tend to have rounded contours and flat surfaces on the frame. More expensive knives will have beveling around the slab edges and design enhancements such as sculpting and inlays (like the Micarta inserts found on the Inkosi). While the overwhelming majority of pocket clips like those found on the Eris are stamped stainless steel, the Inkosi has a Titanium one to match the frame. Such aesthetic value and features add to the cost of the knife due to the added time and materials they add to the manufacturing process, but these upscale elements are expected in an upscale knife.

However, the Kershaw Eris has design features the Reeve knife doesn't, and these should not be overlooked. The Eris folder opens by way of a blade flipper that protrudes out the top rear of the frame. Many prefer this over the somewhat dated thumb stud because it can be located quicker by the index finger (as opposed to the thumb) and takes only a quick flick to engage the blade. The icing on the Eris' cake is the addition of Kershaw's SpeedSafe spring-assisted opening mechanism, which can employ

(above) The small things used in construction of a folder, such as screws, pivots and spacers, affect both its price and durability. The Kershaw Eris uses stainless steel components, which cost less and are not as durable as Titanium.

(left) The Kershaw Eris has features that the higher-priced Inkosi does not, such as the flipper opener shown here. It also employs spring assist to roll the blade out in a flash.

U.S. versus offshore.

Folding knives require many steps from start to finish, all of which determine the final product. The differences between the equipment used cutting, shaping, sanding and finishing parts for a knife make a difference for the simple reason that some machines hold tolerances better than others. Likewise, the workers running the equipment, inspecting the parts and doing any manual assembly are a factor as well. A manufacturer making thousands of low-budget knives in a single run can't be expected to have the same quality controls as one making smaller batches of higher-priced ones. In a nutshell, high-end knives cost more, and are better made, because superior equipment and more human hands-on time are spent in their fabrication.

PARTS SPECIFICATION EQUATION

Parts specifications, such as the thickness of blade steel and frame rails, play a large role in fabrication and determines the efficiency and cost of the folder. For instance, the Reeve Inkosi has a blade thickness of 0.140 inch and 0.1505-inch thick frame slabs. The Kershaw Eris' blade is 0.11-inch thick and its frame slabs are 0.09-inch thick. A beefier knife will outperform a lesser one but will cost more, which is the case with our subjects. Granted, the Inkosi is a slightly larger knife, but there are knives closer in size to the Eris with materials that spec closer to our Reeve subject. It should also be noted that Integral Locks with thicker frame slabs like the Inkosi's offer more surface area on the locking leaf, making for a stronger lock-up

The Reeve Inkosi utilizes Titanium in most of its fabrication. Here you can see the pivot, blade stop, and thumb stud — all made of the superior alloy. Note also that the pivot is much beefier than its lower-priced counterpart.

the blade in the blink of an eye — an important feature on any everyday carry blade for tactical or self-defense use.

Both knives have a comfortable grip with the wider frame on the Reeve Inkosi offering more comfort and better purchase. Both are good for everyday carry

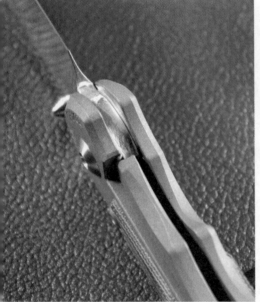

and are very adequate for self-defense, but the beefier Inkosi is more than willing to step out into the field for serious camp duty. Indeed, the forerunner Reeve Sebenza model, which shares many of the same traits as the Inkosi, has been serving military field operators for well over 25 years.

The Inkosi will have no trouble with field chores like carving and shaving seasoned wood. Like its older sibling the Chris Reeve Sebenza Model, these knives are made for hard use and have a lifetime guarantee.

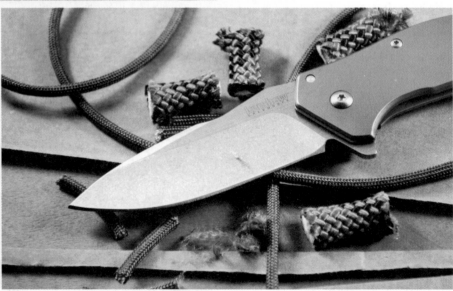

(top) Thicker, beefier frame slabs like those found on the Inkosi, which includes the locking leaf for the blade, offer more surface area on the locking leaf, making for a solid lock-up as greater surface area blocks the tang of the blade.

(above) The Kershaw Eris will serve you well for everyday chores, having no trouble slicing corrugated board, paracord and 3/8-inch rappelling rope during light testing.

DESIGNER LABELS

Interestingly, you'll find a greater selection of collaborations with popular custom knifemakers among the lower-priced knives. While the Kershaw Eris is an in-house design — and a darn good one at that — the company has had great success with custom knifemaker Rick Hinderer's designs in its standard line and in the more upscale Zero Tolerance line under the same KAI USA Ltd. corpo-

rate umbrella. Collaborations are a huge bonus for the knife customer who can't afford a custom knife by the same maker. The manufacturers also benefit by increased sales from designer collaborations. How popular are they? In this day and age you'd be hard-pressed to find a cutlery manufacturer who is not offering collaborations with custom knifemakers. Custom knifemakers are also well served as it gives them added exposure and royalty checks to pad their wallets.

Custom knifemaker Jim Hammond is familiar with such collaborations. "As President Kennedy once said, 'When the tide comes in, all the ships will rise.' This has proven true with benefits to everyone in the knife industry with the inflow of custom knifemakers now working with production companies. It's far easier to utilize creative vision, design understanding and proven manufacturing experience from a maker who's done it for over 40 years, such as myself, than to train someone for decades to hopefully achieve the same end. It brings expertise to the moment and ramps up every aspect of the process into real time from initial concepts to placing the finished knife into the customer's hand."

In the case of Chris Reeve, he is a legendary knifemaker dating back to when he only offered custom fare. His manufacturing designs have been popular

SPECIFICATIONS

MODEL: Kershaw Eris

BLADE STEEL: 8Cr13MoV stainless steel

OVERALL LENGTH: 7.50 in.

HANDLE LENGTH: 4.50 in.

HANDLE THICKNESS: 0.38 in.

BLADE TYPE: Modified drop point

BLADE LENGTH: 3.0 in.

HANDLE MATERIAL: Stainless steel

SPECIAL FEATURES: Flipper opener/ Spring assist

CARRY: Pocket clip/tip-up carry

WEIGHT: 4.70 oz.

MSRP: $49.99

COUNTRY OF MANUFACTURE: China

SPECIFICATIONS

MODEL: Chris Reeve Large Inkosi

BLADE STEEL: S35VN Crucible stainless steel

OVERALL LENGTH: 8.40 in.

HANDLE LENGTH: 4.80 in.

HANDLE THICKNESS: 0.46 in.

BLADE TYPE: Drop point

BLADE LENGTH: 3.60 in.

HANDLE MATERIAL: Titanium/Micarta

SPECIAL FEATURES: Micarta inlays/ lanyard

CARRY: Pocket clip/tip-up carry

WEIGHT: 4.96 oz.

MSRP: $515

COUNTRY OF MANUFACTURE: USA

The Middle Budget Blade: The $250 Sweet Spot

There are hundreds of folding knives to be had in the $50 or lower price range, but the air thins to only a handful around the $500 mark as the price begins to approach the custom knife category. There is, however, a very good selection of folders in the $250 range worth a close look, such as the stunning Zero Tolerance 0055.

Zero Tolerance is under the same Kai USA Ltd. corporate umbrella as Kershaw and is its upscale knife division. Designed by custom knifemaker Gus T. Cecchini of GTC Knives, the 0055 is a production version of his stealthy Airborne model and features a 3.75-inch premium S35VN stainless steel blade hooked up to a sculpted, 5.0-inch Titanium handle. Simple stated, the ZT 0055 is a knockout. The folder's slick SLT "hidden" flipper tab works very similar to a two-stage trigger and won't hang up in the pocket when being accessed. MSRP for the ZT 0055 falls just above the sweet spot at $275 MSRP.

The Zero Tolerance 0055, designed by Gus T. Cecchini of GTC Knives, is loaded with premium materials and innovative features — and the price is right.

dating back nearly 30 years when he introduced the Sebenza, which still sells like hotcakes along with other additions such as the Inkosi. Reeve is also considered the father of the integral lock design, which rules the roost among not only folder manufacturers but custom knifemakers as well.

A PLACE FOR BOTH

Despite such broad differences between low- and high-budget knives there is a strong case to be made for each. Budget knives offer a great opportunity for entry-level knife customers to use and enjoy a competent knife at an affordable price, and the selection from the manufacturers is almost endless. Even counting average materials in low-end models compared to high-end knives, budget blades perform perfectly fine for the average user's everyday needs. And their fixed-blade brethren do well

in the field as well. In fact, some knife users carry a budget folder as their EDC and switch to a more upscale option for special occasions. Budget knives don't offer the endurance of high-end knives, but many users will take that trade-off.

High-end folders are for those who prefer the best and can afford to pay the price. They have complete confidence in their knife and know with no uncertainty that it will perform to the extreme, will be less prone to fail, and will cut like a house afire with an edge that will hold its sharpness longer.

Better yet, there are a plethora of knives to be had between the low- and high-budget folders featured here. For a taste, check out the sidebar on the Zero Tolerance 0055 accompanying this fea-

ture. The cutlery market is burgeoning with knives for any budget, any taste and any need. You'll have no trouble finding one made just for you! **TGD**

SOURCES

Chris Reeve Knives, 2949 S. Victory View Way, Boise, ID 83709. 208-375-0367 chrisreeve.com

Jim Hammond Knives & Designs, LLC, 104 Owens Parkway Suite M, Birmingham, AL 35244. 256-651-1376 jimhammondknives.com

Kershaw/Kai USA, 18600 Teton Avenue, Tualatin, OR 97062. 800-325-2891 kershawknives.com

KnifeArt.com, 13301 Pompano Drive, Little Rock, AR 72211. 800-564-3327 knifeart.com

PROTECTING YOUR OWN SIX

Four major self-defense insurance programs are now available to the millions of Americans who carry concealed. BY **DAVE WORKMAN**

According to a recent estimate by the Crime Prevention Research Center (CPRC), more than 15 million Americans are now licensed to carry a firearm in the United States.

With that many and more legally licensed citizens — including those who keep guns strictly in the home for domestic protection, along with people who open carry or live in one of the dozen states that do not require licenses — the odds are increasing that someone will have to use their firearm to defend against a serious crime.

Realizing this possibility, at least four organizations have recognized the need for some type of coverage plans for the armed citizen who might someday act in self-defense. Unlike television, stopping a villain with lethal force isn't the end of the drama — it's often just the beginning.

Stepping up to the plate with protection programs are the United States Concealed Carry Association (USCCA), the Armed Citizens Legal Defense Network (ACLDN), U.S. Law Shield and the National Rifle Association. Each has a slightly different approach to the challenge, because in this game, there are problems and there are solutions.

The hard truth is that most armed citizens simply have no idea of the legal minefield they step into the second they press the trigger. As more than one of the people we interviewed explained, from that moment, your life is changed forever.

Even if no criminal charge is filed, because we live in a litigious society, there are attorneys just chomping at the bit to make life miserable for armed citizens in civil court. That's the reality. Defending a life with a firearm can break people — it can destroy life savings, families and jobs.

THE UNITED STATES CONCEALED CARRY ASSOCIATION (USCCA)

Tim Schmidt, USCCA founder and president, told Gun Digest that he founded the organization in June 2011, because he had heard horror stories about law-abiding citizens who had defended themselves and subsequently found themselves in legal trouble.

"I didn't think they should have been in trouble," he recalled.

Schmidt discovered quickly that a lot of mainstream insurance companies did not want to be involved in providing coverage for such people, especially since there was limited data available. Today, 6 years later, that data exists.

"If you're a typical gun-owning American and own a house, you're likely to have an insurance claim one-third as often as a home claim," Schmidt said. "But that claim on average will cost seven times as much as a home insurance claim."

Schmidt then added, "Who doesn't have insurance on their home?"

USCCA also has a training program, featuring qualified trainers who teach firearms and self-defense. Presently, there are hundreds of USCCA trainers across the country, and the program is growing.

Additionally, USCCA holds an annual Concealed Carry Expo. Next year's event is slated in Louisville, Kentucky. There are training classes, firearms companies exhibiting and accessories manufacturers represented.

The USCCA program provides three levels of coverage for members:

The Silver level, costing $13 monthly, or a $147 annual payment provides up to $300,000 in protection, including $250,000 for civil lawsuit defense and damages, and firearm theft protection. Also included is $50,000 for an immediate attorney retainer and up-front criminal defense, $2,500-$25,000 immediate bail bonding and $250 a day compensation while in civil court.

USCCA's Gold level provides up to $575,000 in protection, including $500,000 in civil suit defense and damages, plus firearm protection, and

$75,000 for the attorney retainer and criminal defense. There's $5,000 to $50,000 immediate bail bonding and $350 a day compensation while in civil court. All this is covered by a $247 annual membership or $22 monthly.

The Platinum level offers up to $1,150,000 in total protection, including $1,000,000 for civil defense and damages, and gun protection, plus $150,000 for an immediate attorney retainer, $25,000 to $250,000 for immediate bail bonding and $500 per day compensation while in civil court. This membership level costs $347 annually or $30 per month.

For that, Schmidt said, "You are going to have one of the best pre-screened pro-Second Amendment criminal and civil defense attorneys." This representation continues through the entire process.

ARMED CITIZENS LEGAL DEFENSE NETWORK (ACLDN)

When veteran firearms instructor Marty Hayes created the ACLDN as a membership organization, he had already been teaching firearms and self-defense courses for several years. He started back in 1988 and has built a reputation not only as an instructor, but also as an expert witness.

As the founder and proprietor of the Firearms Academy of Seattle (FAS), Hayes has a background in law enforcement and a law degree. It was during the 4 years of law school that he formed the idea of creating "the network." What was lacking, he recalled, was a funding mechanism.

However, that was solved with the participation of FAS students. Hayes set aside 25 percent of each fee to establish the ACLDN. His plan worked, and today there is more than $1 million in the network's legal war chest.

An ACLDN membership costs $135 for the first year and $95 for renewals. For that, the network provides up to $25,000 to post bail in the event of an arrest following a self-defense incident. The

Each of these providers offers different coverage options, but each has value to the armed citizen.

network also forwards up to $25,000 to a member's attorney after an incident.

Unlike other plans, there are no different levels of coverage for ACLDN members. Everyone has the same coverage, Hayes said. Each member's legal fees associated with a legitimate use of self-defense force are covered, including pre-trial, trial, appeals and civil court.

A portion of the annual member dues is deposited in the Legal Defense Fund's account. The ACLDN has an advisory board that consists of noted experts in

the field of firearms and self-defense: John Farnam, Massad Ayoob, Jim Fleming, Emanuel Kapelsohn, Tom Givens and Dennis Tueller.

"People need to be able to defend their actions in court," Hayes explained. "You hope you never get involved in an incident. But if you do, you're going to want a network, and you will get an attorney and [be able to] pay for an attorney."

Of particular interest is the network affiliates, which include gun shops across the country. There are also corporate

sponsors, affiliated attorneys and affiliated instructors.

Like Schmidt, Hayes said that in today's legal environment, every armed citizen should consider the kinds of programs that the various plans provide to be essential. What happens after a self-defense incident can quickly become a minefield. This is why ACLDN provides updates to its members.

U.S. LAW SHIELD

A dire need for protection was evident to Kirk Evans and P.J. Hermosa, the president and executive director, respectively, at U.S. Law Shield, a Texas-based program that actually started in the Lone Star State and has expanded. Now operating in 15 states with more expansion on the horizon, U.S. Law Shield is popular with its 235,000-plus members for a number of reasons.

An attorney by profession, Evans said people enroll "to have full legal defense in the event they have to use a firearm."

"The foundation of our program is education," Evans explained. "Last year we put on about 4,500 seminars on the ins and outs of lawful gun ownership."

Seminars are offered wherever there's an adequate facility, such as a gun shop with a classroom, a gun range — even a restaurant banquet room.

Hermosa said the program promotes tactical training and live-fire shooting.

"We're here to train and educate, based on laws in the states," he said. "We want people to be comfortable in the law."

This information offers state-specific content that people need to know, Hermosa said.

The program started in 2009 as Texas

Law Shield following a self-defense event that exposed what people can go through in the legal system, even if they are in the right.

"We are about empowering people every day," Hermosa added.

U.S. Law Shield has attorneys in each of its states of operation, and each is heavily vetted to ensure the highest quality of legal expertise.

In the event of a self-defense incident for a member, everything is covered "from start to finish," Evans said. There's a hotline for members, and Evans said the group receives one or two calls every day dealing with a specific incident. For this level of service, members pay $10.95 per month or an annual payment of $131.40, and coverage for minor children is an additional $24 annually or $2 per month.

There's also a rate for couples of $21.90 per month or $240 annually. For an additional $2.95 a month or $35.40 per year, each member can get multi-state protection.

Across the 15 active states, there are about 2,400 different gun ranges, stores and facilities that recommend the U.S. Law Shield program, he added. Members can pay either by the month or an annual fee, and there are a couple of options.

Member benefits include coverage whether the gun is fired or not, and there's an emergency hotline answered 24/7 by an attorney. Members receive legal representation for both criminal and civil cases and firearms law updates, according to their website.

NRA CARRY GUARD

Unveiled at the April gathering of the National Rifle Association in Atlanta, the NRA Carry Guard program is an ambitious undertaking considering the already well-established competition.

According to Josh Powell, NRA chief of staff and executive director of general operations, he had discussed the project with Executive Vice President Wayne LaPierre. It made sense because the NRA has been on the front lines to expand concealed carry in the United States for more than 3 decades. Powell estimated that there are approximately 18 million people who carry, including those who lawfully carry without a permit.

"We needed to be the place to come as it relates to concealed carry," Powell added. "If you carry, you need to be with the NRA."

"This is critical," Powell explained, "because people don't understand what your exposure is as a citizen if, God forbid, you use a firearm in self-defense."

"Depending upon where you live," he stressed, "your life is going to be turned upside-down. Most people don't understand that."

There are three levels of coverage in the NRA Carry

Involvement in a defensive shooting doesn't end once the threat is stopped. A great deal happens after the fact, including civil litigation in some cases.

An aspect common to many of these coverage plans is a training program, or at least a major emphasis on receiving the proper training and education to be a responsible armed citizen.

NRA | G CARRY GUARD™

Guard program:

The Bronze level provides $250,000 in coverage for $154.95 annually or $13.95 per month, according to the Carry Guard website.

The Silver membership comes with $500,000 in insurance, for an annual fee of $254.95 or $21.95 per month.

NRA Carry Guard's Gold membership level comes with $1 million in insurance for $359.95 annually or a monthly premium of $31.95.

There's much more to this than peace of mind, Powell assured.

"We've hired the dream team of instructors," he said.

The instructor team includes people with military and law enforcement backgrounds, and the course of instruction covers all the bases.

"There really isn't anything out there quite like this," Powell said, noting that he has gone through the course.

This course includes an introductory section, range time that includes moving and shooting and working under pressure. Powell noted that there are no participation ribbons. Students are graded on their performance.

There are force-on-force scenarios and exercises that teach how to respond to carjackings or incidents in a convenience store. All of this is designed to help armed citizens make decisions in fractions of a second.

Like USCCA, the NRA will be holding an annual expo, with the inaugural event Aug. 25-27, 2017, in Milwaukee, Wisconsin, at the Wisconsin Center. The event will feature exhibitors, plus education opportunities.

"We've generated a tremendous network of attorneys," Powell added. "You will have an advocate who will be advocating on your behalf from the beginning to the end of the process."

CONCLUSION

That, essentially, is what each of these plans offer: an advocate rather than just a public defender who might, or might not, have a full grasp of self-defense, much less any sympathy for an armed citizen. It might come as no shock at all to many people, but not all attorneys sympathize with gun owners who fire in self-defense.

People can take their chances with a public defender, or they can rely on the experts associated with these membership programs. Clearly, a lot of thought went into each of these efforts, and the ultimate beneficiary is the armed citizen. TGD

ZEROING YOUR AR-15

HERE'S HOW TO GET YOUR AR ZEROED WITH ANY SIGHTING SYSTEM

BY **TIGER MCKEE**

"**Z**eroing" the AR means adjusting the sights so your point of impact – where the bullet strikes the target – is the same as your point of aim – where you are holding the sights. There is a variety of methods or formulas for zeroing the AR. Instead of trying to use different size targets at various distances and flipping back and forth between one aperture and the other on the rear sight – as required by some methods – I prefer to use the simple technique described below. In my opinion, to get a "hard" zero with the AR you have to actually shoot it at the distance you've chosen for your zero, rather than simulate distance by using smaller targets.

Once you've zeroed the AR, it's time to fire it various distances to discover what the difference will be between your point of aim (POA) and the point of impact (POI). This will vary according to barrel length and twist rate, and the type ammo, such as bullet weight and the design or shape of the round. Changing ammo, switching between one type ammo and another – even when they are the same weight or design but different brands – will usually change the trajectory of the round, sometimes dramatically.

When it comes to choosing the distance for your zero there are several factors to consider. First is the offset between the sights and the barrel; the sights are higher than the barrel.

These groups were fired from 15 yards, with a 100–yard zero. The low shots were fired aiming at the center of the diamond. This shows how low your offset is. The group of shots in the center was fired aiming at the top of the diamond.

are adjusted so that at 100 yards the bullet strikes the exact point the sights are holding. A 75-yard zero gives you the least deviation between your POA and POI between 25 and 100 yards. At 25 yards the POI will be roughly one and one half inches lower than your POA. The POI at 100 yards will be and one half inches higher than your POA, which will give you a POI of about an inch or so low at 200 yards.

For zeroing it's important to use the ammunition that you anticipate shooting when using your AR. If you're trying to zero using different types of ammo, it's going to be a frustrating process because each one will have a different POI.

Pick one type of ammo and use it to zero. Later, after getting a zero and learning the fundamentals, you can experiment with different rounds to determine which one provides the best accuracy. Also keep in mind that distance will be a big factor. For example, ammo "A" may produce a tighter group at 100 yards, but at 200 yards ammo "B" is more accurate. A lot of research and then actual field testing is necessary to determine what round is will produce the best results for your application.

For the A2 sights, which have a rear sight that's adjustable for elevation, you want to have the rear sight bottomed out, for example on the 6/3 or 8/3 setting. With the A1 sight there is no elevation adjustment on the rear sight. You should be using the large aperture on the rear sight – unless from previous experience you know the small aperture works better for you. (Remember, if you flip

POINT OF AIM VS. POINT OF IMPACT

	RANGE			
	25	50	75	100
25 ZERO	0	2.5-in. H	4.5-in. H	5.5-in. H
50 ZERO	1-in. L	0	1.5-in. H	2-in. H
75 ZERO	1.5-in. L	.25-in. L	0	1.5-in. H
100 ZERO	2.5-in. L	1-in. L	.5-in. L	0

At distances less than 25 yds, regardless of zero the point of impact will be approx. 2.5-in. low
Actual figures will vary according to barrel length, twist rate and bullet weight and design.

(top) Different ammo will change your point of impact according to the weight of the bullet and its velocity. Plus, your barrel length and twist will affect accuracy.

(above) This chart gives you a rough idea of what the difference will be between point of aim and point of impact according to the distance at which the AR is zeroed.

This offset comes into play especially at close distances, where the POI will be lower than the POA. You have to aim or hold high for your round to hit where you need it to go. You also have to consider the trajectory of the round. For example, with a 55-grain bullet firing with a one hundred yard zero the POI will be approximately two inches low at 200 yards.

Before beginning the zero process you need to pick the distance for your zero. I use a 100-yard zero. The sights

When zeroing, work in the most stable position you can, using rests or supports to create stability.

New versions of the AR have rear sights with elevation adjustments. When zeroing, make sure to start with the drum on its lowest setting, 6/3 or 8/3.

The rear sight on early versions of the AR requires a sight tool or bullet tip to adjust. The newer versions have a drum that can be adjusted by hand.

between the large and small aperture you'll be changing the bullet's POI.) To adjust the actual elevation while zeroing use the front sight, moving it up or down as needed. Moving it down, turning it clockwise, will raise your POI. Turning it counter-clockwise raises the front sight, which will lower the bullet's POI. To turn or adjust the front sight you have to depress the detent that holds the sight in place. A sight tool will make adjustments easy, or you can use the tip of a bullet. The front sight will have either four or five slots for the detent; the sight tool must have the same number of prongs to match the front sight.

Windage, moving the bullet right or left, is adjusted with the rear sight. The A1 rear sight requires the use of a sight tool or the tip of a bullet for adjustment. The A2 rear sight has a drum that you turn with your fingers; no tool required.

Take your time during the zeroing process. This isn't something you can do quickly. For the best results, work from a bench, with rests or bags for support. Make sure the handguard is supported, as opposed to the actual barrel touching or resting on the bags. If the barrel is making contact with your rest, it will throw the shots off. For example, when the bottom of the barrel is touching the rest it will throw the shots high. Your goal is to create a solid, stable position – consistency – and apply the fundamentals of marksmanship for every shot.

Start the zeroing process at 25 yards. Make sure you have a steady position, using a rest in order to take out as much

of the human element as possible. Normally I'll fire five or six shots, enough to satisfy myself that I've got a good group established. By firing several rounds, even if you have one or two shots that weren't good, you're still going to have a solid group to work with.

After establishing a good group you're ready to adjust the sights, but first unload the AR. Do not get into the habit of adjusting or doing any work on your firearm while it's loaded. Unload, check and check again to confirm it's clear, and then remember the safety rules are still in effect. After making adjustments you load and start again. The additional benefit of all this is that you're getting in practice on your manipulations.

As mentioned earlier, at 25 yards your bullets should be hitting lower than where you are aiming. This low POI is necessary because of the offset between the sights and barrel. (Don't get too worried about exact measurements here; you're just looking to get it close, and will fine tune the sights as you move back, creating more distance.)

Once you have a rough zero at 25, again with the bullets striking about two inches below your point of aim, move back to 50 yards. Fire a good group, and adjust as necessary. At this distance your point of impact will be closer to the center of the target where you're aiming. As you increase the distance the POI will move upward towards your POA. For example, if you've decided to work with a 100-yard zero, at 50 yards the bullets should be hitting about an inch below where you are aiming.

Fire a good group, and then adjust the sights as needed. Normally I will only adjust one direction at a time. For example, I'll adjust the elevation with the front sight until getting that right, then adjust windage to get it in the right spot. Trying to adjust both the elevation and windage at the same time can sometimes get a little complicated, for example as you adjust the windage it can change the elevation slightly. You may find that after adjusting the front sight and then the rear sight for windage that you have to go back to the front sight for final adjustments.

After getting close at 50 yards, move back to 75 and repeat the process. If you want a 75-yard zero your bullets should be hitting where you're aiming. Point of aim and point of impact are the same. For a 100-yard zero you'll need to move back to that distance and repeat the process one last time, adjusting until your POI is spot on for where you are aiming.

When you have the opportunity, shoot your AR at longer distances to find out how much the bullet will drop. (This will vary, sometimes greatly, according to barrel length, twist and bullet design and weight.) For general-purpose use, you're holding high, aiming above the point you want the shot to go so when the bullet drops it's hitting the target. The other end of the spectrum is High Power competition, where you're adjusting the rear sight to compensate for extended distances so you're always aiming at the center of the target.

You'll also need to shoot it at distances closer than your zero, again to find out the difference between your point of aim and the point of impact. Remember, the sights are offset, higher than the barrel, so as you move closer

You need to zero your iron sights and the red-dot.

When using a red-dot sight, adjust it so your shots are hitting the center of target, and learn your bullet drop and rise from point blank to reasonable combat distances.

than your zero the point of impact will begin to drop. At distances closer than 25 yards you'll be aiming about two and one half inches high to compensate for this offset. (XS Sights have a modified rear sight that has a notch on top of the peep sight that you use for aiming at close distances that compensates for the offset.)

For zeroing a red-dot sight or a more traditional optic with magnification I use the same process. I start at 25, get a rough zero with the point of impact two to two and one half inches lower than the point of aim. Don't' worry about an exact measurement, you'll have to be making more adjustments as you increase the distance.

With red-dot sights, work on getting the shots where they are hitting in the center of the dot, as opposed to somewhere in the dot.

Remember the dot's "size" will vary according to distance. A two minute dot covers up two inches at 100 yards. At 200 yards the two minute dot covers up four inches of target, and at 300 the dot is covering six inches of the target. If you zero with the shots hitting at the top of the dot, this means your point of impact is going to vary according the distance you're shooting. Regardless of distance and the "size" of the dot, center is always

center. Adjust until your hits are in the center of the dot for the distance you've chosen to zero.

There are a lot of optics available that have graduated reticles, varied points for aiming that compensate for distance and trajectory. These are good, but the only way to confirm these "holds" is to actually fire the AR at the distances indicated. As mentioned previously, barrel length and twist and the type round you're firing will all affect the bullet's trajectory. The only way to know where your AR is going to shoot is by firing it at those distances.

Another factor to deal with is the actual adjustment of the optic. One click on the elevation knob is supposed to adjust the POI one quarter of an inch, or one-quarter minute of angle, at 100 yards. But, again, the length of the barrel and its rate of twist and type ammunition you're shooting may mean that one click is greater or less than a quarter inch of movement in the bullet's point of impact.

Any time you change anything on your AR it will be necessary to recheck your zero. The AR is a surgical instrument and modifying anything is going to change what happens when the shot is fired. Something like changing the stock can affect where the bullet hits. Changing ammo is definitely a reason to check your zero. There might not be much difference, and then again there may be

a drastic shift in the bullet's point of impact.

Zeroing the AR requires application of the fundamentals of marksmanship. Your goal is to be as machine-like as possible, trying to repeat the process the same way for every shot. If your eyes get tired then stop, take a rest and start again. The same thing goes for your body. Anytime the body gets tired or stressed it's going to affect your ability to hold steady. Remember to control your breathing. You need to shoot accurately, produce consistent results – a good tight group – then you can move that group wherever it needs to be by adjusting the sights. **TGD**

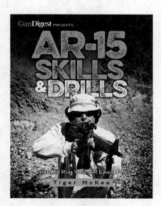

This article is an excerpt from AR-15 Skills & Drills, by Tiger Mckee. To get your copy visit GunDigestStore.com.

Special-purpose rifles are made to shoot as accurately as possible.

Everyone who owns a precision rifle keeps a dope or data book on that weapon – at least they do if they are serious shooters. Typical information includes details on cold bore shots. Normally the point of impact on the first shot fired from a clean, cold barrel will be slightly different from shots fired after that. You record each cold shot, building up enough data to know exactly where that first shot is heading. By gathering and recording data, you know the difference between a shot fired when the air temp is a chilly 15 degrees and the humidity is low vs. a hot day of 95 degrees with humidity to match. You have a record of the changes that will occur if you switch from a 55 grain bullet to one weighing 75 grains. I recommend doing the same thing for every firearm you own.

Most of the people I know who get into firearms, no matter the reason, eventually end up with a small collection of weapons. After all, you need a few pistols for carry, a variety of rifles and carbines, and of course probably a dose of shotguns. At some point it becomes difficult to keep track of everything, especially like when you changed out a buffer spring, how many rounds have been fired through a specific barrel, or what make bolt group is in a particular AR. The solution is to develop a log or data book for each firearm you own.

In my spec sheets I include detailed information about what parts were used to assemble that weapon. There is a record of when it's been cleaned, how many rounds it's fired, or when the recoil spring was last changed. I keep track of when the battery was changed in the red-dot sight. When a part breaks I know what

brand it was, how long it lasted and what to replace it with. There are targets in the file so I know what group to expect from that particular weapon with specific type or brand ammo.

Keeping targets gives me a reference to look back at. If all the sudden AR #3 is shooting three-inch groups at 100 yards instead of one-inch groups, I know there's a problem I need to look at. Keeping this information is also good if you need to take your AR to a gunsmith for repairs or modifications. This way they don't have to try guess about anything; it's all written down and recorded for reference.

I'm an old school guy and keep written records. Plus, if I have a clean sheet of paper I can draw out illustrations for documenting a certain point, or attach pictures to the file. Yes, you could keep your notes on a computer, but remember that the act of writing something down helps implant it in the mind. Typing or entering data on a computer spreadsheet provides you with a record, but it doesn't make the same mental connections.

For the average AR, you probably don't need to record every shot or the weather conditions and the amount of info you would with a precision rifle. Unless of course your precision rifle is an AR, a Special Purpose Rifle, or SPR. But you do need to keep a record of all the different modifications made, bullet trajectory for different distances – including wind shifts – and other major details of that weapon.

Owning and using a firearm is serious business, especially if we're talking about possibly using it for self-defense. Approach all the different aspects of this accordingly. Document everything about your weapons, just as you do with your training and practice.

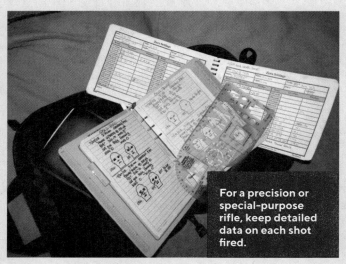

For a precision or special-purpose rifle, keep detailed data on each shot fired.

LIGHT 'EM UP!

TACTICAL WEAPON LIGHTS AND FLASHLIGHTS

The Lucid C3 weapon light features a unique dual-LED system that produces 300 lumens of bright light and is best mounted on an AR side rail.

Advancements in Tactical Lights Allow You to Own the Night

BY **SCOTT W. WAGNER**

In 2009, when I wrote the book, *Own the Night — Selection and Use of Tactical Lights and Laser Sights* for *Gun Digest*, handheld and weapon-mounted LED tactical lighting systems were just starting to become an effective alternative to incandescent lights. By then, LEDs were already more durable and longer lasting than incandescent bulbs, but they weren't up to the power levels of some of the better incandescent systems, such as Surefire's M3 Combat Light (225 lumens). When the manuscript was sent in for publication, I already knew that the 120-lumen limit of the best LED lights would be exceeded before any print copies of the book made it to consumers' hands. But that is the name of the game when it comes to technology of any sort.

Today, there are handheld LED tactical lights that exceed 1,000 lumens, with many models of handheld and weapon-mounted lights putting out 600-800 lumens. Compared to the old police Kel-Lights that I started out my law enforcement career with, the current levels of LED illumination are astounding. Here are some of the best and brightest lights that fulfill the Tactical Light Triad concept — Illuminate, Identify, and Incapacitate by causing disorientation.

FIRST LIGHT USA TORQ

A First Light USA TORQ light has been riding on a MOLLE holster on the external armor carrier I wear while on duty for some time. In fact, it was just a few weeks ago that I used it while taking down a felony sex offender at his home. It worked perfectly.

The First Light USA TORQ's finger ring provides solid control, direction, and retention of the light while wielding a handgun with one or both hands.

The polymer TORQ light, like the aluminum Tomahawk model, is an angle-head design with a finger retention loop. Both lights are designed to work in concert with a two-hand shooting grip on the handgun or as stand-alones. The TORQ's head rotates 360 degrees for best adjustment. It's powered by two AA alkaline penlight batteries. White light output is 155 lumens. According to First Light, 155 lumens is the "sweet spot" — sufficiently bright, but less likely to splash light back in your eyes in close quarters.

Both the law enforcement and civilian versions of the TORQ utilize color LEDs that surround the primary light. The law enforcement version uses red and blue LED. Holding switch "1" down for three seconds switches the primary light to strobe while the reds and blues flash around it. The civilian version uses red and green LEDs. For tactical, emergency, or utility use, the TORQ excels. It can be purchased as a specialized "Kit" or as a stand-alone, with accessories that can be bought separately. It is a great light that I stake my life on whenever I am on patrol. MSRP for the TORQ alone is $99.
firstlight-usa.com

LASERMAX SPARTAN ADJUSTABLE FIT LIGHT AND LASER

The Lasermax Spartan Laser and Light Combo represents a unique departure from standard laser/light combination products in a number of ways. First, it is extremely lightweight (due in part to its polymer construction) tipping the scales at only 1.3 ounces. It also maintains low weight due to the generally small size of

The Lasermax SPS Spartan combines a bright green laser for sighting with a 120-lumen "Mint Green" target identification LED for superior illumination.

the LED lamp used for the light source.

Light output is 120 lumens — relatively low by today's standards, but still nothing to sneeze at — and powerful enough for home defense situations. Lasermax boosts the effectiveness of the 120-lumen output by using a "Mint Green" LED, which according to their website utilizes "the most visible wavelength in the color spectrum" to provide a perceivable boost in performance over a standard white LED. What I was really surprised by is that the light is powered by only one AAA alkaline battery, and that two were included. The light has a sticker warning against the use of lithium batteries.

My Spartan sample came with a green laser to complement the Mint Green LED — although a red laser version is available for $40 less. The laser and LED are controlled individually by ambidextrous paired switching. All switches are "click on" types — one-touch "on," one touch "off." The top switches turn the laser on and off, the bottom switches turn on the light and all operate independently.

The rail mounting system is unique and allows mounting on either Picatinny or Weaver rails. Read the directions before mounting. MSRP is $205.00.

lasermax.com

LUCID C3 WEAPONS LIGHT

Lucid, which is known for fine optics at very reasonable prices, has been branching out into other areas as well — including C3 Weapons lights. Of the weapon lights I've tested, the Lucid C3 is the only one using dual LED lamps, mounted side by side in a 6061 aluminum body. Powered by three AAA alkaline cells, the twin LED's put out a combined total of 300 lumens in a circular beam that covers a wider swatch than a single 300 lumen LED should. A hinged latching switch holds the cells in place. The C3 is 2.75 inches long and weighs 2.25 ounces.

Lucid placed the single control switch on the underside of the light, making it accessible by either hand when mounted. While that placement is unique in terms of making the switch truly ambidextrous in operation, it limits this C3 to long gun mounting. Mounting the C3 on a pistol would require way too much modification of a safe shooting grip to access. An optimal mounting point on a quad rail might be on a side rail. This way the support hand thumb could punch the button off and on. One push for full power on. There is no true momentary position. The strobe setting is activated

by pushing and holding the switch in for approximately 3 seconds. For best tactical applications, 3 seconds is a long time. Strobes need to be activated immediately. However, activation of the primary beam is quick and efficient. MSRP is a reasonable $149.00.

mylucidgear.com

MAG-LITE MAG-TAC CR123 LED FLASHLIGHT

I have a very strong affinity for Mag-Lites. A six C-Cell incandescent Mag-Lite doubled as my patrol flashlight and emergency nightstick and served me well in the 1980s. One of the early Mini-Mag two cell AA penlight flashlights served as my first backup flashlight. Mag-Lite, which has always proudly manufactured its product line in Ontario, California, still makes the Mini-Maglight — but it also makes some of the most up-to-date tactical handheld lights on the market. One of those is the Mag-Tac CR123 LED flashlight.

Powered by two CR123 batteries, and with an output of 320 lumens, the solid aluminum light features a surface with raised knurling that makes it easy to grasp. Also included is a pocket clip that can be attached if you desire. A wrench to accomplish that task is included. I prefer mine without the clip. The beam has a 320-meter reach, and a total run time of four hours.

The tail cap switching system is well-designed, simple, and easily operated with one hand. The pressure switch is very slightly recessed without a "fence." (The "fence" I am referring to is the protective barrier around the base of tactical lights with tail cap switches that prevents accidental activation, particularly when the light is carried in the pocket.) Pressing and holding — or a quick press and release — activates the momentary setting. A quick double-tap locks the beam on — pressing once releases it. Three rapid taps turn on the strobe. There is no low power setting,

Maglite's Mag-Tac CR123 handheld tactical light throws a 320-lumen beam and is heavy duty enough for use on tough SWAT missions.

as it isn't really needed. 320 lumens is an excellent power level, plenty bright for any critical task, but not too bright to compromise your vision for close tasks. MSRP only $95.

maglite.com

STREAMLIGHT POLYTAC X/USB MULTI-FUEL HANDHELD LIGHT

With 600 lumens on tap and a compact 5.46-inch overall length, the Polytac X is what most users desire in a handheld tactical light: powerful light output, ruggedness and easy operation. But there is more to the Polytac X than just the basic features that are the foundation of a good tactical light.

The Polytac X is, as Streamlight terms it, a "multi-fuel" light. In the case of the Polytac X, this means it will run off two standard CR123 lithium cells or Streamlight's new 18650 USB battery. The 18650 is a very cool development in the world of compact power supplies. Externally, it looks like an AA alkaline penlight battery. At the positive end is the USB charging port. When the power is low, simply remove the battery and connect to the USB. Two CR123s are included for power. The 18650 battery is a separate purchase, but it runs the LED lamp three-quarters of an hour longer than do the CR123s, while on high.

The switch is mounted in the tail cap. It's capable of momentary operation with a light touch or can be locked on by fully depressing the switch at any of the operating settings. As the Polytac X comes from the factory, it's set up in an operating pattern of High (600 lumens), Strobe (600 lumens) and Low (35 lumens). But these settings can be changed through Streamlight's Ten Tap programming system. The Polytac X is currently available online for $48.99.

streamlight.com

STREAMLIGHT TLR-7 AND TLR-8 WEAPONLIGHT

I have long been a fan of the Streamlight TLR-1 and especially the TLR-2 HL with its green laser and 800-lumen output. While the TLR-1 is relatively compact, its overall length is 3.39 inches and it weighs 4.18 ounces. Both are

powered by two CR123 lithium cells. While Streamlight has the more compact TLR-3, its body is polymer and the light output is only 125 lumens.

The new TLR-7 and TLR-8 combine the best features of the TLR-1 and TLR-2, with the more compact dimensions of the TLR-3.

STREAMLIGHT POLYTAC X

One of the few true tactical handheld lights with a polymer body, Streamlight's Polytac X puts out a 600-lumen beam and is available with an externally rechargeable battery.

The Streamlight TLR7 and laser-equipped TLR 8 are potent 800-lumen micro-weapon lights that take very little space and are equally at home on rifles, shotguns and handguns.

The TLR-7 and TLR-8 are the new breed of micro-weapon lights. Previously, micro-sized lights meant micro-sized power. The TLR-7 and TLR-8 put out a blistering 500 lumens and throw a light beam 430 feet — from just one CR123. Runtime is 1.5 hours. The TLR-7 and TLR-8 measure only 2.15 inches in length. The TLR-7 weighs only 2.4 ounces, while the TLR-8 with the laser module weighs 2.64 ounces. Each have ambidextrous switching. Pushing the switch just once and holding it turns the light on in momentary mode. A quick press and release keeps the light on; tapping either switch rapidly twice locks the strobe on.

The TLR-7 and TLR-8 beam is a nice, rounded spotlight type with soft edges. It is just right for use on a handgun for room clearing, or when securing perimeter areas outside the home, and its small size makes it easily concealable. MSRP: $109.99.

streamlight.com

SUREFIRE M300C MINI-SCOUT

Surefire is the firm that started the "tactical light revolution" with its compact 6P tactical handheld incandescent light — one of the first I ever saw powered by the equally revolutionary CR123 battery. In addition to handheld lights, Surefire produces a wide range of weapon-mounted lights for both handguns and long guns. One of the newest is the M300C Mini-Scout.

The original Scout, which I tested back in 2009, was an excellent option for mounting on a rail-equipped rifle or shotgun, and is still available as the M600AA Scout light, which has a 200-lumen output. The new M300C is much more compact than the original Scout — 4.10 inches vs. 6.85 inches. That is because the M300C uses only one CR123, rather than two AA cells. Light output of the M300C is 500 lumens, which is more than adequate for a rifle-mounted light. Manufactured from light-weight aerospace aluminum, the M300C weighs in at only 4.1 ounces, which includes the integral built-in mount. The mounting system locks into place via a conveniently sized thumbscrew with diamond pattern knurling.

The circular beam it sends is ideal for close- to mid-range operations. The power switch is in the tail cap and can replaced by a remote pressure switch. The momentary/constant-on power switch operation is simple. A light touch activates the momentary mode. Pushing the switch down to "click" locks the light on. There is no reduced power setting or strobe. Just simple, solid and delivering lifetime tactical performance. MSRP is $299.

surefire.com

setting — pushing down harder activates the 1,200-lumen mode. To switch the light to "constant on," the tail cap switch assembly needs to be rotated clockwise to lock it into place. As you rotate it, first lock on the 5-lumen setting, turning clockwise activates and locks the 1,200 lumen setting in. It takes a fair amount of pressure to activate the momentary switch — therefore no "fence" is needed around the switch to prevent accidental activation while in a pocket, pouch or purse.

The bezel diameter is only 1.125 inches, which means the ECCL2-T slips easily into a front pants pocket. A spring steel clip helps hold it in place. MSRP is $179. **surefire.com**

TERRALUX TT4-EX MAKHAIRA

The Terralux TT4-EX Makhaira is an outstanding handheld (and weapon-mountable) tactical light, which was designed for law enforcement or civilian use in conjunction with the Makhaira (Training) Group.

CNC machined from 6061 T6 aluminum with an intense output of 785 lumens, the TT4-EX Makhaira is more than powerful enough for any low-light task that it is called upon to perform. The TT4-EX Makhaira has one of the most well thought out tail cap power switch setups in the industry — actually, there are two switches on the tail cap. Both switches are protected by a partial "fence" that protects against accidental activation. The tactical main switch button is round and works in both momentary and constant on modes. The second switch is half-moon shaped and is known as the Dedicated Mode Switch (DMS). The DMS acts as the momentary strobe

The Surefire M300C Mini Scout weapon light is greatly improved over the original model, much smaller in size, and with a 500–lumen output. Remote pressure switching is available.

The ECCL2-T uses Surefire's traditional operating switch system. The traditional switch features "momentary on" push-button operation in the tail cap. Since there are two power levels available, pushing down lightly on the momentary push button activates the 5-lumen

SUREFIRE EDCL (EVERYDAY CARRY LIGHT) 2-T HANDHELD

The Everyday Carry concept refers to critical gear that is compact, lightweight and effective, and will be on your person every time you leave your home — no matter the occasion. The Surefire EDCL2-T is an ultra-bright, ultra-compact handheld designed to be added to your everyday carry kit. Powered by two CR123 batteries, the aerospace aluminum, mil-spec hard anodized ECCL2-T puts out a rather incredible 1,200 lumens of lighting power on its full power setting, while its low power setting cranks out 5 lumens. It is the most compact light of this intensity I have ever handled.

SUREFIRE EDCL-2T

The Surefire EDCL-2T is one of the most compact and powerful "Everyday Carry" pocket-sized tactical handheld lights available. Output is an amazing 1,200 lumens.

The Terralux TT4 is a compact 785-lumen powerhouse ideal for EDC or duty use. A separate strobe switch and rotating finger stop for "syringe grip" make it a standout.

switch when the main switch is off and controls the intensity of light when the light is locked in the "on" position, cycling progressively through high (785 Lumens), medium (200 lumens) and low (10 lumens) settings. Pressing and holding the DMS while the TT4-EX is locked on activates the strobe but does not lock it on.

The TT4-EX Makhaira features a rotating finger stop for a syringe grip that has a hole to attach the included lanyard. There is a removable crenelated bezel for defensive strikes and a movable pocket clip. A remote tail cap switch is available for weapon mounting. The TT4-EX Makhaira is priced at $89.99.

lightstarproducts.com

TUFF PRODUCTS T2 AND T180 COMPACT EDC (EVERYDAY CARRY) LIGHTS

TUFF makes two very useful EDC lights that are versatile and powerful, yet small enough so that there is never an excuse not to have one with you. Technically three power sources can be used with both lights: AA penlight, AA rechargeable penlight, and CR123 lithium cells. Only one cell is needed for power.

Both the T2 and T180 come equipped with a threaded sleeve that increases the overall length of the lights to accommodate the longer AA power cell. The T2 flashlight is the more compact of the two, with an overall length of 3.75 inches with a CR123 cell, and 4.25 inches with a AA cell, while the T180 is 3.75 inches long with the CR123 and 4.5 inches long with the AA. Light output with the CR123 is 130 lumens — with an AA cell in place, the output drops to 85 lumens.

The T180 has a 180-degree rotating head. Thus it can be used as a linear or angle headlight by loosening an Allen screw and moving the light head to the desired position. Light output of the T180 is 170 lumens with a CR123 or 120 lumens with an AA cell.

These lights are very small when using CR123s. I have found that I prefer using AA cells with both as it gives me the best control in my hands. One AA and one CR123 are included. MSRP of the T2 is $59.99, while the T180 is $69.99. **TGD**

tuffproducts.com

The Tuff T180 is a micro-handheld utility light with a full 180 lumens of tactical power. The adjustable lighting head can be angled by the user for increased utility.

AFFORDABLE
1,000-YARD TACTICAL
RIFLES

The Rise Armament 1121XR features precision-machined 7075 aluminum billet receivers, a Magpul PRS stock and a smooth Cerakote finish.

THESE LONG-RANGE RIFLES WILL GET THE JOB DONE AND WON'T BREAK THE BANK

BY **TODD WOODARD**

Today's shooters like to go long — that is, they enjoy the challenge of reaching out and touching targets at advanced ranges. Sometimes, the capability of firing accurately at 600-plus yards costs a lot of money, and sometimes it costs less. But the basics of enjoyable long-distance riflery don't change: A good, straight barrel sitting in front of a durable, precise action, and a good trigger. Here are a few rifles that contain those basic elements and more, with the "more" meaning those extra dollars that bring bling to the targets you seek to ring.

BERGARA PREMIER HMR PRO

The Premier Series from Bergara has Custom Series features that are standardized for greater efficiencies in parts production and assembly. The Premier Pro upgrades the 2017 HMR (Hunting and Match Rifle) line, including a Cerakote stainless steel action and barrel with a threaded muzzle and a TriggerTech primary trigger. All Premier Series rifles are capable of producing sub-MOA accuracy with quality factory match-grade ammunition. Weights range from 9.2 to 9.7 pounds, and the line is available in .223 Remington with a 1:8 twist, .22-250 Remington with a 1:9 twist, 6mm and 6.5mm Creedmoor with a 1:8 twist, and .308 Winchester with a 1:10 twist. All the chamberings above have 5/8x24-inch threaded barrels.

(above) The Bergara HMR Pro's injection-molded stock includes a full-length integrated mini-chassis system. Bergara's Premium 416 stainless steel barrels receive a proprietary honing process at the company's barrel making facility in Bergara, Spain. Then, once in the U.S. factory, the barrel receives a Cerakote finish and is coupled with a proprietary Bergara Premier action, with a nonrotating gas shield, coned bolt nose and sliding plate extractor.

(left) From top, the Bergara Premier HMR Pro rifles include 5/8x24-in. threaded muzzles with knurled thread protector; 5-round AICS-style detachable magazines; drilled and tapped receiver that accepts Remington 700 bases with 8x40 screws; a full-length integrated mini-chassis; and a rear buttstock with adjustable cheek piece and length-of-pull panels.

SPECIFICATIONS

MODEL:	Bergara Premier HMR Pro
WEIGHT:	9.2 lbs. (.22-250 Rem.), 9.4 lbs. (.223 Rem., .308 Win., 450 BM), 9.6 lbs. (6.5 CM), 9.7 lbs. (6mm CM)
OVERALL LENGTH:	39.5 in. (.223 Rem., .308 Win.), 43.5 in. (6.5 CM, .22-250 Rem.), 45.5 in. (6mm CM)
BARREL LENGTH:	20 in. (.223 Rem., .308 Win.), 24 in. (6.5 CM, .22-250 Rem.), 26 in. (6mm CM)
MAGAZINE:	AICS-style detachable
MAG CAPACITY:	5-round mag
TRIGGER:	TriggerTech Frictionless Release Technology
BARREL TAPER:	No. 5.5
MUZZLE:	Threaded 5/8x24 in. with knurled thread protector
STOCK:	Bergara HMR molded with mini-chassis
SCOPE MOUNT:	Remington 700 bases with 8x40 screws. Integrated QD flush cup sling mounts and swivel mounts
REAR BUTTSTOCK:	Adjustable cheek piece and length-of-pull. Full-length integrated mini-chassis for repeatable bedding and supports fully free- floated barrel

This action has a two-lug system that features a separate floating bolt head to ensure contact with the lug abutments in the action. It features a cone-shaped bolt nose for smooth feeding of the cartridge, and a spring-loaded sliding plate extractor located in the front of the lower locking lug. The one-piece bolt body is stainless steel with a pad at the rear to accept the threaded-in bolt handle. The HMR Pro offers fully free-floated barrels in 20-, 24- and 26-inch lengths.

The stock on the Bergara Premier HMR Pro has an integrated mini-chassis for repeatable bedding. Suggested retail is $1,715.

BROWNING

In men's clothing, a custom suit is individually hand-fit to the customer, a la John Wick's Italian-cut day and dinner suits with "tactical" carbon-fiber lining, as depicted in *John Wick II.* Of course, these cost top dollar. "Semi-custom" in men's suits means that some components, such as the basic cut, fabrics, and liners, are standard across several styles, so they cost about half or less of what a custom suit commands.

The same's true with Browning's new X-Bolt Pro and X-Bolt Pro Long Range rifles. By the manufacturer's description, they are "semi-custom rifles" with specialized finishing touches and higher-end

construction than the X-Bolt family of hunting rifles. An example is the rifles' carbon-fiber stock, which is lightweight and rigid, sports a palm swell and Inflex recoil pad, and is filled with a noise-dampening foam. Barrels and receivers are stainless steel-coated in Cerakote burnt bronze. The Cerakote finish on the action and barrel is also on the exterior of the stock for added protection, and the Cerakote's burnt-bronze hue tones down the color of the stock for better concealability. The barrel features a new proprietary lapping process to provide consistent accuracy and easier bore cleaning. Other features include a spiral-fluted bolt, enlarged bolt handle, and

rotary magazine feeds the action. The trigger is the adjustable feather model with a top-tang safety. Of course, sling swivel studs allow for easy attachment of a bipod. Suggested retail prices start at $2,070 for the X-Bolt Pro and $2,100 for the X-Bolt Pro Long Range.

A little more spendy (suggested retail starts at $2,130) is the X-Bolt Hell's Canyon Long Range rifle, which features a McMillan Game Scout stock with aluminum pillars, a vertical pistol grip, and a medium-width fore-end. Like the Pro and the Pro Long Range models, it has a Cerakote burnt bronze finish on the metalwork, while the stock sports an A-TACS AU Camo, Dura-Touch Armor Coat finish. Its tube is a 26-inch fluted, free-floating, hand-chambered barrel with a muzzle brake. A 20-MOA Picatinny rail is standard. Available in 6mm Creedmoor, 6.5 Creedmoor, .300 WSM, .26 Nosler, 7mm Remington Magnum, .28 Nosler, and .300 Winchester Magnum.

The X-Bolt Pro, Pro Long Range, and Hell's Canyon Long Range rifles from Browning employ carbon-fiber stocks finished with Inflex recoil pads and are filled with noise-dampening foam. The Cerakote burnt bronze finish on the action and barrel is carried over to the exterior of the stock for added protection and concealability.

threaded muzzle with a muzzle brake or thread protector cap.

Rifles are hand-chambered and come standard with a target crown and threaded muzzle. Barrels are either 22 or 26 inches in length in 6mm Creedmoor, 6.5 Creedmoor, .308 Winchester, .300 WSM, 26 Nosler, .270 Winchester, .30/06 Springfield, 7mm Remington Magnum, 28 Nosler, and .300 Winchester Magnum, or 23 inches in .300 WSM.

The stainless steel receiver is glass bedded into the stock, and on top it's drilled and tapped for X-Lock scope mounts. The stainless steel barrel on the Pro Long Range has a heavy sporter contour and a threaded muzzle brake, with thread protector in case you want to remove the brake. At the tip is a target-style crown. The bolt action features a 60-degree bolt lift, and a detachable

Pro Long Range rifles have 22-, 23-, or 26-inch barrels and are chambered in 6mm Creedmoor, 6.5 Creedmoor, .308 Winchester, .300 WSM, .26 Nosler, .270 Winchester, .30/06 Springfield, 7mm Remington Magnum, .28 Nosler, and .300 Winchester Magnum.

The X-Bolt Hell's Canyon Long Range rifle features a McMillan Game Scout stock, 26-inch, fluted, free-floating and hand-chambered barrel with a muzzle brake, and an A-TACS AU Camo, Dura-Touch Armor Coat finish stock. The 20-MOA rail provides additional long-range sighting options.

CMMG MKW ANVIL XLR2

The all-new MkW ANVIL XLR2 from CMMG is chambered in 6.5 Grendel and fitted with a 22-inch medium-taper barrel, producing enough energy to take out varmints and other critters at distances out to 800 yards. Since its introduction in 2004, the 6.5 Grendel has proven to be an effective round for long-range shooting in both hunting and tactical situations. Bullet weights range from 90 to 130 grains.

The rifle also includes a Geissele Automatics SSA two-stage trigger, ambidextrous CMMG charging handle and safety selector, a CMMG SV Muzzle Brake, and RML15 MLOK handguard. Furniture is a Magpul Moe pistol grip and PRS stock.

According to Chris Reinkemeyer, CEO of CMMG, "The 6.5 Grendel is a great round. It has minimal recoil and is also flat shooting out to 500 yards and beyond. It's great for hunting medium-sized game such as deer and pigs, and best of all, you can find ammo for it that is relatively inexpensive. In building the ANVIL XLR2 with a 22-inch barrel, along with some of our other finest components, we designed this rifle to help shooters achieve the best possible results with this caliber."

A defining feature of the Anvil is CMMG's Powerbolt design, which allows the rifle to utilize a modified AR-10-sized bolt for increased durability. This is important because large-diameter cartridges such as 6.5 Grendel would require material to be milled out of a standard AR15-sized bolt to function.

The MkW Anvil is built on an AR-10-sized frame with the upper receiver shortened by three-quarters of an inch to minimize weight and increase ergonomics. Although the frame is based on the AR-10 platform, the mag well on the lower receiver has been designed to accept standard AR-15 magazines. This allows the rifle to utilize the durable AR-10-sized bolt with calibers such as 6.5 Grendel, which have a case diameter larger than 5.56 NATO.

For those who already own a CMMG MkW Anvil in .458 SOCOM, CMMG will also offer 6.5 Grendel upper-receiver groups compatible with any MkW Anvil lower.

SPECIFICATIONS

MODEL:	CMMG MkW ANVIL XLR2
CALIBER:	6.5 Grendel
BARREL:	22 in., 1:8 Twist, medium taper, 416SS SBN
MUZZLE:	CMMG SV Muzzle Brake, Threaded 5/8x24
HANDGUARD:	CMMG RKM15 KeyMod
UPPER RECEIVER:	Billet 7075-T6 AL Mid-Size
LOWER RECEIVER:	Billet 7075-T6 AL Mid-Size
TRIGGER:	Geissele SSA Two-Stage Trigger
FURNITURE:	Magpul MOE pistol grip and PRS Stock, CMMG's ambidextrous charging handle and safety selector
GAS PORT LOCATION:	Rifle length
WEIGHT:	10.5 lbs. (Unloaded)
LENGTH:	43 in. (Stock collapsed)
MSRP:	$2,300

SHAW RIFLES MARK X BOLT-ACTION RIFLE

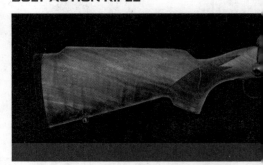

America's largest independent manufacturer of gun barrels is now offering the new Mark X Bolt Action, a custom, made-to-order rifle. You can order online and choose between barrel lengths from 16.25 to 26 inches. You can also select one of 90 chamberings in calibers from .17 through .458. The Savage AccuTrigger is standard, but a Timney is an option.

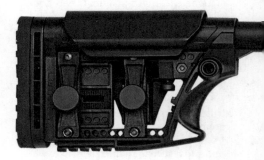

MOSSBERG MVP PRECISION TACTICAL BOLT RIFLE

Mossberg's MVP Precision is a tactical bolt rifle with an all-new chassis and a Luth-AR MBA-3 adjustable stock. The long-range tactical platform is chambered in 6.5mm Creedmoor and 7.62mm NATO (308 Win).

Major elements of the MVP Precision include:

• Mossberg-designed aluminum chassis and slim-profile handguard

• Luth-AR MBA-3 adjustable stock

• Magpul MOE+ grip

• Mag well accepts both M1A/M14 and AR-10/SR25-style magazines

Constructed of lightweight aluminum with an anodized finish, the Mossberg

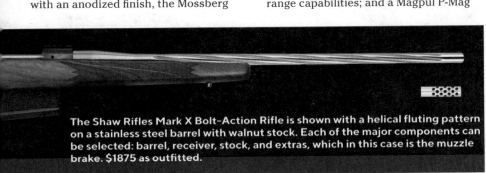

The Shaw Rifles Mark X Bolt-Action Rifle is shown with a helical fluting pattern on a stainless steel barrel with walnut stock. Each of the major components can be selected: barrel, receiver, stock, and extras, which in this case is the muzzle brake. $1875 as outfitted.

chassis provides a solid base for repeatable accuracy. The slim-profile, matte blue-finished aluminum handguard features Magpul's M-LOK modular mounting system for easy attachment of compatible accessories. The free-floating medium bull barrel is threaded 5/8x24 TPI to attach suppressors or muzzle brakes. A thread cap is included.

The button-rifled barrel is constructed of 4140 carbon steel with 5R rifling (6.5mm Creedmoor only). The MVP Precision rifle has a 24-inch barrel with 1:8 twist rate for the 6.5mm Creedmoor and 20-inch barrel length and 1:10 twist rate for the 7.62mm NATO (.308 Win.) chambering. Both barrel and receiver feature a matte blue finish as well.

Mossberg's Lightning Bolt Action (LBA) Trigger System is adjustable from 3 to 7 pounds by the user. It's machined from aircraft-grade aluminum and hard-coat anodized to military spec, preventing corrosion and minimizing wear. Additional design features include an oversized tactical-style bolt handle; oversized trigger guard; 20-MOA Picatinny top rail for maximizing long-range capabilities; and a Magpul P-Mag 10-round magazine.

The MOE+ grip is constructed of reinforced polymer and features a wrap-around rubber overmolding for control. The MOE+ grip accepts optional Storage Cores for gear stowage and includes a basic grip cap. The Luth-AR MBA-3 carbine buttstock has a fully-adjustable, 6-position design (12.5- to 16.5-inch LOP

range). Features include additional cheek height adjustment up to 1 inch; 3-axis buttplate, which provides for 1 1/16-inch length-of-pull adjustment as well as vertical and lateral adjustments to fit the curvature of your shoulder and adjustment for right or left cast.

On the bottom rear of the stock body is a Picatinny rail to attach accessories. An index screw allows you to secure the stock in your favorite position. Other niceties include a soft rubber recoil pad and the ability to easily remove the stock via a screw attachment for ease of transporting or storing the rifle in a compact case.

REMINGTON 700 MDT TACTICAL CHASSIS RIFLE

The new Remington 700 MDT Tactical Chassis rifle, utilizing a Modular Driven Technologies, Inc. chassis, is available with a 24- or 26-inch barrel and is chambered for .308 Winchester (84474), .300 Winchester Magnum (84475) or .338 Lapua Magnum (84477). It has a stainless steel-barreled action, Magpul MAG307 PRS adjustable stock, oversize bolt handle, AAC muzzle brake and ships in a hard case. Counter prices are around $2,550.

RISE ARMAMENT 1121XR RIFLE

The Rise Armament 1121XR rifle in .308 Winchester was designed for shooters seeking more out of a heavy-caliber, gas-driven gun. The button-rifled 20-inch 416R stainless steel barrel is air-gauged and tested, has a 1:11.25-inch twist, and is free-floated for guaranteed sub-MOA accuracy. The 15-inch slim, streamlined billet aluminum handguard is MLOK-

Mossberg's MVP Precision tactical rifle sports an all-new chassis and a Luth-AR MBA-3 adjustable stock.

compatible with a Picatinny upper rail system. The RA-535 Advanced-Performance Trigger has a 3.5-pound single-stage pull with no overtravel and a short reset for fast follow-up shots. It features precision-machined 7075 aluminum billet receivers, a Magpul PRS stock, and a smooth Cerakote finish. It weighs 9.5 pounds and ships in a hard case with two magazines. Available in three standard color schemes — black, foliage green, or flat dark earth (FDE). Retail price: $2,449 at RiseArmament.com.

SAVAGE

The Savage Model 110 Model 110 Big Game and Specialty series has received a full complement of new and improved features addressing fit, trigger pull and bedding. The all-new user-adjustable AccuFit system/stock allows you to customize length of pull and comb height. Inserts included with the rifle can be installed in seconds with a Phillips screwdriver. The new AccuStock also has a rigid chassis embedded in the stock. The standard adjustable AccuTrigger allows out-of-the-stock adjustment down to 2.5 pounds. To look at one model in

The "MDT" in the name of Remington's new M700 Tactical Chassis stands for Modular Driven Technologies, a supplier of chassis for several manufacturers. Other features include an X-Mark Pro externally user-adjustable trigger and a Magpul MAG307 PRS adjustable stock.

The Steyr Pro THB has a cold-hammer-forged, 16-, 20-, or 26-inch threaded heavy barrel chambered in .308 Winchester, finished in a durable Mannox coating. Suggested retail price is $1,265.

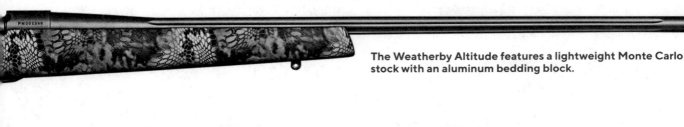

The Weatherby Altitude features a lightweight Monte Carlo stock with an aluminum bedding block.

The Weatherby KCR has a Krieger 26-inch, No. 3 contour custom barrel, which is cut rifled and expertly hand-lapped from cryogenically relieved steel.

more detail, the Savage 110 Long Range Hunter comes with a 26-inch barrel and is chambered for the 6.5 Creedmoor, .260 Remington, .308 Winchester, .300 WSM, .338 Federal, 6.5x284 Norma, 7mm Remington Magnum, .300 Winchester Magnum and .338 Lapua Magnum. Suggested retails start at $1,099.

The 10/110 Stealth Evolution chassis rifle is chambered for six distance-delivering cartridges, including the 6mm Creedmoor. The rifle blends pinpoint precision with torture-tested toughness, and pairs a heavy fluted barrel, blueprinted 10/110 action, 5R rifling, and an AccuTrigger, with a monolithic aluminum chassis finished in rugged bronze Cerakote. It starts with a suggested retail of $1,800.

STEYR PRO TACTICAL HEAVY BARREL .308 WINCHESTER

The Pro THB (Tactical Heavy Barrel) is a complement to Steyr's traditional platforms. The Pro THB's heavy barrel is available in 16-, 20-, or 26-inch lengths with 5/8x24 right-hand muzzle threads topped with a Mannox finish. A tactical bolt knob fits your hand well, and the receiver is topped with a 20-MOA Picatinny rail for built-in elevation when your optic lacks enough up-ticks. It has a durable synthetic stock with removable spacers in the buttstock to adjust length of pull.

The Pro THB likewise includes the Safe Bolt System (SBS), which offers three safety settings operated by a wheel switch on the tang. The Fire mode is indicated by a red dot; the first level of Safe mode disables the firing mechanism, while the second level locks the bolt down against the stock.

WEATHERBY MARK V KCR AND MARK V ALTITUDE

If you're willing to climb the price scale, the Mark V KCR features a Krieger 26-inch, No. 3 contour custom barrel, which is cut rifled and expertly hand-lapped from cryogenically-relieved steel. Of course, it carries the Sub-MOA accuracy guarantee of shooting three-shot groups smaller than 0.99 inch at 100 yards when used with Weatherby factory or premium ammunition. The stock itself has a slimmer forearm and the grip diameter has been reduced. There's also a slight right-hand palm swell on the hand-laminated, raised-comb Monte Carlo composite stock. Inside is an aluminum bedding block.

Chamberings include the Weatherby Magnum cartridges in .257, 6.5-300, .300, and .30-378 sizes. The rifle includes an Accubrake to reduce felt recoil by up to 50 percent. A LXX trigger, oversize bolt knob, composite Monte Carlo stock, and flat dark earth and graphite black Cerakote finish round out the features on this rifle.

In addition to the Weatherby magnums, the new Altitude is available in 6.5 Creedmoor, .270 Winchester, .308 Winchester and .30/06 Springfield. So, what makes it special? It weighs 5.75 pounds with the six-lug action, 6.75 pounds with the nine-lug magnum version. That's due to a lightweight Monte Carlo stock with an aluminum bedding block. Other features include a fluted stainless steel barrel, Kryptek Altitude camo and a Tungsten Cerakote finish. **TGD**

Todd Woodard is editor of Gun Tests magazine, Cartridges of the World, 16th Edition, *and a contributor to numerous firearms publications.*

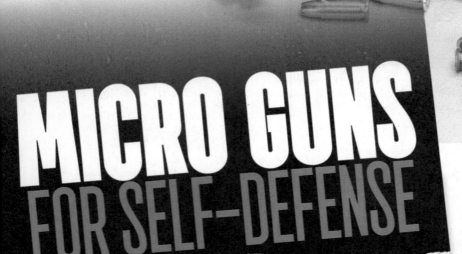

MICRO GUNS FOR SELF-DEFENSE

The .25 ACP is ultra-compact, but also ultra-unpowerful. Yes, it can kill, and no, I wouldn't want to be shot with one. But that doesn't make it a good choice for a defensive caliber.

Small-caliber handguns are attractive for everyday carry, but will they pass muster when needed?

BY **PATRICK SWEENEY**

The .22 LR bullet (left), compared to a .32 and a .380 JHP. This is not the Hammer of Thor, so don't expect miracles.

The subject of a .22, .22 magnum or .25 Auto for defense is controversial. They are not stoppers, period, end of story. However, they are still lethal weapons. The reason they exist is twofold: compactness and low recoil. The smallest handgun to be had is an ultra-compact .22 LR, or a .25 Auto. The lowest-recoiling handgun

you can shoot is a standard-sized pistol chambered in .22 LR, like one of the smaller-sized Ruger Mk I, II, III or IV.

The .25 ACP/auto is not much different from the .22 LR, with the exception that the bullet, almost always a full metal jacket, can be counted on to feed more reliably than the lead-bullet .22 LR. But, that can also be a matter of maintenance

(a lint-choked pistol isn't going to feed anything reliably) and handling.

.25 ACP

I will just pass right over the .25. Despite the compactness of some of the pistols that use it, it offers nothing the .22 LR doesn't, ballistically, and does so at greater cost, less availability, and fewer options for pistol choices.

The .22 LR will sometimes expand, and sometimes not. The bullet on the left is a hollow point, and you can see how much (not) it expanded. The middle one is a regular round–nose, and the loaded cartridge is to the right. The big advantage is the low cost.

.22 LR

The standard .22 LR offers only a straight, bullet-diameter permanent wound, with a depth of 14-15 inches. There may be some expansion with hollowpoint bullets, but that comes at the expense of a couple of inches of penetration. Also, some bullets may yaw and end up stopping base-first in the wound track. When traveling sideways, it does create a marginally larger permanent wound than a simple cylinder, but hardly something to boast about.

The .22 LR is not a big stick when it comes to defense, but it is better than a knife or a club. Especially for someone who can't handle heavier recoil.

The trick to its use in defense is to realize two points. First, you will have to depend on more than one shot. In fact,

(left) You can see the loaded .22 LR, scaled up to the size of a mortar round.

(above) The priming compound in a .22 LR is in the rim. This makes it inexpensive to manufacture, but complicates magazine design for feeding.

the standard response when shooting in defense with a .22 LR should be to empty the magazine and immediately reload. Second, placement matters. The hits have to be high center of mass or else the effort is wasted.

This combination of needs does not make the .22 LR a high-percentage option, even in the handgun realm. But, for those with no other choice, there is no other choice.

.22 MAGNUM

Stepping up, you have the .22 Magnum, which is a longer case than the .22 LR and designed to contain the bullet inside the case. The jacketed bullet offers the promise of expansion, but not always the realization. You see, a .22 Magnum out of a rifle generates plenty of velocity. Out of a handgun, it is often no faster (or not enough faster to matter) than a .22 LR.

The expansion of any of these bullets is not a reliable outcome. Even if they do expand, the degree is not great. An expanding .22 LR, all 40 grains of it, could bump up to .27-inch in diameter.

Hornady has lead the way here, offering a defensive-use .22 Magnum loading,

(right) The .22 Magnum offers a better bullet at higher velocity, but at more cost and noise. (Recoil is still pretty minimal.)

No, this is not the pistol to be carrying daily, concealed. But, if it's the only pistol you have and you are at home, this will be your tool. Learn to shoot, learn the law, and learn to stay calm. The police are coming, but you have to deal with your problem until they arrive.

(right) The Kel-Tec PMR-30 may not look like the Hammer of Thor, but it is soft in recoil, it holds 30 rounds of .22 WMR, and a spare magazine gives you another 30 in a couple of seconds. 30 or 60 rounds of .22 WMR is very comforting, for those who find recoil hard to deal with.

(below) The 5.7, next to a .22 Magnum, and on the left, a .22 LR.

expect a good outcome. Part of that is the improved performance of the .22 Magnum over the .22 LR, and the other is capacity. A standard .22 LR pistol has a 10-round magazine. The PMR-30 magazine holds 30 rounds.

Nine to ten inches isn't FBI-passing performance, but it also doesn't offer anything like the recoil of an FBI-compliant load. This is part of the compromise.

5.7X28 FN

The outlier here is the FN 5.7x28 cartridge. This centerfire cartridge uses a jacketed bullet, longer than a .22 LR or .22 Magnum. Out of the firearms for which it was intended it works reasonably well. That is, out of an SMG-sized firearm like the P90, with a 10.4-inch barrel, it can generate enough velocity to work. The PS90, with its 16.1-inch barrel, really delivers the goods, but that isn't a handgun. Put into a handgun, it comes in a bit ahead of the .22 Magnum in velocity.

There is not a lot of data for the 5.7. It has been adopted by some law enforcement agencies, and has been used in shootings by them. Getting

with a bullet designed to expand at velocities the .22 Magnum can deliver. Called their Critical Defense, it gives 9-10 inches of penetration in ballistic gelatin out of a handgun.

Speer also makes their Gold Dot line of ammunition in the .22 Magnum. If you want as much performance as you can get, in a pistol that isn't going to kick much, then the .22 Magnum can be a good choice.

Combined with a handgun such as the Kel-Tec PMR-30, someone who can't handle a larger caliber can reasonably

information out of those sources is difficult. The only one we have that offers a reasonable data set is the shooting at Fort Hood. There, Major Nidal Hasan fatally shot 13 people and wounded 32 more. He used an FN FiveseveN pistol and two ammo types: the FN SS192 and SS197SR. The SS192 is (or was, FN stopped making it in 2004) a jacketed hollowpoint with an aluminum core. Not much expansion, and not armor-piercing. The SS197SR is loaded with the Hornady V-max bullet, using a blue polymer tip to indicate a slightly higher velocity than the SS196SR.

The ability of the rounds to stop fights was out of proportion from what

The FN FiveseveN pistol holds 20 (or 30) rounds of 5.7 ammunition. It is a bit larger in the grip than .22 LR and .22 Magnum pistols would be, so if that matters, be sure and test before you buy.

There are a lot of loadings for the 5.7x28. Make sure which you have so you are using the right ammo.

one would expect with such a small cartridge. Three of the victims valiantly charged the shooter, attempting to stop him. They were shot for their efforts, were stopped and subsequently died. They charged from close range (the incident happened indoors, so there were not long distances to cover) and yet failed to close the distance due to the gunshot received.

Those wounded with hits to the extremities were unable, in many instances, to flee or fight, due to broken bones. When a "mere" .22 handgun cartridge can break a femur, there's something going on that must be explained. That shot was received by one of the first responders, an in-base civilian security person. She took a hit to her wrist which made that arm unable to function, and a hit to the upper leg that broke her femur.

The drawback to the FiveseveN approach to low-recoil defense is cost. A FiveseveN lists for around $1,180, compared to the Kel-Tec PMR-30 at $455. The FN pistol holds 20 rounds (optional extensions make it a 30-round magazine) compared to the Kel-Tec at 30 rounds standard. An FN magazine is $35, with the extension costing another $18-20, while the Kel-Tec is $31.

5.7x28 ammunition costs (at the moment) $28 per box of 50 rounds, while .22 Magnum can be had for as little as $10 per box of 50 practice FMJs, up to $15 for a box of Hornady Critical Defense.

The last hurdle for the 5.7 is size.

The grip is a bit larger than that of the Kel-Tec, and even if the recoil is mild, if you (or the person you are coaching in this situation) can't get a hand or hands around it, it isn't a good choice.

RECOMMENDATIONS

If you already have a .22 LR pistol and need it for defense, then use the most accurate, readily available .22 LR ammunition to be found. Practice getting as many hits out of a full magazine, on a playing-card-sized target at 7 yards, as quickly as you can. Volume and accuracy need to be your focus here.

A better choice would be either Hornady Critical Defense or Speer Gold Dot in .22 Magnum in the Kel-Tec. The PMR-30 isn't going to cost much, if anything, more than a good .22 LR pistol. Use whichever of these two loads shoots reliably and accurately out of your Kel-Tec. As with the .22 LR, practice hitting a playing card at 7 yards, as quickly as possible, and train yourself to keep shooting on the target until it (he, she, they) goes down.

If you have the hands and the budget, but not the recoil resistance, for something bigger in caliber, then go for the FN FiveseveN in 5.7x28, the 40-grain FMJ. The V-Max is accurate, but is designed as a varmint-level bullet. I'd be much more confident with an FMJ in this situation, than with a readily-expanding bullet of only 40 grains.

While the effect is likely to be better

than the .22 LR or the .22 Magnum, the process should be the same: playing card accuracy, 7 yards, continuous fire until the bad guy goes down.

CAVEATS

There will be those who want to throw me under the bus for recommending the various .22s for defense. I have attempted to be clear: a rimfire is better than anything not a firearm; and for those who cannot handle more recoil, this is perhaps the only choice. I would rather someone who needs a firearm for defense has a weak one than none at all, as long as they realize the limitations of the tool they are using.

There are no .25s I can recommend. For the cost, you can easily acquire .22 LR or .22 Magnum ammo that will perform better. And since you have to depend on volume and speed of fire, the ultra-compact .25s are poor choices, as clever as some of the designs might be. **TGD**

This article is an excerpt from Choosing Handgun Ammo: The Facts That Matter Most for Self-Defense, *available at gundigeststore.com.*

BA

Even rifles designed more for competition, like this Armalite M-15 3-Gun, are well suited for survival use.

TITLE
RIFLES!

From AR-15s to big-Bore AR-10s, these battle-tested guns are built for survival BY **JORGE AMSELLE**

When it comes to survival guns, the rifle is man's best friend. If you need to reach out and make contact, there is no better choice. It is accurate and powerful like no other weapon. At close ranges, it allows you to make a precision shot. At long distances, it can keep bad guys away or take down game animals. The rifle allows you to handle more powerful cartridges with comfort and ease. If I could only own one gun, it would be a rifle.

AR-15: THE ULTIMATE SURVIVAL GUN?

When it comes to survival, the best choice is a rifle that combines power, speed, accuracy, capacity and reliability, ease of use, versatility, accessories, and light weight. To me, there is only one choice: the AR rifle. Its popularity ensures the availability of plenty of spare parts for repairs. Its modularity makes it easy to repair and work on. This modularity allows the versatility to change barrels and cartridges within a certain range.

SURVIVAL SNAPSHOT: RIFLES

PROS: Mid- to long-range accuracy, powerful cartridges, larger magazine capacity.

CONS: Limited use in very confined spaces, weight, recoil.

AMMO TO STOCKPILE: Min. 10,000 rounds.

AUTHOR'S TOP PICK: Any quality Mil-Spec AR Carbine in .223/5.56. **MSRP:** $599-$1,200

SPARE PARTS TO STOCK: Magazines, spring and pin kit, stock, handguards.

REQUIRED ACCESSORIES: Red-dot sight and/or scope, sling, magazine pouches, cleaning kit.

OPTIONAL ACCESSORIES: Bipod, lights, laser.

The AR is the single most versatile rifle available. It can be adapted to fire over a dozen different rifle and pistol calibers. The design makes it easy to install optics and scopes; the collapsible stock allows the length to be adjusted so different-stature shooters can comfortably use the same rifle. All of these features help explain why it is so popular.

The AR serves primarily for self-defense, used to quickly and accurately engage multiple assailants should the need arise. You could certainly use other rifles for such tasks, and I will recommend many, but the AR stands above them all. It is true that the AR may not be the best firearm to use in all defensive situations. Sometimes a shotgun or a pistol will be better suited for specific jobs.

The AR is traditionally chambered in the 5.56x45mm NATO (interchangeable with the .223 Remington caliber) cartridge. Some have questioned the effectiveness of this cartridge, but the U.S. Military has been using this round as their primary rifle caliber for 60 years, through many wars and other interventions. If it were not effective, we would not still have it. As with any firearm, the weight and type of bullet can be easily changed to deliver better performance, and while not all loadings may be ideal for hunting, many are used effectively on deer, feral hogs, coyote, and other game animals.

Some have argued that a 5.56mm AR is bad for home defense because the round will over penetrate and pass through walls, endangering other occupants or neighbors. Yet Police SWAT teams are increasingly switching from 9mm submachine guns to 5.56mm ARs exactly because they penetrate less than the 9mm, especially with proper ammunition selection.

The AR is extremely weather resistant and was designed that way from the start for military use. The receiver is aluminum, the stock polymer, the barrel and bolt carrier chrome lined and phosphate finished. The rifle is not completely rust or corrosion resistant, but it is almost as close as it gets. It was designed to be lightweight at about 6.5 lbs. The carbine version is very compact and can be easily broken down into two parts for ease of transport.

When it comes to parts and accessories, manufacturers are busy producing almost anything you can imagine. It is very easy to take a 6.5-lb. AR carbine and turn it into a futuristic 11-lb. powerhouse. There are many AR manufacturers, and most of their guns are built to Mil-Spec, meaning that they have complete parts interchangeability. I will include a few full reviews below, but first I'll give a round-up of some of the popular AR manufacturers.

Note: When it comes to survival, don't try to get fancy. Many ARs are sold specifically for competition, varmint hunting, in odd calibers, or with non-standard features to appeal to select shooters. That is not what you want. You want the standard Mil-Spec AR carbine. Keep it simple. When it comes to accessories, add only what you think you really need and will actually use. Special coatings or treatments are fine and even the use of custom drop-in trigger kits is OK, as these can be easily replaced with Mil-Spec trigger kits.

The author believes the AR is the single most versatile and practical survival rifle there is, and there are many excellent models like the BCM HSP Jack Carbine here.

AR-15 REVIEWS: A LOOK AT THE BEST SURVIVAL GUN MODELS

DPMS TAC2 AR CARBINE

With the huge and growing interest in AR rifles among competitors, hunters, and recreational shooters — yes, even survival — DPMS offers an incredibly varied catalog of options to satisfy most every AR-related desire. In the competition/tactical/recreation category, they recently introduced the TAC2 carbine, which offers many unique and welcome features.

The DPMS TAC2 is a semi-automatic AR carbine chambered for 5.56 NATO with a traditional direct gas impingement system. And it is this gas system that represents its most distinct feature. Unlike most carbines, the TAC2 has a rifle-length gas system that places the front of the gas tube only about three inches from the muzzle on the 16-inch barrel.

As the bullet passes the gas hole, excess gas is diverted back down the gas tube to put pressure on the gas key and operate the bolt, thus cycling the action. Too little gas and the action will not cycle properly, resulting in short stroking and misfeeds — or failures to eject. Too much gas and the recoil signature is increased, and you end up with more fouling and heat in the receiver, plus more wear and tear on the internal parts. The longer that the bullet is in the barrel after it passes the gas hole, the more gas is pushed back through the gas tube and back into the gas key. This is called dwell time. By lengthening the gas system and shortening the barrel, the dwell time is greatly reduced. While it is still properly timed and sufficient to reliably operate the TAC2, it is shortened to the point that the recoil signature is a much softer push. Of course, less recoil means it is easier to keep the rifle on target for faster follow-up shots, which can be very important in survival situations.

This rifle-length gas system is surrounded by the DPMS M111 modular handguard system. This one-piece aluminum handguard is free floated, so there is no contact with the barrel, and it features a full length of Picatinny rail on top that meets up with the flattop upper receiver for more than 18 inches of uninterrupted rail. This much rail space makes for the easy installation of more advanced optics, including night vision and thermal extenders as well as

The DPMS TAC2 is a semi-automatic AR carbine chambered for 5.56 NATO with a traditional direct gas impingement system. What's unique is its rifle-length gas system.

top-mounted laser units.

The modular handguard has a rounded and fairly smooth profile for comfort, and it provides multiple rail attachment locations at 45-degree angles all around, making it a simple matter to add rail extensions where you need them while leaving the rest of the handguard bare. Plus, it comes standard with one 4-inch rail section under and two shorter rails at the 6 and 9 o'clock positions for mounting lights, lasers, or a bipod.

A free-floated handguard avoids contact with the barrel and improves accuracy since it prevents the application of uneven stress. The barrel itself is made from 4140 steel, which has slightly less carbon content than Mil-Spec, but retains significant durability and corrosion resistance. The carbine's 16-inch barrel is chrome-lined and has a lightweight contour throughout, which is still significantly heavier than a pencil barrel and somewhat smaller than an AR bull barrel. The TAC2 barrel has a 1 in 9-inch twist rate, allowing it to stabilize a wider range of bullet weights, including very low weight expanding ammunition. This twist rate adequately stabilizes heavier bullet weights, too, although for the heaviest .223 ammunition, you may prefer a faster twist rate, such as 1:8 or 1:7.

The barrel is topped off with a very distinctive Panther flash suppressor that significantly reduces muzzle flash to preserve night vision. This steel muzzle device has a Mil-Spec phosphate finish and features four long ports and an aggressively scalloped front with some sharp edges. These can be effective as a glass breaker or standoff device in close quarter survival situations.

Internally, the rear of the barrel extension features M4 feed ramps that are cut wider and lower than those found on a standard AR rifle and are designed to improve reliable feeding of rounds from the magazine into the chamber. This can be especially important in carbines under less than ideal conditions where dirt, grime, and moisture can be introduced.

The bolt and bolt carrier are phosphate finished and chrome-lined, and the bolt carrier has a standard commercial contour. The gas carrier key has been properly staked, which helps to ensure that the gas key does not become loose under fire. All manufacturers will stake their gas keys in some way, but a sure sign of quality is a properly staked one that shows that a hammer and punch has been used with enough force to move sufficient metal into the carrier key screws.

Both the upper and lower receiver are manufactured from forged 7075 T6 aluminum and feature a well-applied hardcoat black anodized finish. The controls on both upper and lower receivers, dust cover, forward assist, bolt release, magazine release, charging handle, and safety selector are all located in the familiar places with nothing ambidextrous. The finish is excellent and has a smooth, almost satin texture. The lower receiver features very nice, deep engraving, and the fire and safe setting are marked on both sides of the receiver. The safety selector has a distinct tab on the right side of the rifle so you can visually ensure the rifle is in the fire or safe position.

DPMS has significantly upgraded the usual Mil-Spec furniture by adding the Magpul MOE polymer grip. This grip is wider than the standard one and includes a palm swell for the web of your hand, and that places your hand lower on the receiver and directly in line with the trigger. Moreover, it has internal storage space for extra batteries or spare parts and is covered in an aggressive texturing for a more ergonomic grip in inclement conditions. The buttstock has been upgraded with a six-position collapsible Magpul ACS stock. This unit allows for easy length of pull adjustments for use by differently statured individuals or when wearing heavy clothing or body armor. Its frame design and position lock prevent unintentional adjustments of your preferred length setting, and it has a significant amount of internal storage space. The ACS has a reversible quick-detach sling attachment point and a rubber buttpad for a non-slip, much more secure shoulder engagement. There is a standard sling attachment point, and the stock has extended check welds on both sides that provide internal storage space and increase comfort.

Other Magpul upgrades on the TAC2 include the polymer extended trigger guard, which is significantly more comfortable than a standard one and enlarges the area for easier use with gloves. The rear sight is the Magpul MBUIS folding sight, which is windage adjustable, deploys very quickly when needed, and folds away when not. It provides a good sight picture, although I personally prefer a larger aperture. The front sight is of the standard AR variety, adjustable for elevation. Another advantage of using a rifle-length gas system as found on the TAC2 is that it maximizes the distance between the rear and front sight, providing you a longer sight radius and making accurate shooting easier.

The TAC2 has a standard Mil-Spec single-stage trigger that broke at just over 6 lbs. with a fair amount of creep, but this is actually better than most AR triggers. Creep is the distance that the trigger moves under tension before it breaks and the gun fires. Too much creep can make it difficult to tell when the shot will break and affects precision shooting. My own preference is for a lighter and crisper trigger, like the many drop-in models available from aftermarket manufacturers like Timney or Geissele.

On the range, the rifle performed well with not a single malfunction over several days of shooting and with no maintenance performed between sessions. The rifle is a bit longer than the most compact carbine because of the Panther flash hider and ACS stock. It is a tad on the heavy side for a carbine at 8.5 lbs. empty. This is likely due to the full-length gas system and handguard. Still, it felt very well balanced and handled easily.

SPECIFICATIONS

DPMS TAC2 AR

CALIBER: 5.56mm NATO
BARREL: 16 in. chrome-lined 1:9 twist
OA LENGTH: 38 in. stock extended, 34.25 in. collapsed
WEIGHT: 8.5 lbs. empty
STOCK: M111 modular handguard with Magpul grip and stock
SIGHTS: Magpul MBUIS
ACTION: Semi-auto
FINISH: Black hardcoat anodized
CAPACITY: 30-round magazine
PRICE: $1,299
320-345-9223
dpmsinc.com

The extra weight and shorter dwell time noticeably reduced the perceived recoil. The 5.56mm cartridge does not have a lot of recoil normally, but with the further reduced recoil, staying on target was easier, and the rifle was a joy to shoot. For accuracy testing, I used a bench rest at 100 yards. The final results were between 1 and 2 MOA (Minute of Angle, or about 1 inch at 100 yards), which is quite good for this type of rifle. My best group, using Black Hills 60-grain V-Max, measured 1.24 inches.

The TAC2 barrel has a 1 in 9-inch twist rate, which allows the barrel to stabilize a wider range of bullet weights including very low weight expanding ammunition.

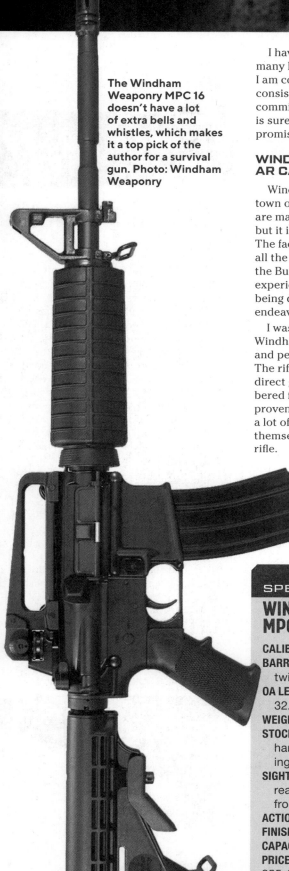

The Windham Weaponry MPC 16 doesn't have a lot of extra bells and whistles, which makes it a top pick of the author for a survival gun. Photo: Windham Weaponry

I have had the opportunity to shoot many DPMS rifles over the years, and I am continually impressed with their consistent quality, innovation, and commitment to the shooter. The TAC2 is sure to please and delivers all that it promises.

WINDHAM WEAPONRY MPC AR CARBINE

Windham Weaponry, named after the town of Windham, Maine where the guns are made, may be an unfamiliar name, but it is far from a new manufacturer. The factory, machinery, owner, and most all the employees were formerly under the Bushmaster name. Now, that same experience and attention to detail are being devoted wholeheartedly to this endeavor.

I was quite eager to see how the new Windham Weaponry MPC 16 would look and perform, and I was not disappointed. The rifle is an M4-style carbine with a direct gas impingement system chambered for 5.56 NATO. The rifle's solid, proven design and features — without a lot of extra bells and whistles — lend themselves ideally for use as a survival rifle.

Both the upper and lower receiver are manufactured from forged 7075 T6 aluminum and have a hardcoat black anodized finish.

The upper receiver has a flattop design with a removable carry handle and A4 dual aperture sights that are elevation and windage adjustable. There are no indexing marks on the top Picatinny rail; so, you would need to take care when removing and replacing optics in order to maintain proper zero.

The 16-inch chrome-lined barrel has an M4 profile and is made from Mil-Spec 4150 chrome-moly vanadium steel. Chrome-moly results in increased carbon content in the steel and adds significant strength and durability, both very desirable features in a duty rifle. The barrel has a fairly standard 1 in 9-inch twist rate, which does a good job of stabilizing a wide range of bullet weights, including very low weight projectiles.

Another Mil-Spec feature is the addition of M4 feed ramps at the back of the chamber. The standard threaded muzzle is topped off with a removable A2 flash hider, and the front sight base is elevation adjustable. Some folks are sticklers for properly F-marked bases on carbines; the Windham Weaponry AR is not so marked, but this is a distinction with very little real world application. Because of the difference in sight radius of a carbine over a rifle, an F-marked sight base is infinitesimally lower than a standard base. This is only an issue when using iron sights at distances past 200 yards, and it can easily be corrected by installing a taller front sight post.

The CAR black plastic handguards have double aluminum heat shields and were extremely effective at protecting the carbine-length gas tube (as well as my hand) from a hot barrel during a full day of range testing. The bolt and bolt carrier are phosphate finished and chrome-lined. The bolt carrier has a Mil-Spec M16 contour (as opposed to a cheaper commercial bolt), which is stronger and heavier to ensure longer and more reliable operation — and it's paired off with a standard carbine buffer. It should be noted that Mil-Spec M-16 bolt carriers are legal to install in semi-auto rifles.

The controls on both upper and lower receivers, dust cover, forward assist, bolt release, magazine release, charging handle, and safety selector are all located in the familiar places with nothing ambidextrous. The trigger guard is the fold down aluminum type for use with gloves.

The M4-type collapsible buttstock has six positions for length of pull to adjust for shooters of varying stature

---

SPECIFICATIONS

WINDHAM WEAPONRY MPC 16

CALIBER: 5.56mm/.223 Rem.
BARREL: 16-inch chrome-lined 1:9 twist
OA LENGTH: 36.25 in. stock extended, 32.5 in. collapsed
WEIGHT: 6.9 lbs. empty
STOCK: M4 double heat shield handguards/6-position telescoping buttstock
SIGHTS: Removable A4 adjustable rear sight and A2 standard base front
ACTION: Semi-auto
FINISH: Black hardcoat anodized
CAPACITY: 30-round magazine
PRICE: $1,086
855-808-1888
windhamweaponry.com

or with use while wearing body armor, and it features the Windham Weaponry logo. The stock was well installed and exhibited excellent fit with very little play. Also, the fit between the upper and lower receiver was excellent with only the slightest amount of play between the two. The lower receiver comes with a standard military-type plastic pistol grip with finger grooves and a slightly flared magazine well.

The trigger is of the standard, single-stage AR variety with the typical utilitarian feel I have come to expect. Unfortunately, that means it's not great, and the trigger exhibited a fair amount of noticeable creep that felt quite gritty, but mercifully avoided any stacking or over-travel. It did break consistently at 7.5 lbs., and it should be noted that this was not developed as a sniper-grade rifle but rather as a utility survival gun. And in that regard, it should serve well.

At 6.9 pounds, this isn't the lightest AR carbine one can purchase, but it is lighter than some of the feature-laden alternatives out there, and its short over-all length and excellent balance make it easy to handle and pleasant to shoot. During my entire range session, I never experienced a single malfunction of any sort, and the rifle performed admirably. Accuracy from a bench rest at 100 yards was about what one should expect from a Mil-Spec rifle, with groups measuring from the best of the day at 1 MOA to the worst at 4 MOA and averaging in

The 16-inch chrome-lined barrel on the Windham AR has an M4 profile and is made from Mil-Spec 4150 chrome-moly vanadium steel. Photo: Windham Weaponry

between. With the right ammunition and a better trigger, this rifle is certainly capable of pinpoint accuracy.

Windham Weaponry ships their rifles in a black hard plastic case with one 30-round magazine, a sling, and a well-illustrated operators manual. Currently, the company's offerings include state-compliant models.

THE DEL-TON .308 AR HEAVY HITTER

I have had the good fortune of testing and reviewing several AR rifles from Del-Ton over the years, and they have all had several things in common: impeccable build quality, solid accuracy, and absolute reliability. They have been traditionally chambered in 5.56mm/.223 Rem. That is, until the company decided to produce one in .308 Win/7.62x51mm.

The new Del-Ton DTI .308 rifle is the company's first big-bore AR, clearly designed for hunters. It is a fact that the latest trend in AR rifles is toward ones chambered in the powerful .308 Win. (or 7.62 NATO) round. However, the .308 AR has not been embraced by the military, and as a result, there is no such thing as a Mil-Spec .308 AR like there is for the .223 variety. The result can be a mishmash of different designs with non-interchangeable parts, but the industry does seem at least to have settled on some basics. Del-Ton's DTI .308 thankfully fits firmly within these unofficial standards. With a few exceptions, the vast majority of ARs chambered in .308 Win. will accept a standard magazine, with the most popular being produced by Magpul and Lancer.

Parts interchangeability is also a priority, and the DTI .308 will accept many parts that fit the standard and plentiful .223 ARs, such as the buffer tube, stock, grips, trigger, and safety. This rifle follows the "common" pattern of the Gen I DPMS .308 ARs for which several

The Del-Ton DTI .308 rifle is the company's first foray into the big-bore AR market. It's a heavy hitter that appeals to hunters, but has obvious survival gun application.

manufacturers now produce aftermarket parts such as handguards.

Like most AR owners, I like to try to use my rifle as much as possible, including for hunting. ARs, despite the way they are portrayed in the media, are gaining more and more popularity as hunting guns thanks to their versatility and ease of use, as well as their accuracy. This just happens to make them ideal all-around survival guns. Unfortunately, in some states such as Virginia where I live, a larger caliber than .223 is required for big game hunting, which includes deer. Del-Ton fielded enough calls for a .308 AR specifically for hunting deer, hogs, and bear that they decided to follow through. The new rifle maintains clean lines and a basic design with features to appeal to hunters, such as a short overall length and low weight for its class, making it easy to lug to your stand.

The DTI .308 is a carbine-length AR with a direct gas impingement system. The 16-inch chrome-moly vanadium barrel features a heavy profile and a 1 in 10-inch twist rate, preferred for the widest variety of bullet weights. It has a carbine-length gas system. The muzzle is threaded and topped with an A2-style flash hider that can be removed and replaced with a different style muzzle device or a direct thread suppressor (which are also gaining popularity among hunters).

The barrel features a durable and weather resistant manganese phosphate finish, including under the front sight base/gas block (which sometimes gets overlooked on less professional builds). The elevation-adjustable A-frame front sight is standard for an AR and includes a sling swivel and a bayonet lug (just in case). At the rear of the barrel, Del-Ton made sure to include M4 feed ramps to improve reliability and feeding.

Del-Ton has done a smart thing with this rifle's handguards: instead of a heavy and unnecessary tactical quad rail, they have plain circular aluminum handguards with an aggressively knurled texture. These allow the barrel to remain free floating, which improves accuracy, while the basic design keeps the rifle's weight down to a minimum. The texture helps keep the rifle firmly in the hand even under inclement conditions. Frankly, you don't want to add a bunch of unnecessary accessories to a hunting rifle regardless, although the DTI .308 is amenable to customizing for a more tactical use.

The gun's forged 7075 T6 aluminum upper receiver is of a flattop design with Picatinny rail. As .308 upper receivers are longer than those on the .223 you get almost a full 7 inches of rail to comfortably mount an optic. The rifle does not include backup rear sights, but these can easily be installed. The charging handle is robust and easy to operate even with an optic mounted, and the upper receiver includes a fully functional forward assist (which some hunters prefer for a quieter chambering), as well as a steel dust cover to keep dirt and debris out of the action when in the field. Both the upper and lower receivers are

Parts interchangeability is a priority and the DTI .308 will accept many parts that fit the standard and plentiful .223 ARs, such as the buffer tube, stocks, grips, triggers and safety. Photo: DTI

hardcoat anodized in a smooth and consistent black.

The lower receiver, likewise forged from Mil-Spec aluminum, has an enlarged integral trigger guard that makes gloved use (especially on those cold mornings) much easier. The beveled magazine well makes for easy magazine changes if needed, and the rifle features all the standard right-handed controls common to all ARs, including the magazine release, bolt catch, and safety selector. Incidentally, the safety selector is not ambidextrous (although one could be easily installed) but it does have "safe" and "fire" markings on both sides for easy status identification.

The furniture on the DTI .308 is very much Mil-Spec with an A2 grip and M4 buttstock. These are functional, but with so many high quality and frankly more comfortable aftermarket grips and stocks available, it is one of the few upgrades that I would make. Fortunately, the buffer tube is standard Mil-Spec diameter for a .223 rifle and will readily accept any stock designed for an AR-15. It comes with a heavy H buffer to compensate for the heavier recoil and bolt carrier needed.

The bolt carrier itself is made from durable, phosphate-finished 8620 steel with a 9310 steel bolt. Both have been heat-treated and plated, and the carrier interior is chrome lined for durability and corrosion resistance. The carrier key is chrome lined, too, and secured

SPECIFICATIONS

DEL-TON DTI 308

CALIBER: .308 Win.
BARREL: 16-inch chrome-moly vanadium. 1:10 twist
OA LENGTH: 37.25 in. stock extended, 34 in. collapsed
WEIGHT: 8 lbs. empty
STOCK: M4 stock and free-float handguard
SIGHTS: A2 front and rail
ACTION: Semi-auto
FINISH: Black hardcoat anodized
CAPACITY: 20-round magazine
PRICE: $947.62
910-645-2172
del-ton.com

with grade 8 screws that have been staked and sealed.

The Mil-Spec single-stage trigger is not bad as far as such triggers go, and it broke at 6 pounds with quite a bit of travel. This is fine for a survival rifle, but for hunting and more precision shooting, I prefer a crisper and lighter trigger. Fortunately, the rifle's design allows for the use of any of a number of drop-in trigger assemblies that offer a lighter trigger and/or a two-stage design preferred by many hunters — one upgrade that is well worth the investment in terms of more comfortable shooting and improved accuracy.

On the range, the Del-Ton DTI .308 was light, short, and easy to handle. At only 8 pounds empty, it's an impressively lightweight .308 AR. You certainly notice the difference in recoil between this and a standard .223 AR, and the rifle requires a more aggressive forward leaning stance in order to keep your balance during rapid fire drills. The recoil is not at all uncomfortable, however, or difficult to manage.

I tested the Del-Ton .308 right out of the box with no maintenance performed over two days of shooting. I did experience two failures to eject during this process, but that is typical and acceptable within any break-in period and while running a rifle dry. Most direct gas impingement ARs far prefer to run with a good supply of lubricant on the bolt and bolt carrier. This is especially the case with ARs chambered in .308, in my experience.

For accuracy testing, I fired the DTI

The average five-shot group size across all types of ammunition tested in the DTI .308 was sub 2 MOA — very good for a .308 carbine of this type.

.308 from a sturdy bench rest. The average five-shot group size across all types of ammunition was sub 2-MOA, which is very good for a .308 carbine of this type. The rifle did exhibit a slight preference for the lighter 155-grain ammunition with my best group measuring 1.16 inches. Match-grade ammunition is typically not recommended for hunting, and my preferred hunting load, the Federal Fusion 180-grain soft point, still averaged just over 2 MOA. Given that most of my deer hunting in the heavy woods of the Shenandoah Valley takes place between 50 and 75 yards, the group sizes would be more than adequate. It should be noted that the heavier bullets produce lower velocities overall, but the difference is less than 200 fps — not enough to make a terminal difference.

As a dedicated hunting rifle, the DTI .308 has much to recommend it, not least of which is that Del-Ton has succeeded in keeping the retail price below $1,000, which is not an easy thing to do for a .308-chambered AR. The rifle comes ready for use with a Magpul 20-round magazine. The only thing you need to change is a preferred optic and any upgrades such as trigger and stock, which are minimal and easy to install. The Del-Ton DTI .308 is an outstanding American made rifle with a lifetime warranty for the original purchaser.

FN FAL

The FN FAL (Fusil Automatique Léger) is as iconic a rifle as the AR or the AK, or at least it should be. I would describe it as the AK of the West. It was used by more than 90 countries throughout the Cold War and fielded by every NATO country except the United States. It was so widely used by Western nations that it earned the moniker of the "Right Arm of the Free World."

The FN-FAL is a semi-automatic rifle using a short-stroke gas piston system and is almost always chambered in 7.62mm NATO/.308 Win. It's a robust and reliable battle-proven rifle that employs a standard 20-round magazine with a non-reciprocating left-side charging handle. Civilian versions are available in the U.S. and are manufactured by Century Arms as well as by DSA Arms, the latter of which makes several tactical and survival variants.

The original rifle was designed for select fire, so it can be found with light or heavy barrels, and it has its own proprietary bipod. Most models come with a top mounted folding carry handle. This seems unnecessary except when using the rifle in full auto. A downside of the carry handle is that it cannot be used with longer optics. As the rifle is all steel and very sturdy, it is on the large and heavy side. This helps tame the recoil significantly, but it can be burdensome to carry for long periods and difficult for smaller shooters to handle.

As the FAL was produced in so many different countries, there is a difference between inch- and metric-patterned rifles. Not all parts will interchange between the two, including the magazines. Metric-pattern rifles are the most commonly seen in the States. Standard FAL have a bolt with a recoil spring assembly that extends into the stock, but other models have been redesigned with folding stocks. Most notable, however, is the gas adjustment system that allows you to adjust for a specific load or in case of fouling. The Century Arms version is fairly standard and economical, while DSA Arms offers more variants.

FN-SCAR

FN, or Fabrique Nationale, has been the main supplier of small arms to the U.S. military for some time now. They manufacture the M-16 and M4 rifles as well as the M240 and M249 general purpose machine gun and squad automatic weapon, or SAW. They also produce the SCAR 16 in 5.56mm and SCAR 17 in 7.62mm for the U.S. Special Forces.

The SCAR 16 and 17 are available as semi-automatic only civilian rifles and use a short-stroke gas piston system of operation that is adjustable for use

SPECIFICATIONS

DSA SA58 PARA CONGO

CALIBER: 7.62x51mm NATO
BARREL: 18 in.
OA LENGTH: 37.5 in./folded 28.5 in.
WEIGHT: 8.76 lbs. (without magazine)
SIGHTS: Iron with rail
SIGHT RADIUS: 22 in.
GRIPS: Plastic
ACTION: Semi-automatic
FINISH: Parkerized
CAPACITY: 20+1 rounds
PRICE: $1,975
dsarms.com

More than 90 countries throughout the Cold War used the FN FAL. It earned the moniker of the "Right Arm of the Free World." Photo: SSGT J.R. Ruark

The FN SCAR 16S FDE shown here, and its larger cousin the SCAR 17, are in use by the U.S. Special Forces. Photo: FN

with or without a suppressor. The free-floated barrel improves accuracy, and all controls are fully ambidextrous with a reversible reciprocating forward charging handle. Note that the charging handle can be used as a forward assist. The polymer stock is both adjustable for length of pull and folding (to the right) and can be fired in the folded position. There is a very handy adjustable cheek riser for use with optics. The rifle comes with an integrated standard top rail for optics and additional accessory rails. The rifle's receiver is made of aluminum to reduce weight, while the lower unit is polymer.

The folding sights are fully adjustable, and the controls, with the exception of the charging handle, are essentially identical to an AR, so transition from one system to the other is easy. The SCAR 16 is lightweight, extremely reliable, and available in black or flat dark earth color. It uses standard AR magazines, so compatibility is not an issue.

SIG556XI TACTICAL MODULAR RIFLE

The SIG556xi rifle from SIG SAUER has a strong military pedigree and offers many modular features that make it a great survival rifle. The SIG556xi is based on the SG550, the standard issue rifle for the Swiss military, and it keeps the modular abilities of its predecessor but adds touches that will be more appreciated by an American audience. In particular, the new rifle uses standard AR magazines instead of the expensive and hard to find proprietary translucent SIG mags.

Unlike the standard AR to which it will undoubtedly be compared, the SIG556xi is a gas piston-operated semi-automatic rifle, although select fire models are available for sale to government agencies. A rotating bolt ensures proper lock up and very much resembles the bolt found on an AK. The basic principle and accompanying reliability is the same. Its gas system has three settings to control the amount of gas that is fed into the gas tube and piston.

If the rifle becomes extremely fouled to the point that reliability suffers, the second setting directs more gas into the system to increase reliable cycling. This is only a temporary measure, and the system should be returned to the normal first setting as soon as it is convenient. The extra gas from position two places more wear and tear on the rifle and

increases recoil. The third position provides the proper amount of gas force for proper cycling with suppressor use.

The SIG556xi's 16-inch steel barrel is not chrome lined; instead, it is nitride treated. The result is an extremely corrosion resistant barrel with improved wear and fatigue resistance and lubricity. This dispenses with the need for a chrome lining and can actually improve accuracy, as chrome lining can be unevenly applied. One of the modular features of the SIG is that the barrel can be removed without tools in the field and replaced with different length barrels that are available in 10-, 14.5-, and 16-inch lengths. Switching calibers is also very easy, and using either 5.56 NATO or .300 Blackout requires only a barrel change. Plus, the 556xi allows for the use of 7.62x39 ammunition. This requires changing the barrel, bolt, and lower receiver to accommodate AK magazines. You can very easily accomplish all of these changes in the field, and since only the upper receiver is serialized, you can have as many unrestricted lower receivers as you like.

The ability to switch between 5.56 NATO and 7.62x39mm is a great boon to anyone in the field, since you should always be able to find one of these two cartridges in abundant supply (along with AR and AK magazines). SIG tested several varieties of AK magazines to check for reliable functioning and report-

accustomed. However, there are optional receiver end plates that allow for the use of standard AR extension tubes and your choice of the vast array of AR stocks.

The upper receiver is steel and made from a stamping, like the AKM. It is the serialized part. The nearly 16 inches of Picatinny rail on top are actually one piece and part of the top handguard, which is made from aluminum. There is plenty of room for extended optics, night vision devices, and laser units. Steel and aluminum flip up diopter sights are stan-

SPECIFICATIONS

SIG SAUER 556xi

CALIBER: 5.56mm
BARREL: 16 in. Nitride 1:7 twist
OA LENGTH: 35.8 in. extended,
26 in. folded
WEIGHT: 7.1 lbs. empty
STOCK: Folding polymer
SIGHTS: Folding adjustable
ACTION: Semi-auto
FINISH: Black
CAPACITY: 30-round magazine
PRICE: $1,466 - $1,599
603-772-2302
sigsauer.com

The SIG556xi rifle from SIG SAUER has a strong military pedigree and offers many modular features that make it a great survival rifle.

edly encountered no issues. The 16-inch 5.56 model tested here had a 1 in 7-inch twist rate and was topped off with a removable three pronged flash hider. The rifle in 7.62x39 has a 1 in 9.5-inch twist.

The handguards are replaceable to fit survival needs. The sample rifle tested was equipped with smooth, lightweight polymer ones. These will readily accept Magpul rail kits and accessories for adding additional mission critical equipment, such as IR lasers or lights. The optional aluminum or carbon fiber handguards are readily adaptable to different length rails.

The side-folding stock makes transport much easier and brings the size of the rifle down to very compact dimensions. A removable polymer cheek rest is attached in order to raise the eye elevation up to optics more comfortably. However, I found that with the stock folded, this cheek rest interfered with the operation of the charging handle. You could switch the ambidextrous charging handle to the left side of the rifle or remove the cheek rest. By the way, the standard folding stock does not have any length of pull adjustments, a feature to which AR users have become

Switching calibers in the SIG556xi is very easy. And changing to either 5.56 NATO or .300 Blackout requires only a barrel change. The 556xi allows for the use of 7.62x39 ammunition, too. This requires changing the barrel, bolt and lower receiver to accommodate AK magazines.

dard, with windage adjustments on the rear sight and elevation on the front. The sights flip up easily and lock into place with a push button retention system.

The charging handle can be reversed from the standard right side to the left; however, cases will continue to eject to the right regardless. At the rear of the charging handle port there are rubber gaskets on both sides of the receiver that allow for the operation of the handle while doing an excellent job of keeping out dust and debris from the action. The lower receiver is made from aluminum and features ambidextrous safety selector and magazine releases. The safety selector has a short 45-degree downward rotation for the fire mode, at least in the semi-automatic model tested. The left-side bolt release is a lever that operates in the opposite fashion from those found on pistols. To lock the bolt to the rear, the bolt hold/release tab must be pushed down. To release it, you must push up on the bolt release or use

the charging handle.

The receiver has an integral extended trigger guard for use with gloves, and the polymer pistol grip has built-in internal storage space for spare batteries or parts and a very aggressive texture on the sides for a firm grip. The SIG556xi weighs and handles very similar to an AR. It is light and handy, and the reliability over two days of testing was impeccable. The rifle features a two-stage trigger, which may seem odd at first if you're used to the Mil-Spec single-stage AR or AK trigger. According to SIG, the trigger pull should be a standard 7.5 pounds combined.

Reloading spent brass is a concern here for the survivalist, as the SIG556xi has a distinct tendency to leave ejected cases with dents to the case mouth.

For accuracy testing, I used a 3-9x Trijicon scope from a stable bench rest position at 100 yards, firing five-shot groups. The results were good, especially with the heavier HPR ammunition that the 1 in 7-inch twist rate barrels generally prefer; this 75-grain round produced sub-MOA results. Standard Mil-Spec 62-grain

ammunition should be capable of respectable accuracy from the SIG556xi.

SIG SAUER has produced an excellent, completely modular and versatile battle rifle for the modern warrior. The ability to quickly and easily adapt the rifle to meet various needs and conditions in the field, including the use of both 5.56 NATO and 7.62x39 ammunition and magazines, is impressive.

ALTERNATIVE RIFLES

No state, however, restricts non-semi-automatic rifles. This includes bolt-, pump-, and lever-action rifles. While these may not be ideal for a survival situation, they are certainly effective for hunting and self-defense. Several manufacturers have recognized this and produced rifles that are very effective survival guns. Here's a look at a few of the best ones.

MOSSBERG

The Mossberg MVP (Varmint and

The Mini-14 is chambered in 5.56mm, the Mini-30 in 7.62x39mm AK. Both, however, use proprietary magazines. Photo: Jan Hrdonka

The Mossberg MVP (Varmint and Predator) is a standard bolt-action rifle that uses AR magazines. Photo: Mossberg

Predator) rifle is a standard bolt-action rifle that uses AR magazines. It's available in both .308 and .223 and will accommodate high-capacity mags. It can be had in several configurations. This offers the versatility of using common AR magazines in an unrestricted bolt action. You will not be able to shoot as fast, but you will have better reliability (thanks to fewer moving parts) and accuracy.

The MVP FLEX features a polymer stock with a pistol grip and an AR-style collapsible stock. It has Mossberg's quick-detach system that allows the stock to be removed for easy and compact transport. The MVP Scout has a full polymer stock and features a threaded barrel with an A2-style flash hider (which makes it easier to install a suppressor), fiber optic sights, and a Picatinny rail for optics. You also get a tactical oversized bolt handle and forward-mounted side rails for extra accessories. To

learn more, visit mossberg.com.

REMINGTON

The Remington Model 7615P is a pump-action rifle that uses standard AR mags, and is designed for law enforcement. Although Remington only sells it to police and government agencies, there is no restriction on private ownership, and they are available on the used market. This rifle is lightweight with a polymer stock and is fast shooting. Not as fast as semi-auto, mind you, but as fast as any bolt action. It's available in several configurations, including versions with pistol grips and collapsing stocks. It has a 16.5-inch barrel with a Parkerized finish. Visit remingtonle.com for more info.

RUGER MINI-14 AND MINI-30

Ruger does make two semi-automatic magazine-fed rifles that are very well suited for survival and may fly under the radar of

some "assault weapons" laws. The Ruger Mini-14 and Mini-30 Ranch Rifles have no pistol grip and sport plain muzzles without flash hiders or threads. The Mini-14 is chambered in 5.56mm, while the Mini-30 is chambered in the 7.62x39mm AK round. Both, however, use proprietary magazines with either a 5-round capacity or, where allowed, a 20-round capacity. These are light and handy rifles.

Ruger's Minis are available in a standard wood stock and blued barrel or what I would recommend — synthetic stock and stainless steel. They are also available in different barrel lengths, and I would opt for the shorter 16-inch barrel models. The Ruger Ranch Rifle is based on the extremely tough and reliable military M1 Garand-style action. It uses a self-cleaning gas piston system of operation that keeps on working even in the worst conditions. Both rifles come

This article is an excerpt from the book, Modern Survival Guns: The Complete Preppers' Guide to Dealing with Everyday Threats, *available at GunDigestStore.com.*

optics ready and include a Picatinny rail and scope rings.

SPECIFICATIONS

RUGER MINI-14 MODEL 5820

CALIBER: 5.56mm
BARREL: 16.12 in.
OA LENGTH: 34.75 in.
WEIGHT: 6.6 lbs. empty
STOCK: Polymer
SIGHTS: Ghost ring
ACTION: Semi-auto
FINISH: Stainless
CAPACITY: 5- or 20-round magazine
PRICE: $1,139
ruger.com

PHOTO ESSAY:

INSIDE THE IDPA

Photographer Yamil Sued captures the fast-paced world of IDPA competition!

BY **YAMIL SUED**

Rain won't stop Jerry Miculek from tackling an IDPA stage.

IDPA – THE INTERNATIONAL DEFENSIVE PISTOL ASSOCIATION – WAS ESTABLISHED IN 1996 OUT OF THE DESIRE OF SHOOTERS WORLDWIDE FOR A SHOOTING SPORT THAT SIMULATED SELF-DEFENSE SCENARIOS AND REAL-LIFE ENCOUNTERS. CREATED BY BILL WILSON, LARRY VICKERS, JOHN SAYLE, WALT RAUCH, KEN HACKATHORN AND DICK THOMAS, THE NEW REALITY-BASED SHOOTING SPORT WAS GEARED MORE TOWARD SELF-DEFENSE AND THE EVER-GROWING NUMBER OF STATES PASSING CONCEALED CARRY LEGISLATION.

Safariland's Bobby McGee sprints while keeping the muzzle of his pistol in a safe direction.

IN THE MID-1990S, ACTION SHOOTERS FELT THAT BOTH IPSC AND USPSA HAD MOVED AWAY FROM PRACTICAL SITUATIONS AND MORE INTO A SPEED GAME WHERE FANCY AND VERY EXPENSIVE HIGH-CAPACITY RACE GUNS WERE NEEDED TO STAY COMPETITIVE; MEANWHILE, IT SEEMED THAT PRODUCTION GUNS, REVOLVERS AND EVEN THE VENERABLE 1911 WERE NO LONGER BEING USED. THIS DROVE THE FOUNDING FATHERS OF IDPA TO CRAFT THE NEW SPORT TO CATER TO ANY LEVEL OF SHOOTER.

A BEGINNING SHOOTER COULD GO TO THEIR LOCAL GUN STORE, PICK UP THE PISTOL OF THEIR CHOICE, THREE MAGAZINES IN TOTAL, A GOOD HOLSTER, AND A DOUBLE MAG POUCH, AND COULD JOIN THE INTERESTING AND FUN ACTION SHOOTING SPORT THAT IS IDPA. FOR MORE INFORMATION VISIT IDPA.COM.

IDPA Revolver Division is still very popular, even with all the other divisions for semi-automatic pistols.

Team Smith & Wesson's Josh Lentz tips a prop table over to use as cover.

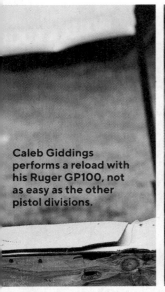

Caleb Giddings performs a reload with his Ruger GP100, not as easy as the other pistol divisions.

Puerto Rico's Alberto De Leon shields his eyes from the early morning sun during a "Standards" course of fire.

(right) Safety Officer Debbie Singer uses her Browning Hi Power in ESP Division.

Randi Rogers safely moves her cover garment to perform the draw.

Targets in all directions and distances is something you see in some IDPA courses of fire.

Running is something that rarely happens in IDPA stages, but some stages can require a bit of a sprint.

When is a Glock not a Glock? When it's manufactured by Lone Wolf Distributors with proprietary custom parts.

Terry Burba uses cover during an IDPA course of fire.

Norma Judith Legados competes in ESP Division with a Springfield Armory XDm 5.25 pistol.

Randi Rogers performs a "slide-lock" reload and reaches for her new magazine from under a cover garment.

Caleb Giddings shoots his Ruger GP100 with a bobbed hammer in Revolver Division.

(above) Gun scribe Massad Ayoob shoots his Springfield Armory XDm 5.25 in ESP Division, note the cover garment.

(right) Arizona's Nils Jonasson turns, then flips his cover garment out of the way to perform his draw. Safety is number one.

TGD

THE SCOUT RIFLE REDEFINED: RUGER GUNSITE SCOUT

Back in the early 1980s, Jeff Cooper believed there was a place for what he described as a "general purpose rifle" — one that could be used both in hunting and tactical situations as needed. What he developed was the concept for a new class of rifle he coined the "scout rifle." Cooper envisioned it as having specific characteristics such as light weight, compact length, ability for fast follow-up shots and chambered in cartridges that are powerful enough to kill a living target of reasonable size. Reasonable size in Cooper's mind was 1,000 pounds.

Though the term scout rifle was new, the concept was not. As far back as World War II, designated marksman of the German Wehrmacht used Mauser K98ks with forward-mounted ZF-41 scopes. The compact, bolt-action Mauser chambered in 8mm no doubt helped

spark the idea of a scout rifle. Hunters in the early 20th century used compact rifles with potent calibers. Cooper was a hunter and no doubt these hunting rifles helped shape the modern idea.

The most unusual characteristic of the scout rifle is that the optic is mounted forward of the receiver instead of on top of it. Mounting the scope forward gives you faster target acquisition since you can keep both eyes open and on the target — as well as on the scope reticle. This setup allows easy access to the action for reloading an internal box magazine, clearing a jam or loading a single round at a time. In hand, the balance of the rifle is slightly changed, putting weight more forward on the non-shooting hand. Austrian rifle manufacturer Steyr worked closely with Cooper to create the first true scout rifle, and the Steyr Scout is the benchmark

(above) A student at Gunsite Academy with a Steyr Scout Rifle during training. Photo: Gunsite Academy

(opposite inset)   A variant of the original, the Ruger Gunsite Scout Rifle is employed by a student at Gunsite Academy. Photo: Gunsite Academy

Among a busy field of do-everything tactical rifles, the Ruger Scout stands out.

BY **ROBERT SADOWSKI**

(left) The concept of a forward-mounted optic is not new. During World War II, some designated marksmen in the German Wehrmacht sported Mauser K98k rifles with forward-mounted ZF-41 scopes. (right) A Mauser K98k rifle from Mitchell's Mausers with a forward-mounted reproduction ZF-41 scope proved to be fast on target but is heavier than what Cooper envisioned.

for all modern spin-offs. The Steyr Scout is Cooper's idea of what a Scout rifle should be: compact, lightweight, and with the ability to reach out to targets with a heavy bullet. At only 6.6 pounds it is very light, features a built-in bipod, has length of pull (LOP) adjustment, spare magazine storage in the stock and flip-up BUIS (backup iron sight) system. The design meets all of Cooper's requirements. Compared to traditional hunting rifles and military rifles of the day, the Steyr Scout looked different, but so do all scout rifles that closely follow Cooper's definition, even today's latest models.

Since then, other firearms manufacturers have developed variations of the scout rifle. The Mossberg MVP Scout features a unique drop-push bolt design that is compatible with both M1A- and AR-style magazines. A combo model pairs the MVP with a UTG Accushot, 1-4x28 extended eye relief optic. Other features include iron sights and a long Picatinny-style rail that allows numerous optics mounting options. Savage has one, too, based on its short action Model 11. The Savage Scout 10 FCM has a detachable high-capacity

traditional route to the scout system, it could be argued Marlin and Springfield Armory used some creative license. The Marlin Model 1895SBL is a lever-action rifle — not the traditional scout rifle action. It is a short and compact rifle chambered in the big-bore .45-70 caliber. The Springfield Armory M1A SOCOM 16, SOCOM II, and Scout Squad don't exactly follow Cooper's definition of a scout rifle either, since these short rifles use

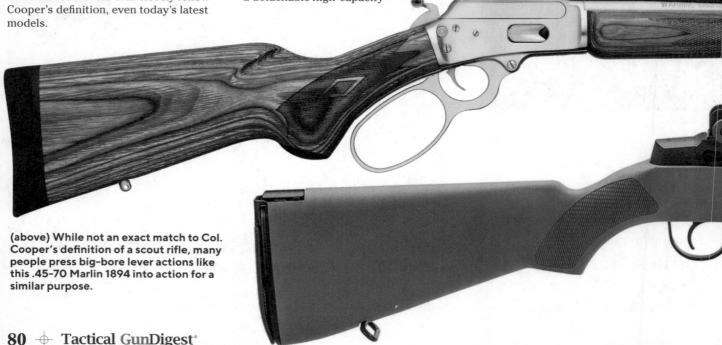

(above) While not an exact match to Col. Cooper's definition of a scout rifle, many people press big-bore lever actions like this .45-70 Marlin 1894 into action for a similar purpose.

a semi-automatic action. The SOCOM rifles takes some design cues from the traditional scout rifle, such as the short 16.2-inch barrel and 37.2-inch length, plus sport a synthetic stock and use a forward scope mount position. The CQB variant even has an adjustable stock. At 10 pounds they are not lightweights, and are heavier than Cooper envisioned.

Ruger has introduced various scout rifle models over the years: the Model 77 Mark II Frontier debuted in 2005, and in 2011 the Gunsite Scout Rifle. The Gunsite rifle was developed in conjunction with the famous shooting academy that bears its name. The Gunsite Scout Rifle was a credible rendition of Cooper's vision, but to me it still isn't exactly what he intended. I thought the laminated wood variant was too heavy and not that accurate. It gave me flashbacks to an Enfield jungle carbine that my dad had sporterized — close but no cigar, as they say. What piqued my interest was when Ruger introduced the Scout Rifle with a lightweight synthetic stock, in my opinion a truer interpretation of Cooper's scout rifle.

The Ruger Scout Rifle is chambered in .308 Winchester, 5.56 NATO and .450 Bushmaster (a 6.5 Creedmoor variant is available as a Davidson's Exclusive) and runs the bullets down a free-floated, 16.5-inch cold-hammer forged alloy steel

(top) With the forward-mounted scope, there is more access to the Ruger Gunsite Scout Rifle's action.

(above) A large magazine release paddle is located just outside the triggerguard, so dumping an empty magazine is fast and efficient.

Some shooters opt for the semi-auto capability of rifles like this Springfield Armory SOCOM, though the author believes the synthetic-stocked Ruger bolt action comes much closer in configuration.

The muzzle brake helps control barrel rise while the front sight is protected by a pair of wings.

(below) The 3-position safety — Fire, Load-Unload, Safe — allows the bolt handle to be raised and lowered only when the safety selector is in either the "Fire" or the "Load-Unload" position. When the safety selector is in the "Safe" position, the bolt handle is locked in the closed position.

(botom) The Hi-Lux LER is equipped with a bullet drop compensated (BDC) reticle that is calibrated to .308 Win. with either 150- or 168-grain bullets at velocities measured from barrels of shorter length.

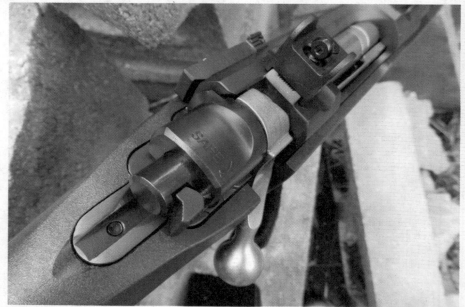

barrel with a 5/8-24 threaded muzzle that wears an efficient brake. The lightweight synthetic stock is equipped with forward aluminum bedding and rear aluminum pillar that lock the receiver into the stock and free float the barrel. At 6.2 pounds this lightweight synthetic stock model is in line with Cooper's thinking — a fast-to-the-shoulder rifle that offers plenty of bullet. The LOP is adjustable via a stack of spacers; add or remove any of the three .5-inch spacers to lengthen or shorten the stock. A soft rubber recoil pad dissipates felt recoil from the .308 Winchester cartridge.

Other traditional scout rifle features include rugged iron sights with a rear ghost ring aperture and a front post with protective wings. A forward, factory-mounted Picatinny rail allows you to mount a long eye relief optic the way Cooper envisioned. This optic setup allows you to shoot with both eyes open and provides better access to the action. The more field of view you have, the better you can engage multiple targets. The Ruger Scout feeds off a steel, detachable box magazine that holds 10 rounds that feed cartridges from the center of the magazine for more reliable and smoother operation. The magazine is manufactured by AM Products.

I mounted a Hi-Lux LER 2-7x32 scope. LER stands for long eye relief, and this scope offers 8 to 14 inches of eye relief. The Hi-Lux LER is equipped with a BDC reticle that is calibrated to .308 Win. cartridges with either 150- or 168-grain bullets at velocities measured from a

(left) A set of Weaver See-Thru rings clamped the Hi-Lux to the Ruger and allowed the author to use the factory iron sights as back-up.

(below) Length of pull on the Ruger Scout can be adjusted by adding or removing stock spacers.

short-barreled rifle. When zeroed at 200 yards, the extra aiming points on the vertical strata are calibrated for 300, 400, 500, and 600 yards, but they only work when the magnification is cranked to 7x power. The magnification ring has a protruding knob that makes adjusting the magnification fast. A set of Weaver See-Thru rings clamped the Hi-Lux to the Ruger and allowed me to use the factory iron sights as back-up.

The Mauser-style action uses a non-rotating controlled round feed extractor and fixed blade-type ejector. The one-piece bolt is made of stainless steel and features a three-position safety lever. Not the push feed like Cooper's Steyr, but practical. You can even load cartridges single fashion with the magazine removed. I fired the rifle off sandbags with two target loads and one hunting load and discovered the Ruger Scout was quite capable of sub-MOA accuracy. Black Hills Gold and Hornady Match groups were a ragged hole with 0.54- and 0.53-inch groups, respectively. Not that the Norma USA ammo was lacking. It produced 0.90-inch groups. That's not bad for a compact, general purpose rifle. Sub-MOA is all well and fine when you have time and sandbags from which to shoot, but offhand shooting is what a scout rifle was designed for. Snap shooting from 25 out to 50 yards showed the Ruger Scout was fast to the shoulder. With both eyes open it was easy to aim with the forward-mounted Hi-Lux scope and the disruptive motion of quickly racking the bolt for a fast follow-up shot meant I got back on target quickly. I used High Speed Gear TACO magazine pouches to practice mag reloads and found the TACO easily adapted to the Scout magazine and kept just the right tension on it so I could easily pull it free from the pouch. The Scout accepts flush-fit 3-round AM steel and Al-style polymer mags as well as 5- and 10-round configurations. A large magazine release paddle is located just outside the trigger guard so dumping an empty magazine is fast and efficient even in the prone position.

Indeed, if I only had one rifle for both hunting and defense the Ruger Gunsite Scout would be it. **TGD**

Special thanks to Eastern Outfitters (easternoutfitter.com) in Hampstead, NC.

SPECIFICATIONS

MODEL: Ruger Scout Rifle

ACTION: Controlled feed, bolt

CALIBERS: .308 Win., 5.56 NATO, .450 Bushmaster, 6.5 Creedmoor

BARREL LENGTH: 16.1 in.

OVERALL LENGTH: 37–38.5 in.

WEIGHT: 6.2 lbs.

STOCK: Synthetic, adj. LOP

SIGHTS: Picatinny rail/ghost ring

FINISH: Matte black

CAPACITY: 10+1

MSRP: $1,139

This shows the non-rotating, Mauser-type controlled round feed extractor in action on the Ruger.

PERFORMANCE: RUGER SCOUT RIFLE

.308 Winchester	Velocity (fps)	Muzzle Energy (ft-lbs)	Best Accuracy (in.)	Average Accuracy (in.)
Norma USA 150-gr. FMJ	2,507	2,094	0.40	0.90
Black Hills Gold 150-gr. GMX	2,598	2,248	0.37	0.54
Hornady Match 178-gr. BTHP	2,395	2,267	0.34	0.53

Bullet weight measured in grains, velocity in fps, muzzle energy in ft-lbs, and accuracy in inches for best three-shot groups at 100 yards.

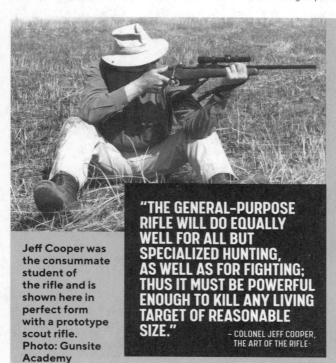

Jeff Cooper was the consummate student of the rifle and is shown here in perfect form with a prototype scout rifle. Photo: Gunsite Academy

"THE GENERAL-PURPOSE RIFLE WILL DO EQUALLY WELL FOR ALL BUT SPECIALIZED HUNTING, AS WELL AS FOR FIGHTING; THUS IT MUST BE POWERFUL ENOUGH TO KILL ANY LIVING TARGET OF REASONABLE SIZE."

– COLONEL JEFF COOPER, THE ART OF THE RIFLE

Specific Scout Rifle Characteristics According to Cooper:

- Overall length of less than 1 meter (39.3 in.)
- Weight of less than 3 kilograms (6.6 lbs.)
- Both iron and optical sights. Typically a ghost ring rear sight with a square post front sight and a 2–3x, long eye relief scope mounted forward of the action to allow easy access to the action for rapid reloading. If the scope is damaged it can easily be removed and the iron sights employed.
- A sling to use as a shooting aid and carrying the rifle
- 2 MOA accuracy consisting of a three-shot group at 200 yards
- The ideal caliber is .308 Winchester/7.62x51mm NATO, with 7mm–08 and .243 Winchester as alternate chamberings.
- A synthetic stock for better durability and no negative impact on the barrel.
- Optional features include a bipod, detachable magazine, butt magazine, and accessory rail for accessories.

The Scout Rifle Evolves: AM Products Chassis System

AM Products, the manufacturer of steel magazines for the Ruger Scout, has built an aluminum chassis system that evolves the Scout rifle concept. The chassis allows you to drop in a barreled Ruger Scout action (Am Products also produces a chassis for Remington and Savage actions) with minimal effort. The AM Scout rifle chassis is lightweight and makes the Ruger Scout barreled action easier to use. I wouldn't think twice about taking the AM chassis-equipped Ruger Scout into the backcountry. In my opinion, AM Products has succeeded in improving the scout concept while maintaining the characteristics of Cooper's original rifle.

Installation is literally drop-in. The chassis is made of forged 7075 aluminum with relief cuts to reduce weight. The fore-end has full relief cuts so the barrel free floats and allows attachment of a bipod. It's sculpted around the bolt knob for fast and easy operation. The trigger guard is enlarged so firing the rifle while wearing heavy winter gloves is not a problem. The chassis is compatible with AR-style grips and stocks. I used an Ergo pistol grip — I like the texture and nice palm swell — and a Mission First Tactical (MFT) BUST Utility stock and BACP cheek piece.

If you can disassemble a stock from a barreled action, then you can easily assemble this chassis system. The fit is perfect and tight. No gaps. No wiggle. Shouldering the AM Scout chassis is a lot like shouldering an AR-15. The stock comb is straight and directly from the rear of the action, so I used high rings to mount an optic. AM offers a custom Picatinny rail, so you can mount a scope in the normal position over the action without having to remove the Ruger's rear sight. According to AM Products, they have extensively tested short barrel .308 Win. rifles with 17-inch heavy barrels in the Scout chassis and they easily performed out to 800 yards with ease.

In my testing of the chassis, I found the upgrade worthy of the scout concept, as the upgrade only helps with long-range accuracy.

The AM Products chassis system for the Ruger Scout Rifle.

TACTICAL REVOLVERS TODAY

The Best Revolvers for Serious Work and How to Use Them

BY **ROBERT CAMPBELL**

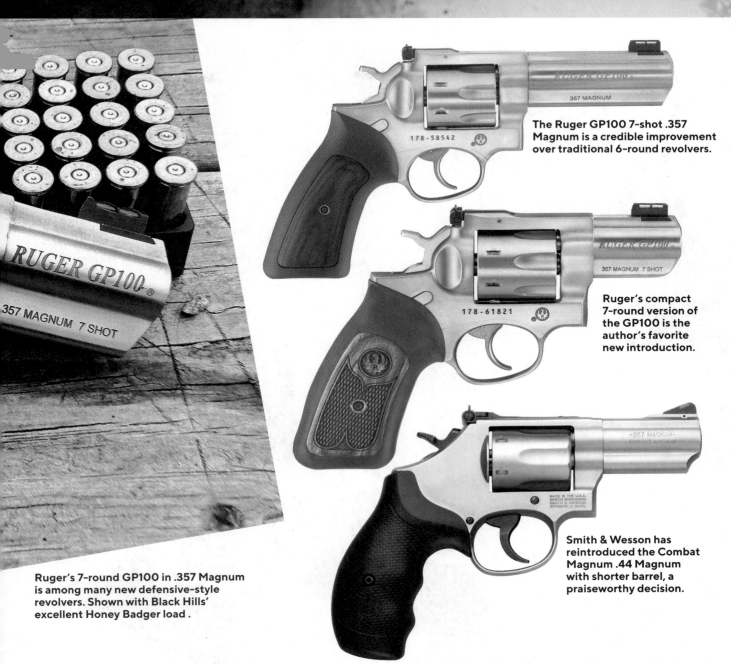

The Ruger GP100 7-shot .357 Magnum is a credible improvement over traditional 6-round revolvers.

Ruger's compact 7-round version of the GP100 is the author's favorite new introduction.

Smith & Wesson has reintroduced the Combat Magnum .44 Magnum with shorter barrel, a praiseworthy decision.

Ruger's 7-round GP100 in .357 Magnum is among many new defensive-style revolvers. Shown with Black Hills' excellent Honey Badger load .

The term tactical is defined as gaining an advantage over an adversary or situation. The revolver is a tactical tool with many advantages. A firearm that has remained viable for so many years and has saved so many lives is worth your consideration. Revolvers are far from outdated for personal defense and, in some situations, may be a better fit for your situation than self-loading pistols.

If you use a revolver for personal defense there are many good choices. As with any handgun the weight or heft of the piece, its balance and the level of recoil you are willing to master are important considerations. Reliability is the baseline for performance. Only after reliability is confirmed are other features considered. During the past few months there have been several interesting revolvers introduced to the buying public. The viability of the revolver is worth weighing in the balance. The greater maintenance demands and complication of semi-automatic handguns may be daunting to the occasional shooter. The revolver is simple — load, holster, draw, fire.

The new revolvers covered here are designed for home and personal defense, and in some cases protection against large animals. Ruger firearms have led the way with new introductions, most based on the GP100 frame. But the Ruger Redhawk has also been given a home defense makeover. Kimber and Smith & Wesson have introduced wheelguns that are sure to fill many needs. The revolver offers many choices and real versatility, and you must carefully consider your situation and make the best choice.

RUGER ADDS MORE POWER, MORE ROUNDS

Among the most interesting recent introductions is the Ruger Redhawk .357 Magnum. The Redhawk is proven and has long chambered the powerful

recoil is light — no more than firing a .38 Special cartridge in a small frame revolver. Muzzle blast is more pronounced than with longer barrel revolvers but the package is controllable. The Redhawk is famously accurate. It would make for a fast handling revolver for animal defense. The Redhawk .357 Magnum can be fired with affordable low-recoil .38 Special loads or powerful magnum ammunition.

Ruger introduced two new revolvers based on the GP100 frame. The first is a .44 Special version. This revolver features a non-fluted 5-round cylinder. The lockwork is adapted to manage the five rounds. Part of the energy expended as we manipulate the trigger is used to cock and drop the hammer, while part of the energy is used to rotate the cylinder. The feel of the action is different than the

Ruger's Redhawk revolver is well made of good material and very strong. A new .357 Magnum variant handles the hot cartridge with ease.

.44 Magnum and .454 Casull cartridges. Chambering the Redhawk in .357 Magnum results in a revolver that is massively overbuilt compared to lightweight revolvers that take a beating from the .357 Magnum cartridge. The Redhawk features an 8-round cylinder. This makes for a good reserve of cartridges. The .357 Mag. Redhawk is a large handgun at over 45 ounces even with the 2.75-inch barrel. In this configuration the Redhawk is exceptionally well balanced. The weight helps absorb the recoil of the powerful .357 Magnum cartridge.

The Redhawk is on the large side for carry under covering garments but well suited to home defense. No handgun is too large to fight with and the short barrel Redhawk's grip frame is smaller than the .44 Magnum version and well-shaped for most hands. Subjectively speaking,

Among Ruger's recent introductions are a 5-shot .44 Special and the 7-round .357 Magnum on the GP100 frame.

Revolvers with 5-, 6-, and 7-round capacities offer many options for the modern shooter.

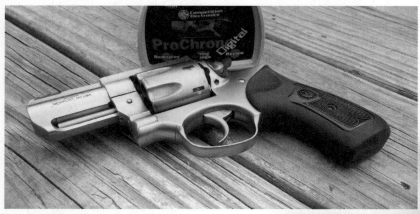

Despite its short barrel, the Ruger GP100 .357 demonstrated real power during ammunition testing.

6-shot revolver, perhaps a bit longer and smoother. This revolver features Hogue's recoil absorbing Monogrip. These grips make for good comfort and control. The .44 Special features a 3-inch barrel. The front sight is a fiber-optic unit. The rear is Ruger's standard fully adjustable sight. All of this adds up to make the .44 Special GP100 an excellent personal defense handgun.

The .44 Special cartridge has been called one of the most inherently accurate of the revolver cartridges. Part of this reputation rests in the first-class revolvers in which the cartridge is chambered. As an example, the GP100 features a rock-solid lockup with a ball and detent located in the crane. The .44 Special is docile with standard pressure loads. A 240-grain lead bullet at 750 fps isn't very difficult to control. There are much faster loads with greater energy. The Hornady 165-grain Critical Defense breaks over 900 fps and offers good wound potential. Buffalo Bore's 200-grain all copper hollowpoint breaks 990 fps. The .44 Special GP100 is among the most accurate factory revolvers I have fired with several loads grouping smaller than 2 inches for five shots at 25 yards. The new GP100 can be concealed under draping covering garments with the proper leather holster choices. While the .357 Magnum enjoys an excellent reputation against motivated adversaries, some prefer the surety of a big-bore cartridge. The .44 Special offers that advantage and the Ruger GP100 is an excellent vehicle for it.

While the Ruger GP100 .44 Special dropped one round in capacity in return for a big-bore cartridge, Ruger was also working on increasing the capacity of the Ruger GP100 .357 Magnum. The result is

The Model 69 .44 Magnum is a hard kicker with real power.

the GP100 7-shooter. As of this writing, 4-inch barrel versions are beginning to ship but the initial batch featured compact wood grips and a 2.5-inch barrel. The new GP100 feels and handles like a smaller revolver. While it is only slightly smaller than the 3-inch-barrel .44 Special version, the overall impression is of a smaller handgun. I have fired the GP100 7-shooter extensively and adopted it as one of my most important personal defense handguns.

The versatility of this wheelgun is unequaled by semi-autos. For example, with mild .38 loads, the GP100 is a pleasant plinker. With .38 Special +P loads, anyone in the family can use the revolver for home defense. When I deploy the piece concealed with .357 Magnum de-

With smaller grips and a .5-inch shorter barrel, the GP100 .357, top, gives the impression of a smaller revolver than the Hogue-stocked .44, bottom.

fense loads I have a handgun with proven wound ballistics. If traveling in the wild, the GP100 is relatively light on the hip, and when loaded with hardcast SWC loads is useful for defense against wild animals. It's accurate from a solid bench rest, as accurate as any GP100 revolver I have fired, and that is saying something. In my experience, the only revolver that is consistently as accurate as the GP100 is the Colt Python and it is only slightly so and it takes a good hand to prove it. In my opinion, the GP100's lockwork in the 7-shot version cycles more quickly than the 6-shot variant. I have shot this revolver extensively with full power Magnum loads and find that I am able to shoot seven magnums as quickly and accurately as six from the 6-shot model. This is an estimable revolver and my favorite among the new introductions.

KIMBER UPS THE GAME

A development that has gained a

(above) Kimber's double-action trigger is possibly the smoothest on the market.

(right) Kimber's addition of high-profile sights to the small-frame K6S revolver is a welcome modification.

The L frame Model 69 Combat Magnum is a great revolver for those willing to master the heavy recoil.

pattern on the target as the 9mm shooter will but rather they prefer a single hard hit and a cessation of action. While I am a fan of classic Smith & Wesson revolvers, the newer guns are more durable and more accurate. The frames are strengthened in critical places. The steel is stronger than ever. Modern CNC machinery ensures that the throat and barrel dimensions are a good match and provide for excellent practical accuracy.

These revolvers are the best of the breed and arguably among the finest handguns ever made. They have the advantages of the revolver. They can be left loaded for long periods and come up shooting.

good reputation quickly is the Kimber K6S. The Kimber .357 Magnum is a light wheelgun that gives those carrying the J frame revolver an option to move up in both caliber and capacity. The K6S accepts six cartridges in its cylinder. Yet, the stainless double-action-only revolver is only fractionally wider than the archetypical 5-shot. The high-profile sights provide an excellent sight picture. The Kimber is accurate enough to take advantage of these sights. The internals are no surprise; the revolver is based on proven lockwork. Kimber took the J-frame action and moved the hammer spring about five degrees and changed the pivot of the hammer. The result is a shorter throw than other revolvers and a smoother feel. This action allows accurate work well past what is assumed to be snubnose ranges. While the Kimber has a short sight radius, an excellent trigger action and modern sights make for a superior shooter.

NEW SMITHS FOR THE TACTICIAN

A few years ago, Smith & Wesson introduced the Model 69 .44 Magnum revolver. The L frame has been offered in a 7-shot .357 Magnum version for some time. The 5-round .44 Magnum is designed as an outdoors handgun for defense against large animals such as the big cats and bears. It isn't for hunting or long-range competition, but gives you a lot of power in a relatively light package. Smith recently introduced an even lighter version of the Model 69: The Combat Magnum Model 69 in .44 Magnum features a 2.75-inch barrel and round butt grip. (All Smith & Wesson revolvers in modern production are round butt frame, but the grips may be offered in either round or square butt configuration.)

This revolver is more suited to concealed carry than the 4-inch version. With an excellent set of sights and the smooth Smith & Wesson action, it has much to recommend. I think most of us will carry it with .44 Special ammunition. But then there are .44 Magnum loads that are not full power and which can be controlled in the Model 69. The person carrying a Magnum revolver isn't going to fire a 50-round course and find a neat

A revolver shoved into the adversary's body at intimate range will fire time and again, whereas a self-loader will jam. Most are more powerful than common semi-auto pistol cartridges. Some shooters will flinch or jerk the trigger with a light semi-auto trigger; the double-action revolver, with its long rolling action, aids in managing recoil. You won't flinch if you don't know exactly when the handgun is going to fire. The revolver is well suited to a novice but also the choice of many seasoned shooters.

Now let's look at how to use the revolver and the best accessories for tactical use.

(left) The Ruger GP100 7-shooter is one fast revolver to fire! (right) The author is staging the trigger from a solid brace. This makes for excellent accuracy.

TACTICAL REVOLVER TECHNIQUES

Double-action revolvers are not terribly complicated to make but do require precision manufacture. The crane must sit flush with the frame and the barrel cylinder gap must be tight; there should be no end shake. The entire lockwork must be timed properly. Modern revolvers are tight and very accurate. Actions are smooth. Most of the magnums feature adjustable sights while the small frame Kimber features quality fixed sights.

Learning to quickly line up the sights is accomplished with hours of dry fire practice. Bring the revolver to eye level and align the sights on target. The trigger action must be pressed smoothly to the rear. The hammer drops, and the trigger is allowed to reset during recoil. Sight picture is important but not as important as the trigger press. If you jerk the trigger you will be off the target completely even at 7 yards, typical personal defense engagement range. The trigger is pressed in stages, hence the term "staging the trigger." The trigger is pressed as you feel the bolt lock into the cylinder and you continue pressing the trigger until the hammer falls. Practice this trigger press until the action becomes automatic and you don't have to think about what is going on. Press, fire, reset, and fire again. Very accurate work can be done with the revolver in this manner. Another advantage is that the barrel can be placed against cover for stability as the revolver is fired.

Reloading the revolver quickly is a useful skill. The process goes like this: The revolver is fired empty and then switched to the non-dominant hand,

When using a speedloader, use your fingers to guide the cartridges into the chamber.

With the cartridges seated, the speedloader knob is turned to release them.

opening the cylinder with the firing hand thumb. The revolver must be held with the muzzle up to allow spent cartridge cases to eject properly. Three fingers go around the frame and press the cylinder completely out of the frame as the non-dominant side thumb strikes the ejector rod and dumps the spent cases. Most fired cases will simply fall out unless the chambers are rough or dirty. After the cases are ejected, the revolver is turned muzzle down to facilitate speed loading. The firing hand accesses the speedloader, which is moved quickly to the cylinder. It's important that you grasp the speedloader properly by running your fingertips to the end of the cartridge nose and guiding them into the chambers. The speedloader knob is then twisted to release the cartridges and the speedloader is allowed to drop away. I use HKS speedloaders and have never had a complaint. They are affordable and useful. Attempting to load a revolver with loose cartridges or a speed strip is far less satisfactory.

REVOLVER AMMO DEVELOPMENTS

There have been interesting developments in self-defense ammunition, much of it directed toward revolvers. I am not going to quote a press release or catalog. I have personally tested the loads discussed. Among the most interesting is the Black Hills Honey Badger. The Honey Badger's advantage is an all-copper bullet with sharp cutting flutes. The projectile doesn't depend on expansion for wound potential. The bullet rips and tears tissue immediately, not after the bullet has begun to expand, and cuts tissue rather than pushing it aside as will a round nose bullet. When it comes

The Black Hills Honey Badger load is a good option for revolvers.

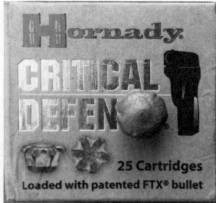

Hornady's 125-grain .357 Magnum Critical Defense load offers ideal expansion.

Buffalo Bore's Tactical Short Barrel Lower Recoil loads are excellent additions to the company's line.

Federal's Hydra-Shok .38 Special load offers good ballistic efficiency and excellent expansion.

to short barrel revolvers that may not generate enough velocity for reliable hollowpoint expansion, the Honey Badger makes a lot of sense. For an all-around defense load, the Honey Badger is a viable alternative. The 100-grain .38 Special has proven accurate in the new Kimber. The newest addition to the Honey Badger line is a .44 Magnum version. I have fired this loading in the Smith & Wesson Model 69 and found it accurate, clean burning, and not too difficult to control in double-action pairs.

Hornady offers its Critical Defense in popular revolver calibers including .32 Magnum, .38 Special, .357 Magnum, .44 Special and .45 Colt. I have the most experience with the .38, .357 and .44 loads. The .357 Magnum is sensibly down-loaded from the 1,450 fps 125-grain standard. At 1,380 fps from a 4-inch barrel and 1,220 fps from the 2.75-inch barrel GP100, this load offers excellent expansion and wound potential. The .44 Special and .45 Colt loads breathe new life into older cartridges.

Buffalo Bore offers powerful hunting loads. A standard for animal defense is the 180-grain hardcast flatpoint .357 Magnum. This load generates 1,380 fps in a 4-inch barrel sixgun. Buffalo Bore recognizes the need for a controllable .357 Magnum loading that offers real power but also low flash and less recoil. The Tactical loads include my personal favorite, the 158-grain JHP Low Flash Low Recoil. This one breaks 1,258 fps from my personal 4-inch Combat Magnum and is plenty accurate.

One of the most interesting additions is sure to be a popular choice for snubnose .38 Special revolvers: Federal's .38 Special 130-grain Hydra-Shok loading. This bullet is loaded deep into the case to maintain a clean powder burn and limit muzzle flash. The Hydra-Shok features modest recoil, good accuracy and excellent expansion. This is an outstanding loading for light revolvers well worth your exploration.

PACKING THE REVOLVER

Among the most important choices you will make is how you will carry your revolver. The holster must keep the handgun secure, offer fast access and real speed. There are holsters that are too soft, inaccessible under the clothing, and which collapse after the handgun is drawn, making holstering the piece without loosening the belt impossible. Revolver holsters differ considerably from semi-auto holsters in both design

The Galco Hornet is an excellent cross-draw holster.

The Urban Carry Revo system is comprised of a backing that allows the attachment of different holsters. The same backing can be used for a number of handgun "shells," making it a very versatile system.

Lobo Gun Leather offers a first-class IWB holster well-suited to revolvers.

holster keeps the handgun cinched in close to the body by use of a proven belt loop design. The butt is angled into the draw and a strong holstering welt is designed to allow ease of holstering. Another good choice is the cross-draw. Crossdraw holsters offer access while you're seated or driving and afford real speed for those that understand how to properly execute the draw. Among the best cross-draw designs is the Galco Hornet.

The Hornet is stitched of quality steerhide and has excellent fit. The DM Bullard Combat is a well-designed strongside holster that I own in several models. Its supple construction keeps the handgun comfortably against the body. It's well suited to heavy, short-barrel handguns such as the Ruger GP100 .44 Special.

The default design for concealed carry is the IWB holster. This design keeps your handgun concealed by riding between your body and trousers. The inside-the-waistband holster allows the use of a larger handgun as the main part of the handgun is buried in the pants. IWB holsters must be firmly attached to the belt. Dual belt loops or a strong belt clip is needed. The holstering welt must allow holstering the handgun after it's drawn, without removing the holster from the inside-the-pants position. Lobo Gunleather offers IWB designs ideal for revolvers. I especially like Lobo's rear clip IWB. This holster keeps the handgun tight against the body and offers a sharp draw. Another design from Lobo Gun-

leather features dual belt loops that spread the weight of the handgun out across the belt line. This holster keeps the handgun high on the belt for a fast draw, with the gun butt angled into the draw.

A new design from Urban Carry is among the most interesting to come along in decades. This holster system, called the Revo Rig, is comprised of a backing that allows the attachment of different holsters. The same backing can be used for a number of handgun shells. The Revo is available for popular revolvers including one of my favorites, the Smith & Wesson Model 442 .38 Special. The backing features dual snaps that lock into the back of the holster. The holster is secured by Velcro as well. It can be adjusted for forward or backward cant. It's a design we are certain to be hearing more about.

Revolvers are more advanced and more suited for tactical use than ever. With proper training and modern accessories, the revolver is not only a viable choice — it is the right choice for many. **TGD**

and balance. A revolver holster must keep the cylinder off the belt line. A high riding holster will keep the revolver close to the body and angled into the draw for real speed. The holster should be tightly fitted to the revolver along the cylinder and barrel for retention. The primary choices include cross-draw, inside-the-waistband (IWB) and strong-side carry.

The strongside holster should always be the first choice. If a covering garment is worn, the strongside scabbard affords good access and speed. A strong choice is the Nelson Holsters Avenger. This

WEB CONTACTS

Kimberusa.com
Smith-wesson.com
Ruger.com
Black-Hills.com
Buffalobore.com
Hornady.com
Nelsonholsters.com
Galcogunleather.com
Dmbullard.com
Logogunleather.com
Urbancarryholsters.com

ABM *Ammo*

20 Cent...
Rifle Car...

300 Winchester Magn...
230gr Berger Match Hybrid OTM Targ...
P/N 70090   Lot # 0061

my 5 favorite
long-range
CARTRIDGES

The Right Cartridge Can Make Your Long-Range Game

BY **PHIL MASSARO**

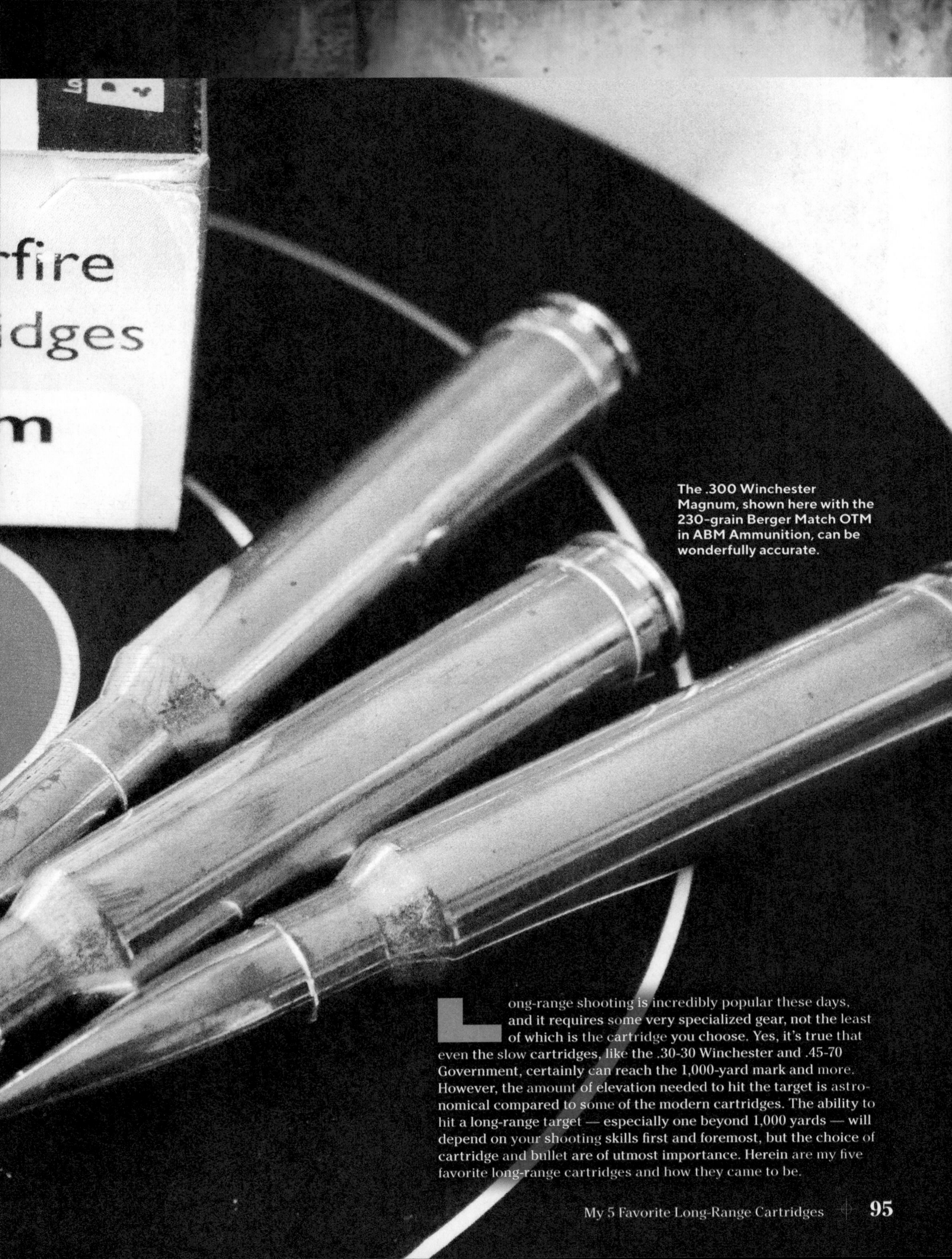

rfire
idges
m

The .300 Winchester Magnum, shown here with the 230-grain Berger Match OTM in ABM Ammunition, can be wonderfully accurate.

ong-range shooting is incredibly popular these days, and it requires some very specialized gear, not the least of which is the cartridge you choose. Yes, it's true that even the slow cartridges, like the .30-30 Winchester and .45-70 Government, certainly can reach the 1,000-yard mark and more. However, the amount of elevation needed to hit the target is astronomical compared to some of the modern cartridges. The ability to hit a long-range target — especially one beyond 1,000 yards — will depend on your shooting skills first and foremost, but the choice of cartridge and bullet are of utmost importance. Herein are my five favorite long-range cartridges and how they came to be.

appetite for barrels. The severe friction, attributed to the huge powder column in the big magnum case, really heats up the throat of the barrel creating erosion in a relatively short time. The 6.5-284 Norma, on the other hand, with a case capacity of roughly 84 percent of that of the .264 Winchester Magnum, backs the velocity off just enough to extend throat and barrel life. The first iteration of the 6.5-284 had the Winchester moniker and a shorter throat (requiring bullets to be seated deeper into the case) but the Norma version — receiving CIP approval in 2000 — changed the throat specification, allowing those long bullets to be seated out farther, increasing case capacity.

The 6.5-284 sends the 140- to 150-grain bullets out of the muzzle at velocities

6.5-284 NORMA

The 6.5-284 Norma is my personal favorite of the 6.5mm cartridges, as it offers what I consider to be the best balance of case capacity, long-range performance and barrel life. Based on the .284 Winchester, it's designed to offer the performance of the .270 Winchester and .280 Remington in a short-action cartridge. It came to life when the wildcatters necked the .284 Win. case down to hold 6.5mm bullets. While the 6.5-284 is not the only wildcat based on the .284 Win., it quickly created a huge buzz in the long-range community. Much of that had to do with the fantastic ballistic coefficient of the 6.5mm bullets — they are virtually unparalleled — but the case capacity also helped considerably.

The .264 Winchester Magnum, introduced in 1959, certainly had the muscle to launch those long, lean 6.5mm bullets. But as a target cartridge. where numerous shots are fired throughout the day, the fast .264 showed a healthy

(above) The 6.5-284 Norma at the SAAM Shooting School in Texas ringing steel out to 1,500 yards.

(right) Mated with a Kestrel anemometer, the 6.5-284 Norma has the capability to truly reach out to long distances, making the shooter's life easier.

(bottom left) Nosler's 142-grain AccuBond bullet. One glance at the length of this bullet will give a good idea as to why it offers such good long-range performance with its very high ballistic coefficient.

(bottom right) The 6.5-284 has large enough case capacity to launch the high ballistic coefficient 6.5mm bullets at very respectable velocities.

from 2,700 to 2,900 fps, depending on barrel length, giving more than enough oomph to make hitting distant targets no issue at all. Benchrest competitors prefer barrels of 28 to 30 inches, to wring all the velocity they can out of the case. I can see the wisdom of this decision, especially with a gun that you don't need to carry around in the field. However, as a long-range tactical or hunting gun, I like to see a bit less barrel length to make things more manageable, yet still take advantage of the case capacity. My own 6.5-284 Norma is set up as a long-range hunting gun, yet still can reach out and touch distant steel targets. It is from the Savage Custom Shop, built on the Model 116 long-action platform (to give me all the room in the magazine I'd ever want), with a 25-inch barrel.

I've used lots of factory ammunition and haven't come across a load that wasn't at least 1 MOA, with some even better. The rifle really shines with my handloads. A 140-grain Hornady ELD Match over a suitable charge of H4831SC in Norma brass, sparked by a Federal GM210M primer, will hold 1/3 MOA out to 500 yards. I've used the rifle at the FTW Ranch — with its multitude of shooting ranges, tricky winds and incredible distances. I was soon hitting steel out to 1,500 yards and would've went farther if not for the limitations of my scope.

The cartridge offers superb wind deflection values, mainly because of the length and conformation of the bullet, with very manageable recoil, which is another of the 6.5-284 Norma's benefits. The recoil is nowhere near that of the faster 6.5s like the .26 Nosler, .264 Winchester Magnum or 6.5-300 Weatherby Magnum. That easy manner allows you to run through an afternoon of shooting without beating the snot out of your shoulder. There are 6.5mm cartridges with less recoil and less speed, and faster ones that can get really snappy when fired from the prone or from the bench, but in my opinion the 6.5-284 Norma is the consummate blend of both, making it my favorite 6.5mm cartridge. It isn't as readily available as the Swede or Creedmoor, but there is good factory ammunition available from Norma and Nosler, and plenty of components available to the handloader.

.300 WINCHESTER MAGNUM

America's love affair with .30-caliber bullets dates back to the 19th century, and with good reason: they have an excellent blend of good trajectory,

Massaro lights up the .300 Winchester Magnum on 1,000-yard steel.

retained energy, and terminal performance, wrapped up in a package that most shooters will handle effectively. They were (and are) employed by the U.S. military, launched from the .30-40 Krag, .30-06 Springfield and 7.62x51mm NATO cartridges, and the sporting world has seen one of the widest selections of cartridges for this bore diameter. In 1963, Winchester introduced the fourth cartridge in its series based on a shortened .375 H&H Belted Magnum: the .300 Winchester. Most folks were expecting the cartridge to follow suit

with the previous three — the .458, .338 and .264 Winchester Magnums – using a 2.500-inch case length, but the earlier release of the .308 Norma Magnum, which is extremely close to that exact formula, muddied up the waters a bit. Winchester instead decided to elongate the case and move the shoulder forward to maximize case capacity. The resulting cartridge measured 2.620 inches, with a neck length of 0.264 inch. That short neck — cartridge designers usually use a neck dimension of at least one caliber in length — has been criticized by some,

Even in a hunting rifle, the .300 Winchester makes an excellent long-range cartridge.

but I've never had an issue with it, as it gives plenty of neck tension to even the longest bullets. The goal was to achieve the ballistics of the .300 Holland & Holland Magnum in a cartridge that used the long-action of the .30-06 Springfield. Winchester did that and more.

The .300 Winchester Magnum will equal or better the Super .30s' velocities, and the departure from a magnum-length action makes the rifle even more affordable. Couple that with the huge marketing capabilities of the Winchester brand, and the .300 Holland was soon pushed off the stage, replaced by the .300 Winchester Magnum in the fabulous Model 70.

Driving a 180-grain bullet to 2,960 fps, the .300 Winchester was an immediate hit with the hunting community, as the striking power and flat trajectory made for an excellent combination, suitable for hunting nearly all of the North American game, as well as a good portion of African species. But it wasn't long before the target community realized exactly what Winchester had concocted: a serious long-range cartridge, worthy of that nearly indefinable term 'inherently accurate.' A well-tuned .300 Winchester is capable of fantastic accuracy, easily sub-MOA, especially in a target rifle. Yes, the recoil can be a bit much, but once you become proficient with the cartridge it won't take long until you realize just how effective the .300 Winnie can be.

The cartridge is most accurate with bullets of 165 grains or heavier, with the best long-range performance coming with the heavies for the caliber, usually between 190 and 240 grains. It has been adopted by the U.S. military and numerous law enforcement agencies for use in sniper rifles, based on its accuracy capabilities and the long-range performance of the cartridge. It will, when loaded with a suitably aerodynamic bullet, maintain supersonic flight out to 1,400 yards, and that gives the .300 a definite advantage over the .308 Winchester, in spite of the additional recoil. Using a 25-degree shoulder for good headspacing — the belt on the cartridge is nothing more than a throwback to the parent cartridge, the .375 H&H Magnum — the cartridge design itself is very efficient, providing a barrel of at least 24 inches is used, and I personally prefer 25 or 26 inches.

Look to the heavy Sierra MatchKing bullets and the Hornady ELD Match, as well as the Berger Hybrid Target and VLD bullets for the best long-range

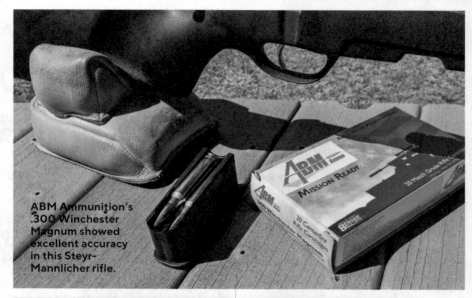

ABM Ammunition's .300 Winchester Magnum showed excellent accuracy in this Steyr-Mannlicher rifle.

Winchester Expedition Long Range .300 Winchester Magnum ammunition, with the 190-grain Nosler AccuBond.

ballistics, as these will retain as much energy as possible, minimizing the effects of wind deflection and extending the supersonic range as far as possible. While most .300 Winchester barrels will be equipped with a 1:10-inch twist rate, there are enough new bullet designs available to warrant a 1:8-inch twist, and were I building a target rifle in this caliber, I'd opt for the latter. There are some great target loads with bullets perfectly suitable for true long-distance work. I especially like the ABM factory loads and the Hornady Match ammo. Top your .300 with the best-quality riflescope you can afford, and watch the magic happen.

to fit perfectly in the AR-10 magazine, giving those who shoot that platform a low-recoiling, uber-accurate choice for long-range work.

However, the 6.5 Creedmoor would find its niche in the bolt-action community. Without a doubt, the bolt-action rifles — with their rigid one-piece stocks and heavier actions — offer a higher level of accuracy (not that some of the semi-autos can't be wonderfully accurate), and in the bolt gun the Creedmoor shows its full potential. These bolt guns are built as short-action rifles, in which the added rigidity of the action only enhances the

6.5 Creedmoor ammunition from the Nosler Match Grade line, using Nosler's 140-grain Custom Competition hollowpoint boattail bullet easily surpasses the performance of .308 Win. on the long-range competition course.

(below) Federal's Gold Medal Match 6.5 Creedmoor with the 140-grain Sierra MatchKing makes an excellent choice for serious long-range work.

(above) Hornady's Precision Hunter ammo built around the 143-grain ELD-X in 6.5 Creedmoor is light-recoiling and laser-accurate.

6.5 CREEDMOOR

Creedmoor. It has become all the rage in the last decade, and with good reason: it was designed for exactly the purpose we are discussing — long-range shooting. Introduced by Hornady in 2007, the Creedmoor is named for the location of some famous international shooting matches in the 1870s. Based on the nearly obscure .30 T/C cartridge (in turn a derivation of the .308 Winchester), the Creedmoor was bred to give optimal long-range performance from the AR-15 platform. Its case was cut down enough to allow the longer 6.5mm bullets to be seated properly, yet still function in the AR's magazine. The result was an efficient yet compact case that will drive the 140-grain bullets to a muzzle velocity of just about 2,700 fps. A cartridge overall length (COL) of 2.825 inches allows it

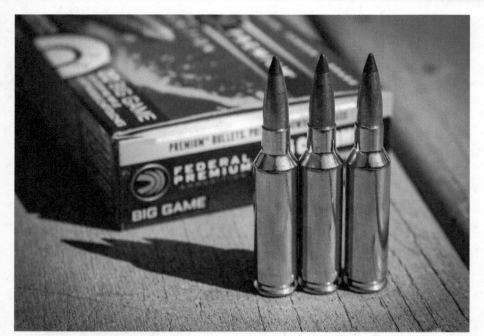

Federal Premium 6.5 Creedmoor ammo, loaded with the 140-grain Trophy Copper bullet, is a sound choice for the long-range deer hunter.

Norma Magnum, in an indoor 500-meter range, each shooter took four shots. The best three were counted, the goal being the tightest group size, and the best group of the day won a Swedish moose hunt with the folks from Norma Precision. The shots were taken off a bipod, on a concrete bench that stood about four feet high. Yes, that's right, it was a rifle none of us had fired, in a cartridge unfamiliar to us all, from a rather awkward shooting position. The day wore on, and I viewed the other numerous products unveiled that day while waiting for the opportunity to shoot my own 500-meter group. When my turn arrived, I met a couple of friends from Norma who were running the competition, and they had the look of pity in their eyes.

"What?!" I inquired.

"Jens Ulrik Hogh has printed a group virtually unbeatable."

accuracy potential of the design. With a 1:8-inch twist rate, bullets from 120 to 140 grains are usually employed, and even with the relatively moderate muzzle velocities (3,000 fps with the 120s and 2,700 fps with the 140s) the 6.5 Creedmoor will maintain supersonic flight out past 1,300 yards, giving it a definite advantage over the .308 Winchester, which even with the 175-grain Sierra MatchKing will start to go transonic at somewhere around 1,000 yards. Wind deflection values are considerably less than that of the similarly proportioned .308 Win., giving the Creedmoor yet another advantage.

And for those longer shooting sessions, the felt recoil of the 6.5 Creedmoor is noticeably less than that of the .308, so for the same weight of rifle, you can easily see why the cartridge is creating such a buzz around the shooting industry. I've used it to punch steel out to 1,500 yards and can tell you it's one of the most pleasant cartridges to shoot.

Virtually every ammunition maker offers a good target load for the 6.5 Creedmoor, and I've had great results with the Hornady Match load using the 140-grain ELD Match, and the Federal Gold Medal Match load with the 140-grain Sierra MatchKing. Trust me when I tell you, the Creedmoor isn't going anywhere; when a cartridge is described by respected long-range shooters as "boringly accurate," it's a winner.

.338 NORMA MAGNUM

I was invited to Range Day at the RWS factory in Nuremberg, Germany, the day prior to the opening of the IWA Show, and they were holding a friendly little shooting competition among the gun writers. Being the only American invited, I had every intention of representing my countrymen as best as possible, though I knew the competition was fierce. There were 42 of us, and I drew the second-to-last position. The rules were: Using a Steyr rifle chambered in the new .338

The .338 Norma Magnum, an update of the .338 Lapua, will most definitely handle long-range duties, with plenty of striking power at truly long range.

I bellied up to the bench and assumed the best position I could. First shot printed at 12 0'clock, about four inches above the bull. Ok, so I shot another. My buddy Kenneth put his index and middle fingers together, indicating the shots were touching. Oh boy, the pressure was on. I asked not to be informed of the next shots, letting the chips fall where they may. The overall result was a three-shot group measuring 1.700 inches, with a four-shot group of just over 2 inches. But, their initial statement proved to be correct: Hogh beat my group by a quarter-inch, taking the prize! I proudly took second-place and congratulated Jens on his excellent shooting. What I did come away from the experience with was great respect for the .338 Norma, which held better than 1/3 MOA at 500 meters in the hands of two different shooters.

Based on a shortened .338 Lapua case — which in turn is based on the century-plus-old .416 Rigby design — the .338 Norma Magnum is one bad hombre. It uses the same COL as does the .338 Lapua (3.681 inches) but in a bit of a different configuration. The .338 Norma Magnum's case is trimmed down to 2.492 inches, roughly the same as the .30-06 Springfield's, but that's not to make it fit in the long-action receivers, it's to allow the longest .338 bullets — those with the seriously long o-gives — to be seated properly in the case. Powder capacity runs roughly 6 percent less, yet velocities are so close that the shooter will be hard pressed to notice the difference.

Now, please don't take this as a slight to the .338 Lapua, as that design is a sound one, and it is plenty accurate, but I'd like to point out a trend in recent cartridge development: the case length is being shortened, in relationship to the action length, to allow for the proper seating of bullets that grow increasingly longer as time goes on. The .338 Norma Magnum and 6.5 Creedmoor are both perfect examples of this concept, and you'll see the same thing in the .224 Valkyrie in just a moment.

Launching a 300-grain Sierra MatchKing at over 2,600 fps (actually a wee-bit faster than the Lapua's advertised velocity with the same bullet), the .338 Norma Magnum will stay supersonic out to 1,500 yards, so it's easily understandable why the U.S. military has adopted it for its sniper cartridge, at least for certain applications. As a target cartridge, the .338 Norma Magnum puts an exclamation point at the end of the sentence, delivering a flat trajectory and excellent wind deflection values, and generates over 4,700 ft-lbs of energy at the muzzle. That'll reach out and touch someone!

.224 VALKYRIE

The newest of the long-range cartridges, introduced by Federal at the 2018 SHOT Show in Las Vegas, the .224

Federal's new .224 Valkyrie (right), shown next to the .223 Remington. Using a shorter, fatter case, the .224 is designed around the 90-grain Sierra MatchKing, and remains supersonic to 1,300 yards with very little recoil.

Valkyrie is another specialty option. In a vein similar to the .22 Nosler, the .224 Valkyrie is designed to give optimum long-range performance from the AR-platform rifles. Where the Nosler was designed to handle the 77-grain .224-inch bullet, the .224 Valkyrie was specifically built around the 90-grain Sierra MatchKing. Now we're talking about a seriously long, high BC bullet, which will — when launched at a decent velocity — stay supersonic out to 1,300 yards or more.

The Valkyrie does exactly that, driving the MatchKing to a muzzle velocity of 2,700 fps from the AR-10 platform. While that may not seem like a monumental combination, it truly shines outside of 500 yards, especially in the gas guns.

I got to spend a bit of time with the Valkyrie in Las Vegas, at the SHOT Show's Industry Day at the Range. Using a Savage MSR rifle and the Federal Gold Medal Match factory load featuring the 90-grain MatchKing, a steel target was set up just over 800 yards away. I talked to the Federal tech guys about how the cartridge performed, and where the rifle was zeroed. "Dial seven mils and send it." I did exactly that and was amazed that between the mild recoil of the cartridge itself, and the amount of recoil taken out by the action, I could watch my own vapor trail as the bullet hit at about 8 o'clock, 4 inches outside the center of the bull. I looked up at my buddy J.J.

Reich and returned the grin he already had on his face. "This is one sweet little cartridge, bud!" Reich just nodded.

I was amazed as to how well the Valkyrie performed in the desert winds, it was certainly less susceptible to the effects of wind deflection than a .308 Winchester would be, and what a pleasure it was to shoot — with what I would describe as a complete lack of recoil! The Valkyrie is most certainly designed for the AR platform, but I'm very excited to try the cartridge in a bolt action. Nonetheless, if you're looking for a great new choice for long-range shooting with your gas gun — either a new rifle, or a conversion to .224 Valkyrie — would be money well spent.

CONCLUSION

These are by no means the only available choices for the long-range shooter, as there is a wide array of choices that will fit the bill, but these represent the cartridges I've either come to depend upon, or will very soon, for my own long-range work. If you handload ammunition, the floodgates open, removing the need for factory ammunition. Even if you don't, the cartridges listed above will offer a wide range of performance levels, and I'd be willing to bet you could spend a considerable amount of time learning how they each perform downrange. **TGD**

AK-12: THE

The AK-12 features improved ergonomics and modularity over the AKM, AK-74 and AK-74M. BY MARCO VOROBIEV

FINAL AK?

The new and perhaps final version of the AK-12 is very different from the gun the Russians unveiled in 2012.

As the AK evolution continues, it will reach critical mass when drastic gun re-design must occur to guide further development of the AK. The AK-12 Avtomat is the newest version of the Kalashnikov-designed rifle, created in 2012. It is a promising product developed by the Kalashnikov Concern at its Izhevsk Plant.

The main feature of the AK-12 is improved ergonomics and modularity in comparison with its predecessors, the AKM, AK-74 and AK-74M. According to the gun designers, they improved the service life, reliability and accuracy of the gun.

The AK-12 demonstrates excellent characteristics during initial testing. It has less recoil, better cooling, is lighter and shorter, and can be reloaded with one hand. That's why in 2015 the AK-12 Kalashnikov Avtomat was adopted and will be used as the main personal weapon for the Russian individual soldier equipment complex Ratnik.

The newer version of the AK-12 in its design was brought back to the original Kalashnikov system. However, it now also included most of the ergonomic, handling and modular features of the previous model.

Is it the same AK-12 they demonstrated in 2012? Not really. In fact, not at all. The development of the new machine started in June 2011 under the leadership of the well-known chief designer of Izhmash, Vladimir Viktorovich Zlobin. It was entirely an Izhmash initiative.

The new AK was based on the work and experience accumulated over the last 10 years. In 2011, the prototype was completed and testing of the fifth-generation Avtomat with the name AK-12 began. The AK-12 is designed to replace the previous versions of the AK-103, AK-74M, AK-74 and early AKM, AKMS and all other AKs still in service.

For the first time, the AK-12 was shown to the public in January 2012, hence its index "12." The main goals in the development of the AK-12 were to:

• Increase the universality of the gun.

• Improve the ergonomic characteristics.

• Preserve and possibly improve the gun's main performance characteristics (accuracy of fire, survivability, reliability in different modes).

The Russian government was not eager to provide any support to development of the new Avtomat, citing the success of old AKs. So, they didn't. During the period of 2013 and 2014, the AK-12 encountered some opposition from the Russian military under the pretext of many shortcomings, so state financing of the trials was denied. Nevertheless, on February 21, 2015, the Ministry of Defense evaluated the characteristics of

To match the look and most importantly the functionality of the AK-12 stock and pistol grip, the author used the FAB Defense M4–AK P folding plastic AR tube, MagPul's CTR stock and a FAB Defense AG–47S grip.

the newly upgraded AK-12.

As a result, it was adopted as the main weapon for the Ratnik individual equipment complex, alongside its more expensive and heavier competitor, the A-545. It also received a preferential role over the balanced automatics Avtomat.

In 2015, after preliminary tests, the fifth-generation Avtomat, already adopted for service, got a number of upgrades. The high-lighted deficiencies were not critical to the design and would be corrected within a year. After the new Avtomat was tested again and passed the government tests with flying colors, its arrival in the Russian armed forces was slotted for 2016.

The AK-12 has the following tactical and technical character-istics:

- Caliber: 5.45x39mm
- Length: 730/940 mm (29.75/37 inches) with stock folded/unfolded
- Weight (without cartridges): 3.2 kg (7.1 lbs.)
- Barrel length: 415mm (16.3 inches)
- Bullet velocity: 900m/s (2,952 fps)
- Rate of fire: 650 rds/min.
- Max. aiming range: 1,000 m.
- Max. effective range: 600 m.
- Magazine capacity: 95 rounds for drum magazine, 30 or 60 rounds for box-type mags
- Firing modes: automatic, fixed 3-shot burst and single shot

All of this is in line with its previous model. You do not have to be an experienced firearms designer or famous gunsmith to see that the new AK-12, though it is a clearly a new weapon type, is still an AK. In fact, it appears to be a compromise between the original AK-12 and the modernization kit.

It appears to have the standard AK-74 stamped receiver, which encompasses the standard trigger and bolt groups. It takes a slight departure from the norm in a copy of the Krebs enhanced safety lever, which is not what the highly publicized original AK-12 had. There is no button mag release. Instead, the regular AK latch is used.

The AR-style telescopic stock is installed instead of the multi-functional stock of the original gun. The stock-folding mechanism is identical to the AK-74. My very own AKS had the same one 30 years ago. The pistol grip is more ergonomic, and similar to one from Israel's FAB Defense or CAA.

The top cover is hinged, using completely new mounting and retention mechanisms, but similar to the modernization kit none-theless. The rear sight block is modified and no longer supports the rear sight. Instead, it is now used for the top cover hinge and to retain the upper handguard more firmly.

The rear sight block is now removable and can be installed anywhere along the Picatinny rail that runs the entire length of the top cover and aligns perfectly with the section atop the upper handguard. The upper handguard has two mounting spots for small Picatinny rail sections, one on each side. The matching lower handguard has the rail at the bottom. The length of the handguards is about the same of those on the AK-74 with excep-tion of the upper.

The differences begin forward of the handguards. Although the gas tube appears to have the same length and similar design, minus the upper handguard brackets, the gas block is a different story. It is a gas/front sight block combination of new design. It is higher than the standard AK and has the gas chamber going all the way forward, where it is topped with a gas regulator. The accessory lug is at the bottom of the combination block for

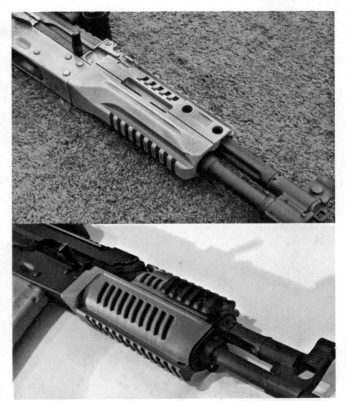

The FAB Defense AKL–47/74 handguards proved to be a pretty good match for the AK-12 guards.

The Russian-made Red Heat AK dust cover provided by Legion USA with full-length Picatinny rail section in combination with original Russian safety/selector lever were a spot-on match.

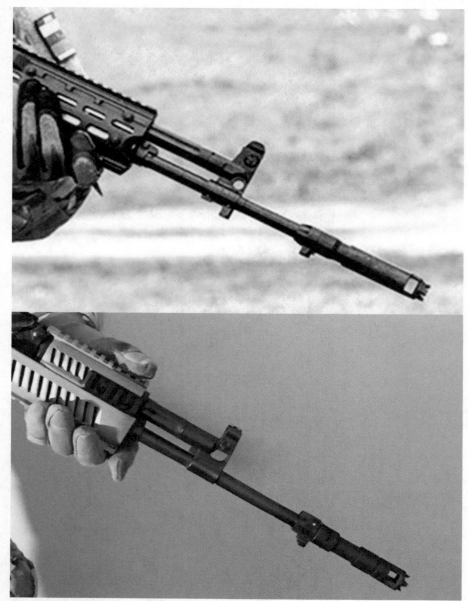

The earlier version of the AK-12 muzzle device was a departure from the standard AK-74 type brake. It resembled the Polish Tantal device, affording the ability to launch rifle grenades.

mounting a grenade launcher.

The muzzle of the upgraded AK-12 is tipped with a threaded block that sports a detent pin and bayonet lug. The gun uses two different muzzle devices. One is a modified version of the AK-74 brake and the other is similar to that of the Polish Tantal rifle.

It is slimmer than the original AK-74 brake and much longer. According to AK-12 designers, this was done for use with foreign rifle grenades. I like the idea. I also think that the Polish Tantal muzzle brake is very effective.

That's it. That's what the AK evolved

into. I don't know why the Russians didn't go with the original AK-12 design and instead settled for this one. Most likely, it was a question of funds needed for retooling the plant and more complicated (read more expensive) manufacturing process. However, I rather like it.

It is intimately familiar to AK fans, it has all the features that a modern gun should have, it's lightweight and looks like a comfortable rifle. In addition, if you believe the designers, it is a better shooting AK than its predecessors. I would not mind owning one. However, since there is no possibility of the AK-12 in its Saiga livery ever making it here, I have to build one.

BUILDING YOUR OWN AK-12

By now you know I had to see if the latest solutions employed by the Kalashnikov Concern's gun designers could be replicated. I had to build one of my own to find out if it handles or shoots as claimed. I once more embarked on the exciting journey of replicating something I cannot have otherwise.

My biggest challenge initially was to find a donor gun in the proper caliber. There were two ways to do this. One was to find a complete gun with gas/front sight combination in 5.45x39mm. The other was to get a standard AK-74 and press off the gas block and front sight and replace them with the combo. I spent a week looking around and considering my options.

The solution was an I.O., Inc., prototype rifle. The new rifle the company was working on was a combination of its M214 rifle and the AK-74. The new rifle had a combination block and threaded barrel. Exactly what I needed.

Having obtained a donor rifle, it was time to collect the rest of the components. By analyzing images of the new Russian AK-12, I came up with a list. Yet again, I tapped into FAB Defense, Brownells, Geissele Automatics, Legion USA and K-Vary Corp. as sources for the needed components. Additionally, I anticipated some actual gunsmithing work would need to be done to finish this project.

As always, I started with the buttstock because it is the easiest thing to replace. By looking at the new AK-12 stock, I could not help but notice that it bears an uncanny resemblance to MagPul's CTR model. Telescopic and folding features for the AK-12 were easier to copy. Out of consideration for weight, I went with the FAB Defense plastic joint M4-AK P folding tube and MagPul CTR stock, once more provided by Brownells.

Just like the earlier model AK-12 and the modernization kit, the new gun's pistol grip is essentially a copy of CAA's ergonomic grip, the G47. FAB Defense was gracious enough to provide its AG-47S grip for the project; it is similar in design and fits perfectly on the gun.

I had to ponder which handguards to use on my AK-12 clone this time. The new Russian AK has handguards that are matching in length and parallel, with rails at the top and bottom. The clue came from the way the side rail sections mount the handguards.

The AK-12's Picatinny side rails mount

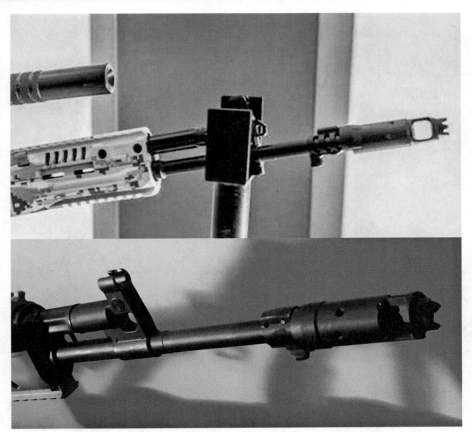

to the upper handguard, instead of the more traditional way to the lower. FAB Defense makes its AKL-47/74 guards with the same mounting option. After taking a closer look at these handguards I thought they were very similar to the originals. I got the FAB Defense handguards and installed them on my gun using standard AK brackets and hardware. I chose the dark earth color for my accessories to most closely resemble the original.

The next step turning the I.O., Inc., gun into the newest Russian AK was the hinged top cover. As previously noted, I have considerable experience with these and used them on previous builds. My preferred railed top cover was the Parabellum AKARS.

Except this time I wanted something else. My search revealed the Russian Red Heat AK dust cover with rail from Legion USA. It installed into the rear side leaf hinge and dropped into place as if it was an original part. Once on the gun, I noticed that it matched the upper handguard rail height perfectly. My rifle was starting to look like the original AK-12. Nevertheless, there was still plenty to do.

The later version of the AK-12 sported a familiar muzzle device, though slightly modified for flash and sound suppressor installation.

In the end, the author was successful in cloning the newest Russian AK Avtomat. The clone gun appears to have a longer barrel. This was dictated by the location of the gas port on the original Bulgarian barrel.

It was not possible to match the new gun's entire list of features, like the adjustable gas system or additional accessory lug. However, the author came pretty darn close.

One more part that came from Legion USA was the Russian version of the Krebs Enhanced Safety lever. I thought I would stay as authentic as I could and used it on my clone along with the Geissele ALG AK High Energy Hammer Spring and the two-zone compression return spring.

I decided to try a different trigger group for the AK-12 this time. I opted for the FIME Group's (affiliated with K-Var Corp. and Arsenal USA) FM-922US trigger group. It was a drop-in replacement and had the look of the regular AK trigger, but with definite performance improvement.

The main body of the gun was done with the updates and, from the front sight/gas block back, it looked pretty close to the AK-12 Avtomat.

It was time for gunsmithing. I needed to find a block with detent pin and bayonet lug that would be pressed over the threaded barrel. Also, there was the matter of which muzzle brake to use. After a search, I decided to go with Polish Tantal parts. The Tantal's front sight had the bayonet lug and detent pin I needed. All I had to do was cut it, grind it and press it on. The Tantal muzzle device is highly effective as a brake and happens to be one of my favorite brakes.

Additionally, there was an issue with the gun's open sights. Since I had to

I.O. Inc.'s rifle had two very important features: the front sight/gas block combination and the 14mm left-hand thread at the muzzle.

remove the original rear sight, I had to find a substitute to go on top of the receiver cover with one caveat, it had to be very low. There was only one that I knew about, the TWS peephole sight, and I got it. The front sight also presented a problem that required some milling. The original I.O. front sight had a circle hood over the sight post. The higher-sitting handguards and a rail on the top of the receiver cover rendered the original

sight useless. I needed to mill the top off the sight to provide more room for the post.

With my unfinished gun and with several parts in tow, I headed to the Erie Ordnance Depot (EOD) shop in Portage, Northern Ohio. Jim Weishuhn, owner of EOD, is a master gunsmith I often call upon when I reach the limits of my gunsmithing abilities. Having a full shop, he often helps me with my projects. This time was not different. We cut the Tantal front sight, creating a detent pin block, ground it into shape and pressed it on the barrel of my AK-12 clone, past the threaded tip exposing enough thread to install a muzzle brake.

Jim pinned the block in place with a working detent pin. Next, he machined an opening in the enclosed front sight hood, making it more suitable for front sight adjustment and better looking. With the gun nearly complete, we moved on to the two muzzle brakes. All we had to do was modify the tips of both brakes to mimic the Russian parts. After Jim machined both muzzle brakes, all that was left was to refinish the modified parts of the gun.

It was done. Stepping back and looking at my creation, I was very satisfied with the way the AK-12 looked. It looked very close to the original. I did try to use most of the accessories in Dark Earth color to match the Russian AK-12, but stopped short of painting the whole gun, instead retaining the option of reconfiguring it later.

Nevertheless, my AK-12 felt light and had an aura of "niftiness" about it. I

Choosing a gun for the AK-12 build was a challenge. Needing an AK-74 with front sight/ gas block combination, the solution came in the form of I.O., Inc.'s hybrid of a Bulgarian kit–built AK-74 and the M214 rifle.

(above) Not only did the author's AK-12 clone closely resemble the Russian Avtomat, it also shot exceptionally well.

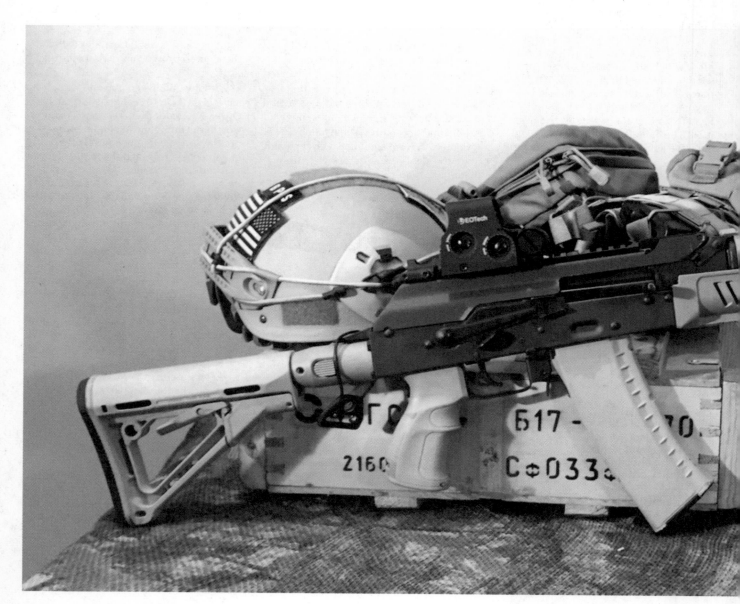

have shouldered it several times and it felt almost intuitive. The ergonomics were improved and, at the same time, it retained the AK familiarity. Other than that, it looked and felt like a foreign gun and it also looked and felt like an AK. It cycled very well with no hang-ups. All controls worked as they should, and the two-stage FIME Group trigger group felt very crisp. The only question was, would it shoot and would it shoot well?

At the range, I set up at 50 yards, as I was more interested in the gun's function than accuracy. I would check that later. For the first series of tests I installed the modified AK-74 brake to see if there was a difference between the standard AK-74 and my newly minted clone.

First shots did not disappoint. The clone worked great and, in the best AK-74 tradition, was easy to shoot with no appreciable recoil.

I switched the muzzle devices, installing the modified Tantal brake. With the Polish-design brake, the next series of shots was surprising. The gun was noticeably smoother and its already almost negligible recoil was reduced even further. I was impressed to say the least. So far, the gun was working well. Of course, I could not compare it the original. However, assumptions could be made. And, if the Russians did similar internal upgrades as I'd done, the new AK-12 is better than the AK-74M.

I'm not putting myself in the same group with Russian firearm designers, engineers and gun makers. Even though I'm a mechanical engineer, I don't know the intricacies of the firearm design. All I can do is wrap my head around the mechanics of it, add some physics principles, and try to replicate a result, sort of a "proof of a concept," if you will.

So, as far as I was concerned, it worked. My AK-12 clone looked very similar to the Russian AK-12 Avtomat and shot exceptionally well, enough for me to adopt it as one of my work rifles.

At the range, I continued to test my new gun. I used its open sights to see if it would produce a decent group and it did. All 30 rounds nestled in a tight group at the 1 o'clock spot, approximately 1 inch off the bull's eye of the target. At 100 yards, my group opened up some, but was still way within my expectations.

In my hands, I had a gun that not only looked and felt great, but also worked well.

After installing a generic red-dot sight, I went to work on steel silhouette targets set up at 50 and 100 yards. It was a pleasure to put it mildly. The AK-12 clone's meager recoil allowed me to maintain a dot on the target while firing at all times and at both distances.

Rapid semi-auto fire was an easy task. The gun felt like something you want to fire on the move during a carbine course or competition. I love the fact that I was able once more to build a gun that closely mimics the appearance and possibly the performance of the newest Russian Avtomat, and I did it with parts available in the U.S. at reasonable prices.

Is the AK-12 the last AK, the last link in its evolution? I don't know. In fact, no one does. As the "Old Guard" gun makers die off or retire, more and more voices in Russia today call for a completely new firearms system. It is time to replace the ancient technology, they say. **TGD**

Here it is, the author's very own, the latest in the AK Evolution species, the AK-12 that he built mostly in his basement, with a little help from friends.

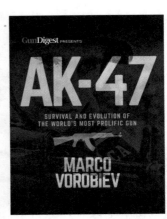

Editor's Note: This excerpt is from AK-47: Survival and Evolution of the World's Most Prolific Gun, *available now at GunDigestStore.com.*

knew right from the start that Ken was trying to prove a point, but I was curious just how far he was willing to push this little "test" he had organized.

Ken Hagen had me stretched prone at the heel of a new H&H Precision custom build he'd recently completed, and before me lay a myriad of targets — each at exponentially increasing distances — scattered across the foothills of the Pacific's Northwest's Mt. Olympus. This rifle, built on a platform of black, was short and stout and chiseled for mid-range service duty. Everything about the gun screamed "urban tactical," and it nearly felt out of place next to the other precision rifles stretch out on either side along the shooting line.

As any rifleman knows, barrel length increases velocities, promoting accuracy at extended distances. That's as much common knowledge as is the fact that the pointy end of a rifle cartridge goes forward when loading. But according to Hagen, increased barrel length can also be used as a crutch when other components of a rifle are, um … lacking.

And to prove his point, Ken intended to have me work over a 1,270-yard target with this .308 — a .308 Win. that sported a 16-inch barrel. And again, as nearly every rifleman knows, the .308 Win. has long been the standard upon which long-range ballistics have been applied. But the 16-inch barrel on a long-range bolt rifle? That's a little less standard.

I began familiarizing myself with the rifle's intricacies with some "gimme" shots at 550 yards on a 12-inch steel plate. As expected from a top-end custom rifle, every shot became slightly more additive than the one prior. I've heard gun writers refer to working a bolt as "effortless," but this was different: It seemed impossible that two pieces of metal could work in unison with such

DEFINING
'CUSTOM'

How H&H Precision Guarantees 1/4 MOA Accuracy BY **LUKE HARTLE**
PHOTOS BY TRACER X

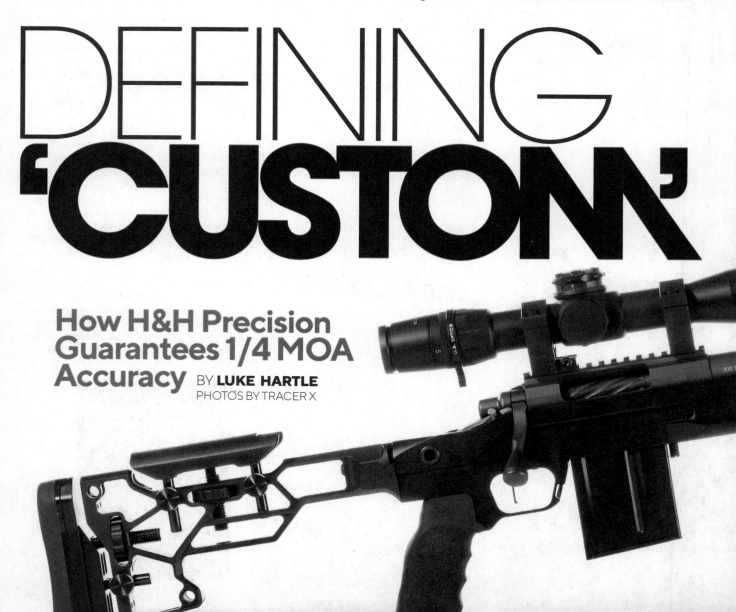

From bolt to muzzle, each component of an H&H Precision barreled action is held to scrupulous tolerances.

> **I've heard gun writers refer to working a bolt as 'effortless,' but this was different: It seemed impossible that two pieces of metal could work in unison with such grace.**

grace. Once that target was thoroughly demoralized, I stopped to send a handful of rounds at a 725-yard target before settling the crosshairs on the clean white paint of the 1,270-yard gong.

My first shot sailed just wide of the gong — a misinterpreted wind call on my part that was embellished by Ken's beady eyes piercing my concentration from over my shoulder. This was the test he was determined to have me pass with his rifle, and I'd allowed my concentration to drift away from the fundamentals … which allowed the bullet to drift away from the intended impact point.

I resettled on the gun, ran a quick mental diagnostic of my body position and waited on the wind call. At the rifle's report, I had time to properly follow though and still get back on target to watch the paint splatter from the collision — a bullet that drops more than 4 stories out of the air will do that for ya. On the heels of that visual verification, I ran the bolt and sent another, and another … and another. And by the time the magazine ran dry, that 1,270-yard white steel plate looked like the cap of a pepper shaker.

For years, Ken has built the H&H Precision brand upon the guarantee that any rifle purchased from him is capable of shooting ¼ MOA. And that's a bold stance in an industry that hangs its hat on producing MOA-guaranteed rifles every day of the week.

THE CUSTOM TOUCH

When I was a kid, Grandma always made the best cookies. Mom's cookies were fine and Auntie did a decent job, too — but none were close to the quality of what Grandma could whip up. Of course, when I inquired to the reasoning behind this phenomenon, I was always told that Granny's cookies taste best because "they were made with love."

I could tell you that Ken Hagen can build a gun on a ¼-MOA guarantee because of the love he incorporates into the gun, but that implies a bit of magic, and the detailed machining work done at H&H Precision is much more surgical in nature.

We've all heard the tale of two friends who walked into the sporting goods store and bought the exact same rifle on the exact same day — but at the range, those two "identical" rifles behave nothing alike when scores are tallied on the target. So, what gives?

STACKING TOLERANCES

Like a chain, any rifle in question is only as accurate as its weakest link. Parts are milled, machined and fitted to a specific set of tolerance parameters. The more finite the tolerances, the better each link in the rifle chain works with the other links.

For example, let's say that when Rifle A was built, the barrel-to-receiver threading was off by one-thousandth of an inch. In reality, that's a pretty small number and it falls within the tolerance allotment determined by the manufacturing company of Rifle A. Let's also say that the bolt face is one-thousandth of an inch out of alignment with the front of the receiver, as is the shoulder of the muzzle brake when secured to the business end of the barrel.

Law enforcement municipalities along the entire coast of Washington State have started shooting H&H Precision rifles exclusively.

Keep in mind that all metal is malleable, and it's very possible to overcome that tiny one-thousandth of an inch by tightening the barrel threads with enough force that the barrel's shoulder aligns perfectly with the front of the receiver. After all, no one is going to buy a gun that wears a tiny gap between the barrel shoulder and the receiver.

However, that "force fitting" has just introduced stress into that rifle. Compound that with the stress it takes to perfectly align the muzzle brake — or any other similar components — thus building stress into that entire barreled action. Forcing the pieces to fit takes advantage of that malleable metal, and it stacks one tolerance deviation on another.

Stress plus heat (as introduced to the barrel by rapid, consecutive shots) equals barrel walking. Simply put, metal stress is what causes bullets to string out as the barrel heats up. And that's why those two identical guns I referenced earlier have the potential to perform so differently: Sometimes, luck has it that everything lines up and a particular gun is nearly stress free — and it drives tacks. Sometimes, luck swings the other way.

Eliminating stress is all but impossible, but Hagen takes the extra time to trim his tolerances down to the ten-thousandth decimal place in an exhausting effort to minimize the stress incorporated to the build. A rifle with no stress will not walk as the barrel heats, and it's also the foundation upon which a ¼-MOA guarantee is built.

BOLT AND RECEIVER TRUING

As we started working up a rifle in Hagen's shop, it's was almost aggravating to watch and wait as Ken measured and re-measured the bolt face and the bolt head against the front of the receiver, but I knew well what he was doing: It's impossible to achieve exceptional accuracy from a rifle whose bolt doesn't perfectly align with its receiver. There was no guesswork here: It had to be checked and cycled — and then checked again — and then check and cycled again to confirm complete compatibility.

BARREL TIMING

After a day in the H&H Precision shop, it's impossible for me to view a barrel as anything but an elbow macaroni noodle. Yes, elbow macaroni. According to Hagen, every single bore in every single barrel that's ever been made has a curve to it. Sure, the macaroni analogy is a bit extreme, but when a rifle bore is drilled, it's impossible to keep the resulting hole from developing a rainbow-like arc to it inside a perfectly straight barrel (according to outside dimensions), regardless of how slight.

So, how is that overcome? It's not — but it is accounted for. Hagen implements a series of surgical steps that help him determine the exact path of the bore curve, and he then aligns the barrel with the receiver so that the curve always points exactly straight up at the muzzle

The Benchmark in Barrels

As with his receivers, Hagen is meticulous when it comes to selecting the components he works into his custom builds. And because the foundation of an H&H Precision rifle is built around the bore, it's arguable that the barrel blank is the most important piece. His choice: Benchmark Barrels.

While studying with Hagen at H&H, we took a day to spend some time understanding the differences between what it takes to make a good barrel, and what it takes to make a great barrel. And although I was sworn to secrecy on a lot of the processes that Benchmark implements, it quickly became obvious that its attention to details that most machinists overlook is what helps it achieve a product that most can only hope to attain. Benchmark is a lot like H&H Precision in that way.

But amid the surgical-like processes is woven a bit of magic: the hand-lapping of the bores. There are no machines that can be tuned fine enough to mirror the learned craft those hand-lappers were practicing. And a job that's done "by feel" is something that's not easily replicated by competition.

–Luke Hartle

This H&H Precision build features a Killer Innovations Orias chassis and a Benchmark barrel.

"Stacking tolerances" refers to compounding deviations when asembling machined parts. True long-range accuracy demands meticulous machining practices.

... like an inverted rainbow, if you will. This helps minimize bullet drop from line-of-sight and keeps bullet travel perfectly aligned with line-of sight as well.

"Imagine if that curve were spitting bullets up and right," said Hagen. "Have fun tracking with that rifle."

BUILT FROM THE BORE OUT

Just as barrel timing references the curvature of a barrel's bore, Hagen references the bore for every other piece of machining (truing the barrel shoulder, cutting the barrel threads, truing the muzzle) — never the exterior of the barrel.

Think about that for just a moment: If a gun is built so that the barrel is perfectly aligned with the receiver instead of the bore being perfectly aligned with the receiver, the chambered cartridge is likely out of alignment with the bore from the very beginning of the shot cycle. This adds more stress to the

The Guns of H&H Precision

Located just outside of Seattle, Ken Hagen of H&H Precision has been building his brand one rifle at a time in the foothills to Mt. Rainier — country perfectly made for testing the art of precision rifle building.

Though not yet a household name, H&H Precision has silently landed contracts with all the major law enforcement municipalities of the Washington coast — and those guys are damn picky about what they choose to shoulder when lives are on the line.

The .308 Win. sporting a 16-inch barrel is a new build for Hagen, custom designed to meet the demands of his growing law enforcement clientele. Still, the H&H menu has an abundance of chassis and hunting models upon which the consumer can build. The rifles don't come cheap — but then again, hand building each and every rifle to ¼-MOA spec does take time and talent.

–Luke Hartle

system, and we already know what that does to accuracy.

As Ken explained the process to me, it almost made me squeamish that many of the concepts he was explaining were so obvious — and apparently he was able to ready that on my face.

"I'm not saying I'm doing the impossible here," Hagen said. "I'm simply say-ing that I'm doing things and attending to details that most rifle manufacturers — big and small — don't do. You can buy a $1,200 precision rifle that shoots well; there are plenty out there under a lot of different brands. H&H Precision is all about the shooter who appreciates what it takes to achieve ¼-MOA accuracy and understands what a gun like that is capable of doing at long ranges."

This article appeared in the August 15, 2018 issue of Gun Digest the Magazine. *Luke Hartle is the Editor-in-Chief of the publication.*

GOING THE DISTANCE

H&H Precision pairs with the Orias Chassis. The result: A rifle boasting a ¼-MOA guarantee and exceptional diversity.

What does it take to elevate a rifle's capabilities to an exceptional level of accuracy? High-quality materials fed into top-precision machines operated by heavily experienced technicians? Maybe. But I'd argue that every single firearm brought to market should have all those qualifications.

I'm not talking about "minute-of-whitetail" accuracy or a gun capable of ringing a 10-inch steel plate at 600 yards. I'm talking about a level of accuracy that was all but inaccessible — barely even fathomable — to civilian shooters a few years ago.

There are a few trends abuzz right now in the shooting world wildly unparalleled in both form and function. On one hand, you've got long-standing, well-respected firearms manufacturers that are kicking out sub-$400 rifles capable of producing consistent sub-MOA groups even when operated by riflemen of moderate skillsets. Think Ruger's American rifles, the Savage Axis, Mossberg's Patriot and Remington's Model 783. And there are others.

For shooters whose version of success is measured in punched big-game tags as much as tightly perforated paper, these guns — and this entire trending category — is a dream come true both in regard to performance and price.

And then there are "the freaks" — a growing fraternity of those who, by definition, create a "very unusual and unexpected event or situation." These are the gunsmiths, engineers, machinists and shooters who demand — and are willing to pay for — perfection that's measured by thousandths of an inch in the shop and by fractions of MOA on the line.

Imagine a precision rifle that can produce ¼-MOA groups. Every shot. From every gun that rolls out of that shop. Yeah, that's freaky.

Defining Precision

Ken Hagen's passion for the shooting sports bloomed at very young age and took roots with a family that was heavily involved in outdoor activities. From age 2 and beyond, Hagen was never left behind when his family headed afield.

"I can remember standing in the front seat of an old 60s Chevy pickup and watching my grandmother shoot antelope and deer," said Hagen. "She stretched across the hood in true redneck fashion, wearing hair curlers and a cigarette hanging out of her mouth. Much like a Labrador retriever with a strong desire to chase and retrieve, I found myself consumed with the passion to hunt and shoot, too."

Admittedly, Hagen didn't do well in grade school because of his daydreams about hunting and shooting while in class. Nothing was more important to him than hunting and shooting, and it wasn't until he lost his hunting privileges due to poor grades that he found the motivation to start paying a bit more attention in class.

"My grandfather had me on a sliding scale when it came to school grades," added Hagen. "An 'A' got me in on elk, deer, antelope and small-game hunts. 'Bs' got me in on deer and antelope. A 'C' got me in on small game. If I came home with a 'D,' I lost my rifle and my hunting privileges. And an 'F' ... well, I didn't dare go there."

Hagen's grandfather was also a builder, and at age 8, the pair built Hagen's first high-power rifle together in his shop — a sporterized Springfield .30-06. The stock was honed from an old block of walnut, which was hand-carved and with jade inlays.

And that's the proverbial spark that lit the passion of rifle building for Hagen.

The unique configuration and incredible machining precision of this Orias Chassis allows for the removal and re-installation of the receiver with a zero point–of-impact shift when torqued to the proper sequence.

From Passion To Profession

"Shooting and building rifles have always been my passion," said Hagen, "but my drive is fueled even further when I can become part of peoples' experience. It's not just about building rifles — it's about being part of something people are proud to own. It's a privileged honor when people select my products and services."

Every H&H Precision rifle is built one at a time, from start to finish. Hagen's attention to detail and devotion to build the best rifle for that customer is solely set aside for that customer, and it's his one-at-a-time devotion that allows him to do it. With each rifle, Hagen promises himself to build to his best ability and never cut any corners, regardless of timelines and production schedules.

"There are hundreds of custom rifle manufacturers on the market producing exceptional rifles," added Hagen. "So when a customer picks H&H Precision over the others, I owe it to them to do my best work. I build for special operations groups who're called to duty when lives are at stake and failure is not an option. I'm not a first-responder or a soldier on the battlefield, but I help serve to protect and defend in other ways."

Every H&H Precision rifle is tested under video to prove ¼-MOA accuracy with a Target Cam System and two cameras. Each customer gets a video of their rifle shooting the groups. Not only is that unparalleled proof of Ken's commitment to perfection, it's almost as if the customer is standing next to Hagen when he's testing their rife — every shot and every bullet hole develops on the screen and is captured by that video.

"My philosophy is simple: If a manufacturer never proved a rifle can shoot ¼-MOA, then how can they guarantee it?" said Hagen. "I hear stories of manufacturers who say it but never

prove it — and we all know talk is cheap. The H&H Precision slogan is as simple as my business philosophy: 'We don't just say it — we prove it!'

"Customer satisfaction is priority No. 1," added Hagen. "If, for any reason, a customer doesn't like one of my rifles within a reasonable timeline, I will refund or replace the rifle. I will never stick a customer with a rifle they're not satisfied with. H&H Precision is the safest bet in town when investing in a high-end rifle."

Even in the current, highly competitive landscape of precision rifle shooters and builders, Ken Hagen's intuition and gunsmithing experience is largely unparalleled. He's also equipped with the latest technologies and machine shop equipment and is backed by years of experience to provide a full service operation. The circle of people who know Hagen's top-secret processes of precision gunsmithing is incredibly tiny, but Hagen accredits much of his success — and his ability to guarantee ¼-MOA — on the Orias Chassis.

Orias Chassis

The Orias Chassis system, developed and built by Killer Innovations and Mega Arms, has quickly evolved into one of the most advanced chassis systems available.

Developed around the patent-pending self-adjusting recoil lug alignment system, the Orias Chassis has a free-floating half-round on the backside of the recoil lug that's held in place by two small magnets. The half-round is free to rotate to perfectly match the angularity of the recoil lug on the receiver as the wedge clamp in the front of the recoil lug forces back into the half-round.

This proprietary system eliminates any minute angularity differences between the receiver's recoil lug and the Orias chassis, which can cause serious accuracy problems at long ranges. The configuration of this system also allows for the removal and reinstallation of the receiver with a zero point-of-impact shift when torqued to the proper sequence.

The Orias Chassis is cut from a solid block of 7075-T651 aluminum. Although 7075 is nearly twice the cost of 6061 aluminum, it's roughly 40 percent stronger and notably lighter, creating an incredibly strong yet lightweight platform for precision rifle shooters who appreciate and demand the attention to detail that can set a rifle apart from the crowd.

Weighing 2.1 pounds and topped off in a Mil-Spec Type 3 hard-anodized finish, each Orias Chassis is equipped with a removable rear trunnion that accepts an AR-style buttstock. To complete the customizing attributes of the Orias, a quick-detach accessory rail, located over the barrel, is available as an optional accessory.

The Bottom Line

"The Orias Chassis gives H&H Precision rifles an incredibly unique, maneuverable, light and highly functioning feel," said Hagen. "The palm swell provides the feel of a competition rifle, while the forend creates the feel of a lightweight, quick-handling hunting rifle. A rifle is only as good as its weakest link, and nothing else on the market comes close to performing

There's a bit of each major long-range shooting demographic — hunters, competitive shooters, long-range marksmen, military personnel or law enforcement snipers — crafted into each H&H Precision rifle.

like the Orias Chassis."

Essentially, with decades of gunsmithing experience from Hagen and hundreds of hours of machining work to perfect the Orias Chassis, comes perfection through time. Hunters, competitive shooters, long-range marksmen, military personnel or law enforcement snipers — there's a bit of each of these shooting disciplines crafted into each H&H Precision rifle. Rare is the rifle capable of delivering such incredible accuracy while still offering so much diversity. You might even call it freaky. TGD
— Luke Hartle

A quick-detach accessory rail, located over the barrel is available as an optional accessory.

AT A GLANCE: THE ORIAS CHASSIS

- Compatible with Remington Model 700 short-action and long-action pattern receivers
- Cut from a solid block of lightweight 7075-T651 billet aluminum
- No bedding required due to patent-pending self-adjusting recoil-lug locking system
- Compatible with Accuracy International-style box magazines
- Removable rear trunnion is compatible with all AR-style buffer tubes and buttstocks
- Available in KEYMOD and M-LOK
- Quick-detach inserts made from steel, black nitrite coated for strength and reliability
- Ambidextrous magazine release
- Quick-detach night vision mount available
- Left-hand short-action and long-action versions now available

AR-15

The Christensen Arms
CA-15 VTAC is designed
with the input of Kyle Lamb.
It has a button-rifled carbon
fiber-wrapped 416 stainless
barrel and a .223 Wylde
match chamber.

ROUNDUP

BY **PATRICK SWEENEY**

To some, the ideal AR-15 is simply about value, the one that provides the most bang for the buck. For others, it is the most bang, period. Since we could never whittle down the entire universe of AR-15 rifles, carbines and pistols to ten, and flatly declare, "these are the only ones you need to look at," here is the next best thing: A roundup of the top candidates for bargain, performance and appearance.

The LWRCI Personal Defense Weapon has a collapsed length of just 20 inches, an 8.6-inch barrel. Of course, that makes it an NFA weapon requiring an ATF tax stamp.

(below) The Primary Weapons Systems Mk116 Mod 1-M is a tack-driver of an AR in the mid-sized category.

LWRCI IC-PDW

If you want a compact, high-performance, no-nonsense carbine that will fit into any storage space or carry bag, then the IC-PDW is smokin.' At just under 6 pounds, and with a collapsed length of just over 20 inches, the PDW (Personal Defense Weapon) with its 8.6-inch barrel delivers the goods. Oh, it isn't a long-range tool, that's for sure, but you can get consistent hits out to 300 meters with something this small, don't doubt it. Ambi controls for selector, mag release and bolt release, and your choice of anodized black or three different Cerakote colors. All this with a cold hammer forged 1/7-inch twist barrel, which is free-floated inside the LWRC Monoforge upper receiver. The bolt and carrier have a slick, easy to clean Nickel-boron plating, and the action is driven by means of the LWRC piston system. Add in the LWRC folding sights, 4-prong flash hider, and ambi charging handle and you have the apex predator of PDWs. Fair warning: the IC-PDW is a short-barreled rifle, an SBR. That means you'll have to apply for a tax stamp for the transfer. That will take some time, and cost an extra $200, but I think it is well worth the hassle and cost. lwrci.com

PRIMARY WEAPONS SYSTEMS MK116 MOD 1-M

PWS has evolved so far beyond the mil-spec threshold that it's a dusty image in their rear-view mirror. The Mk116 Mod 1-M rifle is the most popular one in the line. The PWS piston system is a long-stroke type in which the piston is attached directly to the carrier. This provides extra reciprocating mass to control cyclic rate, and the long piston combats carrier tilt. The barrel is given a 1/8-inch twist to accurately fire heavy .223 bullets, and the chamber is the .223 Wylde, which is a hybrid of the .223 and 5.56mm. This combination is meant to deliver the accuracy of the .223 with the reliability of the 5.56, and it does. The gas system has three settings so you can dial in the gas flow you need for ammunition differences or when mounting a suppressor. The handguard is a full-length free-float design with M-Lok slots. Even in a carbine size with a 16-inch barrel, the weight is just under 7 pounds. The receivers are forged, and the furniture is from Bravo Company. PWS includes its own muzzle brake on the end of the barrel to keep the sights on target, and they also include the most-excellent Lancer 30-round magazine with each Mk116 Mod 1-M rifle or carbine. For a tack-driving AR in the mid-size category, you need only remember PWS. primaryweapons.com

DEL-TON SIERRA 3G

The Del-Ton Sierra 3G rifle is a perfect tool for 3-Gun or multi-gun competition. Starting with forged upper and lowers, Del-Ton has installed a 16-inch chrome-moly vanadium barrel, with a .223 Wylde chamber and 1/8-inch twist. They've threaded on a muzzle brake to dampen recoil. Not that the .223 kicks much, but when you're trying to win matches (or learn how) you want as little felt recoil as possible. Around this barrel, they've placed a Samson Evolution free-float handguard all the way out to the back of the muzzle brake and covering the Samson low-profile gas block. The bolt and carrier are full mil-spec, as are the forged upper and lower receivers. All the parts are made of the correct aluminum or steel alloys, no corner-cutting here. Del-Ton even goes so far as to enthusiastically stake the gas key screws, for which you should thank them. The 3G is set off by means of a CMC single-stage match trigger, a packet trigger that is a self-contained unit. No need to fuss over it, it's ready to go even before Del-Ton slides it into place. On the back end is a Magpul CTR tele-stock, and there's a Magpul PMag30 in the box with your rifle, right from the start. For someone who wants to get into 3-Gun or multi-gun competition, and not break the bank, the Sierra 3G is just the ticket. All you need is a red-dot sight and you're ready to get started. del-ton.com

to hold it. As if that wasn't enough, they made the lower so that it accepts all standard 7.62x39 magazines. That's right, an AR that takes AK magazines. The barrel is 4140 ordnance steel, with a 1/10-inch twist, normal for the AK, and it's threaded 5/8X24 for muzzle devices or suppressor mounts. With Magpul stock, pistol grip and magazine, and CMMG Keymod free-float handguard, you'll get all the accuracy your 7.62x39 ammo can deliver. (Hey, if it's commie ammo, what are you expecting?) The receivers are carved from pre-heat-treated 7075-T6 billets, and all of this comes in at just a bit over 7 pounds. The weight helps dampen the recoil of AK ammo, and CMMG puts an SV muzzle brake on the end. You can order yours in one of 11 different Cerakote colors, opt for a Keymod or M-Lok handguard and be the envy of your gun club buddies. cmmginc.com

(above) The Del-Ton Sierra 3G rifle is fitted at the factory with a CMC single-stage trigger — no need to upgrade it.

The CMMG Mk47 was designed to shoot the 7.62x39mm cartridge. The unique Mk47 lower receiver readily accepts all standard AK mags.

CMMG MK47 AKM

OK, you want something different. How about a mutant? The CMMG MK47 AKM is just that. Combining the ergonomics of the AR-15 with the cartridge of the AK-47, the CMMG is not a kludge or compromise. Most AR-15 rifles in 7.62x39 use the same bolt-lug dimensions as the 5.56 model, and this leaves the bolt weaker than it should be. CMMG made the bolt the size it needed to be, then scaled up the upper receiver

SIG SAUER MCX VIRTUS PISTOL

The SIG MCX Virtus pistol is the choice you should make if you want a compact but powerful handgun. Yes, handgun. The arm brace on the MCX Virtus puts it in the handgun category, and that is good for us. Mechanically, the MCX Virtus pistol has the same SIG piston system as the regular Virtus carbine. This system is designed to play well with the SIG suppressor, but it would play well with any suppressor. In 5.56, it has an 11.5-inch barrel, and in .300 Blackout a 9-inch barrel. The free-float M-Lok handguard is held in place by the

The SIG MCX Virtus pistol is available in 5.56mm NATO and .300 AAC Blackout.

takedown pin of the receiver, and it's easy to slide the handguard off to clean or otherwise work on the barrel and gas system. Since the recoil spring system is in the upper, the Virtus arm brace can be folded, making it even more compact for storage. Because of the MCX design, the cold hammer-forged barrels can easily be swapped out, so if you wanted to have a Virtus pistol with barrels in both 5.56 and .300 Blackout, you can do that. And swap them at the range, once the one you had just been using cooled off enough to handle. Cool and high-tech doesn't come cheap, but then no one accuses SIG of doing anything on the cheap. The MCX Virtus pistol will likely set you back by twenty Benjamins, but it's worth every penny. sigsauer.com

SAVAGE MSR PATROL

Savage? Since when did Savage make AR-15s? Since America decided that the AR-15 was the rifle for the 21st century, the Modern Sporting Rifle. The Savage MSR Patrol is the very definition of value for money. The heart of it is a carbine-length barrel with a .223 Wylde

The MSR Patrol from Savage is loaded with features, which makes it a steal and must-have with an MSRP of under $900.

chamber, 5R rifling and Melonite surface treatment. The receivers are forged to mil-spec dimensions, the trigger is mil-spec but enhanced with improved engagement surfaces. The gas system is mid-length, meaning it's in-between the length of a carbine and rifle, delivering a softer-shooting experience. It has the Blackhawk Knoxx pistol grip and Axiom adjustable carbine stock mounted. The A-frame front sight is matched with a folding rear, in case you want to mount an optic and need to get the rear sight down out of the way. The Blackhawk handguard is full-length and covers the front sight housing, so your hand is protected from the heat of the gas block if you use the extended-arm shooting

stance so popular today. The barrel is threaded for your choice of muzzle devices, or you can leave the Savage flash hider in place. All this with an MSRP well under $900, which means a bunch less than that at your local gun shop. You can opt out of the enhanced trigger and go with an upper lacking the forward assist to save another $14. Don't skimp, get the full Patrol. savagearms.com

CHRISTENSEN ARMS CA-15 VTAC

If you want a no-holds-barred, made from unobtainium and crafted by ballistic elves in the light of a full moon AR-15, then you need to go to Christensen Arms. The CA-15 VTAC is all of that and then some. Designed with the input of Kyle Lamb, the VTAC has a carbon fiber-wrapped 416 stainless barrel, which is button-rifled and sports a .223 Wylde match chamber and a 1/8-inch twist. This barrel is light, accurate and shrugs off heat. This barrel is also part of the sub-MOA guarantee that Christensen Arms builds into the sporty AR. The upper and lowers are milled from pre-hardened billets of 7075-T6 aluminum and given additional weight-reducing cuts in the design. The handguard is a free-float design, made of carbon fiber, and runs up to the back of the Titanium flash hider on the stainless barrel. You have

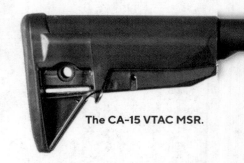

The CA-15 VTAC MSR.

your choice of Keymod or M-Lok slots on the handguard. The trigger is tuned to a crisp pull of 3 ½ to 4 ½ pounds, and the ready-to-be-finished weight is 5.7 pounds. You'll need to put your own aiming system on it, such as irons or optics of some kind, but unless you go crazy, the starting weight of the CA-15 VTAC should keep you under 7 pounds, total. High-tech and lightweight don't come cheap, as the MSRP of the CA-15 is $2,845. But what a rifle! christensenarms.com

SWORD INTERNATIONAL MK16 JÄGER KARABINER

You want style and performance? You can have it from SWORD. In direct gas (5.56) or piston (5.56 & .300 Blk) SWORD makes handy, durable carbines that look good. The top of the carbine fleet is the Mk16 Jäger Karabiner, a piston-driven handy emergency tool. It comes with ambi bolt catch/release, magazine release and selector. The piston will keep powder residue and hot gases out of your receivers, making cleaning easier. The barrel is button-rifled and nitride coated and sports a Warfighter PC Comp V2 on the muzzle to dampen recoil. The gas system is self-regulating, so whatever .223 or 5.56 ammo you feed it will run.

The SWORD Mk16 Jäger Karabiner can be had in 5.56mm or .300 AAC Blackout. A Warfighter PC Comp V2 on the muzzle slashes recoil.

The free-float handguard has M-Lok slots to mount any accessories you might desire. The recoil spring and buffer weight have been tuned for ultra-reliable function. And on top of all this (literally) you get mil-spec Type III anodizing in black, Coyote or Regnar green. The full-length top rail allows you to mount whatever sighting system you feel is best, from irons to optics, to NVG to, well, anything. Each rifle and carbine are tested at SWORD, and deliver 1 MOA or better accuracy, or aren't shipped. sword-int.com

CORE RIFLE SYSTEMS HARDCORE C9

If you want something quiet, plenty handy and that won't make you a pariah at your indoor range in the wintertime, then Core 15 has the perfect AR. The Hardcore C9 uses 9mm Glock magazines, and new this year it can be had as a pistol, a pistol with brace or a carbine. Threaded, of course, for muzzle devices such as a suppressor, the flat-top C9

receiver is built for irons or optics. Both upper and lower are machined from pre-hardened billets of 7075-T6 aluminum and given a Black Cerakote finish over anodized exteriors. The handguard is a Samson M-Lok SX series, and is 7 inches long — long enough to hold, but not so long it interferes with mounting your suppressor. If you're not in the market for a suppressor, the Hardcore C9 comes with the Core 15 muzzle brake, allowing you to keep the sights on target when hammering out 9mm ammo in a match. It comes with the SB Tactical PDW arm brace, and you can adjust its length for your arm length. Who doesn't have Glock 9mm magazines on hand? You? Why not? They are dirt cheap, so get a bunch, because this will be fun.   core15rifles.com

An excellent value, the Devil Dog KRP comes with a superb ALG Defense QMS trigger package. Available in 5.56/.223 Rem. and .308 Win.

DEVIL DOG ARMS KRP (KEYMOD RIFLE PACKAGE)

The Devil Dog Arms KRP, or Keymod Rifle Package, is a whole lot of rifle for not a lot of cash. Oh, it costs more than a plain-jane basic carbine, but what you get is mil-spec or better. Starting with billet 7075-T6 receivers that are given the proper Type III anodizing, DDA puts on a 1/7 twist barrel of a chrome-moly-vanadium alloy, 16 inches and a fraction long. The bolt is properly magnetic particle inspected, the furniture, beside the DDA Keymod free-float handguard, is Magpul, and inside the lower they install an ALG Defense QMS trigger package. The full-length flat-top rail gives you all the rail estate you need to mount iron

Available as a carbine or pistol, the CORE hardcore C9 is fed from Glock 9mm mags.

sights, optics, NVGs, laser, and if there isn't enough room up top, the Keymod handguard gives you an embarrassing number of extra locations. The DDA KRP comes with iron sights at no extra charge, so you have choices. They also offer a bigger brother in .308, and if you want to complete your ensemble, DDA also makes 1911s. devildogarms.com

There you have it, prices from high to low, sizes from ultra-compact to full size. Defensive-use tools, competition rifles and just-fun plinking bullet hosers that will make even your jaded gun club buddies giggle when they get a chance to shoot them. The AR-15, it isn't your grandfather's rifle anymore. TGD

The Hudson H9A 9mm is lighter and less expensive than many similar polymer handguns, but with the same large capacity and superb recoil-reduction system.

10 BEST NEW SEMI-AUTO HANDGUNS

BY **PATRICK SWEENEY**

When it comes to tactical semi-auto pistols, how does one define "best"? Most capacity or power? Best new features? Most bling? If there was truly one best of anything, there would not be so many car makers, camera makers and gunmakers. If you truly want to find the best of something, you have to make sure you really have the variables you are going to consider nailed down. And then you must test the samples, pretty much to destruction. We can't do that, so we're going with the non-destructive route — what's new, cool and well-built by reputable makers. With the full knowledge that I risk the wrath of readers for not selecting anything they deem to be "best," here are ten candidates for that title.

HUDSON H9A

The original Hudson H9 was engineered to diminish felt recoil, provide a clean, crisp trigger, sports good ergonomics and come with high capacity. The grip angle, unlike some hi-cap pistols, is 1911-friendly, and the re-engineered recoil system changes recoil so there is less muzzle rise. Accurate, reliable, quick in function and mild in recoil, the H9 was the must-have item of the SHOT Show when it first appeared. So, how to improve it? Replace the steel frame with one of aluminum, taking 8 ounces off the weight. And replace the Trijicon sights with a fiber-optic front and blade rear, taking $200 off the MSRP. With 15 rounds of 9mm, you get to choose thumb safety or not, and striker-fired. What's not to like? hudsonmfg.com

SIG 365

Compact carry guns are all the rage, and with good reason. Yes, a big gun, with lots of ammo, is comforting, but not exactly comfortable. So, SIG took a look at 9mm cartridges and pistols as its starting point and made the smallest possible magazine that could hold ten rounds. Then they built the smallest possible pistol around that magazine. The SIG 365 (because that's how many days a year you can pack it) holds ten rounds of 9mm, and yet is as compact as competitors' pistols that hold only six or seven. When your life depends on the 9mm, more is better. Heck, more is always better. It is a smidge fatter (to hold its ten rounds) but not enough so that you will be inconvenienced by the extra capacity. The 365 is rated for +P ammo, which it will handle a lot better than you probably will. sigsauer.com

The SIG 365 is a little carry gun that packs 10 big rounds of 9mm.

EVOLVE

Tired of your boring old Glock? Wish you had something that not only looked better, but shot better? Evolve to the rescue. Trigger, frame stippling and non-slip grip treatments, slide sculpting and more can be had in a standard pattern, or custom designs. Want a red-dot on your Glock, but don't want the iron (or plastic) sights gone? They can do that. Tired of the casual accuracy, or the "I hate lead bullets" factory Glock barrel? They can take care of that, too. Want to be able to screw on a suppressor? They have a barrel for that.

And, your choice of slide sculpting combined with color scheme to make your Glock, your Glock. And one really neat part about this is that Glocks are everywhere, and can often be found cheap, used, maybe even a little abused. Evolve can inspect and replace, rebuild, modify and alter, pretty much to your heart's content.

This from a small shop dedicated to quality, and you can talk to the guys building your gun. (If they aren't too busy building the guns that came in ahead of yours. Pistolsmiths can be like that. I know, I was one for a bunch of years.) evolveweaponssystems.com

The new CZ P10 C will come ready to accept a red-dot reflex sight, making it ideal for competition, but it'll also be at home as an EDC concealed carry option.

The Arsenal Firearms Strike One.

STRIKE ONE

OK, take a Glock and then ditch everything about it but the polymer frame. Then build up from there. Make the grip ergonomic. Move the bore axis lower. Modify the locking mechanism into a non-Browning design that doesn't raise the bore axis and design it to withstand a steady diet of 9mm +P+ ammunition. Give it a magazine that holds 17 rounds and equip it with a 5-inch barrel made out of alloy steel that is cold hammer forged for as much oomph as the 9mm load will deliver. That's how you get an Archon Type B and make all your gun club buddies jealous.

Some might be put off by the odd look and lines. Others will want it if only because it doesn't look like anything else out there. Me, I want something that performs, and this one promises to perform. arsenalfirearms.com

CZ P10 C

Compact 9mm, but holding a bunch of ammo? Check. Polymer frame with striker-fired system? Check. Made in the Czech Republic, with a long history of top-notch firearms production? Check. An adapter plate to equip with a red-dot

sight of your choice? Check. Wait, what? That's right, the not-so-big P-10, the mid-sized pistol from CZ, will soon be available with an adapter plate for mounting a red-dot sight. That'll make it possible to shoot at the speed and with the accuracy of an Open pistol, while still being able to use the P-10 as an EDC gun. And, the red-dot sight won't mean losing the irons, as CZ has figured out how to move the rear sight from the back end of the slide to a location between the RDS and the ejection

port — so you'll be able to see the sights through the viewscreen of the optic. All this and the Czech quality we have come to expect can be yours. According to CZ, the new P10 should be available before the end of 2018. cz-usa.com

COONAN

Some handguns fire cartridges that claim ".357 Magnum performance" but there is one pistol that truly does — the Coonan. The idea is simple, if difficult to engineer: Start with the 1911 and design the magazine, barrel, breechface and feed ramp to accommodate a .357 Magnum cartridge. OK, it doesn't sound so simple, really. But Coonan did it, and they have been making the .357 ever

Does the .357 Magnum Coonan 1911 need any introduction?

since. The Classic uses a linkless barrel system, has a pivoting trigger, and if you want to take a break from the recoil and muzzle blast of the .357, you can simply install the .38 Special recoil spring, and voila! you're good to go with softer ammo. For those who want more, there is a compensated .357, a 10mm, a .45 ACP and even a compact .357. All these in stainless steel, and for those who must have it, plain and camo patterns in Duracoat. coananinc.com

TBA SICARIO

Any tactical dude or dudette worth their salt knows the value of low-cost handgun practice. So, in a complete departure from the usual, I'm including the TBA Sicario integrally suppressed pistol. Chambered in .22LR, and built on the Ruger Mk IV pistol, the Sicario uses a barrel inside a sleeve, which encloses a monocore baffle stack built around the barrel. You can take the whole thing apart, dump it into an ultrasonic cleaner, and let the vibrations scour the gunk off the internals. Monocore? That means the baffle part of the suppressor comes out as a single piece. No worries about cor-

The TBA Sicario is an integrally suppressed .22LR built on the Ruger Mark IV pistol. It makes a lot of sense for working on low-cost handgun drills.

Whether you're crushing a home invader or taking on Han Solo and Luke Skywalker, you'll want this all-white Imperial blaster AR pistol, the Model C4 from Doublestar.

rectly assembling the baffle stack after cleaning. It only fits one way, and it's one piece. The whole thing comes apart in 30 seconds or less, and putting it back together is just as easy. The end cap doesn't need a special wrench, you use the base plate of your magazine as the wrench. For super-quiet plinking, this is just the ticket. tbasuppressors.com

DOUBLESTAR C4

OK, I had to include an AR pistol in the best handguns, and this one gets the nod because of Doublestar's sense of humor. Plus, it's a good pistol. The C4 is an AR pistol in 5.56, has a 7.5-inch barrel inside of a Samson 7-inch Evo handguard. Yes, it will be a bit blasty, but you can't get the handiness of a 7.5-inch barrel without a bit of muzzle blast. (Unless you put a suppressor on it, of course.) On top are folding iron sights, either as your main aiming option, or backups to an optic or red-dot. On the back end there is a pistol tube with the

The .44 Magnum Automag is back, with engineering improvements big-bore handgunners will like.

Doublestar Strongarm arm brace, and the part that makes it giggle-worthy: the Cerakote finish by Valkyrie Combat, in battle-worn Imperial White. That's right, an Imperial blaster, for those who are still trying to get the taste of the "Solo" experience out of their movie-plex popcorn. star15.com

THE NEW .44 AUTOMAG

There was a time when you could buy a self-loading pistol that had the power of the .44 Magnum. A pistol that wasn't an anvil, a bulky, shoe-box-sized monster of a handgun. Granted, the one you could have wasn't exactly compact, but it wasn't really big. It was the Automag, and for a short time, you could buy one. The last one was built in 1982, but now they are back. The New Automag company isn't just building clones of the old guns. You see, the old guns, while they were powerful, had some problems. Big problems.

So, the New Automag Company is re-engineering pretty much everything about the design. Magazines, feed ramp geometry, every part is looked at, con-sidered, tested and improved. The plan is to make it right, and then make it in the original calibers and some new ones as well. But first, make it work, and make it in .44 Automag. Tactical applications for this big-bore semi-auto? How about bear defense, outdoor survival and hunt-ing? Tactical dudes must eat, too. I can hardly wait. automag.com

SIG 938

OK, I have two SIGs on the list, so sue me. The SIG 938 is a super-compact, powerful little pistol. A single-stack 9mm, it holds 6 rounds, but you can get an extended magazine that holds seven. The model in question, the P938 Emperor Scorpion, is wrapped in a Flat Dark Earth PVD finish. That is a physical vapor deposition process. Thin, tough, and durable, PVD is hard to beat. And PVD stands up to being beaten on. The grips are made of G10, impervious to all known solvents, and given an aggressive, machined, non-slip surface.

SIG installed an extended, threaded barrel, so you can put a suppressor on your super-compact 9mm pistol. I know what you're thinking: suppressed? Why not? It is compact (ultra-compact) reliable, accurate and handy. Why not put a suppressor on it? And all this for a not-unreasonable $978 MSRP. sigsauer.com

We've run the gamut from the ultra-compact to the big and strong. Not sur-prisingly, six of the ten are chambered in 9mm. Shooters have figured out that becoming good with a handgun requires practice. Practice requires ammo, which costs you in both recoil and money. The 9mm works for a whole host of applica-tions, it costs less and kicks less than many other calibers and can be found everywhere.

Pick yours from this list, or pick one that isn't listed, test, report, discuss. This is America, you have choices, go exercise some. **TGD**

The SIG P938 is an ultra-compact single-stack 9mm. And in FDE finish, looks good.

EMPEROR SCORPION | P93...

REVOLVER ROUNDUP: 10 PICKS FOR SELF-DEFENSE

BY **TODD WOODARD**

The Charter Arms Off Duty in .38 Special offers excellent accuracy and value.

shoot a lot of revolvers each year in a variety of shapes, sizes and power ranges because I enjoy the simplicity and safety of a wheelgun. In fact, my everyday carry firearms are either a Smith & Wesson 642 in .38 Special +P or my wife's S&W Model 332 in .32 H&R Magnum, a titanium-frame test gun from 1999 that delivers a lickin' and keeps on tickin' almost two decades after I first shot it. Both are equipped with Crimson Trace laser grips; mine as a factory offering and hers as an aftermarket add-on. If you dig revolvers like I do, you're always on the lookout for wheelguns that fit your lifestyle.

Many shooters who want to defend themselves and their families rely on the time-proven mechanical action of a revolver. Reason: They're easy to understand, easy to operate, and easy to deploy, even under stress. Here's a selection of top revolvers to consider adding to your "active" collection.

SMITH & WESSON MODEL 686 .357 MAGNUM

The classic 686 stainless steel L-frame is a worthy choice for nearly every bedroom nightstand, because even after years of use it will stay very tight. Look for one with a 2.5-inch barrel and a full underlug that completely shrouds the ejector rod. My favorite versions have a red-ramp front

The Smith & Wesson Model 686 in .357 Magnum packs a wallop, yet is still concealable.

sight machined into the barrel and an adjustable matte-black rear sight with no white outline.

The cylinders will be fluted, and one thing to add would be a better chamfer on the front edge of the cylinder to aid holstering. The cylinder locks up via the end of the ejector rod. That ejector rod is knurled so it won't skid against the skin when ejecting empties. It's easy to reload quickly. Even without the chamfers the rounds slide into the chambers faster using a speedloader.

The backstrap is exposed and has serrations that help you grip the revolver. The wood finger-groove grips are smooth, and the left side is scooped out to allow use of a speedloader, and they have a nice palm swell. The trigger is smooth on most samples and has a nice, consistent pull. The hammer has a full-size spur with a toothy checkered texture. Thumbing back the hammer gives you a confident feeling in its action. The 686 feels better in hand than many other handguns because it's slender

and doesn't stand as tall as an N-frame. Felt recoil with the 686 is tolerable, and it's easy to fall into a 6-shot rhythm naturally.

I like Tuff Products Quickstrips and HKS speedloaders. I carry a Quickstrip since it lays flat in a pants pocket. If I'm wearing a jacket or coat, then I might opt for the bulkier HKS speedloader.

It's possible, though not easy, to find a used 686 for a good price. But it is a classic wheelgun that can outlive you and still be ready to go two generations hence. It's a good investment in the future. smith-wesson.com

RUGER LCR 9MM

The Ruger LCR (Light Compact Revolver) is a different breed of snubnose made of polymer, aluminum and steel. A polymer fire-control housing is the grip and triggerguard portion of the revolver, while the frame assembly is aluminum with a stainless steel barrel sleeve in the frame. The cylinder is stainless steel and is traditionally fluted, unlike the radically fluted cylinder of the LCR .38 Special +P model. The LCR uses a transfer bar safety system that enables the hammer to hit the firing pin only when the trigger is pulled all the way to the rear. So, it's safe to carry fully loaded.

The trigger is smooth and feels much lighter than 10.5 pounds due to the friction-reducing cam-fire system. The cylinder latch on the LCR is squeezed rather than pushed forward like on a Taurus or S&W revolver. The end of the ejector rod on the Ruger LCR 9mm engages a pin in the shroud, locking up the front and via the ejector in the rear. Lockup is tight, and there is little play side to side or front to rear.

The ramped front-sight blade is pinned in place and replaceable or can be modified for a certain load. It also sports a white strip so it's easier to acquire. The rear sight is a groove along the topstrap that seamlessly blends into the arched portion of the frame covering the hammer. The Hogue Tamer grip has a pebbled texture on the sides, palm swells for both left- and right-hand shooters and finger grooves. Where the web of your hand contacts the grip is embellished with the Ruger logo. There's a section of squishy blue rubber on the inside of the grip that absorbs more recoil. The grip feels good in hand, but is slightly larger than some grips, something that might make the LCR print or hinder a draw from a pants pocket holster, depending on the size of your pocket. The rubber-

your hand, reducing felt recoil. Indeed, the LCR shoots softer and produces less muzzle flip, particularly in rapid fire, than many other revolvers. If you already have 9mm pistols or carbines, this non-traditional revolver makes a great addition to the arsenal. ruger.com

RUGER GP100 .44 SPECIAL

The Ruger GP100 in .44 Special is a distinctive revolver. The cylinder is un-fluted, and the grips are a special model from Hogue, designed to combat recoil and offer excellent hand fit. The barrel is 3 inches long. The rear sight is the standard Ruger adjustable sight. The range of adjustment is good, sight picture clean and sharp. The front sight is a bright-green fiber optic. This is a burly handgun at 36 ounces unloaded. The satin stain-less steel finish is well polished with no tool marks. Pebble-grain grips offer a good grasping

The Ruger LCR in 9mm is lightweight and ideal for concealed carry. Its trigger is heavy, but Ruger's friction-reducing cam-fire system makes it feel lighter than it is.

5 inch

Accuracy from the .44 Special GP100 was notable using a variety of ammo.

Moon clips aren't mandatory to fire 9mm cartridges in the Ruger LCR, but they'll make case extraction go more smoothly, and reloads faster.

to-metal fit of the grip is excellent.

The ejector rod pushes empties to the very edge of the chamber; a gravity assist is needed to completely eject the cases. The LCR will fire 9mm cartridges without moon clips, but it will not eject the empty cases. A pencil or some other long, skinny object is needed to eject spent shells.

At the range, the LCR allows a higher grip on the revolver, which means plac-ing the center line of the bore closer to

Ruger's GP100 in .44 Special is a shootable big-bore that carries some serious firepower for personal protection.

SMITH & WESSON PERFORMANCE CENTER MODEL 627 .357 MAGNUM

There's something about the N-frame .357 Magnum that endears itself to users, and the Model 627 is one of those revolvers. Constructed of stainless steel with a matte finish, it's a heavy firearm, more than 40 ounces. The Performance Center's attention to detail — tight fitting, clean metalwork, smooth woodwork — is all over the handgun.

The 2.6-inch-long barrel is slab-sided, which gives the revolver less bulk. The muzzle is nicely crowned. The full ejector shroud has a cutout to relieve some material and weight as well as allow any debris like mud or snow to be removed easily. The top of the barrel is serrated to cut glare, and the front sight is dovetailed into the barrel. The dovetail front sight could easily be swapped out, but the original red ramp front sight is quick to acquire. The rear sight is fully adjustable and matte black. The rear blade's notch has a white outline.

In hand, the small grip is slim and fit me well. The grip of the 627 ended at the revolver's frame, and the frame's backstrap is exposed. Nicely checkered sections of wood are on each grip panel. The left panel is scooped out for ease of use with a speedloader. For concealability, this gets an approving nod. The trigger is smooth-faced, and the 11-pound pull actually feels lighter than the scale indicated. A trigger stop is built into the

surface. The GP100 balances well. It's neither handle heavy nor barrel heavy.

The cylinder locks up at the front and rear and by use of a detent in the crane. As for the action, the trigger is smooth in double-action fire with no hitches or hard spots. The single-action trigger breaks at 4 pounds even.

I fired this gun with HSM 240-grain lead loads, Double Tap 180-grain Controlled Expansion JHPs, Buffalo Bore 200-grain Barnes TAC XP, HSM 200-grain flat points, HSM 240-grain JHP, and the Double Tap 200-grain JHP bonded core. These loads covered a range of power from Cowboy Action loads to personal defense to maximum-effect hunting loads. For defense use at 7 and 10 yards, the testing is fast double-action work. Firing for accuracy happens at 25 yards, using both a braced firing position and a Bullshooters rest. Some of the loads are very light, intended for Cowboy Action and general use. They are very pleasant to fire and were found to be accurate.

The heavier loads, such as the Buffalo Bore 200-grain Barnes, are maximum-effect loads for the .44 Special.

The Ruger proved to be a comfortable handgun to handle in rapid fire. Even with the heavy Buffalo Bore 200-grain load the revolver is comfortable to fire. Tested from the Bullshooters shooting rest, the short-barreled GP100 .44 Special grouped five shots into less than 2 inches more often than not. The smallest group fired for record with the same Buffalo Bore load was 1.1 inches at 25 yards. That is with a short barrel and a fiber-optic front sight.

The GP100 is an accurate revolver, capable in combat shooting and comfortable to fire. ruger.com

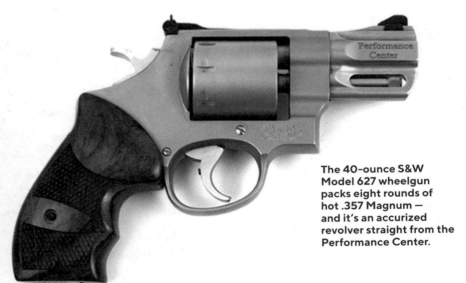

The 40-ounce S&W Model 627 wheelgun packs eight rounds of hot .357 Magnum — and it's an accurized revolver straight from the Performance Center.

trigger. The hammer is teardrop-shaped and has an aggressive texture that assists cocking. Both trigger and hammer have a chrome-flashed finish that matches the stainless finish on the rest of the revolver. The double-action trigger span isn't too big, so even shooters with small hands can easily fire the Model 627 revolver in double action.

The cylinder latch is the newer type, cut for ease of use with speedloaders. Chambers are chamfered to aid in reloading, while the ejector and the rear of the cylinder are cut to allow use of moon clips. The ejector rod is long enough to purge empty brass from the cylinder. This rod length allows 8 rounds to be ejected all at once. A detail that separates the Performance Center revolvers from the standard 686 is a ball detent built into the front of the crane. The ball bearing locks into a V-shaped groove in the frame. This is an accuracy enhancement long used by PPC shooters customizing revolvers for competition.

Before shooting the 627, I thought it was going to be a handful with .357 Magnum loads. In fact, it is very tolerable due to the excellent grip and weight. At 15 yards, it was fired for accuracy using a rest with Winchester White Box .357 Magnum 110-grain JHPs, .38 Special +P 125-grain JHP ammo, as well as Federal Tactical 128-grain Hydra-Shok JHPs. Looking at past ballistic and accuracy data from 4-inch revolvers, the Winchester .357 Magnum ammo is about 200 to 300 fps slower out of snubnose revolvers. Felt recoil is noticeable with all ammunition fired. In DA mode, firing for speed, the 627 is easy to keep on target due to its heft and sights. There is a ramp-up time to get used to pulling the trigger eight times, not a hard thing to learn.

For concealed carry, the 627 is comparable in weight to a 1911 steel frame fully loaded, but the wheelgun is slightly thicker than a typical 1911, 1.7 inches compared to 1.3 inches, respectively. That extra girth is noticeable, so consider carrying the 627 in an outside-the-waist-band holster. www.smith-wesson.com

CHARTER ARMS OFF DUTY .38 SPECIAL

The Off Duty is a small, light, inexpensive revolver. It's of a hammerless design, meaning the hammer is enclosed within the frame, making it smooth and snag-free. The frame is made of aluminum and has a bright matte finish.

The Charter Arms Duty in .38 special is affordable, accurate and sized for deep concealment.

The barrel, crane and cylinder are of stainless steel with a grayish matte finish. As a result, the gun has a subtle two-tone look.

The black rubber grip is minimalist, with finger grooves that position your hand in a high, comfortable spot. The sides of the grips have a slight palm swell and are ribbed for a better grasp. In addition, the grips fill that space behind the triggerguard, providing a high grip hold to control muzzle flip and perform a fast second shot. When shooting the Off Duty, curl your small finger under the grip.

The Charter's cylinder lockup has no wiggle, locking the cylinder in the front and rear. The ejector rod, which is nested and in two pieces, telescopes to snap back into the frame. The cylinder latch is well serrated and large. It's pushed forward to swing out the five-shot cylinder. Both the grips and latch are speedloader friendly. The front edge of the cylinder has a slight chamfer, which aids one-handed holstering.

The Off Duty employs a one-piece frame, which makes the small revolver strong yet slightly smaller than those of two-piece design. The 2-inch barrel uses a full lug that encloses the ejector rod. The lug is tapered so holstering is easier. The ramp front sight is milled into the top of the barrel and serrated to minimize glare. The rear sight is a groove along the top, notched so the aluminum rear sight contrasts nicely with the stainless front sight. The trigger is serrated in the middle, allowing you to keep the position of your trigger finger the same, even during recoil.

Due to the compact size and light weight of the Off Duty, recoil is most noticeable, whacking the web of the hand at the top position of the grip. The rear of the rubber grips are squared off, so you'll feel those edges slap the palms. In terms of accuracy, expect 2 inches for five shots at 15 yards. The smallish grip and stacking on the last bit of trigger press hinder accuracy. Empty cases eject smartly out of the Charter Arms.

In concealed carry, the Off Duty shines. It could be carried in a holster designed for a Smith & Wesson J-frame or dropped into a cargo pants pocket. charterfirearms.com

SMITH & WESSON PERFORMANCE CENTER MODEL 929 9MM

The M929 from Smith & Wesson is an 8-shot 9mm all-stainless steel N-frame

With eight rounds of 9mm on tap, the Smith & Wesson Model 929 Performance Center wrings out the cartridge's velocity with its 6.5-inch barrel.

Chambers come chamfered in the refined Model 929's cylinder.

Loading moon clips with 9mm ammo keeps fresh firepower always at the ready.

revolver designed from the grip up for action pistol competition (Revolver minor), and it comes with the Jerry Miculek signature. For the record, Miculek made a 1,000-yard shot with the 929 on an episode of Shootout Lane. It's just a fun gun to shoot, and as a companion to your 9mm semi-auto pistol or carbine, both sharing the same ammo, it offers capability in the field far beyond what any concealed carry defensive snubnose models can deliver.

This revolver is tight and well made, with no cylinder movement. The cylinder gap is 0.006 inch, well within spec. Since it's an N-frame — designed for long cartridges like the .44 Mag. — the barrel is screwed deeply into the frame. This means 9mm bullets have less free flight in the cylinder before engaging the forcing cone and bore.

The 929 sports a 6.5-inch barrel with a full-length, tapered underlug to help reduce the effects of felt recoil and a compensator to minimize muzzle flip. The compensator can quickly and easily

be removed and replaced with a false muzzle. On top of the barrel is an adjustable rear sight with a plain, matte-black notch. The front Patridge sight is also matte black. On a black target, these sights do get lost. On cardboard and painted steel, they show up much better. The front sight is pinned, so it could be replaced with a sight more suited to your application. Under the rear sight, the 929 is drilled and tapped, so a reflex or red-dot sight could be mounted. The finish of the frame and barrel is a matte stainless with no glare when used in bright sunlight.

The 8-shot cylinder is constructed of lightweight titanium. The ejector is cut for use with moon clips, and all the chambers are chamfered. Although 9mm cartridges can be loaded into the chambers and fired, the ejector doesn't shuck them out. A rod is required to eject the case. However, the moon clips are easy to load and unload without the use of a tool. The crane has a ball detent that snaps into a V-shaped groove in the frame. This setup locks up the 929 consistently tight and is a common gunsmithing modification for competition revolvers. The cylinder latch is the type cut for use with a speedloader, and since the 929 uses moon clips, it's out of the way and doesn't impede a fast reload. It does take slightly longer to load this 8-shot 9mm compared to a 6-shot .45 ACP. That's because the holes in the cylinder of a .45 ACP are larger, with more space in between chambers.

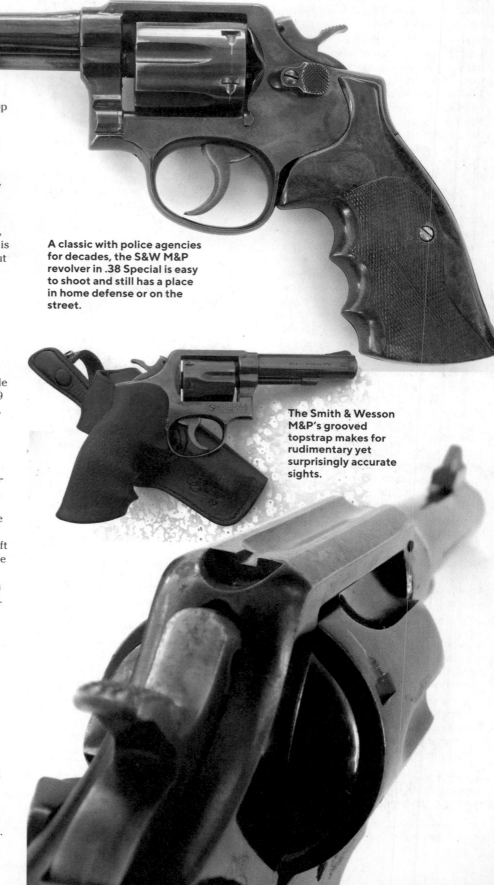

Both the trigger and hammer are chrome-plated. The hammer is tear-drop shaped and offers plenty of traction to thumb cock the 929. The smooth-faced trigger includes a trigger stop. The 929 has a nice trigger, to be expected from the Performance Center. In double action, the pull seems less than the 10.7 pounds it measures.

The grip is typical of a large-frame S&W of late, rubber with finger grooves, which shooters either like or hate. This is a feature that is easily user modified, but at additional cost.

At the range, with an assortment of ammo from Hornady, Winchester, and Atlanta Arms, the 929 preferred 147-grain Atlanta Arms ammo, giving a 5-shot group as small as 0.25 inch at 15 yards. On tombstone-style NRA D-1 targets, where the drill is to shoot eight rounds, reload and shoot two more while keeping hits in the 8-inch A-ring, the 929 is smooth to shoot, with little felt recoil, even with the heavy 147-grain Atlanta Arms ammo. Winchester and Hornady 115-grain ammo is much easier for all shooters to fire fast and accurately.

The trigger is excellent, with no stacking, smooth and consistent throughout the pull — again, what shooters expect from the Performance Shop. Overall, the revolver is fast on target, has a smooth DA trigger pull, and provides enough heft to dampen felt recoil. The 929 is a unique revolver that fills the bill for action shooting or any other situation in which you want a top-notch, fast-shooting tool. smith-wesson.com

SMITH & WESSON MILITARY & POLICE .38 SPECIAL

Many shooters have a mental picture of a revolver they've always wanted to own, and for many a vintage Smith & Wesson Military & Police .38 Special is one such gun. So why venture back in time to get one of these? Price. Because they look old, you can sometimes score a great deal on one. And for a sample in good condition, the Military & Police .38 Special is a great choice.

On good samples, the action is very tight and smooth in operation. The bore and chambers are in excellent condition.

A classic with police agencies for decades, the S&W M&P revolver in .38 Special is easy to shoot and still has a place in home defense or on the street.

The Smith & Wesson M&P's grooved topstrap makes for rudimentary yet surprisingly accurate sights.

The sights are good examples of the fixed type. The front sight is a blade that allows accurate fire when lined up with the grooved topstrap. The Smith & Wesson action lends itself well to staging the trigger, bringing the hammer almost to the firing point and then continuing with the press.

The cylinder release presses forward to open the cylinder. The cylinder rotates right to left. On a good sample, the finish of the M&P revolver is generally good, and most will show some muzzle wear. It carries recoil-soaking weight at 34 ounces, not too heavy for occasional carry. As a truck gun or in the bedroom, it rewards the shooter with good weight and balance, a 4-inch barrel for decent downrange performance, and has a smooth action.

On the firing range, results were excellent in combat fire. The revolver is more comfortable to fire than many current models. Combat accuracy can be excellent, with five-shot groups shot using Black Hills Ammunition 148-grain wadcutters at 25 yards settling into 1.75 inches.

A veteran Military & Police revolver is affordable and offers excellent intrinsic accuracy. It's easy to use well and is powerful enough for personal defense. smith-wesson.com

RUGER LCRX .357 MAGNUM

The Ruger LCRx is an evolution of the LCR series, which incorporates an external hammer for single-action firing. The addition of the hammer to fire the LCRx in SA mode turns out to be a good feature, with plenty of hammer spur exposed to cock the revolver safely, yet the hammer itself is enclosed.

To swing out the cylinder, press the latch. The 5-shot cylinder is fluted to whittle away weight. The crane fits inside the front of the frame. The Ruger wears a Hogue Tamer Monogrip, which is small but offers pronounced finger grooves and palm swells. The grip is compact yet feels substantial in hand. The grip design of the LCRx, like the LCR series, places your grip higher up to better manage recoil — and there is plenty recoil with hot magnum loads — and provides better leverage on the trigger. There is no grip frame on the LCRx, just a grip peg. The Hogue grip offers concealability and recoil protection.

The frame is an aluminum alloy, the barrel a stainless steel insert. The LCRx loaded weighs 17.9 ounces, or 8 ounces less than a Colt Cobra and 6 ounces

The Ruger LCRx features an external hammer, making slow, deliberate longer-range shots more attainable in single action.

The hammered version of the Ruger LCR sports the series' typical space-age looks and construction. Chambered in .357 Magnum, cartridge effectiveness will never be a worry.

less than a Kimber K6s. Of course, light weight and hot loads translate into more recoil. Even so, shooting the LCRx is tolerable with .357 Magnum ammunition, but you must realize how a 17.9-ounce revolver will react when a 158-grain bullet is launched from it at high speeds. Saving grace: The grip is wider, so recoil is spread out more in the palm of your hand.

The trigger face is smooth, and so is the pull, which uses a friction-reducing cam that has no stacking. I would probably replace the pinned front ramp with a fiber optic or tritium dot like the XS Sight. The ramp wears a white strip that is not easy to aim. The LCRx carries well in a Galco Triton Kydex appendix holster. ruger.com

TAURUS PUBLIC DEFENDER POLYMER .410/.45 COLT

The Taurus Polymer Public Defender is an awkward-looking revolver until you pick it up and hold it. It has nice balance and, unlike the Judge from which it's derived, the Public Defender is as compact a revolver as you can get with a cylinder that is chambered for 2.5-inch .410 shotshells. The barrel is a stubby 2 inches, and the ribbed rubber grip is as compact as Taurus's CIA J-frame clone. The revolver's crane has a detent ball that snaps into place in the metal frame.

As the name implies, the Polymer Public Defender is constructed with a polymer frame and grip, which dramatically reduces the weight of the revolver compared to the steel-frame Judge. A steel barrel and cylinder window are embedded into the polymer. The frame and grip are screwed together similar to

the Ruger LCR. The Public Defender is a large snubnose but is very manageable in tight spaces, like the inside of a vehicle. Of course, it is versatile, firing both .410-bore shotshells and .45 Long Colt cartridges. The Taurus has a windage-adjustable rear sight. The front sight is a fiber-optic unit that provides a suitable sight picture for a gun in this class.

To load the Public Defender the cylinder latch, which is built into the oversized recoil shield, is pressed forward. The latch is serrated, flush with the shield, and positioned on the bottom portion of the shield, so pay attention and get a good purchase on it to operate. Expect the trigger weight to measure about 13 pounds in double action and 6 pounds in single-action mode. The

trigger has a smooth face. The hammer is easy to cock back and is mostly concealed by the large recoil shield. Taurus made an effort to ensure the Public Defender is snag free. The tiny compact grip is ribbed and has finger grooves. Most shooters must curl the small finger under the butt. It feels good in hand and is very pointable.

At 25 yards using a rest, .45 Colt cartridges fell into 5-shot groups of 1.6 inches with Federal American Eagle 225-grain JSP ammo. With Hornady Critical Defense 185-grain FTX bullets and Winchester PDX1 Defender 225-grain JHP, expect just under 3-inch averages for 5-shot groups. The gun's versatility includes shooting defensive .410-bore shotshells, such as Hornady Critical De-

The polyer-framed Taurus Public Defender is a large snubnose for close-in defensive work.

The Taurus Public Defender can pack any combination of .45 Colt or .410 shotshell.

fense, which use one .41-caliber FTX slug and two .35-caliber ball projectiles. PDX1 Defender from Winchester is loaded with three discs and 12 BBs. Federal Personal Defense shotshells are loaded with 7/16 oz. of #4 shot. At close range, the defense loads produce some tight patterns. At 5 yards, the Hornady Critical Defense shoots a 1.7-inch pattern. The large projectiles in Winchester PDX1 Defender shotshells pattern nicely on a threat target at 1.1 inches. The BBs create an 11-inch pattern. Be aware that at longer distances shotshell loads disperse and are less effective on the intended target and may accidentally hit bystanders.

It's worth noting that Aguila and Federal shotshells had to be pressed into the chambers, while the Winchester and Hornady shells dropped into the chambers like a cartridge. Shells not fully seated in the chamber did not allow the cylinder to be closed or, if partially seated, did not allow the cylinder to rotate. When ejecting the shells, the defense loads were the easiest to expel. The target loads, however, required you to tap the ejector rod against the wooden shooting bench to pop them out of the chamber. Also, since the shells are so long, the shell closest to the grip when the cylinder is open gets hung up, requiring rotation of the cylinder to remove the shell.

If you're looking for a large-bore revolver for concealed carry, the Taurus may be too large for the job. However, it does make sense for vehicle and night-stand use. taurususa.com

SMITH & WESSON MODEL 649 .357 MAGNUM

The Smith & Wesson Model 649 is built on a J frame, which limits this .357 Magnum to a five-round capacity. The

The Smith & Wesson Model 649 is built of sturdy stainless steel and has a 2.125-inch barrel.

model is a variation of the Model 49 Bodyguard and is still currently produced. There is a reason for its longevity. The Model 649 offers a good compromise on size, round capacity, sights, weight and bulk.

The finish is bright stainless, and even with the 2.125-inch barrel, the 649 has some heft. If it were lighter, no doubt the revolver would batter your palms. The barrel has a full underlug that shrouds the ejector rod. The hammer is shrouded; there is no hammer spur to snag on clothing during a draw, but the knurled hammer still allows the revolver to be cocked and fired in single-action mode. The front-blade sight is blued steel and pinned and could be replaced to match a certain load. The rear sight is a groove in the topstrap of the bright stainless steel frame and offers good contrast.

The grip is made of rubber with finger grooves, and feels thin, which makes it easier to conceal but also inflicts more felt recoil, although it is tolerable with most .357 Magnum loads. Shooting from a bench at 25 yards, the S&W is easy to fire well because of its trigger — no stacking and a smooth, consistent double-action pull. The single-action pul

is light and crisp. The snag-free exterior of the 649 means it can be drawn from a pocket smoothly, and because it's thin, it's easy to carry in an IWB holster.

This firearm can be found new or used, so if you want a concealable, dependable, powerful pistol, then look around for a bargain in the $450 range. smith-wesson.com

Todd Woodard is editor of Gun Tests *magazine and* Cartridges of the World, 16th Edition. *He has carried revolvers for going on 20 years now and hasn't yet been convinced to change to a pistol.* TGD

Smith's J-frame Model 649 is tiny but manages to cram five rounds of .357 Magnum into its diminutive cylinder.

Note the Model 649's shrouded hammer, ideal for concealed carry.

TACTICAL SHOTGUNS

The Benelli M2 with pistol grip is not inexpensive, but the author believes it's one of the best you can get and can meet any tactical task.

BY **SCOTT W. WAGNER**

n my book *Gun Digest Tactical Shotguns*, I asked the question, what exactly is a "tactical shotgun"? Simply put, it's a shotgun modified to be more effective for defensive or combat use. Nearly every conventional tactical shotgun has been modified from what was originally a hunting weapon. Some colonial troops in the early days of the American Revolution were forced to face British soldiers with what was known as a "fowling piece" — a flintlock shotgun designed for bird hunting.

One of the earliest was the short double-barreled "coach shotgun." This was basically a hunting shotgun with the barrels cut down to make it handy to carry on a stagecoach by the fellow "riding shotgun" next to the driver. By World War I, we saw the creation of a short-barreled pump shotgun — the "trench gun" issued to certain American troops for fighting in the close confines and horrid conditions in the dirt trenches. Contrary to popular belief, the advantage of the trench gun wasn't delivering a wide spread of pellets across the width of the trench, but rather unleashing a tremendous close range payload of 00 buckshot rapidly due to the capability of the pump action and 20-inch barrel versus the 24-inch barrel length of the 1903 Springfield rifle. The development of the trench shotgun — regardless of manufacturer — effectively ushered in the era of the modern tactical shotgun. Here are some of the latest tactical shotguns for police, military and armed citizens.

BENELLI M2 TACTICAL SEMI-AUTOMATIC WITH PISTOL GRIP

The Benelli M2 Tactical 12-gauge with the pistol grip stock is, in my opinion, the finest semi-automatic tactical shotgun available on the market today — and I really don't even like pistol grip shotguns all that much. The M2 Tactical is everything I believe a tactical shotgun should be: lightweight

at 6.7 pounds with great pointability, drop-dead reliability and excellent accuracy thanks in part to the prominent ghost ring sights. But what makes the M2 Tactical really stand out is the Inertia-Driven recoil operating system. Inertial drive uses the recoil energy of the shotgun shells to cycle the action much like a semi-automatic pistol's recoil operating system — and it does it very cleanly. There is no gas and carbon blowing around the operating systems like that of traditional gas systems. Think of the M2 Tactical as a self-cleaning oven that shoots!

One thing I noticed about the M2 is that recoil is slightly greater than heavier gas-operated guns. This is why I like the pistol grip stock on the M2. Some of the recoil is diverted through the shooting hand into the non-support side of the body, dividing the energy. If you don't like the pistol grip stock, a black synthetic tactical or ComforTec stock — the latter reduces recoil by 48 percent — are also options.

The Benelli M2 Tactical ships with a set of Flush Crio Chokes and wrench. You get Cylinder, Improved Cylinder, Modified, Improved Modified, and Full chokes. MSRP is $1,359. benelliusa.com

BENELLI NOVA H20 TACTICAL PUMP

The Benelli Nova Tactical Pump is an innovative design that uses an over-molded one-piece polymer stock and receiver, which simplifies manufacture, increases corrosion resistance and improves stability. The H20 variant of the Nova is the saltwater corrosion-resistant version designed for use aboard ships, or in areas where humidity is high, and maintenance low.

Magazine capacity of the Nova H20 Tactical is four rounds. All Novas accept 2 3/4-, 3- or 3 1/2-inch magnum shells. Unless you're seeking protection against grizzly bears, 3- or 3 1/2-inch magnum shells are overkill, and brutal on the sending end as well. Stick with 2

The Benelli Nova H20 is resistant to fresh and saltwater corrosion, but it's a capable tactical scattergun for home defense use, too.

3/4-inch loads for most defensive needs in the lower 48 — 00 buckshot or #1 buckshot loads work great for indoor home defense.

I found there was only one thing I would change on the Nova H20. The rifle sights are low profile and nickel plated. While I would like to see black nitride sights instead for better contrast, the lack of them is certainly not a disqualifier. MSRP is $669. benelliusa.com

The Benelli M2 Tactical.

Inland Manufacturing's Model 37 Trench Gun is based on the Ithaca Model 37 action, sports a heat shield and bayonet lug.

ITHACA MODEL 37 HOME-DEFENSE SHOTGUN

For a tactical shotgun to be effective it must get onto target quickly. There are a lot of tactical shotguns so weighted down with modifications that they simply don't point well. The Ithaca Model 37 Home Defense Shotgun is the definition of outstanding shotgun "pointability." This is the tactical version of the original Model 37 sporting shotgun, which was adopted in World War II as one of the U.S. military's official "trench shotguns" that proved effective in close jungle combat.

Ithaca's Model 37 Defense shotgun ejects from the bottom, making it handy for all members of the family, even southpaws.

The Model 37 Home Defense, like the standard Model 37, features the same trim action that loads and ejects through the bottom port, thus minimizing entry points for dirt and debris. The operation of the 37's pump action is particularly slick. Magazine capacities of 4+1 and 7+1 and choice of 12- or 20-gauge versions are available. I favor the 4-round magazine for best

handling. The 37 Home Defense has a Parkerized finish. Its barrel is cylinder bored and available in 18.5- or 20-inch lengths and accepts 3-inch shells. Synthetic or black walnut stocks are available. Synthetic stocks are checkered, and a new pistol grip version will also be available. Sights are a traditional brass bead that works very well for any confrontation within buckshot range.

The Ithaca Model 37 is the basis for Inland Manufacturing's (www.inland-mfg.com) Model 37 Trench Gun — complete with heat shield and bayonet lug. Prices of the Model 37 Home Defense range from $880 to $1,040. ithaca-gunworks.com

MOSSBERG 20-GAUGE 590 SHOCKWAVE

The Mossberg 590 Shockwave represents a unique departure from the standard "pistol grip only" type of pump-action shotgun, such as Mossberg's own 500 JIC (Just in Case). The 500 JIC, by the way, features a standard

angle pistol grip without the buttstock affixed. The 590 Shockwave represents a bit more radical departure, making it a much more effective and easy to use ultra-close range defensive arm. This is accomplished by the Raptor Bird's Head pistol grip.

Traditional pistol grip shotguns use the standard vertical pistol grip. This limits their use as one-handed firearms in an emergency — making them difficult to point, shoot, and control if only one hand is available for firing.

The Raptor polymer pistol grip is gently angled away from the receiver with nearly the same angle as one would find on a traditional shotgun stock. Its "bird's head" shape keeps your hand from slipping off when firing and allows for much more effective pointing and control with one or two hands. The Mossberg tang-mounted safety makes the 590 the perfect candidate for this type of treatment. A strapped forend is included to keep the support hand clear of the muzzle.

The Mossberg 590 Shockwave in 20 gauge makes a lot of sense for tactical applications: It's short and maneuverable and can be shot fast with relatively light recoil.

The 20-gauge version is plenty powerful, but often overlooked — it saves several ounces of weight while lowering recoil. Limit the 20-gauge Shockwave to 10 yards or so, and you have an easy to maneuver arm with more effectiveness than a standard pistol. MSRP is $455. mossberg.com

The Mossberg 590 Shockwave JIC, or "Just In Case," with supplied tube.

MOSSBERG MAVERICK THUNDER RANCH OVER/UNDER

The Mossberg Maverick Thunder Ranch Over/Under (O/U) was developed in conjunction with Clint Smith and the Thunder Ranch training facility. With Thunder Ranch's input, I was certain that the full tactical potential of this two-shooter would be achieved.

Developed by Clint Smith of Thunder Ranch and Mossberg, the Maverick O/U is snappy to the shoulder and on target and can unload two shotshells quickly.

The Thunder Ranch O/U's 18.5-inch cylinder bore barrels have been given a matte blue finish. The tactical shotgun has three segments of Picatinny railing — one over the receiver, and one on the sides of the barrels. I found the Hi-Viz front sight setup works very well without the need for optics, especially in a close range gun. I liked the operation of the tang-mounted safety. On sporting O/U's, the safety is automatically engaged when the action is closed, requiring you to take the safety off during each reload — not something you want to have to do during a combat situation. The safety also doubles as the barrel selector. It would benefit from a traditional red dot marking the "fire" position.

The Thunder Ranch utilizes a single trigger that launches both shots lighting fast. There are no shell ejectors, only extractors. This means that you must pluck out the empties. Test firing at 25 feet showed that both barrels impacted to the point of aim. Recoil was stout but manageable.

If you want one of the simplest operating, most effective close-range shotguns on the market, look no further than the Mossberg Maverick Thunder Ranch O/U. MSRP is $594. mossberg.com

MOSSBERG 930 SPX TACTICAL PISTOL GRIP SEMI-AUTOMATIC 12 GAUGE

One of the advantages of a semi-automatic tactical shotgun is that the length of pull issue is not as critical since your support hand is not part of the operating system — a good thing for smaller-statured individuals. Another major advantage of a gas-operated semi-auto is that the piston system reduces felt recoil.

The Mossberg 930 is set up very well for either sport shooting or self-defense. Available with either a pistol grip or standard fixed synthetic stock, the 590 shoulders and points naturally. Its 7.25-pound weight helps with quick target acquisition. Magazine capacity is 7+1 rounds with 2 3/4-inch shells. The barrel has a cylinder bore choke — great for shot and slugs. The ghost ring sights are excellent. The prominent front sight features a red light-gathering pipe and protective wings. The rear sight is fully adjustable, protected by wings, and mounted on a Picatinny rail. Try the ghost ring sights first before considering an optic. Other features include sling studs, a large knurled charging handle, and a checkered bolt release button easily

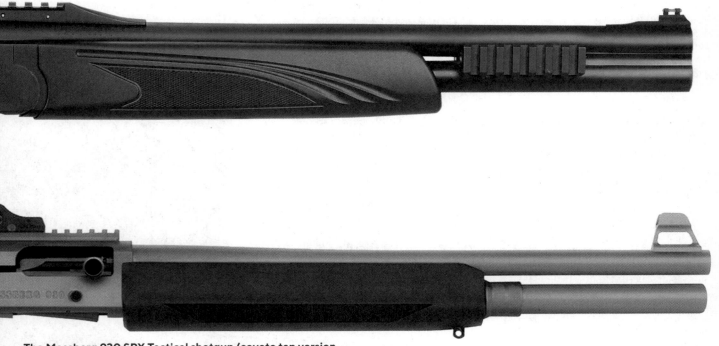

The Mossberg 930 SPX Tactical shotgun (coyote tan version shown) has a capacity of 7+1 and is soft-recoiling, thanks to its gas-operated semi-auto action. Optics options abound with its Picatinny rail, but the supplied ghost ring sights are ready to rock from the box.

The Mossberg SA 20 is an affordable small-gauge alternative produced for Mossberg in Turkey. It's a reliable gas gun that can put heavy payload on target fast.

accessed by the support hand.

A small problem with pistol grip stocks is that accessing the tang-mounted safety is awkward. With the standard synthetic stock, access to the safety is naturally accomplished by the shooting thumb. The 930 SPX is a smooth-shooting and reliable choice. MSRP is $878 for the standard stock and $985 for the pistol grip version. mossberg.com

MOSSBERG INTERNATIONAL SA 20 PISTOL GRIP RAILED TACTICAL SEMI-AUTOMATIC

The SA 20 Pistol Grip Railed Tactical Shotgun from Mossberg may be just the defensive gun for folks who are wary of 12-gauge recoil. The 20 gauge is too

frequently overlooked as a defensive option by many people because its case is smaller and it packs fewer pellets. While less powerful than the 12 gauge, the 20 is powerful enough for deer hunting — and certainly powerful enough for defensive use against humans. Because it has less recoil, shooters are more likely to want to practice more often.

The SA 20 is manufactured by Kayhan Armsen in Turkey and holds 5 shells in the magazine. Weight is only 5.75 pounds, making it faster on target than any of the other shotguns in this review. It literally snaps — rather than swings — onto target. The SA 20's ghost ring sights are like those on the 930 SPX. The rear is adjustable, the

front features a green fiber optic. The sights are mounted on a Picatinny rail. Three rail segments are mounted on the magazine end cap for accessories.

The SA 20 safety departs from the traditional Mossberg design and is mounted on the trigger guard rather than on the tang. This makes it easier to use on a pistol grip gun. The slide release button is on the left rear of the trigger guard.

Quality of the SA 20 is quite good and rapid fire is far more pleasant than with 12-gauge shotguns. MSRP is $574. mossberg.com

REMINGTON 870 EXPRESS TACTICAL SERIES

The Remington 870 is the tactical

pump shotgun with which I am most familiar, having started with it as a deputy sheriff in 1980. In 1986, I qualified as a police firearms instructor with the 870, and carried one daily while working patrol. As an instructor, I've trained or qualified hundreds of police cadets and officers with it.

BASIC MODEL 870 EXPRESS SYNTHETIC TACTICAL

The author is no stranger to the basic Model 870 Express Tactical. Like many police officers, he cut his teeth on the ubiquitous scattergun. The no-frills model still gets the job done.

The 870 has many positive attributes. In sheer volume, it's the number one sales leader when it comes to pump guns, which is why so many different models are available. Its design is adaptable to any purpose — from sporting clays to wingshooting to deer and larger game and for personal defense — the 870 does it all. Reliable service is the hallmark of the Model 870. Twin action bars assure smooth operation for any task, and it's easily fieldstripped for cleaning. Barrels are simple to exchange.

For a solid entry-level tactical shotgun there is the Express Synthetic Tactical series. The base model has an 18.5-inch cylinder bore barrel, 4-round magazine, matte finish, synthetic stocks and bead sight. MSRP is $420. For an additional $23, you can get a 6-shot version of the same gun. This model adds a Picatinny receiver rail for optics, a set of excellent XS Ghost Ring Sights, and extended ported Tactical Rem Choke. Any of these three Express models will give a lifetime of service. remington.com

REMINGTON 870 EXPRESS TACTICAL MAGPUL AND 870 EXPRESS SIX POSITION

Built on the Express Tactical 6-shot 870s with bead sights, these two variations showcase the versatility of the 870. By using advanced stock designs, you can adjust each shotgun to your physical build and needs without resorting to visiting a shotgun "fitter" to make permanent stock alterations.

The Tactical Magpul stock provides you with the ultimate in user-adjustment to achieve a personal fit. Adjustable stocks are important to me as shoulder deterioration over the years has reduced my capability of handling standard shotgun stock lengths of pull — especially with pump guns — making them more difficult to operate. The Tactical Magpul stock utilizes an incremental spacer system that changes the length by 1/2-inch per

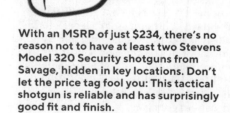

With an MSRP of just $234, there's no reason not to have at least two Stevens Model 320 Security shotguns from Savage, hidden in key locations. Don't let the price tag fool you: This tactical shotgun is reliable and has surprisingly good fit and finish.

The Remington 870 Express Tactical Magpul sports a proven stock option that's a common aftermarket upgrade.

Remington's 6-shot Tactical Magpul model.

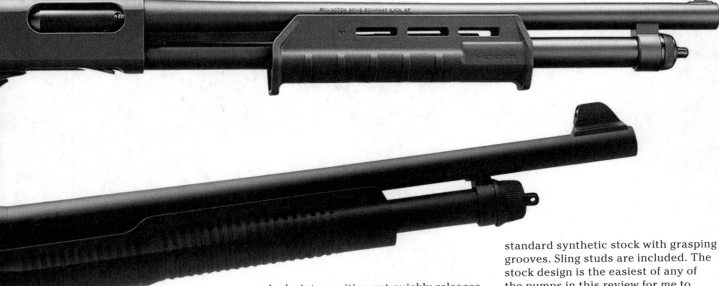

spacer. Range of adjustment is from 14.5 down to 12.5 inches. Optional cheek risers are available to provide the best cheek weld if optics are used, and the buttstock pad is designed for increased recoil reduction. The Magpul fore-end is designed to keep the hand from slipping while working the action. MSRP is $565.

The Six Position Express Tactical uses a rapid adjustment 6-position Magpul Stock, which is the 870 version of Magpul's "M4 Type" stock. I favor this mode the best as adjustments can be made quickly, which comes in handy when wearing different types of clothing, or when sharing the gun with different shooters. The Magpul stock locks into position yet quickly releases. It's my favorite M4 stock. MSRP is $601. remington.com

STEVENS 320 SECURITY BY SAVAGE

Not everyone who wants a defensive shotgun can afford the top end guns. That's why it's important for those on a tight budget to look at models without the expensive options. The Stevens 320 Security is a pump action available in 12 or 20 gauge that uses a rotary bolt design that was originally seen on the Winchester 1200. The rotary bolt system partially disengages with recoil, facilitating rapid cycling. The 320 is built by Sun City Machinery in China, which explains the $234 MSRP!

Several model variations are available. The one I worked with featured a standard synthetic stock with grasping grooves. Sling studs are included. The stock design is the easiest of any of the pumps in this review for me to shoulder and operate. A pistol grip variant is also available. The ghost ring sights are prominent and adjustable, with a green fiber optic up front. Bead sights are available. There's no railing, which helps keep the cost down. The 320 Security utilizes a cross-bolt safety at the rear of the trigger guard, the left rear houses the slide release button. The length of pull for me is excellent, and that is saying something. If I was purchasing this gun I would not need the stock cut down to fit.

The action is surprisingly smooth for a gun with a price tag so low. While lacking bells and whistles, the Stevens 320 Security is a solid design with decent sights, suitable for self-defense, and backed by Savage Arms. savagearms.com **TGD**

TACTICAL RIFLES

The Kimber Advanced Tactical SOC II accepts Accuracy International 5- and 10-round detachable box magazines.

Accurate Rifles for Serious Work
BY TODD WOODARD

Today's tactical rifles have achieved accuracy levels at price points that bring long-range shooting to within reach of more and more shooters. The downside? With so many great choices, tt's now hard to know where to begin. To help you sort it all out, here are 10 tactical rifles for your consideration that have specialized application, unusually superb accuracy or are another option for your long-range toolbox.

FN MODEL PS90 STANDARD 5.7X28MM

FN PS90s sell for $1,450+, and they can be hard to find. Reason: The PS90 takes the bullpup design to the next level. It's lightweight, ambidextrous, compact and has great ergonomics. The PS90 is chambered in 5.7x28mm, a high-velocity small-caliber cartridge similar to the .22 Hornet. The P90 was designed in the mid–1980s and has been in use with

military and police forces in more than 40 nations since 1991. It was designed as a PDW (Personal Defense Weapon) along with the 5.7x28mm cartridge to replace the 9mm used in pistols and submachine guns. FN also chambers this round in the Five-seveN pistol. We found this round to be very accurate with minimal recoil and not a lot of muzzle blast.

The PS90 is a semi-automatic civilian version of the P90. To field strip it, pull

(below) The FN PS90 PDW, or Personal Defense Weapon, is chambered in the very interesting 5.7x28mm cartridge.

Cartridges from the PS90's mag are rotated 90 degrees as they're chambered from above. This magazine was easy to load and held 30 rounds.

the barrel and optic-support group out of the polymer frame/trigger group, aka the stock. The hammer group is pulled from the rear of stock butt. Simple. Integrated into the stock are two hand grips. The rear firing grip is similar to a thumbhole stock. The front grip allows you to grasp the grip and place your thumb inside the triggerguard. That may sound confusing, until you shoulder the PS90 and see how natural it feels. The front grip also has a lip, so your support hand doesn't get near the barrel. This is important with the PS90 because the bare, unprotected barrel is close to your support hand. I'd suggest using gloves, when possible, just in case you fall into AR mode and try to grasp the barrel thinking it's an AR handguard.

Our sample had a 16-inch barrel with a slotted muzzle brake. The optics bridge is metal; it holds the barrel and positions the magazine. It also features a Picatinny rail to mount an optic, and in the bridge are backup iron sights, basically a peep sight paired with a rear hole and post that are small but usable. Controls consist of ambidextrous magazine latches, cocking handles and safety selector. The cocking handles are rounded ears on either side of the weapon, which are effortless to cock. The safety selector is a disc under the trigger that rotates to Safe or Fire. The magazine is a rectangular, clear polymer box that lays on the top of the PS90 and inside the optics bridge. Cartridges from the magazine are rotated 90 degrees as they're chambered from above, unlike many other magazines, which keep the

The PS90's odd-looking grip is surprisingly comfortable and ergonomic.

hook type. There is a separate ejector. The controls are simple. A bolt release is located at the right front of the receiver. The magazine release is under the receiver. It's fast to operate and offers easy reloading, which is done simply by opening the hinged magazine. To make the rifle ready to fire, rack the bolt to the rear and release. The bolt holds open on the last shot fired. The safety is a push-button type in the triggerguard. We rated the safety fast and positive in operation.

Firing this .308 Winchester-chambered rifle off a solid bench rest to confirm

stack of cartridges parallel and below the chamber. This magazine was easy to load and held 30 rounds. We liked the magazine setup because we could easily see the remaining round count while still keeping the rifle in the ready position. Both 10- and 50-round mags are available. Empty brass is ejected from the bottom of the stock (like the Kel-Tec RDB). When the magazine is empty, simply use your support hand to press the magazine catch, pull the empty magazine out, insert a loaded magazine and snap it into place. It takes slightly longer than loading an AR-15 mag.

Going hot with the PS90 at 25 yards we found this bullpup excels in rapid fire. It's easy to shoot with negligible recoil, similar to shooting a rimfire cartridge. The short length of pull — 13.5 inches — means it shoulders quickly. Trigger pull measured about 6 pounds, and it was mushy but serviceable. It is by no means a match-style trigger.

The PS90 is well made, reliable and compact. The cartridge is not as popular as the 5.56mm, but it is proven. If you have a Five-seveN pistol, the PS90 would be a great companion piece. fnamerica.com

BROWNING BAR MK3 STALKER

The Browning Automatic Rifle (BAR), introduced in 1967, uses a short-stroke gas system for operation. It has a 20-inch barrel; the entire gun weighs in at 8.2 pounds scoped. The Stalker features a synthetic one-piece stock. The fit of the

A tactical Browning BAR? The MK3 Stalker in .308 Win. might just qualify, as it packs four rounds and has a synthetic stock that makes it more utilitarian than its wood-stocked cousin.

stock and fore-end is good. The finish is a matte black that is credibly done. The buttstock has a full pistol grip, and the checkering on the pistol grip aids in getting good adhesion when firing.

Operation is simple enough. The bolt head rotates on seven lugs to engage recesses in the barrel. Lockup is tight. When the rifle is fired, the bolt head rotates on a cam pin in the bolt sleeve or bolt carrier. The extractor is a strong

accuracy potential with Hornady ELD Match 168-grain polymer tips, the BAR MK3 fired an average group size of 1.5 inches for three-shot groups at 100 yards. With Federal Trophy Bonded 165-grain polymer tips, it shot an average group size of 1.7 inches, and with Gorilla Ammunition 175-grain Sierra MatchKings it averaged 1.6-inch groups.

If handloading is important, the BAR action works brass more, so some loads

Mfg. (not the original Inland Mfg., but a new company). Inland's current price for the rifle is $1,139. It was built like Uncle Sam intended, using a gas-operated, short-stroke piston system with a rotating bolt and chambered in .30 Carbine. Because the carbine is a mid–20th-century design, there are a few features that might seem dated to the modern shooter, because they are. The crossbolt safety is located outside the triggerguard, which is common on many shotguns and rimfire rifles, but less true for centerfires. The magazine release button, which is larger, sits just forward of the safety button. Initially, testers new to the carbine had to pay attention so they didn't press the wrong button, but they soon learned and could determine by touch which button was which.

may not be suitable for the BAR, including very light or very heavy loads. Just the same, with factory loads or standard handloads, the rifle should prove useful and accurate. browning.com

INLAND MANUFACTURING M1 1945 CARBINE

The M1 Carbine was adopted during World War II, then became a common arm among our soldiers during the Korean and Vietnam Wars, making it one of the most widely produced of all U.S. military rifles. Millions were produced, and at one time surplus models were quite common and inexpensive. Try finding a vintage M1 Carbine today and you will pay close to $1,000 for a well-used specimen. Costs, however, will vary dramatically depending on which manufacturer produced it, the model, features, and its condition.

We tested an M1 Carbine reproduction, the M1 1945 Carbine from Inland

Iron sights on the Inland M1 are rugged, simple.

The new Inland Manufacturing Company's M1 1945 Carbine is a faithful reproduction of the World War II-era gun, and still makes a good home defense option.

Another feature of the design requires the magazines to be loaded straight into the magazine well. Today's modern rifles typically have a flared mag well that funnels the magazine home and offers you a bit of wiggle room when inserting a magazine. Those testers with AR-15 experience found it took slightly more effort to insert and seat the magazine.

Ammo can be found readily online. We purchased Hornady Critical Defense with 110-grain FTX bullets, Hornady .30 Carbine with 110-grain full metal jacket (FMJ) bullets, Aguila 110-grain FMJs, and steel-case TulAmmo rounds, also with 110-grain

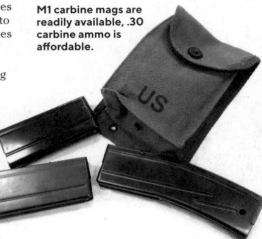

M1 carbine mags are readily available, .30 carbine ammo is affordable.

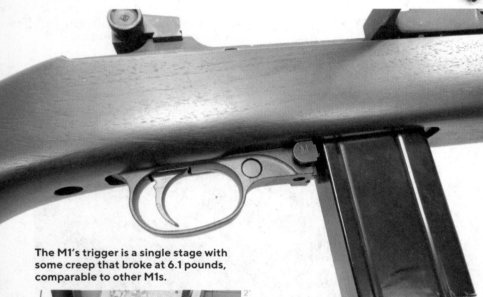

The M1's trigger is a single stage with some creep that broke at 6.1 pounds, comparable to other M1s.

M1 carbine accuracy with Hornady 110-grain full metal jacket (FMJ) bullets was respectable at 100 yards.

FMJs. If you see the trend, the .30 Carbine's sweet spot is the 110-grain bullet. Military ammo was loaded to a muzzle velocity of 1,990 fps and muzzle energy of 967 ft-lbs. Of the four ammo types tested, the Hornady Critical Defense ammo was loaded to 2,000 fps, while the TulAmmo, IMI, Hornady standard, and Aguila were at military velocity of about 1,990 fps. The TulAmmo had the lowest velocity of all ammo tested. The cost is about 4 cents a round, making .30 Carbine ammo slightly less expensive than .223 Remington.

The .30 Carbine has a reputation as being an anemic cartridge, and that is true if you compare it to the .30-06 Springfield. The .30 Carbine round was designed as an intermediate cartridge between the .30-06 Springfield in the M1 Garand and .45 ACP in the M1911A1

pistol. The .30 Carbine fits the role, but push it too far, and naturally it will underperform because it was not designed to replace the .30-06. As a hunting round, it can kill up to deer-size game if used at medium distances down to inside 100 yards. Magazines — new and surplus — are quite easy to acquire and inexpensive, from $8 to $35 depending on manufacturer and capacity.

The M1 1945 Carbine is modeled after the last one the original Inland company manufactured in 1945. Inland Manufacturing was founded in 2013. The company purchased the rights to use the Inland Manufacturing name, which during World War II was a division of General Motors. Back in the day, Inland produced most of the M1 Carbines for the government in Dayton, Ohio, and the new Inland is also located in Dayton, but it has no affiliation with GM. All parts are made in the U.S. According to Inland, all the parts of a new M1 are interchangeable with parts from an original.

Opening the box, the owner finds the Inland M1 set into die-cut foam and sees that it comes with a canvas sling, oiler (which is used to hold the sling into the stock) and one 15-round magazine. The M1 1945 Carbine is made with an investment-cast receiver mated to an 18-inch barrel with four grooves and a 1:20-inch twist rate. The features that make the Inland historically accurate are numerous, including the type-3 bayonet lug and barrel band. Early original production rifles had no bayonet lug. The lug was later incorporated into the design. Original M1s also have simplified sights, which includes a flip-up aperture with two settings — one for 150 yards and the second for 300 yards. Later models used a modified sight with a sliding ramp, and so does the new Inland.

The new Inland also has a pushbutton safety. Late-model originals changed the safety from a pushbutton to a rotating lever. Elsewhere, original M1s had a flat bolt — basically, the top of the bolt was milled flat. Later models used a rounded bolt to reduce manufacturing time. These features were also incorporated into the new Inland.

The walnut stock is referred to as a "low wood" stock, which means it is relieved next to the operating slide. Early M1s had wood nearly covering the slide, and the wood was prone to splitting in this area. From a historical perspective, we felt the Inland is a good facsimile of the original carbine. The stock is a plain piece of walnut with an Inland cartouche on the right side near the metal buttpad. The metal on the action wears a nice Parkerized finish. The steel magazine is blued. The trigger is a single stage with some creep that broke at 6.1 pounds, comparable to other M1s we fired at the same time for reference — typical service-style trigger. In hand, the Inland is lively and comes to the shoulder fast.

At 100 yards, the Aguila ammo performed well, and we were able to shoot our tightest three-shot group, which measured 2.05 inches. The TulAmmo rounds and Hornady Critical Defense also gave good accuracy, averaging close to 2.75 inches. In fact, we were quite pleased with the results because we were using iron sights and a mil-spec-comparable trigger. Recoil was mild with not a lot of muzzle blast. Those new to the carbine easily took to it and found it easy to shoot. At 25 yards, fast follow-up shots were quick because recoil was minimal. Since the rifle is only 36 inches long, it's easy to maneuver. With an unloaded carbine, we maneuvered through rooms and hallways with ease. In our opinion, at the distances typically encountered in a home invasion, the carbine offers plenty of punch. There are less expensive options available, but the Inland could serve as a good home-defense firearm.

The M1 1945 was pleasant to shoot and historically accurate. Collectors of original M1 Carbines would do themselves a service by shooting a new repro like it rather than wearing out an original and reducing the value. It's an expensive home-defense option, but we wouldn't mind using it in that role, if push came to shove. inland-mfg.com

STEYR MODEL AUG A3 M1 W/3X OPTIC

The Steyr AUG is the benchmark by which all other bullpups are judged. It's modular in design and has a reputation for reliability and minimal maintenance. This iconic bullpup has been in service with a variety of police forces and at least 20 militaries since 1978. The AUG has a long history of proven performance. Even though the design is nearly 40 years old, it still looks futuristic. The AUG A3 M1 Optics is the latest variant, which features a traditional AUG scope plus the addition of three Picatinny rail sections on which to mount accessories. This AUG, chambered in 5.56mm NATO, is also made in the U.S.

The AUG features a short-stroke gas-piston system with exhaust gas venting out of the front of the rifle. The piston has an adjustable valve so it can run on all types of ammo and with a suppressor. The action is smooth and easy to manipulate with the non-reciprocating cocking handle. There's plenty of leverage to cock the weapon and lock the handle in a notch in the receiver. You can then slap the handle down to allow the bolt to spring forward and load the chamber. We liked the simplicity of use. The bolt carrier rides on two stainless-steel guide rods in the receiver, which attach to the fiberglass-reinforced polymer stock. The AUG disassembles quickly, what Steyr calls "expedited disassembly," meaning the barrel can be removed in seconds without the use of tools. The AUG quickly fieldstrips into six main components. Barrels with longer lengths are available. Our sample had a 16-inch, cold-hammer-forged barrel with 1:9-inch-twist rifling and a slotted flash

The AUG A3 M1's action is smooth and easy to manipulate with the non-reciprocating cocking handle. There's plenty of leverage to cock the weapon and lock the handle in a notch in the receiver.

A variety of .223 ammo was tested in the Steyr AUG A3 M1, and at 100 yards the author's five-shot groups averaged less than 2 inches.

The Steyr AUG A3 M1 is an iconic bullpup chambered in 5.56 NATO. This new variant is optics ready.

hider. The vertical foregrip can be folded up or rotated down to a vertical grip. We liked this setup and ensured we grasped the vertical grip when shooting offhand. Another feature is the ability to convert to left-hand operation, which requires replacing of the right-hand bolt with the optional left-hand bolt (SteyrArms.com, $249) and swapping the ejection port cover.

This newest AUG is equipped with a Picatinny rail on the top side if you want to mount a second optic. Our sample had an integrated 3X optic, which was bright and clear. Like an optic for an AR, the one on the AUG needs to be mounted high. The scope was positioned 1.95 inches over the stock comb and was easy to aim, with a solid cheek weld. The turret requires a coin or flat screwdriver to make windage and elevation changes. The reticle is a medium crosshair with a rangefinding circle, which we thought was well suited for this bullpup. The scope itself has a topside Picatinny rail so you could mount a CQB red-dot or reflex sight. On the right side of the receiver is another short rail. Also different from previous AUGs is the front sling swivel. This new variant features a Vltor quick-detach sling swivel.

Our sample used Steyr proprietary magazines, though a NATO version of the AUG accepts standard STANAG (AR-15) mags. We liked the clear AUG magazine with the waffle texture, but we could see the NATO version would be more practical for a shooter who already has AR-15 mags. Additional magazines are available in 10-, 30- or 42-round configurations from SteyrArms.com for $45 to $48.

The fastest way to perform magazine changes is to use your support hand like you would with an AR-15, except grab a fresh magazine first, then press the magazine-catch release and strip out the empty mag, then insert the loaded one. Your workspace is more cramped when running a bullpup, and that is one of the trade-offs. Another trade-off is the trigger. The AUG trigger is large and flat as well as glove friendly. It slides rearward with some take-up. Not crisp, but serviceable. The firing grip is also protected by a handguard. At 25 yards the AUG was surgical and spit out brass to the right through the ejection port. Using a rest and shooting to 100 yards, we could squeeze out five-shot groups that averaged less than 2 inches. The AUG had no malfunctions.

The Steyr AUG A3 M1 w/3X optic is a well-made rifle with great ergonomics. steyrarms.com

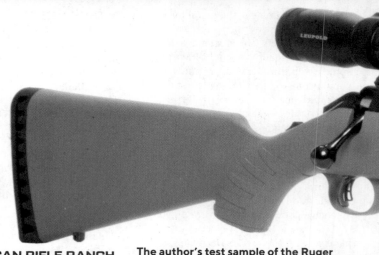

RUGER AMERICAN RIFLE RANCH

The Ruger Ranch Rifle comes in several chamberings, including our .300 Blackout test gun with a five-round rotary magazine. If you're interested in the cartridge more than the rifle, Ruger also chambers an upper for the SR-556 Takedown in .300 BLK, as well as the Mini-14 Tactical Rifle.

The Ranch Rifles come stocked with Flat Dark Earth synthetic units paired with a 16.12-inch-long alloy steel barrel (muzzle diameter of 0.748 inch) and the muzzle threading of 5/8x24. It comes with a 5-inch short-action aluminum scope rail installed. The Ranch has a 1:7-inch

The author's test sample of the Ruger American Ranch Rifle was chambered in .300 AAC Blackout. Shooting unsuppressed, the 220-grain subsonic round from Remington shot 1.8-inch average groups and suppressed 0.8-inch groups.

A 16.12-inch-long alloy steel barrel (muzzle diameter of 0.748 inch) and muzzle threading of 5/8x24 for a muzzle brake complement the Ruger Ranch.

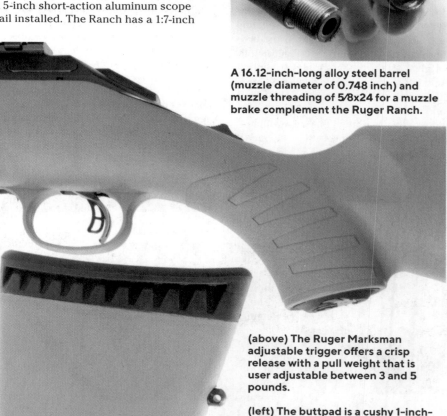

(above) The Ruger Marksman adjustable trigger offers a crisp release with a pull weight that is user adjustable between 3 and 5 pounds.

(left) The buttpad is a cushy 1-inch-thick model that is very comfortable on the shoulder.

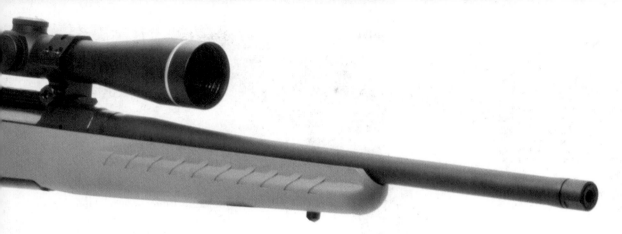

right-hand twist with traditional six grooves/lands. The rifle's hammer-forged barrel is mated to the steel action with a barrel-nut system that ensures perfect headspace. This barreled action sits on a pair of V-notch supports that bed the action. The rifle holds five rounds in its rotary black-polymer magazine, which snaps smoothly into the stock.

But it is the physical dimensions, as well as its accuracy, that makes the Ranch interesting. This rifle out of the box weighs only 6.2 pounds (0.3 pounds more than the manufacturer's specs, however). Overall length is a handy 36 inches, with a longish 14-inch length of pull and a straight comb with a middling amount of drop. After handling and testing the Ranch, our shooters said that in and around a vehicle, even with a 9-inch suppressor aboard, the rifle was easy to move from the driver's seat out the window.

The stock is a sporter shape, which makes it roll around on the shooting bags a little more. The stock has two sling-swivel studs, one in the butt and one in the fore-end. The buttpad is a cushy 1-inch-thick model that is very comfortable on the shoulder. The pistol grip has a grooved texture molded into it. Underneath the action is the company's patent-pending Power Bedding feature, an integral bedding block system that holds the receiver.

Our test ammunition included both supersonic and subsonic rounds. The .300 AAC Blackout rounds were Remington UMC 120-grain OTFB Supersonic, Remington UMC 220-grain Open-Tip Flat Base (OTFB) Subsonic, and Sellier & Bellot 147-grain full metal jacket. In the Ruger, one of the rounds performed significantly better than the rest. Shooting the Remington 120-grain load, the Ruger fired 1.4-inch unsuppressed average

groups and 1.2-inch suppressed average groups. Average velocities were 2,210 fps unsuppressed and 2,229 fps suppressed in the Ruger. Things improved markedly shooting the Sellier & Bellot .300 AAC 147-grain FMJs, with the Ruger firing 1.0-inch groups unsuppressed and 0.8-inch average groups. Average velocities were 2,096 fps suppressed and 2,064 fps unsuppressed. Shooting unsuppressed, the 220-grain subsonic round from Remington shot 1.8-inch average groups and suppressed 0.8-inch groups. Average velocities were all safely below supersonic, producing 1,073 fps and 1,089 fps unsuppressed and suppressed, respectively.

The Ruger was easier to run because its three-lug bolt requires 70 degrees of throw compared to 90 degrees on many other rifles. That left ample scope clearance. The full-diameter bolt body and dual-cocking cams offer smooth, easy cycling from the shoulder. The five-shot magazine loads easily, and the cartridges feed smoothly. Only one rotary magazine comes with the rifle. It's an all-polymer piece that fits flush with the bottom of the stock, reducing the chance of it hanging on clothing or car parts. All ammunition tested functioned perfectly.

The Ruger has a two-position tang safety. The safety selector is located behind the bolt sleeve. The safety selector can be moved from the Fire position to the Safe position only when the firing pin is cocked. Fully raising the bolt handle cocks the firing pin. The cocking piece will protrude from the bolt shroud when the firing pin is cocked. This safety is visible, accessible and easy to operate.

The Ruger Marksman adjustable trigger offers a crisp release with a pull weight that is user adjustable between 3 and 5 pounds. There's about six full turns of adjustment. Turning the screw in

no more than half-revolution increments, we tuned the trigger pull weight down to 3 pounds.

If you're looking for a lightweight suppressed solution with mid-range punch and excellent accuracy, the Ranch Rifle is an easy winner. ruger.com

TIKKA T3X TAC A1 PRECISION BOLT-ACTION RIFLE

Introduced in 2017, Tikka's T3x TAC A1 is a tactical bolt action with a host of innovations that long-distance shooters will appreciate. I'll start with the trigger first. It's unusual to find a two-stage trigger in a factory rifle, but the Finnish T3x TAC A1 is outfitted with one that is adjustable. Two-stage triggers are common on competition rifles, wherein the first stage is set to pull some of the overall trigger weight, allowing the second stage to break with only minimal additional pressure. For instance, this trigger's pull weight can be adjusted to between 2 and 4 pounds. Assume that you want a 2-pound break weight; this trigger will allow you to put the first pound of pressure on the first stage, allowing the second stage to break with only 1 pound of additional press.

The sexy chassis body is a one-piece, reduced receiver-port T3x aluminum middle action fitted to a cold-forged barrel chambered in .308 Win., .260 Rem. or 6.5 Creedmoor. Barrels for the .308 Win. chambering are all 1:11 twist and come in the 16-inch (#JRTAC316SB, $1,899, LE/MIL only), 20-inch (#JRTAC316, $1,899), and 24-inch lengths (#JRTAC316L, $1,899; and a left-hand action, #JRTAC416L, $1,999). The 6.5 Creedmoor models are both 1:8-twist 24-inch models, with the #JRTAC382L listing for $1,899 and the left-hand version, #JRTAC482L, carrying an MSRP of $1,999. The barrel specs are the same for the .260 Rem. and 6.5CM,

The Tikka T3X TAC A1 chassis is a one-piece, reduced receiver-port T3x aluminum middle action fitted to a cold-forged barrel. Chamberings are .308 Win., .260 Rem. and 6.5 Creedmoor.

The Tikka T3X TAC A1 uses an aluminum handguard with M-LOK ports. That's a zero-MOA Picatinny rail on top. The rifle comes with two 10-round detachable magazines that extend from the bottom of the receiver.

listing for $1,899. The muzzle is threaded 5/8X24 to accept suppressors or muzzle brakes.

The chassis system offers an adjustable cheekpiece (height and angle) and length of pull, the latter being changed by adding or subtracting spacers between the buttpad and buttstock frame. The Tikka's stock also folds. The system includes an aluminum handguard with M-LOK ports, a 0 MOA Picatinny rail on top, and several QD sockets and sling clip points. The chassis is compatible with AR-style stocks, pistol grips and handguards. In the action, the two-lug bolt is Teflon coated and is run with an oversized bolt handle.

Other vitals include weights of 10.36 pounds for the 16-inch-barrel model; 10.8 pounds for the 20-inch variant, and 11.24 pounds for the 24-inch-barrel rifle. Respective overall lengths with the stock open are 35.83 inches, 39.80 inches and 43.46 inches. OALs with the stock folded are, respectively, 26.57, 30.55 and 34.21 inches. The Tikka ships with two 10-round detachable box magazines. tikka.fi/en-us

REMINGTON 700 PRECISION CHASSIS RIFLE (PCR)

A lot of the rifles that are dominating long-range shooting events are chassis models, because the rigid aluminum-alloy stocks are basically inert and can resist warping due to humidity and temperature. But machining those chassis requires high-quality aluminum and a lot of time on CNC machines, so they tend to be costly. That's not the case with Remington's Model 700 PCR (Precision Chassis Rifle), now available at retail locations nationwide.

The 24-inch free-floated barrel has 5R rifling and is protected by an aluminum handguard with SquareDrop, a proprietary 100% free-float attachment system that allows adjustable mounting positions for any Keymod or SquareDrop accessory. The SquareDrop handguard has extended alignment flanges to ensure a repeatable fit, eliminating torque and rotational force movement. A turnbuckle mounting design means you can install and remove the rail system. The smooth, snag-free design doesn't "cheesegrate" your hands.

The Model 700 PCR pairs the well-tested Model 700 action with an exclusive aircraft-grade aluminum-alloy chassis whose rigidity and atmospheric immunity create a stable and consistent platform for launching long-distance hits on targets. Other accurizing upgrades include a 24-inch barrel with 5R rifling that's free-floated in an aluminum handguard, plus a user-configurable Magpul PRS Gen 3 stock. And if you can't produce sub-MOA groups, then it's probably you, because every PCR's ability to shoot three shots under an inch is confirmed with Remington's Computer Aided Targeting System (CATS) before it leaves the factory.

Other features include threaded muzzle with protector, tactical bolt knob, X-Mark Pro externally adjustable trigger, aluminum handguard with SquareDrop, Picatinny rail for attaching your optics of choice, 5-round Magpul detachable magazine and a Magpul pistol grip.

The 700 PCR is available in three chamberings: Model No. 84583 in 260 Remington, No. 84586 in 6.5 Creedmoor and No. 84587 in 308 Win. List is $1,199, but an online check found several locations selling them for substantially less. remington.com

(above) That's a tactical bolt knob above the X-Mark Pro externally adjustable trigger. The rifle is topped with a Picatinny rail for attaching optics, a 5-round Magpul detachable magazine and a Magpul pistol grip.

(below) Remington's Model 700 PCR (Precision Chassis Rifle) houses a Model 700 action in an aircraft-grade aluminum-alloy chassis.

Magpul's PRS (Precision Rifle/Sniper) GEN3 stock features tool-less length-of-pull and cheekpiece-height adjustments using aluminum detent knobs. It includes a cant- and height-adjustable rubber buttpad and rotation-limiting QD sling swivel cups, as well as M-LOK slots on the bottom for rear monopod mounting.

BERGARA MATCH PRECISION B-14 BMP RIFLE

The B-14 Series is Bergara's affordable line of rifles built in Spain, but the basics of the company's accurate products is continued, with a coned bolt nose and breech ensuring smooth feeding and a sliding plate extractor for proper alignment. On the Bergara Match Precision (BMP) Chassis rifle specifically, there's also a 4140CrMo steel barrel finished in matte blue with a No. 6 barrel taper and a muzzle threaded 5/8X24 inch with knurled thread protector. The whole outfit sits in a machined aluminum chassis stock. All B-14 rifles are guaranteed to produce 100-yard groups of 1.0 MOA or better with quality factory ammunition.

Specifications for the Bergara BMP vary by barrel length. The 1:10-twist 20-inch barrel on the .308 Win. produces an overall length of 39.5 inches and a dry weight of 10.15 pounds. The 24-inch 1:8-twist rate barrel for the 6.5 Creedmoor produces a rifle that's 43.5 inches long and weighs 11 pounds. The 26-inch barrel on the 6mm CM likewise has a 1:8 twist, and weighs in at 11.1 pounds and measures 45.5 inches in length overall.

Lengths and contours vary by model. In .308 Win, overall length is 39.5 inches with a 20-inch barrel; in 6.5 Creedmoor, 43.5 inches with a 24-inch barrel; and in 6mm CM, 45.5 inches with a 26-inch barrel. The .308 weighs 10.15 pounds, the 6.5 Creedmoor 11 pounds and the 6mm Creedmoor checks in at 11.1 lbs. Twist rates are 1:8 for the 6.5 Creedmoor, 1:10 for the .308 Win. and 1:8 for the 6mm Creedmoor. The bolt itself has a spring-

The BMP's rear buttstock enables you to adjust the cheek piece height and the stock's length of pull. Also, a standard AR–style buffer tube can be installed, and the pistol grip can be replaced with any AR-style grip.

The Bergara BMP's bolt is a one-piece design with two locking lugs and a 90-degree bolt throw angle. The AICS-style detachable magazine holds 5 rounds. The Bergara curved trigger comes set at about 3 pounds. The receiver top is factory drilled and tapped to accept Remington 700 scope bases.

ASHBURY PRECISION MRCS-AR

Ashbury Precision Ordnance (APO) Manufacturing's SABER Modular Rifle Chassis System, or MRCS-AR, utilizes the same Center Chassis Section module as all other SABER rifle chassis platforms while giving you the ability to attach a variety of commercial AR shoulder stocks and handguards.

The MRCS-AR is designed for the carbine shooter desiring to set up their bolt gun like a favorite gas gun, or the bolt-gun shooter can use the chassis as a modular compact lightweight rifle with AR features.

The SABER MRCS-AR rifle shoulder stock deploys a mil-spec six-position buffer tube and a Magpul MOE shoulder stock and cheekpiece riser. The retractable MOE shoulder stock assembly is attached to the SABER Center Chassis Section with a tension-adjustable double locking alloy hinge, making it both retractable and foldable. You can easily install other aftermarket AR shoulder stocks along with APO signature shoulder stocks.

loaded ejector, a side-mounted bolt stop, a one-piece body with two locking lugs and a 90-degree bolt throw angle. The magazine is an AICS-style detachable 5-round unit.

All B-14 Rifles feature a Bergara Performance Trigger, wherein the two-position safety is part of the trigger assembly. With it, the rifle can be unloaded while in the Safe position. The Bergara curved trigger comes set at about three pounds. The chassis on the Bergara BMP has been factory drilled and tapped to accept Remington 700 scope mount bases, has an integrated QD flush cup sling mounts and swivel mounts. The rear buttstock provides an adjustable cheekpiece and length of pull adjustment, and a standard AR-style buffer tube can be installed.

The pistol grip can be replaced with any AR-style grip, allowing for your own customizations. The B-14 BMP starts at $1,699. bergarausa.com

The MRCS-AR is available for the popular short-action Savage Model 10 bolt-action rifle in right- and left-hand operation and a long-action model. The MRCS-AR uses the Magpul PMAG 5 7.62AC 5-round detachable box magazines for the 308 Win. family of cartridges and features an ambidextrous paddle lever release. The MOE pistol grip is attached to the Center Chassis Section with a 17.5-degree Grip Angle Adapter (just like a M1911-A1) and includes an adjustable hand grip-to-trigger distance feature for shooters with long or short fingers.

The MRCS-AR employs a rugged APO-designed octagonal aluminum-alloy handguard that uses the Magpul M-LOK accessory attachment system at the 3, 6, 9, and 12 o'clock positions and a bipod stud located at the front of the hand-guard. The fore-end can accommodate barrel shank diameters and contours measuring 1.250 inches. An optional carbon-fiber handguard with similar features is available as an upgrade. For professional marksmen and predator hunters desiring to maximize downrange precision using clip-on night vision and thermal imaging weapon sights, Ashbury also makes a one-piece 20-MOA monolithic rail.

The modular MRCS-AR rifle chassis system is manufactured to ISO:9001-2008 standards from aerospace-grade aluminum alloys and carbon-reinforced composites. The base model has a standard hardcoat-anodized black finish. A range of Cerakote ceramic coating colors are available from the APO Custom Shop.

The SABER MRCS-AR short-action model weighs only 3.9 pounds. A tactical-hunter version, using a Savage Model 10 FCP with a 24-inch medium-contour barrel and Bushnell 2.5-16x42mm Elite riflescope, weighs in under 10 pounds. This chassis can be found for $700, and barreled actions with the chassis come as Savage Model 10 Ashbury models and trade for around $1,050. ashburyprecisionordnance.com

The MRCS-AR is available for the short-action Savage Model 10 bolt-action rifle in right- and left-hand operation and a long-action model. The MRCS-AR uses Magpul PMAG 5 7.62AC 5-round detachable box magazines.

(below) The SABER MRCS-AR rifle shoulder stock has a mil-spec six-position buffer tube and a Magpul MOE shoulder stock and cheekpiece riser.

Ashbury Precision Ordnance (APO) Manufacturing's SABER Modular Rifle Chassis System, or MRCS-AR, comes on Savage Model 10 Ashbury models. The chassis alone often sells for about $700. The APO-designed octagonal aluminum-alloy handguard features the Magpul M-LOK accessory attachment system at the 3, 6, 9, and 12 o'clock positions and a bipod stud located at the front of the handguard. The fore-end can accommodate barrel shank diameters and contours measuring 1.250 inches.

The Kimber Advanced Tactical SOC II comes in FDE (flat dark earth, top) and SG (sniper gray) finishes. The SOC II is chambered in 6.5 Creedmoor and .308 Win. (Item Nos. 3000855 and 3000856 respectively in FDE coloring, and Item Nos. 3000857 and 3000858 in SG coloring), and the short-barrel SRC II is offered in .308 Win. (Item No. 3000859 in FDE).

KIMBER ADVANCED TACTICAL SOC II AND SRC II PRECISION RIFLES

Kimber has upped its game in the long-range market with the new Kimber Advanced Tactical SOC II and Advanced Tactical SRC II precision rifles. Both come with the eye-popping half-MOA accuracy guarantee.

Common to both the Advanced Tactical SOC II and SRC II is Kimber's 8400 action, which includes a full-length Mauser claw extractor for controlled-round feeding and extraction. The SOC II and SRC II also have 3-position wing safeties, a match-grade trigger tuned to break at 2.5 pounds, and muzzles that are 5/8X24 threaded to accept standard brakes or suppressors.

Barreled actions are mounted in a McRees Precision G10 Standard aluminum lightweight chassis system. Side-folding stocks adapt to the shooter, as they are adjustable for comb height, butt height, length of pull and have M-LEV embedded cant indicators. Some shooters like to use a bit of cant when cast in the stock isn't available to get the gun to come to the face, but the cant must be repeatable or bullet impact can vary. So the level is a nice touch.

Other details include the SOC II's 22-inch barrel, the SRC II's 16-inch barrel, 1913 MIL-STD forward 20-MOA night vision mount, bipod mount and MLOK side mounts. Both rifles accept Accuracy International 5- and 10-round detachable box magazines. The Advanced Tactical

SOC II is available with a sniper gray or flat dark earth chassis system, and the Advanced Tactical SRC II comes in a flat dark earth colored chassis. The rifles ship with a nylon stock pack and drag bag suitable for both storage and deployment.

The Kimber Advanced Tactical SOC II is chambered in 6.5 Creedmoor and .308 Win., and the SRC II is offered in .308 Win. The precision rifles are available from Kimber Master Dealers with very reasonable MSRPs of $2,449. kimberamerica.com TGD

Todd Woodard is editor of Gun Tests *magazine,* Cartridges of the World, 16th Edition, *and a contributor to numerous firearms publications.*

The Kimber Advanced Tactical SOC II and SRC II rifles come with a half-minute accuracy guarantee, if the shooter is up to it.

Side-folding stocks on the Advanced Tactical SOC II and SRC II rifles are adjustable for comb height, butt height and length of pull.

Kimber's 8400 action, proven in its sporter rifles with a full-length Mauser claw extractor, also appears in the Advanced Tactical SOC II and SRC II rifles.

The Kimbers ship with a detachable nylon stock pack and drag bag suitable for both storage and deployment.

Optics
ROUNDUP

From Scopes to Red-Dots, Optics to Bet Your Life On
BY **TODD WOODARD**

The Aimpoint C5 — smaller, but just as rugged and precise as previous generations.

For those who stack up the round count comes the insight that what's on top of the gun matters as much as the gun itself. That is, you can't hit what you can't see, or more accurately, you can't hit what you can't target. Following are ten recommendations for a variety of optics that have proven themselves as reliable in dozens of firearms evaluations.

NIKON M-223 SERIES 3-12X42MM

Nikon's M-223 Series 3-12X42mm uses a BDC (bullet-drop compensating) system with its lower half of the vertical reticle wire showing a series of open circles and hash marks that can quickly be put over a target. Though the scope circles are set up for an optimum 55-grain 223 Rem. loading, Nikon's Spot

With a bullet-drop compensating (BDC) reticle that syncs with a smartphone app, the Nikon M-223 proved versatile and easy to set up.

(above) Tactile adjustment clicks gave the expected quarter-inch of bullet impact at 100 yards during testing of the Nikon M-223.

(right) Establishing holdovers for the author's test ammo was simple using Nikon's Spot On Ballistics Match Technology iPhone app.

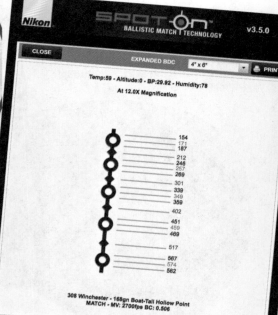

On Ballistics Match Technology iPhone app gives you access to instant data specific to your shooting equipment. Simply enter your BDC-equipped Nikon model, load data, and preferred zero range, and the program will show the precise range for the crosshairs and each ballistic circle.

At the range, we used an iPhone 7 Plus to consult Spot On and move from a 100-yard zero to shoot center shots at 300 and 600 yards with no come-up adjustment. For example, with a Savage Model 10PT-SR chambered in .308 Winchester using a 168-grain Hornady load, the second hash mark from the top offered a 301-yard point of impact.

Elsewhere, the scope is equipped with a side-focus turret for parallax correction and a one-piece 1-inch main tube that's nitrogen-filled and O-ring-sealed. The glass lens elements are fully multi-coated and offer sharp target images. Adjustment clicks give the expected quarter-inch of bullet impact at 100 yards, and we could adjust the click-stops while keeping our heads on the stock because the adjustments have tactile clicks. Eye relief is 3.9 inches. It runs $460. nikonsportoptics.com

SWAROVSKI BTX SPOTTING SCOPE

The Swarovski BTX is a unique system combining the features and benefits of a spotting scope and binocular. The BTX offers both-eye viewing through all objective modules in the Swarovski

Swarovski's BTX system gives you both-eye viewing for spotting scopes, reducing eye strain during long glassing sessions.

ATX/STX series. It simply attaches to the objective. The BTX also features an adjustable forehead rest, which can be retracted for more comfortable viewing, and an aiming aid is integrated above the right eyepiece. If you're spotting a lot of long-distance targets for your team, this is an excellent piece of glass that your body will thank you for by reducing eyestrain and headaches. Suggested retail, $2,988. swarovski.com

The Viridian R5–G42 Reactor Green Laser for the Glock 42 automatically turns on when drawn from a holster.

VIRIDIAN R5-G42 REACTOR GREEN LASER

The function of carry guns such as the Glock 42 in .380 ACP is as portable self-defense sidearms. Stock sights aren't made to win matches. How much aiming does a concealed-carrier have to do with a bad guy 15 feet away? The open sights on the Glock 42 aren't bad, but a laser enabled us to shoot it on par with bigger guns with better sights.

We added a Viridian R5-G42 Reactor Green Laser for the Glock 42. This laser automatically turns on when drawn from

(below) Shooting Hornady Critical Defense 90-grain FTEs, the Glock and Viridian laser sight closed group sizes to 1.7 inches as compared with open sights, which grouped at 3.3 inches.

a supplied leather and polymer holster. Additional holster options are available from many holster manufacturers.

Unquestionably, the laser helped our shooters' accuracy. Shooting Winchester 95-grain FMJs, the average group size with a laser was 1.2 inches for the Glock, noticeably better than we could do with open sights (1.7 inches.) We saw the same group-size decrease with the Prvi Partizan 94-grain FMJs, with the Glock at a laser-aided 1.2 inches compared to open sights at 3.7 inches. The trend continued with Hornady Critical Defense 90-grain FTEs, with the Glock and laser sight at 1.7 inches and open sights at 3.3 inches. The G42 is big enough to shoot well and small enough to hide well. With the laser, it is very accurate. viridianweapontech.com

ZEISS VICTORY SF BINOCULAR LASER RANGEFINDER SERIES

The premium Victory SF binocular laser rangefinder series is available in four models: 8x42, 10x42, 8x54 and 10x54. These binos are designed with enhanced ergonomics for comfortable operation over extended periods. Range capability is out to 2,500 yards. They can also connect to the Zeiss B.I.S. II Ballistic Calculator via Bluetooth technology, so with one click the range, angle, equivalent horizontal distance and holdover values can be quickly displayed. These are elegant tools with the best-possible glass and function, and they enable you or your spotter to get distance and firing solutions prior to sending one downrange. Suggested retail prices start at $3,250. zeiss.com

Bushnell's Elite 6-24X50mm riflescope is a bargain for the long-range shooter demanding precision and features at a fraction of the cost of competing brands.

BUSHNELL ELITE 6-24X50MM RIFLESCOPE

Tactical scopes are bred to provide an advantage over multiple targets at short to moderate distance, or an adversary at long range. Typically, the difference between tactical scopes is the reticle pattern and degree of magnification, depending on the application for which they were designed.

If you're looking for a bargain long-range optic, the Bushnell Elite 4200 Tactical 6-24X50 (No. 42-6245T) might be your deal. Now discontinued and supplanted by the 4500 series, the Bushnell Elite 4200 Tactical's magnification ring is bold, easy to turn, and offers the largest numbers from 6 to 24. The adjustment turret shows you which direction is up, down, right, and left, but the top of each adjustment knob is left blank. The knobs themselves are bulbous and grooved for grip. The numbers (0-11, for a total of 12 MOA) are large and clear. Turning the knobs offers well-defined clicks for each one-quarter MOA. The Elite offers the same amount of adjustment for both windage and elevation (186 clicks). Traditional cup-like lens covers connected by elastic are supplied. The total of these features make the Bushnell Elite scopes very easy to use.

In our hold-off test, we landed groups 4.0 inches to the left and 3.7 inches to the right. The variation in height was almost nil. To measure the differential between distances from point of aim in our windage knob test, we had to go two columns right of the decimal point. Sixteen clicks left moved point of impact 2.3 inches. Thirty-two clicks right pushed point of impact 2.2 inches right of our original

Zeiss' Victory SF Laser Rangefinder binos not only provide crystal-clear glass, they can range out to 2,500 yards.

You can connect to the Zeiss B.I.S. II Ballistic Calculator via Bluetooth technology, so with one click the range, angle, equivalent horizontal distance and holdover values can be quickly displayed.

The Trijicon RMR (Rugged Miniature Reflex) Dual Illumination sight operates without batteries. It uses tritium to illuminate the reticle in low-light conditions, along with fiber optics that automatically adjust brightness of the reticle level and contrast to available light conditions. An RMR pistol mount plate kit ($102) is required to mount the RMR to a Glock 20

Large 12-MOA turrets provide 186 clicks of adjustment — plenty to handle most long-range applications.

TRIJICON DUAL ILLUMINATED RMR

Adding a red-dot sight to a carry pistol has pros and cons. First, the cons. The total cost of the weapon system nearly doubles as the sights are almost as expensive as the pistol; the sights have a larger footprint than the typical rear sight; battery life must be monitored; and foul weather can diminish the capability of the sight. The pros are faster target acquisition and ease of aiming. The ability to shoot faster and more accurately in situations under 25 yards are strong reasons to make the switch from irons to a reflex sight.

zero. Returning the scope to our original zero was almost perfect, close enough to be blamed on shooter error.

The most challenging aspect of our test was to move the point of impact up 4 MOA from our zero after having been lowered 4 MOA and have the resulting groups land equidistant from center. The Bushnell scope was able to raise the point of impact 2.4 inches above zero after dropping it 2.4 inches downward.

After calling out distances to our shooter, we think the side focus does a better job of matching clarity to calibration. The adjustment knobs have plenty of feedback and solid detent. With "only" 98 clicks of adjustment available in either direction, we might wish for more vertical space or choose to build in more elevation via the mount. But for clearance or used prices at or below $400, you can pay more for several scopes that offer a lot less. bushnell.com

The Trijicon RMR runs without batteries, and automatically adjusts to outside ambient light conditions.

Gen4 10mm, bringing the cost up to $679. A hex wrench is supplied. The RMR's housing is made of forged aluminum with a sight window that's square on the bottom with an arc on top. No special tools are required to adjust the sight; in fact, in a pinch you can use the rim of a fired case. The clicks are audible and precise. The brightness of the reticle aiming point adjusts automatically when going from bright to dim light and vice versa.

The sight window is thick and that tended to block the view slightly when aiming with both eyes. The top edge of the sight window houses a translucent band that gathers light to power the aiming point. Its ruggedness gives a higher level of confidence to take abuse. Testers used the sight to rack the slide by grabbing it with their hand or catching it on the edge of a shooting table or holster. The sight stayed dead on, no change in zero. This optic is bank vault secure. The battle-tested Trijicon RMR is expensive, but for many people, the convenience of not using batteries outweighs the cost. trijicon.com

AIMPOINT COMPM5

The CompM5 is a compact red-dot sight — in fact, it's the smallest in the Comp series — powered by a single AAA battery, which gives it up to five years of continuous power at position seven. An advanced wedged lens system offers dot clarity and makes the sight parallax-free. The CompM5 is compatible with Aimpoint 3XMag-1 and 6XMag-1 magnifiers as well as all generations of night-vision devices. The sight is offered in standard height for MSR mounting and absolute co-witness configurations. Suggested retail $1,068. aimpoint.com

The Aimpoint CompM5 is the smallest in Aimpoint's Comp Series, operates on one AAA battery.

(above) The RMR's housing is made of forged aluminum with a sight window that's square on the bottom with an arc on top.

RUGER LCP-LM

The LCP-LM mashed together Ruger's tiniest pistol with LaserMax's triggerguard laser sight. The laser is nicely integrated into the pistol. To turn the laser on, the button is pressed from either the right or left side. To turn it off, press the button from the opposite side to center it.

The laser battery is accessed via screws to remove a sideplate. One 1/3 N-cell lithium battery provides power. The laser can be removed, but there are polymer tabs that look like they could easily be broken if the laser is snapped on and off the gun numerous times. The LCP-LM is adjusted via two tiny hex screws. The Ruger pistol (.380 ACP) has minimal sights that make it easily slipped into almost any size pocket.

The Ruger LCP-LM is a good choice for deep concealed carry, and the factory-installed laser gives you the ability to fire it from nearly any position without having to bring the paltry sights into alignment with the eyes. ruger.com

TRIJICON ACCUPOINT TR23-2G 5-20X50

The Trijicon AccuPoint TR23-2G scope is built on a 30mm-diameter tube with a 50mm objective lens and a mil-dot reticle. The reticle is in the first focal plane, and the knobs offer .25-MOA click adjustment. The reticle pattern can be used to range the target at any level of magnification using the following equation:

Height or width of target in yards multiplied by 1000; divided by the size of the target as measured against the mil-dot reticle, equals distance. As you can see, you must know the approximate size of the target. When military or police snipers deal with the human torso, the mea-

The .380 ACP–chambered Ruger LCP with LaserMax triggerguard laser is ideal for deep concealment.

to fight wind drift becomes much easier with the additional visual aid of the mil dots. This makes visualizing a hold that changes both windage and elevation much easier. Also, holding off center by, say, one mil dot can also be effective when engaging a moving target.

The Trijicon AccuPoint presents a green dot at dead center of the reticle. Wrapped around the eyepiece just behind the heavily grooved rubber-coated magnification ring is a separate ring with handy grip lines. Cut into this ring is a window covering a little less than 180 degrees of the tube. Behind the window is a light-gathering filament measuring about 0.30-inch wide. Moving this ring regulates intensity by determining how much light is getting to the filament, which powers a tritium-phosphor lamp. The result is a 0.5-MOA illuminated green dot at the center of the reticle (an amber-colored dot is also available). The dot is cube-shaped, which helps maintain the reticle grid. With the filament window shuttered in daylight, the reticle appears to be a solid intersection of black cross-hairs. The dot best responds to ambient light. In dim overcast light, we found that a pinhole of light was available at the center of the reticle.

surement they typically use is 30 inches, or 0.833 yards. The mil-dot reticle comes into play when you look through the scope and determine how tall the target appears when measured against the reticle. Once distance is determined, elevation can be adjusted according to published data, such as a range card.

In addition to its ranging ability, the mil-dot reticle offers another advantage over common crosshairs: Holding over for added elevation or holding off

Large turrets on the big Trijicon give you 12 MOA of adjustment per revolution.

Trijicon's AccuPoint TR23-2G 5-20X50mm optic proved clear, adjustments precise and is outfitted with an expansive mid-dot grid reticle.

Aside from the illumination feature, our staff was impressed with the overall clarity of the AccuPoint scope. There was also more space between mil-dots, giving you a bright, seemingly wider field of view.

The construction of the AccuPoint is robust and confidence-inspiring. Side focus is marked from 40 yards to infinity with regular hashmarks, but no other corresponding numbers. Rotation is very easy, with perhaps too little detent to hold the dial in place. This is suitable for the lone shooter who's merely looking for focus but would make following the instructions of a spotter more difficult. Fine focus is available by rotating the eyepiece. A section of the rear tube is grooved for grip, but so long as the scope is mounted the magnification and eyepiece focus rings are easily turned without affecting the other.

The windage and elevation dials are marked from 0 to 11, for 12 MOA per revolution. The clicks may not be audible, but the ratchets are well defined. Directional arrows for both windage and elevation are clearly visible from behind the scope, as well as from above and to the side. The lines on the elevation and windage towers are not numbered.

In a 2-dot holdoff test, the point of impact averaged about 3.9 inches from the center. This would be ideal, but the variation was as large as 3.8 inches to the left and 4.2 inches to the right. The center of each group was level with our zero group in the center. Cranking the knobs 4 MOA in either direction for a windage test, there was about a .5-inch difference in placement of the point of impact. Average displacement was close to perfect (2.07 inches), but this time the left-side group was farther away, 2.4 inches from center versus 1.8 inches to the right.

In terms of adjustment for elevation, a total of 206 clicks are available from top to bottom. Dead center is 103 clicks from the bottom or the top. (We counted 195 clicks of windage adjustment.) Sixteen clicks moves the point of impact about 2.9 inches below point of aim. But 32 clicks up from this point moves the point of impact only 1.8 inches above point of aim.

Shooters liked the airy view and expansive grid presented by the reticle. The larger mil dots made it easier to perform visual measurements, but the giveback was that they blocked more target area. trijicon.com

LEUPOLD DELTAPOINT REFLEX SIGHT

A reflex sight enables you to keep both eyes open and view a target through a small curved glass lens, onto which a reticle is projected. A light-emitting diode projects a red dot, amber chevron, or other aiming point, giving you an unlimited field of view since there is no magnification and the aiming point projects out to infinity. This means that parallax will not affect sighting; place the aiming point on a target, and if zeroed properly, the target will be hit. Think of it as a mini heads-up display for your pistol.

There are two ways to attach the reflex sight to a pistol. One option is to mill an area near the rear sight on the slide and drill and tap it. This option allows you to keep iron sights as backup and it places the reflex sight closer to the bore's center axis. In this configuration, you can use iron sights that are taller — like those used with a suppressor — so they clear the reflex sight. Some mount the rear BUIS in front of the reflex, others behind it. The second method of attachment is to use the rear sight dovetail with a mounting plate. We chose the second option because it was less expensive and we wanted to be able to mount the reflex ourselves. The tools needed to mount the sight, other than the ones included with the optic, were a hammer and brass punch.

Leupold's DeltaPoint reflex sight proved rugged following all sorts of ammo testing and even slide-racking.

At the range, we tested the sight's ruggedness by shooting a variety of ammo: PMC 200-grain FMJ-TC, Hornady 165-grain FTX, Buffalo Bore 180-grain JHP and American Eagle 180-grain FMJ. These rounds offered a variety of bullets and muzzle velocities, from the mild American Eagle to the hot Buffalo Bore. Hands down, the red-dot was faster to acquire than open sights. Place the dot on the target, press the trigger, hole in target. Simple. There was, however, a learning curve to find the aiming point in the sight window. At the beginning, it took time. The pistol needed to be held slightly lower than when using the open sights. Ramp up time was short, but a switch to the DeltaPoint will require training to become acclimated to the sight. Also, since the sight is attached directly to the slide, it does whatever the slide does. The sights being parallax free mean that the aiming point doesn't need to be centered within the sight window. We fired the handgun with the dot uncentered to see if parallax had any effect, and for the distance tested out to 25 yards there were no issues. The accuracy was more than adequate for action-shooting competition and defensive purposes. The DeltaPoint sights are made to be mounted and zeroed with no in-the-field adjustments, but we did shoot, move the sight to the right a few clicks or turns, then several clicks to the left, then back to the right to test

the accuracy of the adjustment system. All were within factory spec and to our satisfaction.

The DeltaPoint is powered by a battery and is motion activated. It'll shut down if left at complete rest for five minutes, which saves battery power. Once moved, the sight automatically turns on. A rubber cover puts the sight at its lowest illumination setting, also reserving battery life. The battery should last 9,000 hours, or more than a year.

Included with the Leupold are 10 different mounting plates that fit everything from Smith & Wesson revolvers to numerous semi-automatics pistols, except for the big Glock 20 Gen 4 chambered in 10mm. (Note that today's Glock MOS system makes mounting the DeltaPoint a breeze.) A plate was included for the standard-frame Glocks, but not the .45 ACP and 10mm models. Another $40 was required for a mounting plate from JP Enterprises, totaling $605. A mount for Weaver/Picatinny-style rails is also included for those wanting to mount it on a long gun. Though the mounting plate was not included for our Glock, the assortment of bases that came with the sight was a real plus. A rubber cover and a battery were also included.

Mounting the DeltaPoint, we first slid a dovetail mounting plate into the slide's dovetail, then secured it with a screw. The sight was then bolted to the plate.

Sight acquisition was indeed faster than iron sights using the Leupold DeltaPoint, and accuracy significantly better.

The optic needs to be removed from the mounting plate to change the battery, and we thought the sight would lose zero once removed. We found it was still zeroed after removing it from the base, though we would recheck it every time we replaced the battery.

A tiny supplied Torx wrench was required to adjust windage and elevation. Locking set screws need to be loosened with the same wrench prior to zeroing the sight. The sight window of the DeltaPoint is oval with flat sides. The sight window frame is thin, so there is little field-of-view obstruction. The optic also has little reflection signature and the lens is crystal clear.

The DeltaPoint system is always ready, though it requires a battery. The extra mounting plates are a plus. leupold.com **TGD**

Todd Woodard is editor of Gun Tests *magazine,* Cartridges of the World, 16th Edition, *and a contributor to numerous firearms publications.*

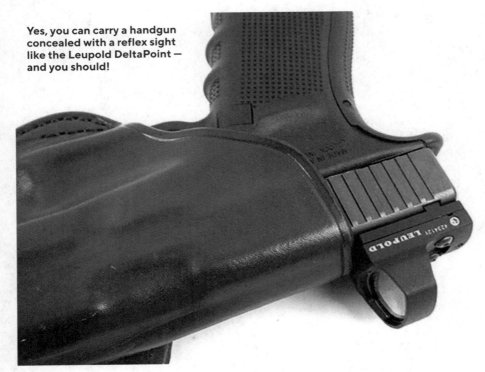

Yes, you can carry a handgun concealed with a reflex sight like the Leupold DeltaPoint — and you should!

TACTICAL BLADES

The **Best** in Tactical Knives for Utility, Survival and Everyday Carry

BY **JOE KERTZMAN**

The Santa Fe Stoneworks Custom #01 Buttonlock has a titanium body that weighs a slight 2.3 ounces and a VG-10 steel blade. This one's a looker.

There's a lot to be said for evolution in tactical knife design — trends becoming standard features, experience dictating form and function, and what was once new becoming standard issue.

BUCK INERTIA

Such is the case with the Buck 293 Inertia everyday carry flipper folder. What I love about this knife is that it takes a few of the best innovations over the past 20 years and melds them into one handy and ultimately useful folder.

The Buck Inertia carries a 3 1/8-inch drop-point 420HC stainless steel blade, works off a fast-opening flipper mechanism. A nice 3 1/8-inch, drop-point 420HC stainless steel blade, complete with a swedge (slight false edge) along the spine, works off a fast-opening flipper mechanism. For those unfamiliar with a "flipper," it's an extended tang that protrudes from the handle when the folder is in the closed position. A flick of the forefinger on the flipper sets the spring of the assisted-opening mechanism in motion and the blade flies open with a snap. It's fast and smooth, and there's also a one-hand thumb hole in the blade if you prefer to open the folder that way. A locking liner holds the blade open and at the ready.

The nylon handle is grooved and textured, as well as skeletonized, with holes machined through it to reduce weight. It feels good in the average hand. And there's a deep-carry pocket clip. The knife only weighs 3.8 ounces. The manufacturer's suggested retail price (MSRP): $60, and this model is made in the USA. buckknives.com

PRO-TECH

Alright, this one is not for the faint of heart. But, man, it sure is a fun and useful folder, whether you consider it a "tactical" piece or just an everyday carry knife. No matter, it's built for speed, sport and spot-on cutting.

I must like the drop-point blades, as I tend toward them and high, hollow-ground edges. And I'm not alone — for folks who use knives regularly, it seems the drop-point blades that R.W. "Bob" Loveless made so popular in his day are the most common, though certainly not exclusive. By the way, this one is a short 1.99 inches long, of a little higher-class 154CM stainless steel with a satin finish, and plain edged (no serrations).

But why only 1.99 inches long? Because the Pro-Tech "CAL-MIGO" (friend of California?) automatic (yes, switchblade) folder is "California Legal," with a sub-2-inch blade. Sure bet, it's a friend of California. Check out the black 6061-T6 aluminum handle, nothing fancy, but it fills the hand, and sports a push button opener, a slide safety, pass-through lanyard hole, plunge lock and tip-up pocket clip.

The popularity of these small auto folders has gone way up over the years, well beyond the California borders. A lot of folks see the value of having a small, quick-to-open, quality knife in their pocket. MSRP: $170. protech knives.com

The 1.99-inch long Pro-Tech CALMIGO.

The ESEE Knives CR 2.5 sports a (you guessed it) 2.5-inch 1095 high-carbon steel blade, and weighs just 2.5 ounces.

ESEE KNIVES

Quite frankly, there's nothing handier than a little bird-and-trout knife with a well-thought-out design, quality materials and uncompromised cutting ability. This one comes in a traditional leather pouch sheath and is a fine specimen.

Part of the ESEE Knives Camp Lore series, the CR 2.5 fixed blade is aptly named for its 2.5-inch 1095 high-carbon steel blade, and the fact that it weighs 2.5 ounces. Though high carbon, the blade features a stonewashed black oxide finish, so it won't rust quite as easily as an untreated non-stainless steel blade.

Designed by Cody Rowen as a lightweight bird-and-trout knife, it's intended to dress small game and perform light chores, but come on, guys, anyone who knows how to handle a knife knows by looking at it, and feeling its solid build, this one can be used to dress and skin larger game, with some good reports already coming back from camp. Honestly, the slim CR 2.5 can go from peeling an apple to separating joints on an elk, and don't worry, it won't break. It's a full-tang model with bolted canvas Micarta grips. You'd have to put it through destruction tests to bend it.

Many hunters are not only carrying the CR 2.5 into the field to dress game, but on their hips in the pouch sheath for ordinary daily cutting chores, as well as bragging rights, of course.

I can't tell you for sure, but the company claims the CR 2.5 is sold in 24 countries. MSRP: $143.50. eseeknives.com

SPYDERCO

Sometimes refinement costs a few bucks, but in this case it's worth it in my own humble opinion. Let's start with the leaf-shaped, fully flat-ground 2.95-inch CPM S90V stainless steel blade of the Spyderco Native 5 folder. As far as blade steels go, the particle-metallurgy proprietary alloy is top of the line, with a high, hard vanadium carbide content, and the tip of this knife and cutting edge are equal parts pointy and sharp.

It will puncture and slice cutting media with aplomb. Small details, too, like the thumb and finger notches in and above the choil are not left off, nor merely afterthoughts.

Then there's the rounded and fluted carbon fiber handle with patterning that splays out from the center like rays emitting from the sun; the hourglass-shaped four-position pocket clip with rounded-off edges; back lock on the hump of the handle; and thong hole through the handle butt.

The grip has an integral fingerguard and is shaped to fit the hand — imagine that. It's also backed by full, skeletonized stainless steel liners, which, in concert with the stainless back spacer, are structurally solid and balanced, and properly anchor the back-lock mechanism.

Whether you're a believer or not, anyone who has met the Spyderco crew, and particularly founder Sal Glesser, knows the company is constantly committed to improving quality and design. If you ask me, the Native 5 nails it. MSRP: $359.95. spyderco.com

BEAR & SON CUTLERY

Check out the olive-drab green G-10 handle of the Bear Edge Model 61102 — not only is it handsome, with grooves along the top and finger indents on the bottom, it's a functional design, meant to be gripped and squeezed a little.

I like it, and it's not just a lanyard hole on the handle butt,

either, but an extended steel, screw-on strap slot for a nice thong to trail behind.

It might surprise some that the 61102 is the flagship model of the Bear Edge brand from Bear & Son Cutlery, which is aimed toward knife owners who carry and use their knives daily but are on a tight budget. When people think of budget lines, they don't often equate quality, yet the flipper folder has a 3.38-inch, recurved 440 stainless steel blade with a high, hollow grind and a swedge on the spine, and the curvaceous cutter comes to a nice point and has an integral fingerguard.

My favorite feature isn't visible, but instead takes the form of ball bearing washers. Folding knife fanatics will tell you that ball bearing and Teflon washers and the like make for smoother folder action, and they're correct in saying so.

An ambidextrous tip-up pocket clip and milled inner handle that houses hidden liners complete the piece, which weighs in at 3.1 ounces. For the price, you can't really go wrong.

MSRP: $59.99. bearandsoncutlery.com

The Spyderco Native 5 Carbon Fiber is the epitome of tactical flipper refinement.

BOKER USA

The love affair with locking folders is not going away anytime soon — it's a longtime affair, a relationship, and it's intimate. They're handy, easy to carry, and if held to high-quality standards, workmanship and materials, they're safe and exhibit the most high-tech features.

The "intimate" part comes from holding and using them, examining the cutting edges, handles and, in the case of the Boker Plus 01BO730 "Urban Trapper," the flipper mechanisms and sturdy frame locks.

Few who experience a well-made frame-lock folder ever go back to other locking mechanisms or folding knife patterns. With the right amount of handle frame heft and tight lockup interface, it's as sturdy a folding knife as a folder gets.

Designed by Brad Zinker, the Urban Trapper is named for its traditional trapper-pattern VG-10 blade and is one of the thinnest titanium frame locks in profile I've seen on the market. The large holes milled through the titanium grip make it extremely lightweight, at only 1.7 ounces, so it's easy to carry in a suit, slacks or trousers pocket.

Of minimalist design, the flipper mechanism is smooth and there's plenty of handle frame to lock the VG-10 blade tightly. And, of course, it comes with a pocket clip.

This one must be held to understand the easy functionality of the opening mechanism. It can't be "grasped" by text alone. Pun intended. MSRP: $125.95. bokerusa.com

The Boker Plus Urban Trapper flipper is a tough little frame-lock folder, and affordable!

BLADE-TECH INDUSTRIES

If curves are more pleasant to hold and behold, then the Blade-Tech Pro Hunter Folder, designed by Tim Wegner, is a sight for sore eyes and a respite for sore hands. This one is a radius-ramp LinerLock folder with a choice of black or orange G-10 handle and a 3.625-inch CPM S30V steel blade — one of the most technically advanced edge-holding steels on the market today.

From what I understand, the Taiwan-made Pro Hunter was developed as a more affordable version of the Professional Hunter Magnum, which is manufactured in the United States. In use, though, the Taiwanese version is a tough, multi-tasking knife, especially in chores a hunter requires.

The big-belly blade in a modified drop-point pattern is a skinner and game dresser, and while the elongated one-hand-opening "V hole" in the blade makes it easy to access, the devil is in the details — like the thumb and finger notches at intervals along the spine of the blade so you can choke up on it, as well as index the cutting edge and tip so you always know where they are, even in low light. And I did, and this puppy performed!

Because it was designed to cut flesh, I'd imagine the Pro Hunter Folder would make a great defensive tactics knife. The handle is ergonomically shaped and comfortable in all grip configurations. MSRP: $119.95. blade-tech.com

The Blade-Tech Pro Hunter Folder, designed by Tim Wegner, comes with your choice of black or orange G-10 handle and a 3.625-inch CPM S30V steel blade.

BERETTA USA CORP.

When a person has handled enough knives, and guns for that matter, you tend to be a little wary of phrases such as "air light." Then, when you come to understand that a hunting buddy of yours, as well as the local cop, have employed and been satisfied with the Beretta Serrated Airlight II knife, you say, "Alright, I'll give it a try."

I admit, I was still wary. The large holes milled through the blade and the partial edge serrations aren't my cup of tea on a folding knife. I did like the looks of the black Sure Grip finish of the aluminum handle frame, and sure enough, it was comfortable to handle.

The locking-liner folder integrates a thumb stud for opening the 3.12-inch semi-serrated AUS-6 steel blade. The blade I tested was nicely heat treated and held up well, and you know, I didn't mind the serrations at all. And they, of course, came in handy for tearing through sinew and fibers. There's enough plain-edge blade and belly for all other tasks.

It's a lightweight everyday carry knife, and I have to say, it comes in handy. I kept reaching for it over others because the Serrated Airlight II proved easy to use, feels flat and unobtrusive in the hand, and it's an attractive design. Made in Seki City, Japan, the MSRP is $85. berettausa.com

SANTA FE STONEWORKS

You won't meet a nicer family than the Wirtels, owners of Santa Fe Stoneworks, nor will you come across a more interesting knife company business plan. The Wirtels and Santa Fe Stoneworks specialize in fashioning precious stone grips and stone-handle knives of all configurations.

Owner Bill Wirtel has passed down valuable skill and knowledge to his kids, and talking to him, the pride escapes from his every pore.

The Santa Fe Stoneworks Custom #01 Buttonlock is the first design from Anna and Miles Wirtel. It showcases a titanium body that weighs a slight 2.3 ounces and a VG-10 steel blade. The knife is 3 1/2 inches closed with a 3-inch blade for an overall length of 6 1/2 inches open.

But let's get to the attractive specialty stuff. The #01 Buttonlock is available in all the company's fossilized handle materials — woolly mammoth tooth, tusk and bone — as well as in gemstone grips, exotic woods and "brain coral."

With a deep pocket clip and full attention to detail, fit, form and finish, this one's a no-brainer. The Wirtels call the knife "Tesoro," which is Italian for beautiful or treasured.

The knife truly is light, beautiful and functional for everyday carry, and one that any owner would be proud to use and show off! MSRP circa $280, varying by handle material. santafestoneworks.com

KERSHAW

A business owner must satisfy every customer — some of whom like their knives made in the U.S., while others desire a quality knife at a price point they can afford without the slightest thought as to country of manufacturing origin.

Isidora Forrest of Kershaw told me some customers wanted the Kershaw Natrix made in the United States, so their wishes were granted with the new Bare-knuckle Model 7777, based on the style of the Natrix, but with a slimmed-down profile and upgraded materials.

All I can say is, right off the bat, it's a looker. I absolutely love the matte-gray anodized-aluminum handle with all the character of a bridge troll, as well as the way the integral fingerguard leads right into the flipper mechanism of the folder and how the Sandvik 14C28N blade has a high grind and thoughtfully designed thumb ramp. The blade has a handsome stonewash finish, and I mean that, and anyone who has used Sandvik steel knows it's hard, holds an edge and doesn't stain.

The folder comes with a sub-frame lock, and the blade rides on the company's KVT ball bearing system and rotates on an oversized pivot. A reversible deep-carry pocket clip completes the piece. Could it possibly cut as good as it looks? Did I mention the Sandvik steel blade? MSRP: $109.99. kaiusaltd.com **TGD**

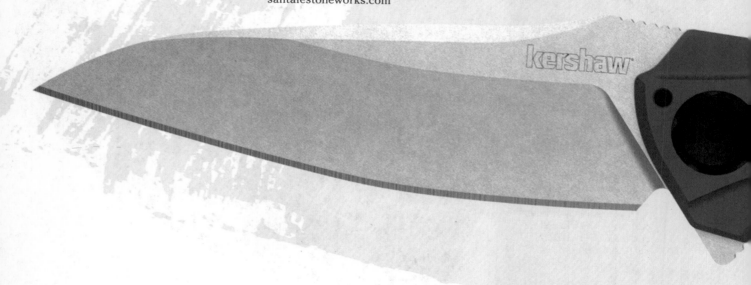

The Kershaw Bareknuckle
Model 7777 is made in the
USA, has a Sandvik 14C28N
blade with a high grind
and thoughtfully designed
thumb ramp.

SELF-DEFENSE
AMMO
ROUNDUP

BY **TODD WOODARD**

With shooting tons of commercial ammunition each year comes the realization that some of it really is better — at least in my test guns — than other brands. Worldwide, ammunition manufacturers churn out billions of rounds each year to satisfy the pew-pew needs of expectant shooters. Here's a rundown of self-defense ammo choices that are worth looking at to feed into your firearms' chambers.

The author found that Remington
UMC 10mm 180-grain FMJs hit
hard, were accurate and affordable.

Self-Defense Ammo Roundup

SELLIER & BELLOT .300 AAC BLACKOUT

I recently bought and shot a Ruger American Rifle Ranch Model chambered in .300 AAC Blackout. I admit I'm a latecomer to the Blackout because it seemed many other rounds were already doing the same job, so what was the point? Well, the point is, the cartridge has excellent range manners and good accuracy, as I learned.

I purchased several hundred rounds of Sellier & Bellot .300 AAC 147-grain full metal jacket for about $13 per 20-round box. In a comparison of the Ruger American Ranch Rifle against a Remington M700 SPS Tactical (also chambered in .300 BLK), and a Savage 10PT-SR in .308 Winchester, the idea was to pit three threaded-barrel bolt-action rifles head to head, with and without a suppressor. I fired them unsuppressed and suppressed with a Rugged Suppressors Surge 7.62 from SilencerShop.com, a modular 30-caliber rifle silencer that enables you to change the size and configuration of your silencer from a full-size 9-inch one to a shorter 7.5-inch unit. It produces a sound reduction level from 134 to 138.4dB.

The S&B round is supersonic, 2,064 fps unsuppressed and 2,096 fps suppressed, out of the Ruger, and 2,099/2,110 fps respectively from the SPS Tactical. From the Ruger and Remington, I was impressed with the low recoil these FMJs produced and was more surprised with the downrange results. In the Ruger at 100 yards, the S&B fired unsuppressed 1-MOA three-shot groups (1-inch), and with the Surge 7.62 can attached, those groups shrunk to 0.8-inch, on average. At the same time, the round also shot well in the SPS-T, with so-so groups unsuppressed of 1-inch average size, but eye-popping 0.4-inch groups suppressed.

Sellier & Bellot .300 AAC 147-grain full metal jacket ammo will make a lot of friends with that kind of accuracy combined with a price per round of only $.65 cents. At that price, it's worth trying some in your tactical guns. sellierbellot.us

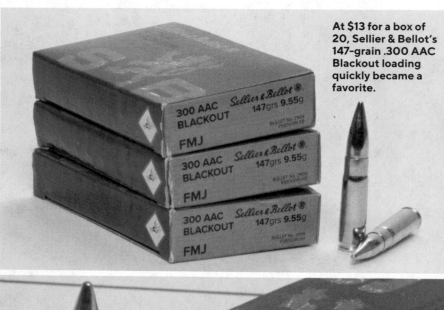

At $13 for a box of 20, Sellier & Bellot's 147-grain .300 AAC Blackout loading quickly became a favorite.

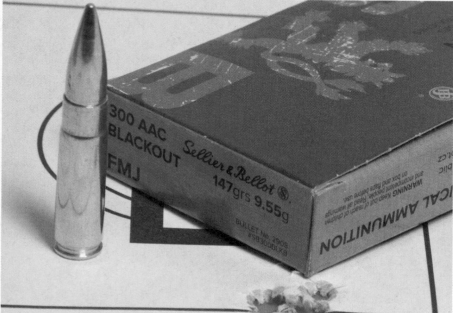

Accuracy from the Ruger Ranch Rifle was excellent with the affordable Sellier & Bellot 147-grain .300 Blk. Ammo: Unsuppressed groups were 1 MOA but with the Surge 7.62 suppressor attached, those groups shrunk to 0.8-inch, on average.

With a Rugged Suppressors Surge 7.62 can, the author's test rifle, a Remington SPS Tactical, shot the Sellier & Bellot .300 AAC Blackout 147-grainers into a 0.4-inch group at 100 yards.

BUFFALO BORE .38 SUPER 147-GRAIN JHP

Author Bob Campbell tested 16 .38 Super loads recently, and I was intrigued by the results because I like the Super. Several rounds earned Grade-A recommendations in that test, but one in particular caught my attention. The .38 Super was once a handloading proposition for maximum performance, with handgunners using 9mm JHP bullets and hardcast lead .38 Special bullets. Today, Cor-Bon, Buffalo Bore, and DoubleTap offer high-performance loads rivaling some of the hotter handloads of the past, so I wouldn't be surprised if the .38 Super sees an upsurge in popularity. If you're looking for penetration, full metal jacket loads don't expand or shed weight, and shot through 24+ inches of water.

On the hollowpoint side, we tested 115-, 124- and 147-grain loads from Buffalo Bore with the Hornady XTP bullet. The Buffalo Bore 147-grain load cost $28.79/20 rounds and was the heaviest load in the test. It came out the muzzle of a 1911-style pistol at 1,099 fps, or about 100 fps faster than many 9mm loads with this bullet. The 147-grain XTP load penetrated a deep 24 inches in water — the greatest penetration of any

hollowpoint load tested. It generated 394 ft-lbs of energy and shot 2.2-inch groups at 25 yards. It retained 100 percent of its weight and expanded to a 0.54-inch diameter. That's downrange performance most shooters would be happy with when things get serious. buffalobore.com

AGUILA 1.75-INCH #4 BUCK/ #1 BUCK SHOTSHELLS

When we fired the then-newish Mossberg 590 Shockwave, it came with a determination letter from the Bureau of Alcohol, Tobacco, Firearms and Explosives (ATF) defining the pump-action as a "Non-NFA Firearm." The 590 Shockwave comes from the factory with a 14-inch barrel, Shockwave Technologies Raptor grip and overall length of 26.5 inches. Because the Shockwave can't be shoulder mounted and meets the overall length requirement of 26 inches, it's defined as a "firearm" under the federal Gun Control Act of 1968 (GCA). Part of the legal definition of a "shotgun" means it must be made to be fired from the shoulder. Further, since Mossberg manufactures it with a new receiver and pistol grip at the factory, it falls under the definitions as a Pistol Grip Only (PGO) firearm. That's why the Shockwave doesn't fall under the National Firearms Act rules and doesn't require a tax stamp. PGO firearms can include certain shotguns having barrels

38 SUPER +P

☐ Item 33A/20	115 gr.	J.H.P.	1450 F.P.S./ME 537 ft. lbs
☐ Item 33B/20	124 gr.	J.H.P.	1350 ME 502 ft. lbs
☐ Item 33C/20	124 gr.	F.M.J.-FN	1350 ME 502 ft. lbs
☐ Item 33D/20	125 gr.	Hard Cast FN	1375 525 ft. lbs
☑ Item 33E/20	147 gr.	J.H.P.	1150 432 ft. lbs

STRICTLY BUSINESS.

(above) Aguila's standard 2.75-inch shell with the 1.75-inch Minishell next to it in correct proportion. When used in the Shockwave, proper function required the addition of an accessory added to the mag well, the OPSol Texas Mini-Clip.

Buffalo Bore's 147-grain JHP is a formidable choice in .38 Super. These things drilled 24 inches into water, produced a crushing 394 ft-lbs of energy.

of less than 18 inches in length. The final reason why the Shockwave can have a 14-inch barrel is the NFA definition of a "firearm," the overall length must exceed 26 inches. The Shockwave, from muzzle to grip, measures 26.37 inches. Some state regulations prohibit the sale of such PGO firearms, so be mindful of your local regulations.

But how easy was it to shoot a shotgun with a 14-inch barrel loaded with 2.75-inch shells? Not all that pleasant. At the range, we had an assortment of Aguila 1.75-inch and Winchester 2.75-inch shells. We also fired a few 3-inch shells through the Shockwave just for the experience. Recoil was brutal with 3-inchers. With Aguila's 1.75-inch minishells, the Shockwave has an 8+1 capacity. These minishells produce mild recoil, but typically do not cycle in a shotgun's action because repeaters are designed to use a shell with a minimum length of 2.75 inches. The OPSol Texas Mini-Clip (opsolmini-clip.com) is an aftermarket accessory that facilitates reliable cycling with Aguila minishells. We acquired a Mini-Clip to see if this inexpensive adapter would enable us to run the Shockwave with 1.75-inch minishells. It did. The Mini-Clip is compatible with all Mossberg 500, 590 and 590A1 models.

We found the Shockwave gave us tight patterns at 10 yards, not what we expected from a 14-inch barrel with a cylinder bore choke. The Aguila buckshot minishell averaged a 10-inch pattern on an 18-inch wide target. Recoil was mild. We really liked shooting the minishells through the Shockwave. For home defense or a handy truck gun, check this combination out. aguilaammo.com

FEDERAL PREMIUM .410 HANDGUN PERSONAL DEFENSE 2.5-INCH 000 BUCK

When author Ralph Winingham tested a Taurus Judge (handles .410-bore shotshells and .45 Colt), a Smith & Wesson Governor (takes .410, 45 Colt, and .45 ACP), and a Mossberg Model 500 Cruiser that fires .410-bore shotshells head to head for self-defense use, we learned which type of close-range firearm is the most effective with the diminutive .410 loads, including those that have recently been developed with short-barreled revolvers in mind. The focus was on the handling ability of the three firearms and their patterning performance at close-quarters ranges. We attempted to walk the fine line that divides ease of handling with putting the pattern in the

Federal Premium .410 Handgun Personal Defense 2.5-Inch 000 Buck Shotshell ammo penetrated 18 inches into water.

right place to evaluate the two revolvers and the pump action.

Our favorite load in that test was Federal Premium .410 Handgun Personal Defense 2.5-Inch 000 Buck Shotshell Ammo, which we bought for $16/20. This is a formidable loading. While the payload is smaller than 12- or 20-gauge buckshot, penetration is on the par with the larger shells. Results were very consistent at 18 inches of water penetration from the handgun. The load gained some 400 fps in velocity from the shotgun and 2 more inches in penetration. Penetration is ideal, and we feel that a well-centered pattern should prove effective. The copper-coated projectiles flattened to an extent in water. federalpremium.com

REMINGTON UMC 180-GRAIN 10MM AUTO

In a test of 10mm semi-autos, author Robert Sadowski used three different loads from SIG SAUER, Armscor and Federal. After the test, I held on to one of the firearms and shot it quite a bit. All three pistols, a Kimber Custom TLE II, Dan Wesson Bruin Bronze (1911 platforms) and a Tanfoglio Witness (CZ 75 type) delivered at least some sub-2-inch five-shot groups at 25 yards. The Federal American Eagle 180-grain FMJ was not as hot as the SIG load. The SIG ammo factory data shows a muzzle velocity of 1,250 fps; we got 1,243 fps. The Federal is factory speed stamped at 1,030 fps, and that lighter load (1,043 fps to 1,072 fps chronograph readings) made it easier to shoot. About 750 rounds of Remington UMC ammo, held over from a previous test, was likewise well mannered, coming in between the SIG and Federal in terms of handling and on par with the Federal in accuracy.

Using a rest and open sights and firing at targets placed 25 yards downrange, the Remington will remind you that a 10mm Auto is not a learner's pistol or for those who are sensitive to recoil. The smallest groups with the Federal load

USING A REST AND OPEN SIGHTS AND FIRING AT TARGETS PLACED 25 YARDS DOWNRANGE, THE REMINGTON WILL REMIND YOU THAT A 10MM AUTO IS NOT A LEARNER'S PISTOL OR FOR THOSE WHO ARE SENSITIVE TO RECOIL.

from the SIG, Dan Wesson, and Witness were 1.9, 1.5, and 1.4 inches, respectively. Average groups were 2.3, 1.7, and 1.8 inches, respectively. Going hot with the Witness and the UMCs, we shot on par with the Federal load and still have a hefty reservoir on hand. It was recently priced at $37.57/50. remington.com

Remington UMC 10mm ammo is affordable, but it's no slouch and hits hard enough for serious consideration for use in a tactical pistol.

BLACK HILLS .357 MAGNUM 125-GRAIN JHP

Priced at $40.90 online, the Black Hills load was packaged in a 50-round box at an attractive price, earning it the best buy nod in a showdown of .357 Magnum loads. This load exhibits modest recoil for the performance, while maintaining penetration in the ideal range at 14 inches, along with good expansion (0.72 inch) and 100 percent weight retention. Velocity isn't at the top of the list at 1,370 fps, so this load is controllable in double-action pairs and offers all of the power most shooters will wish to handle in a 35-ounce revolver.

Penetration and expansion from the Black Hills .357 Magnum 125–grain JHP load plowed 14 inches and opened up to .72 inch.

When it comes to the .357 Magnum cartridge, the consensus is the round is a great performer. It's taken deer, bears and even larger game. However, the rub is that these exploits were made with larger revolvers, often with barrels of at least 6 inches. When it comes to personal defense, most folks are going to carry 2-, 3- or 4-inch-barrel revolvers. So, for those shooters who prefer the wheelgun, the Magnum needs to work in a shorter barrel.

When you consider the flash, blast, and recoil inherent in the Magnum cartridge, the question must be asked: Is the .357 Magnum the best choice for personal defense over other revolver cartridges? It offers excellent performance in a relatively compact package that the big-bore revolvers can't match for speed and packing ability. The Magnum is superior to the .38 Special, no matter how hot the Special is loaded. If you use the Black Hills .357 Magnum 125-Grain JHP for personal defense you can mitigate the offsets of this powerful round. black-hills.com

AR CARTRIDGE ROUND UP

In a tactical book like this one, I'll have to pick more than one 5.56/.223 Remington round to account for the different barrel twist rates out there. When Gun Tests Magazine compared more than two dozen such rounds, winners in three common weight classes came up.

COR-BON DPX X BULLET 53-GRAIN .223 REMINGTON

Beginning with the lightest first, the .223 Remington 53-grain Cor-Bon DPX X Bullet was the first combination that reached the critical penetration depth that is acceptable for personal defense, in our view. In fact, it was among the best loads tested. The Cor-Bon DPX, loaded with a Barnes Triple-Shock X Bullet, was reliable and accurate, and the performance of the all-copper Barnes bullet was good in water, reaching a 17-inch depth. The bullet expanded to about twice its original diameter (0.42 inch) and retained 74 percent of its weight (39 grains). Velocity was 3,201 fps, producing 1,205 ft-lbs of energy and shooting half-inch groups at 25 yards. These all-copper bullets are expensive items from a custom maker, but their performance cannot be faulted. corbon.com

Cor-Bon's 53-grain DPX X Bullet was the lightest of the .223 loads tested, and penetrated like gangbusters.

IN FACT, IT WAS AMONG THE BEST LOADS TESTED. THE COR-BON DPX, LOADED WITH A BARNES TRIPLE-SHOCK X BULLET, WAS RELIABLE AND ACCURATE, AND THE PERFORMANCE OF THE ALL-COPPER BARNES BULLET WAS GOOD IN WATER, REACHING A 17-INCH DEPTH.

COR®BON

223 Rem 53gr DPX

Velocity 3000fps Energy 1059ft/lbs

NOSLER MATCH BALLISTIC TIP 60-GRAIN .223 REMINGTON

Nosler's Match Ballistic Tip .223 Remington load is a 60-grain choice that puts out 2,850 fps and 1,081 ft-lbs. We were surprised to find Nosler ammunition at an affordable price ($24/20 rounds), as this is top-quality ammunition, as the testing proved. The 60-grain weight trounced the lighter bullet loads in penetration, gaining 19 inches in water penetration, expanding to 0.40 inches in diameter, and shooting 0.5-inch groups at 25 yards. It kept 83 percent (50 grains) of its starting weight. nosler.com

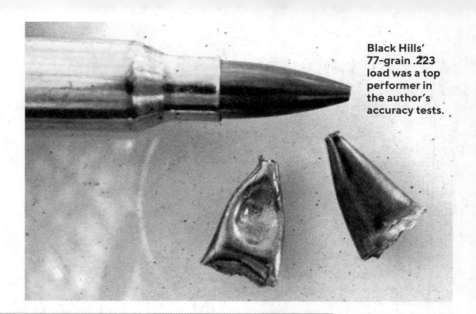

Black Hills' 77-grain .223 load was a top performer in the author's accuracy tests.

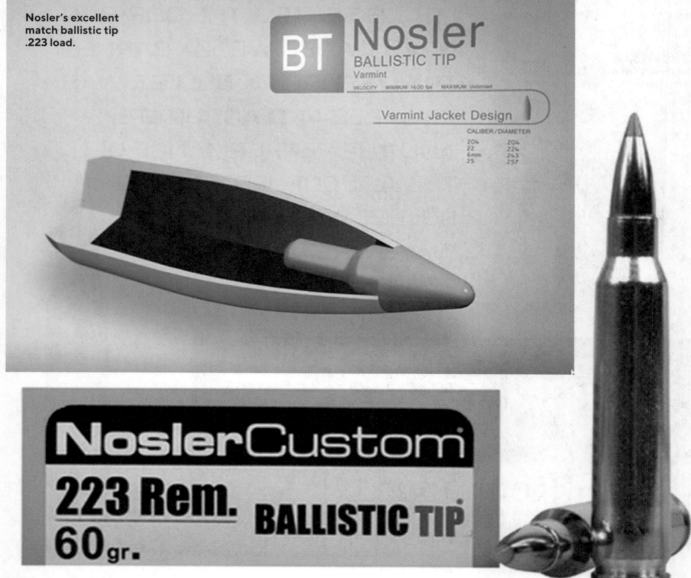

Nosler's excellent match ballistic tip .223 load.

BLACK HILLS 77-GRAIN MATCHKING HPBT

The 77-grain Black Hills MatchKing HPBT was the heaviest load in the test, developing 2,666 fps and 1,215 ft-lbs of muzzle energy, and shooting lights-out at 25 yards — a 0.2-inch group average. It penetrated 11 inches in water and kept 40 grains of its starting weight (52 percent) and expanded to 0.38 inch in diameter. Of all of the loads tested, the Black Hills 77-grain Open Tip has the only undeniable world-class record for unquestioned effect by our long-range military shooters and is a top choice for special law enforcement teams. Black Hill's military contracts have proven this load's performance. The single most accurate load tested, the Black Hills Open Tip, is a winner on all counts. This number is a best buy when purchased in the blue 50-round box. black-hills.com

WINCHESTER .308 WIN. 185-GRAIN HOLLOWPOINT

The .308 Winchester is usually loaded, for good downrange effect, to supersonic speeds and isn't that often thought of as a subsonic round. However, Winchester's Super-X 85-grain Power-Point JHP Subsonic .308 Win. load has a massive

Accuracy with the Winchester subsonic load was excellent. Groups like this will get the job done.

hollowpoint and true subsonic speeds. Average velocity was 1,109 fps unsuppressed and 1,079 fps suppressed. It has shot OK for me unsuppressed (1.4 inches), and did a little better suppressed (1.2 inches) in the Savage Arms 10PT-SR. What's nice about the Savage, of course, is that it comes from the factory with a 5/8X24 threaded muzzle, so slipping on a Surge 7.62 from SilencerShop.com is easy peasy.

What was remarkable about the combination was how quiet and soft the Super-X Subsonic shot.

The Savage Model 10PT comes factory-threaded for a muzzle brake or suppressor.

Under 300 yards, we could expect 3.5-inch groups with a suppressor on the rifle, and that's small enough to hit most targets the tactical shooter needs to hit — and really not leave much of a sonic mark to point out where the shot came from. Also, we'd consider using the Super-X Subsonic as a teaching round for shooters who needed some range time with a big bolt gun, but who might not have the experience of getting pushed by a .30-caliber round. Recoil of the round in the 9.6-pound Savage was much more like a .243 Winchester in a normal Hill Country deer rifle. winchester.com TGD

The author used this Savage Model 10PT in .308 to test Winchester's 185-grain subsonic load out to 300 yards.

WHAT WAS REMARKABLE ABOUT THE COMBINATION WAS HOW QUIET AND SOFT THE SUPER-X SUBSONIC SHOT. UNDER 300 YARDS, WE COULD EXPECT 3.5-INCH GROUPS WITH A SUPPRESSOR ON THE RIFLE, AND THAT'S SMALL ENOUGH TO HIT MOST TARGETS THE TACTICAL SHOOTER NEEDS TO HIT.

DEFENSIVE AMMO

What Matters? What Doesn't?
Get the Answers Here!

Caliber controversies and endless debates swirl around handgun caliber and cartridge selection. Now, leading Gun Digest author Patrick Sweeney brings a clear voice of reason to the discussion, with data and expert insight to help you choose the right ammo for your needs.

Product No. R6058

Revealed here:

- **Results of ballistics testing for popular handgun rounds**
- **The truth about so-called "stopping power"**
- **The best 9mm rounds for concealed carry**
- **Effectiveness of small calibers for personal defense**
- **Studying the heavy hitters: .357 Magnum, .45 ACP and 10mm**

Choosing Handgun Ammo is a must to help you make smart decisions about concealed carry, home defense, and personal protection ammunition.

A pistol chosen by the U.S. Army should be good enough for most shooters. As the author's range test proved, it is indeed.

SIG M17 REVIEW

Range Testing the SIG M17 Civilian Variant

BY **ROBERT CAMPBELL**

The U.S. military recently completed a rigorous test of 9mm high-capacity handguns. The winner likely will serve for a decade or more. SIG's P320 won the contest and was adopted as the U.S. M17. Several upgrades and modifications were undertaken to meet military standards.

The SIG M17 is a great shooter with many good features, including a 17-round capacity and short, fast trigger.

Its modular design was among its most notable strong suits. The firing module is contained in the frame. The steel chassis can be removed and placed into a smaller frame. The slide and barrel can be changed as well. This makes for versatility. In an institutional environment, the modular design makes for easy accommodation of shooters with small and large hands. The pistol is competitively priced. Recently, SIG introduced a civilian version of the U.S. Army's new pistol: The P320 M17. As range testing proved, it's an interesting and effective handgun.

SIG M17 DETAILS

The SIG M17 pistol is a service-size handgun at 8 inches long, 5.5 inches high, 1.3 inches wide and 29 ounces unloaded. It ships with two 17-round magazines. The M17 features an ambidextrous slide lock and a well-designed ambidextrous safety. The teardrop-shaped magazine release isn't ambidextrous but works well for those who practice. The pistol is finished in PVD coyote brown. The frame is polymer and the slide is stainless steel beneath the coating. An advantage of the M17 is that the rear sight cover is a night

sight unit (it is removable for red-dot use). The front sight is a SIGLITE tritium dot. Disassembly is simple and doesn't require the trigger to be pressed. The technology is cutting edge. How it shoots is the question I wanted to answer.

FIRING LINE

The pistol feels good in the hand with a slightly sharper grip angle than some polymer pistols. The grip feels solid and fits my average-size hands well. The sights provide an excellent sight picture. Many polymer pistols are slide heavy. The M17 is less so than most. The pistol operates like most striker-fired handguns, but the striker isn't initially prepped as much as the Glock when the slide is racked. This results in a heavier trigger action. The SIG M17 trigger broke at 6.5 pounds on the Lyman electronic trigger-pull gauge. The trigger press is very short, however, and this makes for

excellent speed. Reset is rapid. The pistol points well compared to most polymer-frame handguns. A 29 ounces, this 9mm handgun doesn't kick much and the grip spreads recoil across the hand. Grip pebbling makes for good adhesion.

My range test put more than 2,000 rounds through the SIG P320 M17. It never failed to feed, chamber, fire or

(above) The M17 offers real speed in reloading due to a well-designed magazine release and slide lock.

The M17 is a clean and uncluttered design. It features an ambidextrous safety lever, an ambidextrous slide lock and a light rail.

The M17 responds well to a trained shooter. Reliability was excellent with all of the ammo tested in it.

The M17 is comfortable to shoot from all firing positions.

eject. It is lively in the hand and tracks well — responding perfectly to a trained shooter. When you are firing at multiple targets, the rule is always the same: fire, allow trigger reset during recoil and fire again as soon as you regain the sight picture. The SIG allows fast hits. Among the training loads I have used is the Federal Syntech in both 115- and 124-grain weights. This load is useful in indoor ranges as it is lead-free and requires less cleaning when used in large quantities.

Accuracy is more than adequate for training well past 25 yards. There are two types of accuracy — practical and intrinsic. Very few people are capable of shooting to the mechanical or intrinsic accuracy level of a pistol. The practical accuracy of the M17 is high.

I proofed the pistol with modern defense loads including Federal's 124-grain HST, Federal 135-grain Deep Penetrator and Federal HST 147-grain +P. I particularly like the 147-grain +P load. This is an overlooked combination that adds enough velocity to the 147-grain bullet to ensure expansion, yet it isn't a hard kicker. Like all quality firearms, the M17 prefers one load to others but has demonstrated useful accuracy with all ammo tested. When firing high-recoil defense loads, the P320 M17 remained controllable. The cadence of fire isn't set by how fast you are able to press the trig-

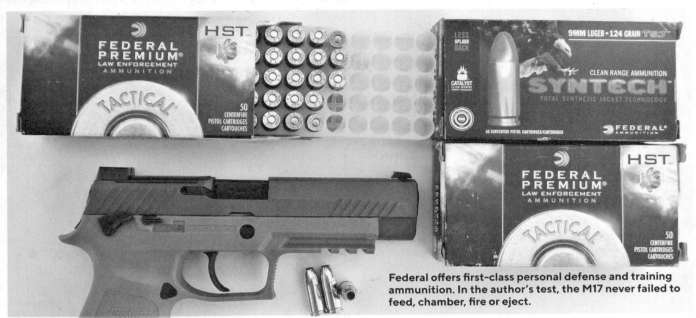

Federal offers first-class personal defense and training ammunition. In the author's test, the M17 never failed to feed, chamber, fire or eject.

Groups like this one, printed by the SIG P320 M17 in the hands of a trained shooter, inspire confidence.

ger but by how quickly you are able to regain the sights after recoil. As for absolute accuracy, the pistol was fired from a solid bench using the Bullshooters pistol rest from Brownells. Five-shot groups at 25 yards ranged from 2.5 to 3.5 inches. The pistol is clearly accurate enough for personal defense or service use.

The SIG P320 M17 9mm offers a considerable advantage over the standard P320 in the sights and finish. The pistol responds well to a trained shooter, but you must remain well-practiced. The M17 trigger, once learned, produces excellent results. The M17 is a credible defense and duty handgun with much to recommend. TGD

SPECIFICATIONS

MODEL: SIG P320 M17
CALIBER: 9mm Luger
ACTION: Semi-auto
GRIP TYPE: Modular polymer
FRAME: Full-size
FRAME MATERIAL: Stainless steel
FRAME FINISH: Stainless steel
SLIDE FINISH: Coyote PVD
SLIDE MATERIAL: Stainless steel
BARREL MATERIAL: Carbon steel
ACCESSORY RAIL: M1913
TRIGGER: Striker
TRIGGER TYPE: Standard
BARREL LENGTH: 4.7 in. (119mm)
OVERALL LENGTH: 8 in. (203mm)
OVERALL WIDTH: 1.3 in. (33mm)
HEIGHT: 5.5 in. (140mm)
WEIGHT: 29.6 oz. (840g)

Table A: SIG P320 9mm Accuracy and Ballistics		
Load	Velocity (fps)	5-Shot 25-Yard Group (in.)
Federal 124-gr. HST	1,190	2.5
Federal 147-gr. HST	980	3.0
Federal 135-gr. Deep Penetrator	1,099	2.8
Federal 124-gr. Syntech	1,100	3.5
Velocity recorded with a RCBS Ammomaster chronograph.		

The Ruger Officer-Style .45 ACP Compact 1911 pistol is a 21st-century take on the M15 .45 that was produced for general officers in the U.S. military from 1972 to 1981. Produced by the Rock Island Military Arsenal (not to be confused with the modern commercial manufacturer Rock Island Armory) the M15 General Officers Model was created by cutting down and modifying existing 1911A1 pistols to make the new gun. The M15 was created because certain generals at the time wanted a full-power combat pistol that was more easily carried than the 1911A1. The new M15 would replace the .32 and .380 M1903 pistols that were carried at times even by the likes of George S. Patton.

In the not too distant past, I would have said that manufacturing a compact .45-caliber combat pistol was a somewhat questionable project for personnel who were generally located outside of active combat zones. After all, even Gen. Patton never fired his silver Colt .45 Peacemaker or Smith & Wesson Model 27 .357 Magnum in combat during World War II — although Patton did shoot at a German plane with a .380.

Around October 18, 2018, Brigadier General Jeffrey Smiley was shot and wounded during a meeting in Kandahar, Afghanistan in a Taliban attack at the governor's compound. Two Afghan leaders were killed. The top military commander in Afghanistan, General Scott Miller, was also present but not injured. It was not known if the generals were armed with handguns or if they returned fire. Because of that I can see the need for the M15 General Officer's pistol considering the type of warfare we have engaged in since 2001.

The M15 was sized the same as a Colt Commander. The Colt company would eventually introduce what we now know as the "Officer's Model" .45 in 1985. Equipped with a 6- or 7-round magazine in .45 ACP, the Officer's Model, and the later aluminum-framed Lightweight Officer's Model, featured a shorter grip frame than the Colt Commander and a shorter 3.5-inch barrel.

The Colt Officer's series always seemed to me to be a cool pistol. One of the detectives I worked with years ago carried a nickel-plated Officer's Model as his duty sidearm. The original Colt Officer's handguns had developed a reputation for being unreliable. However, I owned a M1991A1 Compact .45, which was a budget-priced version of the Officer's Model and never had a problem with it. The Officer's concept still lives on today with Colt in its Defender Series and the longer-barreled Wiley Clap CCO (Concealed Carry Officer's) Series, neither of which seem to have reliability issues.

Now, Ruger has added an "Officer-Style" pistol to its fine SR1911 lineup that picks up where the original Colt Officer's Model left off — and it has no reliability issues. The Ruger SR1911 Officer-Style pistol is an all-stainless steel compact 1911 that brings the original concept into the 21st century. Equipped with a 3.6-inch barrel, this impressive pistol comes equipped with two 7-round magazines, giving up nothing in defensive capability over its full-size brethren — yet it is sized for all day carry.

When I took the Officer-Style pistol out of the box, I was pleasantly surprised by the appearance of the matte stainless steel finish of the slide and frame. It appears to have a slight gold hue to it, reminiscent of the brushed-nickel finishes applied to various handguns in the 1980s, including the Colt Officer's Model. It gives the Ruger a richer tone than standard matte-finished stainless steel.

The weight of the Officer-Style is 31 ounces, which is important in terms of soaking up recoil from the powerful .45 ACP cartridge. The overall length is 7.25 inches and the height is 5 inches. The Ruger has many features favored by today's 1911 shooter. Starting at the top, it features a set of black, drift-adjustable Novak 3-dot sights. Novak sights are the gold-standard in combat handgun sights and are designed not to snag on clothing during a rapid draw. There are many manufacturers that make copies of the original design, but the Officers-Style Ruger uses the real deal.

The slide features wide, slanted grasping grooves at the rear only — the barrel is too short to perform a press check from the front. If you need to make sure of the Ruger's loaded status, there is a large circular viewing port at the rear of the chamber.

The Officer-Style has a black-accented, oval-shaped skeletonized hammer mated with a titanium firing pin in the slide for

Retired Ohio probation officer and Colt 1911 aficionado Michael Skeen tests the Ruger .45 ACP Officer-Style 1911 pistol. The solid stainless steel frame and slide keep recoil controllable even when firing SIG's 230-grain Elite V-Crown .45 ACP ammo. Empties were ejected smartly forward and to the right of the shooter.

RUGER
OFFICER-STYLE 1911
.45 ACP

A Compact-Size Full-Power Defender
BY **SCOTT W. WAGNER**

faster lock times. There is also a black-accented oversize beavertail grip safety to protect your hand from hammer bite. The mainspring housing, also black, is rounded and is a nice compromise between a flat and traditionally arched type.

The black manual thumb safety is extended and easily reached. While Ruger's website states that the black slide lock lever (which I refer to as the slide release) is also extended, it didn't appear that way on my test sample. More so than the thumb safety, the slide release needs to have a rear extension so that it can be released during a rapid reload without having to twist the pistol in the shooting hand to reach it. My thumb just can't quite reach it without twisting.

The black-checkered magazine release is prominent enough to be operated easily by the shooting hand thumb, but not so prominent as to be accidentally activated.

The replaceable G10 grip panels feature the Ruger logo on both sides, which is textured to enhance the gripping service. Their gray-black color blends in well. If you haven't yet figured this out, the Ruger Officer-Style .45 is one sharp-looking pistol. The handgun has a skeletonized aluminum trigger adjustable for overtravel, which, when combined with the "Series 70" operating system, makes for a crisp trigger pull. There was no need for any adjustment.

I took the Ruger to a friend's private

The Ruger SR1911 Officer-Style .45 features modern enhancements preferred by law enforcement in a 1911-type pistol. These enhancements include a beavertail grip safety, genuine Novak 3-dot drift-adjustable combat sights, rounded mainspring housing and skeletonized hammer and trigger. It is a lot of .45 for the money (and size).

The Ruger SR1911 9mm Officer-Style pistol's aluminum frame offers a significant weight savings over the stainless steel .45 ACP version for increased all-day carry comfort. Note the dark frame contrast and the distinctive V-shaped rear slide grasping grooves.

With a weight of 27.2 ounces, the 9mm Luger chambering of the lightweight Officer-Style pistol may prove to be a better caliber choice for the average concealed carry permit holder than the heavier-recoiling .45 ACP.

thing. I was not disappointed by the Ruger's reliability.

I had forgotten how pleasant it is to shoot a properly fitted and balanced .45 ACP — especially an all-steel one. I often test .40- and 9mm-caliber pistols, and I'd forgotten about the .45's pleasant muzzle blast — at least with standard pressure loads. It's not the push of a recoiling gun in the hand that bothers new shooters most, it's the muzzle blast. This is especially true if the handgun is being fired in an indoor range.

Skeen and I both averaged 3- to 4-inch groups at 30 feet shooting two-handed standing. The sights were regulated dead on to the point of aim. Switching to the SIG Elite .45 ball ammo produced the same results, as did SIG's Elite 230-grain

SPECIFICATIONS

MODEL: Ruger Officer-Style
CHAMBERINGS: 9mm and .45 ACP
CAPACITY: 7+1
SLIDE: Stainless steel
BARREL LENGTH: 3.60 in.
GRIP FRAME: Low-glare stainless
GRIP PANELS: Deluxe checkered G10
WIDTH: 1.34 in.
SIGHTS: Drift-adjustable Novak 3-Dot
WEIGHT: 31 oz.
OVERALL LENGTH: 7.25 in.
HEIGHT: 5 in.
GROOVES: 6
TWIST: 1:16 RH
www.ruger.com

V-Crown load — which felt the same as the practice loads in terms of recoil and blast. With a muzzle velocity of 830 FPS from a full-size pistol (which is actually 20 FPS slower than SIG's practice load), the V-Crown should still be traveling around 750 FPS or more from the short barrel of the Ruger (weather was not conducive to chronograph testing that day). There were no malfunctions of any kind.

In our opinion, the Ruger Officer-Style .45 ACP is a great defensive and carry pistol. If you desire a lighter-weight version, there is an aluminum-frame 9mm variant that weighs in at only 27.2 ounces. Both have an MSRP of $979. **TGD**

Despite its smaller size, the SR1911 Officer-Style .45 is sweet handling, as officer Michael Skeen discovered from his test-firing session. Skeen found Ruger's take on the compact .45 to be more refined and shooter friendly than the original Colt Officer's Model .45 he owned and carried on duty in the 1980s.

range for testing along with an assortment of ball ammunition and SIG's Elite 230-grain FMJ practice .45s and 230-grain Elite V-Crown defensive ammo. I enlisted the help of a fellow police firearms instructor Probation Officer Mike Skeen (ret.) to help evaluate the Ruger. Skeen is a long-time aficionado of 1911 .45 autos.

Skeen was just as enamored with the look and feel of the Ruger as I was. We tested it right out of the box with no pre-cleaning or additional lubrication. I started out with the assorted brands of 230-grain FMJ ball. The reason I do my tests that way is that I believe many purchasers of new guns will do the same

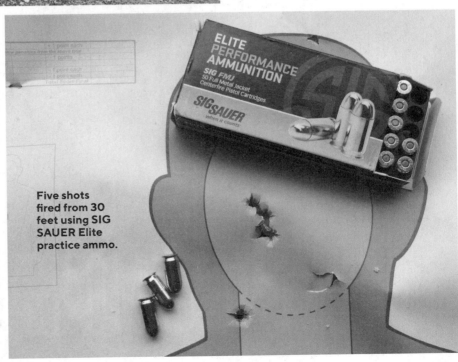

Five shots fired from 30 feet using SIG SAUER Elite practice ammo.

GLOCK 40 MOS:
10MM AMMO REVIEW

In this evaluation, the author tested the Glock 40 MOS with a variety of 10mm ammo to find out what's best for any given application. The system proved extremely versatile.

Gun Digest Tests Today's Best 10mm Ammo in a Glock 40 MOS

BY **COREY GRAFF**

The resurgence of interest in the 10mm Auto cartridge is attended by a fanciful and ever-growing myth of legendary stopping power. Along with these fantasies flows a mountain of steamy bunk, served like dung on shiny china.

Regardless of what the bespectacled gun counter guy may claim, the 10mm Auto is not "the .44 Magnum of semi-autos." Not even close. Nor is it the .41 Magnum of semi-autos. The way many people talk about the 10mm Auto cartridge, you'd think they're describing the lesser-known but related 10mm Magnum, which was first chambered by Harry Sanders in some of his early Automag pistols and later by Smith & Wesson in the Model 610. That load is a hammer that is not produced commercially today. The 10mm Magnum, of course, bested the standard 10mm Automatic by at least 300 fps and did indeed make .41 Magnum territory.

However, as we discovered in this ammo test, the standard 10mm Automatic, the .40-caliber brainchild of the late Col. Jeff Cooper, is no pussycat. And true to its reputation, it hits like a Mike Tyson uppercut. Testing a Glock 40 MOS (Modular Optics System) — a 6-inch long-slide 10mm and reigning king of hand cannons in the company's lineup — with a Burris FastFire 3 reflex-style sight, I lit off a bunch of the best 10mm ammunition made today to see what takes the cake for range practice, hunting and personal protection loads. Here are the results.

TRIGGER NOTES

Glock's striker-fired mechanism feels like a rough double-action trigger, but you must keep the pistol design in context. Glocks are typically used for everyday carry and personal defense, so I can understand a tough trigger. After all, when it comes to self-defense, it makes sense to have a heavy trigger that only trips when it's intended to be pulled.

But since I wanted a handgun that could also be used for a wider range of tactical and survival scenarios, a lighter, smoother trigger pull to facilitate long-range accuracy was desired. On a hunting handgun, the trigger can't hinder accuracy on shots that could range from 25 to 50, or even 100 yards. There's a case to be made for long-range handgun accuracy in a tactical handgun. You never know what you might encounter.

Thankfully, I was able to improve the trigger dramatically by installing a 3.5-lb. connector and spring kit, doing some judicious hand polishing of key mating parts and finishing up with a deburring job that would have made the old machine shop teachers proud. A little elbow grease transformed the Glock trigger into a 3.4-lb. beauty. Considering the Glock's stellar out-of-the-box accuracy and reliability, it is now fully capable of unleashing hellfire on targets from point blank to 50 yards with alarming precision.

BURRIS FASTFIRE 3

The little Burris Fastfire 3 reflex-style red-dot sight looks tiny sitting on top of the G40's massive slide, but don't judge a book by its cover. How Burris engineered it to not only keep from flying into the wild blue yonder under the heavy recoil of powerful 10mm loads is beyond me, but what really impresses is how well it holds zero shot after shot after shot. I tried to break it by shooting hundreds of rounds of the hottest loads I could get my hands on. It kept working, didn't budge. That inspired confidence.

The optic uses a 3 MOA red-dot, which has three manual brightness settings and one automatic brightness sensor, which is what I used. Elevation and windage adjustments are accomplished using a small, standard screwdriver in the slots on the top and back. Adjustments are responsive and precise. The Fastfire 3 is a simple 1x magnification and was completely parallax free.

The sight was left in the off position

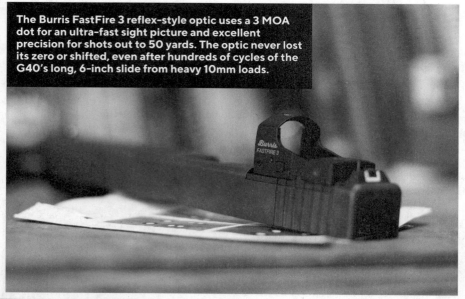

The Burris FastFire 3 reflex-style optic uses a 3 MOA dot for an ultra-fast sight picture and excellent precision for shots out to 50 yards. The optic never lost its zero or shifted, even after hundreds of cycles of the G40's long, 6-inch slide from heavy 10mm loads.

Range practice ammo proved surprisingly accurate in the Glock 40 MOS. Samples included Federal American Eagle 180-gr. FMJ, Blaser 200-gr. FMJ and the accuracy winner, DoubleTap Colt National Match 180-gr. FMJ. There were no failures to feed or eject from any of the ammunition tested, which is typical of Glock reliability.

while carried, and I practiced activating the left-side On button with my left-hand thumb during the draw cycle. There were no hiccups using this technique, but still uncertainty exists among some shooters. So they install tall suppressor sights on reflex-equipped handguns. The idea is to provide a "co-witness" through the red-dot's screen and serve as a backup in case of optics failure. I chose not to do that. Instead, I found that for shots at normal defensive ranges of 7 yards and under, you can simply use the screen itself with the optic turned off to bracket an IDPA target. The result is an ultra-fast sight picture — even quicker than obtaining the red-dot — and remarkably accurate. It seems to act as a sort of extra-large rear peep sight. For longer shots, Burris has provided a vertical white line on the back edge of the Fast-Fire 3, which functions as a makeshift rear sight should a backup be needed.

With all these features, such a rig places a tremendous amount of firepower in your hands. You can dump 15 rounds of heavy 10mm, jack a reload home, unleash another volley and whistle Dixie … all without skipping a beat. That might be a bit overkill on whitetails, but two-

(above) DoubleTap's Colt National Match 180-grain FMJ load proved exceptionally accurate, printing an average 1.32-inch group, and a best .60-inch group at 25 yards from a solid rest.

(below) The selection of 10mm ammo from Hornady gave a solid performance in the personal protection category. The Hornady Custom 180-grain XTP load printed a 2.12-inch average group at 25 yards.

(left) The real surprise in the test was the performance of the 180-grain Trophy Bonded JSP load from Federal. This load scoots a flat-meplat bullet along at 1,355 fps, putting 734 ft-lbs. on target. On top of that, its accuracy was second best of all lots tested — 1.50-in. average and .44-inch best groups at 25 yards.

(below) The overall winner of our 10mm Auto ammo test was the Underwood 150-grain Xtreme Hunter load. It yielded 1.24-inch average and .53-inch best groups at 25 yards. Best of all, it's doing 1,415 fps for 667 ft-lbs of muzzle energy. That level of accuracy and horsepower can dominate for hunting, survival, home defense and everyday carry.

legged attackers deserve every bit of it. In case you're wondering, the era of reflex sights on handguns is here to stay. The technology is ready for prime time. However, when carried all day under a shirt concealed, the little screen on the reflex sight attracts dust like Yogi Bear to a pic-a-nic basket. It's not worth crying about, though — simply blast it clear every few days with a can of compressed air and use the fleece scratch-free cloth provided by Burris to safely wipe the screen clean.

10MM RANGE REVIEW

For the range test, I shot a selection of 10mm ammo through the Glock 40 MOS. That included practice, personal protection and hunting loads. Representing the range/target loads were Federal 180-grain American Eagle FMJ, Blaser 200-grain FMJ and DoubleTap Colt National Match 180-grain FMJ. Among this group, DoubleTap's Colt NM loading produced the most consistent accuracy

The TR Holsters Inside-the-Waistband holster is remarkably comfortable and versatile. It perfectly secures and conceals the big Glock 40 10mm — including the Burris FastFire 3 reflex sight.

Underwood's 140-grain Xtreme Penetrator load ranked very high as tested in the Glock 40 MOS. The load uses the Lehigh Defense bullet and penetrates like an anti-aircraft shell. It's carried by many Alaskans for bear encounters.

Recoil from the Glock 40 MOS is no walk in the park but is easily controllable thanks to the ergonomics of the Gen 4 Glock's slimmer pistol grip and long, 6-inch slide.

TR HOLSTERS: GLOCK 40 MOS EDC SOLUTION

THERE AREN'T MANY SUITABLE CONCEALED CARRY HOLSTERS AVAILABLE FOR THE MASSIVE GLOCK 40 MOS, SCABBARDS THAT'LL ACCOMMODATE A RED-DOT SIGHT ON SUCH A BEAST OF A HANDGUN. ONE THAT DOES SO WITH EASE IS THE TR KYDEX IWB CUSTOM. WITH THE SIMPLICITY OF A SINGLE BELT CLIP, IT ALLOWS THE HOLSTERED HANDGUN TO BE REMOVED QUICKLY WHEN NEEDED. BEST OF ALL, THE THING IS COMFORTABLE, CARRIES HUGE HANDGUNS EFFORTLESSLY. TR OFFERS THIS CUSTOM BUILD IN A BEWILDERING RANGE OF COLORS. BE SURE TO CHOOSE THE "RMR OPTICS" OPTION TO ACCOMMODATE A REFLEX SIGHT. AT $82 IT'S A GREAT VALUE.

TRHOLSTERS.COM

The Guide's Choice Chest Holster from Diamond D Custom keeps the big Glock 40 MOS positioned front and center for an easy draw. It has a mag pouch to carry extra ammo, and a slide strap to secure the pistol.

DIAMOND D GUIDE'S CHOICE CHEST HARNESS

WHEN OPERATING IN COLD WEATHER, YOU CAN'T ALWAYS ACCESS YOUR SIDEARM EASILY UNDER A HEAVY COAT. THAT'S WHEN YOU WANT A CHEST HARNESS LIKE THE GUIDES'S CHOICE FROM DIAMOND D CUSTOM LEATHER, OF WASILLA, ALASKA. IT'S AVAILABLE FOR THE GLOCK 40 MOS (AND MANY POPULAR BIG-BORE REVOLVERS AND SEMI-AUTO PISTOLS) AND KEEPS THE HEFTY 10MM FRONT AND CENTER FOR A QUICK DRAW — WHETHER YOU'RE TARGETING WHITETAILS OR NEED TO ESTABLISH PECKING ORDER QUICKLY WITH AN UPPITY BEAR.

THE THING THAT SETS THE GUIDE'S CHOICE CHEST RIG APART FROM THE COMPETITION IS ITS SIMPLICITY: IT HAS ONE SHOULDER STRAP THROUGH WHICH YOU PUT YOUR ARM, AND THEN YOU SIMPLY BRING THE CHEST STRAP AROUND AND CLICK IT INTO PLACE. IT TAKES ABOUT 10 SECONDS AND IS ROCK SOLID.

"WE WANTED SOMETHING THAT WAS EASY TO PUT ON REALLY QUICKLY, AND WAS FUNCTIONAL, YET STILL MAKES THE GUN — NO MATTER HOW BIG OR HEAVY IT IS — FEEL LIGHTWEIGHT," SAID MIKE BARRETT OF DIAMOND D CUSTOM. "WHEN YOU'RE OUT THERE HIKING, YOU SHOULDN'T NEED THREE OF YOUR BUDDIES TO HELP YOU PUT ON A STRAP SYSTEM FOR A HOLSTER. IT SHOULD BE AS QUICK AND EASY AS OURS HAS BEEN DESIGNED."

THE HOLSTERS ARE HANDMADE BY DAVID JOHNSTON FROM THE BEST RODEO-GRADE LEATHER. JOHNSTON IS A FORMER BULL RIDER AND LEATHER CRAFTSMAN WHO MADE SADDLES AND HARD-USE GEAR TO CONTROL ORNERY BOVINE. THE GEAR IS STITCHED AND ASSEMBLED BY JOHNSTON'S CREW, WHO TEST THE RIGS IN THE TOUGHEST CLIMATES OF ALASKA.

DIAMONDDCUSTOMLEATHER.COM

The author shot this rapid-fire group from 7 yards ... with the Burris FastFire 3 *turned off* to simulate a battery or switch failure (no such failure ever occurred). The technique uses the window of the reflex sight to bracket the target. It's fast and accurate enough.

from the Glock 40, with a 1.32-inch average, and a .60-inch best group at 25 yards from a rest. Personal defense choices tested included Hornady's 180- and 155-grain XTP, and Hornady Critical Duty with a 175-grain FlexLock bullet. Federal's 180-grain Hydra-Shok, DoubleTap's 135-grain Controlled Expansion JHP and the Underwood 115-grain Xtreme Defender rounded out the best choices for concealed carry. When it comes to EDC — considering accuracy and sheer foot pounds of energy — it was a dead heat between DoubleTap's 135-grain JHP and Underwood's 115-grain Extreme Defender, both of which kept average groups just over an inch at 25 yards and crushed the 700 fps barrier (725 fps and 788 fps, respectively).

For the hunting/survival category, there was naturally some overlap with some of the personal defense loads already mentioned, especially the DoubleTap 135-grain JHP load. Federal's 180-grain Trophy Bonded JSP was a real humdinger. It proved accurate and hard-hitting, with a best 25-yard group of .44 inch and 734 ft-lbs, making it a must-try for whitetails and everyday carry. Underwood's two screamers — a 140-grain Xtreme Penetrator (a favorite for grizzly bear protection) and 150-grain Xtreme Hunter — were the cat's meow. The 140-grain load printed very consistent groups that averaged 1.34 inches at 25 yards, with 738 ft-lbs of energy. Even more impressive was Underwood's 150-grain Xtreme Hunter, the second-most accurate ammunition of the entire test (1.24 average, .53-inch best groups at 25 yards) and still hitting with 667 ft-lbs of muzzle energy. Note that the Underwood loads use the CNC-machined all-copper Lehigh Defense Xtreme Defense bullet, which employs radial flutes that force hydraulic energy outward to build pressure and carve a nasty wound channel without sacrificing penetration.

CONCLUSION

Between today's hot, full-power 10mm Auto factory loads, and easy-shooting platforms such as the Glock 40 MOS, the effectiveness of truly powerful, high-pressure cartridges can fully be harnessed. For survival against man or beast, hand cannons like these should have a prominent place in your tactical handgun toolbox. **TGD**

While gun owners may argue about the effectiveness of the .45 ACP vs. 9mm for self-defense, no one disputes the 10mm's chops. It is a decisive fight stopper.

Table 1. 10mm Ammunition Test Results					
LOAD	VELOCITY (fps)	ENERGY (ft-lbs)	25-YARD GROUP AVG. (in.)	BEST 25-YARD GROUP (in.)	50-YARD GROUP AVG. (in.)
Federal American Eagle 180-gr. FMJ	1,011	484	4.93	.66	–
Blaser 200-gr. FMJ	1,023	465	1.72	.49	–
DoubleTap Colt National Match 180-gr. FMJ	1,179	556	1.32	.60	–
Hornady Custom 180-gr. XTP	1,210	585	2.12	1.84	–
Hornady 155-gr. XTP Custom	1,321	601	2.20	1.79	–
Hornady Critical Duty 175-gr. FlexLock	1,137	502	3.86	1.15	–
Federal 180-gr. Hydra-Shok JHP	1,071	459	2.22	1.525	–
DoubleTap 135-gr. Controlled Expansion JHP	1,555	725	1.82	1.16	–
Federal 180-gr. Trophy Bonded JSP	1,355	734	1.50	.44	–
Underwood 115-gr. Xtreme Defender	1,757	788	1.41	1.25	–
Underwood 140-gr. Xtreme Penetrator	1,541	738	1.80	1.34	4.73
Underwood 150-gr. Xtreme Hunter	1,415	667	1.24	.53	3.95

A Palmetto Armory upper and Mossberg Tactical lower made up the author's .224 Valkyrie test rifle. The rifle and ammo shot sub-half MOA at 100 yards. The 1:7 twist barrel likes bullets of 60 grains and heavier.

Up-Gunning the AR-15 Platform with Federal's .224 Valkyrie

BY L.P. BREZNY

With so many specialty cartridges for the AR platform in the field already, developing a cartridge to beat the .223/5.56mm NATO round was no small task. But Federal did just that, resulting in the new and very interesting .224 Valkyrie cartridge.

Based on the 6.8 Remington case, the .224 Valkyrie is a larger fuel cell than the .223 and uses an overly long and heavy, high-ballistic coefficient (BC) bullet. Tack on a fast 1:7 twist rifling and the new cartridge is able to handle bullets ranging from 60 to 90 grains with ease in the basic AR-15/M16 receiver. It makes for an ideal urban sniper round when more range and power are needed. The .224 Valkyrie's tactical possibilities are endless. With no change in the AR's action or upper design, save for magazine modification due to the larger circumference of the cartridge, we now have a souped-up AR-15 cartridge for the police officer, border patrol agent or even special operations military sniper.

After writing three books on long-range shooting with specialized rifles and loads, I know what is required of a dedicated, hard-hitting, extended-range gunning system.

.224 VALKYRIE FOR TACTICAL APPLICATIONS

from available parts, thereby cutting the cost about 30 percent. I matched a Mossberg AR-15 tactical lower with a Palmetto State Armory upper. All that remained was to chase down a 6.8-style 5-round magazine, add a scope base riser on the Weaver rail for an elevated optics system and my 21-inch target-weight stainless steel test rifle would be ready. After the rifle was completed, a Nikon Prostaff target scope with sunshade was the final element.

DOWN RANGE

The rifle was zeroed at 100 yards. The load was Nosler 60-grain bullets at 3,300 fps, which produced a 100-yard group of .788 inch. On the 600-yard steel target, I used the Federal Cartridge computer database for my firing solutions and ran the data to 1,000 yards using the 60-, 75-, 88- and 90-grain bullets.

I pressed the Valkyrie to the 600-yard AT Steel Target by walking my bullets out every 100 yards from the 200-yard marker, and then running up the elevating clicks accordingly. The Nikon MOA reticle did not have subtensions but was accurate when I used the top turret adjustments. In effect, 600-yard shooting was effortless. Most shooting was done with the Federal Premium 60-grain Nosler BT load, while the Federal American Eagle 75-grain load was used to punch through the high, midday winds. The variety of bullet weights available in commercial .224 Valkyrie factory loadings make it a good choice for tactical applications.

"Green man" targets represent life-size criminals that need to be stopped — headshot when hostage situations, and center-mass body hits at long range. The .224 Valkyrie passed this test with flying colors.

(right) A variety of bullet weights and styles are already in stores for the .224 Valkyrie.

Also, with 23 years' experience as a police officer on the street and being able to train with class-one city cops in special operations shooting drills, my learning curve with this high-velocity barn burner of a .22-caliber cartridge came quickly.

THE RIFLE

You need the proper firearm for testing, so I elected to build my own rifle

The Palmetto Armory/Mossberg Tactical AR proved itself with better than half MOA accuracy. The extremely flat-shooting .224 Valkyrie cartridge made hits out to 600 yards a breeze.

Steel torso targets are used here when shooting the .224 Valkyrie in one-shot stop scenarios.

With the first round of testing complete, I headed to the long-distance range to engage warm targets (prairie dogs at 500 yards). Other targets in this location included my "green man" and "blue man" portable panels. These represent real-world shooting for tactical applications. On call here were the 90-grain Federal Fusion and the 88-grain Hornady ELD Match loads.

With a 30-percent value blowing from left to right — based on observing moving grass — the wind was building intensity out to 300 yards across a shallow draw. I had to dope my shots with both elevation clicks and Kentucky windage. At 200 yards, headshots were commonplace, and at 300 to 400 yards center mass was the clear objective. Shooting the heavier bullets produced some very solid performance profiles of both cartridges that were tested. Shooting the hostage impact shot was clearly possible to 200 yards on a green man target. That is beyond maximum range as directed by police fire control when special operations are assigned to eliminate a threat. As a rule, shot placement in a hostage situation needs to put the bullet between the upper lip (cleft shot) and the nose. This initiates a no-flop stone-dead subject that will not retain any level of trigger control, or the ability to move an arm or finger.

THE TACTICAL TESTS

To put the .224 Valkyrie through its paces, I set up shooting scenarios using paper targets that were situated behind an old junk stock car that doubles as a target on the range. The first fictitious example was based on a rural State Highway Patrol threat encounter. After pulling over a driver on a routine traffic stop, a gunfight ensued leaving the officer wounded and taking cover behind his patrol car's rear wheel. A responding squad was quickly dispatched, and with the responding officer expecting his partner to be pinned down by a handgun-wielding perp, he proceeded to approach the scene and close to 125 yards using his squad as a shield. Returning fire as the assailant appeared around his vehicle, the officer delivers a center mass vital shot from the .224 Valkyrie-chambered AR-15 — thereby dispatching the threat with a single round. Using the old dilapidated stock car as the bad guy's getaway vehicle, I placed a blue man target to duplicate the shot as closely as possible. My results were three rounds downrange with three positive mid-torso hits. The bullets were Hornady 88-grain Match ELD's. The shot was, for all intents and purposes, a walk in the park, a testimony to the Valkyrie's effectiveness.

In the second role play scenario, the bad guy is using an AK-47 against

an officer after a country traffic stop. The officer has taken cover in an old grain bin built of brick near the road. A second officer has responded to the shots fired call. Seeing that the bad guy is armed with a long-range weapon clearly capable of penetrating his unit, he drops back 250 yards, then takes cover using the far side of the squad's driver side, thereby putting the engine and front wheels in front of himself for barrier protection. Setting up his .224 Valkyrie AR-15 (chambering the heavy, 88-grain bullet) he takes his shot from the safer long-range position. The target was engaged, ending the threat with a single round to the bad guy's vitals.

CONCLUSION

When shooting these controlled scenarios in real time it is clear to me that the .224 Valkyrie is quite capable of performing the role of a squad officer's precision sniper rifle. I've reported on officer training programs that dealt with shooting through vehicle window glass and other barricade materials, and long-range sniper shooting tactics as applied to police officers facing situations much like those I tested.

It is my opinion that the .224 Valkyrie — especially considering its full range of factory-loaded ammunition — could meld nicely into an urban-, rural- or counter-sniper weapon in the future. TGD

Table A: Performance .224 Valkyrie				
Load	Muzzle Velocity (fps)	500-Yard Velocity (fps)	Drop at 300 yards (in.)	Drop at 500 yards (in.)
Federal Nosler BT 60 gr.	3,300	1,710	8.4	35.8
Federal Fusion SP 90 gr.	2,700	1,919	14.9	45.9
American Eagle FMJ 75 gr.	3,000	2,124	12.0	45.0
Hornady Match ELD 88 gr.	2,675	1,920	8.3	47.4
Note: Bullets do not go transonic until 1,400 yards.				

Table B. Ballistic Tracking: Federal FMJ 75 gr. Zero 100 yards						
Scope Turret Settings/Sub-tensions (MOA)						
200 yds.	300 yds.	350 yds.	400 yds.	450 yds.	500 yds.	550 yds.
1.5	3.7	4.9	6.3	7.8	9.4	11.1

Source: Federal Cartridge ballistics program.
*Accuracy notes: In general, the .224 Valkyrie printed group sizes ranging from .669 inch at 100 yards (best) to 3.211 inches at 600 yards.

The author's homebuilt AR-15 in .224 Valkyrie. With lower and optics, it put him back only about $500 and some change.

TACTICAL KNIFE REVIEW:

THE SCORPION STRIKES!

Hogue's SIG SAUER Emperor Scorpion Tactical Blade is one Wicked Companion

BY **PAT COVERT**

The SIG SAUER Emperor Scorpion pistol needs little introduction to most handgun aficionados, and if you own one of these superb upscale semi-autos you'll be delighted to know there's a little sting

Manufactured by Hogue Knives, SIG
SAUER's X5 Emperor Scorpion tactical
folders, are perfect companions for their
handgun counterparts. At top is the
Wharncliffe model, at bottom the Spear
Point.

The two X5 Emperor Scorpion models' blades are strikingly different. The Wharncliffe (top) leans to the combat/self-defense side, while the Spear Point (bottom) offers a bit more utility.

The SIG SAUER X5 Emperor Scorpion series of knives consists of two tactical folders licensed and manufactured by Hogue Knives. All the things you like about your pistol are right here — from its Flat Dark Earth accents to its black G10 grips. The designs are collaborations with custom knife-maker Allen Elishewitz, who has been on board with Hogue from the initial launch of its cutlery line — and is a key reason Hogue was so successful right out of the gate. Elishewitz is a legend in the custom knife world.

A strong synergy between SIG and Hogue is evident in the way the two companies collaborate. Hogue manufactures the G10 grips found on SIG's Emperor Scorpion handguns, and they have gone to great lengths to make sure the finishes on knife and pistol match. According to Hogue President Jim Bruns, "We send our blades to the same house back east that SIG uses for its frames and slides. They match the color for us with the same process and ship them back to us. This is the only way to guarantee the perfect pair — pistol and knife. The finish is done by Ion Bond and is simply called FDE (Flat Dark Earth) PVD."

Two versions of the X5 Emperor Scorpions are available, the only difference being in blade styles: one a spear point and the other a Wharncliffe. We'll be testing the Spear Point model here because the spear blade style offers a bit

Here you can appreciate the mechanical functions of the knife. The blade opens via the index finger activating the flipper. The round button is the blade release, and the sliding safety affords added protection when the folder is not in use.

The Emperor's blade was tested for its carving ability on a block of seasoned Basswood. The blade was able to take off 1/8-inch shavings like butter.

more utility than the Wharncliffe, which leans more to the self-defense/combat side. MSRP for both is $249.95.

THE SCORPION SPEAR POINT

The X5 Emperor Scorpion Spear Point is 8.15 inches in length fully opened. The blade is 3.5 inches long and features CPM154 stainless steel with the Flat Dark Earth PVD coating. On the spine is a 'harpoon' kick-up with a swedge-grind (false edge) to enhance penetration. CPM154 is a proprietary blade steel made by Crucible Industries, LLC and is a modernized, finer-grained version of the old 154CM ball bearing steel many custom knifemakers latched onto early on in the modern tactical knife era of the 1990s. Though not as flashy as some of the newer exotic blade steels, CPM154 is highly respected and some noted custom knifemakers prefer it over the newer blends. The blade opens via an index finger-activated flipper, which protrudes out of the back of the handle and doubles as a fingerguard when the blade is fully deployed.

Elishewitz's penchant for excellent design is evident in the X5 Emperor Scorpion's 4.75-inch handle, exhibiting many hallmarks of his custom knives. The wicked curves give the handle an aggressive look, but also have purpose. There's an index finger groove, which makes for a tight grip. On the top of the handle spine there's a notch in the blade for the thumb to lock into. The handle is T6 aluminum, matte black anodized with checkered G10 inlays for enhanced purchase. An inset SIG logo in the Flat Dark Earth color scheme makes for a nice touch. At the handle base is a metal color-keyed plate that adds strength to the pommel, which can serve as a hammering weapon.

The X5 Emperor Scorpion's blade is razor sharp right out of the box and tackled slicing this 1/16-inch suede skiving with ease.

On the forward portion of the handle the guts of the knife are displayed: an easy to locate push-button blade release and slide safety to keep things "tidy" in the pocket. Most folders don't have a safety, but it's a good option to have. If you've ever had a folder open in your pocket you can relate. On the back is a 2-inch deep, discreet carry pocket clip (color-keyed also) and repetition of the checkering and SIG logo. For storage, the X5 Emperor Scorpion comes with a black canvas pouch sporting the SIG monogram.

THE SCORPION BITES

The X5 Emperor Scorpion's 4.75-inch handle length qualifies it as a full-size tactical folder, able to accommodate those with large mitts. Its weight is a comfortable 4.66 ounces — relatively lightweight for its size. The tactile feel of the nicely curved handle is excellent, the finger groove and thumb notch boosting the value. Little things like the matte finish and checkering add to the purchase. Both the fencers and pistol grip feel natural and the finger groove works well for both. The blade locks up tightly and the push-button release is quick and easy to access.

The X5 Emperor Scorpion's spear blade is razor sharp right out of the box. I started out testing that blade on some 1/16-inch suede skiving. On a flat wood surface, the blade glided through the suede with little effort and sliced easily on handheld pull-throughs as well. The tough, fleshy material was no match for the spear point's fine-tuned factory edge.

Next, I turned to some 3/8-inch rappelling rope, a test medium that tends to wreak havoc on blade edges. On a flat surface, the blade sliced through the rope in single strokes using medium pressure. Given that I've tested quite a few knives that have required two or three sawing motions to cut through the same rope that's a very good grade. With heavy pressure I was able to pull through the looped rope in one firm stroke, another good sign the blade is up to the task.

Lastly, the blade was given the "chunk test" to see how well it could dig into a block of cured Basswood. This a wood commonly used by carvers and on musical instruments such as electric guitar bodies for its excellent density to weight ratio. Using downward strokes, I was able to consistently shave off lengths of the Basswood 1/8-inch thick or better. In the field, the blade would no doubt be even more effective on softer, greener

SPECIFICATIONS

MODEL: SIG SAUER Emperor Scorpion

BLADE LENGTH: 3.5 in.

OVERALL LENGTH: 8.125 in.

CLOSED LENGTH: 4.625 in.

WEIGHT: 4.6 oz.

MECHANISM: Automatic button deployment with manual safety

HANDLE MATERIAL (FRAME): Matte black 6061-T6 anodized aluminum with G10 inserts

POCKET CLIP: Stainless steel ambidextrous deep pocket carry

BLADE STYLE: Spear Point or Wharncliffe

BLADE THICKNESS: 0.15 in.

BLADE MATERIAL: CPM154 Stainless steel

BLADE HARDNESS: RC 57-59

BLADE TREATMENT: Cryogenically treated

BLADE FINISH: Flat Dark Earth PVD

(above) A length of tough 3/8-inch rappelling rope was used to test the Emperor Scorpion's cutting power. The blade had no trouble slicing through the rope in clean, single strokes.

(right) The handle has the same checkered G10 inlays and SIG Sauer monogram as the front.

wood. After all testing was done, the PVD blade coating showed no noticeable scuffs or chipping. A quick wipe with a little light oil and it was good as new.

The Emperor Scorpion's cutting, slicing and carving ability fared very well in all three tests. When a knife performs this well on utilitarian chores, you can bet it will do the same in a well-trained hand for self-defense. Considering the quality of build and features such as its wicked sharp blade, excellent ergonomics, push-button release, and safety options, the SIG SAUER X5 Emperor Scorpion is well worth its $249.95 price tag. There are over fifteen SIG SAUER-branded folders and fixed blades in the Hogue line, all well worth your consideration. **TGD**

For more information on the X5 Emperor Scorpion visit Hogue Knives at hogueinc.com/knives/SIGsauer

GSG MP40P
REVIEW

A Modern Semi-Auto "Schmeisser" MP 40 Provides Heavy 9mm Firepower BY L.P. BREZNY

With a history longer than my arm, the MP 40 is still regarded as one of the most collectible and functional machine pistols ever built. And while there may not be a massive amount of tactical work for a weapon as old as the MP 40, even after decades of production it is still very much sought after. That goes for current German production semi-automatics, and original full-auto German military variants harvested from World War II. A friend of mine recently sold an original one for the grand sum of $18,000, while another one went at auction with a closing price of $45,000 and change. With that information, I rest my case in terms of both the value and interest that is generated among shooters and collectors of the German MP 40 Schmeisser.

If there was ever a symbol of "spray and pray," the MP 40 fills the bill.

During the Second World War, my father latched on to an MP 40 when he was a railroad engineer. Yes, we had them in the U.S. Army, in addition to the 742ROB in France, and later Germany. He ditched his M1 carbine in favor of the Schmeisser, after he saw firsthand what the machine pistols could do in a combat setting.

During the 1950's, an acquaintance brought back an MP 40 he took off a very willing German in combat. He got it home, and it was fully functional. Always wanting the gun when they became available through German Sport Guns GmbH, Ense-Hoingen Germany, I tried for a long time to land a semi-automatic model in the typical German military wood shipping crate. But after some time searching, I gave up on that idea. That is when I came across the GSG MP40P while attending the 2017 SHOT Show. It was sold by American Tactical, of Summerville, South Carolina.

AMERICAN TACTICAL GSG MP40P

While not going into extreme detail, as I am no expert on German arms, I can say that the MP40P makes use of the 9mm Luger round and stacks these nasty little cartridges in a 25-round stick magazine that also acts as the forward handgrip. While some would suggest that the 9mm Luger cartridge is a weak sister to many current handgun rounds, I can attest that — based on many years of service in law enforcement and from carrying a Smith & Wesson Model 5906 9mm for at least half of those years on the street — there is more to the 9mm than meets the untrained eye.

Starting with the outstanding Winchester Black Talon load that was outlawed but has since come back

Training on an A/T torso steel target is great training. The author getting the feel for basic handling is front and center here.

Defense is the keyword when it comes to the MP40P. You can emerge from a vehicle with a high rate of firepower and own the situation.

The GSG MP40P from American Tactical Imports (ATI) as sold out of the box. The sling is not German standard-issue. The wire stock is not included and requires an ATF NFA tax stamp before installing. The MP40P as sold as a machine pistol is semi-automatic and is not a Class III machine gun (again, unless a shoulder stock is attached).

in many varied forms, there is also the Federal Hydra-Shok, Gold Dot by Speer, SIG SAUER V-Crown, Winchester Silvertip and even a cold tracer from G2 Research/VIP Technology. While that brief list barely scratches the surface of available 9mm loads, it's an indication as to where the small German-based round is heading in the 21st century. And it seems that the very well-designed MP 40 is going right along for the ride.

In this review, I am discussing the MP40P Model C/D. This means semi-auto, closed bolt design, versus the full-auto open-bolt type as has been used by the militaries of almost 50 countries. Save for that small detail, the two machine pistols are so similar you could not tell the difference with bolts closed.

The MP40P is war-industry manufactured, but as offered today is not a cheap pile of junk by any means. Designed and built from 1938 to 1945 in Germany, it can make use of a 32-round mag or a 64-duel-round magazine system (military production). It has an effective range of about 200 yards, and a maximum range of 250 yards. The MP40P is obviously a close support system, and best used in house-to-house fighting, or in police hands when taking down barricaded shooters. As a rule, troops like the machine pistol very much, and it was even used as late as the Vietnam War by our Special Forces when hunting VC in the north of the country.

Coming in at a weight of 7.8 pounds empty, the MP 40 makes use of machined steel polymer (Bakelite plastic) and stamped parts — the same material used in the construction of the German P-38 9mm pistol. It is robust, can take punishment and has good balance and easy-handling qualities.

The MP40P's sights are partridge style in the rear and a heavy hooded post at the front. The underside of the barrel has a steel strip for additional reinforcement should the gun be used as a club. Sling attachment loops are built into the frame.

Using the sights without the wire stock attachment in place is a bit useless, but with a buttstock attached the MP40P becomes a longer-range combat tool. Regarding the stock attachment, the federal ATF form "Making a Firearm" must be applied for and received before a stock can be attached to the MP40P. This application with paperwork will cost you an additional $200.00 for the federal tax stamp.

The MP40P retains a magazine release

The underside of the barrel is supported by a steel rail, and a heavy steel hood protects the front sight. This styling is a dead giveaway for an MP 40-style machine pistol.

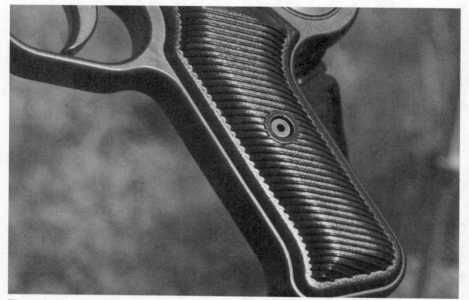

The poly pistol grip is the same material found on German P–38s. It's extremely tough and battle hard. The grip feels solid and functional.

loose a runaway, thereby emptying the magazine in one short burst. Thankfully that didn't happen.

However, a problem surfaced during the loading of the magazine. It is one tough customer to drop a 9mm round into. Even when using the provided loading aid, the whole deal was slow, tough on the fingers and just not fun at all. Once the mag was loaded, however, she clicked off rounds like any good German production gun should.

Shooting triple taps resulted in a very fast recovery and a solid aiming platform when not using sights. The GSG MP40P functioned flawlessly, and total control was a snap with each round sent downrange. The bottom line is that the MP 40 was well-designed from day one, and it really shows under live-fire conditions. It is little wonder why it was adapted for both military and police use.

If there is any additional area save for that nasty magazine loading system that comes up short, it is the instruction

on the left-side front, which consists of a large button that can be activated inadvertently during firing. I did just that when testing the weapon and had to learn to keep my hand back and away from that control feature.

The safety is nothing more than a round turning button. When arrows are aligned with the stock's length, it is in the fire mode. Turning the button with arrows crossing the stock puts it on safe. It is not a fancy safety system, but these tactical guns were not designed for Sunday plinking, but full-time combat applications. As a second safety, however, the breech bolt retains a striker safety that blocks the bolt. This will stop the bolt from engaging, preventing the gun from firing. Some of the early MP

40s had no safety at all. I talked with a Russian supply truck driver who, during the Battle for Stalingrad, had one go off several times behind his driver's seat while bouncing around on rough roads. Like some U.S. troops, the Russians liked to use the MP 40 when they could get their hands on one.

FIRING FUNCTION

When testing the MP40P I elected to shoot diamond plate and Action/Target surface-hardened plate steel on my club range. Using a loading block over the stick mag provided with the weapon, I first loaded six-round strings of 9mm to get a working feel for the machine pistol. It would not have been the first semi-auto weapon I have ever tested that turned

SIG Elite 9mm ammo performed excellent in the MP40P. Fired from a longer-barreled machine pistol, the old Luger round has a lot of zip and banged steel with authority.

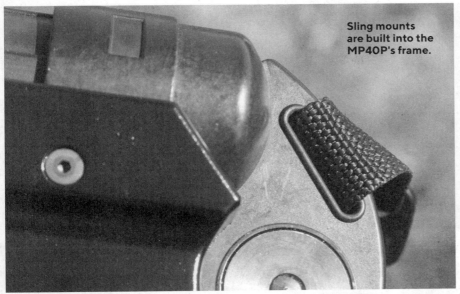

Sling mounts are built into the MP40P's frame.

This rear sight and heavy return spring illustrate the robust construction of the GSG MP40P.

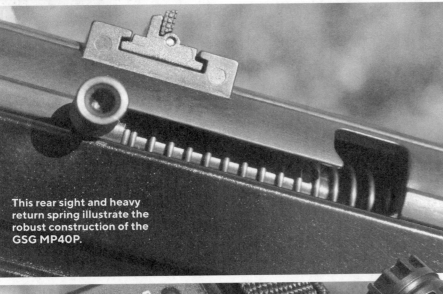

The left-side forward magazine latch is large and easy to activate.

SPECIFICATIONS

MODEL: ATI GSG MP40P

OVERALL LENGTH: 24.5 in.

HEIGHT: 7 in.

FRAME: Zamak 5 with polymer accents

WEIGHT: w/ Magazine unloaded - 7.8 lbs. (9.80 with folding stock attached)

CALIBER: 9x19mm

BARREL LENGTH: 10 in.

MAGAZINE: Detachable 25-round - all metal

MSRP: S579.95

americantactical.us

800-290-0065

manual. It informs the buyer to see the "expert" for disassembly of the MP40P for service and cleaning. Assuming that means a gunsmith specializing in German military guns, that's not exactly workable in the middle of South Dakota where I live.

Now I pack the MP40P behind my truck seat along with a couple of sticks of 9mm ammo when crossing the back-country. During ink-black nights in areas with little or no population, it gives me a warm, fuzzy feeling — regardless of the temperature outside. TGD

Changing out the front sight requires the removal of this ring. The manufacturer provides four height options for the front sight. If the one installed is too high or low, you can buy a replacement sight from ATI. In effect, lacking the wire stock, it won't make a whole lot of difference, and the rear adjustable sight will fill in nicely if a dead zero is the objective of the shooter.

MOLOT VEPR 12 REVIEW

Don't Fear the Vepr: Banned Russian 12-Gauge

BY **ROBERT SADOWSKI**

hanks to arbitrary importation restrictions, the Russian-made Vepr 12 can only be imported into the U.S. with a fixed stock and a 5-round magazine. Obviously, these unnecessary gun controls are draconian. Thankfully, FIME Group, located in Las Vegas, imports Vepr 12 shotguns and then replaces some of the Russian components with U.S. parts to pass 922r compliance, making them legal to own. FIME offers fixed-stock models, but a fully functional folding stock makes the Vepr 12 more adaptable and easier to use in confined spaces. When you handle a Vepr, you soon realize you have some serious equipment in your hands.

The Vepr is based on the Russian RPK light machine gun. The RPK and Vepr are similar to an AK with almost identical controls and operating systems, except that they use a larger, more heavy-duty trunnion block and receiver — making

them beefier, tougher and more rugged weapons. It also makes them heavy, but the weight is an asset since it helps you better manage the recoil from stout 12-gauge loads. At 9.7 pounds, the Vepr is heavy. Other semi-automatic shotguns, like the Benelli A4, weigh closer to 7.8 pounds. Pump-action shotguns are closer to 6.5 pounds. And while we are all well-versed in running a tube-fed shotgun — be it a pump or semi-auto — the Vepr is in a class all by itself.

Box magazine-fed, semi-automatic shotguns require a different mindset. Running a Vepr 12 is a lot like running an AR or AK. The typical semi-auto shotgun uses a tube magazine and is slow to reload. Shotguns like the Vepr 12 challenge conventional thinking about defensive shotguns. Instead of thumbing a single round one at a time into a tubular magazine, the Vepr 12 takes separate mags, which are available in 2-, 5-, 8-,

A fully functional folding stock makes the Vepr 12 shotgun more adaptable and easier to use in confined spaces.

10- and 12-round capacities. The 5-round magazine is about the size of an AR-10 mag, only fatter. There is no rocking and locking the magazine like on an AK. With the Vepr 12 you insert the magazine into the magazine well just like you do with an AR. From that point on, the Vepr 12 is pure AK.

It incorporates an AK paddle-type magazine that requires you to swipe away the spent magazine like you would with an AK rifle. The magazine well is polymer, so mag insertion is slick and fast.

In addition to the magazine system, there are other unique features that separate the Vepr 12 from other Asian-made 12 gauges that feed from a box mag. The Vepr 12 includes an ambidextrous safety selector and, my favorite, the bolt hold-open mechanism that greatly simplifies reloading. That feature can be engaged via a small button on the right side and rear of the trigger, which also sends the

At 25 yards, the Vepr 12 is capable of surgical precision with slugs; this group is from Federal Maximum Hydra-Shot 1-oz. slugs.

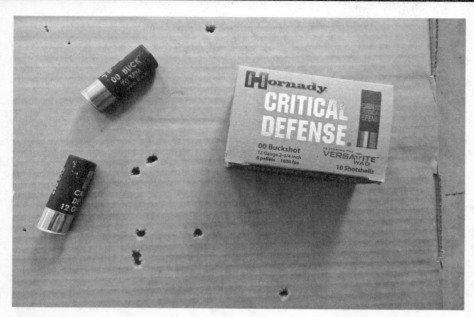

Hornady Critical Defense 00–buck punched a 7-inch pattern at 25 yards.

bolt forward. The button looks a lot like a slide release on a pump-action shotgun.

The Vepr 12 variant I tested incorporates a left-side folding tubular buttstock. The stock locks in place when extended and folded. Overall length with the stock folded is 28.7 inches, which is only 3 inches longer than a Shockwave-type pump shotgun. You can run the Vepr with the stock folded or extended. A textured button on the side of the receiver is depressed to fold the stock, and another textured button on the rear of the receiver is depressed to extend the stock. Attached to the comb of the tubular stock is a small padded cheek piece that can be adjusted for left- or right-handed shooters. There is also a rubber recoil pad to mitigate recoil.

The Vepr sports a 19-inch barrel that is choked cylinder bore, and the muzzle is threaded so you can attach muzzle devices like comps, brakes or choke tubes. It's equipped with rifle-style sights; an elevation-adjustable front sight is protected by wings and a windage-adjustable rear. If you want to mount a red-dot sight the dust cover is hinged with an integrated Picatinny rail.

The safety is different from the typical AK type. It is ambidextrous with an additional tab at the lower rear portion above the pistol grip, as well as on the other side of the receiver above the pistol grip. The pistol grip is rubber with serrations for texture. They help reduce felt recoil and allow you to control the Vepr when it is chewing through shells. The handguard is made of polymer and is ribbed — protecting your hand from heat during extended shooting sessions. And that feature offers a sure grip.

The trigger pull measured a heavy 7.9 pounds, not exactly match quality, but I was able to group slugs so at least two out of three holes touched at 25 yards. For throwing slugs that's great performance in my book.

The matte black finish on the Vepr is what I like to refer to as typical Natasha and Boris: all business, military-grade former Soviet-bloc style. If it gets scratched, simply use a black Sharpie to cover it up.

I assembled a bunch of 2 3/4-inch 12-gauge defense ammo, from Winchester PDX1 Defender, which is loaded with a slug and 00 buck, to Hornady Critical Defense and military-grade 00 buck. I also tried Federal Maximum Hydra-Shok 1-oz. hollowpoint slugs and Winchester Supreme High-Velocity Turkey with a payload of 1 1/2 ounces of #5 shot. The Vepr was immune to any differences in ammo and ran exceptionally well. I shot it from the hip with the stock folded and extended. And I shouldered it using both stock positions. I could not trip it up. It chopped through everything I loaded into it even with mixed ammo in the magazine — just the kind of tactical-capable firearm I like. It's not picky about what it shoots.

The Ve pr operates like an AK. Its long-stroke piston works the action with reliability. The bolt carrier operated smoothly. The padded cheek piece provides a nice cheek weld, which, along with the butt pad, reduces felt recoil. Magazine reloads are fast — a lot faster

The Vepr 12 is based on the Russian RPK light machine gun.

than a tube magazine shotgun. Between the Vepr's weight and its ergonomics, it is a pleasure to shoot.

What I did notice was how well it grouped the Winchester and Hornady Defense loads at 25 yards: 11 and 7 inches respectively. That is the surgical precision I like with home defense shotguns. I want to be sure my assorted payload of 00 buck hits the intended target, reducing liability concerns. With slugs, three-shot groups at 25 yards averaged 3.5 inches. With a red-dot sight, group size would shrink dramatically.

The mag-fed Vepr requires a different mindset. It made me change my mind. **TGD**

The 5-round magazine is about the size of an AR-10 mag, only thicker. Box magazine-fed, semi-automatic shotguns require a different mindset.

SPECIFICATIONS

MODEL: Molot Vepr 12

ACTION TYPE: Semi-automatic

GAUGE: 12; 3-in. chamber

OVERALL LENGTH (STOCK EXTENDED): 38.5 in.

OVERALL LENGTH (STOCK FOLDED): 28.7 in.

CAPACITY: 5+1

WEIGHT UNLOADED: 9.7 lbs.

BARREL: 19 in., threaded muzzle

RECEIVER: Matte black steel

CHOKE: Cylinder bore

STOCK: Folding tubular buttstock with cheek rest

GRIP: Textured rubber

FRONT SIGHT: Winged, adj. post

REAR SIGHT: Adj. RPK style

TRIGGER PULL WEIGHT: 7.5 lbs.

SAFETY: Manual 2-position

702-215-3600

fimegroup.com

Fieldstripping the Vepr 12 is the same as tearing down an AK.

Table A. Slug Performance: Molot Vepr 12	
12-Gauge Slugs	25-Yard 3-Shot Average Accuracy (in.)
Federal Maximum Hydra-Shok 1-oz. HP	3.5
Winchester PDX1 Defender 1-oz. Slug w/300 Buck Shot	11.0

Table B. Shot Performance: Molot Vepr 12	
12-Gauge Shot	25-Yard Average Pattern (in.)
Hornady Critical Defense 00 Buck	7.0
Winchester Military Grade 00 Buck	22.0
Winchester Supreme High-Velocity Turky Load #5	25.0

The magazine well is polymer, making magazine insertion fast and easy.

The Vepr 12 features an ambidextrous safety selector and a bolt hold-open mechanism that greatly simplifies reloading.

The Howa KRG Bravo is a fusion between chassis-style precision rifles and field guns. It's fully capable of hunting or long-range tactical applications.

ACCESSIBLY ACCURATE: HOWA KRG BRAVO REVIEW

BY **COREY GRAFF**

Combined with a Nightforce ATACR 4–16x42 F1 scope, the Howa KRG Bravo smashed expectations.

My first long-range rifle took a chunk out of my savings to the tune of nearly $6,000 buckaroos, and so did the second one I had built. These custom rifles also took better than six months to complete from the time ordered. Since those days — just a few short years ago — the cost of entry into long-range shooting has come way, way down.

It's benefitted from the repeatability of CNC machine tools and innovations in stock-to-action fit that promote accuracy. Partnerships between rifle makers and the burgeoning aftermarket stock industry help, too. Expectations of sub-minute-of-angle (MOA) precision are now assumed. The message from the shooting public: Make my groups small and keep my rifle around a thousand dollars. And companies like the Japanese concern Howa, imported and distributed by Legacy Sports International of Reno, Nevada, have delivered. Case in point: The Howa KRG Bravo.

HOWA KRG BRAVO .308 REVIEW

Built on Howa's 1500 barrel-action, which has come to be regarded as one of the best in the industry, the KRG Bravo

was introduced at the 2018 SHOT Show and features the Kinetic Research Group (KRG) Bravo stock. Clearly competing with crossover models like the Bergara HMR (Hunting Match Rifle), Howa's

KRG Bravo bridges the gap between benchrest, tactical, law enforcement, Precision Rifle Series (PRS) competition and hunting. All polymer, the stock is not really a true "chassis" type, but

Saving money on the affordable Howa, you can put more into best-of-class optics, such as the Nightforce ATACR 4–16x42 F1 scope. The first focal plane scope uses extra-low dispersion (ED) glass and has a massive 34mm tube to suck light in like a black hole. It offers a total of 89 MOA or 26 mils of elevation adjustment.

After having used it, it's difficult to imagine life at the long-distance range without the Nightforce TS-82 spotting scope. With its 20-70x magnification range and tack-sharp resolution, seeing black holes on black bullseyes after calling shots was critical in the long-range accuracy evaluation.

more of a hybrid design with just enough modularity so you can customize to your heart's content. Yet, it still feels like a traditional stock. The stock has a full-length aluminum spine that gives it backbone rigidity while keeping the weight down. Since I'm accustomed to bedded rifle actions in heavier fiberglass stocks, like those from H-S Precision and McMillan, I found the Howa KRG to have a somewhat top-heavy feel, but I quickly got used to it.

The Howa 1500 KRG Bravo is available in black or Flat Dark Earth (FDE) color schemes and is packed with features. For one thing, the barrel comes threaded to accept a muzzle brake. The KRG Bravo stock has an in-built grip storage compartment that would be a good spot for small tools and a Bore Snake-type cleaner. A removable section under the buttstock comes off with the turn of an Allen screw and reveals a grip hook to pull the rifle snugly into your shoulder while shooting. In addition, M-LOK slots adorn the forend section for even more customization. The stock also includes

The Bravo stock from Kinetic Research Group (KRG) is completely modular. Its 12.5- to 15-inch length-of-pull adjustable stock, easy-to-set cheek riser, buttstock grip hook and M-LOK compatible forend open up endless possibilities for customization.

(above) Federal's 175-grain Gold Medal Match ammo was a solid performer in the Howa 1500 rifle. It produced a .81-inch best group at 100 yards; average was 1.14 inches before barrel break-in.

(below) The Nightforce ATACR 4-16x42 F1 scope is an ideal match for the KRG Bravo in .308 Win. Thanks to its cavernous 34mm tube it has a wide range of internal adjustment — up to 26 mils or 89 MOA — and its ZeroHold elevation turret lock lets you set your zero but also adjust below zero.

a quick-release stud that fits into a milled recess near the top-right side of the buttstock, just in front of the recoil pad. I took advantage of this feature and installed a Magpul quick-detach sling swivel. That made it simple to attach a Rhodesian sling from Andy's Custom Leather to support field operations (hunting). The system was flawless.

Speaking of the recoil pad, the modular system includes three spacers to customize the length of pull (LOP). The rifle came without them installed, and the out-of-box 12.5-inch LOP was way too short for me. To rectify this, I simply removed two Allen screws accessible via holes in the recoil pad, added the three spacers and put it all back together for a final LOP of 15 inches. The adjustable cheek riser gives you an instantly perfect cheek weld and eye alignment through the scope.

The Howa's action and bolt throw are remarkably smooth for a factory rifle. The two-position safety is located next to the action and is operated easily with your thumb. The trigger is exceptional, breaking cleanly at an average 3 lbs., 10 oz., as measured with the Lyman trigger-pull gauge.

OPTICS AND ACCESSORIES

When it comes to optics, there are two ways to think about a "budget" precision rifle build. There are now a lot of excellent riflescopes in the $500–$800 price range that would make an ideal and affordable match for a rifle system such as the Howa KRG Bravo. Indeed, many shooters go this route and it's a winning combination — even in competition. The other way to think about it is to use the money saved on the rifle and put it into high-end optics. That was my thinking behind contacting Nightforce, which supplied an ATACR 4-16x42 F1 scope with the Mil-C reticle. They also sent along the excellent Nightforce TS-82 spotting scope, which allows you to count nose hairs on flies at 500 paces (and spot black holes on black targets at 300 yards or more — exceptional resolution).

The ATACR scope's features would require a full dedicated review to even begin to do it justice. This first focal plane scope has glass that stands with any of the premier German makers in edge-to-edge clarity, resolution and light transmission. Clicks are solid and precise and the built-in illumination — activated by a simple push of the gold button

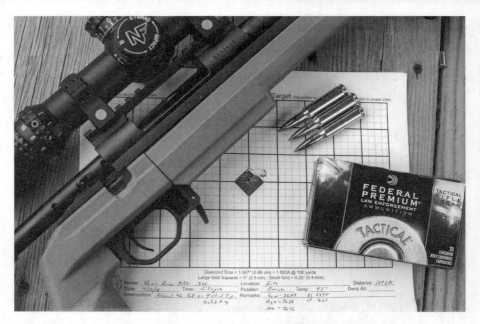

(above) A new addition to Federal's lineup, the Law Enforcement 168-grain Tactical Tip MatchKing load took top prize in the 100-yard accuracy test with a .98-inch average and .49-inch best group.

(below) The Howa KRG Bravo put Federal Gold Medal 185-grain Berger Juggernaut OTM rounds into a best .69-inch group and averaged .92 inch at 100 yards. The new high ballistic coefficient (.552) load from Federal makes the .308 Win. a genuine 1,000-yard option.

SPECIFICATIONS

MODEL: Howa KRG Bravo

CALIBERS: 6mm Creedmoor, 6.5mm Creedmoor, .308 Win.

BARRELS: 20-, 24-, or 26-in. heavy barrel

BARREL TWIST: 1:7.5 (6mm CM); 1:9 (6.5 CM); 1:10 (.308 Win.)

MAGAZINE: 10-round AICS

COLOR OPTIONS: Black or Flat Dark Earth (FDE)

STOCK FEATURES: Built-in buttstock grip hook for rear bag use; grip storage compartment; M-LOK compatible fore-end

LENGTH OF PULL: 12.5–15 in.

WEIGHT: 9.9–10.2 lbs.

MSRP: $1,279–$1,339

legacysports.com

Table A. Howa KRG Bravo .308 Win. Ballistics and Accuracy Test				
Load	Velocity (fps)	Energy (ft.-lbs.)	100-Yard Group Avg. (in.)	100-Yard Group Best (in.)
Hornady TAP 168-gr.	2,575	2,474	1.16	.83
Federal Gold Berger 185-gr.	2,530	2,630	.92	.69
Federal LE Tactical Tip MatchKing 168 gr.	2,646	2,612	.98	.49
Federal Gold Medal Match 175 gr.	2,570	2,567	1.14	.81
Velocities measured 10 ft. from muzzle using a Shooting Chrony Beta Master chronograph.				

on the left parallax turret — makes this military-grade optic extremely versatile for any tactical application one might face.

While there have been many advancements in bipods in recent years, the gold standard remains the Harris S-BRM 6-9 in. notched model, which provided all the support and adjustment needed for bench and field shooting.

BENCHREST TEST RESULTS

One note about the Howa 1500 barreled-action: While it is often compared to the Remington 700 (it is indeed very similar), the scope base hole pattern on the receiver is uniquely Howa and you will need a Howa base.

I tested four selections of ammo from 100 yards. Those included the Federal Gold Medal 185-grain Berger Jugernaught OTM, Federal LE 168-grain Tactical Tip MatchKing, Federal Gold Medal Match 175 grain and Hornady TAP in 168 grains. The table below details the results; averages came in around 1 MOA or under from a pre-broken-in barrel. I am quite certain those groups would shrink further after a barrel break-in period. Best groups ranged from .49 to .83 inch — meeting Howa's .5 MOA guarantee.

During shot strings, groups remained consistent as the Howa's heavy barrel shrugged off heat. From the bench and prone positions, the Howa KRG Bravo came to shoulder quickly and printed tiny groups as the action spit spent brass like a champ. What didn't I like? The AICS steel mag gouged brass as rounds were fed, and it was rougher to feed than a rusty old military bring-back caked in Cosmoline. Thankfully, the solution was easy. A switch to the Magpul PMAG AICS 5-round polymer magazine slicked up round extraction and ejection, made it feel like a completely different rifle.

CONCLUSION

On the range and in the woods the Howa KRG Bravo is an impressive rifle system for the price. Its affordable accuracy was a nice break from the custom rifle option costing several times more. My only complaint is that, due to time constraints, I didn't have a chance to really wring the system out to 1,000 yards. It would have been nice to let the Howa's

The KRG Bravo's modular stock made it easy to establish perfect cheek weld and eye-to-scope alignment for prone shooting.

accuracy and the Nightforce scope's exceptionally high-resolution glass flex their combined muscle while perched on some western draw. Even so, at the modest distances found here in the Midwest, the combination of Howa KRG Bravo, Nightforce ATACR and Federal match ammo made drilling bullseyes as easy as shooting fish in a barrel. TGD

The Critical Duty load from Hornady has been thoroughly tested and has emerged at the top of the heap among modern loads for self-defense.

SELF-DEFENSE AMMO TEST:
HORNADY
CRITICAL
DUTY

The Hornady FlexLock bullet optimizes expansion and penetration, traits born from years' worth of research and development.

Hornady Critical Duty Ammo is a Winner for Armed Citizens

BY **ROBERT CAMPBELL**

t was big news recently when the FBI contract for handgun ammunition was, for the first time ever, won by Hornady Manufacturing. After years of the contract being traded back and forth by the big three ammo makers — Remington, Federal and Winchester — Hornady finally sealed the deal. The contract was awarded based on quality control, reliability, accuracy and ballistic performance. The improved handgun loads from Hornady make the most of a handgun cartridge.

Among the author's favorite combinations is the SIG P220 and Critical Duty ammunition.

(right) The author tests and carefully catalogs ammunition performance for reference. The 135-grain 9mm Critical Duty load meets all criteria for service pistol use.

The Critical Duty bullet features a specially formulated nose plug and a jacket design that locks the core to the bullet.

Hornady competed in the FBI testing, which first required the loading to be proofed for reliability. After that, the load was fired for accuracy and had to demonstrate a clean powder burn. If reliability isn't proven, there is little point in proceeding to expensive ballistic testing. The FBI tests included firing into obstacles and then measuring penetration and expansion after the bullet exited these barriers. A study some years ago noted that up to half of the felons faced by the FBI and other law enforcement agencies were behind cover, most often vehicle sheet metal or car glass. That is why total penetration, maximum wound cavity and expansion are tested. The bullet is fired into bare gelatin, heavy clothing covering bare gelatin, sheet steel, wallboard, plywood and vehicle glass. These tests are difficult on a handgun bullet. Bullet design is more important than caliber or velocity.

In the recent past, the only means of increasing wound potential was to increase the weight and diameter of the bullet. For example, moving from a .38- to a .45-caliber bullet, or by increasing velocity, such as moving up to the .357 Magnum from .38 Special, or 9mm +P+ from standard 9mm loads. The FBI did a study several decades ago that deter-mined that a service pistol heavier than 35 ounces becomes a burden on the belt and is difficult to conceal. Recoil is a factor given the frequency of training most agencies can maintain. The FBI needed a load that would produce enough damage to stop the pressurized blood system of the body from operating. Penetration was the primary concern. If the bullet doesn't penetrate to the vitals it is worthless. Velocity is important as it enables this penetration. Velocity also instigates expansion, which increases the frontal diameter of the bullet and makes the projectile less likely to push flesh aside, instead cutting flesh and creating a larger wound.

Hornady Critical Duty ammo is a development that isn't related to the

(below) The 10mm Critical Duty load is powerful and accurate.

Even in compact handguns the 135-grain 9mm is pleasant to fire and is controllable.

company's earlier XTP. And while it uses the same technology as the Critical Defense load, it is a different animal. The Critical Duty loading uses a specially formulated plug in the hollow nose cavity that presses into the nose sump and instigates expansion. This load penetrates auto glass, building material, and sheet metal and exits to penetrate at least 13 inches in ballistic gelatin. During institutional and industry testing, expansion was found to be 1.2 to 1.6 times larger than the original diameter. The nose of the FlexLock bullet does not tend to become clogged. Expansion isn't as dependent on velocity. The FlexLock features a jacket locked solidly to the lead core — the bullet will not separate in tough material. There is no tradeoff between expansion and penetration as the FlexLock excels at both, a testimony to Hornady's extensive research and development.

The FBI found during its testing that the Hornady 135-grain 9mm adopted by the agency was the most accurate 9mm loading ever tested. I've shot the Hornady 135-grain FlexLock extensively and performed my own ballistic testing, including assessing expansion and penetration in water, wet newsprint and gelatin. This makes for a broad understanding of handgun performance. The Hornady FlexLock is a great load for the dedicated men and women of the FBI. The FBI contract for the 9mm load was a hard contest, and Hornady has earned the contract by excellence of design and quality control. For the armed citizen, it will perform equally well. TGD

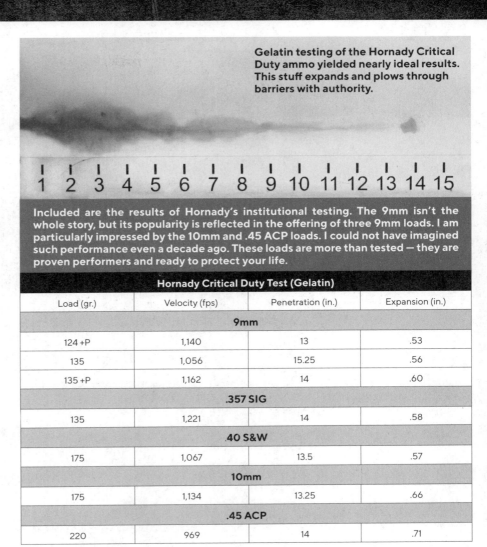

Gelatin testing of the Hornady Critical Duty ammo yielded nearly ideal results. This stuff expands and plows through barriers with authority.

Included are the results of Hornady's institutional testing. The 9mm isn't the whole story, but its popularity is reflected in the offering of three 9mm loads. I am particularly impressed by the 10mm and .45 ACP loads. I could not have imagined such performance even a decade ago. These loads are more than tested — they are proven performers and ready to protect your life.

Hornady Critical Duty Test (Gelatin)			
Load (gr.)	Velocity (fps)	Penetration (in.)	Expansion (in.)
9mm			
124 +P	1,140	13	.53
135	1,056	15.25	.56
135 +P	1,162	14	.60
.357 SIG			
135	1,221	14	.58
.40 S&W			
175	1,067	13.5	.57
10mm			
175	1,134	13.25	.66
.45 ACP			
220	969	14	.71

A primary concern with service ammunition is control, reliability and modest muzzle signature.

The Wilson Combat Recon Tactical WC-10 platform is chambered for short-action cartridges, including the .243 Winchester, .260 Remington, .308 Winchester, .338 Federal, .358 Winchester, 6mm Creedmoor, 6.5mm Creedmoor and the 7mm-08 Remington.

WILSON COMBAT
RECON TACTICAL

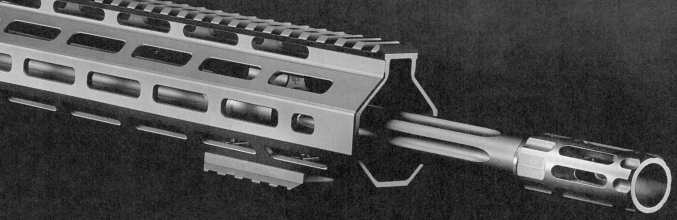

Chambered in .338 Federal, the Recon Tactical is a featherlight heavyweight

BY **JAMES PINSKY**

Plenty has been written about the .338 Federal as a hunting cartridge. Yet, there's so much this .308 Winchester-on-steroids can do, especially when you entertain the idea of the .338-caliber round for tactical applications.

The first step to proving a cartridge's worth for any application is making sure it's matched with the right weapon, and there are none better than the AR platform. One of the best examples of today's modern AR comes from Wilson Combat, which has been making world-class firearms for decades.

The Recon Tactical can be configured with a threaded muzzle brake, or with an Accu-Tac or QComp flash hider.

Led by all-world shooter Bill Wilson, the Arkansas-based firearms manufacturer is famous for top-of-the-line 1911s, tactical shotguns, knives, AR-15s and, of course, AR-10s. I recently tested the Wilson Combat Recon Tactical AR-10 (known within Wilson Combat circles as the WC-10) chambered in .338 Federal. Earlier in 2018, I had already proven the cartridge more than capable for hunting by taking a South Texas Nilgai — a large-bodied Indian antelope — with an identical WC-10 in .338 Federal. I had topped that AR with a Nightforce 2.5-10x42 compact riflescope. What's unique about the Nightforce, aside from its world-class construction and svelte size, is the fact that you can illuminate the reticle in red or green to suit your tactical needs. Optics-wise, I also used a SIG SAUER ROMEO3 reflex sight and an ATN X-Sight II HD 3-14x Day/Night optic.

Before we look closer at the Recon Tactical, let's define what a tactical rifle is: A hunting rifle's job is to make sure there is honor in how an animal's life is taken. A tactical rifle's honor comes from making sure its operator's life isn't taken. Many will argue that the specifications for both roles are identical, but at the end of the day when the rifle you select can mean the difference between you coming home under your own power, or under the power of six of your closest friends, quite a few rifles good enough to hunt with won't make your final cut. To me, a Wilson Combat firearm is a top pick — for hunting or tactical use.

WC-10 RECON TACTICAL

The WC-10 Recon Tactical is built to be light, reliable and accurate. It starts with a billet upper and lower receiver. The 18-inch barrel is a Wilson Combat Recon Tactical Match Grade, which is paired with a mid-length gas system and a Lo-Profile gas block that is capped with a threaded barrel end. Mine was finished with a QComp flash hider. The top of the rifle and barrel is finished with a Picatinny rail courtesy of a "tactical rail interface, modular," or T.R.I.M., for a variety of optics from adjustable iron sights, daylight scopes, reflex sights, thermal optics and of course light-intensified night vision optics. The rifle is operated by a Wilson Combat TTU (Tactical Trigger Unit) set at 4 pounds and sports a premium bolt carrier group made from S7 steel that is NP3 coated, with both the upper and lower receivers finished in Armor-Tuff, which is applied over a mil-spec hard-anodized surface. Bringing up the rear of the rifle is an adjustable Rogers/Wilson Super-Stoc. The entire rifle weights about 8 pounds without any optics or ammunition. My rifle measured 40 inches from end to stock extended fully, and 36.5 inches with the rifle stock fully collapsed. "The primary goals of the (AR-10) project was to make the rifles as light as possible while still retaining stellar accuracy," said Bill Wilson.

The rifle doesn't need any upgrades. Wilson Combat believes its firearms leave the factory as well-built and designed as possible, which is a point of personal pride for Bill Wilson. "We have spared no expense in development, testing and production of these rifles," said Wilson. "If we could build a better one, we would. A big advantage Wilson

The Recon Tactical
comes with an adjustable
Rogers/Wilson Super-Stoc.

Combat has is the fact that I've been a serious hunter since the early '70s and have a very keen personal interest in Wilson Combat making the very best ARs on the market whether for hunting or tactical use. I'm shooting and testing AR products virtually on a daily basis. Here at the (Wilson Combat) ranch we are fortunate to have shooting ranges out to 800 yards for extensive accuracy testing. Also, I hog hunt at least 325 days out of the year and I'm also deer hunting over 120 days a year … with annual harvests of 200-plus hogs and 50-plus deer, all with ARs. Who else proves out their product like that?"

I used a variety of .338 Federal factory loads during my review of the Recon Tactical, and none of the ammunition failed to deliver in accuracy, reliability or cost-effectiveness. The .338 Federal, relatively speaking, isn't an expensive AR-10 cartridge to shoot, especially when you consider the amount of power you're getting. Wilson himself is a big fan of the necked-up .308 family of cartridges, which includes not only the .338 Federal

but its slightly larger brother, the .358 Winchester. "The .338 Federal, and the .358 (Winchester), are substantially more powerful than the .308," said Wilson. "Both are underrated for what they're capable of, and I don't know why they're not more popular."

The question everyone wants to have answered is, what can a .338 Federal do that a .308 Winchester isn't already capable of, tactically? Put simply — it makes a bigger hole and hits harder. In fact, the beauty of the .338 Federal as a tactical choice, especially in a lightweight, accurate, and ultra-reliable platform like the Recon Tactical semi-automatic rifle isn't what it can do differently than the combat-proven .308 Winchester, but what it can do the same. You see, the .338 Federal uses the same magazine, and it uses the same parent case, primer and basic firearms configuration profile. The .338 Federal is nothing more than a .308 Winchester bulked up. Yet it's remained flexible and full of endurance.

Need a firearm for short- to medium-range sniping? The .338 Federal works

and it can hit harder than the .308 Winchester. Need a .308 with a bit more breeching presence? Boom — meet the far more robust .338 Federal and its bigger 200-plus-grain bullets. Here's some basic math based on factory loads to show you how similar yet slightly better the .338 Federal is when compared to the .308 Winchester at the distance of 500 yards. At 500 yards, a .308 Winchester shooting the 175-grain Sierra MatchKing gives us a 51.8-inch drop with 1,264 ft-lbs of energy going 1,803 fps. Now, add 25 more grains to the non-match 200-grain soft-point bullet of the Federal Power-Shok .338 Federal load and you get 52.2 inches of drop at 500 yards going a bit slower at 1,721 fps but hitter harder with 1,315 ft-lbs of energy.

Most people don't invest in a .338 Federal for long-range work, but in a pinch it certainly can do some damage at 500 yards. It only goes faster and hits harder the closer it is to the target coming from a rifle with the same size, weight, magazine, ergonomics and barrel profile as the all-world tactically proven

Like all AR-10 configurations, a Wilson Combat WC-10 rifle can be broken down into key parts for easy cleaning, storage and portability.

.308 Winchester. Ultimately, however, Wilson will remind any operator, hunter or target shooter that the biggest impact to the success or failure of a firearm isn't the cartridge. It's the operator and his or her skillset. "People always think caliber, but the first thing they need to think about is bullet selection and shot placement," Wilson said. "Can you get a bullet to do what you want it to do, and can you put it where it needs to be?" If the answer to these questions is as emphatic as the downrange energy of a .338 Federal 200-grain bullet, then things can end well for you.

Wilson Combat makes rifles that can be — and are — trusted daily with human lives at stake. Wilson makes them in the pesky AR-15 platform, and they make them in the bigger, stronger, more powerful AR-10 platform. Wilson Combat can build you a rifle chambered in .338 Federal for any situation you may face. If you need a reliable rifle that can accurately deliver bigger, heavier, more powerful bullets than your standard .308 Winchester, then I urge you to consider the .338 Federal in a Wilson Combat Recon Tactical. The rifle will work, it will be accurate, it will be light, and it will give you that little extra punch you might need some day to make sure you come home under your own power and not by that of six of your closest friends. **TGD**

Ballistics Table. .338 Federal/Wilson Combat Recon Tactical				
Manufacturer	Bullet	Muzzle Velocity (fps)	Muzzle Energy (ft-lbs)	Average 100-yd. Group (in.)
Federal Fusion MSR	185-gr. BRN	2,550	2,687	1.12
Federal Power-Shok	200-gr. SP	2,490	2,769	1.24
Federal American Eagle	185-gr. JSP	2,600	2,793	1.44
DoubleTap	200-gr. Scirocco II	2,360	2,609	1.11

(above) Bill Wilson was heavily involved in the development of the WC-10 rifles. He personally tested the guns for the best configuration, barrel twist rate and overall accuracy.

(below) The author used a Wilson Combat .338 Federal to harvest this Nilgai in Texas. Nilgai are robust animals weighing more than 500 pounds and can prove tough to kill. The .338 Federal was more than adequate for the task.

MOSSBERG 590 SHOCKWAVE

Mossberg's 590 Shockwave is a pump-action, close-quarters blaster.

BY **ROBERT SADOWSKI**

When Mossberg rolled out the 590 Shockwave in 2017, it created waves that continue to reverberate even today. But is it a shotgun or a pistol? You can bet that the ATF bureaucrats are scrutinizing that question. All I know is, the Shockwave offers 12-gauge power in a super small, compact package. Depending on whether you stoke it with shot or slugs, the Shockwave is an intense weapon. And it's perfectly legal, no NFA tax stamp required.

When hurricane Florence blew through the Carolinas in September 2018, puking feet of water in my neck of the woods, my family and I needed to evacuate, and fast. At the time, it was a Category 4 storm and we were in her bullseye. My bug-out bag was a simple and indiscrete gym duffel that held the 590 Shockwave along with boxes of birdshot, buckshot and slugs. I took Aguila Minishells in birdshot, buckshot, and slugs, and military-grade Winchester 2 3/4-inch shells in 00 buck. Not knowing what the storm would deal us, I knew that the power outages, dwindling gasoline supplies and lack of a warm shower and hot food

For a short-range defense weapon in cramped conditions like a vehicle, as a bug-out option, or for home defense, the 590 Shockwave offers compact and effective 12-gauge firepower.

Firing from the hip, the author braced the grip on his hip and pumped as fast as he could. Doing so, he easily maintained control using Aguila Minishells, and achieved good accuracy out to 10 yards.

can turn people ugly. Looters were a concern. The birdshot was for snakes. In knee-deep water, any living thing is looking to claim a high, dry spot. We needed to prepare for anything.

The Shockwave uses Mossberg's proven Model 590 action. Like all 590s, it is built to last and take a beating. The difference between the Shockwave and the rest of the Model 590 series of shotguns is obvious. The Shockwave comes from the factory with a heavy-walled 14-inch barrel and a Shockwave Technologies Raptor grip. It has an overall length of

26.5 inches and that is the reason why it has a 14-inch barrel. Because the 590 Shockwave is not capable of being shoulder-mounted and meets the overall length requirement of 26 inches, it is defined as a "firearm" under the Federal Gun Control Act (GCA).

It comes from the factory with the receiver fitted with a bird's head grip and fore-end strap, which is manufactured by Shockwave. The polymer grip has a fine texture. My personal Shockwave is an early model; current models come with a sling swivel post in the grip butt. The sling swivels make the Shockwave well-suited for carry on a one-point sling.

The controls are like any Model 590 shotgun. There is an easy-to-manipulate ambidextrous safety button located at the top-rear of the aluminum-alloy receiver. Regardless of whether you're a left- or right-handed shooter, your shooting hand thumb will fall directly on top of it. The action incorporates double-action bars so the slide pumps smoothly, and the polymer fore-end is coarsely ribbed to provide a good gripping surface. The strap is also very helpful, as the Shockwave can be a beast, producing significant recoil depending on the loads used. The nylon strap is attached to the fore-end to keep your hand in place when shooting. The heavy-wall barrel is like Mossberg military 590A1 models. It is a plain barrel with a brass bead for rough sighting. In use, the Shockwave is compact and highly maneuverable, but it does take some ramp-up time to shoot it proficiently.

At the range, I ran an assortment of Aguila 1 3/4- and Winchester 2 3/4-inch shells through the Shockwave. Still, I couldn't resist firing a few 3 inchers just to check that off my bucket list. Spoiler alert: Recoil was brutal with the 3-inch

shells. Magazine capacity is the same as a standard Model 590: With 2 3/4-inch shells, the capacity is 5+1 and 4+1 with 3 inchers.

I'd opt for the OPSol Texas Mini-Clip and pack it with Aguila 1 3/4-inch Minishells. With these, the capacity jumps to 8+1. Minishells produce mild recoil, but typically do not cycle in autoloading shotguns, which are designed to use shells with a minimum length of 2 3/4 inches. The OPSol Texas Mini-Clip (opsolmini-clip.com) is an aftermarket accessory that allows you to reliably cycle Aguila Minishells in all Mossberg 500, 590 and 590A1 models as well as Maverick 88 shotguns. The Mini-Clip costs $17 and is made of a flexible polymer that snaps into the loading port of the Shockwave receiver. Just push the Mini-Clip into the loading port so it's flush at the rear and bottom of the port, then rack the slide a few times to make sure it's secured in position (it can be quickly removed without tools). The Mini-Clip reduces the size of the loading port so a Minishell is perfectly positioned as it moves from the magazine tube to the elevator assembly. To remove the Mini-Clip, unload the shotgun, engage the safety and retract the slide. Use your thumb to push the Mini-Clip out through the ejection port. I like the ease of installing the Mini-Clip. If you run out of Minishells, just push the clip out and load 2 3/4-inch shotshells.

Shooting the Shockwave is a lot like shooting an AR pistol or a lever-action 'Mare's Leg. It feels awkward at first. You don't have the steady aim like with a typical shotgun, nor is it as small as a handgun. I could shoot it one-handed, but follow-up shots were slow since I needed two hands to cycle the action. With a two-hand hold and using the

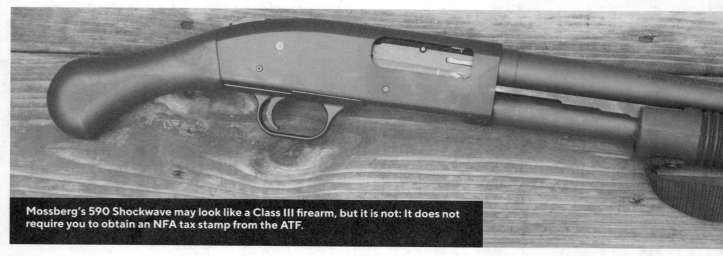

Mossberg's 590 Shockwave may look like a Class III firearm, but it is not: It does not require you to obtain an NFA tax stamp from the ATF.

(above) **The receiver is fitted with the Raptor "bird's head" grip from Shockwave Technologies.**

SPECIFICATIONS

MODEL: Mossberg 590 Shockwave

ACTION: Pump

CHAMBER SIZE: 3.5 in.

OVERALL LENGTH: 26.37 in.

CAPACITY: 5+1 (2 3/4-in.); 4+1 (3-in.); 8+1 (1 3/4 in.)

WEIGHT UNLOADED: 5.2 lbs.

WEIGHT LOADED: 6 lbs.

BARREL: 14 in. heavy wall, matte blued steel

RECEIVER: Matte blued steel

CHOKE: Cylinder bore

GRIP: Bird's head, textured polymer

FRONT SIGHT: Brass bead

TRIGGER PULL WEIGHT: 6 lbs.

SAFETY: Ambidextrous thumb

800-363-3555

mossberg.com

The strap is very helpful, as the Shockwave can be a beast, producing significant recoil depending on the loads used.

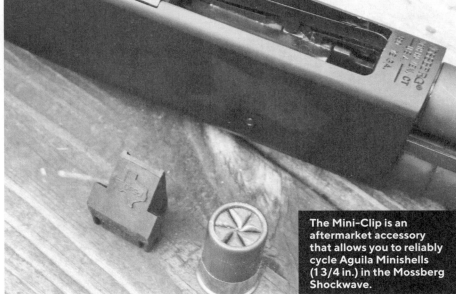

The Mini-Clip is an aftermarket accessory that allows you to reliably cycle Aguila Minishells (1 3/4 in.) in the Mossberg Shockwave.

brass bead to aim, I fired the Shockwave at eye level. This gave me the best accuracy. It is a close-quarter weapon for fast point shooting. I fired it from the hip and, with the grip tucked to the side of my chest, I could fire fast follow-up shots with good accuracy out to 10 yards. With my support hand secured in place by the strap, and firing hand on the grip, it cycled smoothly. The strap keeps your hand in place, especially with standard 2 3/4-inch military buckshot loads. By bracing the grip on my hip and pumping as fast as possible, I could easily maintain control using Minishells. I achieved good accuracy out to 10 yards.

At 10 yards the Shockwave patterned tightly, which was not what I expected from a 14-inch barrel and a cylinder-bore choke. Don't fool yourself into thinking the Shockwave is a hall sweeper. It will clear a hallway but is much more surgical in its approach. With Aguila buckshot Minishells I averaged a 10-inch pattern on an 18-inch-wide target. Recoil was mild with Minishells and more noticeable with 2 3/4-inch shells. Loaded with 2 3/4-inch Winchester military-grade buckshot, 10-yard patterns averaged a 4.5-inch spread. The 3-inch birdshot loads dished out brutal recoil and printed an 18-inch pattern. I also tested Aguila Minishell 7/8-ounce slugs using a rest and firing offhand. At 10 yards, my 3-shot groups averaged 4 inches. The Shockwave performed flawlessly with all ammo making it good to go right out of the box.

For a short-range defensive weapon in cramped conditions like a vehicle, as a bug-out option, or for home defense, the 590 Shockwave offers compact and effective 12-gauge firepower. **TGD**

Many manufacturers do not supply suggested retail prices. Others did not get their pricing to us before press time. All pricing can vary dependent on the exact brand and style of ammo selected and/or the retail outlet from which you make your purchase. Pricing has been rounded to the nearest dollar and represents our best estimate of average pricing.
An * after the cartridge means these loads are available with Nosler Partition or Swift A-Frame bullets. Listed pricing may or may not reflect this bullet type.
** = these are packed 50 to box, all others are 20 to box. Wea. Mag.= Weatherby Magnum. Spfd. = Springfield. A-Sq. = A-Square. N.E.=Nitro Express.

Cartridge	Bullet Wgt. Grs.	VELOCITY (fps)					ENERGY (ft. lbs.)					TRAJ. (in.)				Est. Price/box
		Muzzle	100 yds.	200 yds.	300 yds.	400 yds.	Muzzle	100 yds.	200 yds.	300 yds.	400 yds.	100 yds.	200 yds.	300 yds.	400 yds.	
17, 22																
17 Hornet	15.5	3860	2924	2159	1531	1108	513	294	160	81	42	1.4	0.0	-9.1	-33.7	NA
17 Hornet	20	3650	3078	2574	2122	1721	592	421	294	200	131	1.10	0.0	-6.4	-20.6	NA
17 Hornet	25	3375	2842	2367	1940	1567	632	448	311	209	136	1.4	0	24.8	56.3	NA
17 Remington Fireball	20	4000	3380	2840	2360	1930	710	507	358	247	165	1.6	1.5	-2.8	-13.5	NA
17 Remington Fireball	25	3850	3280	2780	2330	1925	823	597	429	301	206	0.9	0.0	-5.4	NA	NA
17 Remington	20	4200	3544	2978	2477	2029	783	558	394	272	183	0	-1.3	-6.6	-17.6	NA
17 Remington	25	4040	3284	2644	2086	1606	906	599	388	242	143	+2.0	+1.7	-4.0	-17.0	$17
4.6x30 H&K	30	2025	1662	1358	1135	1002	273	184	122	85	66	0	-12.7	-44.5	—	NA
4.6x30 H&K	40	1900	1569	1297	1104	988	320	218	149	108	86	0	-14.3	-39.3	—	NA
204 Ruger (Hor)	24	4400	3667	3046	2504	2023	1032	717	494	334	218	0.6	0	-4.3	-14.3	NA
204 Ruger (Fed)	32 Green	4030	3320	2710	2170	1710	1155	780	520	335	205	0.9	0.0	-5.7	-19.1	NA
204 Ruger	32	4125	3559	3061	2616	2212	1209	900	666	486	348	0	-1.3	-6.3	—	NA
204 Ruger	32	4225	3632	3114	2652	2234	1268	937	689	500	355	.6	0.0	-4.2	-13.4	NA
204 Ruger	40	3900	3451	3046	2677	2336	1351	1058	824	636	485	.7	0.0	-4.5	-13.9	NA
204 Ruger	45	3625	3188	2792	2428	2093	1313	1015	778	589	438	1.0	0.0	-5.5	-16.9	NA
5.45x39mm	60	2810	2495	2201	1927	1677	1052	829	645	445	374	1.0	0.0	-9.2	-27.7	NA
221 Fireball	40	3100	2510	1991	1547	1209	853	559	352	212	129	0	-4.1	-17.3	-45.1	NA
221 Fireball	50	2800	2137	1580	1180	988	870	507	277	155	109	+0.0	-7.0	-28.0	0.0	$14
22 Hornet (Fed)	30 Green	3150	2150	1390	990	830	660	310	130	65	45	0.0	-6.6	-32.7	NA	NA
22 Hornet	34	3050	2132	1415	1017	852	700	343	151	78	55	+0.0	-6.6	-15.5	-29.9	NA
22 Hornet	35	3100	2278	1601	1135	929	747	403	199	100	67	+2.75	0.0	-16.9	-60.4	NA
22 Hornet	40	2800	2397	2029	1698	1413	696	510	366	256	177	0	-4.6	-17.8	-43.1	NA
22 Hornet	45	2690	2042	1502	1128	948	723	417	225	127	90	+0.0	-7.7	-31.0	0.0	$27**
218 Bee	46	2760	2102	1550	1155	961	788	451	245	136	94	+0.0	-7.2	-29.0	0.0	$46**
222 Rem.	35	3760	3125	2574	2085	1656	1099	759	515	338	213	1.0	0.0	-6.3	-20.8	NA
222 Rem.	50	3345	2930	2553	2205	1886	1242	953	723	540	395	1.3	0	-6.7	-20.6	NA
222 Remington	40	3600	3117	2673	2269	1911	1151	863	634	457	324	+1.07	0.0	-6.13	-18.9	NA
222 Remington	50	3140	2602	2123	1700	1350	1094	752	500	321	202	+2.0	-0.4	-11.0	-33.0	$11
222 Remington	55	3020	2562	2147	1773	1451	1114	801	563	384	257	+2.0	-0.4	-11.0	-33.0	$12
222 Rem. Mag.	40	3600	3140	2726	2347	2000	1150	876	660	489	355	1.0	0	-5.7	-17.8	NA
222 Rem. Mag.	50	3340	2917	2533	2179	1855	1238	945	712	527	382	1.3	0	-6.8	-20.9	NA
222 Rem. Mag.	55	3240	2748	2305	1906	1556	1282	922	649	444	296	+2.0	-0.2	-9.0	-27.0	$14
22 PPC	52	3400	2930	2510	2130	NA	1335	990	730	525	NA	+2.0	1.4	-5.0	0.0	NA

Cartridge	Bullet Wgt. Grs.	VELOCITY (fps)					ENERGY (ft. lbs.)					TRAJ. (in.)				Est. Price/box
		Muzzle	100 yds.	200 yds.	300 yds.	400 yds.	Muzzle	100 yds.	200 yds.	300 yds.	400 yds.	100 yds.	200 yds.	300 yds.	400 yds.	
223 Rem.	35	3750	3206	2725	2291	1899	1092	799	577	408	280	1.0	0	-5.7	-18.1	NA
223 Rem.	35	4000	3353	2796	2302	1861	1243	874	607	412	269	0.8	0	-5.3	-17.3	NA
223 Rem.	64	2750	2368	2018	1701	1427	1074	796	578	411	289	2.4	0	-11	-34.1	NA
223 Rem.	75	2790	2562	2345	2139	1943	1296	1093	916	762	629	1.5	0	-8.2	-24.1	NA
223 Remington	40	3650	3010	2450	1950	1530	1185	805	535	340	265	+2.0	+1.0	-6.0	-22.0	$14
223 Remington	40	3800	3305	2845	2424	2044	1282	970	719	522	371	0.84	0.0	-5.34	-16.6	NA
223 Remington (Rem)	45 Green	3550	2911	2355	1865	1451	1259	847	554	347	210	2.5	2.3	-4.3	-21.1	NA
223 Remington	50	3300	2874	2484	2130	1809	1209	917	685	504	363	1.37	0.0	-7.05	-21.8	NA
223 Remington	52/53	3330	2882	2477	2106	1770	1305	978	722	522	369	+2.0	+0.6	-6.5	-21.5	$14
223 Remington (Win)	55 Green	3240	2747	2304	1905	1554	1282	921	648	443	295	1.9	0.0	-8.5	-26.7	NA
223 Remington	55	3240	2748	2305	1906	1556	1282	922	649	444	296	+2.0	-0.2	-9.0	-27.0	$12
223 Remington	60	3100	2712	2355	2026	1726	1280	979	739	547	397	+2.0	+0.2	-8.0	-24.7	$16
223 Remington	62	3000	2700	2410	2150	1900	1240	1000	800	635	495	1.60	0.0	-7.7	-22.8	NA
223 Remington	64	3020	2621	2256	1920	1619	1296	977	723	524	373	+2.0	-0.2	-9.3	-23.0	$14
223 Remington	69	3000	2720	2460	2210	1980	1380	1135	925	750	600	+2.0	+0.8	-5.8	-17.5	$15
223 Remington	75	2790	2554	2330	2119	1926	1296	1086	904	747	617	2.37	0.0	-8.75	-25.1	NA
223 Rem. Super Match	75	2930	2694	2470	2257	2055	1429	1209	1016	848	703	1.20	0.0	-6.9	-20.7	NA
223 Remington	77	2750	2584	2354	2169	1992	1293	1110	948	804	679	1.93	0.0	-8.2	-23.8	NA
223 WSSM	55	3850	3438	3064	2721	2402	1810	1444	1147	904	704	0.7	0.0	-4.4	-13.6	NA
223 WSSM	64	3600	3144	2732	2356	2011	1841	1404	1061	789	574	1.0	0.0	-5.7	-17.7	NA
5.56 NATO	55	3130	2740	2382	2051	1750	1196	917	693	514	372	1.1	0	-7.3	-23.0	NA
5.56 NATO	75	2910	2676	2543	2242	2041	1410	1192	1002	837	693	1.2	0	-7.0	-21.0	NA
224 Wea. Mag.	55	3650	3192	2780	2403	2057	1627	1244	943	705	516	+2.0	+1.2	-4.0	-17.0	$32
22 Nosler	55	3350	2965	2615	2286	1984	1370	1074	833	638	480	0	-2.5	-10.1	-24.4	
22 Nosler	77	2950	2672	2410	2163	1931	1488	1220	993	800	637	0	-3.4	-12.8	-29.7	
224 Valkyrie	90	2700	2542	2388	2241	2098	1457	1291	1140	1003	880	1.9	0	-8.1	-23.2	NA
224 Valkyrie	75	3000	2731	2477	2237	2010	1499	1242	1022	833	673	1.6	0	-7.3	-21.5	NA
224 Valkyrie	60	3300	2930	2589	2273	1797	1451	1144	893	688	522	1.3	0	-6.5	-19.8	NA
225 Winchester	55	3570	3066	2616	2208	1838	1556	1148	836	595	412	+2.0	+1.0	-5.0	-20.0	$19
22-250 Rem.	35	4450	3736	3128	2598	2125	1539	1085	761	524	351	6.5	-4.1		-13.4	NA
22-250 Rem.	40	4000	3320	2720	2200	1740	1420	980	660	430	265	+2.0	+1.8	-3.0	-16.0	$14
22-250 Rem.	40	4150	3553	3033	2570	2151	1530	1121	817	587	411	0.6	0	-4.4	-14.2	NA
22-250 Rem.	45 Green	4000	3293	2690	2159	1696	1598	1084	723	466	287	1.7	1.7	-3.2	-15.7	NA
22-250 Rem.	50	3725	3264	2641	2455	2103	1540	1183	896	669	491	0.89	0.0	-5.23	-16.3	NA
22-250 Rem.	52/55	3680	3137	2656	2222	1832	1654	1201	861	603	410	+2.0	+1.3	-4.0	-17.0	$13
22-250 Rem.	60	3600	3195	2826	2485	2169	1727	1360	1064	823	627	+2.0	+2.0	-2.4	-12.3	$19
22-250 Rem.	64	3425	2988	2591	2228	1897	1667	1269	954	705	511	1.2	0	-6.4	-20.0	NA

Cartridge	Bullet Wgt. Grs.	VELOCITY (fps)					ENERGY (ft. lbs.)					TRAJ. (in.)				Est. Price/box
		Muzzle	100 yds.	200 yds.	300 yds.	400 yds.	Muzzle	100 yds.	200 yds.	300 yds.	400 yds.	100 yds.	200 yds.	300 yds.	400 yds.	
220 Swift	40	4200	3678	3190	2739	2329	1566	1201	904	666	482	+0.51	0.0	-4.0	-12.9	NA
220 Swift	50	3780	3158	2617	2135	1710	1586	1107	760	506	325	+2.0	+1.4	-4.4	-17.9	$20
220 Swift	50	3850	3396	2970	2576	2215	1645	1280	979	736	545	0.74	0.0	-4.84	-15.1	NA
220 Swift	50	3900	3420	2990	2599	2240	1688	1298	992	750	557	0.7	0	-4.7	-14.5	NA
220 Swift	55	3800	3370	2990	2630	2310	1765	1390	1090	850	650	0.8	0.0	-4.7	-14.4	NA
220 Swift	55	3650	3194	2772	2384	2035	1627	1246	939	694	506	+2.0	+2.0	-2.6	-13.4	$19
220 Swift	60	3600	3199	2824	2475	2156	1727	1364	1063	816	619	+2.0	+1.6	-4.1	-13.1	$19
22 Savage H.P.	70	2868	2510	2179	1874	1600	1279	980	738	546	398	0	-4.1	-15.6	-37.1	NA
22 Savage H.P.	71	2790	2340	1930	1570	1280	1225	860	585	390	190	+2.0	-1.0	-10.4	-35.7	NA

6mm (24)

Cartridge	Bullet Wgt. Grs.	Muzzle	100 yds.	200 yds.	300 yds.	400 yds.	Muzzle	100 yds.	200 yds.	300 yds.	400 yds.	100 yds.	200 yds.	300 yds.	400 yds.	Est. Price/box
6mm BR Rem.	100	2550	2310	2083	1870	1671	1444	1185	963	776	620	+2.5	-0.6	-11.8	0.0	$22
6mm Norma BR	107	2822	2667	2517	2372	2229	1893	1690	1506	1337	1181	+1.73	0.0	-7.24	-20.6	NA
6mm Creedmoor	108	2786	2618	2456	2299	2149	1861	1643	1446	1267	1106	1.5	0	-6.6	-18.9	$26
6mm PPC	70	3140	2750	2400	2070	NA	1535	1175	895	665	NA	+2.0	+1.4	-5.0	0.0	NA
243 Winchester	55	4025	3597	3209	2853	2525	1978	1579	1257	994	779	+0.6	0.0	-4.0	-12.2	NA
243 Win.	58	3925	3465	3052	2676	2330	1984	1546	1200	922	699	0.7	0	-4.4	-13.8	NA
243 Winchester	60	3600	3110	2660	2260	1890	1725	1285	945	680	475	+2.0	+1.8	-3.3	-15.5	$17
243 Win.	70	3400	3020	2672	2350	2050	1797	1418	1110	858	653	0	-2.5	-9.7	—	NA
243 Winchester	70	3400	3040	2700	2390	2100	1795	1435	1135	890	685	1.1	0.0	-5.9	-18.0	NA
243 Winchester	75/80	3350	2955	2593	2259	1951	1993	1551	1194	906	676	+2.0	+0.9	-5.0	-19.0	$16
243 Win.	80	3425	3081	2763	2468	2190	2984	1686	1357	1082	852	1.1	0	-5.7	-17.1	NA
243 Win.	87	2800	2574	2359	2155	1961	1514	1280	1075	897	743	1.9	0	-8.1	-23.8	NA
243 Win.	95	3185	2908	2649	2404	2172	2140	1784	1480	1219	995	1.3	0	-6.3	-18.6	NA
243 W. Superformance	80	3425	3080	2760	2463	2184	2083	1684	1353	1077	847	1.1	0.0	-5.7	-17.1	NA
243 Winchester	85	3320	3070	2830	2600	2380	2080	1770	1510	1280	1070	+2.0	+1.2	-4.0	-14.0	$18
243 Winchester	90	3120	2871	2635	2411	2199	1946	1647	1388	1162	966	1.4	0.0	-6.4	-18.8	NA
243 Winchester*	100	2960	2697	2449	2215	1993	1945	1615	1332	1089	882	+2.5	+1.2	-6.0	-20.0	$16
243 Winchester	105	2920	2689	2470	2261	2062	1988	1686	1422	1192	992	+2.5	+1.6	-5.0	-18.4	$21
243 Light Mag.	100	3100	2839	2592	2358	2138	2133	1790	1491	1235	1014	+1.5	0.0	-6.8	-19.8	NA
243 WSSM	55	4060	3628	3237	2880	2550	2013	1607	1280	1013	794	0.6	0.0	-3.9	-12.0	NA
243 WSSM	95	3250	3000	2763	2538	2325	2258	1898	1610	1359	1140	1.2	0.0	-5.7	-16.9	NA
243 WSSM	100	3110	2838	2583	2341	2112	2147	1789	1481	1217	991	1.4	0.0	-6.6	-19.7	NA
6mm Remington	80	3470	3064	2694	2352	2036	2139	1667	1289	982	736	+2.0	+1.1	-5.0	-17.0	$16
6mm R. Superformance	95	3235	2955	2692	2443	3309	2207	1841	1528	1259	1028	1.2	0.0	-6.1	-18.0	NA
6mm Remington	100	3100	2829	2573	2332	2104	2133	1777	1470	1207	983	+2.5	+1.6	-5.0	-17.0	$16
6mm Remington	105	3060	2822	2596	2381	2177	2105	1788	1512	1270	1059	+2.5	+1.1	-3.3	-15.0	$21
240 Wea. Mag.	87	3500	3202	2924	2663	2416	2366	1980	1651	1370	1127	+2.0	+2.0	-2.0	-12.0	$32

Cartridge	Bullet Wgt. Grs.	VELOCITY (fps)					ENERGY (ft. lbs.)					TRAJ. (in.)				Est. Price/box
		Muzzle	100 yds.	200 yds.	300 yds.	400 yds.	Muzzle	100 yds.	200 yds.	300 yds.	400 yds.	100 yds.	200 yds.	300 yds.	400 yds.	
240 Wea. Mag.	100	3150	2894	2653	2425	2207	2202	1860	1563	1395	1082	1.3	0	-6.3	-18.5	NA
240 Wea. Mag.	100	3395	3106	2835	2581	2339	2559	2142	1785	1478	1215	+2.5	+2.8	-2.0	-11.0	$43
25-20 Win.	86	1460	1194	1030	931	858	407	272	203	165	141	0.0	-23.5	0.0	0.0	$32**
25-45 Sharps	87	3000	2677	2385	2112	1859	1739	1384	1099	862	668	1.1	0	-7.4	-22.6	$25
25-35 Win.	117	2230	1866	1545	1282	1097	1292	904	620	427	313	+2.5	-4.2	-26.0	0.0	$24
250 Savage	100	2820	2504	2210	1936	1684	1765	1392	1084	832	630	+2.5	+0.4	-9.0	-28.0	$17
257 Roberts	100	2980	2661	2363	2085	1827	1972	1572	1240	965	741	+2.5	-0.8	-5.2	-21.6	$20
257 Roberts	122	2600	2331	2078	1842	1625	1831	1472	1169	919	715	+2.5	0.0	-10.6	-31.4	$21
257 Roberts+P	100	3000	2758	2529	2312	2105	1998	1689	1421	1187	984	1.5	0	-7.0	-20.5	NA
257 Roberts+P	117	2780	2411	2071	1761	1488	2009	1511	1115	806	576	+2.5	-0.2	-10.2	-32.6	$18
257 Roberts+P	120	2780	2560	2360	2160	1970	2060	17 50	1480	1240	1030	+2.5	+1.2	-6.4	-23.6	$22
257 R. Superformance	117	2946	2705	2478	2265	2057	2253	1901	1595	1329	1099	1.1	0.0	-5.7	-17.1	NA
25-06 Rem.	87	3440	2995	2591	2222	1884	2286	1733	1297	954	686	+2.0	+1.1	-2.5	-14.4	$17
25-06 Rem.	90	3350	3001	2679	2378	2098	2243	1790	1434	1130	879	1.2	0	-6.0	-18.3	NA
25-06 Rem.	90	3440	3043	2680	2344	2034	2364	1850	1435	1098	827	+2.0	+1.8	-3.3	-15.6	$17
25-06 Rem.	100	3230	2893	2580	2287	2014	2316	1858	1478	1161	901	+2.0	+0.8	-5.7	-18.9	$17
25-06 Rem.	117	2990	2770	2570	2370	2190	2320	2000	1715	1465	1246	+2.5	+1.0	-7.9	-26.6	$19
25-06 Rem.*	120	2990	2730	2484	2252	2032	2382	1985	1644	1351	1100	+2.5	+1.2	-5.3	-19.6	$17
25-06 Rem.	122	2930	2706	2492	2289	2095	2325	1983	1683	1419	1189	+2.5	+1.8	-4.5	-17.5	$23
25-06 R. Superformance	117	3110	2861	2626	2403	2191	2512	2127	1792	1500	1246	1.4	0.0	-6.4	-18.9	NA
25 WSSM	85	3470	3156	2863	2589	2331	2273	1880	1548	1266	1026	1.0	0.0	-5.2	-15.7	NA
25 WSSM	115	3060	2844	2639	2442	2254	2392	2066	1778	1523	1398	1.4	0.0	-6.4	-18.6	NA
25 WSSM	120	2990	2717	2459	2216	1987	2383	1967	1612	1309	1053	1.6	0.0	-7.4	-21.8	NA
257 Wea. Mag.	87	3825	3456	3118	2805	2513	2826	2308	1870	1520	1220	+2.0	+2.7	-0.3	-7.6	$32
257 Wea. Mag.	90	3550	3184	2848	2537	2246	2518	2026	1621	1286	1008	1.0	0	-5.3	-16.0	NA
257 Wea. Mag.	100	3555	3237	2941	2665	2404	2806	2326	1920	1576	1283	+2.5	+3.2	0.0	-8.0	$32
257 Wea. Mag.	110	3330	3069	2823	2591	2370	2708	2300	1947	1639	1372	1.1	0	-5.5	-16.1	NA
257 Scramjet	100	3745	3450	3173	2912	2666	3114	2643	2235	1883	1578	+2.1	+2.77	0.0	-6.93	NA

6.5

Cartridge	Bullet Wgt. Grs.	VELOCITY (fps)					ENERGY (ft. lbs.)					TRAJ. (in.)				Est. Price/box
		Muzzle	100 yds.	200 yds.	300 yds.	400 yds.	Muzzle	100 yds.	200 yds.	300 yds.	400 yds.	100 yds.	200 yds.	300 yds.	400 yds.	
6.5 Grendel	123	2590	2420	2256	2099	1948	1832	1599	1390	1203	1037	1.8	0	-8.6	-25.1	NA
6.5x47 Lapua	123	2887	NA	2554	NA	2244	2285	NA	1788	NA	1380	NA	4.53	0.0	-10.7	NA
6.5x50mm Jap.	139	2360	2160	1970	1790	1620	1720	1440	1195	985	810	+2.5	-1.0	-13.5	0.0	NA
6.5x50mm Jap.	156	2070	1830	1610	1430	1260	1475	1155	900	695	550	+2.5	-4.0	-23.8	0.0	NA
6.5x52mm Car.	139	2580	2360	2160	1970	1790	2045	1725	1440	1195	985	+2.5	0.0	-9.9	-29.0	NA
6.5x52mm Car.	156	2430	2170	1930	1700	1500	2045	1630	1285	1005	780	+2.5	-1.0	-13.9	0.0	NA
6.5x52mm Carcano	160	2250	1963	1700	1467	1271	1798	1369	1027	764	574	+3.8	0.0	-15.9	-48.1	NA
6.5x55mm Swe.	93	2625	2350	2090	1850	1630	1425	1140	905	705	550	2.4	0.0	-10.3	-31.1	NA

Cartridge	Bullet Wgt. Grs.	VELOCITY (fps)					ENERGY (ft. lbs.)					TRAJ. (in.)				Est. Price/box
		Muzzle	100 yds.	200 yds.	300 yds.	400 yds.	Muzzle	100 yds.	200 yds.	300 yds.	400 yds.	100 yds.	200 yds.	300 yds.	400 yds.	
6.5x55mm Swe.	123	2750	2570	2400	2240	2080	2065	1810	1580	1370	1185	1.9	0.0	-7.9	-22.9	NA
6.5x55mm Swe.*	139/140	2850	2640	2440	2250	2070	2525	2170	1855	1575	1330	+2.5	+1.6	-5.4	-18.9	$18
6.5x55mm Swe.	140	2550	NA	NA	NA	NA	2020	NA	NA	NA	NA	0.0	0.0	0.0	0.0	$18
6.5x55mm Swe.	140	2735	2563	2397	2237	2084	2325	2041	1786	1556	1350	1.9	0	-8.0	-22.9	NA
6.5x55mm Swe.	156	2650	2370	2110	1870	1650	2425	1950	1550	1215	945	+2.5	0.0	-10.3	-30.6	NA
260 Rem.	100	3200	2917	2652	2402	2165	2273	1889	1561	1281	1041	1.3	0	-6.3	-18.6	NA
260 Rem.	130	2800	2613	2433	2261	2096	2262	1970	1709	1476	1268	1.8	0	-7.7	-22.2	NA
260 Remington	125	2875	2669	2473	2285	2105	2294	1977	1697	1449	1230	1.71	0.0	-7.4	-21.4	NA
260 Remington	140	2750	2544	2347	2158	1979	2351	2011	1712	1448	1217	+2.2	0.0	-8.6	-24.6	NA
6.5 Creedmoor	120	3020	2815	2619	2430	2251	2430	2111	1827	1574	1350	1.4	0.0	-6.5	-18.9	NA
6.5 Creedmoor	120	3050	2850	2659	2476	2300	2479	2164	1884	1634	1310	1.4	0	-6.3	-18.3	NA
6.5 Creedmoor	140	2550	2380	2217	2060	1910	2021	1761	1527	1319	1134	2.3	0	-9.4	-27.0	NA
6.5 Creedmoor	140	2710	2557	2410	2267	2129	2283	2033	1805	1598	1410	1.9	0	-7.9	-22.6	NA
6.5 Creedmoor	140	2820	2654	2494	2339	2190	2472	2179	1915	1679	1467	1.7	0.0	-7.2	-20.6	NA
6.5 C. Superformance	129	2950	2756	2570	2392	2221	2492	2175	1892	1639	1417	1.5	0.0	-6.8	-19.7	NA
6.5x52R	117	2208	1856	1544	1287	1104	1267	895	620	431	317	0	-8.7	-32.2	—	NA
6.5x57	131	2543	2295	2060	1841	1638	1882	1532	1235	986	780	0	-5.1	-18.5	-42.1	NA
6.5 PRC	143	2960	2808	2661	2519	2381	2782	2503	2248	2014	1800	1.5	0	-6.4	-18.2	NA
6.5 PRC	147	2910	2775	2645	2518	2395	2764	2514	2281	2069	1871	1.5	0	-6.5	-18.4	NA
6.5-284 Norma	142	3025	2890	2758	2631	2507	2886	2634	2400	2183	1982	1.13	0.0	-5.7	-16.4	NA
6.5-284 Norma	156	2790	2531	2287	2056	-	2697	2220	1812	1465	-	1.9	0	-8.6	-	NA
6.71 (264) Phantom	120	3150	2929	2718	2517	2325	2645	2286	1969	1698	1440	+1.3	0.0	-6.0	-17.5	NA
6.5 Rem. Mag.	120	3210	2905	2621	2353	2102	2745	2248	1830	1475	1177	+2.5	+1.7	-4.1	-16.3	Disc.
264 Win. Mag.	100	3400	3104	2828	2568	2322	2566	2139	1775	1464	1197	1.1	0	-5.4	-16.1	NA
264 Win. Mag.	125	3200	2978	2767	2566	2373	2841	2461	2125	1827	1563	1.2	0	-5.8	-16.8	NA
264 Win. Mag.	130	3100	2900	2709	2526	2350	2773	2427	2118	1841	1594	1.3	0	-6.1	-17.6	NA
264 Win. Mag.	140	3030	2782	2548	2326	2114	2854	2406	2018	1682	1389	+2.5	+1.4	-5.1	-18.0	$24
6.5 Nosler	129	3400	3213	3035	2863	2698	3310	2957	2638	2348	2085	0.9	0	-4.7	-13.6	NA
6.5 Nosler	140	3300	3118	2943	2775	2613	3119	2784	2481	2205	1955	1.0	0	-5.0	-14.6	NA
6.71 (264) Blackbird	140	3480	3261	3053	2855	2665	3766	3307	2899	2534	2208	+2.4	+3.1	0.0	-7.4	NA
6.5-300 Weatherby Magnum	127	3531	3309	3099	2898	2706	-	3088	2707	2368	2065	0	-1.68	-6.98	-16.43	NA
6.5-300 Weatherby Magnum	130	3476	3267	3084	2901	2726	-	3097	2746	2430	2145	0	-1.74	-7.14	-16.68	NA
6.5-300 Weatherby Magnum	140	3395	3122	2866	2624	2394	-	3030	2552	2139	1781	0	-2.04	-8.24	-19.36	NA
6.8 REM SPC	90	2840	2444	2083	1756	1469	1611	1194	867	616	431	2.2	0	-3.9	-32.0	NA
6.8 REM SPC	110	2570	2338	2118	1910	1716	1613	1335	1095	891	719	2.4	0.0	-6.3	-20.8	NA
6.8 REM SPC	120	2460	2250	2051	1863	1687	1612	1349	1121	925	758	2.3	0	-10.5	-31.1	NA
6.8mm Rem.	115	2775	2472	2190	1926	1683	1966	1561	1224	947	723	+2.1	0.0	-3.7	-9.4	NA

Cartridge	Bullet Wgt. Grs.	VELOCITY (fps)					ENERGY (ft. lbs.)					TRAJ. (in.)				Est. Price/box
		Muzzle	100 yds.	200 yds.	300 yds.	400 yds.	Muzzle	100 yds.	200 yds.	300 yds.	400 yds.	100 yds.	200 yds.	300 yds.	400 yds.	
27																
270 Win. (Rem.)	115	2710	2482	2265	2059	NA	1875	1485	1161	896	NA	0.0	4.8	-17.3	0.0	NA
270 Win.	120	2675	2288	1935	1619	1351	1907	1395	998	699	486	2.6	0	-12.0	-37.4	NA
270 Win.	140	2940	2747	2563	2386	2216	2687	2346	2042	1770	1526	1.8	0	-6.8	-19.8	NA
270 Win. Supreme	130	3150	2881	2628	2388	2161	2865	2396	1993	1646	1348	1.3	0.0	-6.4	-18.9	NA
270 Win. Supreme	150	2930	2693	2468	2254	2051	2860	2416	2030	1693	1402	1.7	0.0	-7.4	-21.6	NA
270 W. Superformance	130	3200	2984	2788	2582	2393	2955	2570	2228	1924	1653	1.2	0.0	-5.7	-16.7	NA
270 Winchester	100	3430	3021	2649	2305	1988	2612	2027	1557	1179	877	+2.0	+1.0	-4.9	-17.5	$17
270 Winchester	130	3060	2776	2510	2259	2022	2702	2225	1818	1472	1180	+2.5	+1.4	-5.3	-18.2	$17
270 Winchester	135	3000	2780	2570	2369	2178	2697	2315	1979	1682	1421	+2.5	+1.4	-6.0	-17.6	$23
270 Winchester*	140	2940	2700	2480	2260	2060	2685	2270	1905	1590	1315	+2.5	+1.8	-4.6	-17.9	$20
270 Winchester*	150	2850	2585	2336	2100	1879	2705	2226	1817	1468	1175	+2.5	+1.2	-6.5	-22.0	$17
270 WSM	130	3275	3041	2820	2609	2408	3096	2669	2295	1564	1673	1.1	0.0	-5.5	-16.1	NA
270 WSM	140	3125	2865	2619	2386	2165	3035	2559	2132	1769	1457	1.4	0.0	-6.5	-19.0	NA
270 WSM	150	3000	2795	2599	2412	2232	2997	2601	2250	1937	1659	1.5	0	-6.6	-19.2	NA
270 WSM	150	3120	2923	2734	2554	2380	3242	2845	2490	2172	1886	1.3	0.0	-5.9	-17.2	NA
270 Wea. Mag.	100	3760	3380	3033	2712	2412	3139	2537	2042	1633	1292	+2.0	+2.4	-1.2	-10.1	$32
270 Wea. Mag.	130	3375	3119	2878	2649	2432	3287	2808	2390	2026	1707	+2.5	-2.9	-0.9	-9.9	$32
270 Wea. Mag.	130	3450	3194	2958	2732	2517	3435	2949	2525	2143	1828	1.0	0	-4.9	-14.5	NA
270 Wea. Mag.*	150	3245	3036	2837	2647	2465	3507	3070	2681	2334	2023	+2.5	+2.6	-1.8	-11.4	$47
7mm																
7mm BR	140	2216	2012	1821	1643	1481	1525	1259	1031	839	681	+2.0	-3.7	-20.0	0.0	$23
275 Rigby	140	2680	2455	2242	2040	1848	2233	1874	1563	1292	1062	2.2	0	-9.1	-26.5	NA
7mm Mauser*	139/140	2660	2435	2221	2018	1827	2199	1843	1533	1266	1037	+2.5	0.0	-9.6	-27.7	$17
7mm Mauser	139	2740	2556	2379	2209	2046	2317	2016	1747	1506	1292	1.9	0	-8.1	-23.3	NA
7mm Mauser	154	2690	2490	2300	2120	1940	2475	2120	1810	1530	1285	+2.5	+0.8	-7.5	-23.5	$17
7mm Mauser	175	2440	2137	1857	1603	1382	2313	1774	1340	998	742	+2.5	-1.7	-16.1	0.0	$17
7x30 Waters	120	2700	2300	1930	1600	1330	1940	1405	990	685	470	+2.5	-0.2	-12.3	0.0	$18
7mm-08 Rem.	120	2675	2435	2207	1992	1790	1907	1579	1298	1057	854	2.2	0	-9.4	-27.5	NA
7mm-08 Rem.	120	3000	2725	2467	2223	1992	2398	1979	1621	1316	1058	+2.0	0.0	-7.6	-22.3	$18
7mm-08 Rem.	139	2840	2608	2387	2177	1978	2489	2098	1758	1463	1207	1.8	0	-7.9	-23.2	NA
7mm-08 Rem.*	140	2860	2625	2402	2189	1988	2542	2142	1793	1490	1228	+2.5	+0.8	-6.9	-21.9	$18
7mm-08 Rem.	154	2715	2510	2315	2128	1950	2520	2155	1832	1548	1300	+2.5	+1.0	-7.0	-22.7	$23
7-08 R. Superformance	139	2950	2857	2571	2393	2222	2686	2345	2040	1768	1524	1.5	0.0	-6.8	-19.7	NA
7x64mm	173	2526	2260	2010	1777	1565	2452	1962	1552	1214	941	0	-5.3	-19.3	-44.4	NA
7x64mm Bren.	140	2950	2710	2483	2266	2061	2705	2283	1910	1597	1320	1.5	0.0	-2.9	-7.3	$24.50
7x64mm Bren.	154	2820	2610	2420	2230	2050	2720	2335	1995	1695	1430	+2.5	+1.4	-5.7	-19.9	NA

Cartridge	Bullet Wgt. Grs.	VELOCITY (fps)					ENERGY (ft. lbs.)					TRAJ. (in.)				Est. Price/box
		Muzzle	100 yds.	200 yds.	300 yds.	400 yds.	Muzzle	100 yds.	200 yds.	300 yds.	400 yds.	100 yds.	200 yds.	300 yds.	400 yds.	
7x64mm Bren.*	160	2850	2669	2495	2327	2166	2885	2530	2211	1924	1667	+2.5	+1.6	-4.8	-17.8	$24
7x64mm Bren.	175	2650	2445	2248	2061	1883	2728	2322	1964	1650	1378	2.2	0	-9.1	-26.4	$24.50
7x65mmR	173	2608	2337	2082	1844	1626	2613	2098	1666	1307	1015	0	-4.9	-17.9	-41.9	NA
275 Rigby	139	2680	2456	2242	2040	1848	2217	1861	1552	1284	1054	2.2	0	-9.1	-26.5	NA
284 Winchester	150	2860	2595	2344	2108	1886	2724	2243	1830	1480	1185	+2.5	+0.8	-7.3	-23.2	$24
280 R. Superformance	139	3090	2890	2699	2516	2341	2946	2578	2249	1954	1691	1.3	0.0	-6.1	-17.7	NA
280 Rem.	139	3090	2891	2700	2518	2343	2947	2579	2250	1957	1694	1.3	0	-6.1	-17.7	NA
280 Remington	140	3000	2758	2528	2309	2102	2797	2363	1986	1657	1373	+2.5	+1.4	-5.2	-18.3	$17
280 Remington*	150	2890	2624	2373	2135	1912	2781	2293	1875	1518	1217	+2.5	+0.8	-7.1	-22.6	$17
280 Remington	160	2840	2637	2442	2556	2078	2866	2471	2120	1809	1535	+2.5	+0.8	-6.7	-21.0	$20
280 Remington	165	2820	2510	2220	1950	1701	2913	2308	1805	1393	1060	+2.5	+0.4	-8.8	-26.5	$17
280 Ack. Imp.	140	3150	2946	2752	2566	2387	3084	2698	2354	2047	1772	1.3	0	-5.8	-17.0	NA
280 Ack. Imp.	150	2900	2712	2533	2360	2194	2800	2450	2136	1855	1603	1.6	0	-7.0	-20.3	NA
280 Ack. Imp.	160	2950	2751	2561	2379	2205	3091	2686	2331	2011	1727	1.5	0	-6.9	-19.9	NA
7x61mm S&H Sup.	154	3060	2720	2400	2100	1820	3200	2520	1965	1505	1135	+2.5	+1.8	-5.0	-19.8	NA
7mm Dakota	160	3200	3001	2811	2630	2455	3637	3200	2808	2456	2140	+2.1	+1.9	-2.8	-12.5	NA
7mm Rem. Mag.	139	3190	2986	2791	2605	2427	3141	2752	2405	2095	1817	1.2	0	-5.7	-16.5	NA
7mm Rem. Mag. (Rem.)	140	2710	2482	2265	2059	NA	2283	1915	1595	1318	NA	0.0	-4.5	-1.57	0.0	NA
7mm Rem. Mag.*	139/140	3150	2930	2710	2510	2320	3085	2660	2290	1960	1670	+2.5	+2.4	-2.4	-12.7	$21
7mm Rem. Mag.	150/154	3110	2830	2568	2320	2085	3221	2667	2196	1792	1448	+2.5	+1.6	-4.6	-16.5	$21
7mm Rem. Mag.*	160/162	2950	2730	2520	2320	2120	3090	2650	2250	1910	1600	+2.5	+1.8	-4.4	-17.8	$34
7mm Rem. Mag.	165	2900	2699	2507	2324	2147	3081	2669	2303	1978	1689	+2.5	+1.2	-5.9	-19.0	$28
7mm Rem Mag.	175	2860	2645	2440	2244	2057	3178	2718	2313	1956	1644	+2.5	+1.0	-6.5	-20.7	$21
7 R.M. Superformance	139	3240	3033	2836	2648	2467	3239	2839	2482	2163	1877	1.1	0.0	-5.5	-15.9	NA
7 R.M. Superformance	154	3100	2914	2736	2565	2401	3286	2904	2560	2250	1970	1.3	0.0	-5.9	-17.2	NA
7mm Rem. SA ULTRA MAG	140	3175	2934	2707	2490	2283	3033	2676	2277	1927	1620	1.3	0.0	-6	-17.7	NA
7mm Rem. SA ULTRA MAG	150	3110	2828	2563	2313	2077	3221	2663	2188	1782	1437	2.5	2.1	-3.6	-15.8	NA
7mm Rem. SA ULTRA MAG	160	2850	2676	2508	2347	2192	2885	2543	2235	1957	1706	1.7	0	-7.2	-20.7	NA
7mm Rem. SA ULTRA MAG	160	2960	2762	2572	2390	2215	3112	2709	2350	2029	1743	2.6	2.2	-3.6	-15.4	NA
7mm WSM	140	3225	3008	2801	2603	2414	3233	2812	2438	2106	1812	1.2	0.0	-5.6	-16.4	NA
7mm WSM	160	2990	2744	2512	2081	1883	3176	2675	2241	1864	1538	1.6	0.0	-7.1	-20.8	NA
7mm Wea. Mag.	139	3300	3091	2891	2701	2519	3361	2948	2580	2252	1958	1.1	0	-5.2	-15.2	NA
7mm Wea. Mag.	140	3225	2970	2729	2501	2283	3233	2741	2315	1943	1621	+2.5	+2.0	-3.2	-14.0	$35
7mm Wea. Mag.	140	3340	3127	2925	2732	2546	3467	3040	2659	2320	2016	0	-2.1	-8.2	-19	NA
7mm Wea. Mag.	150	3175	2957	2751	2553	2364	3357	2913	2520	2171	1861	0	-2.5	-9.6	-22	NA
7mm Wea. Mag.	154	3260	3023	2799	2586	2382	3539	3044	2609	2227	1890	+2.5	+2.8	-1.5	-10.8	$32
7mm Wea. Mag.*	160	3200	3004	2816	2637	2464	3637	3205	2817	2469	2156	+2.5	+2.7	-1.5	-10.6	$47

Cartridge	Bullet Wgt. Grs.	VELOCITY (fps)					ENERGY (ft. lbs.)					TRAJ. (in.)				Est. Price/box
		Muzzle	100 yds.	200 yds.	300 yds.	400 yds.	Muzzle	100 yds.	200 yds.	300 yds.	400 yds.	100 yds.	200 yds.	300 yds.	400 yds.	
7mm Wea. Mag.	165	2950	2747	2553	2367	2189	3188	2765	2388	2053	1756	+2.5	+1.8	-4.2	-16.4	$43
7mm Wea. Mag.	175	2910	2693	2486	2288	2098	3293	2818	2401	2033	1711	+2.5	+1.2	-5.9	-19.4	$35
7.21(.284) Tomahawk	140	3300	3118	2943	2774	2612	3386	3022	2693	2393	2122	2.3	3.2	0.0	-7.7	NA
7mm STW	140	3300	3086	2889	2697	2513	3384	2966	2594	2261	1963	0	-2.1	-8.5	-19.6	NA
7mm STW	140	3325	3064	2818	2585	2364	3436	2918	2468	2077	1737	+2.3	+1.8	-3.0	-13.1	NA
7mm STW	150	3175	2957	2751	2553	2364	3357	2913	2520	2171	1861	0	-2.5	-9.6	-22	NA
7mm STW	175	2900	2760	2625	2493	2366	3267	2960	2677	2416	2175	0	-3.1	-11.2	-24.9	NA
7mm STW Supreme	160	3150	2894	2652	2422	2204	3526	2976	2499	2085	1727	1.3	0.0	-6.3	-18.5	NA
7mm Rem. Ultra Mag.	140	3425	3184	2956	2740	2534	3646	3151	2715	2333	1995	1.7	1.6	-2.6	-11.4	NA
7mm Rem. Ultra Mag.	160	3225	3035	2854	2680	2512	3694	3273	2894	2551	2242	0	-2.3	-8.8	-20.2	NA
7mm Rem. Ultra Mag.	174	3040	2896	2756	2621	2490	3590	3258	2952	2669	2409	0	-2.6	-9.9	-22.2	NA
7mm Firehawk	140	3625	3373	3135	2909	2695	4084	3536	3054	2631	2258	+2.2	+2.9	0.0	-7.03	NA
7.21 (.284) Firebird	140	3750	3522	3306	3101	2905	4372	3857	3399	2990	2625	1.6	2.4	0.0	-6.0	NA
.28 Nosler	160	3300	3114	2930	2753	2583	3883	3444	3049	2693	2371	1.1	0	-5.1	-14.9	$78

30

Cartridge	Bullet Wgt. Grs.	VELOCITY (fps)					ENERGY (ft. lbs.)					TRAJ. (in.)				Est. Price/box
		Muzzle	100 yds.	200 yds.	300 yds.	400 yds.	Muzzle	100 yds.	200 yds.	300 yds.	400 yds.	100 yds.	200 yds.	300 yds.	400 yds.	
300 ACC Blackout	110	2150	1886	1646	1432	1254	1128	869	661	501	384	0	-8.3	-29.6	-67.8	NA
300 AAC Blackout	125	2250	2031	1826	1636	1464	1404	1145	926	743	595	0	-7	-24.4	-54.8	NA
300 AAC Blackout	220	1000	968	-	-	-	488	457	-	-	-	0	-	-	-	-
30 Carbine	110	1990	1567	1236	1035	923	977	600	373	262	208	0.0	-13.5	0.0	0.0	$28**
30 Carbine	110	2000	1601	1279	1067	—	977	626	399	278	—	0	-12.9	-47.2	—	NA
300 Whisper	110	2375	2094	1834	1597	NA	1378	1071	822	623	NA	3.2	0.0	-13.6	NA	NA
300 Whisper	208	1020	988	959	NA	NA	480	451	422	NA	NA	0.0	-34.10	NA	NA	NA
303 Savage	190	1890	1612	1327	1183	1055	1507	1096	794	591	469	+2.5	-7.6	0.0	0.0	$24
30 Remington	170	2120	1822	1555	1328	1153	1696	1253	913	666	502	+2.5	-4.7	-26.3	0.0	$20
7.62x39mm Rus.	123	2360	2049	1764	1511	1296	1521	1147	850	623	459	3.4	0	-14.7	-44.7	NA
7.62x39mm Rus.	123/125	2300	2030	1780	1550	1350	1445	1125	860	655	500	+2.5	-2.0	-17.5	0.0	$13
30-30 Win.	55	3400	2693	2085	1570	1187	1412	886	521	301	172	+2.0	0.0	-10.2	-35.0	$18
30-30 Win.	125	2570	2090	1660	1320	1080	1830	1210	770	480	320	-2.0	-2.6	-19.9	0.0	$13
30-30 Win.	140	2500	2198	1918	1662	—	1943	1501	1143	858	—	2.9	0	-12.4	—	NA
30-30 Win.	150	2390	2040	1723	1447	1225	1902	1386	989	697	499	0.0	-7.5	-27.0	-63.0	NA
30-30 Win. Supreme	150	2480	2095	1747	1446	1209	2049	1462	1017	697	487	0.0	-6.5	-24.5	0.0	NA
30-30 Win.	160	2300	1997	1719	1473	1268	1879	1416	1050	771	571	+2.5	-2.9	-20.2	0.0	$18
30-30 Win. Lever Evolution	160	2400	2150	1916	1699	NA	2046	1643	1304	1025	NA	3.0	0.2	-12.1	NA	NA
30-30 PMC Cowboy	170	1300	1198	1121	—	—	638	474	—	—	—	0.0	-27.0	0.0	0.0	NA
30-30 Win.*	170	2200	1895	1619	1381	1191	1827	1355	989	720	535	+2.5	-5.8	-23.6	0.0	$13
300 Savage	150	2630	2354	2094	1853	1631	2303	1845	1462	1143	886	+2.5	-0.4	-10.1	-30.7	$17
300 Savage	150	2740	2499	2272	2056	1852	2500	2081	1718	1407	1143	2.1	0	-8.8	-25.8	NA

Cartridge	Bullet Wgt. Grs.	VELOCITY (fps)					ENERGY (ft. lbs.)					TRAJ. (in.)				Est. Price/box
		Muzzle	100 yds.	200 yds.	300 yds.	400 yds.	Muzzle	100 yds.	200 yds.	300 yds.	400 yds.	100 yds.	200 yds.	300 yds.	400 yds.	
300 Savage	180	2350	2137	1935	1754	1570	2207	1825	1496	1217	985	+2.5	-1.6	-15.2	0.0	$17
30-40 Krag	180	2430	2213	2007	1813	1632	2360	1957	1610	1314	1064	+2.5	-1.4	-13.8	0.0	$18
7.65x53mm Arg.	180	2590	2390	2200	2010	1830	2685	2280	1925	1615	1345	+2.5	0.0	-27.6	0.0	NA
7.5x53mm Argentine	150	2785	2519	2269	2032	1814	2583	2113	1714	1376	1096	+2.0	0.0	-8.8	-25.5	NA
308 Marlin Express	140	2800	2532	2279	2040	1818	2437	1992	1614	1294	1207	2.0	0	-8.7	-25.8	NA
308 Marlin Express	160	2660	2430	2226	2026	1836	2513	2111	1761	1457	1197	3.0	1.7	-6.7	-23.5	NA
307 Winchester	150	2760	2321	1924	1575	1289	2530	1795	1233	826	554	+2.5	-1.5	-13.6	0.0	Disc.
7.5x55 Swiss	180	2650	2450	2250	2060	1880	2805	2390	2020	1700	1415	+2.5	+0.6	-8.1	-24.9	NA
7.5x55mm Swiss	165	2720	2515	2319	2132	1954	2710	2317	1970	1665	1398	+2.0	0.0	-8.5	-24.6	NA
30 Remington AR	123/125	2800	2465	2154	1867	1606	2176	1686	1288	967	716	2.1	0.0	-9.7	-29.4	NA
308 Winchester	55	3770	3215	2726	2286	1888	1735	1262	907	638	435	-2.0	+1.4	-3.8	-15.8	$22
308 Win.	110	3165	2830	2520	2230	1960	2447	1956	1551	1215	938	1.4	0	-6.9	-20.9	NA
308 Win. PDX1	120	2850	2497	2171	NA	NA	2164	1662	1256	NA	NA	0.0	-2.8	NA	NA	NA
308 Winchester	150	2820	2533	2263	2009	1774	2648	2137	1705	1344	1048	+2.5	+0.4	-8.5	-26.1	$17
308 W. Superformance	150	3000	2772	2555	2348	1962	2997	2558	2173	1836	1540	1.5	0.0	-6.9	-20.0	NA
308 Win.	155	2775	2553	2342	2141	1950	2650	2243	1887	1577	1308	1.9	0	-8.3	-24.2	NA
308 Win.	155	2850	2640	2438	2247	2064	2795	2398	2047	1737	1466	1.8	0	-7.5	-22.1	NA
308 Winchester	165	2700	2440	2194	1963	1748	2670	2180	1763	1411	1199	+2.5	0.0	-9.7	-28.5	$20
308 Winchester	168	2680	2493	2314	2143	1979	2678	2318	1998	1713	1460	+2.5	0.0	-8.9	-25.3	$18
308 Win. Super Match	168	2870	2647	2462	2284	2114	3008	2613	2261	1946	1667	1.7	0.0	-7.5	-21.6	NA
308 Win. (Fed.)	170	2000	1740	1510	NA	NA	1510	1145	860	NA	NA	0.0	0.0	0.0	0.0	NA
308 Winchester	178	2620	2415	2220	2034	1857	2713	2306	1948	1635	1363	+2.5	0.0	-9.6	-27.6	$23
308 Win. Super Match	178	2780	2609	2444	2285	2132	3054	2690	2361	2064	1797	1.8	0.0	-7.6	-21.9	NA
308 Winchester*	180	2620	2393	2178	1974	1782	2743	2288	1896	1557	1269	+2.5	-0.2	-10.2	-28.5	$17
30-06 Spfd.	55	4080	3485	2965	2502	2083	2033	1483	1074	764	530	+2.0	+1.9	-2.1	-11.7	$22
30-06 Spfd. (Rem.)	125	2660	2335	2034	1757	NA	1964	1513	1148	856	NA	0.0	-5.2	-18.9	0.0	NA
30-06 Spfd.	125	2700	2412	2143	1891	1660	2023	1615	1274	993	765	2.3	0	-9.9	-29.5	NA
30-06 Spfd.	125	3140	2780	2447	2138	1853	2736	2145	1662	1279	953	+2.0	+1.0	-6.2	-21.0	$17
30-06 Spfd.	150	2910	2617	2342	2083	1853	2820	2281	1827	1445	1135	+2.5	+0.8	-7.2	-23.4	$17
30-06 Superformance	150	3080	2848	2617	2417	2216	3159	2700	2298	1945	1636	1.4	0.0	-6.4	-18.9	NA
30-06 Spfd.	152	2910	2654	2413	2184	1968	2858	2378	1965	1610	1307	+2.5	+1.0	-6.6	-21.3	$23
30-06 Spfd.*	165	2800	2534	2283	2047	1825	2872	2352	1909	1534	1220	+2.5	+0.4	-8.4	-25.5	$17
30-06 Spfd.	168	2710	2522	2346	2169	2003	2739	2372	2045	1754	1497	+2.5	+0.4	-8.0	-23.5	$18
30-06 M1 Garand	168	2710	2523	2343	2171	2006	2739	2374	2048	1758	1501	2.3	0	-8.6	-24.6	NA
30-06 Spfd. (Fed.)	170	2000	1740	1510	NA	NA	1510	1145	860	NA	NA	0.0	0.0	0.0	0.0	NA
30-06 Spfd.	178	2720	2511	2311	2121	1939	2924	2491	2111	1777	1486	+2.5	+0.4	-8.2	-24.6	$23
30-06 Spfd.*	180	2700	2469	2250	2042	1846	2913	2436	2023	1666	1362	-2.5	0.0	-9.3	-27.0	$17

Cartridge	Bullet Wgt. Grs.	VELOCITY (fps)					ENERGY (ft. lbs.)					TRAJ. (in.)				Est. Price/box
		Muzzle	100 yds.	200 yds.	300 yds.	400 yds.	Muzzle	100 yds.	200 yds.	300 yds.	400 yds.	100 yds.	200 yds.	300 yds.	400 yds.	
30-06 Superformance	180	2820	2630	2447	2272	2104	3178	2764	2393	2063	1769	1.8	0.0	-7.6	-21.9	NA
30-06 Spfd.	220	2410	2130	1870	1632	1422	2837	2216	1708	1301	988	+2.5	-1.7	-18.0	0.0	$17
30-06 High Energy	180	2880	2690	2500	2320	2150	3315	2880	2495	2150	1845	+1.7	0.0	-7.2	-21.0	NA
30 T/C	150	2920	2696	2483	2280	2087	2849	2421	2054	1732	1450	1.7	0	-7.3	-21.3	NA
30 T/C Superformance	150	3000	2772	2555	2348	2151	2997	2558	2173	1836	1540	1.5	0.0	-6.9	-20.0	NA
30 T/C Superformance	165	2850	2644	2447	2258	2078	2975	2560	2193	1868	1582	1.7	0.0	-7.6	-22.0	NA
300 Rem SA Ultra Mag	150	3200	2901	2622	2359	2112	3410	2803	2290	1854	1485	1.3	0.0	-6.4	-19.1	NA
300 Rem SA Ultra Mag	165	3075	2792	2527	2276	2040	3464	2856	2339	1898	1525	1.5	0.0	-7	-20.7	NA
300 Rem SA Ultra Mag	180	2960	2761	2571	2389	2214	3501	3047	2642	2280	1959	2.6	2.2	-3.6	-15.4	NA
300 Rem. SA Ultra Mag	200	2800	2644	2494	2348	2208	3841	3104	2761	2449	2164	0	-3.5	-12.5	-27.9	NA
7.82 (308) Patriot	150	3250	2999	2762	2537	2323	3519	2997	2542	2145	1798	+1.2	0.0	-5.8	-16.9	NA
300 RCM	150	3265	3023	2794	2577	2369	3550	3043	2600	2211	1870	1.2	0	-5.6	-16.5	NA
300 RCM Superformance	150	3310	3065	2833	2613	2404	3648	3128	2673	2274	1924	1.1	0.0	-5.4	-16.0	NA
300 RCM Superformance	165	3185	2964	2753	2552	2360	3716	3217	2776	2386	2040	1.2	0.0	-5.8	-17.0	NA
300 RCM Superformance	180	3040	2840	2649	2466	2290	3693	3223	2804	2430	2096	1.4	0.0	-6.4	-18.5	NA
300 WSM	150	3300	3061	2834	2619	2414	3628	3121	2676	2285	1941	1.1	0.0	-5.4	-15.9	NA
300 WSM	180	2970	2741	2524	2317	2120	3526	3005	2547	2147	1797	1.6	0.0	-7.0	-20.5	NA
300 WSM	180	3010	2923	2734	2554	2380	3242	2845	2490	2172	1886	1.3	0	-5.9	-17.2	NA
300 WSM	190	2875	2729	2588	2451	2319	3486	3142	2826	2535	2269	0	3.2	-11.5	-25.7	NA
308 Norma Mag.	180	2975	2787	2608	2435	2269	3536	3105	2718	2371	2058	0	-3	-11.1	-25.0	NA
308 Norma Mag.	180	3020	2820	2630	2440	2270	3645	3175	2755	2385	2050	+2.5	+2.0	-3.5	-14.8	NA
300 Dakota	200	3000	2824	2656	2493	2336	3996	3542	3131	2760	2423	+2.2	+1.5	-4.0	-15.2	NA
300 H&H Mag.	180	2870	2678	2494	2318	2148	3292	2866	2486	2147	1844	1.7	0	-7.3	-21.6	NA
300 H&H Magnum*	180	2880	2640	2412	2196	1990	3315	2785	2325	1927	1583	+2.5	+0.8	-6.8	-21.7	$24
300 H&H Mag.	200	2750	2596	2447	2303	2164	3357	2992	2659	2355	2079	1.8	0	-7.6	-21.8	NA
300 H&H Magnum	220	2550	2267	2002	1757	NA	3167	2510	1958	1508	NA	-2.5	-0.4	-12.0	0.0	NA
300 Win. Mag.	150	3290	2951	2636	2342	2068	3605	2900	2314	1827	1424	+2.5	+1.9	-3.8	-15.8	$22
300 WM Superformance	150	3400	3150	2914	2690	2477	3850	3304	2817	2409	2043	1.0	0.0	-5.1	-15.0	NA
300 Win. Mag.	165	3100	2877	2665	2462	2269	3522	3033	2603	2221	1897	+2.5	+2.4	-3.0	-16.9	$24
300 Win. Mag.	178	2900	2760	2568	2375	2191	3509	3030	2606	2230	1897	+2.5	+1.4	-5.0	-17.6	$29
300 Win. Mag.	178	2960	2770	2588	2413	2245	3463	3032	2647	2301	1992	1.5	0	-6.7	-19.4	NA
300 WM Super Match	178	2960	2770	2587	2412	2243	3462	3031	2645	2298	1988	1.5	0.0	-6.7	-19.4	NA
300 Win. Mag.*	180	2960	2745	2540	2344	2157	3501	3011	2578	2196	1859	+2.5	+1.2	-5.5	-18.5	$22
300 WM Superformance	180	3130	2927	2732	2546	2366	3917	3424	2983	2589	2238	1.3	0.0	-5.9	-17.3	NA
300 Win. Mag.	190	2885	1691	2506	2327	2156	3511	3055	2648	2285	1961	+2.5	+1.2	-5.7	-19.0	$26
300 Win. Mag.	195	2930	2760	2596	2438	2286	3717	3297	2918	2574	2262	1.5	0	-6.7	-19.4	NA

300 Win. Mag.*	200	2825	2595	2376	2167	1970	3545	2991	2508	2086	1742	-2.5	+1.6	-4.7	-17.2	$36
300 Win. Mag.	220	2680	2448	2228	2020	1823	3508	2927	2424	1993	1623	+2.5	0.0	-9.5	-27.5	$23
30 Nosler	180	3200	3004	2815	2635	2462	4092	3606	3168	2774	2422	0	-2.4	-9.1	-20.9	NA
30 Nosler	210	3000	2868	2741	2617	2497	4196	3836	3502	3193	2906	0	-2.7	-10.1	-22.5	NA
300 Rem. Ultra Mag.	150	3450	3208	2980	2762	2556	3964	3427	2956	2541	2175	1.7	1.5	-2.6	-11.2	NA
300 Rem. Ultra Mag.	150	2910	2686	2473	2279	2077	2820	2403	2037	1716	1436	1.7	0.0	-7.4	-21.5	NA
300 Rem. Ultra Mag.	165	3350	3099	2862	2938	2424	4110	3518	3001	2549	2152	1.1	0	-5.3	-15.6	NA
300 Rem. Ultra Mag.	180	3250	3037	2834	2640	2454	4221	3686	3201	2786	2407	2.4	0.0	-3.0	-12.7	NA
300 Rem. Ultra Mag.	180	2960	2774	2505	2294	2093	3501	2971	2508	2103	1751	2.7	2.2	-3.8	-16.4	NA
300 Rem. Ultra Mag.	200	3032	2791	2562	2345	2138	4083	3459	2916	2442	2030	1.5	0.0	-6.8	-19.9	NA
300 Rem. Ultra Mag.	210	2920	2790	2665	2543	2424	3975	3631	3311	3015	2740	1.5	0	-6.4	-18.1	NA
30 Nosler	180	3200	3004	2815	2635	2462	4092	3606	3168	2774	2422	0	-2.4	-9.1	-20.9	NA
30 Nosler	210	3000	2868	2741	2617	2497	4196	3836	3502	3193	2906	0	-2.7	-10.1	-22.5	NA
300 Wea. Mag.	100	3900	3441	3038	2652	2305	3714	2891	2239	1717	1297	+2.0	+2.6	-0.6	-8.7	$32
300 Wea. Mag.	150	3375	3126	2892	2670	2459	3794	3255	2786	2374	2013	1.0	0	-5.2	-15.3	NA
300 Wea. Mag.	150	3600	3307	3033	2776	2533	4316	3642	3064	2566	2137	+2.5	+3.2	0.0	-8.1	$32
300 Wea. Mag.	165	3140	2921	2713	2515	2325	3612	3126	2697	2317	1980	1.3	0	-6.0	-17.5	NA
300 Wea. Mag.	165	3450	3210	3000	2792	2593	4360	3796	3297	2855	2464	+2.5	+3.2	0.0	-7.8	NA
300 Wea. Mag.	178	3120	2902	2695	2497	2308	3847	3329	2870	2464	2104	+2.5	-1.7	-3.6	-14.7	$43
300 Wea. Mag.	180	3330	3110	2910	2710	2520	4430	3875	3375	2935	2540	+1.0	0.0	-5.2	-15.1	NA
300 Wea. Mag.	190	3030	2830	2638	2455	2279	3873	3378	2936	2542	2190	+2.5	+1.6	-4.3	-16.0	$38
300 Wea. Mag.	220	2850	2541	2283	1964	1736	3967	3155	2480	1922	1471	+2.5	+0.4	-8.5	-26.4	$35
300 Pegasus	180	3500	3319	3145	2978	2817	4896	4401	3953	3544	3172	+2.28	+2.89	0.0	-6.79	NA
300 Norma Magnum	215	3017	2881	2748	2618	2491	4346	3963	3605	3272	2963	NA	NA	NA	NA	$85
300 Norma Magnum	230	2934	2805	2678	2555	2435	4397	4018	3664	3334	3028	NA	NA	NA	NA	$85
300 Norma Magnum	225	2850	2731	2615	2502	2392	4058	3726	3417	3128	2859	1.6	0	-6.7	-18.9	NA

31

32-20 Win.	100	1210	1021	913	834	769	325	231	185	154	131	0.0	-32.3	0.0	0.0	$23**
303 British	150	2685	2441	2211	1993	1789	2401	1985	1628	1323	1066	2.2	0	-9.3	-27.4	NA
303 British	180	2460	2124	1817	1542	1311	2418	1803	1319	950	687	+2.5	-1.8	-16.8	0.0	$18
303 Light Mag.	150	2830	2570	2325	2094	1884	2667	2199	1800	1461	1185	+2.0	0.0	-8.4	-24.6	NA
7.62x54mm Rus.	146	2950	2730	2520	2320	NA	2820	2415	2055	1740	NA	+2.5	+2.0	-4.4	-17.7	NA
7.62x54mm Rus.	174	2800	2607	2422	2245	2075	3029	2626	2267	1947	1664	1.8	0	-7.8	-22.4	NA
7.62x54mm Rus.	180	2580	2370	2180	2000	1820	2650	2250	1900	1590	1100	+2.5	0.0	-9.8	-28.5	NA
7.7x58mm Jap.	150	2640	2399	2170	1954	1752	2321	1916	1568	1271	1022	+2.3	0.0	-9.7	-28.5	NA
7.7x58mm Jap.	180	2500	2300	2100	1920	1750	2490	2105	1770	1475	1225	+2.5	0.0	-10.4	-30.2	NA

8mm

Cartridge	Wt.														Price
8x56 R	205	2400	2188	1987	1797	1621	2621	2178	1796	1470	1196	+2.9	0.0	-11.7	-34.3	**NA**
8x57mm JS Mau.	165	2850	2520	2210	1930	1670	2965	2330	1795	1360	1015	+2.5	+1.0	-7.7	0.0	**NA**
32 Win. Special	165	2410	2145	1897	1669	NA	2128	1685	1318	1020	NA	2.0	0.0	-13.0	-19.9	**NA**
32 Win. Special	170	2250	1921	1626	1372	1175	1911	1393	998	710	521	+2.5	-3.5	-22.9	0.0	**$14**
8mm Mauser	170	2360	1969	1622	1333	1123	2102	1464	993	671	476	+2.5	-3.1	-22.2	0.0	**$18**
8mm Mauser	196	2500	2338	2182	2032	1888	2720	2379	2072	1797	1552	2.4	0	-9.8	-27.9	**NA**
325 WSM	180	3060	2841	2632	2432	2242	3743	3226	2769	2365	2009	+1.4	0.0	-6.4	-18.7	**NA**
325 WSM	200	2950	2753	2565	2384	2210	3866	3367	2922	2524	2170	+1.5	0.0	-6.8	-19.8	**NA**
325 WSM	220	2840	2605	2382	2169	1968	3941	3316	2772	2300	1893	+1.8	0.0	-8.0	-23.3	**NA**
8mm Rem. Mag.	185	3080	2761	2464	2186	1927	3896	3131	2494	1963	1525	+2.5	+1.4	-5.5	-19.7	**$30**
8mm Rem. Mag.	220	2830	2581	2346	2123	1913	3912	3254	2688	2201	1787	+2.5	+0.6	-7.6	-23.5	**Disc.**

33

Cartridge	Wt.														Price
338 Federal	180	2830	2590	2350	2130	1930	3200	2670	2215	1820	1480	1.8	0.0	-8.2	-23.9	**NA**
338 Marlin Express	200	2565	2365	2174	1992	1820	2922	2484	2099	1762	1471	3.0	1.2	-7.9	-25.9	**NA**
338 Federal	185	2750	2550	2350	2160	1980	3105	2660	2265	1920	1615	1.9	0.0	-8.3	-24.1	**NA**
338 Federal	210	2630	2410	2200	2010	1820	3225	2710	2265	1880	1545	2.3	0.0	-9.4	-27.3	**NA**
338 Federal MSR	185	2680	2459	2230	2020	1820	2950	2460	2035	1670	1360	2.2	0.0	-9.2	-26.8	**NA**
338-06	200	2750	2553	2364	2184	2011	3358	2894	2482	2118	1796	+1.9	0.0	-8.22	-23.6	**NA**
330 Dakota	250	2900	2719	2545	2378	2217	4668	4103	3595	3138	2727	+2.3	+1.3	-5.0	-17.5	**NA**
338 Lapua	250	2900	2685	2481	2285	2098	4668	4002	2416	2899	2444	1.7	0	-7.3	-21.3	**NA**
338 Lapua	250	2963	2795	2640	2493	NA	4842	4341	3881	3458	NA	+1.9	0.0	-7.9	0.0	**NA**
338 Lapua	285	2745	2616	2491	2369	2251	4768	4331	3926	3552	3206	1.8	0	-7.4	-21	**NA**
338 Lapua	300	2660	2544	2432	2322	-	4715	4313	3940	3592	-	1.9	0	-7.8	-	**NA**
338 RCM Superformance	185	2980	2755	2542	2338	2143	3647	3118	2653	2242	1887	1.5	0.0	-6.9	-20.3	**NA**
338 RCM Superformance	200	2950	2744	2547	2358	2177	3846	3342	2879	2468	2104	1.6	0.0	-6.9	-20.1	**NA**
338 RCM Superformance	225	2750	2575	2407	2245	2089	3778	3313	2894	2518	2180	1.9	0.0	-7.9	-22.7	**NA**
338 WM Superformance	185	3080	2850	2632	2424	2226	3896	3337	2845	2413	2034	1.4	0.0	-6.4	-18.8	**NA**
338 Win. Mag.	200	3030	2820	2620	2429	2246	4077	3532	3049	2621	2240	1.4	0	-6.5	-18.9	**NA**
338 Win. Mag.*	210	2830	2590	2370	2150	1940	3735	3130	2610	2155	1760	+2.5	+1.4	-6.0	-20.9	**$33**
338 Win. Mag.*	225	2785	2517	2266	2029	1808	3871	3165	2565	2057	1633	+2.5	+0.4	-8.5	-25.9	**$27**
338 WM Superformance	225	2840	2758	2582	2414	2252	4318	3798	3331	2911	2533	1.5	0.0	-6.8	-19.5	**NA**
338 Win. Mag.	230	2780	2573	2375	2186	2005	3948	3382	2881	2441	2054	+2.5	+1.2	-6.3	-21.0	**$40**
338 Win. Mag.*	250	2660	2456	2261	2075	1898	3927	3348	2837	2389	1999	+2.5	+0.2	-9.0	-26.2	**$27**
338 Ultra Mag.	250	2860	2645	2440	2244	2057	4540	3882	3303	2794	2347	1.7	0.0	-7.6	-22.1	**NA**
338 Lapua Match	250	2900	2760	2625	2494	2366	4668	4229	3825	3452	3108	1.5	0.0	-6.6	-18.8	**NA**
338 Lapua Match	285	2745	2623	2504	2388	2275	4768	4352	3966	3608	3275	1.8	0.0	-7.3	-20.8	**NA**
33 Nosler	225	3025	2856	2687	2525	2369	4589	4074	3608	3185	2803	0	-2.8	-10.4	-23.4	**NA**

Cartridge	Grains														Price
33 Nosler	265	2775	2661	2547	2435	2326	4543	4167	3816	3488	3183	0	-3.4	-12.2	-26.8	NA
33 Nosler	300	2550	2445	2339	2235	2134	4343	3981	3643	3327	3033	0	-4.3	-15	-32.6	NA
8.59(.338) Galaxy	200	3100	2899	2707	2524	2347	4269	3734	3256	2829	2446	3	3.8	0.0	-9.3	NA
340 Wea. Mag.*	210	3250	2991	2746	2515	2295	4924	4170	3516	2948	2455	+2.5	+1.9	-1.8	-11.8	$56
340 Wea. Mag.*	250	3000	2806	2621	2443	2272	4995	4371	3812	3311	2864	+2.5	+2.0	-3.5	-14.8	$56
338 A-Square	250	3120	2799	2500	2220	1958	5403	4348	3469	2736	2128	+2.5	+2.7	-1.5	-10.5	NA
338-378 Wea. Mag.	225	3180	2974	2778	2591	2410	5052	4420	3856	3353	2902	3.1	3.8	0.0	-8.9	NA
338 Titan	225	3230	3010	2800	2600	2409	5211	4524	3916	3377	2898	+3.07	+3.8	0.0	-8.95	NA
338 Excalibur	200	3600	3361	3134	2920	2715	5755	5015	4363	3785	3274	+2.23	+2.87	0.0	-6.99	NA
338 Excalibur	250	3250	2922	2618	2333	2066	5863	4740	3804	3021	2370	+1.3	0.0	-6.35	-19.2	NA

34, 35

Cartridge	Grains														Price
348 Winchester	200	2520	2215	1931	1672	1443	2820	2178	1656	1241	925	+2.5	-1.4	-14.7	0.0	$42
357 Magnum	158	1830	1427	1138	980	883	1175	715	454	337	274	0.0	-16.2	-33.1	0.0	$25**
35 Remington	150	2300	1874	1506	1218	1039	1762	1169	755	494	359	+2.5	-4.1	-26.3	0.0	$16
35 Remington	200	2080	1698	1376	1140	1001	1921	1280	841	577	445	+2.5	-6.3	-17.1	-33.6	$16
35 Remington	200	2225	1963	1722	1505	—	2198	1711	1317	1006	—	3.8	0	-15.6	—	NA
35 Rem. Lever Evolution	200	2225	1963	1721	1503	NA	2198	1711	1315	1003	NA	3.0	-1.3	-17.5	NA	NA
356 Winchester	200	2460	2114	1797	1517	1284	2688	1985	1434	1022	732	+2.5	-1.8	-15.1	0.0	$31
356 Winchester	250	2160	1911	1682	1476	1299	2591	2028	1571	1210	937	+2.5	-3.7	-22.2	0.0	$31
358 Winchester	200	2475	2180	1906	1655	1434	2720	2110	1612	1217	913	2.9	0	-12.6	-37.9	NA
358 Winchester	200	2490	2171	1876	1619	1379	2753	2093	1563	1151	844	+2.5	-1.6	-15.6	0.0	$31
358 STA	275	2850	2562	2292	2039	NA	4958	4009	3208	2539	NA	+1.9	0.0	-8.6	0.0	NA
350 Rem. Mag.	200	2710	2410	2130	1870	1631	3261	2579	2014	1553	1181	+2.5	-0.2	-10.0	-30.1	$33
35 Whelen	200	2675	2378	2100	1842	1606	3177	2510	1958	1506	1145	+2.5	-0.2	-10.3	-31.1	$20
35 Whelen	200	2910	2585	2283	2001	1742	3760	2968	2314	1778	1347	1.9	0	-8.6	-25.9	NA
35 Whelen	225	2500	2300	2110	1930	1770	3120	2650	2235	1870	1560	+2.6	0.0	-10.2	-29.9	NA
35 Whelen	250	2400	2197	2005	1823	1652	3197	2680	2230	1844	1515	+2.5	-1.2	-13.7	0.0	$20
358 Norma Mag.	250	2800	2510	2230	1970	1730	4350	3480	2750	2145	1655	+2.5	+1.0	-7.6	-25.2	NA
358 STA	275	2850	2562	229*2	2039	1764	4959	4009	3208	2539	1899	+1.9	0.0	-8.58	-26.1	NA

9.3mm

Cartridge	Grains														Price
9.3x57mm Mau.	232	2362	2058	1778	1528	NA	2875	2182	1630	1203	NA	0	-6.8	-24.6	NA	NA
9.3x57mm Mau.	286	2070	1810	1590	1390	1110	2710	2090	1600	1220	955	+2.5	-2.6	-22.5	0.0	NA
370 Sako Mag.	286	3550	2370	2200	2040	2880	4130	3570	3075	2630	2240	2.4	0.0	-9.5	-27.2	NA
9.3x62mm	232	2625	2302	2002	1728	-	2551	2731	2066	1539	-	2.6	0	-11.3	-	NA
9.3x62mm	250	2550	2376	2208	2048	—	3609	3133	2707	2328	—	0	-5.4	-17.9	—	NA
9.3x62mm	286	2360	2155	1961	1778	1608	3537	2949	2442	2008	1642	0	-6.0	-21.1	-47.2	NA
9.3x62mm	286	2400	2163	1941	1733	—	3657	2972	2392	1908	—	0	-6.7	-22.6	—	NA

9.3x64mm	286	2700	2505	2318	2139	1968	4629	3984	3411	2906	2460	+2.5	+2.7	-4.5	-19.2	**NA**
9.3x72mmR	193	1952	1610	1326	1120	996	1633	1112	754	538	425	0	-12.1	-44.1	—	**NA**
9.3x74mmR	250	2550	2376	2208	2048	—	3609	3133	2707	2328	—	0	-5.4	-17.9	—	**NA**
9.3x74Rmm	286	2360	2136	1924	1727	1545	3536	2896	2351	1893	1516	0.0	-6.1	-21.7	-49.0	**NA**

375

375 Winchester	200	2200	1841	1526	1268	1089	2150	1506	1034	714	527	+2.5	-4.0	-26.2	0.0	**$27**
375 Winchester	250	1900	1647	1424	1239	1103	2005	1506	1126	852	676	+2.5	-6.9	-33.3	0.0	**$27**
376 Steyr	225	2600	2331	2078	1842	1625	3377	2714	2157	1694	1319	2.5	0.0	-10.6	-31.4	**NA**
376 Steyr	270	2600	2372	2156	1951	1759	4052	3373	2787	2283	1855	2.3	0.0	-9.9	-28.9	**NA**
375 Dakota	300	2600	2316	2051	1804	1579	4502	3573	2800	2167	1661	+2.4	0.0	-11.0	-32.7	**NA**
375 N.E. 2-1/2"	270	2000	1740	1507	1310	NA	2398	1815	1362	1026	NA	+2.5	-6.0	-30.0	0.0	**NA**
375 Flanged	300	2450	2150	1886	1640	NA	3998	3102	2369	1790	NA	+2.5	-2.4	-17.0	0.0	**NA**
375 Ruger	250	2890	2675	2471	2275	2088	4636	3973	3388	2873	2421	1.7	0	-7.4	-21.5	**NA**
375 Ruger	260	2900	2703	2514	2333	—	4854	4217	3649	3143	—	0	-4.0	-13.4	—	**NA**
375 Ruger	270	2840	2600	2372	2156	1951	4835	4052	3373	2786	2283	1.8	0.0	-8.0	-23.6	**NA**
375 Ruger	300	2660	2344	2050	1780	1536	4713	3660	2800	2110	1572	2.4	0.0	-10.8	-32.6	**NA**
375 Flanged NE	300	2400	2103	1829	NA	NA	3838	2947	2228	NA	NA	0	-6.4	-	-	**NA**
375 H&H Magnum	250	2890	2675	2471	2275	2088	4636	3973	3388	2873	2421	1.7	0	-7.4	-21.5	**NA**
375 H&H Magnum	250	2670	2450	2240	2040	1850	3955	3335	2790	2315	1905	+2.5	-0.4	-10.2	-28.4	**NA**
375 H&H Magnum	270	2690	2420	2166	1928	1707	4337	3510	2812	2228	1747	+2.5	0.0	-10.0	-29.4	**$28**
375 H&H Mag.	270	2800	2562	2337	2123	1921	4700	3936	3275	2703	2213	1.9	0	-8.3	-24.3	**NA**
375 H&H Magnum*	300	2530	2245	1979	1733	1512	4263	3357	2608	2001	1523	+2.5	-1.0	-10.5	-33.6	**$28**
375 H&H Mag.	300	2660	2345	2052	1782	1539	4713	3662	2804	2114	1577	2.4	0	-10.8	-32.6	**NA**
375 H&H Hvy. Mag.	270	2870	2628	2399	2182	1976	4937	4141	3451	2150	1845	+1.7	0.0	-7.2	-21.0	**NA**
375 H&H Hvy. Mag.	300	2705	2386	2090	1816	1568	4873	3793	2908	2195	1637	+2.3	0.0	-10.4	-31.4	**NA**
375 H&H Mag.	350	2300	2052	1821	-	-	4112	3273	2578	-	-	0	-6.7	-	-	**NA**
375 Rem. Ultra Mag.	270	2900	2558	2241	1947	1678	5041	3922	3010	2272	1689	1.9	2.7	-8.9	-27.0	**NA**
375 Rem. Ultra Mag.	260	2950	2750	2560	2377	—	5023	4367	3783	3262	—	0	-3.8	-12.9	—	**NA**
375 Rem. Ultra Mag.	300	2760	2505	2263	2035	1822	5073	4178	3412	2759	2210	2.0	0.0	-8.8	-26.1	**NA**
375 Wea. Mag.	260	3000	2798	2606	2421	—	5195	4520	3920	3384	—	0	-3.6	-12.4	—	**NA**
375 Wea. Mag.	300	2700	2420	2157	1911	1685	4856	3901	3100	2432	1891	+2.5	-.04	-10.7	0.0	**NA**
378 Wea. Mag.	260	3100	2894	2697	2509	—	5547	4834	4199	3633	—	0	-4.2	-14.6	—	**NA**
378 Wea. Mag.	270	3180	2976	2781	2594	2415	6062	5308	4635	4034	3495	+2.5	+2.6	-1.8	-11.3	**$71**
378 Wea. Mag.	300	2929	2576	2252	1952	1680	5698	4419	3379	2538	1881	+2.5	+1.2	-7.0	-24.5	**$77**
375 A-Square	300	2920	2626	2351	2093	1850	5679	4594	3681	2917	2281	+2.5	+1.4	-6.0	-21.0	**NA**
38-40 Win.	180	1160	999	901	827	764	538	399	324	273	233	0.0	-33.9	0.0	0.0	**$42****

40, 41

Cartridge	Bullet Wt.	Muzzle	100	200	300	400	Muzzle	100	200	300	400					Price
400 A-Square DPM	400	2400	2146	1909	1689	NA	5116	2092	3236	2533	NA	2.98	0.0	-10.0	NA	NA
400 A-Square DPM	170	2980	2463	2001	1598	NA	3352	2289	1512	964	NA	2.16	0.0	-11.1	NA	NA
408 CheyTac	419	2850	2752	2657	2562	2470	7551	7048	6565	6108	5675	-1.02	0.0	1.9	4.2	NA
405 Win.	300	2200	1851	1545	1296		3224	2282	1589	1119		4.6	0.0	-19.5	0.0	NA
450/400-3"	400	2050	1815	1595	1402	NA	3732	2924	2259	1746	NA	0.0	NA	-33.4	NA	NA
416 Ruger	400	2400	2151	1917	1700	NA	5116	4109	3264	2568	NA	0.0	-6.0	-21.6	0.0	NA
416 Dakota	400	2450	2294	2143	1998	1859	5330	4671	4077	3544	3068	+2.5	-0.2	-10.5	-29.4	NA
416 Taylor	375	2350	2021	1722	na	na	4600	3403	2470	NA	NA	0	-7	NA	NA	NA
416 Taylor	400	2350	2117	1896	1693	NA	4905	3980	3194	2547	NA	+2.5	-1.2	15.0	0.0	NA
416 Hoffman	400	2380	2145	1923	1718	1529	5031	4087	3285	2620	2077	+2.5	-1.0	-14.1	0.0	NA
416 Rigby	350	2600	2449	2303	2162	2026	5253	4661	4122	3632	3189	+2.5	-1.8	-10.2	-26.0	NA
416 Rigby	400	2370	2210	2050	1900	NA	4990	4315	3720	3185	NA	+2.5	-0.7	-12.1	0.0	NA
416 Rigby	400	2400	2115	1851	1611	—	5115	3973	3043	2305	—	0	-6.5	-21.8	—	NA
416 Rigby	400	2415	2156	1915	1691	—	5180	4130	3256	2540	—	0	-6.0	-21.6	—	NA
416 Rigby	410	2370	2110	1870	1640	NA	5115	4050	3165	2455	NA	+2.5	-2.4	-17.3	0.0	$110
416 Rem. Mag.*	350	2520	2270	2034	1814	1611	4935	4004	3216	2557	2017	+2.5	-0.8	-12.6	-35.0	$82
416 Rem. Mag.	400	2400	2142	1901	1679	—	5116	4076	3211	2504	—	3.1	0	-12.7	—	NA
416 Rem. Mag.	450	2150	1925	1716	-	-	4620	3702	2942	-	-	0	-7.8	-	-	NA
416 Wea. Mag.*	400	2700	2397	2115	1852	1613	6474	5104	3971	3047	2310	+2.5	0.0	-10.1	-30.4	$96
10.57 (416) Meteor	400	2730	2532	2342	2161	1987	6621	5695	4874	4147	3508	+1.9	0.0	-8.3	-24.0	NA
500/416 N.E.	400	2300	2092	1895	1712	—	4697	3887	3191	2602	—	0	-7.2	-24.0	—	NA
500/416 N.E.	410	2325	2062	1817	-	-	4620	3735	2996	NA	NA	0	-6.7	-	-	NA
404 Jeffrey	400	2150	1924	1716	1525	NA	4105	3289	2614	2064	NA	+2.5	-4.0	-22.1	0.0	NA
404 Jeffrey	400	2300	2053	1823	1611	—	4698	3743	2950	2306	—	0	-6.8	-24.1	—	NA
404 Jeffery	400	2350	2020	1720	1458	—	4904	3625	2629	1887	—	0	-6.5	-21.8	—	NA
404 Jeffery	450	2150	1946	1755	-	-	4620	3784	3078	-	-	0	-7.6	-	-	NA

425, 44

Cartridge	Bullet Wt.	Muzzle	100	200	300	400	Muzzle	100	200	300	400					Price
425 Express	400	2400	2160	1934	1725	NA	5115	4145	3322	2641	NA	+2.5	-1.0	-14.0	0.0	NA
44-40 Win.	200	1190	1006	900	822	756	629	449	360	300	254	0.0	-33.3	0.0	0.0	$36**
44 Rem. Mag.	210	1920	1477	1155	982	880	1719	1017	622	450	361	0.0	-17.6	0.0	0.0	$14
44 Rem. Mag.	240	1760	1380	1114	970	878	1650	1015	661	501	411	0.0	-17.6	0.0	0.0	$13
444 Marlin	240	2350	1815	1377	1087	941	2942	1753	1001	630	472	+2.5	-15.1	-31.0	0.0	$22
444 Marlin	265	2120	1733	1405	1160	1012	2644	1768	1162	791	603	+2.5	-6.0	-32.2	0.0	Disc.
444 Mar. Lever Evolution	265	2325	1971	1652	1380	NA	3180	2285	1606	1120	NA	3.0	-1.4	-18.6	NA	NA
444 Mar. Superformance	265	2400	1976	1603	1298	NA	3389	2298	1512	991	NA	4.1	0.0	-17.8	NA	NA

45

Cartridge	Bullet Wt.	Muzzle	100	200	300	400	Muzzle	100	200	300	400					Price
45-70 Govt.	250	2025	1616	1285	1068	—	2276	1449	917	634	—	6.1	0	-27.2	—	NA

45-70 Govt.	300	1810	1497	1244	1073	969	2182	1492	1031	767	625	0.0	-14.8	0.0	0.0	$21
45-70 Govt. Supreme	300	1880	1558	1292	1103	988	2355	1616	1112	811	651	0.0	-12.9	-46.0	-105.0	NA
45-70 Govt.	325	2000	1685	1413	1197	—	2886	2049	1441	1035	—	5.5	0	-23.0	—	NA
45-70 Lever Evolution	325	2050	1729	1450	1225	NA	3032	2158	1516	1083	NA	3.0	-4.1	-27.8	NA	NA
45-70 Govt. CorBon	350	1800	1526	1296			2519	1810	1307			0.0	-14.6	0.0	0.0	NA
45-70 Govt.	405	1330	1168	1055	977	918	1590	1227	1001	858	758	0.0	-24.6	0.0	0.0	$21
45-70 Govt. PMC Cowboy	405	1550	1193	—	—	—	1639	1280	—	—	—	0.0	-23.9	0.0	0.0	NA
45-70 Govt. Garrett	415	1850	—	—	—	—	3150	—	—	—	—	3.0	-7.0	0.0	0.0	NA
45-70 Govt. Garrett	530	1550	1343	1178	1062	982	2828	2123	1633	1327	1135	0.0	-17.8	0.0	0.0	NA
450 Bushmaster	250	2200	1831	1508	1480	1073	2686	1860	1262	864	639	0.0	-9.0	-33.5	0.0	NA
450 Marlin	325	2225	1887	1587	1332	—	3572	2570	1816	1280	—	4.2	0	-18.1	—	NA
450 Marlin	350	2100	1774	1488	1254	1089	3427	2446	1720	1222	922	0.0	-9.7	-35.2	0.0	NA
450 Mar. Lever Evolution	325	2225	1887	1585	1331	NA	3572	2569	1813	1278	NA	3.0	-2.2	-21.3	NA	NA
457 Wild West Magnum	350	2150	1718	1348	NA	NA	3645	2293	1413	NA	NA	0.0	-10.5	NA	NA	NA
450/500 N.E.	400	2050	1820	1609	1420	—	3732	2940	2298	1791	—	0	-9.7	-32.8	—	NA
450 N.E. 3-1/4"	465	2190	1970	1765	1577	NA	4952	4009	3216	2567	NA	+2.5	-3.0	-20.0	0.0	NA
450 N.E.	480	2150	1881	1635	1418	—	4927	3769	2850	2144	—	0	-8.4	-29.8	—	NA
450 N.E. 3-1/4"	500	2150	1920	1708	1514	NA	5132	4093	3238	2544	NA	+2.5	-4.0	-22.9	0.0	NA
450 No. 2	465	2190	1970	1765	1577	NA	4952	4009	3216	2567	NA	+2.5	-3.0	-20.0	0.0	NA
450 No. 2	500	2150	1920	1708	1514	NA	5132	4093	3238	2544	NA	+2.5	-4.0	-22.9	0.0	NA
450 Ackley Mag.	465	2400	2169	1950	1747	NA	5947	4857	3927	3150	NA	+2.5	-1.0	-13.7	0.0	NA
450 Ackley Mag.	500	2320	2081	1855	1649	NA	5975	4085	3820	3018	NA	+2.5	-1.2	-15.0	0.0	NA
450 Rigby	500	2350	2139	1939	1752	—	6130	5079	4176	3408	—	0	-6.8	-22.9	—	NA
450 Rigby	550	2100	1887	1690	–	–	5387	4311	3425	–	–	0	-8.3	–	–	NA
458 Win. Magnum	400	2380	2170	1960	1770	NA	5030	4165	3415	2785	NA	+2.5	-0.4	-13.4	0.0	$73
458 Win. Magnum	465	2220	1999	1791	1601	NA	5088	4127	3312	2646	NA	+2.5	-2.0	-17.7	0.0	NA
458 Win. Magnum	500	2040	1823	1623	1442	1237	4620	3689	2924	2308	1839	+2.5	-3.5	-22.0	0.0	$61
458 Win. Mag.	500	2140	1880	1643	1432	—	5084	3294	2996	2276	—	0	-8.4	-29.8	—	NA
458 Win. Magnum	510	2040	1770	1527	1319	1157	4712	3547	2640	1970	1516	+2.5	-4.1	-25.0	0.0	$41
458 Lott	465	2380	2150	1932	1730	NA	5848	4773	3855	3091	NA	+2.5	-1.0	-14.0	0.0	NA
458 Lott	500	2300	2029	1778	1551	—	5873	4569	3509	2671	—	0	-7.0	-25.1	—	NA
458 Lott	500	2300	2062	1838	1633	NA	5873	4719	3748	2960	NA	+2.5	-1.6	-16.4	0.0	NA
460 Short A-Sq.	500	2420	2175	1943	1729	NA	6501	5250	4193	3319	NA	+2.5	-0.8	-12.8	0.0	NA
460 Wea. Mag.	500	2700	2404	2128	1869	1635	8092	6416	5026	3878	2969	+2.5	+0.6	-8.9	-28.0	$72

475

500/465 N.E.	480	2150	1917	1703	1507	NA	4926	3917	3089	2419	NA	+2.5	-4.0	-22.2	0.0	NA
470 Rigby	500	2150	1940	1740	1560	NA	5130	4170	3360	2695	NA	+2.5	-2.8	-19.4	0.0	NA

	Wt.	Muzzle	100	200	300	400	Muzzle	100	200	300	400	100	200	300	400	Price
470 Nitro Ex.	480	2190	1954	1735	1536	NA	5111	4070	3210	2515	NA	+2.5	-3.5	-20.8	0.0	**NA**
470 N.E.	500	2150	1885	1643	1429	—	5132	3945	2998	2267	—	0	-8.9	-30.8	—	**NA**
470 Nitro Ex.	500	2150	1890	1650	1440	1270	5130	3965	3040	2310	1790	+2.5	-4.3	-24.0	0.0	**$177**
475 No. 2	500	2200	1955	1728	1522	NA	5375	4243	3316	2573	NA	+2.5	-3.2	-20.9	0.0	**NA**

50, 58

	Wt.	Muzzle	100	200	300	400	Muzzle	100	200	300	400	100	200	300	400	Price
50 Alaskan	450	2000	1729	1492	NA	NA	3997	2987	2224	NA	NA	0.0	-11.25	NA	NA	**NA**
500 Jeffery	570	2300	1979	1688	1434	—	6694	4958	3608	2604	—	0	-8.2	-28.6	—	**NA**
505 Gibbs	525	2300	2063	1840	1637	NA	6166	4922	3948	3122	NA	+2.5	-3.0	-18.0	0.0	**NA**
505 Gibbs	570	2100	1893	1701	-	-	5583	4538	3664	-	-	0	-8.1	-	-	**NA**
505 Gibbs	600	2100	1899	1711	-	-	5877	4805	3904	-	-	0	-8.1	-	-	**NA**
500 N.E.	570	2150	1889	1651	1439	—	5850	4518	3450	2621	—	0	-8.9	-30.6	—	**NA**
500 N.E.-3"	570	2150	1928	1722	1533	NA	5850	4703	3752	2975	NA	+2.5	-3.7	-22.0	0.0	**NA**
500 N.E.-3"	600	2150	1927	1721	1531	NA	6158	4947	3944	3124	NA	+2.5	-4.0	-22.0	0.0	**NA**
495 A-Square	570	2350	2117	1896	1693	NA	5850	4703	3752	2975	NA	+2.5	-1.0	-14.5	0.0	**NA**
495 A-Square	600	2280	2050	1833	1635	NA	6925	5598	4478	3562	NA	+2.5	-2.0	-17.0	0.0	**NA**
500 A-Square	600	2380	2144	1922	1766	NA	7546	6126	4920	3922	NA	+2.5	-3.0	-17.0	0.0	**NA**
500 A-Square	707	2250	2040	1841	1567	NA	7947	6530	5318	4311	NA	+2.5	-2.0	-17.0	0.0	**NA**
500 BMG PMC	660	3080	2854	2639	2444	2248	13688	500 yd. zero				+3.1	+3.9	+4.7	+2.8	**NA**
577 Nitro Ex.	750	2050	1793	1562	1360	NA	6990	5356	4065	3079	NA	+2.5	-5.0	-26.0	0.0	**NA**
577 Tyrannosaur	750	2400	2141	1898	1675	NA	9591	7633	5996	4671	NA	+3.0	0.0	-12.9	0.0	**NA**

600, 700

	Wt.	Muzzle	100	200	300	400	Muzzle	100	200	300	400	100	200	300	400	Price
600 N.E.	900	1950	1680	1452	NA	NA	7596	5634	4212	NA	NA	+5.6	0.0	0.0	0.0	**NA**
700 N.E.	1200	1900	1676	1472	NA	NA	9618	7480	5774	NA	NA	+5.7	0.0	0.0	0.0	**NA**

50 BMG

	Wt.	Muzzle	100	200	300	400	Muzzle	100	200	300	400	100	200	300	400	Price
50 BMG	624	2952	2820	2691	2566	2444	12077	11028	10036	9125	8281	0	-2.9	-10.6	-23.5	**NA**
50 BMG Match	750	2820	2728	2637	2549	2462	13241	12388	11580	10815	10090	1.5	0.0	-6.5	-18.3	**NA**

Notes: Blanks are available in 32 S&W, 38 S&W and 38 Special. "V" after barrel length indicates test barrel was vented to produce ballistics similar to a revolver with a normal barrel-to-cylinder gap. Ammo prices are per 50 rounds except when marked with an ** which signifies a 20 round box; *** signifies a 25-round box. Not all loads are available from all ammo manufacturers. Listed loads are those made by Remington, Winchester, Federal, and others. DISC. is a discontinued load. Prices are rounded to the nearest whole dollar and will vary with brand and retail outlet.

Cartridge	Bullet Wgt. Grs.	VELOCITY (fps)			ENERGY (ft. lbs.)			Mid-Range Traj. (in.)		Bbl. Lgth. (in).	Est. Price/ box
		Muzzle	50 yds.	100 yds.	Muzzle	50 yds.	100 yds.	50 yds.	100 yds.		
22, 25											
221 Rem. Fireball	50	2650	2380	2130	780	630	505	0.2	0.8	10.5"	$15
25 Automatic	35	900	813	742	63	51	43	NA	NA	2"	$18
25 Automatic	45	815	730	655	65	55	40	1.8	7.7	2"	$21
25 Automatic	50	760	705	660	65	55	50	2.0	8.7	2"	$17
30											
7.5mm Swiss	107	1010	NA	NA	240	NA	NA	NA	NA	NA	NEW
7.62x25 Tokarev	85	1647	1458	1295	512	401	317	0	-3.2	4.75	
7.62mmTokarev	87	1390	NA	NA	365	NA	NA	0.6	NA	4.5"	NA
7.62 Nagant	97	790	NA	NA	134	NA	NA	NA	NA	NA	NEW
7.63 Mauser	88	1440	NA	NA	405	NA	NA	NA	NA	NA	NEW
30 Luger	93	1220	1110	1040	305	255	225	0.9	3.5	4.5"	$34
30 Carbine	110	1790	1600	1430	785	625	500	0.4	1.7	10"	$28
30-357 AeT	123	1992	NA	NA	1084	NA	NA	NA	NA	10"	NA
32											
32 NAA	80	1000	933	880	178	155	137	NA	NA	4"	NA
32 S&W	88	680	645	610	90	80	75	2.5	10.5	3"	$17
32 S&W Long	98	705	670	635	115	100	90	2.3	10.5	4"	$17
32 Short Colt	80	745	665	590	100	80	60	2.2	9.9	4"	$19
32 H&R	80	1150	1039	963	235	192	165	NA	NA	4"	NA
32 H&R Magnum	85	1100	1020	930	230	195	165	1.0	4.3	4.5"	$21
32 H&R Magnum	95	1030	940	900	225	190	170	1.1	4.7	4.5"	$19
327 Federal Magnum	85	1400	1220	1090	370	280	225	NA	NA	4-V	NA
327 Federal Magnum	100	1500	1320	1180	500	390	310	-0.2	-4.50	4-V	NA
32 Automatic	60	970	895	835	125	105	95	1.3	5.4	4"	$22
32 Automatic	60	1000	917	849	133	112	96			4"	NA
32 Automatic	65	950	890	830	130	115	100	1.3	5.6	NA	NA
32 Automatic	71	905	855	810	130	115	95	1.4	5.8	4"	$19
8mm Lebel Pistol	111	850	NA	NA	180	NA	NA	NA	NA	NA	NEW
8mm Steyr	112	1080	NA	NA	290	NA	NA	NA	NA	NA	NEW
8mm Gasser	126	850	NA	NA	200	NA	NA	NA	NA	NA	NEW
9mm, 38											
380 Automatic	60	1130	960	NA	170	120	NA	1.0	NA	NA	NA
380 Automatic	75	950	NA	NA	183	NA	NA	NA	NA	3"	$33
380 Automatic	85/88	990	920	870	190	165	145	1.2	5.1	4"	$20
380 Automatic	90	1000	890	800	200	160	130	1.2	5.5	3.75"	$10
380 Automatic	95/100	955	865	785	190	160	130	1.4	5.9	4"	$20
38 Super Auto +P	115	1300	1145	1040	430	335	275	0.7	3.3	5"	$26
38 Super Auto +P	125/130	1215	1100	1015	425	350	300	0.8	3.6	5"	$26
38 Super Auto +P	147	1100	1050	1000	395	355	325	0.9	4.0	5"	NA
38 Super Auto +P	115	1130	1016	938	326	264	225	1	-9.5	-	NA
9x18mm Makarov	95	1000	930	874	211	182	161	NA	NA	4"	NEW
9x18mm Ultra	100	1050	NA	NA	240	NA	NA	NA	NA	NA	NEW
9x21	124	1150	1050	980	365	305	265	NA	NA	4"	NA
9x21 IMI	123	1220	1095	1010	409	330	281	-3.15	—	5.0	NA
9x23mm Largo	124	1190	1055	966	390	306	257	0.7	3.7	4"	NA
9x23mm Win.	125	1450	1249	1103	583	433	338	0.6	2.8	NA	NA
9mm Steyr	115	1180	NA	NA	350	NA	NA	NA	NA	NA	NEW
9mm Luger	80	1445	–	–	–	385	–	–	–	–	NA
9mm Luger	88	1500	1190	1010	440	275	200	0.6	3.1	4"	$24
9mm Luger	90	1360	1112	978	370	247	191	NA	NA	4"	$26
9mm Luger	92	1325	1117	991	359	255	201	-3.2	—	4.0	NA
9mm Luger	95	1300	1140	1010	350	275	215	0.8	3.4	4"	NA
9mm Luger	100	1180	1080	NA	305	255	NA	0.9	NA	4"	NA
9mm Luger Guard Dog	105	1230	1070	970	355	265	220	NA	NA	4"	NA
9mm Luger	115	1155	1045	970	340	280	240	0.9	3.9	4"	$21

Cartridge	Bullet Wgt. Grs.	VELOCITY (fps)			ENERGY (ft. lbs.)			Mid-Range Traj. (in.)		Bbl. Lgth. (in.)	Est. Price/ box
		Muzzle	50 yds.	100 yds.	Muzzle	50 yds.	100 yds.	50 yds.	100 yds.		
9mm Luger	123/125	1110	1030	970	340	290	260	1.0	4.0	4"	$23
9mm Luger	124	1150	1040	965	364	298	256	-4.5	—	4.0	NA
9mm Luger	135	1010	960	918	306	276	253	—	—	4.0	NA
9mm Luger	140	935	890	850	270	245	225	1.3	5.5	4"	$23
9mm Luger	147	990	940	900	320	290	265	1.1	4.9	4"	$26
9mm Luger +P	90	1475	NA	NA	437	NA	NA	NA	NA	NA	NA
9mm Luger +P	115	1250	1113	1019	399	316	265	0.8	3.5	4"	$27
9mm Federal	115	1280	1130	1040	420	330	280	0.7	3.3	4"V	$24
9mm Luger Vector	115	1155	1047	971	341	280	241	NA	NA	4"	NA
9mm Luger +P	124	1180	1089	1021	384	327	287	0.8	3.8	4"	NA
38											
38 S&W	146	685	650	620	150	135	125	2.4	10.0	4"	$19
38 S&W Short	145	720	689	660	167	153	140	-8.5	—	5.0	NA
38 Short Colt	125	730	685	645	150	130	115	2.2	9.4	6"	$19
39 Special	100	950	900	NA	200	180	NA	1.3	NA	4"V	NA
38 Special	110	945	895	850	220	195	175	1.3	5.4	4"V	$23
38 Special	110	945	895	850	220	195	175	1.3	5.4	4"V	$23
38 Special	130	775	745	710	175	160	120	1.9	7.9	4"V	$22
38 Special Cowboy	140	800	767	735	199	183	168			7.5" V	NA
38 (Multi-Ball)	140	830	730	505	215	130	80	2.0	10.6	4"V	$10**
38 Special	148	710	635	565	165	130	105	2.4	10.6	4"V	$17
38 Special	158	755	725	690	200	185	170	2.0	8.3	4"V	$18
38 Special +P	95	1175	1045	960	290	230	195	0.9	3.9	4"V	$23
38 Special +P	110	995	925	870	240	210	185	1.2	5.1	4"V	$23
38 Special +P	125	975	929	885	264	238	218	1	5.2	4"	NA
38 Special +P	125	945	900	860	250	225	205	1.3	5.4	4"V	#23
38 Special +P	129	945	910	870	255	235	215	1.3	5.3	4"V	$11
38 Special +P	130	925	887	852	247	227	210	1.3	5.50	4"V	NA
38 Special +P	147/150	884	NA	NA	264	NA	NA	NA	NA	4"V	$27
38 Special +P	158	890	855	825	280	255	240	1.4	6.0	4"V	$20
357											
357 SIG	115	1520	NA	NA	593	NA	NA	NA	NA	NA	NA
357 SIG	124	1450	NA	NA	578	NA	NA	NA	NA	NA	NA
357 SIG	125	1350	1190	1080	510	395	325	0.7	3.1	4"	NA
357 SIG	135	1225	1112	1031	450	371	319	—	—	4.0	NA
357 SIG	147	1225	1132	1060	490	418	367	—	—	4.0	NA
357 SIG	150	1130	1030	970	420	355	310	0.9	4.0	NA	NA
356 TSW	115	1520	NA	NA	593	NA	NA	NA	NA	NA	NA
356 TSW	124	1450	NA	NA	578	NA	NA	NA	NA	NA	NA
356 TSW	135	1280	1120	1010	490	375	310	0.8	3.5	NA	NA
356 TSW	147	1220	1120	1040	485	410	355	0.8	3.5	5"	NA
357 Mag., Super Clean	105	1650									NA
357 Magnum	110	1295	1095	975	410	290	230	0.8	3.5	4"V	$25
357 (Med.Vel.)	125	1220	1075	985	415	315	270	0.8	3.7	4"V	$25
357 Magnum	125	1450	1240	1090	585	425	330	0.6	2.8	4"V	$25
357 Magnum	125	1500	1312	1163	624	478	376	—	—	8.0	NA
357 (Multi-Ball)	140	1155	830	665	420	215	135	1.2	6.4	4"V	$11**
357 Magnum	140	1360	1195	1075	575	445	360	0.7	3.0	4"V	$25
357 Magnum FlexTip	140	1440	1274	1143	644	504	406	NA	NA	NA	NA
357 Magnum	145	1290	1155	1060	535	430	360	0.8	3.5	4"V	$26
357 Magnum	150/158	1235	1105	1015	535	430	360	0.8	3.5	4"V	$25
357 Mag. Cowboy	158	800	761	725	225	203	185				NA
357 Magnum	165	1290	1189	1108	610	518	450	0.7	3.1	8-3/8"	NA
357 Magnum	180	1145	1055	985	525	445	390	0.9	3.9	4"V	$25
357 Magnum	180	1180	1088	1020	557	473	416	0.8	3.6	8"V	NA
357 Mag. CorBon F.A.	180	1650	1512	1386	1088	913	767	1.66	0.0		NA
357 Mag. CorBon	200	1200	1123	1061	640	560	500	3.19	0.0		NA
357 Rem. Maximum	158	1825	1590	1380	1170	885	670	0.4	1.7	10.5"	$14**

Cartridge	Bullet Wgt. Grs.	VELOCITY (fps)			ENERGY (ft. lbs.)			Mid-Range Traj. (in.)		Bbl. Lgth. (in).	Est. Price/ box
		Muzzle	50 yds.	100 yds.	Muzzle	50 yds.	100 yds.	50 yds.	100 yds.		
40, 10mm											
40 S&W	120	1150	–	–	352	–	–	–	–	–	$38
40 S&W	125	1265	1102	998	444	337	276	-3.0	–	4.0	NA
40 S&W	135	1140	1070	NA	390	345	NA	0.9	NA	4"	NA
40 S&W Guard Dog	135	1200	1040	940	430	325	265	NA	NA	4"	NA
40 S&W	155	1140	1026	958	447	362	309	0.9	4.1	4"	$14***
40 S&W	165	1150	NA	NA	485	NA	NA	NA	NA	4"	$18***
40 S&W	175	1010	948	899	396	350	314	–	–	4.0	NA
40 S&W	180	985	936	893	388	350	319	1.4	5.0	4"	$14***
40 S&W	180	1000	943	896	400	355	321	4.52	–	4.0	NA
40 S&W	180	1015	960	914	412	368	334	1.3	4.5	4"	NA
400 Cor-Bon	135	1450	NA	NA	630	NA	NA	NA	NA	5"	NA
10mm Automatic	155	1125	1046	986	436	377	335	0.9	3.9	5"	$26
10mm Automatic	155	1265	1118	1018	551	430	357	–	–	5.0	NA
10mm Automatic	170	1340	1165	1145	680	510	415	0.7	3.2	5"	$31
10mm Automatic	175	1290	1140	1035	650	505	420	0.7	3.3	5.5"	$11**
10mm Auto. (FBI)	180	950	905	865	361	327	299	1.5	5.4	4"	$16**
10mm Automatic	180	1030	970	920	425	375	340	1.1	4.7	5"	$16**
10mm Auto H.V.	180	1240	1124	1037	618	504	430	0.8	3.4	5"	$27
10mm Automatic	200	1160	1070	1010	495	510	430	0.9	3.8	5"	$14**
10.4mm Italian	177	950	NA	NA	360	NA	NA	NA	NA	NA	NEW
41 Action Exp.	180	1000	947	903	400	359	326	0.5	4.2	5"	$13**
41 Rem. Magnum	170	1420	1165	1015	760	515	390	0.7	3.2	4"V	$33
41 Rem. Magnum	175	1250	1120	1030	605	490	410	0.8	3.4	4"V	$14**
41 (Med. Vel.)	210	965	900	840	435	375	330	1.3	5.4	4"V	$30
41 Rem. Magnum	210	1300	1160	1060	790	630	535	0.7	3.2	4"V	$33
41 Rem. Magnum	240	1250	1151	1075	833	706	616	0.8	3.3	6.5V	NA
44											
44 S&W Russian	247	780	NA	NA	335	NA	NA	NA	NA	NA	NA
44 Special	210	900	861	825	360	329	302	5.57	–	6.0	NA
44 Special FTX	165	900	848	802	297	263	235	NA	NA	2.5"	NA
44 S&W Special	180	980	NA	NA	383	NA	NA	NA	NA	6.5"	NA
44 S&W Special	180	1000	935	882	400	350	311	NA	NA	7.5"V	NA
44 S&W Special	200	875	825	780	340	302	270	1.2	6.0	6"	$13**
44 S&W Special	200	1035	940	865	475	390	335	1.1	4.9	6.5"	$13**
44 S&W Special	240/246	755	725	695	310	285	265	2.0	8.3	6.5"	$26
44-40 Win.	200	722	698	676	232	217	203	-3.4	-23.7	4.0	NA
44-40 Win.	205	725	689	655	239	216	195	–	–	7.5	NA
44-40 Win.	210	725	698	672	245	227	210	-11.6	–	5.5	NA
44-40 Win.	225	725	697	670	263	243	225	-3.4	-23.8	4.0	NA
44-40 Win. Cowboy	225	750	723	695	281	261	242				NA
44 Rem. Magnum	180	1610	1365	1175	1035	745	550	0.5	2.3	4"V	$18**
44 Rem. Magnum	200	1296	1193	1110	747	632	548	-.5	-6.2	6.0	NA
44 Rem. Magnum	200	1400	1192	1053	870	630	492	0.6	NA	6.5"	$20
44 Rem. Magnum	200	1500	1332	1194	999	788	633	–	–	7.5	NA
44 Rem. Magnum	210	1495	1310	1165	1040	805	635	0.6	2.5	6.5"	$18**
44 Rem. Mag. FlexTip	225	1410	1240	1111	993	768	617	NA	NA	NA	NA
44 (Med. Vel.)	240	1000	945	900	535	475	435	1.1	4.8	6.5"	$17
44 R.M. (Jacketed)	240	1180	1080	1010	740	625	545	0.9	3.7	4"V	$18**
44 R.M. (Lead)	240	1350	1185	1070	970	750	610	0.7	3.1	4"V	$29
44 Rem. Magnum	250	1180	1100	1040	775	670	600	0.8	3.6	6.5"V	$21
44 Rem. Magnum	250	1250	1148	1070	867	732	635	0.8	3.3	6.5"V	NA
44 Rem. Magnum	275	1235	1142	1070	931	797	699	0.8	3.3	6.5"	NA
44 Rem. Magnum	300	1150	1083	1030	881	781	706	–	–	7.5	NA
44 Rem. Magnum	300	1200	1100	1026	959	806	702	NA	NA	7.5"	$17
44 Rem. Magnum	330	1385	1297	1220	1406	1234	1090	1.83	0.00	NA	NA
44 Webley	262	850	–	–	–	–	–	–	–	–	NA
440 CorBon	260	1700	1544	1403	1669	1377	1136	1.58	NA	10"	NA

Cartridge	Bullet Wgt. Grs.	VELOCITY (fps)			ENERGY (ft. lbs.)			Mid-Range Traj. (in.)		Bbl. Lgth. (in).	Est. Price/ box
		Muzzle	50 yds.	100 yds.	Muzzle	50 yds.	100 yds.	50 yds.	100 yds.		
45, 50											
450 Short Colt/450 Revolver	226	830	NA	NA	350	NA	NA	NA	NA	NA	NEW
45 S&W Schofield	180	730	NA	NA	213	NA	NA	NA	NA	NA	NA
45 S&W Schofield	230	730	NA	NA	272	NA	NA	NA	NA	NA	NA
45 G.A.P.	165	1007	936	879	372	321	283	-1.4	-11.8	5.0	NA
45 G.A.P.	185	1090	970	890	490	385	320	1.0	4.7	5"	NA
45 G.A.P.	230	880	842	NA	396	363	NA	NA	NA	NA	NA
45 Automatic	150	1050	NA	NA	403	NA	NA	NA	NA	NA	$40
45 Automatic	165	1030	930	NA	385	315	NA	1.2	NA	5"	NA
45 Automatic Guard Dog	165	1140	1030	950	475	390	335	NA	NA	5"	NA
45 Automatic	185	1000	940	890	410	360	325	1.1	4.9	5"	$28
45 Auto. (Match)	185	770	705	650	245	204	175	2.0	8.7	5"	$28
45 Auto. (Match)	200	940	890	840	392	352	312	2.0	8.6	5"	$20
45 Automatic	200	975	917	860	421	372	328	1.4	5.0	5"	$18
45 Automatic	230	830	800	675	355	325	300	1.6	6.8	5"	$27
45 Automatic	230	880	846	816	396	366	340	1.5	6.1	5"	NA
45 Automatic +P	165	1250	NA	NA	573	NA	NA	NA	NA	NA	NA
45 Automatic +P	185	1140	1040	970	535	445	385	0.9	4.0	5"	$31
45 Automatic +P	200	1055	982	925	494	428	380	NA	NA	5"	NA
45 Super	185	1300	1190	1108	694	582	504	NA	NA	5"	NA
45 Win. Magnum	230	1400	1230	1105	1000	775	635	0.6	2.8	5"	$14**
45 Win. Magnum	260	1250	1137	1053	902	746	640	0.8	3.3	5"	$16**
45 Win. Mag. CorBon	320	1150	1080	1025	940	830	747	3.47			NA
455 Webley MKII	262	850	NA	NA	420	NA	NA	NA	NA	NA	NA
45 Colt FTX	185	920	870	826	348	311	280	NA	NA	3"V	NA
45 Colt	200	1000	938	889	444	391	351	1.3	4.8	5.5"	$21
45 Colt	225	960	890	830	460	395	345	1.3	5.5	5.5"	$22
45 Colt + P CorBon	265	1350	1225	1126	1073	884	746	2.65	0.0		NA
45 Colt + P CorBon	300	1300	1197	1114	1126	956	827	2.78	0.0		NA
45 Colt	250/255	860	820	780	410	375	340	1.6	6.6	5.5"	$27
454 Casull	250	1300	1151	1047	938	735	608	0.7	3.2	7.5"V	NA
454 Casull	260	1800	1577	1381	1871	1436	1101	0.4	1.8	7.5"V	NA
454 Casull	300	1625	1451	1308	1759	1413	1141	0.5	2.0	7.5"V	NA
454 Casull CorBon	360	1500	1387	1286	1800	1640	1323	2.01	0.0		NA
460 S&W	200	2300	2042	1801	2350	1851	1441	0	-1.60	NA	NA
460 S&W	260	2000	1788	1592	2309	1845	1464	NA	NA	7.5"V	NA
460 S&W	250	1450	1267	1127	1167	891	705	NA	NA	8.375-V	NA
460 S&W	250	1900	1640	1412	2004	1494	1106	0	-2.75	NA	NA
460 S&W	300	1750	1510	1300	2040	1510	1125	NA	NA	8.4-V	NA
460 S&W	395	1550	1389	1249	2108	1691	1369	0	-4.00	NA	NA
475 Linebaugh	400	1350	1217	1119	1618	1315	1112	NA	NA	NA	NA
480 Ruger	325	1350	1191	1076	1315	1023	835	2.6	0.0	7.5"	NA
50 Action Exp.	300	1475	1251	1092	1449	1043	795	-	-	6"	NA
50 Action Exp.	325	1400	1209	1075	1414	1055	835	0.2	2.3	6"	$24**
500 S&W	275	1665	1392	1183	1693	1184	854	1.5	NA	8.375	NA
500 S&W	300	1950	1653	1396	2533	1819	1298	—	—	8.5	NA
500 S&W	325	1800	1560	1350	2340	1755	1315	NA	NA	8.4-V	NA
500 S&W	350	1400	1231	1106	1523	1178	951	NA	NA	10"	NA
500 S&W	400	1675	1472	1299	2493	1926	1499	1.3	NA	8.375	NA
500 S&W	440	1625	1367	1169	2581	1825	1337	1.6	NA	8.375	NA
500 S&W	500	1300	1178	1085	1876	1541	1308	—	—	8.5	NA
500 S&W	500	1425	1281	1164	2254	1823	1505	NA	NA	10"	NA

Note: The actual ballistics obtained with your firearm can vary considerably from the advertised ballistics.
Also, ballistics can vary from lot to lot with the same brand and type load.

Cartridge	Bullet Wt. Grs.	Velocity (fps) 22-1/2" Bbl.		Energy (ft. lbs.) 22-1/2" Bbl.		Mid-Range Traj. (in.)	Muzzle Velocity
		Muzzle	100 yds.	Muzzle	100 yds.	100 yds.	6" Bbl.
17 Aguila	20	1850	1267	NA	NA	NA	NA
17 Hornady Mach 2	15.5	2050	1450	149	75	NA	NA
17 Hornady Mach 2	17	2100	1530	166	88	0.7	NA
17 HMR Lead Free	15.5	2550	1901	NA	NA	.90	NA
17 HMR TNT Green	16	2500	1642	222	96	NA	NA
17 HMR	17	2550	1902	245	136	NA	NA
17 HMR	17	2650	NA	NA	NA	NA	NA
17 HMR	20	2375	1776	250	140	NA	NA
17 Win. Super Mag.	20 Tipped	3000	2504	400	278	0.0	NA
17 Win. Super Mag.	20 JHP	3000	2309	400	237	0.0	NA
17 Win. Super Mag.	25 Tipped	2600	2230	375	276	0.0	NA
5mm Rem. Rimfire Mag.	30	2300	1669	352	188	NA	24
22 Short Blank	—	—	—	—	—	—	—
22 Short CB	29	727	610	33	24	NA	706
22 Short Target	29	830	695	44	31	6.8	786
22 Short HP	27	1164	920	81	50	4.3	1077
22 Colibri	20	375	183	6	1	NA	NA
22 Super Colibri	20	500	441	11	9	NA	NA
22 Long CB	29	727	610	33	24	NA	706
22 Long HV	29	1180	946	90	57	4.1	1031
22 LR Pistol Match	40	1070	890	100	70	4.6	940
22 LR Shrt. Range Green	21	1650	912	127	NA	NA	NA
CCI Quiet 22 LR	40	710	640	45	36	NA	NA
22 LR Sub Sonic HP	38	1050	901	93	69	4.7	NA
22 LR Segmented HP	40	1050	897	98	72	NA	NA
22 LR Standard Velocity	40	1070	890	100	70	4.6	940
22 LR AutoMatch	40	1200	990	130	85	NA	NA
22 LR HV	40	1255	1016	140	92	3.6	1060
22 LR Silhoutte	42	1220	1003	139	94	3.6	1025
22 SSS	60	950	802	120	86	NA	NA
22 LR HV HP	40	1280	1001	146	89	3.5	1085
22 Velocitor GDHP	40	1435	–	–	–	NA	NA
22LR CCI Copper	21	1850	–	–	–	–	–
22 LR Segmented HP	37	1435	1080	169	96	2.9	NA
22 LR Hyper HP	32/33/34	1500	1075	165	85	2.8	NA
22 LR Expediter	32	1640	NA	191	NA	NA	NA
22 LR Stinger HP	32	1640	1132	191	91	2.6	1395
22 LR Lead Free	30	1650	NA	181	NA	NA	NA
22 LR Hyper Vel	30	1750	1191	204	93	NA	NA
22 LR Shot #12	31	950	NA	NA	NA	NA	NA
22 WRF LFN	45	1300	1015	169	103	3	NA
22 Win. Mag. Lead Free	28	2200	NA	301	NA	NA	NA
22 Win. Mag.	30	2200	1373	322	127	1.4	1610
22 Win. Mag. V-Max BT	33	2000	1495	293	164	0.60	NA
22 Win. Mag. JHP	34	2120	1435	338	155	1.4	NA
22 Win. Mag. JHP	40	1910	1326	324	156	1.7	1480
22 Win. Mag. FMJ	40	1910	1326	324	156	1.7	1480
22 Win. Mag. Dyna Point	45	1550	1147	240	131	2.60	NA
22 Win. Mag. JHP	50	1650	1280	300	180	1.3	NA
22 Win. Mag. Shot #11	52	1000	–	NA	–	–	NA

NOTES: * = 10 rounds per box. ** = 5 rounds per box. Pricing variations and number of rounds per box can occur with type and brand of ammunition. Listed pricing is the average nominal cost for load style and box quantity shown. Not every brand is available in all shot size variations. Some manufacturers do not provide suggested list prices. All prices rounded to nearest whole dollar. The price you pay will vary dependent upon outlet of purchase. # = new load spec this year; "C" indicates a change in data.

10 Gauge 3-1/2" Magnum

Dram Equiv.	Shot Ozs.	Load Style	Shot Sizes	Brands	Avg. Price/box	Velocity (fps)
Max	2-3/8	magnum blend	5, 6, 7	Hevi-shot	NA	1200
4-1/2	2-1/4	premium	BB, 2, 4, 5, 6	Win., Fed., Rem.	$33	1205
Max	2	premium	4, 5, 6	Fed., Win.	NA	1300
4-1/4	2	high velocity	BB, 2, 4	Rem.	$22	1210
Max	18 pellets	premium	00 buck	Fed., Win.	$7**	1100
Max	1-7/8	Bismuth	BB, 2, 4	Bis.	NA	1225
Max	1-3/4	high density	BB, 2	Rem.	NA	1300
4-1/4	1-3/4	steel	TT, T, BBB, BB, 1, 2, 3	Win., Rem.	$27	1260
Mag	1-5/8	steel	T, BBB, BB, 2	Win.	$27	1285
Max	1-5/8	Bismuth	BB, 2, 4	Bismuth	NA	1375
Max	1-1/2	hypersonic	BBB, BB, 2	Rem.	NA	1700
Max	1-1/2	heavy metal	BB, 2, 3, 4	Hevi-Shot	NA	1500
Max	1-1/2	steel	T, BBB, BB, 1, 2, 3	Fed.	NA	1450
Max	1-3/8	steel	T, BBB, BB, 1, 2, 3	Fed., Rem.	NA	1500
Max	1-3/8	steel	T, BBB, BB, 2	Fed., Win.	NA	1450
Max	1-3/4	slug, rifled	slug	Fed.	NA	1280
Max	24 pellets	Buckshot	1 Buck	Fed.	NA	1100
Max	54 pellets	Super-X	4 Buck	Win.	NA	1150

12 Gauge 3-1/2" Magnum

Dram Equiv.	Shot Ozs.	Load Style	Shot Sizes	Brands	Avg. Price/box	Velocity (fps)
Max	2-1/4	premium	4, 5, 6	Fed., Rem., Win.	$13*	1150
Max	2	Lead	4, 5, 6	Fed.	NA	1300
Max	2	Copper plated turkey	4, 5	Rem.	NA	1300
Max	18 pellets	premium	00 buck	Fed., Win., Rem.	$7**	1100
Max	1-7/8	Wingmaster HD	4, 6	Rem.	NA	1225
Max	1-7/8	heavyweight	5, 6	Fed.	NA	1300
Max	1-3/4	high density	BB, 2, 4, 6	Rem.		1300
Max	1-7/8	Bismuth	BB, 2, 4	Bis.	NA	1225
Max	1-5/8	blind side	Hex, 1, 3	Win.	NA	1400
Max	1-5/8	Hevi-shot	T	Hevi-shot	NA	1350
Max	1-5/8	Wingmaster HD	T	Rem.	NA	1350
Max	1-5/8	high density	BB, 2	Fed.	NA	1450
Max	1-5/8	Blind side	Hex, BB, 2	Win.	NA	1400
Max	1-5/8	high density	BB, 2	Fed.	NA	1450
Max	1-5/8	Blind side	Hex, BB, 2	Win.	NA	1400
Max	1-3/8	Heavyweight	2, 4, 6	Fed.	NA	1450
Max	1-3/8	steel	T, BBB, BB, 2, 4	Fed., Win., Rem.	NA	1450
Max	1-1/2	FS steel	BBB, BB, 2	Fed.	NA	1500
Max	1-1/2	Supreme H-V	BBB, BB, 2, 3	Win.	NA	1475

12 Gauge 3-1/2" Magnum *(cont.)*

Dram Equiv.	Shot Ozs.	Load Style	Shot Sizes	Brands	Avg. Price/box	Velocity (fps)
Max	1-3/8	H-speed steel	BB, 2	Rem.	NA	1550
Max	1-1/4	Steel	BB, 2	Win.	NA	1625
Max	24 pellets	Premium	1 Buck	Fed.	NA	1100
Max	54 pellets	Super-X	4 Buck	Win.	NA	1050

12 Gauge 3" Magnum

Dram Equiv.	Shot Ozs.	Load Style	Shot Sizes	Brands	Avg. Price/box	Velocity (fps)
4	2	premium	BB, 2, 4, 5, 6	Win., Fed., Rem.	$9*	1175
4	1-7/8	premium	BB, 2, 4, 6	Win., Fed., Rem.	$19	1210
4	1-7/8	duplex	4x6	Rem.	$9*	1210
Max	1-3/4	turkey	4, 5, 6	Fed., Fio., Win., Rem.	NA	1300
Max	1-3/4	high density	BB, 2, 4	Rem.	NA	1450
Max	1-5/8	high density	BB, 2	Fed.	NA	1450
Max	1-5/8	Wingmaster HD	4, 6	Rem.	NA	1227
Max	1-5/8	high velocity	4, 5, 6	Fed.	NA	1350
4	1-5/8	premium	2, 4, 5, 6	Win., Fed., Rem.	$18	1290
Max	1-1/2	Wingmaster HD	T	Rem.	NA	1300
Max	1-1/2	Hevi-shot	T	Hevi-shot	NA	1300
Max	1-1/2	high density	BB, 2, 4	Rem.	NA	1300
Max	1-1/2	slug	slug	Bren.	NA	1604
Max	1-5/8	Bismuth	BB, 2, 4, 5, 6	Bis.	NA	1250
4	24 pellets	buffered	1 buck	Win., Fed., Rem.	$5**	1040
4	15 pellets	buffered	00 buck	Win., Fed., Rem.	$6**	1210
4	10 pellets	buffered	000 buck	Win., Fed., Rem.	$6**	1225
4	41 pellets	buffered	4 buck	Win., Fed., Rem.	$6**	1210
Max	1-3/8	heavyweight	5, 6	Fed.	NA	1300
Max	1-3/8	high density	B, 2, 4, 6	Rem. Win.	NA	1450
Max	1-3/8	slug	slug	Bren.	NA	1476
Max	1-3/8	blind side	Hex, 1, 3, 5	Win.	NA	1400
Max	1-1/4	slug, rifled	slug	Fed.	NA	1600
Max	1-3/16	saboted	slug	Bren.	NA	1476
Max	7/8	slug, rifled	slug	Rem.	NA	1875
Max	1-1/8	low recoil	BB	Fed.	NA	850
Max	1-1/8	steel	BB, 2, 3, 4	Fed., Win., Rem.	NA	1550
Max	1-1/16	high density	2, 4	Win.	NA	1400
Max	1	steel	4, 6	Fed.	NA	1330
Max	1-3/8	buckhammer	slug	Rem.	NA	1500

Dram Equiv.	Shot Ozs.	Load Style	Shot Sizes	Brands	Avg. Price/box	Velocity (fps)
12 Gauge 3" Magnum *(cont.)*						
Max	1	TruBall slug	slug	Fed.	NA	1700
Max	1	slug, rifled	slug, magnum	Win., Rem.	$5**	1760
Max	1-3/8	buckhammer	slug	Rem.	NA	1500
Max	1	saboted slug	slug	Rem., Win., Fed.	$10**	1550
Max	385 grs.	partition gold	slug	Win.	NA	2000
Max	1-1/8	Rackmaster	slug	Win.	NA	1700
Max	300 grs.	XP3	slug	Win.	NA	2100
3-5/8	1-3/8	steel	BBB, BB, 1, 2, 3, 4	Win., Fed., Rem.	$19	1275
Max	1-1/8	snow goose FS	BB, 2, 3, 4	Fed.	NA	1635
Max	1-1/8	steel	BB, 2, 4	Rem.	NA	1500
Max	1-1/8	steel	T, BBB, BB, 2, 4, 5, 6	Fed., Win.	NA	1450
Max	1-1/8	steel	BB, 2	Fed.	NA	1400
Max	1-1/8	FS lead	3, 4	Fed.	NA	1600
Max	1-3/8	Blind side	Hex, BB, 2	Win.	NA	1400
4	1-1/4	steel	T, BBB, BB, 1, 2, 3, 4, 6	Win., Fed., Rem.	$18	1400
Max	1-1/4	FS steel	BBB, BB, 2	Fed.	NA	1450
12 Gauge 2-3/4"						
Max	1-5/8	magnum	4, 5, 6	Win., Fed.	$8*	1250
Max	1-3/8	lead	4, 5, 6	Fiocchi	NA	1485
Max	1-3/8	turkey	4, 5, 6	Fio.	NA	1250
Max	1-3/8	steel	4, 5, 6	Fed.	NA	1400
Max	1-3/8	Bismuth	BB, 2, 4, 5, 6	Bis.	NA	1300
3-3/4	1-1/2	magnum	BB, 2, 4, 5, 6	Win., Fed., Rem.	$16	1260
Max	1-1/4	blind side	Hex, 2, 5	Win.	NA	1400
Max	1-1/4	Supreme H-V	4, 5, 6, 7-1/2	Win. Rem.	NA	1400
3-3/4	1-1/4	high velocity	BB, 2, 4, 5, 6, 7-1/2, 8, 9	Win., Fed., Rem., Fio.	$13	1330
Max	1-1/4	high density	B, 2, 4	Win.	NA	1450
Max	1-1/4	high density	4, 6	Rem.	NA	1325
3-1/4	1-1/4	standard velocity	6, 7-1/2, 8, 9	Win., Fed., Rem., Fio.	$11	1220
Max	1-1/8	Hevi-shot	5	Hevi-shot	NA	1350
3-1/4	1-1/8	standard velocity	4, 6, 7-1/2, 8, 9	Win., Fed., Rem., Fio.	$9	1255
Max	1-1/8	steel	2, 4	Rem.	NA	1390
Max	1	steel	BB, 2	Fed.	NA	1450
3-1/4	1	standard velocity	6, 7-1/2, 8	Rem., Fed., Fio., Win.	$6	1290
3-1/4	1-1/4	target	7-1/2, 8, 9	Win., Fed., Rem.	$10	1220
3	1-1/8	spreader	7-1/2, 8, 8-1/2, 9	Fio.	NA	1200

Dram Equiv.	Shot Ozs.	Load Style	Shot Sizes	Brands	Avg. Price/box	Velocity (fps)
12 Gauge 2-3/4" *(cont.)*						
3	1-1/8	target	7-1/2, 8, 9, 7-1/2x8	Win., Fed., Rem., Fio.	$7	1200
2-3/4	1-1/8	target	7-1/2, 8, 8-1/2, 9, 7-1/2x8	Win., Fed., Rem., Fio.	$7	1145
2-3/4	1-1/8	low recoil	7-1/2, 8	Rem.	NA	1145
2-1/2	26 grams	low recoil	8	Win.	NA	980
2-1/4	1-1/8	target	7-1/2, 8, 8-1/2, 9	Rem., Fed.	$7	1080
Max	1	spreader	7-1/2, 8, 8-1/2, 9	Fio.	NA	1300
3-1/4	28 grams (1 oz)	target	7-1/2, 8, 9	Win., Fed., Rem., Fio.	$8	1290
3	1	target	7-1/2, 8, 8-1/2, 9	Win., Fio.	NA	1235
2-3/4	1	target	7-1/2, 8, 8-1/2, 9	Fed., Rem., Fio.	NA	1180
3-1/4	24 grams	target	7-1/2, 8, 9	Fed., Win., Fio.	NA	1325
3	7/8	light	8	Fio.	NA	1200
3-3/4	8 pellets	buffered	000 buck	Win., Fed., Rem.	$4**	1325
4	12 pellets	premium	00 buck	Win., Fed., Rem.	$5**	1290
3-3/4	9 pellets	buffered	00 buck	Win., Fed., Rem., Fio.	$19	1325
3-3/4	12 pellets	buffered	0 buck	Win., Fed., Rem.	$4**	1275
4	20 pellets	buffered	1 buck	Win., Fed., Rem.	$4**	1075
3-3/4	16 pellets	buffered	1 buck	Win., Fed., Rem.	$4**	1250
4	34 pellets	premium	4 buck	Fed., Rem.	$5**	1250
3-3/4	27 pellets	buffered	4 buck	Win., Fed., Rem., Fio.	$4**	1325
		PDX1	1 oz. slug, 3-00 buck	Win.	NA	1150
Max	1 oz	segmenting, slug	slug	Win.	NA	1600
Max	1	saboted slug	slug	Win., Fed., Rem.	$10**	1450
Max	1-1/4	slug, rifled	slug	Fed.	NA	1520
Max	1-1/4	slug	slug	Lightfield		1440
Max	1-1/4	saboted slug	attached sabot	Rem.	NA	1550
Max	1	slug, rifled	slug, magnum	Rem., Fio.	$5**	1680
Max	1	slug, rifled	slug	Win., Fed., Rem.	$4**	1610
Max	1	sabot slug	slug	Sauvestre		1640
Max	7/8	slug, rifled	slug	Rem.	NA	1800
Max	400	plat. tip	sabot slug	Win.	NA	1700
Max	385 grains	Partition Gold Slug	slug	Win.	NA	1900
Max	385 grains	Core-Lokt bonded	sabot slug	Rem.	NA	1900
Max	325 grains	Barnes Sabot	slug	Fed.	NA	1900

Dram Equiv.	Shot Ozs.	Load Style	Shot Sizes	Brands	Avg. Price/box	Velocity (fps)
12 Gauge 2-3/4" (cont.)						
Max	300 grains	SST Slug	sabot slug	Hornady	NA	2050
Max	3/4	Tracer	#8 + tracer	Fio.	NA	1150
Max	130 grains	Less Lethal	.73 rubber slug	Lightfield	NA	600
Max	3/4	non-toxic	zinc slug	Win.	NA	NA
3	1-1/8	steel target	6-1/2, 7	Rem.	NA	1200
2-3/4	1-1/8	steel target	7	Rem.	NA	1145
3	1#	steel	7	Win.	$11	1235
3-1/2	1-1/4	steel	T, BBB, BB, 1, 2, 3, 4, 5, 6	Win., Fed., Rem.	$18	1275
3-3/4	1-1/8	steel	BB, 1, 2, 3, 4, 5, 6	Win., Fed., Rem., Fio.	$16	1365
3-3/4	1	steel	2, 3, 4, 5, 6, 7	Win., Fed., Rem., Fio.	$13	1390
Max	7/8	steel	7	Fio.	NA	1440
16 Gauge 2-3/4"						
3-1/4	1-1/4	magnum	2, 4, 6	Fed., Rem.	$16	1260
3-1/4	1-1/8	high velocity	4, 6, 7-1/2	Win., Fed., Rem., Fio.	$12	1295
2-3/4	1-1/8	standard velocity	6, 7-1/2, 8	Fed., Rem. Fio.	$9	1185
2-1/2	1	dove	6, 7-1/2, 8, 9	Fio., Win.	NA	1165
Max	1	Bismuth	4, 6	Rio	NA	1200
Max	15/16	steel	2, 4	Fed., Rem.	NA	1300
Max	7/8	steel	2, 4	Win.	$16	1300
3	12 pellets	buffered	1 buck	Win., Fed., Rem.	$4**	1225
Max	4/5	slug, rifled	slug	Win., Fed., Rem.	$4**	1570
Max	.92	sabot slug	slug	Sauvestre	NA	1560
20 Gauge 3" Magnum						
3	1-1/4	premium	2, 4, 5, 6, 7-1/2	Win., Fed., Rem.	$15	1185
Max	1-1/4	Wingmaster HD	4, 6	Rem.	NA	1185
3	1-1/4	turkey	4, 6	Fio.	NA	1200
Max	1-1/4	Hevi-shot	2, 4, 6	Hevi-shot	NA	1250
Max	1-1/8	high density	4, 6	Rem.	NA	1300
Max	18 pellets	buck shot	2 buck	Fed.	NA	1200
Max	24 pellets	buffered	3 buck	Win.	$5**	1150

Dram Equiv.	Shot Ozs.	Load Style	Shot Sizes	Brands	Avg. Price/box	Velocity (fps)
20 Gauge 3" Magnum (cont.)						
2-3/4	20 pellets	buck	3 buck	Rem.	$4**	1200
Max	1	hypersonic	2, 3, 4	Rem.	NA	Rem.
3-1/4	1	steel	1, 2, 3, 4, 5, 6	Win., Fed., Rem.	$15	1330
Max	1	blind side	Hex, 2, 5	Win.	NA	1300
Max	7/8	steel	2, 4	Win.	NA	1300
Max	7/8	FS lead	3, 4	Fed.	NA	1500
Max	1-1/16	high density	2, 4	Win.	NA	1400
Max	1-1/16	Bismuth	2, 4, 5, 6	Bismuth	NA	1250
Mag	5/8	saboted slug	275 gr.	Fed.	NA	1900
Max	3/4	TruBall slug	slug	Fed.	NA	1700
Max	3/4	TruBall slug	slug	Fed.	NA	1700
20 Gauge 2-3/4"						
2-3/4	1-1/8	magnum	4, 6, 7-1/2	Win., Fed., Rem.	$14	1175
2-3/4	1	high velocity	4, 5, 6, 7-1/2, 8, 9	Win., Fed., Rem., Fio.	$12	1220
Max	1	Bismuth	4, 6	Bis.	NA	1200
Max	1	Hevi-shot	5	Hevi-shot	NA	1250
Max	1	Supreme H-V	4, 6, 7-1/2	Win. Rem.	NA	1300
Max	1	FS lead	4, 5, 6	Fed.	NA	1350
Max	7/8	Steel	2, 3, 4	Fio.	NA	1500
2-1/2	1	standard velocity	6, 7-1/2, 8	Win., Rem., Fed., Fio.	$6	1165
2-1/2	7/8	clays	8	Rem.	NA	1200
2-1/2	7/8	promotional	6, 7-1/2, 8	Win., Rem., Fio.	$6	1210
2-1/2	1	target	8, 9	Win., Rem.	$8	1165
Max	7/8	clays	7-1/2, 8	Win.	NA	1275
2-1/2	7/8	target	8, 9	Win., Fed., Rem.	$8	1200
Max	3/4	steel	2, 4	Rem.	NA	1425
2-1/2	7/8	steel - target	7	Rem.	NA	1200
1-1/2	7/8	low recoil	8	Win.	NA	980
Max	1	buckhammer	slug	Rem.	NA	1500
Max	5/8	Saboted Slug	Copper Slug	Rem.	NA	1500
Max	20 pellets	buffered	3 buck	Win., Fed.	$4	1200

20 Gauge 2-3/4" (cont.)

Dram Equiv.	Shot Ozs.	Load Style	Shot Sizes	Brands	Avg. Price/box	Velocity (fps)
Max	5/8	slug, saboted	slug	Win.,	$9**	1400
2-3/4	5/8	slug, rifled	slug	Rem.	$4**	1580
Max	3/4	saboted slug	copper slug	Fed., Rem.	NA	1450
Max	3/4	slug, rifled	slug	Win., Fed., Rem., Fio.	$4**	1570
Max	.9	sabot slug	slug	Sauvestre		1480
Max	260 grains	Partition Gold Slug	slug	Win.	NA	1900
Max	260 grains	Core-Lokt Ultra	slug	Rem.	NA	1900
Max	260 grains	saboted slug	platinum tip	Win.	NA	1700
Max	3/4	steel	2, 3, 4, 6	Win., Fed., Rem.	$14	1425
Max	250 grains	SST slug	slug	Hornady	NA	1800
Max	1/2	rifled, slug	slug	Rem.	NA	1800
Max	67 grains	Less lethal	2/.60 rubber balls	Lightfield	NA	900

28 Gauge 3"

Dram Equiv.	Shot Ozs.	Load Style	Shot Sizes	Brands	Avg. Price/box	Velocity (fps)
Max	7/8	tundra tungsten	4, 5, 6	Fiocchi	NA	TBD

28 Gauge 2-3/4"

Dram Equiv.	Shot Ozs.	Load Style	Shot Sizes	Brands	Avg. Price/box	Velocity (fps)
2	1	high velocity	6, 7-1/2, 8	Win.	$12	1125
2-1/4	3/4	high velocity	6, 7-1/2, 8, 9	Win., Fed., Rem., Fio.	$11	1295
2	3/4	target	8, 9	Win., Fed., Rem.	$9	1200
Max	3/4	sporting clays	7-1/2, 8-1/2	Win.	NA	1300
Max	3/4	Bismuth	5, 7	Rio	NA	1250
Max	5/8	steel	6, 7	NA	NA	1300
Max	5/8	slug		Bren.	NA	1450

410 Bore 3"

Dram Equiv.	Shot Ozs.	Load Style	Shot Sizes	Brands	Avg. Price/box	Velocity (fps)
Max	11/16	high velocity	4, 5, 6, 7-1/2, 8, 9	Win., Fed., Rem., Fio.	$10	1135
Max	9/16	Bismuth	5, 7	Rio	NA	1175
Max	3/8	steel	6	NA	NA	1400
		judge	5 pellets 000 Buck	Fed.	NA	960
		judge	9 pellets #4 Buck	Fed.	NA	1100
Max	Mixed	Per. Defense	3DD/12BB	Win.	NA	750

410 Bore 2-1/2"

Dram Equiv.	Shot Ozs.	Load Style	Shot Sizes	Brands	Avg. Price/box	Velocity (fps)
Max	1/2	high velocity	4, 6, 7-1/2	Win., Fed., Rem.	$9	1245
Max	1/5	slug, rifled	slug	Win., Fed., Rem.	$4**	1815
1-1/2	1/2	target	8, 8-1/2, 9	Win., Fed., Rem., Fio.	$8	1200
Max	1/2	sporting clays	7-1/2, 8, 8-1/2	Win.	NA	1300
Max		Buckshot	5-000 Buck	Win.	NA	1135
		judge	12-bb's, 3 disks	Win.	NA	TBD
Max	Mixed	Per. Defense	4DD/16BB	Win.	NA	750
Max	42 grains	Less lethal	4/.41 rubber balls	Lightfield	NA	1150

ACCU-TEK AT-380 II ACP
Caliber: 380 ACP. **Capacity:** 6-round magazine. **Barrel:** 2.8 in. **Weight:** 23.5 oz. **Length:** 6.125 in. overall. **Grips:** Textured black composition. **Sights:** Blade front,rear adjustable for windage. **Features:** Made from 17-4 stainless steel, has an exposed hammer, manual firing-pin safety block and trigger disconnect. Magazine release located on the bottom of the grip. American made, lifetime warranty. Comes with two 6-round stainless steel magazines and a California-approved cable lock. Introduced 2006. Made in USA by Excel Industries.
Price: Satin stainless **$289.00**

ACCU-TEK HC-380
Similar to AT-380 II except has a 13-round magazine.
Price: **$330.00**

ACCU-TEK LT-380
Similar to AT-380 II except has a lightweight aluminum frame. **Weight:** 15 ounces.
Price: **$324.00**

AMERICAN CLASSIC 1911-A1
Caliber: .45 ACP. **Capacity:** 7+1 magazine **Barrel:** 5 in. **Grips:** Checkered walnut. **Sights:** Fixed. **Finish:** Blue or hard chromed. A .22 LR version is also available. Other variations include Trophy model with adjustable sights, two-tone finish.
Price: .... **$609.00–$819.00**

AMERICAN CLASSIC COMMANDER
Caliber: .45 ACP. Same features as 1911-A1 model except is Commander size with 4.25-in. barrel.
Price: .... **$624.00–$795.00**

AMERICAN TACTICAL IMPORTS MILITARY 1911
Caliber: .45 ACP. **Capacity:** 7+1 magazine. **Barrel:** 5 in. **Grips:** Textured mahogany. **Sights:** Fixed military style. **Finish:** Blue. Also offered in Commander and Officer's sizes and Enhanced model with additional features.
Price: .... **$500.00–$899.00**

AMERICAN TACTICAL IMPORTS GSG 1911
Caliber: .22 LR. **Capacity:** 10+1 magazine. **Weight:** 34 oz. Other features and dimensions similar to centerfire 1911.
Price: **$299.95**

AUTO-ORDNANCE 1911A1
Caliber: 45 ACP. **Capacity:** 7-round magazine. **Barrel:** 5 in. **Weight:** 39 oz. **Length:** 8.5 in. overall. **Grips:** Brown checkered plastic with medallion. **Sights:** Blade front, rear drift-adjustable for windage. **Features:** Same specs as 1911A1 military guns-parts interchangeable. Frame and slide blued; each radius has non-glare finish. Introduced 2002. Made in USA by Kahr Arms.
Price: 1911PKZSE Parkerized, plastic grips **$688.00**
Price: 1911PKZSEW Parkerized, wood grips... **$705.00**
Price: 1911BKOW Black matte finish, wood grips **$750.00**

BAER H.C. 40
Caliber: 40 S&W. **Capacity:** 18- round magazine. **Barrel:** 5 in. **Weight:** 37 oz. **Length:** 8.5 in. overall. **Grips:** Wood. **Sights:** Low-mount adjustable rear sight with hidden rear leaf, dovetail front sight. **Features:** Double-stack Caspian frame, beavertail grip safety, ambidextrous thumb safety, 40 S&W match barrel with supported chamber, match stainless steel barrel bushing, lowered and flared ejection port, extended ejector, match trigger fitted, integral mag well, bead blast blued finish on lower, polished sides on slide. Introduced 2008. Made in USA by Les Baer Custom, Inc.
Price: **$2,960.00**

BAER 1911 BOSS .45
Caliber: .45 ACP. **Capacity:** 8+1 capacity. **Barrel:** 5 in. **Weight:** 37 oz. **Length:** 8.5 in. overall. **Grips:** Premium Checkered Cocobolo Grips. **Sights:** Low-Mount LBC Adj. Sight, Red Fiber Optic Front. **Features:** Speed Trgr, Beveled Mag Well, Rounded for Tactical. Rear cocking serrations on the slide, Baer fiber optic front sight (red), flat mainspring housing, checkered at 20 LPI, extended combat safety, Special tactical package, chromed complete lower, blued slide, (2) 8-round premium magazines.
Price: **$2,560.00**

BAER 1911 CUSTOM CARRY
Caliber: .45 ACP. **Capacity:** 7- or 10-round magazine. **Barrel:** 5 in. **Weight:** 37 oz. **Length:** 8.5 in. overall. **Grips:** Checkered walnut. **Sights:** Baer improved ramp-style dovetailed front, Novak low-mount rear. **Features:** Baer forged NM frame, slide and barrel with stainless bushing. Baer speed trigger with 4-lb. pull. Partial listing shown. Made in USA by Les Baer Custom, Inc.
Price: Custom Carry 5, blued **$2,190.00**
Price: Custom Carry 5, stainless **$2,290.00**
Price: Custom Carry 4 Commanche-length, blued **$2,190.00**
Price: Custom Carry 4 Commanche-length, .38 Super **$2,550.00**

Prices given are believed to be accurate at time of publication however, many factors affect retail pricing so exact prices are not possible.

BAER 1911 ULTIMATE RECON

Caliber: .45 ACP. **Capacity:** 7- or 10-round magazine. **Barrel:** 5 in. **Weight:** 37 oz. **Length:** 8.5 in. overall. **Grips:** Checkered cocobolo. **Sights:** Baer improved ramp-style dovetailed front, Novak low-mount rear. **Features:** NM Caspian frame, slide and barrel with stainless bushing. Baer speed trigger with 4-lb. pull. Includes integral Picatinny rail and Sure-Fire X-200 light. Made in USA by Les Baer Custom, Inc. Introduced 2006.
Price: Bead blast blued $2,650.00
Price: Bead blast chrome $2,910.00

BAER 1911 PREMIER II

Calibers: .38 Super, 400 Cor-Bon, .45 ACP. **Capacity:** 7- or 10-round magazine. **Barrel:** 5 in. **Weight:** 37 oz. **Length:** 8.5 in. overall. **Grips:** Checkered rosewood, double diamond pattern. **Sights:** Baer dovetailed front, low-mount Bo-Mar rear with hidden leaf. **Features:** Baer NM forged steel frame and barrel with stainless bushing, deluxe Commander hammer and sear, beavertail grip safety with pad, extended ambidextrous safety; flat mainspring housing; 30 LPI checkered front strap. Made in USA by Les Baer Custom, Inc.
Price: 5 in. .45 ACP $2,180.00
Price: 5 in. 400 Cor-Bon $2,380.00
Price: 5 in. .38 Super $2,620.00
Price: 6 in. .45 ACP, 400 Cor-Bon, .38 Super, From $2,390.00
Price: Super-Tac, .45 ACP, 400 Cor-Bon, .38 Super, From $2,650.00

BAER 1911 S.R.P.

Caliber: .45 ACP. **Barrel:** 5 in. **Weight:** 37 oz. **Length:** 8.5 in. overall. **Grips:** Checkered walnut. **Sights:** Trijicon night sights. **Features:** Similar to the F.B.I. contract gun except uses Baer forged steel frame. Has Baer match barrel with supported chamber, complete tactical action. Has Baer Ultra Coat finish. Introduced 1996. Made in USA by Les Baer Custom, Inc.
Price: Government or Commanche Length $2,840.00

BAER 1911 STINGER

Calibers: .45 ACP or .38 Super. **Capacity:** 7-round magazine. **Barrel:** 5 in. **Weight:** 34 oz. **Length:** 8.5 in. overall. **Grips:** Checkered cocobolo. **Sights:** Baer dovetailed front, low-mount Bo-Mar rear with hidden leaf. **Features:** Baer NM frame. Baer Commanche slide, Officer's style grip frame, beveled mag well. Made in USA by Les Baer Custom, Inc.
Price: .45 ACP .... $2,240.00–$2,310.00
Price: .38 Super $2,840.00

BAER 1911 PROWLER III

Caliber: .45 ACP. **Capacity:** 8-round magazine. **Barrel:** 5 in. **Weight:** 34 oz. **Length:** 8.5 in. overall. **Grips:** Checkered cocobolo. **Sights:** Baer dovetailed front, low-mount Bo-Mar rear with hidden leaf. **Features:** Similar to Premier II with tapered cone stub weight, rounded corners. Made in USA by Les Baer Custom, Inc.
Price: Blued $2,910.00

BAER HEMI 572

Caliber: .45 ACP. Based on Les Baer's 1911 Premier I pistol and inspired by Chrysler 1970 Hemi Cuda muscle car. **Features:** Double serrated slide, Baer fiber optic front sight with green insert, VZ black recon grips with hex-head screws, hard chrome finish on all major components, Dupont S coating on barrel, trigger, hammer, ambi safety and other controls.
Price: $2,690.00

BAER ULTIMATE MASTER COMBAT

Calibers: .45 ACP or .38 Super. A full house competition 1911 offered in 8 variations including 5 or 6-inch barrel, PPC Distinguished or Open class, Bullseye Wadcutter class and others. Features include double serrated slide, fitted slide to frame, checkered front strap and trigger guard, serrated rear

of slide, extended ejector, tuned extractor, premium checkered grips, blued finish and two 8-round magazines.
Price: Compensated .45 .... $3,240.00
Price: Compensated. 38 Super $3,390.00

BERETTA M92/96 A1 SERIES

Calibers: 9mm, .40 S&W. **Capacities:** 15-round magazine; .40 S&W, 12 rounds (M96 A1). **Barrel:** 4.9 in. **Weight:** 33-34 oz. **Length:** 8.5 in. **Sights:** Fiber optic front, adjustable rear. **Features:** Same as other models in 92/96 family except for addition of accessory rail.
Price: $775.00

BERETTA MODEL 92FS

Caliber: 9mm. **Capacity:** 10-round magazine. **Barrels:** 4.9 in., 4.25 in. (Compact). **Weight:** 34 oz. **Length:** 8.5 in. overall. **Grips:** Checkered black plastic. **Sights:** Blade front, rear adjustable for windage. Tritium night sights available. **Features:** Double action. Extractor acts as chamber loaded indicator, squared trigger guard, grooved front and backstraps, inertia firing pin. Matte or blued finish. Introduced 1977. Made in USA
Price: $699.00
Price: Inox $850.00

BERETTA M9 .22 LR

Caliber: .22 LR. **Capacity:** 10 or 15-round magazine. **Features:** Black Brunitron finish, interchangeable grip panels. Similar to centerfire 92/M9 with same operating controls, lighter weight (26 oz.).
Price: $430.00

BERETTA MODEL U22 NEOS

Caliber: .22 LR. **Capacity:** 10-round magazine. **Barrels:** 4.5 in. and 6 in. **Weights:** 32 oz.; 36 oz. **Length:** 8.8 in./10.3 in. **Sights:** Target. **Features:** Integral rail for standard scope mounts, light, perfectly weighted, 100 percent American made by Beretta.
Price: Blue $325.00
Price: Inox $350.00

BERETTA MODEL PX4 STORM

Calibers: 9mm, 40 S&W. **Capacities:** 17 (9mm Para.); 14 (40 S&W). **Barrel:** 4 in. **Weight:** 27.5 oz. **Grips:** Black checkered w/3 interchangeable backstraps. **Sights:** 3-dot system coated in Superluminova; removable front and rear sights. **Features:** DA/SA, manual safety/hammer decocking lever (ambi) and automatic firing pin block safety. Picatinny rail. Comes with two magazines (17/10 in 9mm Para. and 14/10 in 40 S&W). Removable hammer unit. American made by Beretta. Introduced 2005.
Price: 9mm or .40 .... $650.00
Price: .45 ACP $700.00
Price: .45 ACP SD (Special Duty) $1,150.00

BERETTA MODEL PX4 STORM SUB-COMPACT

Calibers: 9mm, 40 S&W. **Capacities:** 13 (9mm); 10 (40 S&W). **Barrel:** 3 in. **Weight:** 26.1 oz. **Length:** 6.2 in. overall. **Grips:** NA. **Sights:** NA. **Features:** Ambidextrous manual safety lever, interchangeable backstraps included, lock breech and tilt barrel system, stainless steel barrel, Picatinny rail.
Price: $650.00

BERETTA MODEL M9

Caliber: 9mm. **Capacity:** 15. **Barrel:** 4.9 in. **Weights:** 32.2-35.3 oz. **Grips:** Plastic. **Sights:** Dot and post, low profile, windage adjustable rear. **Features:** DA/SA, forged aluminum alloy frame, delayed locking-bolt system, manual

safety doubles as decocking lever, combat-style trigger guard, loaded chamber indicator. Comes with two magazines (15/10). American made by Beretta. Introduced 2005.
Price: $675.00

BERETTA MODEL M9A1

Caliber: 9mm. **Capacity:** 15. **Barrel:** 4.9 in. **Weights:** 32.2-35.3 oz. **Grips:** Plastic. **Sights:** Dot and post, low profile, windage adjustable rear. **Features:** Same as M9, but also includes integral Mil-Std-1913 Picatinny rail, has checkered front and backstrap. Comes with two magazines (15/10). American made by Beretta. Introduced 2005.
Price: $775.00

BERETTA M9A3

Caliber: 9mm. **Capacity:** 10 or 15. **Features:** Same general specifications as M9A1 with safety lever able to be converted to decocker configuration. Flat Dark Earth finish. Comes with three magazines, Vertec-style thin grip.
Price: $1,100.00

BERETTA NANO

Caliber: 9mm. **Capacity:** 6-round magazine. **Barrel:** 3.07 in. **Weight:** 17.7 oz. **Length:** 5.7 in. overall. **Grips:** Polymer. **Sights:** 3-dot low profile. **Features:** Double-action only, striker fired. Replaceable grip frames.
Price: $475.00

BERSA THUNDER 380 SERIES
Caliber: .380 ACP. **Capacity:** 7 rounds. **Barrel:** 3.5 in. **Weight:** 23 oz. **Length:** 6.6 in. overall. **Features:** Otherwise similar to Thunder 45 Ultra Compact. 380 DLX has 9-round capacity. 380 Concealed Carry has 8-round capacity. Imported from Argentina by Eagle Imports, Inc.
Price: Thunder Matte **$335.00**
Price: Thunder Satin Nickel **$355.00**
Price: Thunder Duo-Tone **$355.00**
Price: Thunder Duo-Tone with Crimson Trace Laser Grips **$555.00**

BERSA THUNDER 9 ULTRA COMPACT/40 SERIES
Calibers: 9mm, 40 S&W. **Barrel:** 3.5 in. **Weight:** 24.5 oz. **Length:** 6.6 in. overall. **Features:** Otherwise similar to Thunder 45 Ultra Compact. 9mm Para. High Capacity model has 17-round capacity. 40 High Capacity model has 13-round capacity. Imported from Argentina by Eagle Imports, Inc.
Price: **$500.00**

BERSA THUNDER 22
Caliber: .22 LR. **Capacity:** 10-round magazine. **Weight:** 19 oz. **Features:** Similar to Thunder .380 Series except for caliber. Alloy frame and slide. Finish: Matte black, satin nickel or duo-tone.
Price: **$320.00**

BERETTA PICO
Caliber: .380 ACP. **Capacity:** 6-round magazine. **Barrel:** 2.7 in. **Weight:** 11.5 oz. **Length:** 5.1 in. overall. **Grips:** Integral with polymer frame. Interchangeable backstrap. **Sights:** White outline rear. **Features:** Adjustable, quick-change. Striker-fired, double-action only operation. Ambidextrous magazine release and slide release. Ships with two magazines, one flush, one with grip extension. Made in the USA.
Price: **$399.00**

BERSA THUNDER 45 ULTRA COMPACT
Caliber: .45 ACP. **Barrel:** 3.6 in. **Weight:** 27 oz. **Length:** 6.7 in. overall. **Grips:** Anatomically designed polymer. **Sights:** White outline rear. **Features:** Double action; firing pin safeties, integral locking system. Available in matte, satin nickel, gold, or duo-tone. Introduced 2003. Imported from Argentina by Eagle Imports, Inc.
Price: Thunder 45, matte blue **$500.00**
Price: Thunder 45, duo-tone **$550.00**

BERSA THUNDER PRO XT
Caliber: 9mm. **Capacity:** 17-round magazine. **Barrel:** 5 in. **Weight:** 34 oz. **Grips:** Checkered black polymer. **Sights:** Adjustable rear, dovetail fiber optic front. **Features:** Available with matte or duo-tone finish. Traditional double/single action design developed for competition. Comes with five magazines.
Price: **$923.00**

BROWNING 1911-22 COMPACT

Caliber: .22 LR **Capacity:** 10-round magazine. **Barrel:** 3.625 in. **Weight:** 15 oz. **Length:** 6.5 in. overall. **Grips:** Brown composite. **Sights:** Fixed. **Features:** Slide is machined aluminum with alloy frame and matte blue finish. Blowback action and single action trigger with manual thumb and grip safeties. Works, feels and functions just like a full-size 1911. It is simply scaled down and chambered in the best of all practice rounds: .22 LR for focus on the fundamentals.
Price: **$600.00**

BROWNING 1911-22 A1

Caliber: .22 LR, **Capacity:** 10-round magazine. **Barrel:** 4.25 in. **Weight:** 16 oz. **Length:** 7.0625 in. overall. **Grips:** Brown composite. **Sights:** Fixed. **Features:** Slide is machined aluminum with alloy frame and matte blue finish. Blowback action and single action trigger with manual thumb and grip safeties. Works, feels and functions just like a full-size 1911. It is simply scaled down and chambered in the best of all practice rounds: .22 LR for focus on the fundamentals.
Price: **$600.00**

BROWNING 1911-22 BLACK LABEL

Caliber: .22 LR. **Capacity:** 10-round magazine. **Barrels:** 4.25 in. or 3.625 in. (Compact model). **Weight:** 14 oz. overall. **Features:** Other features are similar to standard 1911-22 except for this model's composite/polymer frame, extended grip safety, stippled black laminated grip, skeleton trigger and hammer. Available with accessory rail (shown). Suppressor Ready model has threaded muzzle protector, 4.875-inch barrel.
Price: **$640.00**
Price: With Rail.. **$670.00**
Price: Suppressor Ready model... **$740.00**

BROWNING 1911-22 POLYMER DESERT TAN

Caliber: .22 LR. **Capacity:** 10-round magazine. **Barrels:** 4.25 in. or 3.625 in. **Weight:** 13–14 oz. overall. **Features:** Other features are similar to standard 1911-22 except for this model's composite/polymer frame. Also available with pink composite grips.
Price: **$580.00**

BROWNING 1911-380

Caliber: .380 ACP. **Capacity:** 8-round magazine. **Barrels:** 4.25 in. or 3.625 in. (Compact). **Weight:** 16 to 17.5 oz. **Features:** Aluminum or stainless slide, polymer frame with or without rail. Features are virtually identical to those on the 1911-22. 1911-380 Pro has three-dot combat or night sights, G10 grips, accessory rail. Medallion Pro has checkered walnut grips.
Price: **$670.00**
Price: Pro, Medallion Pro...................................... **$800.00–$910.00**

BROWNING HI POWER

No longer in production, although some Hi Powers may still be available at a limited number of dealers. **Caliber:** 9mm. **Capacity:** 13-round magazine. **Barrel:** 4.625 in. **Weight:** 32 oz. **Length:** 7.75 in. **Grips:** Checkered walnut (standard model), textured and grooved polymer (Mark III). **Sights:** Fixed low-profile 3-dot (Mark III), fixed or adjustable low profile (standard model). **Features:** Single-action operation with ambidextrous thumb safety, forged steel frame and slide. Made in Belgium.

Price: Mark III **$1,110.00**
Price: Fixed Sights... **$1,120.00**
Price: Standard, Adjustable sights **$1,200.00**

BROWNING BUCK MARK CAMPER UFX

Caliber: .22 LR. **Capacity:** 10-round magazine. **Barrel:** 5.5-in. tapered bull. **Weight:** 34 oz. **Length:** 9.5 in. overall. **Grips:** Overmolded Ultragrip Ambidextrous. **Sights:** Pro-Target adjustable rear, ramp front. **Features:** Matte blue receiver, matte blue or stainless barrel.

Price: Camper UFX.. **$390.00**
Price: Camper UFX stainless **$430.00**

BROWNING BUCK MARK HUNTER

Caliber: .22 LR. **Capacity:** 10-round magazine. **Barrel:** 7.25-in. heavy tapered bull. **Weight:** 38 oz. **Length:** 11.3 in. overall. **Grips:** Cocobolo target. **Sights:** Pro-Target adjustable rear, Tru-Glo/Marble's fiber-optic front. Integral scope base on top rail. Scope in photo not included. **Features:** Matte blue.

Price: **$500.00**

BROWNING BUCK PRACTICAL URX

Caliber: .22 LR. **Capacity:** 10-round magazine. **Barrels:** 5.5-in. tapered bull or 4-in. slab-sided (Micro). **Weight:** 34 oz. **Length:** 9.5 in. overall. **Grips:** Ultragrip RX Ambidextrous. **Sights:** Pro-Target adjustable rear, Tru-Glo/Marble's fiber-optic front. **Features:** Matte gray receiver, matte blue barrel.

Price: **$479.00**
Price: Stainless **$470.00**
Price: Micro **$470.00**

BROWNING BUCK MARK PLUS UDX

Caliber: .22 LR. **Capacity:** 10-round magazine. **Barrel:** 5.5-in. slab-sided. **Weight:** 34 oz. **Length:** 9.5 in. overall. **Grips:** Walnut Ultragrip DX Ambidextrous or rosewood. **Sights:** Pro-Target adjustable rear, Tru-Glo/Marble's fiber-optic front. **Features:** Matte blue or stainless.

Price: **$550.00**
Price: Stainless.. **$600.00**

BROWNING BUCK MARK FIELD TARGET SUPPRESSOR READY

Caliber: .22 LR. **Capacity:** 10-round magazine. **Barrel:** 5.5-in. heavy bull, suppressor ready. **Grips:** Cocobolo target. **Sights:** Pro-Target adjustable rear, Tru-Glo/Marble's fiber-optic front. Integral scope base on top rail. Scope in photo not included. **Features:** Matte blue.

Price: **$600.00**

CHIAPPA 1911-22

Caliber: .22 LR. **Capacity:** 10-round magazine. **Barrel:** 5 in. **Weight:** 33.5 oz. **Length:** 8.5 in. **Grips:** Two-piece wood. **Sights:** Fixed. **Features:** A faithful replica of the famous John Browning 1911A1 pistol. Fixed barrel design. Available in black, OD green or tan finish. Target and Tactical models have adjustable sights.

Price: From .... **$269.00–$408.00**

CHIAPPA M9-22 STANDARD

Caliber: .22 LR. **Barrel:** 5 in. **Weight:** 2.3 lbs. **Length:** 8.5 in. **Grips:** Black molded plastic or walnut. **Sights:** Fixed front sight and windage adjustable rear sight. **Features:** The M9 9mm has been a U.S. standard-issue service pistol since 1990. Chiappa's M9-22 is a replica of this pistol in 22 LR. The M9-22 has the same weight and feel as its 9mm counterpart but has an affordable 10-shot magazine for the .22 Long Rifle cartridge, which makes it a true rimfire reproduction. Comes standard with steel trigger, hammer assembly and a 1/2x28 threaded barrel.

Price: **$339.00**

CHIAPPA M9-22 TACTICAL

Caliber: .22 LR. **Barrel:** 5 in. **Weight:** 2.3 lbs. **Length:** 8.5 in. **Grips:** Black molded plastic. **Sights:** Fixed front sight and Novak-style rear sights. **Features:** The M9-22 Tactical model comes with a faux suppressor (this ups the "cool factor" on the range and extends the barrel to make it even more accurate). It also has a 1/2x28 thread adaptor that can be used with a legal suppressor.
Price: $419.00

CHRISTENSEN ARMS 1911 SERIES

Calibers: .45 ACP, .40 S&W, 9mm. **Barrels:** 3.7 in., 4.3 in., 5.5 in. **Features:** All models are built on a titanium frame with hand-fitted slide, match-grade barrel, tritium night sights and G10 Operator grip panels.
Price: .... $1,995.00–$3,799.00

CITADEL M-1911

Calibers: .45 ACP, 9mm. **Capacity:** 7 (.45), 8 (9mm). **Barrels:** 5 or 3.5 in (.45 & 9mm only). **Weight:** 2.3 lbs. **Length:** 8.5 in. **Grips:** Checkered wood or Hogue wrap-around polymer. **Sights:** Low-profile combat fixed rear, blade front. **Finish:** Matte black, brushed or polished nickel. **Features:** Extended grip safety, ambidextrous safety and slide release. Built by Armscor (Rock Island Armory) in the Philippines and imported by Legacy Sports.
Price: Matte black $592.00
Price: Matte black, Hogue grips $630.00
Price: Brushed nickel $681.00
Price: Polished nickel... $700.00

CIMARRON MODEL 1911

Caliber: .45 ACP. **Barrel:** 5 in. **Weight:** 37.5 oz. **Length:** 8.5 in. overall. **Grips:** Checkered walnut. **Features:** A faithful reproduction of the original pattern of the Model 1911 with Parkerized finish and lanyard ring. Polished or nickel finish available.
Price: $541.00

CIMARRON MODEL 1911 WILD BUNCH

Caliber: .45 ACP. **Barrel:** 5 in. **Weight:** 37.5 oz. **Length:** 8.5 in. overall. **Grips:** Checkered walnut. **Features:** Original WWI 1911 frame with flat mainspring housing, correct markings, polished blue finish, comes with tanker shoulder holster.
Price: $842.00

COBRA ENTERPRISES FS32, FS380

Calibers: .32 ACP or .380 ACP. **Capacity:** 7 rounds. **Barrel:** 3.5 in. **Weight:** 2.1 lbs. **Length:** 6.375 in. overall. **Grips:** Black molded synthetic integral with frame. **Sights:** Fixed. Made in USA by Cobra Enterprises of Utah, Inc.
Price: .... $138.00–$250.00

COBRA ENTERPRISES PATRIOT SERIES

Calibers: .380, 9mm or .45 ACP. **Capacities:** 6-, 7- or 10-round magazine. **Barrel:** 3.3 in. **Weight:** 20 oz. **Length:** 6 in. overall. **Grips:** Black polymer. **Sights:** Fixed. **Features:** Bright chrome, satin nickel or black finish. Made in USA by Cobra Enterprises of Utah, Inc.
Price: .... $349.00–$395.00

COBRA DENALI

Caliber: .380 ACP. **Capacity:** 5 rounds. **Barrel:** 2.8 in. **Weight:** 22 oz. **Length:** 5.4 in. **Grips:** Black molded synthetic integral with frame. **Sights:** Fixed. **Features:** Made in USA by Cobra Enterprises of Utah, Inc.
Price: $179.00

COLT MODEL 1991 MODEL O

Caliber: .45 ACP. **Capacity:** 7-round magazine. **Barrel:** 5 in. **Weight:** 38 oz. **Length:** 8.5 in. overall. **Grips:** Checkered black composition. **Sights:** Ramped blade front, fixed square notch rear, high profile. **Features:** Matte finish. Continuation of serial number range used on original G.I. 1911A1 guns. Comes with one magazine and molded carrying case. Introduced 1991. Series 80 firing system.
Price: Blue $799.00
Price: Stainless $879.00

COLT XSE SERIES MODEL O COMBAT ELITE

Caliber: .45 ACP. **Capacity:** 8-round magazine. **Barrel:** 5 in. **Grips:** Checkered, double-diamond rosewood. **Sights:** Three white-dot Novak. **Features:** Brushed stainless receiver with blued slide; adjustable, two-cut aluminum trigger; extended ambidextrous thumb safety; upswept beavertail with palm swell; elongated slot hammer.
Price: $1,100.00

COLT LIGHTWEIGHT COMMANDER

Calibers: .45 ACP, 8-shot, 9mm (9 shot). **Barrel:** 4.25 in. **Weight:** 26 oz. alloy frame, 33 oz. (steel frame). **Length:** 7.75 in. overall. **Grips:** G10 Checkered Black Cherry. **Sights:** Novak White Dot front, Low Mount Carry rear. **Features:** Blued slide, black anodized frame. Aluminum alloy frame.
Price: $999.00
Price: Combat Commander w/steel frame.......................... $949.00

Prices given are believed to be accurate at time of publication however, many factors affect retail pricing so exact prices are not possible.

COLT DEFENDER

Caliber: .45 ACP (7-round magazine), 9mm (8-round). **Barrel:** 3 in. **Weight:** 22.5 oz. **Length:** 6.75 in. overall. **Grips:** Pebble-finish rubber wraparound with finger grooves. **Sights:** White dot front, snag-free Colt competition rear. **Features:** Stainless or blued finish; aluminum frame; combat-style hammer; Hi-Ride grip safety, extended manual safety, disconnect safety. Introduced 1998. Made in USA by Colt's Mfg. Co., Inc.
Price: Stainless $899.00
Price: Blue $949.00

COLT SERIES 70

Caliber: .45 ACP. **Barrel:** 5 in. **Weight:** 37.5 oz. **Length:** 8.5 in. **Grips:** Rosewood with double diamond checkering pattern. **Sights:** Fixed. **Features:** Custom replica of the Original Series 70 pistol with a Series 70 firing system, original roll marks. Introduced 2002. Made in USA by Colt's Mfg. Co., Inc.
Price: Blued $899.00
Price: Stainless $979.00

COLT 38 SUPER

Caliber: .38 Super. **Barrel:** 5 in. **Weight:** 36.5 oz. **Length:** 8.5 in. **Grips:** Wood with double diamond checkering pattern. **Finish:** Bright stainless. **Sights:** 3-dot. **Features:** Beveled magazine well, standard thumb safety and service-style grip safety. Introduced 2003. Made in USA. by Colt's Mfg. Co., Inc.
Price: $1,499.00

COLT MUSTANG POCKETLITE

Caliber: .380 ACP. **Capacity:** 6-round magazine. **Barrel:** 2.75 in. **Weight:** 12.5 oz. **Length:** 5.5 in. **Grips:** Black composite. **Finish:** Brushed stainless. **Features:** Thumb safety, firing-pin safety block. Introduced 2012.
Price: $599.00

COLT MUSTANG LITE

Caliber: .380 ACP. Similar to Mustang Pocketlite except has black polymer frame.
Price: $499.00

COLT MUSTANG XSP

Caliber: .380 ACP. **Features:** Similar to Mustang Pocketlite except has polymer frame, black diamond or bright stainless slide, squared trigger guard, accessory rail, electroless nickel finished controls.
Price: Bright Stainless.. $528.00
Price: Black Diamond-Like Carbon finish............................. $672.00

COLT RAIL GUN

Caliber: .45 ACP. **Capacity:** (8+1). **Barrel:** 5 in. **Weight:** 40 oz. **Length:** 8.5 in. **Grips:** Rosewood double diamond. **Sights:** White dot front and Novak rear. **Features:** 1911-style semi-auto. Stainless steel frame and slide, front and rear slide serrations, skeletonized trigger, integral accessory rail, Smith & Alexander upswept beavertail grip palm swell safety, tactical thumb safety, National Match barrel.
Price: $1,199.00

COLT SPECIAL COMBAT GOVERNMENT CARRY MODEL

Calibers: .45 ACP (8+1), .38 Super (9+1). **Barrel:** 5 in. **Weight:** NA. **Length:** 8.5 in. **Grips:** Black/silver synthetic. **Sights:** Novak front and rear night sights. **Features:** 1911-style semi-auto. Skeletonized three-hole trigger, slotted hammer, Smith & Alexander upswept beavertail grip palm swell safety and extended magazine well, Wilson tactical ambidextrous safety. Available in blued, hard chrome, or blued/satin-nickel finish, depending on chambering. Marine pistol has desert tan Cerakote stainless steel finish, lanyard loop.
Price: $2,095.00

COLT GOVERNMENT MODEL 1911A1 .22

Caliber: .22 LR. **Capacity:** 12-round magazine. **Barrel:** 5 in. **Weight:** 36 oz. **Features:** Made in Germany by Walther under exclusive arrangement with Colt Manufacturing Company. Blowback operation. All other features identical to original, including manual and grip safeties, drift-adjustable sights.
Price: $399.00

Prices given are believed to be accurate at time of publication however, many factors affect retail pricing so exact prices are not possible.

Tactical *GunDigest* ⊕ **285**

COLT COMPETITION PISTOL
Calibers: .45 ACP, .38 Super or 9mm Para. Full-size Government Model with 5-inch national match barrel, dual-spring recoil operating system, adjustable rear and fiber optic front sights, custom G10 Colt logo grips.
Price: **$999.00**
Price: 38 Super **$1,099.00**

COLT SERIES 70 NATIONAL MATCH GOLD CUP
Caliber: .45 ACP. **Barrel:** 5 in. national match. **Weight:** 37 oz. **Length:** 8.5 in. **Grips:** Checkered walnut with gold medallions. **Sights:** Adjustable Bomar rear, target post front. Finish: blued. **Features:** Flat top slide, flat mainspring housing. Wide three-hole aluminum trigger.
Price: **$1,299.00**

COLT GOLD CUP TROPHY Calibers: .45 ACP or 9mm. Updated version of the classic Colt target and service pistol first introduced in the late 1950s to give shooters a serious competition pistol out of the box. Features include an undercut trigger guard, upswept beavertail grip safety and dual-spring recoil system. Checkering on the front and rear of the grip strap is 25 LPI with blue G10 grips. The new Gold Cup Trophy is built on the Series 70 firing system. Re-introduced to the Colt catalog in 2017.
Price: **$1,699.00**

CZ 75 B
Calibers: 9mm, .40 S&W. **Capacity:** 10-round magazine. **Barrel:** 4.7 in. **Weight:** 34.3 oz. **Length:** 8.1 in. overall. **Grips:** High impact checkered plastic. **Sights:** Square post front, rear adjustable for windage; 3-dot

---

system. **Features:** Single action/double action; firing pin block safety; choice of black polymer, matte or high-polish blue finishes. All-steel frame. B-SA is a single action with a drop-free magazine. Imported from the Czech Republic by CZ-USA.
Price: 75 B **$625.00**
Price: 75 B, stainless **$783.00**
Price: 75 B-SA **$661.00**

CZ 75 BD DECOCKER
Similar to the CZ 75B except has a decocking lever in place of the safety lever. All other specifications are the same. Introduced 1999. Imported from the Czech Republic by CZ-USA.
Price: 9mm, black polymer **$612.00**

CZ 75 B COMPACT
Similar to the CZ 75 B except has 14-round magazine in 9mm, 3.9-in. barrel and weighs 32 oz. Has removable front sight, non-glare ribbed slide top. Trigger guard is squared and serrated; combat hammer. Introduced 1993. Imported from the Czech Republic by CZ-USA.
Price: 9mm, black polymer **$631.00**
Price: 9mm, dual tone or satin nickel **$651.00**
Price: 9mm. D PCR Compact, alloy frame **$651.00**

CZ P-07 DUTY
Calibers: .40 S&W, 9mm. **Capacity:** 16+1. **Barrel:** 3.8 in. **Weight:** 27.2 oz. **Length:** 7.3 in. overall. **Grips:** Polymer black Polycoat. **Sights:** Blade front, fixed groove rear. **Features:** The ergonomics and accuracy of the CZ 75 with a totally new trigger system. The new Omega trigger system simplifies the CZ 75 trigger system, uses fewer parts and improves the trigger pull. In addition, it allows users to choose between using the handgun with a decocking lever (installed) or a manual safety (included) by a simple parts change. The polymer frame design of the Duty and a new sleek slide profile (fully machined from bar stock) reduce weight, making the P-07 Duty a great choice for concealed carry.
Price: **$524.00**

Prices given are believed to be accurate at time of publication however, many factors affect retail pricing so exact prices are not possible.

CZ P-09 DUTY

Calibers: 9mm, .40 S&W. **Capacity:** 19 (9mm), 15 (.40). **Features:** High-capacity version of P-07. Accessory rail, interchangeable grip backstraps, ambidextrous decocker can be converted to manual safety.

Price: **$544.00**

CZ 75 TACTICAL SPORT

Similar to the CZ 75 B except the CZ 75 TS is a competition ready pistol designed for IPSC standard division (USPSA limited division). Fixed target sights, tuned single-action operation, lightweight polymer match trigger with adjustments for take-up and overtravel, competition hammer, extended magazine catch, ambidextrous manual safety, checkered walnut grips, polymer magazine well, two-tone finish. Introduced 2005. Imported from the Czech Republic by CZ-USA.

Price: 9mm, 20-shot mag. **$1,310.00**
Price: .40 S&W, 16-shot mag. **$1,310.00**

CZ 75 SP-01

Similar to NATO-approved CZ 75 Compact P-01 model. Features an integral 1913 accessory rail on the dust cover, rubber grip panels, black Polycoat finish, extended beavertail, new grip geometry with checkering on front and back straps, and double or single action operation. Introduced 2005. The Shadow variant designed as an IPSC "production" division competition firearm. Includes competition hammer, competition rear sight and fiber-optic front sight, modified slide release, lighter recoil and mainspring for use with "minor power factor" competition ammunition. Includes Polycoat finish and slim walnut grips. Finished by CZ Custom Shop. Imported from the Czech Republic by CZ-USA.

Price: SP-01 Standard **$680.00**
Price: SP-01 Shadow Target II **$1,638.00**

CZ 97 B

Caliber: .45 ACP. **Capacity:** 10-round magazine. **Barrel:** 4.85 in. **Weight:** 40 oz. **Length:** 8.34 in. overall. **Grips:** Checkered walnut. **Sights:** Fixed. **Features:** Single action/double action; full-length slide rails; screw-in barrel bushing; linkless barrel; all-steel construction; chamber loaded indicator; dual transfer bars. Introduced 1999. Imported from the Czech Republic by CZ-USA.

Price: Black polymer **$707.00**
Price: Glossy blue **$727.00**

CZ 97 BD DECOCKER

Similar to the CZ 97 B except has a decocking lever in place of the safety lever. Tritium night sights. Rubber grips. All other specifications are the same. Introduced 1999. Imported from the Czech Republic by CZ-USA.

Price: 9mm, black polymer **$816.00**

CZ 2075 RAMI/RAMI P

Calibers: 9mm, .40 S&W. **Barrel:** 3 in. **Weight:** 25 oz. **Length:** 6.5 in. overall. **Grips:** Rubber. **Sights:** Blade front with dot, white outline rear drift adjustable for windage. **Features:** Single action/double action; alloy or polymer frame, steel slide; has laser sight mount. Imported from the Czech Republic by CZ-USA.

Price: 9mm, alloy frame, 10- and 14-shot magazines **$671.00**
Price: .40 S&W, alloy frame, 8-shot magazine **$671.00**
Price: RAMI P, polymer frame, 9mm, .40 S&W **$612.00**

CZ P-01

Caliber: 9mm. **Capacity:** 14-round magazine. **Barrel:** 3.85 in. **Weight:** 27 oz. **Length:** 7.2 in. overall. **Grips:** Checkered rubber. **Sights:** Blade front with dot, white outline rear drift adjustable for windage. **Features:** Based on the CZ 75, except with forged aircraft-grade aluminum alloy frame. Hammer forged barrel, decocker, firing-pin block, M3 rail, dual slide serrations, squared trigger guard, re-contoured trigger, lanyard loop on butt. Serrated front and backstrap. Introduced 2006. Imported from the Czech Republic by CZ-USA.

Price: CZ P-01 .... **$680.00**

CZ 805 BREN S1

Calibers: 5.56 NATO or .300 AAC Blackout. **Capacity:** 30-round capacity. **Barrel:** 11 in. **Weight:** 6.7 lbs. **Features:** Semi-automatic version of 9mm. 20-round magazine. Semi-automatic version of Czech military large-frame pistol. Uses AR-type magazines. Aluminum frame, adjustable sights, accessory rails.

Price: **$1,799.00**

Prices given are believed to be accurate at time of publication however, many factors affect retail pricing so exact prices are not possible.

Tactical GunDigest® ✛ **287**

CZ SCORPION EVO

Caliber: 9mm. **Capacity:** 20-round magazine. **Features:** Semi-automatic version of CZ Scorpion Evo submachine gun. Ambidextrous controls, adjustable sights, accessory rails.
Price: **$849.00**

DAN WESSON DW RZ-10

Caliber: 10mm. **Capacity:** 9-round magazine. **Barrel:** 5 in. **Grips:** Diamond checkered cocobolo. **Sights:** Bo-Mar-style adjustable target sight. **Weight:** 38.3 oz. **Length:** 8.8 in. overall. **Features:** Stainless steel frame and serrated slide. Series 70-style 1911, stainless steel frame, forged stainless steel slide. Commander-style match hammer. Reintroduced 2005. Made in USA by Dan Wesson Firearms, distributed by CZ-USA.
Price: 10mm, 8+1 .... **$1,558.00**

DAN WESSON DW RZ-45 HERITAGE

Caliber: .45 ACP. **Capacity:** 7-round magazine. **Weight:** 36 oz. **Length:** 8.8 in. overall. Similar to the RZ-10 Auto except in .45 ACP.
Price: 10mm, 8+1 .... **$1,428.00**

DAN WESSON VALOR 1911

Calibers: 9mm, .40 S&W, .45 ACP. **Barrel:** 5 in. **Grips:** Slim Line G10. **Sights:** Heinie Ledge Straight Eight adjustable night sights. **Weight:** 2.4 lbs. **Length:** 8.8 in. overall. **Features:** The defensive-style Valor is a base stainless 1911 with matte black finish. Other features include forged stainless frame and match

barrel with 25 LPI checkering and undercut trigger guard, adjustable defensive night sights, and Slim Line VZ grips. Silverback model has polished stainless slide and matte black frame Made in USA by Dan Wesson Firearms, distributed by CZ-USA.
Price: **$2,012.00**
Price: 10mm **$2,271.00**
Price: Silverback .... **$1,883.00–$2,064.00**

DAN WESSON SPECIALIST

Caliber: .45 ACP. **Capacity:** 8-round magazine. **Barrel:** 5 in. **Grips:** G10 VZ Operator II. **Sights:** Single amber tritium dot rear, green lamp with white target ring front sight. **Features:** Integral Picatinny rail, 25 LPI frontstrap checkering, undercut trigger guard, ambidextrous thumb safety, extended mag release and detachable two-piece mag well.
Price: **$1,701.00**

DAN WESSON V-BOB

Caliber: .45 ACP. **Capacity:** 8-round magazine. **Barrel:** 4.25 in. **Weight:** 34 oz. **Length:** 8 in. **Grips:** Slim Line G10. **Sights:** Heinie Ledge Straight-Eight Night Sights. **Features:** Black matte or stainless finish. Bobtail forged grip frame with 25 LPI checkering front and rear.
Price: **$2,077.00**

DAN WESSON VALKYRIE

Caliber: .45 ACP. **Barrel:** 4.25 in. **Length:** 7.75 in. **Grips:** Slim Line G10. **Sights:** Tritium Night Sights. **Features:** Similar to V-Bob except has Commander-size slide on Officer-size frame.
Price: **$2,012.00**

DAN WESSON POINTMAN

Calibers: 9mm, .38 Super, .45 ACP. **Capacity:** 8 or 9-round magazine. **Barrel:** 5 in. **Length:** 8.5 in. **Grips:** Double-diamond cocobolo. **Sights:** Adjustable rear and fiber optic front. **Features:** Undercut trigger guard, checkered front strap, serrated rib on top of slide.
Price: .45, .38 Super **$1,597.00**
Price: 9mm **$1,558.00**

DAN WESSON A2

Caliber: .45 ACP. **Capacity:** 8-round magazine capacity. Limited production model based on traditional 1911A1 design. **Features:** Modern fixed combat sights, lowered/flared ejection port, double-diamond walnut grips. Introduced 2017.
Price: **$1,363.00**

DESERT EAGLE 1911 G

Caliber: .45 ACP. **Capacity:** 8-round magazine. **Barrels:** 5 in. or 4.33 in. (DE1911C Commander size), or 3.0 in. (DE1911U Undercover). **Grips:** Double diamond checkered wood. **Features:** Extended beavertail grip safety, checkered flat mainspring housing, skeletonized hammer and trigger, extended mag release and thumb safety, stainless full-length guide road, enlarged ejection port, beveled mag well and high-profile sights. Comes with two 8-round magazines.
Price: $904.00
Price: Undercover.. $1,019.00

DESERT EAGLE MARK XIX

Calibers: .357 Mag., 9 rounds; .44 Mag., 8 rounds; .50 AE, 7 rounds. **Barrels:** 6 in., 10 in., interchangeable. **Weight:** 62 oz. (.357 Mag.); 69 oz. (.44 Mag.); 72 oz. (.50 AE) **Length:** 10.25-in. overall (6-in. bbl.). **Grips:** Polymer; rubber available. **Sights:** Blade-on-ramp front, combat-style rear. Adjustable available. **Features:** Interchangeable barrels; rotating three-lug bolt; ambidextrous safety; adjustable trigger. Military epoxy finish. Satin, bright nickel, chrome, brushed, matte or black-oxide finishes available. 10-in. barrel extra. Imported from Israel by Magnum Research, Inc.
Price: .... $1,572.00–$2,060.00

BABY DESERT EAGLE III

Calibers: 9mm, .40 S&W, .45 ACP. **Capacities:** 10-, 12- or 15-round magazines. **Barrels:** 3.85 in. or 4.43 in. **Weights:** 28–37.9 oz. **Length:** 7.25–8.25 overall. **Grips:** Ergonomic polymer. **Sights:** White 3-dot system. **Features:** Choice of steel or polymer frame with integral rail; slide-mounted decocking safety. Upgraded design of Baby Eagle II series.
Price: .... $646.00–$691.00

DESERT EAGLE L5

Caliber: .357 Magnum. **Capacity:** 9+1. **Barrel:** 5 in. **Weight:** 50 oz. **Length:** 9.7 in. **Features:** Steel barrel, frame and slide with full Weaver-style accessory rail and integral muzzle brake. Gas-operated rotating bolt, single-action trigger, fixed sights.
Price: From $1,790.00

DESERT EAGLE MR9, MR40

Caliber: 9mm, (15-round magazine) or .40 S&W (11 rounds). **Barrel:** 4.5 in. **Weight:** 25 oz. **Length:** 7.6 in. overall. **Sights:** Three-dot rear sight adjustable for windage, interchangeable front sight blades of different heights. **Features:** Polymer frame, locked breech, striker-fired design with decocker/safety button on top of slide, three replaceable grip palm swells, Picatinny rail. Made in Germany by Walther and imported by Magnum Research. Introduced 2014.
Price: $559.00

DIAMONDBACK DB380

Caliber: .380 ACP. **Capacity:** 6+1. **Barrel:** 2.8 in. **Weight:** 8.8 oz. **Features:** ZERO-Energy striker firing system with a mechanical firing pin block, steel magazine catch, windage-adjustable sights. Frames available with several color finish options.
Price: .... $290.00–$350.00

DIAMONDBACK DB9

Caliber: 9mm. **Capacity:** 6+1. **Barrel:** 3 in. **Weight:** 11 oz. **Length:** 5.60 in. **Features:** Other features similar to DB380 model.
Price: .... $290.00–$350.00

DIAMONDBACK DB FS NINE

Caliber: 9mm. **Capacity:** 15+1. **Barrel:** 4.75 in. **Weight:** 21.5 oz. **Length:** 7.8 in. **Features:** Double-action, striker-fired model with polymer frame and stainless steel slide. Flared mag well, extended magazine base pad, ergonomically contoured grip, fixed 3-dot sights, front and rear slide serrations, integral MIL-STD 1913 Picatinny rail.
Price: $483.00

Prices given are believed to be accurate at time of publication however, many factors affect retail pricing so exact prices are not possible.

Tactical GunDigest® ✦ **289**

DOUBLESTAR 1911 SERIES

Caliber: .45 ACP. **Capacity:** 8-round magazine. **Barrels:** 3.5 in., 4.25 in., 5 in. **Weights:** 33–40 oz. **Grips:** Cocobolo wood. **Sights:** Novak LoMount 2 white-dot rear, Novak white-dot front. **Features:** Single action, M1911-style with forged frame and slide of 4140 steel, stainless steel barrel machined from bar stock by Storm Lake, funneled mag well, accessory rail, black Nitride finish.
Price: .... $1,364.00–$2,242.00

EAA WITNESS FULL SIZE

Calibers: 9mm, .38 Super. **Capacity:** 18-round magazine; .40 S&W, 10mm, 15-round magazine; .45 ACP, 10-round magazine. **Barrel:** 4.5 in. **Weight:** 35.33 oz. **Length:** 8.1 in. overall. **Grips:** Checkered rubber. **Sights:** Undercut blade front, open rear adjustable for windage. **Features:** Double-action/single-action trigger system; round trigger guard; frame-mounted safety. Available with steel or polymer frame. Also available with interchangeable .45 ACP and .22 LR slides. Steel frame introduced 1991. Polymer frame introduced 2005. Imported from Italy by European American Armory.
Price: Steel frame $607.00
Price: Polymer frame $571.00
Price: 45/22 .22 LR, full-size steel frame, blued $752.00

EAA WITNESS COMPACT

Caliber: 9mm. **Capacity:** 14-round magazine; .40 S&W, 10mm, 12-round magazine; .45 ACP, 8-round magazine. **Barrel:** 3.6 in. **Weight:** 30 oz. **Length:** 7.3 in. overall. **Features:** Available with steel or polymer frame (shown). All polymer frame Witness pistols are capable of being converted to other calibers. Otherwise similar to full-size Witness. Imported from Italy by European American Armory.
Price: Polymer frame $571.00
Price: Steel frame $607.00

EAA WITNESS-P CARRY

Caliber: 9mm. **Capacity:** 17-round magazine; 10mm, 15-round magazine; .45 ACP, 10-round magazine. **Barrel:** 3.6 in. **Weight:** 27 oz. **Length:** 7.5 in. overall. **Features:** Otherwise similar to full-size Witness. Polymer frame introduced 2005. Imported from Italy by European American Armory.
Price: $711.00

EAA WITNESS PAVONA COMPACT POLYMER

Calibers: .380 ACP (13-round magazine), 9mm (13) or .40 S&W (9). **Barrel:** 3.6 in. **Weight:** 30 oz. **Length:** 7 in. overall. **Features:** Designed primarily for women with fine-tuned recoil and hammer springs for easier operation, a polymer frame with integral checkering, contoured lines and in black, charcoal, blue, purple or magenta with silver or gold sparkle.
Price: .... $476.00–$528.00

EAA WITNESS ELITE 1911

Caliber: .45 ACP. **Capacity:** 8-round magazine. **Barrel:** 5 in. **Weight:** 32 oz. **Length:** 8.58 in. overall. **Features:** Full-size 1911-style pistol with either steel or polymer frame. Also available in Commander or Officer's models with 4.25- or 3.5-in. barrel, polymer frame.
Price: $580.00
Price: Commander or Officer's Model................................. $627.00

EAA SAR B6P
Caliber: 9mm. Based on polymer frame variation of CZ 75 design. Manufactured by Sarsilmaz in Turkey. Features similar to Witness series.
Price: .... **$407.00–$453.00**

EAA SAR K2-45
Caliber: .45 ACP. **Barrel:** 4.7 in. **Weight:** 2.5 lbs. **Features:** Similar to B6P with upgraded features. Built by Sarsilmaz for the Turkish military. Features include a cocked and locked carry system, ergonomically designed grip, steel frame and slide construction, adjustable rear sight, extended beaver tail, serrated trigger guard and frame, removable dove-tail front sight, auto firing pin block and low barrel axis for reduced felt recoil.
Price: **$849.00**

ED BROWN KOBRA CARRY LIGHTWEIGHT
Caliber: .45 ACP. **Capacity:** 7-round magazine. **Barrel:** 4.25 in. (Commander model slide). **Weight:** 27 oz. **Grips:** Hogue exotic wood. **Sights:** 10-8 Performance U-notch plain black rear sight with .156-in. notch for fast acquisition of close targets. Fixed dovetail front night sight with high-visibility white outlines. **Features:** Aluminum frame and bobtail housing. Matte finished Gen III coated slide for low glare, with snakeskin on rear of slide only. Snakeskin pattern serrations on forestrap and mainspring housing, dehorned edges, beavertail grip safety. LW insignia on slide, which stands for Lightweight.
Price: Kobra Carry Lightweight **$3,495.00**

ED BROWN CLASSIC CUSTOM
Caliber: .45 ACP. **Capacity:** 7-round magazine. **Barrel:** 5 in. **Weight:** 40 oz. **Grips:** Cocobolo wood. **Sights:** Bo-Mar adjustable rear, dovetail front. **Features:** Single action, M1911 style, custom made to order, stainless frame and slide available. Special mirror-finished slide.
Price: From **$3,695.00**

ED BROWN KOBRA AND KOBRA CARRY
Caliber: .45 ACP. **Capacity:** 7-round magazine. **Barrels:** 5 in. (Kobra); 4.25 in. (Kobra Carry). **Weight:** 39 oz. (Kobra); 34 oz. (Kobra Carry). **Grips:** Hogue exotic wood. **Sights:** Ramp, front; fixed Novak low-mount night sights, rear. **Features:** Snakeskin pattern serrations on forestrap and mainspring housing, dehorned edges, beavertail grip safety.
Price: Kobra K-SS, From **$2,695.00**
Price: Kobra Carry, From.. **$2,945.00**

ED BROWN EXECUTIVE SERIES
Similar to other Ed Brown products, but with 25-LPI checkered frame and mainspring housing. Various finish, sight and grip options.
Price: .... **$2,695.00–$3,395.00**

ED BROWN SPECIAL FORCES
Similar to other Ed Brown products, but with ChainLink treatment on forestrap and mainspring housing. Entire gun coated with Gen III finish. Square cut serrations on rear of slide only. Dehorned. Introduced 2006. Available with various finish, sight and grip options.
Price: From .... **$2,156.00–$4,675.00**

ED BROWN SPECIAL FORCES CARRY
Similar to the Special Forces basic models. Features a 4.5-in. Commander Bobtail frame. Weighs approx. 35 oz. Fixed dovetail 3-dot night sights with high-visibility white outlines.
Price: From **$2,695.00**

EXCEL ARMS MP-22

Caliber: .22 WMR. **Capacity:** 9-round magazine. **Barrel:** 8.5-in. bull barrel. **Weight:** 54 oz. **Length:** 12.875 in. overall. **Grips:** Textured black composition. **Sights:** Fully adjustable target sights. **Features:** Made from 17-4 stainless steel, comes with aluminum rib, integral Weaver base, internal hammer, firing pin block. American made, lifetime warranty. Comes with two 9-round stainless steel magazines and a California-approved cable lock. .22 WMR Introduced 2006. Made in USA by Excel Arms.
Price: $477.00

EXCEL ARMS MP-5.7

Caliber: 5.7x28mm. **Capacity:** 9-round magazine. **Features:** Blowback action. Other features similar to MP-22. Red-dot optic sights, scope and rings are optional.
Price: $615.00
Price: With optic sights.. $685.00
Price: With scope and rings... $711.00

FIRESTORM 380

Caliber: .380 ACP. **Capacity:** 7+1. **Barrel:** 3.5 in. **Weight:** 20 oz. **Length:** 6.6 in. **Sights:** Fixed, white outline system. **Grips:** Rubber. **Finish:** Black matte. **Features:** Traditional DA/SA operation.
Price: $270.00

FMK 9C1 G2

Caliber: 9mm. **Capacity:** 10+1 or 14+1. **Barrel:** 4 in. **Overall length:** 6.85 in. **Weight:** 23.45 oz. **Finish:** Black, Flat Dark Earth or pink. **Sights:** Interchangeable Glock compatible. **Features:** Available in either single action or double action only. Polymer frame, high-carbon steel slide, stainless steel barrel. Very low bore axis and shock absorbing backstrap are said to result in low felt recoil. DAO model has Fast Action Trigger (FAT) with shorter pull and reset. Made in the USA.
Price: $409.95

FN FNS SERIES

Caliber: 9mm. **Capacity:** 17-round magazine, .40 S&W (14-round magazine). **Barrels:** 4 in. or 3.6 in. (Compact). **Weights:** 25 oz. (9mm), 27.5 oz. (.40). **Length:** 7.25 in. **Grips:** Integral polymer with two interchangeable backstrap inserts. **Features:** Striker fired, double action with manual safety, accessory rail, ambidextrous controls, 3-dot night sights.
Price: $599.00

FN FNX SERIES

Calibers: 9mm, .40 S&W. **Capacities:** 17-round magazine, .40 S&W (14 rounds), .45 ACP (10 or 14 rounds). **Barrels:** 4 in. (9mm and .40), 4.5 in. .45. **Weights:** 22–32 oz. (.45). **Lengths:** 7.4, 7.9 in. (.45). **Features:** DA/SA operation with decocking/manual safety lever. Has external extractor with loaded-chamber indicator, front and rear cocking serrations, fixed 3-dot combat sights.
Price: 9mm, .40 .... $699.00
Price: .45 ACP $824.00

FN FNX .45 TACTICAL

Similar to standard FNX .45 except with 5.3-in. barrel with threaded muzzle, polished chamber and feed ramp, enhanced high-profile night sights, slide cut and threaded for red-dot sight (not included), MIL-STD 1913 accessory rail, ring-style hammer.
Price: $1,400.00

FN FIVE-SEVEN

Caliber: 5.7x28mm. **Capacity:** 10- or 20-round magazine. **Barrel:** 4.8 in. **Weight:** 23 oz. **Length:** 8.2 in. **Features:** Adjustable three-dot system. Single-action polymer frame, chambered for low-recoil 5.7x28mm cartridge.
Price: $1,349.00

GLOCK 17/17C

Caliber: 9mm. **Capacities:** 17/19/33-round magazines. **Barrel:** 4.49 in. **Weight:** 22.04 oz. (without magazine). **Length:** 7.32 in. overall. **Grips:**

Black polymer. **Sights:** Dot on front blade, white outline rear adjustable for windage. **Features:** Polymer frame, steel slide; double-action trigger with Safe Action system; mechanical firing pin safety, drop safety; simple takedown without tools; locked breech, recoil operated action. ILS designation refers to Internal Locking System. Adopted by Austrian armed forces 1983. NATO approved 1984. Model 17L has 6-inch barrel, ported or non-ported, slotted and relieved slide, checkered grip with finger grooves, no accessory rail. Imported from Austria by Glock, Inc. USA.

Price: From	$599.00
Price: 17L	$750.00
Price: 17 Gen 4	$649.00
Price: 17 Gen 5	$599.99

GLOCK GEN4 SERIES

In 2010, a new series of Generation 4 pistols was introduced with several improved features. These included a multiple backstrap system offering three different size options, short, medium or large frame; reversible and enlarged magazine release; dual recoil springs; and RTF (Rough Textured Finish) surface. Some recent models are only available in Gen 4 configuration.

GEN 5 SERIES

A new frame design was introduced in 2017 named Generation 5. The finger grooves were removed for more versatility and the user can customize the grip by using different backstraps, as with the Gen 4 models. A flared mag well and a cutout at the front of the frame give the user more speed during reloading. There is a reversible and enlarged magazine catch, changeable by users, as well as the ambidextrous slide stop lever to accommodate left- and right-handed operators. The rifling and crown of the barrel are slightly modified for increased precision. As of 2018, Gen 5 variants are available in Glock Models 17, 19, 26 and 34.

GLOCK 19/19C

Caliber: 9mm. **Capacities:** 15/17/19/33-round magazines. **Barrel:** 4.02 in. **Weight:** 20.99 oz. (without magazine). **Length:** 6.85 in. overall. Compact version of Glock 17. Imported from Austria by Glock, Inc.

Price:	$599.00
Price: 19 Gen 4	$649.00
Price: 19 Gen 5	$749.00

GLOCK 20/20C 10MM

Caliber: 10mm. **Capacity:** 15-round magazine. **Barrel:** 4.6 in. **Weight:** 27.68 oz. (without magazine). **Length:** 7.59 in. overall. **Features:** Otherwise similar to Model 17. Imported from Austria by Glock, Inc. Introduced 1990.

Price: From	$637.00
Price: 20 Gen 4	$687.00

GLOCK MODEL 20 SF SHORT FRAME

Caliber: 10mm. **Barrel:** 4.61 in. with hexagonal rifling. **Weight:** 27.51 oz. **Length:** 8.07 in. overall. **Sights:** Fixed. **Features:** Otherwise similar to the Model 20 but with short-frame design, extended sight radius.

Price:	$637.00

GLOCK 21/21C

Caliber: .45 ACP. **Capacity:** 13-round magazine. **Barrel:** 4.6 in. **Weight:** 26.28 oz. (without magazine). **Length:** 7.59 in. overall. **Features:** Otherwise similar to the Model 17. Imported from Austria by Glock, Inc. Introduced 1991. SF version has tactical rail, smaller diameter grip, 10-round magazine capacity. Introduced 2007.

Price: From	$637.00
Price: 21 Gen 4	$687.00

GLOCK 22/22C

Caliber: .40 S&W. **Capacities:** 15/17-round magazine. **Barrel:** 4.49 in. **Weight:** 22.92 oz. (without magazine). **Length:** 7.32 in. overall. **Features:** Otherwise similar to Model 17, including pricing. Imported from Austria by Glock, Inc. Introduced 1990.

Price: From	$599.00
Price: 22C	$649.00
Price: 22 Gen 4	$649.00

GLOCK 23/23C

Caliber: .40 S&W. **Capacities:** 13/15/17-round magazine. **Barrel:** 4.02 in. **Weight:** 21.16 oz. (without magazine). **Length:** 6.85 in. overall. **Features:** Otherwise similar to the Model 22, including pricing. Compact version of Glock 22. Imported from Austria by Glock, Inc. Introduced 1990.

Price:	$599.00
Price: 23C Compensated	$621.00
Price: 23 Gen 4	$649.00

GLOCK 24/24C

Caliber: .40 S&W. **Capacities:** 10/15/17 or 22-round magazine. **Features:** Similar to Model 22 except with 6.02-inch barrel, ported or non-ported, trigger pull recalibrated to 4.5 lbs.

Price: From	$750.00

GLOCK 26

Caliber: 9mm. **Capacities:** 10/12/15/17/19/33-round magazine. **Barrel:** 3.46 in. **Weight:** 19.75 oz. **Length:** 6.29 in. overall. Subcompact version of Glock 17. Imported from Austria by Glock, Inc.

Price:	$599.00
Price: 26 Gen 4	$649.00
Price: 26 Gen 5	$749.00

GLOCK 27

Caliber: .40 S&W. **Capacities:** 9/11/13/15/17-round magazine. **Barrel:** 3.46 in. **Weight:** 19.75 oz. (without magazine). **Length:** 6.29 overall. **Features:** Otherwise similar to the Model 22, including pricing. Subcompact version of Glock 22. Imported from Austria by Glock, Inc. Introduced 1996.

Price: From	$599.00
Price: 27 Gen 4	$649.00

GLOCK 29 GEN 4

Caliber: 10mm. **Capacities:** 10/15-round magazine. **Barrel:** 3.78 in. **Weight:** 24.69 oz. (without magazine). **Length:** 6.77 in. overall. **Features:** Otherwise similar to the Model 20, including pricing. Subcompact version of the Glock 20. Imported from Austria by Glock, Inc. Introduced 1997.

Price: Fixed sight	$637.00

GLOCK MODEL 29 SF SHORT FRAME
Caliber: 10mm. **Barrel:** 3.78 in. with hexagonal rifling. **Weight:** 24.52 oz. **Length:** 6.97 in. overall. **Sights:** Fixed. **Features:** Otherwise similar to the Model 29 but with short-frame design, extended sight radius.
Price: **$637.00**

GLOCK 30 GEN 4
Caliber: .45 ACP. **Capacities:** 9/10/13-round magazines. **Barrel:** 3.78 in. **Weight:** 23.99 oz. (without magazine). **Length:** 6.77 in. overall. **Features:** Otherwise similar to the Model 21, including pricing. Subcompact version of the Glock 21. Imported from Austria by Glock, Inc. Introduced 1997. SF version has tactical rail, octagonal rifled barrel with a 1:15.75 rate of twist, smaller diameter grip, 10-round magazine capacity. Introduced 2008.
Price: **$637.00**
Price: 30 SF (short frame) **$637.00**

GLOCK 30S
Caliber: .45 ACP. **Capacity:** 10-round magazine. **Barrel:** 3.78 in. **Weight:** 20 oz. **Length:** 7 in. **Features:** Variation of Glock 30 with a Model 36 slide on a Model 30SF frame (short frame).
Price: **$637.00**

GLOCK 31/31C
Caliber: .357 Auto. **Capacities:** 15/17-round magazine. **Barrel:** 4.49 in. **Weight:** 23.28 oz. (without magazine). **Length:** 7.32 in. overall. **Features:** Otherwise similar to the Model 17. Imported from Austria by Glock, Inc.
Price: From **$599.00**
Price: 31 Gen 4 .... **$649.00**

GLOCK 32/32C
Caliber: .357 Auto. **Capacities:** 13/15/17-round magazine. **Barrel:** 4.02 in. **Weight:** 21.52 oz. (without magazine). **Length:** 6.85 in. overall. **Features:** Otherwise similar to the Model 31. Compact. Imported from Austria by Glock, Inc.
Price: **$599.00**
Price: 32 Gen 4 .... **$649.00**

GLOCK 33
Caliber: .357 Auto. **Capacities:** 9/11/13/15/17-round magazine. **Barrel:** 3.46 in. **Weight:** 19.75 oz. (without magazine). **Length:** 6.29 in. overall. **Features:** Otherwise similar to the Model 31. Subcompact. Imported from Austria by Glock, Inc.
Price: From **$599.00**
Price: 33 Gen 4 .... **$614.00**

GLOCK 34
Caliber: 9mm. **Capacities:** 17/19/33-round magazine. **Barrel:** 5.32 in. **Weight:** 22.9 oz. **Length:** 8.15 in. overall. **Features:** Competition version of Glock 17 with extended barrel, slide, and sight radius dimensions. Available with MOS (Modular Optic System).
Price: From **$679.00**
Price: MOS **$840.00**
Price: 34 Gen 4 .... **$729.00**
Price: 34 Gen 5 .... **$899.00**

GLOCK 35
Caliber: .40 S&W. **Capacities:** 15/17-round magazine. **Barrel:** 5.32 in. **Weight:** 24.52 oz. (without magazine). **Length:** 8.15 in. overall. **Sights:** Adjustable. **Features:** Otherwise similar to the Model 22. Competition version of the Glock 22 with extended barrel, slide and sight radius dimensions. Available

with MOS (Modular Optic System). Introduced 1996.
Price: From **$679.00**
Price: MOS **$840.00**
Price: 35 Gen 4 .... **$729.00**

GLOCK 36
Caliber: .45 ACP. **Capacity:** 6-round magazine. **Barrel:** 3.78 in. **Weight:** 20.11 oz. (without magazine). **Length:** 6.77 overall. **Sights:** Fixed. **Features:** Single-stack magazine, slimmer grip than Glock 21/30. Subcompact. Imported from Austria by Glock, Inc. Introduced 1997.
Price: **$637.00**

GLOCK 37
Caliber: .45 GAP. **Capacity:** 10-round magazine. **Barrel:** 4.49 in. **Weight:** 25.95 oz. (without magazine). **Length:** 7.32 in. overall. **Features:** Otherwise similar to the Model 17. Imported from Austria by Glock, Inc. Introduced 2005.
Price: **$614.00**
Price: 37 Gen 4 .... **$664.00**

GLOCK 38
Caliber: .45 GAP. **Capacities:** 8/10-round magazine. **Barrel:** 4.02 in. **Weight:** 24.16 oz. (without magazine). **Length:** 6.85 overall. **Features:** Otherwise similar to the Model 37. Compact. Imported from Austria by Glock, Inc.
Price: **$614.00**

GLOCK 39
Caliber: .45 GAP. **Capacities:** 6/8/10-round magazine. **Barrel:** 3.46 in. **Weight:** 19.33 oz. (without magazine). **Length:** 6.3 overall. **Features:** Otherwise similar to the Model 37. Subcompact. Imported from Austria by Glock, Inc.
Price: **$614.00**

GLOCK 40 GEN 4
Caliber: 10mm. **Features:** Similar features as the Model 41 except for 6.01-in. barrel. Includes MOS optics.
Price: **$840.00**

GLOCK 41 GEN 4
Caliber: .45 ACP. **Capacity:** 13-round magazine. **Barrel:** 5.31 in. **Weight:** 27 oz. **Length:** 8.9 in. overall. **Features:** This is a long-slide .45 ACP Gen4 model introduced in 2014. Operating features are the same as other Glock models. Available with MOS (Modular Optic System).
Price: **$749.00**
Price: MOS **$840.00**

Prices given are believed to be accurate at time of publication however, many factors affect retail pricing so exact prices are not possible.

GLOCK 42 GEN 4
Caliber: .380 ACP. **Capacity:** 6-round magazine. **Barrel:** 3.25 in. **Weight:** 13.8 oz. **Length:** 5.9 in. overall. **Features:** This single-stack, slimline sub-compact is the smallest pistol Glock has ever made. This is also the first Glock pistol made in the USA.
Price: $499.00

GLOCK 43 GEN 4
Caliber: 9mm. **Capacity:** 6+1. **Barrel:** 3.39 in. **Weight:** 17.95 oz. **Length:** 6.26 in. **Height:** 4.25 in. **Width:** 1.02 in. **Features:** Newest member of Glock's Slimline series with single-stack magazine.
Price: $599.00

GRAND POWER P-1 MK7
Caliber: 9mm. **Capacity:** 15+1 magazine. **Barrel:** 3.7 in. **Weight:** 26 oz. **Features:** Compact DA/SA pistol featuring frame-mounted safety, steel slide and frame and polymer grips. Offered in several variations and sizes. Made in Slovakia and imported by Eagle Imports.
Price: $449.99

GUNCRAFTER INDUSTRIES NO. 1
Calibers: .45 ACP or .50 GI. **Capacity:** 7-round magazine. **Features:** 1911-style series of pistols best known for the proprietary .50 GI chambering. Offered in several common 1911 variations. No. 1 has 5-inch heavy match-grade barrel, 7-round magazine, Parkerized or hard chrome finish, checkered grips and frontstrap, Heinie slant tritium sights. Other models include Commander-style, Officer's Model, Long Slide w/6-inch barrel and several 9mm and .38 Super versions.
Price: .... $2,695.00–$4,125.00

HECKLER & KOCH USP
Calibers: 9mm, .40 S&W, .45 ACP. **Capacities:** 15-round magazine; .40 S&W, 13-shot magazine; 45 ACP, 12-shot magazine. **Barrels:** 4.25–4.41 in. **Weight:** 1.65 lbs. **Length:** 7.64–7.87 in. overall. **Grips:** Non-slip stippled black polymer. **Sights:** Blade front, rear adjustable for windage. **Features:** New HK design with polymer frame, modified Browning action with recoil reduction system, single control lever. Special "hostile environment" finish on all metal parts. Available in SA/DA, DAO, left- and right-hand versions. Introduced 1993. .45 ACP Introduced 1995. Imported from Germany by Heckler & Koch, Inc.
Price: USP .45 .... $1,033.00
Price: USP .40 and USP 9mm $952.00

HECKLER & KOCH USP COMPACT
Calibers: 9mm, .357 SIG, .40 S&W, .45 ACP. **Capacities:** 13-round magazine; .40 S&W and .357 SIG, 12-shot magazine; .45 ACP, 8-shot magazine. **Features:** Similar to the USP except the 9mm, .357 SIG and .40 S&W have 3.58-in. barrels, measure 6.81 in. overall and weigh 1.47 lbs. (9mm). Introduced 1996. .45 ACP measures 7.09 in. overall. Introduced 1998. Imported from Germany by Heckler & Koch, Inc.
Price: USP Compact .45 .... $1,040.00
Price: USP Compact 9mm, .40 S&W $992.00

HECKLER & KOCH USP45 TACTICAL
Calibers: .40 S&W, .45 ACP. **Capacities:** 13-round magazine; .45 ACP, 12-round magazine. **Barrels:** 4.90-5.09 in. **Weight:** 1.9 lbs. **Length:** 8.64 in. overall. **Grips:** Non-slip stippled polymer. **Sights:** Blade front, fully adjustable target rear. **Features:** Has extended threaded barrel with rubber O-ring; adjustable trigger; extended magazine floorplate; adjustable trigger stop; polymer frame. Introduced 1998. Imported from Germany by Heckler & Koch, Inc.
Price: USP Tactical .45 .... $1,352.00
Price: USP Tactical .40 .... $1,333.00

Prices given are believed to be accurate at time of publication however, many factors affect retail pricing so exact prices are not possible.

Tactical GunDigest® ⊕ **295**

HECKLER & KOCH USP COMPACT TACTICAL

Caliber: .45 ACP. **Capacity:** 8-round magazine. **Features:** Similar to the USP Tactical except measures 7.72 in. overall, weighs 1.72 lbs. Introduced 2006. Imported from Germany by Heckler & Koch, Inc.
Price: USP Compact Tactical **$1,352.00**

HECKLER & KOCH HK45

Caliber: .45 ACP. **Capacity:** 10-round magazine. **Barrel:** 4.53 in. **Weight:** 1.73 lbs. **Length:** 7.52 in. overall. **Grips:** Ergonomic with adjustable grip panels. **Sights:** Low profile, drift adjustable. **Features:** Polygonal rifling, ambidextrous controls, operates on improved Browning linkless recoil system. Available in Tactical and Compact variations.
Price: USP Tactical .45 .... **$1,193.00–$1,392.00**

HECKLER & KOCH MARK 23 SPECIAL OPERATIONS

Caliber: .45 ACP. **Capacity:** 12-round magazine. **Barrel:** 5.87 in. **Weight:** 2.42 lbs. **Length:** 9.65 in. overall. **Grips:** Integral with frame; black polymer. **Sights:** Blade front, rear drift adjustable for windage; 3-dot. **Features:** Civilian version of the SOCOM pistol. Polymer frame; double action; exposed hammer; short recoil, modified Browning action. Introduced 1996. Imported from Germany by Heckler & Koch, Inc.
Price: **$2,299.00**

HECKLER & KOCH P30 AND P30L

Calibers: 9mm, .40 S&W. **Capacities:** 13- or 15-round magazines. **Barrels:** 3.86 in. or 4.45 in. (P30L) **Weight:** 26–27.5 oz. **Length:** 6.95, 7.56 in. overall. **Grips:** Interchangeable panels. **Sights:** Open rectangular notch rear sight with contrast points. **Features:** Ergonomic features include a special grip frame with interchangeable backstrap inserts and lateral plates, allowing the pistol to be individually adapted to any user. Browning-type action with modified short recoil operation. Ambidextrous controls include dual slide releases, magazine release

levers and a serrated decocking button located on the rear of the frame (for applicable variants). A Picatinny rail molded into the front of the frame. The extractor serves as a loaded-chamber indicator.
Price: P30 .... **$1,099.00**
Price: P30L Variant 2 Law Enforcement Modification
(LEM) enhanced DAO **$1,149.00**
Price: P30L Variant 3 Double Action/Single Action
(DA/SA) with Decocker **$1,108.00**

HECKLER & KOCH P2000

Calibers: 9mm, .40 S&W. **Capacities:** 13-round magazine; .40 S&W, 12-shot magazine. **Barrel:** 3.62 in. **Weight:** 1.5 lbs. **Length:** 7 in. overall. **Grips:** Interchangeable panels. **Sights:** Fixed Patridge style, drift adjustable for windage, standard 3-dot. **Features:** Incorporates features of HK USP Compact pistol, including Law Enforcement Modification (LEM) trigger, double-action hammer system, ambidextrous magazine release, dual slide-release levers, accessory mounting rails, recurved, hook trigger guard, fiber-reinforced polymer frame, modular grip with exchangeable backstraps, nitro-carburized finish, lock-out safety device. Introduced 2003. Imported from Germany by Heckler & Koch, Inc.
Price: **$799.00**

HECKLER & KOCH P2000 SK

Calibers: 9mm, .357 SIG, .40 S&W. **Capacities:** 10-round magazine; .40 S&W and .357 SIG, 9-round magazine. **Barrel:** 3.27 in. **Weight:** 1.3 lbs. **Length:** 6.42 in. overall. **Sights:** Fixed Patridge style, drift adjustable. **Features:** Standard accessory rails, ambidextrous slide release, polymer frame, polygonal bore profile. Smaller version of P2000. Introduced 2005. Imported from Germany by Heckler & Koch, Inc.
Price: **$799.00**

HECKLER & KOCH VP9/VP 40

Calibers: 9mm, .40 S&W. **Capacities:** 10- or 15-round magazine. .40 S&W (10 or 13). **Barrel:** 4.09 in. **Weight:** 25.6 oz. **Length:** 7.34 in. overall. **Sights:** Fixed 3-dot, drift adjustable. **Features:** Striker-fired system with HK enhanced light pull trigger. Ergonomic grip design with interchangeable backstraps and side panels.
Price: **$719.00**

HI-POINT FIREARMS MODEL 9MM COMPACT

Caliber: 9mm. **Capacity:** 8-round magazine. **Barrel:** 3.5 in. **Weight:** 25 oz. **Length:** 6.75 in. overall. **Grips:** Textured plastic. **Sights:** Combat-style

Prices given are believed to be accurate at time of publication however, many factors affect retail pricing so exact prices are not possible.

adjustable 3-dot system; low profile. **Features:** Single-action design; frame-mounted magazine release; polymer frame. Scratch-resistant matte finish. Introduced 1993. Comps are similar except they have a 4-in. barrel with muzzle brake/compensator. Compensator is slotted for laser or flashlight mounting. Introduced 1998. Made in USA by MKS Supply, Inc.
Price: C-9 9mm $199.00

HI-POINT FIREARMS MODEL 380 POLYMER
Caliber: .380 ACP. **Capacities:** 10- and 8-round magazine. **Weight:** 25 oz. **Features:** Similar to the 9mm Compact model except chambered for adjustable 3-dot sights. Polymer frame. Action locks open after last shot. Trigger lock.
Price: CF-380 .... $179.00

HI-POINT FIREARMS 40 AND 45 SW/POLYMER
Calibers: .40 S&W, .45 ACP. **Capacities:** .40 S&W, 8-round magazine; .45 ACP, 9 rounds. **Barrel:** 4.5 in. **Weight:** 32 oz. **Length:** 7.72 in. overall. **Sights:** Adjustable 3-dot. **Features:** Polymer frames, last round lock-open, grip-mounted magazine release, magazine disconnect safety, integrated accessory rail, trigger lock. Introduced 2002. Made in USA by MKS Supply, Inc.
Price: $219.00

HIGH STANDARD HS-22
Caliber: .22 Long Rifle **Capacity:** 10-round magazine. **Barrels:** 5.5-in. bull or slab-sided. **Weight:** 44 oz. **Length:** 9.5 in. **Grips:** Wood. **Sights:** Adjustable. **Finish:** Flat black or Parkerized gray. **Features:** Removable aluminum rib, adjustable trigger, various custom options available.
Price: From $900.00

ITHACA 1911
Caliber: .45 ACP. **Capacity:** 7-round capacity. **Barrels:** 4.25 or 5 in. **Weight:** 35 or 40 oz. **Sights:** Fixed combat or fully adjustable target. **Grips:** Checkered cocobolo with Ithaca logo. Classic 1911A1 style with enhanced features including match-grade barrel, lowered and flared ejection port, extended beavertail grip safety, hand-fitted barrel bushing, two-piece guide rod, checkered front strap.
Price: $1,575.00

IVER JOHNSON EAGLE
Calibers: 9mm, .45 ACP. **Features:** Series of 1911-style pistols made in typical variations including full-size (Eagle), Commander (Hawk), Officer's (Thrasher) sizes in .45 ACP and 9mm. Many finishes available, including Cerakote, polished stainless, pink and several snakeskin variations.
Price: .... $608.00–$959.00

KAHR CM SERIES
Calibers: 9mm, .40 S&W, .45 ACP. **Capacities:** 9mm (6+1), .40 S&W (6+1). .45 ACP (5+1). CM45 Model is shown. **Barrels:** 3 in., 3.25 in. (45) **Weights:** 15.9–17.3 oz. **Length:** 5.42 in. overall. **Grips:** Textured polymer with integral steel rails molded into frame. **Sights:** CM9093, Pinned in polymer sight; PM9093, drift-adjustable, white bar-dot combat. **Features:** A conventional rifled barrel instead of the match-grade polygonal barrel on Kahr's PM series; the CM slide stop lever is MIM (metal-injection-molded) instead of machined; the CM series slide has fewer machining operations and uses simple engraved markings instead of roll marking. The CM series are shipped with one magazine instead of two. The slide is machined from solid 416 stainless with a matte finish, each gun is shipped with one 6-round stainless steel magazine with a flush baseplate. Magazines are U.S.-made, plasma welded, tumbled to remove burrs and feature Wolff springs. The magazine catch in the polymer frame is all metal and will not wear out on the stainless steel magazine after extended use.
Price: $460.00

KAHR MK SERIES MICRO

Similar to the K9/K40 except is 5.35 in. overall, 4 in. high, with a 3.08 in. barrel. Weighs 23.1 oz. Has snag-free bar-dot sights, polished feed ramp, dual recoil spring system, DAO trigger. Comes with 5-round flush baseplate and 6-shot grip extension magazine. Introduced 1998. Made in USA by Kahr Arms.

Price: M9093 MK9, matte stainless steel **$911.00**
Price: M9093N MK9, matte stainless steel, tritium
night sights **$1,017.00**
Price: M9098 MK9 Elite 2003, stainless steel **$991.00**
Price: M4043 MK40, matte stainless steel **$911.00**
Price: M4043N MK40, matte stainless steel, tritium
night sights **$1,115.00**
Price: M4048 MK40 Elite 2003, stainless steel **$991.00**

KAHR P SERIES

Calibers: .380 ACP, 9mm, .40 S&W, 45 ACP. **Capacity:** 7-shot magazine. **Features:** Similar to K9/K40 steel frame pistol except has polymer frame, matte stainless steel slide. Barrel length 3.5 in.; overall length 5.8 in.; weighs 17 oz. Includes two 7-shot magazines, hard polymer case, trigger lock. Introduced 2000. Made in USA by Kahr Arms.

Price: KP9093 9mm **$762.00**
Price: KP4043 .40 S&W **$762.00**
Price: KP4543 .45 ACP **$829.00**
Price: KP3833 .380 ACP (2008).. **$667.00**

KAHR KP GEN 2 PREMIUM SERIES

Calibers: 9mm, .45 ACP. **Capacities:** KP9 9mm (7-shot magazine), KP45 .45 ACP (6 shots). **Barrel:** 3.5 in. **Features:** Black polymer frame, matte stainless slide, Tru-Glo Tritium fiber optic sights, short trigger, accessory rail.

Price: **$976.00**

KAHR TP GEN 2 PREMIUM SERIES

Calibers: 9mm, .45 ACP. **Capacities:** TP9 9mm (8-shot magazine), TP45 .45 ACP (7 or 8 shots). **Barrels:** 4, 5, or 6 in. **Features:** Model with 4-inch barrel has features similar to KP GEN 2. The 5-inch model has front and rear slide serrations, white 3-dot sights, mount for reflex sights. The 6-inch model has the same features plus comes with Leupold Delta Point Reflex sight.

Price: **$976.00**
Price: 5-inch bbl **$1,015.00**
Price: 6-inch bbl **$1,566.00**

KAHR PM SERIES

Calibers: 9mm, .40 S&W, .45 ACP. **Capacity:** 7-round magazine. **Features:** Similar to P-Series pistols except has smaller polymer frame (Polymer Micro). Barrel length 3.08 in.; overall length 5.35 in.; weighs 17 oz. Includes two 7-shot magazines, hard polymer case, trigger lock. Introduced 2000. Made in USA by Kahr Arms.

Price: PM9093 PM9 .... **$810.00**
Price: PM4043 PM40 .... **$810.00**
Price: PM4543 PM45.. **$880.00**

KAHR CT 9/40/45 SERIES

Calibers: 9mm, .40 S&W, .45 ACP. **Capacities:** 9mm (8+1), .40 S&W (6+1) .45 ACP (7+1). **Barrel:** 4 in. **Weights:** 20–25 oz. **Length:** 5.42 in. overall. **Grips:** Textured polymer with integral steel rails molded into frame. **Sights:** Drift adjustable, white bar-dot combat. **Features:** Same as Kahr CM Series.

Price: **$460.00**

KAHR CT 380

Caliber: .380 ACP. **Capacity:** (7+1). **Barrel:** 3 in. **Weight:** 14 oz. Other features similar to CT 9/40/45 models.

Price: **$419.00**

KAHR K SERIES

Calibers: K9: 9mm, 7-shot; K40: .40 S&W, 6-shot magazine. **Barrel:** 3.5 in. **Weight:** 25 oz. **Length:** 6 in. overall. **Grips:** Wraparound textured soft polymer. **Sights:** Blade front, rear drift adjustable for windage; bar-dot combat style. **Features:** Trigger-cocking double-action mechanism with passive firing pin block. Made of 4140 ordnance steel with matte black finish. Contact maker for complete price list. Introduced 1994. Made in USA by Kahr Arms.

Price: K9093C K9, matte stainless steel **$855.00**
Price: K9093NC K9, matte stainless steel w/tritium
night sights **$985.00**
Price: K9094C K9 matte blackened stainless steel **$891.00**
Price: K9098 K9 Elite 2003, stainless steel **$932.00**
Price: K4043 K40, matte stainless steel **$855.00**
Price: K4043N K40, matte stainless steel w/tritium
night sights **$985.00**
Price: K4044 K40, matte blackened stainless steel **$891.00**
Price: K4048 K40 Elite 2003, stainless steel **$932.00**

Prices given are believed to be accurate at time of publication however, many factors affect retail pricing so exact prices are not possible.

KAHR T SERIES

Calibers: 9mm, .40 S&W. **Capacities:** T9: 9mm, 8-round magazine; T40: .40 S&W, 7-round magazine. **Barrel:** 4 in. **Weight:** 28.1–29.1 oz. **Length:** 6.5 in. overall. **Grips:** Checkered Hogue Pau Ferro wood grips. **Sights:** Rear: Novak low-profile 2-dot tritium night sight, front tritium night sight. **Features:** Similar to other Kahr makes, but with longer slide and barrel upper, longer butt. Trigger cocking DAO; locking breech; Browning-type recoil lug; passive striker block; no magazine disconnect. Comes with two magazines. Introduced 2004. Made in USA by Kahr Arms.
Price: KT9093 T9 matte stainless steel **$857.00**
Price: KT9093-NOVAK T9, "Tactical 9," Novak night sight **$980.00**
Price: KT4043 40 S&W...**$857.00**

KAHR CW SERIES

Caliber: 9mm, .40 S&W, .45 ACP. **Capacities:** 9mm, 7-round magazine; .40 S&W and .45 ACP, 6-round magazine. **Barrels:** 3.5 and 3.64 in. **Weight:** 17.7–18.7 oz. **Length:** 5.9–6.36 in. overall. **Grips:** Textured polymer. Similar to P-Series, but CW Series have conventional rifling, metal-injection-molded slide stop lever, no front dovetail cut, one magazine. CW40 introduced 2006. Made in USA by Kahr Arms.
Price: CW9093 CW9 ....**$449.00**
Price: CW4043 CW40 ....**$449.00**
Price: CW4543 CW45 ....**$449.00**

KAHR P380

Caliber: .380 ACP. **Capacity:** 6+1. **Features:** Very small DAO semi-auto pistol. Features include 2.5-in. Lothar Walther barrel; black polymer frame with

stainless steel slide; drift adjustable white bar/dot combat/sights; optional tritium sights; two 6+1 magazines. Overall length 4.9 in., weight 10 oz. without magazine.
Price: Standard sights **$667.00**
Price: Night sights.. **$792.00**

KAHR CW380

Caliber: .380 ACP. **Capacity:** 6-round magazine. **Barrel:** 2.58 in. **Weight:** 11.5 oz. **Length:** 4.96 in. **Grips:** Textured integral polymer. **Sights:** Fixed white-bar combat style. **Features:** DAO. Black or purple polymer frame, stainless slide.
Price: **$419.00**

KAHR TIG SPECIAL EDITION

Caliber: 9mm. **Capacity:** 8 rounds. **Weight:** 18.5 oz. **Barrel:** 4 in. (Sub-compact model). **Features:** Limited Special Edition to support Beyond the Battlefield Foundation founded by John "Tig" Tiegen and his wife to provide support for wounded veterans. Tiegen is one of the heroes of the Benghazi attack in 2012. Kryptek Typhon finish on frame, black Teracote finish on slide engraved with Tiegen signature, Tig logo and BTB logo. Production will be limited to 1,000 pistols. Part of the proceeds from the sale of each firearm will be donated to the Beyond the Battlefield Foundation by Kahr Firearms Group.
Price: **$541.00**

KEL-TEC P-11

Caliber: 9mm. **Capacity:** 10-round magazine. **Barrel:** 3.1 in. **Weight:** 14 oz. **Length:** 5.6 in. overall. **Grips:** Checkered black polymer. **Sights:** Blade front, rear adjustable for windage. **Features:** Ordnance steel slide, aluminum frame. DAO trigger mechanism. Introduced 1995. Made in USA by Kel-Tec CNC Industries, Inc.
Price: From **$340.00**

KEL-TEC PF-9
Caliber: 9mm. **Capacity:** 7 rounds. **Weight:** 12.7 oz. **Sights:** Rear sight adjustable for windage and elevation. **Barrel:** 3.1 in. **Length:** 5.85 in. **Features:** Barrel, locking system, slide stop, assembly pin, front sight, recoil springs and guide rod adapted from P-11. Trigger system with integral hammer block and the extraction system adapted from P-3AT. Mil-Std-1913 Picatinny rail. Made in USA by Kel-Tec CNC Industries, Inc.
Price: From $356.00

KEL-TEC P-32
Caliber: .32 ACP. **Capacity:** 7-round magazine. **Barrel:** 2.68. **Weight:** 6.6 oz. **Length:** 5.07 overall. **Grips:** Checkered composite. **Sights:** Fixed. **Features:** Double-action-only mechanism with 6-lb. pull; internal slide stop. Textured composite grip/frame.
Price: From $326.00

KEL-TEC P-3AT
Caliber: .380 ACP. **Capacity:** 7-round magazine **Weight:** 7.2 oz. **Length:** 5.2. **Features:** Lightest .380 ACP made; aluminum frame, steel barrel.
Price: From $331.00

KEL-TEC PLR-16
Caliber: 5.56mm NATO. **Capacity:** 10-round magazine. **Weight:** 51 oz. **Sights:** Rear sight adjustable for windage, front sight is M-16 blade. **Barrel:** 9.2 in. **Length:** 18.5 in. **Features:** Muzzle is threaded 1/2x28 to accept standard attachments such as a muzzle brake. Except for the barrel, bolt, sights and mechanism, the PLR-16 pistol is made of high-impact glass fiber reinforced polymer. Gas-operated semi-auto. Conventional gas-piston operation with M-16 breech locking system. MIL-STD-1913 Picatinny rail. Made in USA by Kel-Tec CNC Industries, Inc.
Price: Blued $682.00

KEL-TEC PLR-22
Caliber: .22 LR. **Capacity:** 26-round magazine. **Length:** 18.5 in. overall. 40 oz. **Features:** Semi-auto pistol based on centerfire PLR-16 by same maker. Blowback action. Open sights and Picatinny rail for mounting accessories; threaded muzzle.
Price: $400.00

KEL-TEC PMR-30
Caliber: .22 Magnum (.22WMR). **Capacity:** 30 rounds. **Barrel:** 4.3 in. **Weight:** 13.6 oz. **Length:** 7.9 in. overall. **Grips:** Glass reinforced Nylon (Zytel). **Sights:** Dovetailed aluminum with front & rear fiber optics. **Features:** Operates on a unique hybrid blowback/locked-breech system. It uses a double-stack magazine of a new design that holds 30 rounds and fits completely in the grip of the pistol. Dual opposing extractors for reliability, heel magazine release to aid in magazine retention, Picatinny accessory rail under the barrel, Urethane recoil buffer, captive coaxial recoil springs. The barrel is fluted for light weight and effective heat dissipation. PMR30 disassembles for cleaning by removal of a single pin.
Price: $455.00

KIMBER MICRO CDP
Caliber: .380 ACP. **Capacity:** 6-round magazine. **Barrel:** 2.75 in. **Weight:** 17 oz. **Grips:** Double diamond rosewood. Mini 1911-style single action with no grip safety.
Price: $951.00

KIMBER MICRO CRIMSON CARRY
Caliber: .380 ACP. **Capacity:** 6-round magazine. **Barrel:** 2.75 in. **Weight:** 13.4 oz. **Length:** 5.6 in **Grips:** Black synthetic, double diamond. **Sights:** Fixed low profile. **Finish:** Matte black. **Features:** Aluminum frame with satin silver finish, steel slide, carry-melt treatment, full-length guide rod, rosewood Crimson Trace Lasergrips.
Price: $747.00

KIMBER MICRO TLE
Caliber: .380 ACP. **Features:** Similar to Micro Crimson Carry. **Features:** Black slide and frame. Green and black G10 grips.
Price: $734.00

KIMBER MICRO RAPTOR
Caliber: .380 ACP **Capacity:** 6-round magazine. **Sights:** Tritium night sights. **Finish:** Stainless. **Features:** Variation of Micro Carry with Raptor-style scalloped "feathered" slide serrations and grip panels.
Price: $842.00

KIMBER COVERT SERIES
Caliber: .45 ACP **Capacity:** 7-round magazine. **Barrels:** 3, 4 or 5 in. **Weight:** 25–31 oz. **Grips:** Crimson Trace laser with camo finish. **Sights:** Tactical wedge 3-dot night sights. **Features:** Made in the Kimber Custom Shop.

Finish: Kimber Gray frame, matte black slide, black small parts. Carry Melt treatment. Available in three frame sizes: Custom, Pro and Ultra.
Price: **$1,457.00**

KIMBER CUSTOM II
Caliber: 9mm, .45 ACP. **Barrel:** 5 in. **Weight:** 38 oz. **Length:** 8.7 in. overall. **Grips:** Checkered black rubber, walnut, rosewood. **Sights:** Dovetailed front and rear, Kimber low profile adjustable or fixed sights. **Features:** Slide, frame and barrel machined from steel or stainless steel. Match-grade barrel, chamber and trigger group. Extended thumb safety, beveled magazine well, beveled front and rear slide serrations, high ride beavertail grip safety, checkered flat mainspring housing, kidney cut under trigger guard, high cut grip, match-grade stainless steel barrel bushing, polished breechface, Commander-style hammer, lowered and flared ejection port, Wolff springs, bead blasted black oxide or matte stainless finish. Introduced in 1996. Made in USA by Kimber Mfg., Inc.
Price: Custom II **$871.00**

KIMBER CUSTOM TLE II
Caliber: .45 ACP or 10mm. **Features:** TLE (Tactical Law Enforcement) version of Custom II model plus night sights, frontstrap checkering, threaded barrel, Picatinny rail.
Price: .45 ACP **$1,007.00**
Price: 10mm **$1,028.00**

KIMBER STAINLESS II
Same features as Custom II except has stainless steel frame.
Price: Stainless II .45 ACP **$998.00**
Price: Stainless II 9mm **$1,016.00**
Price: Stainless II .45 ACP w/night sights.................................. **$1,141.00**
Price: Stainless II Target .45 ACP (stainless, adj. sight) **$1,108.00**

KIMBER PRO CARRY II
Calibers: 9mm, .45 ACP. **Features:** Similar to Custom II, has aluminum frame, 4-in. bull barrel fitted directly to the slide without bushing. Introduced 1998. Made in USA by Kimber Mfg., Inc.
Price: Pro Carry II, .45 ACP **$837.00**
Price: Pro Carry II, 9mm **$857.00**
Price: Pro Carry II w/night sights **$977.00**

KIMBER SAPPHIRE PRO II
Caliber: 9mm. **Capacity:** 9-round magazine. **Features:** Similar to Pro Carry II, 4-inch match-grade barrel. Striking two-tone appearance with satin silver aluminum frame and high polish bright blued slide. Grips are blue/black G-10 with grooved texture. Fixed Tactical Edge night sights. From the Kimber Custom Shop.
Price: **$1,652.00**

KIMBER RAPTOR II
Caliber: .45 ACP. **Capacities:** .45 ACP (8-round magazine, 7-round (Ultra and Pro models). **Barrels:** 3, 4 or 5 in. **Weight:** 25–31 oz. **Grips:** Thin milled rosewood. **Sights:** Tactical wedge 3-dot night sights. **Features:** Made in the Kimber Custom Shop. Matte black or satin silver finish. Available in three frame sizes: Custom (shown), Pro and Ultra.
Price: .... **$1,434.00–$1,568.00**

KIMBER ULTRA CARRY II
Calibers: 9mm, .45 ACP. **Features:** Lightweight aluminum frame, 3-in. match-grade bull barrel fitted to slide without bushing. Grips 0.4-in. shorter. Light recoil spring. Weighs 25 oz. Introduced in 1999. Made in USA by Kimber Mfg., Inc.
Price: Stainless Ultra Carry II .45 ACP **$919.00**
Price: Stainless Ultra Carry II 9mm **$1,016.00**
Price: Stainless Ultra Carry II .45 ACP with night sights **$1,039.00**

KIMBER GOLD MATCH II
Caliber: .45 ACP. **Features:** Similar to Custom II models. Includes stainless steel barrel with match-grade chamber and barrel bushing, ambidextrous thumb safety, adjustable sight, premium aluminum trigger, hand-checkered double diamond rosewood grips. Barrel hand-fitted for target accuracy. Made in USA by Kimber Mfg., Inc.
Price: Gold Match II .45 ACP.. **$1,393.00**
Price: Gold Match Stainless II .45 ACP **$1,574.00**

Prices given are believed to be accurate at time of publication however, many factors affect retail pricing so exact prices are not possible.

Tactical GunDigest® ◈ **301**

KIMBER CDP II SERIES

Calibers: 9mm, .45 ACP. **Features:** Similar to Custom II but designed for concealed carry. Aluminum frame. Standard features include stainless steel slide, fixed Meprolight tritium 3-dot (green) dovetail-mounted night sights, match-grade barrel and chamber, 30 LPI frontstrap checkering, two-tone finish, ambidextrous thumb safety, hand-checkered double diamond rosewood grips. Introduced in 2000. Made in USA by Kimber Mfg., Inc.

Price: Ultra CDP II 9mm (2008) **$1,359.00**
Price: Ultra CDP II .45 ACP **$1,318.00**
Price: Compact CDP II .45 ACP **$1,318.00**
Price: Pro CDP II .45 ACP **$1,318.00**
Price: Custom CDP II (5-in. barrel, full length grip) **$1,318.00**

KIMBER CDP

Calibers: 9mm, .45 ACP. **Barrel:** 3, 4 or 5 in. **Weight:** 25–31 oz. **Features:** Aluminum frame, stainless slide, 30 LPI checkering on backstrap and trigger guard, low profile tritium night sights, Carry Melt treatment. **Sights:** Hand checkered rosewood or Crimson Trace Lasergrips. Introduced in 2017.

Price: **$1,173.00**
Price: With Crimson Trace Lasergrips **$1,473.00**

KIMBER ECLIPSE II SERIES

Calibers: .38 Super, 10 mm, .45 ACP. **Features:** Similar to Custom II and other stainless Kimber pistols. Stainless slide and frame, black oxide, two-tone finish. Gray/black laminated grips. 30 LPI frontstrap checkering. All models have night sights; Target versions have Meprolight adjustable Bar/Dot version. Made in USA by Kimber Mfg., Inc.

Price: Eclipse Ultra II (3-in. barrel, short grip) **$1,350.00**
Price: Eclipse Pro II (4-in. barrel, full-length grip) **$1,350.00**
Price: Eclipse Custom II 10mm **$1,350.00**
Price: Eclipse Target II (5-in. barrel, full-length grip,
  adjustable sight) **$1,393.00**

KIMBER TACTICAL ENTRY II

Caliber: 45 ACP. **Capacity:** 7-round magazine. **Barrel:** 5 in. **Weight:** 40 oz. **Length:** 8.7 in. overall. **Features:** 1911-style semi-auto with checkered frontstrap, extended magazine well, night sights, heavy steel frame, tactical rail.

Price: **$1,490.00**

KIMBER TACTICAL CUSTOM HD II

Caliber: .45 ACP. **Capacity:** 7-round magazine. **Barrel:** 5 in. match-grade. **Weight:** 39 oz. **Length:** 8.7 in. overall. **Features:** 1911-style semiauto with night sights, heavy steel frame.

Price: **$1,387.00**

KIMBER SUPER CARRY PRO

Caliber: .45 ACP. **Capacity:** 8-round magazine. **Features:** 1911-style semi-auto pistol. Ambidextrous thumb safety; Carry Melt profiling; full-length guide rod; aluminum frame with stainless slide; satin silver finish; super carry serrations; 4-inch barrel; micarta laminated grips and tritium night sights.

Price: **$1,596.00**

KIMBER SUPER CARRY HD SERIES

Caliber: .45 ACP. **Features:** Designated as HD (Heavy Duty), each is chambered in .45 ACP and features a stainless steel slide and frame, premium KimPro II finish and night sights with cocking shoulder for one-hand operation. Like the original Super Carry pistols, HD models have directional serrations on slide, frontstrap and mainspring housing for unequaled control under recoil. A round heel frame and Carry Melt treatment make them comfortable to carry and easy to conceal.

KIMBER SUPER CARRY ULTRA HD

Caliber: .45 ACP. **Capacity:** 7-round magazine. **Barrel:** 3 in. **Weight:** 32 oz. **Length:** 6.8 in. overall. **Grips:** G-10, Checkered with border. **Sights:** Night sights with cocking shoulder radius 4.8 in. **Features:** Rugged stainless slide and frame with KimPro II finish. Aluminum match-grade trigger with a factory setting of approximately 4-5 pounds.

Price: **$1,699.00**

Prices given are believed to be accurate at time of publication however, many factors affect retail prices so exact prices are not possible.

KIMBER SUPER CARRY PRO HD
Caliber: .45 ACP. **Capacity:** 8-round magazine. **Barrel:** 4 in. **Weight:** 35 oz.
Length: 7.7 in. overall. **Features:** Same as Super Carry Ultra HD model.
Price: **$1,699.00**

KIMBER SUPER CARRY CUSTOM HD
Caliber: .45 ACP. **Capacity:** 8-round magazine. **Barrel:** 5. **Weight:** 38 oz.
Length: 8.7 overall. **Grips:** G-10, Checkered with border. **Sights:** Night sights
with cocking shoulder radius 4.8 in. **Features:** Rugged stainless steel slide
and frame with KimPro II finish. Aluminum match grade trigger with a factory
setting of approximately 4-5 pounds.
Price: **$1,625.00**

KIMBER ULTRA CDP II
Calibers: 9mm, .45 ACP. **Capacities:** 7-round magazine (9 in 9mm). **Features:**
Compact 1911-style pistol; ambidextrous thumb safety; carry melt profiling;
full-length guide rod; aluminum frame with stainless slide; satin silver finish;
checkered frontstrap; 3-inch barrel; rosewood double diamond Crimson
Trace laser grips; tritium 3-dot night sights.
Price: **$1,603.00**

KIMBER STAINLESS ULTRA TLE II
Caliber: .45 ACP. **Capacity:** 7-round magazine. **Features:** 1911-style semi-auto
pistol. Features include full-length guide rod; aluminum frame with stainless
slide; satin silver finish; checkered frontstrap; 3-in. barrel; tactical gray double
diamond grips; tritium 3-dot night sights.
Price: **$1,136.00**

KIMBER ROYAL II
Caliber: .45 ACP. **Capacity:** 7-round magazine. **Barrel:** 5 in. **Weight:** 38
oz. **Length:** 8.7 in. overall. **Grips:** Solid bone-smooth. **Sights:** Fixed low
profile. **Features:** A classic full-size pistol wearing a charcoal blue finish
complimented with solid bone grip panels. Front and rear serrations.
Aluminum match-grade trigger with a factory setting of approximately
4–5 pounds.
Price: **$1,785.00**

KIMBER MASTER CARRY SERIES
Caliber: .45 ACP. **Capacity:** 8-round magazine, 9mm (Pro only). **Barrels:** 5 in.
(Custom), 4 in. (Pro), 3 in. (Ultra) **Weight:** 25–30 oz. **Grips:** Crimson Trace
Laser. **Sights:** Fixed low profile. **Features:** Matte black KimPro slide, aluminum
round heel frame, full-length guide rod.
Price: **$1,497.00**

KIMBER WARRIOR SOC
Caliber: .45 ACP. **Capacity:** 7-round magazine. **Barrel:** 5 in threaded for suppression. **Sights:** Fixed Tactical Wedge tritium. **Finish:** Dark Green frame, Flat Dark Earth slide. **Features:** Full-size 1911 based on special series of pistols made for USMC. Service melt, ambidextrous safety.
Price: **$1,392.00**

KIMBER SUPER JAGARE
Caliber: 10mm. **Capacity:** 8+1. **Barrel:** 6 in, ported. **Weight:** 42 oz. **Finish:** Stainless steel KimPro, Charcoal gray frame, diamond-like carbon coated slide. Slide is ported. **Sights:** Delta Point Pro Optic. **Grips:** Micarta. Frame has rounded heel, high cut trigger guard. Designed for hunting.
Price: **$2,688.00**

KIMBER KHX SERIES
Calibers: .45 ACP, 9mm. **Capacity:** 8+1. **Features:** This series is offered in Custom, Pro and Ultra sizes. **Barrels:** 5-, 4- or 3-inch match-grade stainless steel. **Weights:** 25–38 oz. **Finishes:** Stainless steel frame and slide with matte black KimPro II finish. Stepped hexagonal slide and top-strap serrations. **Sights:** Green and red fiber optic and Hogue Laser Enhanced MagGrip G10 grips and matching mainspring housings. Pro and Ultra models have rounded heel frames. Optics Ready (OR) models available in Custom and Pro sizes with milled slide that accepts optics plates for Vortex, Trijicon and Leupold red-dot sights.
Price: Custom OR .45 ACP **$1,087.00**
Price: Custom OR 9mm **$1,108.00**
Price: Custom, Pro or Ultra .45 .... **$1,259.00**
Price: Custom, Pro or Ultra 9mm **$1,279.00**

KIMBER AEGIS ELITE SERIES
Calibers: 9mm, .45 ACP. **Features:** Offered in Custom, Pro and Ultra sizes with 5-, 4.25- or 3-in. barrels. Sights: Green or red fiber optic or Vortex Venom red dot on OI (Optics Installed) models (shown). Grips: G10. Features: Satin finish stainless steel frame, matte black or gray slide, front and rear AEX slide serrations.
Price: .45 ACP **$1,021.00**
Price: 9mm **$1,041.00**
Price: .45 OI **$1,375.00**
Price: 9mm OI... **$1,395.00**

LIONHEART LH9 MKII
Caliber: 9mm. **Capacities:** 15-round magazine. LH9C Compact, 10 rounds. **Barrel:** 4.1 in. **Weight:** 26.5 oz. **Length:** 7.5 in **Grips:** One-piece black polymer with textured design. **Sights:** Fixed low profile. Novak LoMount sights available. **Finish:** Cerakote Graphite Black or Patriot Brown. **Features:** Hammer-forged heat-treated steel slide, hammer-forged aluminum frame. Double-action PLUS action.
Price: **$695.00**
Price: Novak sights **$749.00**

LLAMA MAX-1
Calibers: .38 Super, .45 ACP. **Barrel:** 5 in. **Weight:** 37 oz. **Sights:** Mil-spec. fixed. **Features:** Standard size and features of the 1911A1 full-size model. Lowered ejection port, matte blue or hard chrome finish. Imported from the Philippines by Eagle Imports. Introduced in 2016.
Price: **$565.00**

Prices given are believed to be accurate at time of publication however, many factors affect retail pricing so exact prices are not possible.

LLAMA MICRO MAX
Caliber: .380 ACP. **Capacity:** 7-round magazine. **Weight:** 23 oz. **Sights:** Novak style rear, fiber optic front. **Grips:** Wood or black synthetic. **Features:** A compact 1911-style pistol with 3.75-in. barrel. Skeletonized hammer and trigger, double slide serrations, comes with two 7-shot magazines. Imported from the Philippines by Eagle Imports.
Price: $468.00

MAC 3011 SSD TACTICAL
Caliber: .45 ACP. **Capacity:** 14+1 magazine. **Barrel:** 5-in. match-grade bull. **Sights:** Bomar-type fully adjustable rear, dovetail front. **Weight:** 46 oz. **Finish:** Blue. **Grips:** Aluminum. **Features:** Checkered frontstrap serrations, skeletonized trigger and hammer, flared and lowered ejection port, ambidextrous safety. Imported from the Philippines by Eagle Imports.
Price: $1,136.00

MAC 1911 BOB CUT
Caliber: .45 ACP. **Capacity:** 8+1 magazine. **Barrel:** 4.25 in. Commander-size 1911 design. **Sights:** Novak-type fully adjustable rear, dovetail front. **Weight:** 34.5 oz. **Finish:** Blue or hard chrome. **Grips:** Custom hardwood. **Features:** Stippled frontstrap, skeletonized trigger and hammer, flared and lowered ejection port, bobtail grip frame. Imported from the Philippines by Eagle Imports.
Price: $902.00

MAC 1911 BULLSEYE
Caliber: .45 ACP **Capacity:** 8+1 magazine. **Barrel:** 6-in. match-grade bull. **Sights:** Bomar-type fully adjustable rear, dovetail front. **Weight:** 46 oz. **Finish:** Blue or hard chrome. **Grips:** Hardwood. **Features:** Checkered frontstrap, skeletonized trigger and hammer, flared and lowered ejection port, wide front and rear slide serrations. Imported from the Philippines by Eagle Imports.
Price: $1,219.00

NIGHTHAWK CUSTOM T4
Calibers: 9mm, .45 ACP **Capacities:** .45 ACP, 7- or 8-round magazine; 9mm, 9 or 10 rounds; 10mm, 9 or 10 rounds. **Barrels:** 3.8, 4.25 or 5 in. **Weights:** 28–41 ounces, depending on model. **Features:** Manufacturer of a wide range of 1911-style pistols in Government Model (full-size), Commander and Officer's frame sizes. Shown is T4 model, introduced in 2013 and available only in 9mm.
Price: From .... $3,495.00–$3,695.00

NIGHTHAWK CUSTOM GRP
Calibers: 9mm, 10mm, .45 ACP. **Capacity:** 8-round magazine. **Features:** Global Response Pistol (GRP). Black, Sniper Gray, green, Coyote Tan or Titanium Blue finish. Match-grade barrel and trigger, choice of Heinie or Novak adjustable night sights.
Price: $3,095.00

NIGHTHAWK CUSTOM SHADOW HAWK
Caliber: 9mm. **Barrels:** 5 in. or 4.25 in. **Features:** Stainless steel frame with black Nitride finish, flat-faced trigger, high beavertail grip safety, checkered frontstrap, Heinie Straight Eight front and rear titanium night sights.
Price: $3,795.00

NIGHTHAWK CUSTOM WAR HAWK
Caliber: .45 ACP. **Barrels:** 5 in. or 4.25 in. **Features:** One-piece mainspring housing and mag well, Everlast Recoil System, Hyena Brown G10 grips.
Price: $3,895.00

NIGHTHAWK CUSTOM BOB MARVEL 1911
Calibers: 9mm or .45 ACP. **Barrel:** 4.25-in. bull barrel. **Features:** Everlast Recoil System, adjustable sights, match trigger, black Melonite finish.
Price: $4,395.00

NIGHTHAWK CUSTOM DOMINATOR
Caliber: .45 ACP. **Capacity:** 8-round magazine. **Features:** Stainless frame, black Perma Kote slide, cocobolo double-diamond grips,, front and rear slide serrations, adjustable sights.
Price: $3,595.00

Prices given are believed to be accurate at time of publication however, many factors affect retail pricing so exact prices are not possible.

Tactical GunDigest® ◈ **305**

NIGHTHAWK CUSTOM SILENT HAWK

Caliber: .45 ACP. **Capacity:** 8-round magazine. **Barrel:** 4.25 in. **Features:** Commander recon frame, G10 black and gray grips. Designed to match Silencerco silencer, not included with pistol.
Price: $4,295.00

NIGHTHAWK CUSTOM HEINIE LONG SLIDE

Calibers: 10mm, .45 ACP. **Barrel:** Long slide 6-in. **Features:** Cocobolo wood grips, black Perma Kote finish, adjustable or fixed sights, frontstrap checkering.
Price: $3,895.00

NIGHTHAWK CUSTOM BROWNING HI POWER

Caliber: 9mm. **Capacity:** 13-round magazine. **Features:** Nighthawk hasn't reinvented the classic high-capacity pistol but has improved it. Features include hand textured frame, trigger guard, slide top and rear, extended beavertail, contoured mag well, Heinie slant pro rear sight with a Nighthawk 14K gold bead front, crowned barrel, crisp 4-lb. trigger job, Cerakote Satin finish, select cocobolo checkered grips. Comes with two 13-round magazines.
Price: $3,195.00

NIGHTHAWK CUSTOM BORDER SPECIAL

Caliber: .45 ACP **Capacity:** 8+1 magazine. **Barrel:** 4.25-in. match grade. **Weight:** 34 oz. **Sights:** Heinie Black Slant rear, gold bead front. **Grips:** Cocobolo double diamond. **Finish:** Cerakote Elite Midnight black. **Features:** Commander-size steel frame with bobtail concealed carry grip. Scalloped frontstrap and mainspring housing. Serrated slide top. Rear slide serrations only. Crowned barrel flush with bushing.
Price: $3,650.00

NORTH AMERICAN ARMS GUARDIAN DAO

Calibers: .25 NAA, .32 ACP, .380 ACP, .32 NAA. **Capacity:** 6-round magazine. **Barrel:** 2.49 in. **Weight:** 20.8 oz. **Length:** 4.75 in. overall. **Grips:** Black polymer. **Sights:** Low-profile fixed. **Features:** DAO mechanism. All stainless steel construction. Introduced 1998. Made in USA by North American Arms. The .25 NAA is based on a bottle-necked .32 ACP case, and the .32 NAA is on a bottle-necked .380 ACP case.
Price: .25 NAA, 32 ACP $409.00
Price: .32 NAA, .380 ACP $486.00

PHOENIX ARMS HP22, HP25

Calibers: .22 LR, .25 ACP. **Capacities:** .22 LR, 10-shot (HP22), .25 ACP, 10-shot (HP25). **Barrel:** 3 in. **Weight:** 20 oz. **Length:** 5.5 in. overall. **Grips:** Checkered composition. **Sights:** Blade front, adjustable rear. **Features:** Single action, exposed hammer; manual hold-open; button magazine release. Available in satin nickel, matte blue finish. Introduced 1993. Made in USA by Phoenix Arms.
Price: With gun lock $162.00
Price: HP Range kit with 5-in. bbl., locking case and
      accessories (1 Mag) $207.00
Price: HP Deluxe Range kit with 3- and 5-in. bbls., 2 mags, case $248.00

REMINGTON R1

Caliber: .45 ACP. **Capacity:** 7-round magazine. **Barrels:** 5 in. (Full-size); 4.25 in. (Commander). **Weight:** 38.5 oz., 31 oz. (Ultralite). **Grips:** Double diamond walnut. **Sights:** Fixed, dovetail front and rear, 3-dot. **Features:** Flared and lowered ejection port. Comes with two magazines.
Price: Full-size or Commander $774.00
Price: Stainless $837.00
Price: Ultralite Commander... $849.00

REMINGTON R1 LIMITED

Calibers: 9mm, .40 S&W, .45 ACP (Double-stack only). **Capacity:** 19+1 magazine. **Barrel:** 5 in. **Grips:** G10 VZ Operator. **Weight:** 38 oz. **Features:** Stainless steel frame and slide. Double Stack Model has 19-shot capacity.
Price: $1,250.00
Price: Limited Double Stack... $1,399.00

REMINGTON R1 RECON

Calibers: 9mm, .45 ACP. **Barrel:** 4.25-in. match grade. **Features:** Double-stack stainless steel frame and slide. G10 VZ Operator grips, skeletonized trigger, ambidextrous safety, PVD coating, Tritium night sights, wide front and rear serrations, checkered mainspring housing and frontstrap.
Price: $1,275.00

REMINGTON R1 TACTICAL

Caliber: .45 ACP. **Barrel:** 5-in. **Sights:** Trijicon night sights. **Features:** Single- or double-stack frame. Threaded barrel available on double-stack model. Adjustable trigger. Other features same as Recon.
Price: $1,250.00
Price: Threaded barrel.. $1,275.00

REMINGTON R1 HUNTER

Caliber: 10mm. **Capacity:** 8-round magazine. **Barrel:** 6-in. match grade. **Sights:** Fully adjustable. **Finish:** Stainless steel. Comes with two 8-shot magazines, Operator II VZ G10 grips.
Price: $1,310.00

REMINGTON R1 ENHANCED

Calibers: .45 ACP, 9mm. **Capacities:** Same features as standard R1 except 8-shot magazine (.45), 9-shot (9mm). Stainless satin black oxide finish, wood laminate grips and adjustable rear sight. Other features include forward slide serrations, fiber optic front sight. Available with threaded barrel.
Price: $903.00
Price: Stainless $990.00
Price: Threaded barrel.. $959.00
Price: With Crimson Trace Laser Sight.................... $1,129.00
Price: Enhanced Double Stack $999.00

REMINGTON R1 CARRY

Caliber: .45 ACP. **Capacity:** 8-round magazine. **Barrel:** 5 in. or 4.25 in. (Carry Commander). **Weight:** 35–39 oz. **Grips:** Cocobolo. **Sights:** Novak-type drift-adjustable rear, tritium-dot front sight. **Features:** Skeletonized trigger. Comes with one 8- and one 7-round magazine.
Price: $1,067.00

REMINGTON RM380

Caliber: .380 ACP. **Capacity:** 6-round magazine. **Barrel:** 2.9 in. **Length:** 5.27 in. **Height:** 3.86 in. **Weight:** 12.2 oz. **Sights:** Fixed and contoured. **Grips:** Glass-filled nylon with replaceable panels. **Features:** Double-action-only operation, all-metal construction with aluminum frame, stainless steel barrel, light dual recoil spring system, extended beavertail. Introduced in 2015.
Price: Light blue/black two-tone $348.00
Price: Black finish $436.00
Price: With Crimson Trace Laser Sight................. $638.00

REMINGTON RP9/RP45

Calibers: 9mm, .45 ACP. **Capacities:** 10- or 18-round magazine. **Barrel:** 4.5 in. **Weight:** 26.4 oz. **Sights:** Drift adjustable front and rear. **Features:** Striker-fired polymer frame model with Picatinny rail. Interchangeable backstraps. Smooth, light trigger pull with short reset, trigger safety. Easy loading double-stack magazine.
Price: $418.00

REMINGTON R51

Caliber: 9mm. **Capacity:** 7-round magazine. **Barrel:** 3.4 in. **Sights:** Fixed low profile. **Weight:** 22 oz. **Features:** Skeletonized trigger with crisp, light pull. Aluminum frame with black stainless slide. Redesigned and improved variation of 2014 model, which was recalled. Reintroduced in 2017.
Price: $448.00

REPUBLIC FORGE 1911

Calibers: .45 ACP, 9mm, .38 Super, .40 S&W, 10mm. **Features:** A manufacturer of custom 1911-style pistols offered in a variety of configurations, finishes and frame sizes, including single- and double-stack models with many options. Made in Texas.
Price: From $2,795.00

Prices given are believed to be accurate at time of publication however, many factors affect retail pricing so exact prices are not possible.

Tactical GunDigest ✛ **307**

ROBERTS DEFENSE 1911 SERIES
Caliber: .45 ACP. **Capacity:** 8-round magazine. **Barrels:** 5, 4.25 or 3.5 in. **Weights:** 26–38 oz. **Sights:** Novak-type drift-adjustable rear, tritium-dot or fiber optic front sight. **Features:** Skeletonized trigger. Offered in four model variants with many custom features and options. Made in Wisconsin by Roberts Defense.
Price: Recon.. **$2,370.00**
Price: Super Grade **$2,270.00**
Price: Operator.. **$2,350.00**

ROCK ISLAND ARMORY 1911A1-45 FSP
Calibers: 9mm, .38 Super, .45 ACP. **Capacities:**.45 ACP (8 rounds), 9mm Parabellum, .38 Super (9 rounds**).** **Features:** 1911-style semi-auto pistol. Hard rubber grips, 5-inch barrel, blued, Duracoat or two-tone finish, drift-adjustable sights. Nickel finish or night sights available.
Price: From **$538.00**

ROCK ISLAND ARMORY 1911A1-FS MATCH
Caliber: .45 ACP. **Barrels:** 5 in. or 6 in. **Features:** 1911 match-style pistol. Features fiber optic front and adjustable rear sights, skeletonized trigger and hammer, extended beavertail, double diamond checkered walnut grips.
Price: **$877.00**

ROCK ISLAND ARMORY 1911A1-.22 TCM
Caliber: .22 TCM. **Capacity:** 17-round magazine. **Barrel:** 5 in. **Weight:** 36 oz. **Length:** 8.5 in. **Grips:** Polymer. **Sights:** Adjustable rear. **Features:** Chambered for high velocity .22 TCM rimfire cartridge. Comes with interchangeable 9mm barrel.
Price: **$960.00**

ROCK ISLAND ARMORY PRO MATCH ULTRA "BIG ROCK"
Caliber: 10mm. **Capacity:** 8- or 16-round magazine. **Barrel:** 6 in. **Weight:** 40 oz. **Length:** 8.5 in. **Grips:** VZ G10. **Sights:** Fiber optic front, adjustable rear. **Features:** Two magazines, upper and lower accessory rails, extended beavertail safety.
Price: **$1,187.00**
Price: High capacity model................................ **$1,340.00**

ROCK ISLAND ARMORY MAP & MAPP
Caliber: 9mm. **Capacity:** 16-round magazine. **Barrel:** 3.5 (MAPP) or 4 in (MAP). Browning short recoil action-style pistols with: integrated front sight; snag-free rear sight; single- & double-action trigger; standard or ambidextrous rear safety; polymer frame with accessory rail.
Price: **$500.00**

ROCK ISLAND ARMORY XT22
Calibers: .22 LR, .22 Magnum. **Capacities:** 10- or 15-round magazine. **Barrel:** 5 in. **Weight:** 38 oz. **Features:** The XT-22 is the only .22 1911 with a forged 4140 steel slide and a one piece 4140 chrome moly barrel. Available as a .22/.45 ACP combo.
Price: **$600.00**
Price: .22 LR/.45 combo **$900.00**

ROCK ISLAND ARMORY BABY ROCK 380
Caliber: .380 ACP. **Capacity:** 7-round magazine. **Features:** Blowback operation. An 85 percent-size version of 1911-A1 design with features identical to full-size model.
Price: **$460.00**

ROCK RIVER ARMS LAR-15/LAR-9
Calibers: .223/5.56mm NATO, 9mm. **Barrels:** 7 in., 10.5 in. Wilson chrome moly, 1:9 twist, A2 flash hider, 1/2x28 thread. **Weights:** 5.1 lbs. (7-in. barrel), 5.5 lbs. (10.5-in. barrel). **Length:** 23 in. overall. **Stock:** Hogue rubber grip.

Sights: A2 front. **Features:** Forged A2 or A4 upper, single stage trigger, aluminum free-float tube, one magazine. Similar 9mm Para. LAR-9 also available. From Rock River Arms, Inc.
Price: LAR-15 7 in. A2 AR2115............................ **$1,175.00**
Price: LAR-15 10.5 in. A4 AR2120...................... **$1,055.00**
Price: LAR-9 7 in. A2 9mm2115.......................... **$1,320.00**

ROCK RIVER ARMS TACTICAL PISTOL
Caliber: .45 ACP. **Features:** Standard-size 1911 pistol with rosewood grips, Heinie or Novak sights, Black Cerakote finish.
Price: **$2,200.00**

ROCK RIVER ARMS LIMITED MATCH
Calibers: .45 ACP, 40 S&W, .38 Super, 9mm. **Barrel:** 5 in. **Sights:** Adjustable rear, blade front. **Finish:** Hard chrome. **Features:** National Match frame with beveled magazine well, front and rear slide serrations, Commander Hammer, G10 grips.
Price: **$3,600.00**

ROCK RIVER ARMS CARRY PISTOL
Caliber: .45 ACP. **Barrel:** 5 in. **Sights:** Heinie. **Finish:** Parkerized. **Grips:** Rosewood. **Weight:** 39 oz.
Price: **$1,600.00**

ROCK RIVER ARMS 1911 POLY
Caliber: .45 ACP. **Capacity:** 7-round magazine. **Barrel:** 5 in. **Weight:** 33 oz. **Sights:** Fixed. **Features:** Full-size 1911-style model with polymer frame and steel slide.
Price: **$925.00**

RUGER AMERICAN PISTOL
Calibers: 9mm, .45 ACP. **Capacities:** 10 or 17 (9mm), 10 (.45 ACP). **Barrels:** 4.2 in. (9), 4.5 in. (.45). **Lengths:** 7.5 or 8 in. **Weights:** 30–31.5 oz. **Sights:** Novak LoMount Carry 3-Dot. **Finish:** Stainless steel slide with black Nitride finish. **Grip:** One-piece ergonomic wrap-around module with adjustable palm swell and trigger reach. **Features:** Short take-up trigger with positive re-set, ambidextrous mag release and slide stop, integrated trigger safety, automatic sear block system, easy takedown. Introduced in 2016.
Price: **$579.00**

RUGER AMERICAN COMPACT PISTOL
Caliber: 9mm. **Barrel:** 3.5 in. **Features:** Compact version of American Pistol with same general specifications.
Price: **$579.00**

Prices given are believed to be accurate at time of publication however, many factors affect retail pricing so exact prices are not possible.

RUGER SR9 /SR40
Calibers: 9mm, .40 S&W. **Capacities:** 9mm (17-round magazine), .40 S&W (15). **Barrel:** 4.14 in. **Weights:** 26.25, 26.5 oz. **Grips:** Glass-filled nylon in two color options — black or OD Green, w/flat or arched reversible backstrap. **Sights:** Adjustable 3-dot, built-in Picatinny-style rail. **Features:** Semi-auto in six configurations, striker-fired, through-hardened stainless steel slide brushed or blackened stainless slide with black grip frame or blackened stainless slide with OD Green grip frame, ambidextrous manual 1911-style safety, ambi. mag release, mag disconnect, loaded chamber indicator, Ruger cam block design to absorb recoil, comes with two magazines. 10-shot mags available. Introduced 2008. Made in USA by Sturm, Ruger & Co.
Price: SR9 (17-Round), SR9-10 (SS) $569.00

RUGER SR9C/SR40C COMPACT
Calibers: 9mm, .40 S&W. **Capacities:** 10- and 17-round magazine. **Barrels:** 3.4 in. (SR9C), 3.5 in. (SR40C). **Weight:** 23.4 oz. **Features:** Features include 1911-style ambidextrous manual safety; internal trigger bar interlock and striker blocker; trigger safety; magazine disconnector; loaded chamber indicator; two magazines, one 10-round and the other 17-round; 3.5-in. barrel; 3-dot sights; accessory rail; brushed stainless or blackened allow finish.
Price: $569.00

RUGER SECURITY-9
Caliber: 9mm. **Capacity:** 10- or 15-round magazine. **Barrel:** 4 in. **Weight:** 21 oz. **Sights:** Drift-adjustable 3-dot. Striker-fired polymer-frame compact

model. Uses the same Secure Action as LCP II. Bladed trigger safety plus external manual safety.
Price: $379.00

RUGER SR45
Caliber: .45 ACP. **Capacity:** 10-round magazine. **Barrel:** 4.5 in. **Weight:** 30 oz. **Length:** 8 in. **Grips:** Glass-filled nylon with reversible flat/arched backstrap. **Sights:** Adjustable 3-dot. **Features:** Same features as SR9.
Price: $569.00

RUGER LC9S
Caliber: 9mm. **Capacity:** 7+1. **Barrel:** 3.12 in. **Grips:** Glass-filled nylon. **Sights:** Adjustable 3-dot. **Features:** Brushed stainless slide, black glass-filled grip frame, blue alloy barrel finish. Striker-fired operation with smooth trigger pull. Integral safety plus manual safety. Aggressive frame checkering with smooth "melted" edges. Slightly larger than LCS380. LC9S Pro has no manual safety.
Price: $479.00

RUGER LC380
Caliber: .380 ACP. Other specifications and features identical to LC9.
Price: $479.00
Price: LaserMax laser grips $529.00
Price: Crimson Trace Laserguard $629.00

Prices given are believed to be accurate at time of publication however, many factors affect retail pricing so exact prices are not possible.

RUGER LCP
Caliber: .380. **Capacity:** 6-round magazine. **Barrel:** 2.75 in. **Weight:** 9.4 oz. **Length:** 5.16 in. **Grips:** Glass-filled nylon. **Sights:** Fixed, drift adjustable or integral Crimson Trace Laserguard.
Price: Blued **$259.00**
Price: Stainless steel slide.. **$289.00**
Price: Viridian-E Red Laser sight.................................. **$349.00**
Price: Custom w/drift adjustable rear sight.................... **$269.00**

RUGER LCP II
Caliber: .380. **Capacity:** 6-round magazine. **Barrel:** 2.75 in. **Weight:** 10.6 oz. **Length:** 5.16 in. **Grips:** Glass-filled nylon. **Sights:** Fixed. **Features:** Last round fired holds action open. Larger grip frame surface provides better recoil distribution. Finger grip extension included. Improved sights for superior visibility. Sights are integral to the slide, hammer is recessed within slide.
Price: **$349.00**

RUGER EC9S
Caliber: 9mm. **Capacity:** 7-shot magazine. **Barrel:** 3.125 in. Striker-fired polymer frame. **Weight:** 17.2 oz.
Price: **$299.00**

RUGER MK IV COMPETITION

RUGER MARK IV SERIES
Caliber: .22 LR. **Capacity:** 10-round magazine. **Barrels:** 5.5 in, 6.875 in. Target model has 5.5-in. bull barrel, Hunter model 6.88-in. fluted bull, Competition model 6.88-in. slab-sided bull. **Weight:** 33–46 oz. **Grips:** Checkered or target laminate. **Sights:** Adjustable rear, blade or fiber-optic front (Hunter). **Features:** Updated design of Mark III series with one-button takedown. Introduced 2016. Modern successor of the first Ruger pistol of 1949.
Price: Standard **$449.00**

Price: Target (blue) **$529.00**
Price: Target (stainless) **$689.00**
Price: Hunter .... **$769.00–$799.00**
Price: Competition **$749.00**

RUGER 22/45 MARK IV PISTOL
Caliber: .22 LR. **Features:** Similar to other .22 Mark IV autos except has Zytel grip frame that matches angle and magazine latch of Model 1911 .45 ACP pistol. Available in 4.4-, 5.5-in. bull barrels. Comes with extra magazine, plastic case, lock. Molded polymer or replaceable laminate grips. **Weight:** 25–33 oz. **Sights:** Adjustable. Updated design of Mark III with one-button takedown. Introduced 2016.
Price: **$409.00**
Price: 4.4-in. bull threaded barrel w/rails **$529.00**
Price: Lite w/aluminum frame, rails **$549.00**

RUGER MARK IV TARGET

RUGER 22/45 MARK IV

RUGER SR22
Caliber: .22 LR. **Capacity:** 10-round magazine. **Barrel:** 3.5 in. **Weight:** 17.5 oz. **Length:** 6.4 in. **Sights:** Adjustable 3-dot. **Features:** Ambidextrous manual safety/decocking lever and mag release. Comes with two interchangeable

Prices given are believed to be accurate at time of publication however, many factors affect retail pricing so exact prices are not possible.

rubberized grips and two magazines. Black or silver anodize finish. Available with threaded barrel.

Price: Black **$439.00**
Price: Silver **$459.00**
Price: Threaded barrel **$479.00**

RUGER SR1911

Caliber: .45. **Capacity:** 8-round magazine. **Barrel:** 5 in. (3.5 in. Officer Model) **Weight:** 39 oz. **Length:** 8.6 in., 7.1 in. **Grips:** Slim checkered hardwood. **Sights:** Novak LoMount Carry rear, standard front. **Features:** Based on Series 70 design. Flared and lowered ejection port. Extended mag release, thumb safety and slide-stop lever, oversized grip safety, checkered backstrap on the flat mainspring housing. Comes with one 7-round and one 8-round magazine.
Price: **$939.00**

RUGER SR1911 CMD

Caliber: .45 ACP. **Barrel:** 4.25 in. **Weight:** 29.3 (aluminum), 36.4 oz. (stainless). **Features:** Commander-size version of SR1911. Other specifications and features are identical to SR1911.
Price: Low glare stainless **$939.00**
Price: Anodized aluminum two-tone **$979.00**

RUGER SR1911 TARGET

Calibers: 9mm, .45 ACP. **Capacities:** .45 and 10mm (8-round magazine), 9mm (9 shot). **Barrel:** 5 in. **Weight:** 39 oz. **Sights:** Bomar adjustable. **Grips:** G10 Deluxe checkered. **Features:** Skeletonized hammer and trigger, satin stainless finish. Introduced in 2016.
Price: **$1,019.00**

RUGER SR1911 OFFICER

Caliber: 9mm. **Capacity:** 8-round magazine. **Barrel:** 3.6 in. **Weight:** 27 oz. **Features:** Compact variation of SR1911 Series. Black anodized aluminum frame, stainless slide, skeletonized trigger, Novak 3-dot Night Sights, G10 deluxe checkered G10 grips.
Price: **$979.00**

SCCY CPX

Caliber: 9mm. **Capacity:** 10-round magazine. **Barrel:** 3.1 in. **Weight:** 15 oz. **Length:** 5.7 in. overall. **Grips:** Integral with polymer frame. **Sights:** 3-dot system, rear adjustable for windage. **Features:** Zytel polymer frame, steel slide, aluminum alloy receiver machined from bar stock. DAO with consistent 9-pound trigger pull. Concealed hammer. Available with (CPX-1) or without (CPX-2) manual thumb safety. Introduced 2014. Made in USA by SCCY Industries.
Price: Black carbon **$334.00**
Price: Stainless/blue two-tone **$339.00**

SEECAMP LWS 32/380 STAINLESS DA

Calibers: .32 ACP, .380 ACP. **Capacity:** 6-round magazine. **Barrel:** 2 in., integral with frame. **Weight:** 10.5 oz. **Length:** 4.125 in. overall. **Grips:** Glass-filled nylon. **Sights:** Smooth, no-snag, contoured slide and barrel top. **Features:** Aircraft quality 17-4 PH stainless steel. Inertia-operated firing pin. Hammer fired DAO. Hammer automatically follows slide down to safety rest position after each shot, no manual safety needed. Magazine safety disconnector. Polished stainless. Introduced 1985. From L.W. Seecamp.
Price: .32 .... **$446.25**
Price: .380 .... **$795.00**

SIG SAUER P220

Caliber: .45 ACP, 10mm. **Capacity:** 7- or 8-round magazine. **Barrel:** 4.4 in. **Weight:** 27.8 oz. **Length:** 7.8 in. overall. **Grips:** Checkered black plastic. **Sights:** Blade front, drift adjustable rear for windage. Optional Siglite night sights. **Features:** Double action. Stainless steel slide, Nitron finish, alloy frame, M1913 Picatinny rail; safety system of decocking lever, automatic firing pin safety block, safety intercept notch, and trigger bar disconnector. Squared combat-type trigger guard. Slide stays open after last shot. Introduced 1976. P220 SAS Anti-Snag has dehorned stainless steel slide, front Siglite night sight, rounded trigger guard, dust cover, Custom Shop wood grips. Equinox line is Custom Shop product with Nitron stainless slide with a black hard-anodized alloy frame, brush-polished flats and nickel accents. Truglo tritium fiber-optic front sight, rear Siglite night sight, gray laminated wood grips with checkering and stippling. From SIG SAUER, Inc.

Price:	**$1,087.00**
Price: P220 Elite 10mm	**$1,422.00**
Price: P220 Elite Stainless	**$1,359.00**
Price: P220 Super Match	**$1,467.00**
Price: P220 Combat Threaded Barrel	**$1,282.00**
Price: Legion 10mm	**$1,904.00**

SIG SAUER 1911

Calibers: .45 ACP, .40 S&W. **Capacities:** .45 ACP, .40 S&W. 8- and 10-round magazine. **Barrel:** 5 in. **Weight:** 40.3 oz. **Length:** 8.65 in. overall. **Grips:** Checkered wood grips. **Sights:** Novak night sights. Blade front, drift adjustable rear for windage. **Features:** Single-action 1911. Hand-fitted dehorned stainless steel frame and slide; match-grade barrel, hammer/ sear set and trigger; 25-LPI front strap checkering, 20-LPI mainspring housing checkering. Beavertail grip safety with speed bump, extended thumb safety, firing pin safety and hammer intercept notch. Introduced 2005. XO series has contrast sights, Ergo Grip XT textured polymer grips. STX line available from Sig Sauer Custom Shop; two-tone 1911, non-railed, Nitron slide, stainless frame, burled maple grips. Polished cocking serrations, flat-top slide, mag well. Carry line has Siglite night sights, lanyard attachment point, gray diamondwood or rosewood grips, 8+1 capacity. Compact series has 6+1 capacity, 7.7 OAL, 4.25-in. barrel, slim-profile wood grips, weighs 30.3 oz. Ultra Compact in 9mm or .45 ACP has 3.3-in. barrel, low-profile night sights, slim-profile gray diamondwood or rosewood grips. 6+1 capacity. 1911 C3 is a 6+1 compact .45 ACP, rosewood custom wood grips, two-tone and Nitron finishes. Weighs 30 oz. unloaded, lightweight alloy frame. Length is 7.7 in. Now offered in more than 30 different models with numerous options for frame size, grips, finishes, sight arrangements and other features. From SIG SAUER, Inc.

Price: Nitron	**$1,174.00**
Price: Tacops	**$1,221.00**
Price: XO Black	**$1,010.00**
Price: STX	**$1,244.00**
Price: Nightmare	**$1,244.00**
Price: Carry Nightmare	**$1,195.00**
Price: Compact C3	**$1,010.00**
Price: Ultra Compact	**$1,119.00**
Price: Max	**$1,663.00**
Price: Spartan	**$1,397.00**
Price: Super Target	**$1,609.00**
Price: Traditional Stainless Match Elite	**$1,164.00**

SIG SAUER P225 A-1

Caliber: 9mm. **Capacity:** 8-round magazine. **Barrels:** 3.6 or 5 in. **Weight:** 30.5 oz. **Features:** Shorter and slim-profile version of P226 with enhanced short reset trigger, single-stack magazine.

Price:	**$1,122.00**
Price: Night sights	**$1,236.00**

SIG SAUER SP2022
Calibers: 9mm, .357 SIG, .40 S&W. **Capacities:** 10-, 12-, or 15-round magazines. **Barrel:** 3.9 in. **Weight:** 30.2 oz. **Length:** 7.4 in. overall. **Grips:** Composite and rubberized one-piece. **Sights:** Blade front, rear adjustable for windage. Optional Siglite night sights. **Features:** Polymer frame, stainless steel slide; integral frame accessory rail; replaceable steel frame rails; left- or right-handed magazine release, two interchangeable grips. From SIG SAUER, Inc.
Price: **$642.00**

SIG SAUER P238
Caliber: .380 ACP. **Capacity:** 6-round magazine. **Barrel:** 2.7 in. **Weight:** 15.4 oz. **Length:** 5.5 in. overall. **Grips:** Hogue G-10 and Rosewood grips. **Sights:** Contrast/Siglite night sights. **Features:** All-metal beavertail-style frame.
Price: **$723.00**
Price: Desert Tan **$738.00**
Price: Polished **$798.00**
Price: Rose Gold **$932.00**
Price: Emperor Scorpion **$801.00**

SIG SAUER P226
Calibers: 9mm, .40 S&W. **Barrel:** 4.4 in. **Length:** 7.7 in. overall. **Features:** Similar to the P220 pistol except has 4.4-in. barrel, measures 7.7 in. overall, weighs 34 oz. DA/SA or DAO. Many variations available. Snap-on modular grips. Legion series has improved short reset trigger, contoured and shortened beavertail, relieved trigger guard, higher grip, other improvements. From SIG SAUER, Inc.
Price: From **$1,087.00**
Price: Elite **$1,481.00**
Price: Combat **$1,289.00**
Price: Tactical Operations (TACOPS) **$1,329.00**
Price: Engraved **$1,631.00**
Price: Legion **$1,428.00**
Price: RX w/Romeo 1 Reflex sight **$1,685.00**
Price: MK25 Navy Version **$1,187.00**

SIG SAUER P227
Caliber: .45 ACP. **Capacity:** 10-round magazine. **Features:** Same general specifications and features as P226 except chambered for .45 ACP and has double-stack magazine.
Price: .... **$1,087.00–$1,350.00**

SIG SAUER P229 DA
Caliber: Similar to the P220 except chambered for 9mm (10- or 15-round magazines), .40 S&W, (10- or 12-round magazines). **Barrels:** 3.86-in. barrel, 7.1 in. overall length and 3.35 in. height. **Weight:** 32.4 oz. **Features:** Introduced 1991. Snap-on modular grips. Frame made in Germany, stainless steel slide assembly made in U.S.; pistol assembled in U.S. Many variations available. Legion series has improved short reset trigger, contoured and shortened beavertail, relieved trigger guard, higher grip, other improvements. From SIG SAUER, Inc.
Price: P229, From **$1,085.00**
Price: P229 Legion **$1,413.00**
Price: P229 Select **$1,195.00**

SIG SAUER P320
Calibers: 9mm, .357 SIG, .40 S&W, .45 ACP. **Capacities:** 15 or 16 rounds (9mm), 13 or 14 rounds (.357 or .40). **Barrels:** 3.6 in. (Subcompact), 3.9 in. (Carry model) or 4.7 in. (Full size). **Weights:** 26–30 oz. **Lengths:** 7.2 or 8.0 in overall. **Grips:** Interchangeable black composite. **Sights:** Blade front, rear adjustable for windage. Optional Siglite night sights. **Features:** Striker-fired DAO, Nitron finish slide, black polymer frame. Frame size and calibers are interchangeable. Introduced 2014. Made in USA by SIG SAUER, Inc.
Price: Full size **$679.00**
Price: Carry (shown) **$679.00**

SIG SAUER P320 SUBCOMPACT
Calibers: 9mm, .40 S&W. **Barrel:** 3.6 in. **Features:** Accessory rail. Other features similar to Full-Size and Carry models.
Price: **$679.00**

SIG SAUER MODEL 320 RX
Caliber: 9mm. **Capacity:** 17-round magazine. **Barrels:** 4.7 in. or 3.9 in. **Features:** Full and Compact size models with ROMEO1 Reflex sight, accessory rail, stainless steel frame and slide. XFive has improved control ergonomics, bull barrel, 21-round magazines.
Price: **$952.00**
Price: XFive **$1,005.00**

Prices given are believed to be accurate at time of publication however, many factors affect retail pricing so exact prices are not possible.

Tactical GunDigest ⊕ **313**

SIG SAUER P365
Caliber: 9mm. **Barrel:** 3.1 in. **Weight:** 17.8 oz. **Features:** Micro-compact striker-fired model with 10-round magazine, stainless steel frame and slide, XRAY-3 day and night sights fully textured polymer grip.
Price: $599.00

SIG SAUER MPX
Calibers: 9mm, .357 SIG, .40 S&W. **Capacities:** 10, 20 or 30 rounds. **Barrel:** 8 in. **Weight:** 5 lbs **Features:** Semi-auto AR-style gun with closed, fully locked short-stroke pushrod gas system.
Price: From $2,016.00

SIG SAUER P938
Calibers: 9mm, .22 LR. **Capacities:** 9mm (6-shot mag.), .22 LR (10-shot mag.). **Barrel:** 3.0 in. **Weight:** 16 oz. **Length:** 5.9 in. **Grips:** Rosewood, Blackwood, Hogue Extreme, Hogue Diamondwood. **Sights:** Siglite night sights or Siglite rear with Tru-Glo front. **Features:** Slightly larger version of P238.
Price: .... $760.00–$1,195.00
Price: .22 LR.. $656.00

SMITH & WESSON M&P SERIES
Calibers: .22 LR, 9mm, .357 Sig, .40 S&W. **Capacities, full-size models:** 12 rounds (.22), 17 rounds (9mm), 15 rounds (.40). **Compact models:** 12 (9mm), 10 (.40). **Barrels:** 4.25, 3.5 in. **Weights:** 24, 22 oz. **Lengths:** 7.6, 6.7 in. **Grips:** Polymer with three interchangeable palm swell grip sizes. **Sights:** 3 white-dot system with low-profile rear. **Features:** Zytel polymer frame with stainless steel slide, barrel and structural components. VTAC (Viking Tactics) model has Flat Dark Earth finish, VTAC Warrior sights. Compact models available with Crimson Trace Lasergrips. Numerous options for finishes, sights, operating controls.
Price: $569.00
Price: (VTAC)... $799.00
Price: (Crimson Trace) .... $699.00–$829.00
Price: M&P 22 .... $389.00–$419.00

SMITH & WESSON M&P PRO SERIES C.O.R.E.
Calibers: 9mm, .40 S&W. **Capacities:** 17 rounds (9mm), 15 rounds (.40). **Barrels:** 4.25 in. (M&P9, M&P40), or 5 in. (M&P9L, M&P40L). **Features:**

Based on the Pro series line of competition-ready firearms, the C.O.R.E. models (Competition Optics Ready Equipment) feature a slide engineered to accept six popular competition optics (Trijicon RMR, Leupold Delta Point, Jpoint, Doctor, C-More STS, Insight MRDS). Optics not included. Other features identical to standard M&P9 and M&P40 models.
Price: $769.00

SMITH & WESSON M&P 45
Caliber: .45 ACP. **Capacity:** 8 or 10 rounds. **Barrel length:** 4 or 4.5 in. **Weight:** 26, 28 or 30 oz. **Features:** Available with or without thumb safety. **Finish:** Black or Dark Earth Brown. **Features:** M&P model offered in three frame sizes.
Price: .... $599.00–$619.00
Price: Threaded barrel kit.............................. $719.00

SMITH & WESSON M&P M2.0 SERIES
Calibers: 9mm, .40 S&W, .45 ACP. **Capacities:** 17 rounds (9mm), 15 rounds (.40), 10 rounds (.45). **Barrels:** 4.25, 4.5 or 4.6 in. (.45 only). **Weights:** 25 –27 oz. **Finishes:** Armornite Black or Flat Dark Earth. **Grip:** Textured polymer with 4 interchangeable modular inserts. Second Generation of M&P Pistol series. Introduced in 2017.
Price: $599.00

SMITH & WESSON M&P 9/40 SHIELD
Calibers: 9mm, .40 S&W. **Capacities:** 7- and 8-round magazine (9mm); 6-round and 7-round magazine (.40). **Barrel:** 3.1 in. **Length:** 6.1 in. **Weight:** 19 oz. **Sights:** 3-white-dot system with low-profile rear. Features: Ultra-compact, single-stack variation of M&P series. Available with or without thumb safety. Crimson Trace Green Laserguard available.
Price: $449.00
Price: CT Green Laserguard $589.00

SMITH & WESSON M&P 45 SHIELD
Caliber: .45 ACP. **Barrel:** 3.3 in. Ported model available. **Weight:** 20–23 oz. **Sights:** White dot or tritium night sights. Comes with one 6-round and one 7-round magazine.
Price: $479.00
Price: Tritium night sights................................... $579.00
Price: Ported barrel $609.00

SMITH & WESSON MODEL SD9 VE/SD40 VE
Calibers: .40 S&W, 9mm. **Capacities:** 10+1, 14+1 and 16+1 **Barrel:** 4 in. **Weight:** 39 oz. **Length:** 8.7 in. **Grips:** Wood or rubber. **Sights:** Front: Tritium Night Sight, Rear: Steel Fixed 2-Dot. **Features:** SDT (Self Defense Trigger) for optimal, consistent pull first round to last, standard Picatinny-style rail, slim ergonomic textured grip, textured finger locator and aggressive front and backstrap texturing with front and rear slide serrations.
Price: $389.00

Prices given are believed to be accurate at time of publication however, many factors affect retail pricing so exact prices are not possible.

SPHINX SDP
Caliber: 9mm. **Capacity:** 15-shot magazine. **Barrel:** 3.7 in. **Weight:** 27.5 oz. **Length:** 7.4 in. **Sights:** Defiance Day & Night Green fiber/tritium front, tritium 2-dot red rear. **Features:** DA/SA with ambidextrous decocker, integrated slide position safety, aluminum MIL-STD 1913 Picatinny rail, Blued alloy/steel or stainless. Aluminum and polymer frame, machined steel slide. Offered in several variations. Made in Switzerland and imported by Kriss USA.
Price: From **$999.00**

SMITH & WESSON MODEL SW1911
Calibers: .45 ACP, 9mm. **Capacities:** 8 rounds (.45), 7 rounds (subcompact .45), 10 rounds (9mm). **Barrels:** 3, 4.25, 5 in. **Weights:** 26.5–41.7 oz. **Lengths:** 6.9–8.7 in. **Grips:** Wood, wood laminate or synthetic. Crimson Trace Lasergrips available. **Sights:** Low-profile white dot, tritium night sights or adjustable. **Finish:** Black matte, stainless or two-tone. **Features:** Offered in three different frame sizes. Skeletonized trigger. Accessory rail on some models. Compact models have round-butt frame. Pro Series have 30 LPI checkered frontstrap, oversized external extractor, extended mag well, full-length guide rod, ambidextrous safety.
Price: Standard Model E Series, From **$979.00**
Price: Crimson Trace grips **$1,149.00**
Price: Pro Series .... **$1,459.00–$1,609.00**
Price: Scandium Frame E Series **$1,449.00**

SPRINGFIELD ARMORY EMP ENHANCED MICRO
Calibers: 9mm, 40 S&W. **Capacity:** 9-round magazine. **Barrel:** 3-inch stainless steel match grade, fully supported ramp, bull. **Weight:** 26 oz. **Length:** 6.5 in. overall. **Grips:** Thinline cocobolo hardwood. **Sights:** Fixed low-profile combat rear, dovetail front, 3-dot tritium. **Features:** Two 9-round stainless steel magazines with slam pads, long aluminum match-grade trigger adjusted to 5 to 6 lbs., forged aluminum alloy frame, black hardcoat anodized finish; dual spring full-length guide rod, forged satin-finish stainless steel slide. Introduced 2007. Champion has 4-inch barrel, fiber optic front sight, three 10-round magazines, Bi-Tone finish.
Price: .... **$1,104.00–$1,249.00**
Price: Champion **$1,179.00**

SMITH & WESSON BODYGUARD 380
Caliber: .380 Auto. **Capacity:** 6+1. **Barrel:** 2.75 in. **Weight:** 11.85 oz. **Length:** 5.25 in. **Grips:** Polymer. **Sights:** Integrated laser plus drift-adjustable front and rear. **Features:** The frame of the Bodyguard is made of reinforced polymer, as is the magazine base plate and follower, magazine catch and trigger. The slide, sights and guide rod are made of stainless steel, with the slide and sights having a Melonite hardcoating.
Price: **$449.00**

SPRINGFIELD ARMORY XD(M) SERIES

Calibers: 9mm, .40 S&W, .45 ACP. **Barrels:** 3.8 or 4.5 in. **Sights:** Fiber optic front with interchangeable red and green filaments, adjustable target rear. **Grips:** Integral polymer with three optional backstrap designs. **Features:** Variation of XD design with improved ergonomics, deeper and longer slide serrations, slightly modified grip contours and texturing. Black polymer frame, forged steel slide. Black and two-tone finish options.
Price: .... **$623.00–$779.00**

SPRINGFIELD ARMORY XD SERIES

Calibers: 9mm, .40 S&W, .45 ACP. **Barrels:** 3, 4, 5 in. **Weights:** 20.5-31 oz. **Lengths:** 6.26-8 overall. **Grips:** Textured polymer. **Sights:** Varies by model; Fixed sights are dovetail front and rear steel 3-dot units. **Features:** Three sizes in X-Treme Duty (XD) line: Sub-Compact (3-in. barrel), Service (4-in. barrel), Tactical (5-in. barrel). Three ported models available. Ergonomic polymer frame, hammer-forged barrel, no-tool disassembly, ambidextrous magazine release, visual/tactile loaded chamber indicator, visual/tactile striker status indicator, grip safety, XD gear system included. Introduced 2004. XD 45 introduced 2006. Compact line introduced 2007. Compact is shipped with one extended magazine (13) and one compact magazine (10). XD Mod.2 Sub-Compact has newly contoured slide and redesigned serrations, stippled grip panels, fiber-optic front sight. From Springfield Armory.
Price: Sub-Compact OD Green 9mm/40 S&W, fixed sights **$508.00**
Price: Compact .45 ACP, 4 barrel, Bi-Tone finish **$607.00**
Price: Service Black 9mm/.40 S&W, fixed sights **$541.00**
Price: Service Black .45 ACP, external thumb safety **$638.00**
Price: V-10 Ported Black 9mm/.40 S&W **$608.00**
Price: XD Mod.2 .... **$565.00**
Price: XD OSP w/Vortex Venom Red Dot Sight **$724.00**

SPRINGFIELD ARMORY MIL-SPEC 1911A1

Caliber: .45 ACP. **Capacity:** 7-round magazine. **Barrel:** 5 in. **Weights:** 35.6–39 oz. **Lengths:** 8.5–8.625 in. overall. **Finish:** Stainless steel. **Features:** Similar to Government Model military .45.
Price: Mil-Spec Parkerized, 7+1, 35.6 oz. **$785.00**
Price: Mil-Spec Stainless Steel, 7+1, 36 oz. **$889.00**

SPRINGFIELD ARMORY TACTICAL RESPONSE

Caliber: .45 ACP. **Features:** Similar to 1911A1 except .45 ACP only, checkered frontstrap and main-spring housing, Novak Night Sight combat rear sight and matching dove-tailed front sight, tuned, polished extractor, oversize barrel link; lightweight speed trigger and combat action job, match barrel and bushing, extended ambidextrous thumb safety and fitted beavertail grip safety. Checkered Cocobolo wood grips, comes with two

Prices given are believed to be accurate at time of publication however, many factors affect retail pricing so exact prices are not possible.

Wilson 7-shot magazines. Frame is engraved "Tactical" both sides of frame with "TRP." Introduced 1998. TRP-Pro Model meets FBI specifications for SWAT Hostage Rescue Team.

Price: **$1,646.00**
Price: Operator with adjustable Trijicon night sights...................... **$1,730.00**

SPRINGFIELD ARMORY RANGE OFFICER

Calibers: 9mm, .45 ACP. **Barrels:** 5-in. stainless match grade. Compact model has 4 in. barrel. **Sights:** Adjustable target rear, post front. **Grips:** Double diamond checkered walnut. **Weights:** 40 oz., 28 oz. (compact). **Features:** Operator model has fiber optic sights.

Price: **$936.00**
Price: Compact **$899.00**
Price: Stainless finish... **$1,045.00**
Price: Operator **$1,029.00**

SPRINGFIELD ARMORY CHAMPION OPERATOR LIGHTWEIGHT

Caliber: .45 ACP. **Barrel:** 4-in. stainless match-grade bull barrel. **Sights:** 3-dot Tritium combat profile. **Grips:** Double diamond checkered cocobolo with Cross Cannon logo. **Features:** Alloy frame with integral rail, extended ambi thumb safety and trigger, lightweight Delta hammer.

Price: **$1,050.00**

SPRINGFIELD ARMORY 911

Caliber: .380 ACP. **Barrel:** 2.7-in. stainless steel. **Sights:** 3-dot Tritium combat profile. **Weight:** 12.6 oz. **Grips:** Grooved Hogue G10. **Features:** Alloy frame, stainless steel slide. Springfield Armory's smallest pistol to date.

Price: **$599.00**

STEYR M-A1 SERIES

Calibers: 9mm, .40 S&W. **Capacities:** 9mm (15 or 17-round capacity) or .40 S&W (10-12). **Barrels:** 3.5 in. (MA-1), 4.5 in. (L-A1), 3 in. (C-A1). **Weight:** 27 oz. **Sights:** Fixed with white outline triangle. **Grips:** Black

synthetic. Ergonomic low-profile for reduced muzzle lift. **Features:** DAO striker-fired operation.

Price: M-A1.. **$575.00**
Price: C-A1 compact model.. **$575.00**
Price: L-A1 full-size model **$575.00**
Price: S-A1 subcompact model.................................... **$575.00**

STOEGER COMPACT COUGAR

Caliber: 9mm. **Capacity:** 13+1. **Barrel:** 3.6 in. **Weight:** 32 oz. **Length:** 7 in. **Grips:** Wood or rubber. **Sights:** Quick read 3-dot. **Features:** DA/SA with a matte black finish. The ambidextrous safety and decocking lever is easily accessible to the thumb of a right- or left-handed shooter.

Price: **$469.00**

STI INTERNATIONAL

This company manufactures a wide selection of 1911-style semi-auto pistols chambered in .45 ACP, 9mm, .357 SIG, 10mm and .38 Super. Barrel lengths are offered from 3.0 to 6.0 in. Listed here are several of the company's more than 20 current models. Numerous finish, grip and sight options are available.

Price: 5.0 Trojan **$1,499.00**
Price: 5.0 Apeiro **$2,999.00**
Price: Costa Carry Comp.. **$3,699.00**
Price: H.O.S.T. Single stack....................................... **$2,699.00**
Price: H.O.S.T. Double stack...................................... **$3,199.00**
Price: DVC 3-Gun **$2,999.00**
Price: DVC Limited **$3,199.00**
Price: DVC Open **$3,999.00**
Price: HEXTAC Series **$2,199.00**

Prices given are believed to be accurate at time of publication however, many factors affect retail pricing so exact prices are not possible.

Tactical GunDigest ✛ **317**

TAURUS MODEL 92
Caliber: 9mm. **Capacity:** 10- or 17-round magazine. **Barrel:** 5 in. **Weight:** 34 oz. **Length:** 8.5 in. overall. **Grips:** Checkered rubber, rosewood, mother of pearl. **Sights:** Fixed notch rear. 3-dot sight system. Also offered with micrometer-click adjustable night sights. **Features:** DA, ambidextrous 3-way hammer drop safety, allows cocked and locked carry. Blued, stainless steel, blued with gold highlights, stainless steel with gold highlights, forged aluminum frame, integral key-lock. .22 LR conversion kit available. Imported from Brazil by Taurus International.
Price: 92B $513.00
Price: 92SS $529.00

TAURUS SLIM PT-709
Caliber: 9mm. **Capacity:** 7+1. **Weight:** 19 oz. **Length:** 6.24 in. width less than an inch. **Features:** Compact DA/SA semi-auto pistol in polymer frame; blued or stainless slide; SA/DA trigger pull; low-profile fixed sights.
Price: $319.00
Price: Stainless... $339.00

TAURUS SLIM 740
Caliber: .40 S&W. **Capacity:** 6+1. **Barrel:** 3.2 in. **Weight:** 19 oz. **Length:** 6.24 in. overall. **Grips:** Polymer Grips. **Features:** DA with stainless steel finish.
Price: $319.00
Price: Stainless... $339.00

TAURUS CURVE
Caliber: .380 ACP. **Capacity:** 6+1. **Barrel:** 2.5 in. **Weight:** 10.2 oz. **Length:** 5.2 in. **Features:** Unique curved design to fit contours of the body for comfortable concealed carry with no visible "printing" of the firearm. Double-action only. Light and laser are integral with frame.
Price: $404.00

TAURUS MODEL 1911
Calibers: 9mm, .45 ACP. **Capacities:** .45 ACP 8+1, 9mm 9+1. **Barrel:** 5 in. **Weight:** 33 oz. **Length:** 8.5 in. **Grips:** Checkered black. **Sights:** Heinie straight 8. **Features:** SA. Blued, stainless steel, duotone blue and blue/gray finish. Standard/Picatinny rail, standard frame, alloy frame and alloy/Picatinny rail. Introduced in 2007. Imported from Brazil by Taurus International.
Price: 1911B, Blue $719.00
Price: 1911B, Walnut grips $866.00
Price: 1911SS, Stainless Steel $907.00
Price: 1911SS-1, Stainless Steel w/rail................................ $945.00
Price: 1911 DT, Duotone Blue $887.00

TAURUS SPECTRUM
Caliber: .380. **Barrel:** 2.8 in. **Weight:** 10 oz. **Length:** 5.4 in. **Sights:** Low-profile integrated with slide. **Features:** Polymer frame with stainless steel slide. Many finish combinations with various bright colors. Made in the USA. Introduced in 2017.
Price: .... $289.00–$305.00

Prices given are believed to be accurate at time of publication however, many factors affect retail pricing so exact prices are not possible.

TRISTAR 100 /120 SERIES
Calibers: 9mm, .40 S&W (C-100 only). **Capacities:** 15 (9mm), 11 (.40). **Barrels:** 3.7–4.7 in. **Weights:** 26–30 oz. **Grips:** Checkered polymer. **Sights:** Fixed. **Finishes:** Blue or chrome. **Features:** Alloy or steel frame. SA/DA. A series of pistols based on the CZ 75 design. Imported from Turkey.
Price: From .... **$460.00–$490.00**

TURNBULL MODEL 1911
Caliber: .45 ACP. **Features:** An accurate reproduction of 1918-era Model 1911 pistol. Forged slide with appropriate shape and style. Late-style sight with semi-circle notch. Early-style safety lock with knurled undercut thumb piece. Short, wide checkered spur hammer. Hand-checkered double-diamond American Black Walnut grips. Hand polished with period correct Carbonia charcoal bluing. Custom made to order with many options. Made in the USA by Doug Turnbull Manufacturing Co.
Price: From **$2,625.00**

WALTHER P99 AS
Calibers: 9mm, .40 S&W. **Capacities:** 15 or 10 rounds (9mm), 10 or 8 rounds (.40). **Barrels:** 3.5 or 4 in. **Weights:** 21–26 oz. **Lengths:** 6.6–7.1 in. **Grips:** Polymer with interchangeable backstrap inserts. **Sights:** Adjustable rear, blade front with three interchangeable inserts of different heights. **Features:**

Offered in two frame sizes, standard and compact. DA with trigger safety, decocker, internal striker safety, loaded chamber indicator. Made in Germany.
Price: **$629.00**

WALTHER PK380
Caliber: .380 ACP. **Capacity:** 8-round magazine. **Barrel:** 3.66 in. **Weight:** 19.4 oz. **Length:** 6.5 in. **Sights:** Three-dot system, drift adjustable rear. **Features:** DA with external hammer, ambidextrous mag release and manual safety. Picatinny rail. Black frame with black or nickel slide.
Price: **$399.00**
Price: Nickel slide **$449.00**

WALTHER PPK/S
Caliber: .22 LR. **Capacities:** 10+1 (.22), 7+1 (.380). **Barrel:** 3.3 in **Weight:** 22 oz. **Length:** 6.1 in **Grips:** Checkered plastic. **Sights:** Fixed. Made in Germany.
Price: (.22 blue) **$400.00**
Price: (.22 nickel) **$430.00**

WALTHER PPQ M2
Calibers: 9mm, .40 S&W, .45 ACP, .22 LR. **Capacities:** 9mm, (15-round magazine), .40 S&W (11). .45 ACP, 22 LR (PPQ M2 .22). **Barrels:** 4 or 5 in. **Weight:** 24 oz. **Lengths:** 7.1, 8.1 in. **Sights:** Drift-adjustable. **Features:** Quick Defense trigger, firing pin block, ambidextrous slidelock and mag release, Picatinny rail. Comes with two extra magazines, two interchangeable frame backstraps and hard case. Navy SD model has threaded 4.6-in. barrel. M2 .22 has aluminum slide, blowback operation, weighs 19 ounces.
Price: 9mm, .40 .... **$649.00–$749.00**
Price: M2 .22 .... **$429.00**
Price: .45 .... **$699.00–$799.00**

WALTHER CCP
Caliber: 9mm. **Capacity:** 8-round magazine. **Barrel:** 3.5 in. **Weight:** 22 oz. **Length:** 6.4 in. **Features:** Thumb-operated safety, reversible mag release, loaded chamber indicator. Delayed blowback gas-operated action provides less recoil and muzzle jump, and easier slide operation. Available in all black or black/stainless two-tone finish.
Price: From .... **$469.00–$499.00**

Prices given are believed to be accurate at time of publication however, many factors affect retail pricing so exact prices are not possible.

Tactical GunDigest® ✛ **319**

WALTHER PPS

Calibers: 9mm, 40 S&W. **Capacities:** 6-, 7-, 8-round magazines for 9mm; 5-, 6-, 7-round magazines for 40 S&W. **Barrel:** 3.2 in. **Weight:** 19.4 oz. **Length:** 6.3 in. overall. **Stocks:** Stippled black polymer. **Sights:** Picatinny-style accessory rail, 3-dot low-profile contoured sight. **Features:** PPS — "Polizeipistole Schmal" or Police Pistol Slim. Measures 1.04-in. wide. Ships with 6- and 7-round magazines. Striker-fired action, flat slide stop lever, alternate backstrap sizes. QuickSafe feature decocks striker assembly when backstrap is removed. Loaded chamber indicator. Introduced 2008.
Price: $629.00

WALTHER CREED

Caliber: 9mm. **Capacity:** 16+1. **Barrel:** 4 in. **Weight:** 27 oz. **Sights:** 3-dot system. **Features:** Polymer frame with ergonomic grip, Picatinny rail, pre-cocked DA trigger, front and rear slide serrations with non-slip surface. Comes with two magazines. Similar to the discontinued PPX. Made in Germany.
Price: $349.00

WALTHER P22

Caliber: .22 LR. **Barrels:** 3.4, 5 in. **Weights:** 19.6 oz. (3.4), 20.3 oz. (5). **Lengths:** 6.26, 7.83 in. **Sights:** Interchangeable white dot, front, 2-dot adjustable, rear. **Features:** A rimfire version of the Walther P99 pistol, available in nickel slide with black frame, Desert Camo or Digital Pink Camo frame with black slide.
Price: From $379.00
Price: Nickel slide/black frame, or black slide/camo frame $449.00

WILSON COMBAT ELITE SERIES

Calibers: 9mm, .38 Super, .40 S&W; .45 ACP. **Barrel:** Compensated 4.1-in. hand-fit, heavy flanged cone match grade. **Weight:** 36.2 oz. **Length:** 7.7 in. overall. **Grips:** Cocobolo. **Sights:** Combat Tactical yellow rear tritium inserts, brighter green tritium front insert. **Features:** High-cut frontstrap, 30 LPI checkering on frontstrap and flat mainspring housing, High-Ride Beavertail grip safety. Dehorned, ambidextrous thumb safety, extended ejector, skeletonized ultra light hammer, ultralight trigger, Armor-Tuff finish on frame and slide. Introduced 1997. Made in USA by Wilson Combat. This manufacturer offers more than 100 different 1911 models ranging in price from about $2,800 to $5,000. XTAC and Classic 6-in. models shown. Prices show a small sampling of available models.
Price: Classic, From.. $3,300.00
Price: CQB, From $2,865.00
Price: Hackathorn Special.. $3,750.00
Price: Tactical Carry... $3,750.00
Price: Tactical Supergrade $5,045.00
Price: Bill Wilson Carry Pistol $3,850.00
Price: Ms. Sentinel... $3,875.00
Price: Hunter 10mm, .460 Rowland $4,100.00
Price: Beretta Brigadier Series, From.. $1,095.00
Price: X-Tac Series, From $2,760.00
Price: Texas BBQ Special, From... $4,960.00

BAER 1911 ULTIMATE MASTER COMBAT

Calibers: .38 Super, 400 Cor-Bon, .45 ACP (others available). **Capacity:** 10-shot magazine. **Barrels:** 5, 6 in. Baer National Match. **Weight:** 37 oz. **Length:** 8.5 in. overall. **Grips:** Checkered cocobolo. **Sights:** Baer dovetail front, low-mount Bo-Mar rear with hidden leaf. **Features:** Full-house competition gun. Baer forged NM blued steel frame and double serrated slide; Baer triple port, tapered cone compensator; fitted slide to frame; lowered, flared ejection port; Baer reverse recoil plug; full-length guide rod; recoil buff; beveled magazine well; Baer Commander hammer, sear; Baer extended ambidextrous safety, extended ejector, checkered slide stop, beavertail grip safety with pad, extended magazine release button; Baer speed trigger. Made in USA by Les Baer Custom, Inc.

Price: .45 ACP Compensated $3,240.00
Price: .38 Super Compensated $3,390.00
Price: 5-in. Standard barrel $3,040.00
Price: 5-in. barrel .38 Super or 9mm $3,140.00
Price: 6-in. barrel... $3,140.00
Price: 6-in. barrel .38 Super or 9mm $3,220.00

BAER 1911 NATIONAL MATCH HARDBALL

Caliber: .45 ACP. **Capacity:** 7-round magazine. **Barrel:** 5 in. **Weight:** 37 oz. **Length:** 8.5 in. overall. **Grips:** Checkered walnut. **Sights:** Baer dovetail front with under-cut post, low-mount Bo-Mar rear with hidden leaf. **Features:** Baer NM forged steel frame, double serrated slide and barrel with stainless bushing; slide fitted to frame; Baer match trigger with 4-lb. pull; polished feed ramp, throated barrel; checkered frontstrap, arched mainspring housing; Baer beveled magazine well; lowered, flared ejection port; tuned extractor; Baer extended ejector, checkered slide stop; recoil buff. Made in USA by Les Baer Custom, Inc.

Price: $2,310.00

BAER 1911 PPC OPEN CLASS

Caliber: .45 ACP, 9mm. **Barrel:** 6 in, fitted to frame. **Sights:** Adjustable PPC rear, dovetail front. **Grips:** Checkered Cocobola. **Features:** Designed for NRA Police Pistol Combat matches. Lowered and flared ejection port, extended ejector, polished feed ramp, throated barrel, frontstrap checkered at 30 LPI, flat serrated mainspring housing, Commander hammer, front and rear slide serrations. 9mm has supported chamber.

Price: $2,695.00
Price: 9mm w/supported chamber $3,095.00

BAER 1911 BULLSEYE WADCUTTER

Similar to National Match Hardball except designed for wadcutter loads only. Polished feed ramp and barrel throat; Bo-Mar rib on slide; full-length recoil rod; Baer speed trigger with 3.5-lb. pull; Baer deluxe hammer and sear; Baer beavertail grip safety with pad; flat mainspring housing checkered 20 LPI. Blue finish; checkered walnut grips. Made in USA by Les Baer Custom, Inc.

Price: From $2,390.00

COLT GOLD CUP NM SERIES

Caliber: .45 ACP. **Capacity:** 8-round magazine. **Barrel:** 5-inch National Match. **Weight:** 37 oz. **Length:** 8.5. **Grips:** Checkered wraparound rubber composite with silver-plated medallions or checkered walnut grips with gold medallions. **Sights:** Target post dovetail front, Bomar fully adjustable rear. **Features:** Adjustable aluminum wide target trigger, beavertail grip safety, full-length recoil spring and target recoil spring, available in blued finish or stainless steel.

Price: (blued) $1,299.00
Price: (stainless) $1,350.00

COLT COMPETITION PISTOL

Calibers: .45 ACP, 9mm or .38 Super. **Capacities:** 8 or 9-shot magazine. **Barrel:** 5 in. National Match. **Weight:** 39 oz. **Length:** 8.5 in. **Grips:** Custom Blue Colt G10. **Sights:** Novak adjustable rear, fiber optic front. A competition-ready pistol out of the box at a moderate price. Blue or satin nickel finish. Series 80 firing system. O Series has stainless steel frame and slide with Cerakote gray frame and black slide, competition trigger, gray/black G-10 grips, front and rear slide serrations.

Price: .... $949.00–$1,099.00
Price: Competition O series... $2,499.00

CZ 75 TS CZECHMATE

Caliber: 9mm. **Capacity:** 20-round magazine. **Barrel:** 130mm. **Weight:** 1360 g **Length:** 266mm overall. **Features:** The handgun is custom built, therefore the quality of workmanship is fully comparable with race pistols built directly to IPSC shooters' wishes. Individual parts and components are excellently match fitted, broke-in and tested. Every handgun is outfitted with a four-port compensator, nut for shooting without a compensator, the slide stop with an extended finger piece, the slide stop without a finger piece, ergonomic grip panels from aluminum with a new type pitting and side mounting provision with the C-More red-dot sight. For shooting without a red-dot sight there is included a standard target rear sight of Tactical Sports type, package contains also the front sight.

Price: $3,317.00

CZ 75 TACTICAL SPORTS

Calibers: 9mm, .40 S&W. **Capacities:** 17-20-round magazines. **Barrel:** 114mm. **Weight:** 1270 g **Length:** 225mm overall. **Features:** Semi-automatic handgun with a locked breech. This model is designed for competition shooting in accordance with world IPSC (International Practical Shooting Confederation) rules and regulations. The CZ 75 TS pistol model design stems from the standard CZ 75 model. However, this model features a number of special modifications, which are usually required for competitive handguns: SA trigger mechanism, match trigger made of plastic featuring option for trigger travel adjustments before discharge (using upper screw), and for overtravel (using bottom screw). The adjusting screws are set by the manufacturer — sporting hammer specially adapted for a reduced trigger pull weight, an extended magazine catch, grip panels made of walnut, guiding funnel made of plastic for quick inserting of the magazine into pistol's frame. Glossy blued slide, silver Polycoat frame. Packaging includes 3 magazines.

Price: $1,310.00

DAN WESSON CHAOS
Caliber: 9mm. **Capacity:** 21-round magazine. **Barrel:** 5 in. **Weight:** 3.20 lbs. **Length:** 8.75 in. overall. **Features:** A double-stack 9mm designed for 3-Gun competition.
Price: **$3,829.00**

DAN WESSON HAVOC
Calibers: 9mm, .38 Super. **Capacity:** 21-round magazine. **Barrel:** 4.25 in. **Weight:** 2.20 lbs. **Length:** 8 in. overall. **Features:** The Havoc is based on an "All Steel" Hi-capacity version of the 1911 frame. It comes ready to compete in Open IPSC/USPSA division. The C-more mounting system offers the lowest possible mounting configuration possible, enabling extremely fast target acquisition. The barrel and compensator arrangement pair the highest level of accuracy with the most effective compensator available.
Price: **$4,299.00**

DAN WESSON MAYHEM
Caliber: .40 S&W. **Capacity:** 18-round magazine. **Barrel:** 6 in. **Weight:** 2.42 lbs. **Length:** 8.75 in. overall. **Features:** The Mayhem is based on an "All-Steel" Hi-capacity version of the 1911 frame. It comes ready to compete in Limited IPSC/USPSA division or fulfill the needs of anyone looking for a superbly accurate target-grade 1911. The 6-in. bull barrel and tactical rail add to the static weight, or "good weight." A 6-in. long slide for added sight radius and enhanced pointability, but that would add to the "bad weight" so the 6-in. slide has been lightened to equal the weight of a 5 in. The result is a 6 in. long slide that balances and feels like a 5 in. but shoots like a 6 in. The combination of the all-steel frame with industry leading parts delivers the most well-balanced, softest shooting 6-in. limited gun on the market.
Price: **$3,899.00**

DAN WESSON TITAN
Caliber: 10mm. **Capacity:** 21-round magazine. **Barrel:** 4.25 in. **Weight:** 1.62 lbs. **Length:** 8 in. overall. **Features:** The Titan is based on an "All Steel" Hi-capacity version of the 1911 frame. The rugged HD night sights are moved forward and recessed deep into the slide yielding target accuracy and extreme durability. The Snake Scale serrations' aggressive 25 LPI checkering, and the custom competition G-10 grips ensure controllability even in the harshest of conditions. The combination of the all-steel frame, bull barrel and tactical rail enhance the balance and durability of this formidable target-grade Combat handgun.
Price: **$3,829.00**

EAA WITNESS ELITE GOLD TEAM
Calibers: 9mm, 9x21, .38 Super, .40 S&W, .45 ACP. **Barrel:** 5.1 in. **Weight:** 44 oz. **Length:** 10.5 in. overall. **Grips:** Checkered walnut, competition-style. **Sights:** Square post front, fully adjustable rear. **Features:** Triple-chamber cone compensator; competition SA trigger; extended safety and magazine release; competition hammer; beveled magazine well; beavertail grip. Hand-fitted major components. Hard chrome finish. Match-grade barrel. From EAA Custom Shop. Introduced 1992. Limited designed for IPSC Limited Class competition. Features include full-length dust-cover frame, funneled magazine well, interchangeable front sights. Stock (2005) designed for IPSC Production Class competition. Match introduced 2006. Made in Italy, imported by European American Armory.
Price: Gold Team **$2,406.00**
Price: Stock, 4.5 in. barrel, hard-chrome finish **$1,263.00**
Price: Limited Custom Xtreme.. **$2,502.00**
Price: Witness Match Xtreme.. **$2,335.00**
Price: Witness Stock III Xtreme **$2.252.00**

HIGH STANDARD SUPERMATIC TROPHY TARGET
Caliber: .22 LR. **Capacity:** 9-round mag. **Barrels:** 5.5-in. bull or 7.25-in. fluted. **Weights:** 44–46 oz. **Lengths:** 9.5–11.25 in. overall. **Stock:** Checkered hardwood with thumb rest. **Sights:** Undercut ramp front, frame-mounted micro-click rear adjustable for windage and elevation; drilled and tapped for scope mounting. **Features:** Gold-plated trigger, slide lock, safety-lever and magazine release; stippled front grip and backstrap; adjustable trigger and sear. Barrel weights optional. From High Standard Manufacturing Co., Inc.
Price: 5.5-in. barrel **$1,070.00**
Price: 7.25-in. barrel **$1,205.00**

Prices given are believed to be accurate at time of publication however, many factors affect retail pricing so exact pricing are not possible.

HIGH STANDARD VICTOR TARGET

Caliber: .22 LR. **Capacity:** 10-round magazine. **Barrels:** 4.5 in. or 5.5 in. polished blue; push-button takedown. **Weight:** 46 oz. **Length:** 9.5 in. overall. **Stock:** Checkered walnut with thumb rest. **Sights:** Undercut ramp front, micro-click rear adjustable for windage and elevation. Also available with scope mount, rings, no sights. **Features:** Stainless steel frame. Full-length vent rib. Gold-plated trigger, slide lock, safety-lever and magazine release; stippled front grip and backstrap; polished blue slide; adjustable trigger and sear. Comes with barrel weight. From High Standard Manufacturing Co., Inc.
Price: 4.5- or 5.5-in. barrel, vented sight rib, scope base **$1,050.00**

KIMBER SUPER MATCH II

Caliber: .45 ACP. **Capacity:** 8-round magazine. **Barrel:** 5 in. **Weight:** 38 oz. **Length:** 8.7 in. overall. **Grips:** Rosewood double diamond. **Sights:** Blade front, Kimber fully adjustable rear. **Features:** Guaranteed to shoot 1-in. groups at 25 yards. Stainless steel frame, black KimPro slide; two-piece magazine well; premium aluminum match-grade trigger; 30 LPI frontstrap checkering; stainless match-grade barrel; ambidextrous safety; special Custom Shop markings. Introduced 1999. Made in USA by Kimber Mfg., Inc.
Price: **$2,313.00**

RUGER MARK IV TARGET

Caliber: .22 LR. **Capacity:** 10-round magazine. **Barrel:** 5.5-in. heavy bull. **Weight:** 35.6 oz. **Grips:** Checkered synthetic or laminate. **Sights:** .125 blade front, micro-click rear, adjustable for windage and elevation, loaded chamber indicator; integral lock, magazine disconnect. Plastic case with lock included.
Price: (blued) **$529.00**
Price: (stainless) **$689.00**

SMITH & WESSON MODEL 41 TARGET

Caliber: .22 LR. **Capacity:** 10-round magazine. **Barrels:** 5.5 in., 7 in. **Weight:** 41 oz. (5.5-in. barrel). **Length:** 10.5 in. overall (5.5-in. barrel). **Grips:** Checkered walnut with modified thumb rest, usable with either hand. **Sights:** .125 in. Patridge on ramp base; micro-click rear-adjustable for windage and elevation. **Features:** .375 in. wide, grooved trigger; adjustable trigger stop drilled and tapped.
Price: .... **$1,369.00–$1,619.00**

STI APEIRO

Calibers: 9mm, .40 S&W, .45 ACP. **Features:** 1911-style semi-auto pistol with Schuemann "Island" barrel; patented modular steel frame with polymer grip; high capacity double-stack magazine; stainless steel ambidextrous thumb safeties and knuckle relief high-rise beavertail grip safety; unique sabertooth rear cocking serrations; 5-inch fully ramped, fully supported "Island" bull barrel, with the sight milled in to allow faster recovery to point of aim; custom engraving on the polished sides of the (blued) stainless steel slide; stainless steel mag well; STI adjustable rear sight and Dawson fiber optic front sight; blued frame.
Price: **$2,999.00**

STI EAGLE 5.0, 6.0

Calibers: 9mm, 9x21, .38 & .40 Super, .40 S&W, 10mm, .45 ACP. **Capacity:** 10-round magazine. **Barrels:** 5-, 6-in. bull. **Weight:** 34.5 oz. **Length:** 8.62 in. overall. **Grips:** Checkered polymer. **Sights:** STI front, Novak or Heinie rear. **Features:** Standard frames plus 7 others; adjustable match trigger; skeletonized hammer; extended grip safety with locator pad. Introduced 1994. Made in USA by STI International.

Price: (5.0 Eagle)... $2,099.00

STI STEELMASTER

Caliber: 9mm minor, comes with one 126mm magazine. **Barrel:** 4.15 in. **Weight:** 38.9 oz. **Length:** 9.5 in. overall. **Features:** Based on the renowned STI race pistol design, the SteelMaster is a shorter and lighter pistol that allows for faster target acquisition with reduced muzzle flip and dip. Designed to shoot factory 9mm (minor) ammo, this gun delivers all the advantages of a full-size race pistol in a smaller, lighter, faster-reacting and less violent package. The Steelmaster is built on the patented modular steel frame with polymer grip. It has a 4.15-in. classic slide which has been flat topped. Slide lightening cuts on the front and rear further reduce weight while "Sabertooth" serrations further enhance the aesthetics of this superior pistol. It also uses the innovative Trubor compensated barrel, which has been designed to eliminate misalignment of the barrel and compensator bore or movement of the compensator on the barrel. The shorter Trubor barrel system in the SteelMaster gives an even greater reduction in muzzle flip, and the shorter slide decreases overall slide cycle time allowing the shooter to achieve faster follow-up shots. The SteelMaster is mounted with a C-More, 6-minute, red-dot scope with blast shield and thumb rest. Additional enhancements include aluminum mag well, stainless steel ambidextrous safeties, stainless steel high rise grip safety, STI "Spur" hammer, STI RecoilMaster guide rod system and checkered frontstrap and mainspring housing.

Price: $2,799.00

STI TROJAN

Calibers: 9mm, .38 Super, .40 S&W, .45 ACP. **Barrel:** 5 in., 6 in. **Weight:** 36 oz. **Length:** 8.5 in. **Grips:** Rosewood. **Sights:** STI front with STI adjustable rear. **Features:** Stippled frontstrap, flat-top slide, one-piece steel guide rod.

Price: (Trojan 5) $1,499.00
Price: (Trojan 6, not available in .38 Super) $1,555.00

STI TRUBOR

Calibers: 9mm 'Major', 9x23, .38 Super (USPSA, IPSC). **Barrel:** 5 in. with integrated compensator. **Weight:** 41.3 oz. (including scope and mount) **Length:** 10.5 in. overall. **Features:** Built on the patented modular steel frame with polymer grip, the STI Trubor utilizes the Trubor compensated barrel, which is machined from one piece of 416 rifle-grade stainless steel. The Trubor is designed to eliminate misalignment of the barrel and compensator bore or movement of the compensator along the barrel threads, giving the shooter a more consistent performance and reduced muzzle flip. True to 1911 tradition, the Trubor has a classic scalloped slide with front and rear cocking serrations on a forged steel slide (blued) with polished sides, aluminum mag well, stainless steel ambidextrous safeties, stainless steel high rise grip safety, full-length guide rod, checkered frontstrap and checkered mainspring housing. With mounted C-More Railway sight included with the pistol.

Price: $2,999.00

CHARTER ARMS BULLDOG

Caliber: .44 Special. **Capacity:** 5-round cylinder. **Barrel:** 2.5 in. **Weight:** 21 oz. **Sights:** Blade front, notch rear. **Features:** Soft-rubber pancake-style grips, shrouded ejector rod, wide trigger and hammer spur. American made by Charter Arms.

Price: Blued **$409.00**
Price: Stainless **$422.00**
Price: Target Bulldog, 4 barrel, 23 oz. **$479.00**

CHARTER ARMS CRIMSON UNDERCOVER

Caliber: .38 Special +P. **Capacity:** 5-round cylinder. **Barrel:** 2 in. **Weight:** 16 oz. **Grip:** Crimson Trace. **Sights:** Fixed. **Features:** Stainless finish and frame. American made by Charter Arms.

Price: **$577.00**

CHARTER ARMS BOOMER

Caliber: .44 Special. **Capacity:** 5-round cylinder. **Barrel:** 2 in., ported. **Weight:** 20 oz. **Grips:** Full rubber combat. **Sights:** Fixed.

Price: Blued **$443.00**

CHARTER ARMS POLICE BULLDOG

Caliber: .38 Special. **Capacity:** 6-round cylinder. **Barrel:** 4.2 in. **Weight:** 26 oz. **Sights:** Blade front, notch rear. Large frame version of Bulldog design.

Price: Blued **$408.00**

CHARTER ARMS OFF DUTY

Caliber: .38 Special. **Barrel:** 2 in. **Weight:** 12.5 oz. **Sights:** Blade front, notch rear. **Features:** 5-round cylinder, aluminum casting, DAO with concealed hammer. Also available with semi-concealed hammer. American made by Charter Arms.

Price: Aluminum **$404.00**
Price: Crimson Trace Laser grip **$657.00**

CHARTER ARMS MAG PUG

Caliber: .357 Mag. **Capacity:** 5-round cylinder. **Barrel:** 2.2 in. **Weight:** 23 oz. **Sights:** Blade front, notch rear. **Features:** American made by Charter Arms.

Price: Blued or stainless **$400.00**
Price: 4.4-in. full-lug barrel... **$470.00**
Price: Crimson Trace Laser Grip.. **$609.00**

CHARTER ARMS CHIC LADY & CHIC LADY DAO

Caliber: .38 Special. **Capacity:** 5-round cylinder. **Barrel:** 2 in. **Weight:** 12 oz. **Grip:** Combat. **Sights:** Fixed. **Features:** 2-tone pink or lavender & stainless with aluminum frame. American made by Charter Arms.

Price: Chic Lady **$473.00**
Price: Chic Lady DAO **$483.00**

CHARTER UNDERCOVER LITE

Caliber: .38 Special +P. **Capacity:** 5-round cylinder. **Barrel:** 2 in. **Weight:** 12 oz. **Grip:** Full. **Sights:** Fixed. **Features:** 2-tone pink & stainless with aluminum frame. Constructed of tough aircraft-grade aluminum and steel, the Undercover Lite offers rugged reliability and comfort. This ultra-lightweight 5-shot .38 Special features a 2-in. barrel, fixed sights and traditional spurred hammer. American made by Charter Arms.

Price: **$397.00**

CHARTER ARMS PITBULL

Calibers: 9mm, 40 S&W, .45 ACP. **Capacity:** 5-round cylinder. **Barrel:** 2.2 in. **Weights:** 20–22 oz. **Sights:** Fixed rear, ramp front. **Grips:** Rubber. **Features:** Matte stainless steel frame or Nitride frame. Moon clips not required for 9mm, .45 ACP.

Price: 9mm **$502.00**
Price: .40 S&W **$489.00**
Price: .45 ACP **$489.00**

Prices given are believed to be accurate at time of publication however, many factors affect retail pricing so exact prices are not possible.

Tactical GunDigest® ✛ **325**

CHARTER ARMS SOUTHPAW

Caliber: .38 Special +P. **Capacity:** 5-round cylinder. **Barrel:** 2 in. **Weight:** 12 oz. **Grips:** Rubber Pachmayr style. **Features:** Snubnose, matte black aluminum alloy frame with stainless steel cylinder. Cylinder latch and crane assembly are on right side of frame for convenience of left-hand shooters.
Price: $419.00

CHARTER ARMS PATHFINDER

Calibers: .22 LR or .22 Mag. **Capacity:** 6-round cylinder. **Barrel:** 2 in., 4 in. **Weights:** 20 oz. (12 oz. Lite model). **Grips:** Full. **Sights:** Fixed or adjustable (Target). **Features:** Stainless finish and frame.
Price .22 LR $365.00
Price .22 Mag $367.00
Price: Lite $379.00
Price: Target $409.00

CHARTER ARMS UNDERCOVER

Caliber: .38 Special +P. **Capacity:** 6-round cylinder. **Barrel:** 2 in. **Weight:** 12 oz. **Sights:** Blade front, notch rear. **Features:** American made by Charter Arms.
Price: Blued $346.00

CHARTER ARMS UNDERCOVER SOUTHPAW

Caliber: .38 Spec. +P. **Capacity:** 5-round cylinder. **Barrel:** 2 in. **Weight:** 12 oz. **Sights:** NA. **Features:** Cylinder release is on the right side and the cylinder opens to the right side. Exposed hammer for both SA and DA. American made by Charter Arms.
Price: $419.00

CHIAPPA RHINO

Calibers: .357 Magnum, 9mm, .40 S&W. **Features:** 2-, 4-, 5- or 6-inch barrel; fixed or adjustable sights; visible hammer or hammerless design. **Weights:** 24–33 oz. Walnut or synthetic grips with black frame; hexagonal-shaped cylinder. Unique design fires from bottom chamber of cylinder.
Price: From $1,139.00

COBRA SHADOW

Caliber: .38 Special +P. **Capacity:** 5 rounds. **Barrel:** 1.875 in. **Weight:** 15 oz. Aluminum frame with stainless steel barrel and cylinder. **Length:** 6.375 in. **Grips:** Rosewood, black rubber or Crimson Trace Laser. **Features:** Black anodized, titanium anodized or custom colors including gold, red, pink and blue.
Price: $369.00
Price: Rosewood grips $434.00
Price: Crimson Trace Laser grips.......... $625.00

COLT COBRA

Caliber: .38 Special. **Capacity:** 6 rounds. **Sights:** Fixed rear, fiber optic red front. **Grips:** Hogue rubbed stippled with finger grooves. **Weight:** 25 oz. **Finish:** Matte stainless. Same name as classic Colt model made from 1950–1986 but totally new design. Introduced in 2017.
Price: $699.00

COLT NIGHT COBRA

Caliber; .38 Special. **Capacity:** 6 rounds. **Grips:** Black synthetic VC G10. **Sight:** Tritium front night sight. DAO operation with bobbed hammer. Features a linear leaf spring design for smooth DA trigger pull.
Price: $899.00

COMANCHE II-A

Caliber: .38 Special. **Capacity:** 6-round cylinder. **Barrels:** 3 or 4 in. **Weights:** 33, 35 oz. **Lengths:** 8, 8.5 in. overall. **Grips:** Rubber. **Sights:** Fixed. **Features:** Blued finish, alloy frame. Distributed by SGS Importers.
Price: $220.00

EAA WINDICATOR

Calibers: .38 Special, .357 Mag **Capacity:** 6-round cylinder. **Barrels:** 2 in., 4 in. **Weight:** 30 oz. (4 in.). **Length:** 8.5 in. overall (4 in. bbl.). **Grips:** Rubber with finger grooves. **Sights:** Blade front, fixed rear. **Features:** Swing-out cylinder; hammer block safety; blue or nickel finish. Introduced 1991. Imported from

Germany by European American Armory.
Price: .38 Spec. from **$354.00**
Price: .357 Mag, steel frame from **$444.00**

KIMBER K6S
Caliber: .357 Magnum. **Capacity:** 6-round cylinder. **Barrel:** 2-inch full lug.
Grips: Gray rubber. **Finish:** Satin stainless. Kimber's first revolver, claimed to be world's lightest production 6-shot .357 Magnum. DAO design with non-stacking match-grade trigger. Introduced 2016. CDP model has laminated checkered rosewood grips, Tritium night sights, two-tone black DLC/brushed stainless finish, match grade trigger.
Price: **$878.00**
Price: 3-in. Barrel.. **$899.00**
Price: Deluxe Carry w/Medallion grips................................... **$1,088.00**
Price: Custom Defense Package **$1,155.00**
Price: Crimson Trace Laser Grips **$1,177.00**

KORTH USA
Calibers: .22 LR, .22 WMR, .32 S&W Long, .38 Special, .357 Mag., 9mm.
Capacity: 6-shot. **Barrels:** 3, 4, 5.25, 6 in. **Weights:** 36–52 oz. **Grips:** Combat, Sport: Walnut, Palisander, Amboina, Ivory. **Finish:** German Walnut, matte with oil finish, adjustable ergonomic competition style. **Sights:** Adjustable Patridge (Sport) or Baughman (Combat), interchangeable and adjustable rear w/Patridge front (Target) in blue and matte. **Features:** DA/SA, 3 models, over 50 configurations, externally adjustable trigger stop and weight, interchangeable cylinder, removable wide-milled trigger shoe on Target model. Deluxe models are highly engraved editions. Available finishes include high polish blued finish, plasma coated in high polish or matte silver, gold, blue or charcoal. Many deluxe options available. From Korth USA.
Price: From **$8,000.00**
Price: Deluxe Editions, from **$12,000.00**

KORTH SKYHAWK
Caliber: 9mm. **Barrels:** 2 or 3 in. **Sights:** Adjustable rear with gold bead front.
Grips: Hogue with finger grooves. **Features:** Polished trigger, skeletonized hammer. Imported by Nighthawk Custom.
Price: **$1,699.00**

ROSSI R461/R462
Caliber: .357 Mag. **Capacity:** 6-round cylinder. **Barrel:** 2 in. **Weight:** 26–35 oz.
Grips: Rubber. **Sights:** Fixed. **Features:** DA/SA, +P-rated frame, blue carbon or high polish stainless steel, patented Taurus Security System.
Price: Blue carbon finish.. **$349.00**
Price: Stainless finish.. **$359.00**

ROSSI MODEL R971/R972
Caliber: 357 Mag. +P. **Capacity:** 6-round cylinder. **Barrel:** 4 in., 6 in. **Weight:** 32 oz. **Length:** 8.5 or 10.5 in. overall. **Grips:** Rubber. **Sights:** Blade front, adjustable rear. **Features:** SA/DA action. Patented key-lock Taurus Security System; forged steel frame. Introduced 2001. Made in Brazil by Amadeo Rossi. Imported by BrazTech/Taurus.
Price: Model R971 (blued finish, 4-in. bbl.) **$399.00**
Price: Model R972 (stainless steel finish, 6-in. bbl.) **$429.00**

Prices given are believed to be accurate at time of publication however, many factors affect retail pricing so exact prices are not possible.

Tactical GunDigest® ⊕ **327**

Price: .44 Spl. **$829.00**
Price: 7-round cylinder, 327 Fed or .357 Mag **$899.00**

ROSSI MODEL 351/851

Similar to Model R971/R972, chambered for .38 Special +P. Blued finish, 4-inch barrel. Introduced 2001. Made in Brazil by Amadeo Rossi. From BrazTech/Taurus.
Price: **$349.00**

RUGER GP-100 MATCH CHAMPION

Calibers: 10mm Magnum, .357 Mag. **Capacity:** 6-round cylinder. **Barrel:** 4.2-in. half shroud, slab-sided. **Weight:** 38 oz. **Sights:** Fixed rear, fiber optic front. **Grips:** Hogue Stippled Hardwood. **Features:** Satin stainless steel finish.
Price: Blued **$969.00**

RUGER LCR

Calibers: .22 LR (8-round cylinder), .22 WMR, .38 Special and .357 Mag., 5-round cylinder. **Barrel:** 1.875 in. **Weights:** 13.5–17.10 oz. **Length:** 6.5 in. overall. **Grips:** Hogue Tamer or Crimson Trace Lasergrips. **Sights:** Pinned ramp front, U-notch integral rear. **Features:** The Ruger Lightweight Compact Revolver (LCR), a 13.5 ounce, small frame revolver with a smooth, easy-to-control trigger and highly manageable recoil.
Price: .22 LR, .22 WMR, .38 Spl., iron sights **$579.00**
Price: 9mm, .327, .357, iron sights..................................... **$669.00**
Price: .22 LR, .22WMR, .38 Spl. Crimson Trace Lasergrip **$859.00**
Price: 9mm, .327, .357, Crimson Trace Lasergrip **$949.00**

RUGER GP-100

Calibers: .357 Mag., .327 Federal Mag, .44 Special **Capacities:** 6- or 7-round cylinder, .327 Federal Mag (7-shot), .44 Special (5-shot), .22 LR, (10-shot). **Barrels:** 3-in. full shroud, 4-in. full shroud, 6-in. full shroud. (.44 Special offered only with 3-in. barrel.) **Weights:** 36–45 oz. **Sights:** Fixed; adjustable on 4- and 6-in. full shroud barrels. **Grips:** Ruger Santoprene Cushioned Grip with Goncalo Alves inserts. **Features:** Uses action, frame features of both the Security-Six and Redhawk revolvers. Full-length, short ejector shroud. Satin blue and stainless steel.
Price: Blued **$769.00**
Price: Satin stainless **$799.00**
Price: .22 LR **$829.00**

Prices given are believed to be accurate at time of publication however, many factors affect retail pricing so exact pricing is not possible.

RUGER LCRX
Calibers: .38 Special +P, 9mm, .327 Fed. Mag., .22 WMR. **Barrels:** 1.875 in. or 3 in. **Features:** Similar to LCR except this model has visible hammer, adjustable rear sight. The 3-inch barrel model has longer grip. 9mm comes with three moon clips.
Price: **$579.00**
Price: .327 Mag., .357 Mag., 9mm **$699.00**

RUGER REDHAWK
Calibers: .44 Rem. Mag., .45 Colt and .45 ACP/.45 Colt combo. **Capacity:** 6-round cylinder. **Barrels:** 2.75, 4.2, 5.5, 7.5 in. (.45 Colt in 4.2 in. only.) **Weight:** 54 oz. (7.5 bbl.). **Length:** 13 in. overall (7.5-in. barrel). **Grips:** Square butt cushioned grip panels. TALO Distributor exclusive 2.75-in. barrel stainless model has round butt, wood grips. **Sights:** Interchangeable Patridge-type front, rear adjustable for windage and elevation. **Features:** Stainless steel, brushed satin finish, blued ordnance steel. 9.5 sight radius. Introduced 1979.
Price: **$1,079.00**
Price: Hunter Model 7.5-in. bbl. **$1,159.00**
Price: TALO 2.75 in. model **$1,069.00**

RUGER SP-101
Calibers: .22 LR (6 shot); .327 Federal Mag. (6-shot), .38 Spl, .357 Mag. (5-shot). **Barrels:** 2.25, 3 1/16, 4.2 in (.327 Mag.). **Weights:** 25–30 oz. **Sights:** Adjustable or fixed, rear; fiber-optic or black ramp front. **Grips:** Ruger Cushioned Grip with inserts. **Features:** Compact, small frame, double-action revolver. Full-length ejector shroud. Stainless steel only.
Price: Fixed sights **$719.00**
Price: Adjustable rear, fiber optic front sights **$769.00**

RUGER SUPER REDHAWK
Calibers: 10mm, .44 Rem. Mag., .454 Casull, .480 Ruger. **Capacities:** 5- or 6-round cylinder. **Barrels:** 2.5 in. (Alaskan), 5.5 in., 6.5 in. (10mm), 7.5 in. or 9.5 in. **Weight:** 44–58 oz. **Length:** 13 in. overall (7.5-in. barrel). **Grips:** Hogue Tamer Monogrip. **Features:** Similar to standard Redhawk except has heavy extended frame with Ruger Integral Scope Mounting System on wide topstrap. Wide hammer spur lowered for better scope clearance. Incorporates mechanical design features and improvements of GP-100. Ramp front sight base has Redhawk-style interchangeable insert sight blades, adjustable rear sight. Alaskan model has 2.5-inch barrel. Satin stainless steel and low-glare stainless finishes. Introduced 1987.
Price: .44 Magnum, 10mm.. **$1,159.00**
Price: .454 Casull, .480 Ruger... **$1,199.00**

SMITH & WESSON GOVERNOR
Calibers: .410 Shotshell (2.5 in.), .45 ACP, .45 Colt. **Capacity:** 6 rounds. **Barrel:** 2.75 in. **Length:** 7.5 in., (2.5 in. barrel). **Grip:** Synthetic. **Sights:** Front: Dovetailed tritium night sight or black ramp, rear: fixed. **Grips:** Synthetic. **Finish:** Matte black or matte silver (Silver Edition). **Weight:** 29.6 oz. **Features:** Capable of chambering a mixture of .45 Colt, .45 ACP and .410 gauge 2.5-inch shotshells, the Governor is suited for both close and distant encounters, allowing users to customize the load to their preference. Scandium alloy frame, stainless steel cylinder. Packaged with two full moon clips and three 2-shot clips.
Price: **$869.00**
Price: w/Crimson Trace Laser Grip **$1,179.00**

SMITH & WESSON J-FRAME
The J-frames are the smallest Smith & Wesson wheelguns and come in a variety of chamberings, barrel lengths and materials as noted in the individual model listings.

SMITH & WESSON 60LS/642LS LADYSMITH
Calibers: .38 Special +P, .357 Mag. **Capacity:** 5-round cylinder. **Barrels:** 1.875 in. (642LS); 2.125 in. (60LS) **Weights:** 14.5 oz. (642LS); 21.5 oz. (60LS); **Length:** 6.6 in. overall (60LS). **Grips:** Wood. **Sights:** Black blade, serrated ramp front, fixed notch rear. 642 CT has Crimson Trace Laser Grips. **Features:** 60LS model has a Chiefs Special-style frame. 642LS has Centennial-style frame, frosted matte finish, smooth combat wood grips. Introduced 1996. Comes in a fitted carry/storage case. Introduced 1989. Made in USA by Smith & Wesson.
Price: (642LS) **$499.00**
Price: (60LS) **$759.00**
Price: (642 CT) **$699.00**

SMITH & WESSON MODEL 63
Caliber: .22 LR **Capacity:** 8-round cylinder. **Barrel:** 3 in. **Weight:** 26 oz. **Length:** 7.25 in. overall. **Grips:** Black synthetic. **Sights:** Hi-Viz fiber optic front sight, adjustable black blade rear sight. **Features:** Stainless steel construction throughout. Made in USA by Smith & Wesson.
Price: **$769.00**

SMITH & WESSON MODEL 442/637/638/642 AIRWEIGHT
Caliber: .38 Special +P. **Capacity:** 5-round cylinder. **Barrels:** 1.875 in., 2.5 in. **Weight:** 15 oz. **Length:** 6.375 in. overall. **Grips:** Soft rubber. **Sights:** Fixed, serrated ramp front, square notch rear. **Features:** A family of J-frame .38 Special revolvers with aluminum-alloy frames. Model 637; Chiefs Special-style frame with exposed hammer. Introduced 1996. Models 442, 642; Centennial-style frame, enclosed hammer. Model 638, Bodyguard style, shrouded hammer. Comes in a fitted carry/storage case. Introduced 1989. Made in USA by Smith & Wesson.
Price: From **$469.00**
Price: Laser Max Frame Mounted Red Laser sight **$539.00**

SMITH & WESSON MODELS 637 CT/638 CT
Similar to Models 637, 638 and 642 but with Crimson Trace Laser Grips.
Price: **$699.00**

SMITH & WESSON MODEL 317 AIRLITE
Caliber: .22 LR. **Capacity:** 8-round cylinder. **Barrel:** 1.875 in. **Weight:** 10.5 oz. **Length:** 6.25 in. overall (1.875-in. barrel). **Grips:** Rubber. **Sights:** Serrated ramp front, fixed notch rear. **Features:** Aluminum alloy, carbon and stainless steels, Chiefs Special-style frame with exposed hammer. Smooth combat trigger. Clear Cote finish. Model 317 Kit Gun has adjustable rear sight, fiber optic front. Introduced 1997.
Price: $759.00

SMITH & WESSON MODEL 340/340PD AIRLITE SC CENTENNIAL
Calibers: .357 Mag., 38 Special +P. **Capacity:** 5-round cylinder. **Barrel:** 1.875 in. **Weight:** 12 oz. **Length:** 6.375 in. overall (1.875-in. barrel). **Grips:** Rounded butt rubber. **Sights:** Black blade front, rear notch **Features:** Centennial-style frame, enclosed hammer. Internal lock. Matte silver finish. Scandium alloy frame, titanium cylinder, stainless steel barrel liner. Made in USA by Smith & Wesson.
Price: $1,019.00

SMITH & WESSON MODEL 351PD
Caliber: .22 Mag. **Capacity:** 5-round cylinder. **Barrel:** 1.875 in. **Weight:** 10.6 oz. **Length:** 6.25 in. overall (1.875-in. barrel). **Sights:** HiViz front sight, rear notch. **Grips:** Wood. **Features:** 7-shot, aluminum-alloy frame. Chiefs Special-style frame with exposed hammer. Nonreflective matte-black finish. Internal lock. Made in USA by Smith & Wesson.
Price: $759.00

SMITH & WESSON MODEL 360/360PD AIRLITE CHIEF'S SPECIAL
Calibers: .357 Mag., .38 Special +P. **Capacity:** 5-round cylinder. **Barrel:** 1.875 in. **Weight:** 12 oz. **Length:** 6.375 in. overall (1.875-in. barrel). **Grips:** Rounded butt rubber. **Sights:** Black blade front, fixed rear notch.

Features: Chief's Special-style frame with exposed hammer. Internal lock. Scandium alloy frame, titanium cylinder, stainless steel barrel. Made in USA by Smith & Wesson.
Price: $1,019.00

SMITH & WESSON BODYGUARD 38
Caliber: .38 Special +P. **Capacity:** 5-round cylinder. **Barrel:** 1.9 in. **Weight:** 14.3 oz. **Length:** 6.6 in. **Grip:** Synthetic. **Sights:** Front: Black ramp, Rear: fixed, integral with backstrap. **Plus:** Integrated laser sight. **Finish:** Matte black. **Features:** The first personal protection series that comes with an integrated laser sight.
Price: $539.00

SMITH & WESSON MODEL 640 CENTENNIAL DA ONLY
Calibers: .357 Mag., .38 Special +P. **Capacity:** 5-round cylinder. **Barrel:** 2.125 in. **Weight:** 23 oz. **Length:** 6.75 in. overall. **Grips:** Uncle Mike's Boot grip. **Sights:** Tritium Night Sights. **Features:** Stainless steel. Fully concealed hammer, snag-proof smooth edges. Internal lock.
Price: $839.00

SMITH & WESSON MODEL 649 BODYGUARD
Caliber: .357 Mag., .38 Special +P. **Capacity:** 5-round cylinder. **Barrel:** 2.125 in. **Weight:** 23 oz. **Length:** 6.625 in. overall. **Grips:** Uncle Mike's Combat. **Sights:** Black pinned ramp front, fixed notch rear. **Features:** Stainless steel construction, satin finish. Internal lock. Bodyguard style, shrouded hammer. Made in USA by Smith & Wesson.
Price: $729.00

SMITH & WESSON K-FRAME/L-FRAME
The K-frame series are mid-size revolvers and the L-frames are slightly larger.

SMITH & WESSON MODEL 10 CLASSIC
Caliber: .38 Special. **Capacity:** 6-round cylinder. **Features:** Bright blued steel frame and cylinder, checkered wood grips, 4-inch barrel and fixed sights. The oldest model in the Smith & Wesson line, its basic design goes back to the original Military & Police Model of 1905.
Price: **$739.00**

SMITH & WESSON MODEL 17 MASTERPIECE CLASSIC
Caliber: .22 LR. **Capacity:** 6-round cylinder. **Barrel:** 6 in. **Weight:** 40 oz. **Grips:** Checkered wood. **Sights:** Pinned Patridge front, micro-adjustable rear. Updated variation of K-22 Masterpiece of the 1930s.
Price: **$989.00**

SMITH & WESSON MODEL 48 CLASSIC
Same specifications as Model 17 except chambered in .22 Magnum (.22 WMR) and is available with a 4- or 6-inch barrel.
Price: .... **$949.00–$989.00**

SMITH & WESSON MODEL 64/67
Caliber: .38 Special +P. **Capacity:** 6-round cylinder **Barrel:** 3 in. **Weight:** 33 oz. **Length:** 8.875 in. overall. **Grips:** Soft rubber. **Sights:** Fixed, .125-in. serrated ramp front, square notch rear. Model 67 is similar to Model 64 except for adjustable sights. **Features:** Satin finished stainless steel, square butt.
Price: From .... **$689.00–$749.00**

SMITH & WESSON MODEL 66
Caliber: .357 Magnum. **Capacity:** 6-round cylinder. **Barrel:** 4.25 in. **Weight:** 36.6 oz. **Grips:** Synthetic. **Sights:** White outline adjustable rear, red ramp front. **Features:** Return in 2014 of the famous K-frame "Combat Magnum" with stainless finish.
Price: **$849.00**

SMITH & WESSON MODEL 69
Caliber: .44 Magnum. **Capacity:** 5-round cylinder. **Barrel:** 4.25 in. **Weight:** 37 oz. **Grips:** Checkered wood. **Sights:** White outline adjustable rear, red ramp front. **Features:** L-frame with stainless finish, 5-shot cylinder, introduced in 2014.
Price: **$989.00**

SMITH & WESSON MODEL 617
Caliber: .22 LR. **Capacity:** 10-round cylinder. **Barrel:** 6 in. **Weight:** 44 oz. **Length:** 11.125 in. **Grips:** Soft rubber. **Sights:** Patridge front, adjustable rear. Drilled and tapped for scope mount. **Features:** Stainless steel with satin finish. Introduced 1990.
Price: From **$829.00**

SMITH & WESSON MODEL 686/686 PLUS
Caliber: .357 Mag/.38 Special. **Capacity:** 6 (686) or 7 (Plus). **Barrels:** 6 in. (686), 3 or 6 in. (686 Plus), 4 in. (SSR). **Weight:** 35 oz. (3 in. barrel). **Grips:** Rubber. Sights: White outline adjustable rear, red ramp front. **Features:** Satin stainless frame and cylinder. Stock Service Revolver (SSR) has tapered underlug, interchangeable front sight, high-hold ergonomic wood grips, chamfered charge holes, custom barrel w/recessed crown, bossed mainspring.
Price: 686 .... **$829.00**
Price: Plus **$849.00**
Price: SSR **$999.00**

SMITH & WESSON MODEL 986 PRO
Caliber: 9mm. **Capacity:** 7-round cylinder **Barrel:** 5-in. tapered underlug. **Features:** SA/DA L-frame revolver chambered in 9mm. Features similar to 686 PLUS Pro Series with 5-inch tapered underlug barrel, satin stainless finish, synthetic grips, adjustable rear and Patridge blade front sight.
Price: **$1,149.00**

SMITH & WESSON M&P R8
Caliber: .357 Mag. **Capacity:** 8-round cylinder. **Barrel:** 5-in. half lug with accessory rail. **Weight:** 36.3 oz. **Length:** 10.5 in. **Grips:** Black synthetic. **Sights:** Adjustable v-notch rear, interchangeable front. **Features:** Scandium alloy frame, stainless steel cylinder.
Price: **$1,329.00**

Prices given are believed to be accurate at time of publication however, many factors affect retail pricing so exact prices are not possible.

SMITH & WESSON N-FRAME

These large-frame models introduced the .357, .41 and .44 Magnums to the world.

SMITH & WESSON MODEL 25 CLASSIC

Calibers: .45 Colt or .45 ACP. **Capacity:** 6-round cylinder. **Barrel:** 6.5 in. **Weight:** 45 oz. **Grips:** Checkered wood. **Sights:** Pinned Patridge front, micro-adjustable rear.
Price: **$1,019.00**

SMITH & WESSON MODEL 27 CLASSIC

Caliber: .357 Magnum. **Capacity:** 6-round cylinder. **Barrels:** 4 or 6.5 in. **Weight:** 41.2 oz. **Grips:** Checkered wood. **Sights:** Pinned Patridge front, micro-adjustable rear. Updated variation of the first magnum revolver, the .357 Magnum of 1935.
Price: (4 in.) **$1,019.00**
Price: (6.5 in.) **$1,059.00**

SMITH & WESSON MODEL 29 CLASSIC

Caliber: .44 Magnum **Capacity:** 6-round cylinder. **Barrel:** 4 or 6.5 in. **Weight:** 48.5 oz. **Length:** 12 in. **Grips:** Altamont service walnut. **Sights:** Adjustable white-outline rear, red ramp front. **Features:** Carbon steel frame, polished-blued or nickel finish. Has integral key lock safety feature to prevent accidental discharges. Original Model 29 made famous by "Dirty Harry" character played in 1971 by Clint Eastwood.
Price: .... **$999.00–$1,169.00**

SMITH & WESSON MODEL 57 CLASSIC

Caliber: .41 Magnum. **Capacity:** 6-round cylinder. **Barrel:** 6 in. **Weight:** 48 oz. **Grips:** Checkered wood. **Sights:** Pinned red ramp, micro-adjustable rear.
Price: **$1,009.00**

SMITH & WESSON MODEL 329PD ALASKA BACKPACKER

Caliber: .44 Magnum. **Capacity:** 6-round cylinder. **Barrel:** 2.5 in. **Weight:** 26 oz. **Length:** 9.5 in. **Grips:** Synthetic. **Sights:** Adj. rear, HiViz orange-dot front. **Features:** Scandium alloy frame, blue/black finish, stainless steel cylinder.
Price: From **$1,159.00**

SMITH & WESSON MODEL 625/625JM

Caliber: .45 ACP. **Capacity:** 6-round cylinder. **Barrels:** 4 in., 5 in. **Weight:** 43 oz. (4-in. barrel). **Length:** 9.375 in. overall (4-in. barrel). **Grips:** Soft rubber; wood optional. **Sights:** Patridge front on ramp, S&W micrometer click rear adjustable for windage and elevation. **Features:** Stainless steel construction with .400-in. wide semi-target hammer, .312-in. smooth combat trigger; full lug barrel. Glass beaded finish. Introduced 1989. Jerry

Miculek Professional (JM) Series has .265-in. wide grooved trigger, special wooden Miculek Grip, five full moon clips, gold bead Patridge front sight on interchangeable front sight base, bead blast finish. Unique serial number run. Mountain Gun has 4-in. tapered barrel, drilled and tapped, Hogue Rubber Monogrip, pinned black ramp front sight, micrometer click-adjustable rear sight, satin stainless frame and barrel weighs 39.5 oz.
Price: 625 or 625JM **$1,074.00**

SMITH & WESSON MODEL 629

Calibers: .44 Magnum, .44 S&W Special. **Capacity:** 6-round cylinder. **Barrels:** 4 in., 5 in., 6.5 in. **Weight:** 41.5 oz. (4-in. bbl.). **Length:** 9.625 in. overall (4-in. bbl.). **Grips:** Soft rubber; wood optional. **Sights:** .125-in. red ramp front, white outline rear, internal lock, adjustable for windage and elevation. Classic similar to standard Model 629, except Classic has full-lug 5-in. barrel, chamfered front of cylinder, interchangeable red ramp front sight with adjustable white outline rear, Hogue grips with S&W monogram, drilled and tapped for scope mounting. Factory accurizing and endurance packages. Introduced 1990. Classic Power Port has Patridge front sight and adjustable rear sight. Model 629CT has 5-in. barrel, Crimson Trace Hoghunter Lasergrips, 10.5 in. OAL, 45.5 oz. weight. Introduced 2006.
Price: From **$949.00**

TAURUS MODEL 44SS

Caliber: .44 Magnum. **Capacity:** 5-round cylinder. **Barrel:** 4-in. ported. **Weight:** 34 oz. **Grips:** Rubber. **Sights:** Adjustable. **Features:** Double action. Integral key-lock. Introduced 1994. Finish: Matte stainless. Imported from Brazil by Taurus International Manufacturing, Inc.
Price: From **$769.00**

TAURUS MODEL 65

Caliber: .357 Magnum. **Capacity:** 6-round cylinder. **Barrel:** 4-in. full underlug. **Weight:** 38 oz. **Length:** 10.5 in. overall. **Grips:** Soft rubber. **Sights:** Fixed. **Features:** Double action, integral key-lock. Matte blued or stainless. Imported by Taurus International.
Price: Blued **$519.00**
Price: Stainless **$569.00**

TAURUS MODEL 66

Similar to Model 65, 4 in. or 6 in. barrel, 7-round cylinder, adjustable rear sight. Integral key-lock action. Imported by Taurus International.
Price: Blue **$579.00**
Price: Stainless **$629.00**

TAURUS MODEL 82 HEAVY BARREL

Caliber: .38 Special. **Capacity:** 6-round cylinder. **Barrel:** 4 in., heavy. **Weight:** 36.5 oz. **Length:** 9.25 in. overall. **Grips:** Soft black rubber. **Sights:** Serrated ramp front, square notch rear. **Features:** Double action, solid rib, integral key-lock. Imported by Taurus International.
Price: From **$499.00**

TAURUS MODEL 85FS

Caliber: .38 Special. **Capacity:** 5-round cylinder. **Barrel:** 2 in. **Weights:** 17–24.5 oz., titanium 13.5–15.4 oz. **Grips:** Rubber, rosewood or mother of pearl. **Sights:** Ramp front, square notch rear. **Features:** Spurred hammer. Blued, matte stainless, blue with gold accents, stainless with gold accents; rated for +P ammo. Integral keylock. Some models have titanium frame. Introduced 1980. Imported by Taurus International.
Price: From **$379.00**

TAURUS 380 MINI

Caliber: .380 ACP. **Capacity:** 5-round cylinder w/moon clip. **Barrel:** 1.75 in. **Weight:** 15.5 oz. **Length:** 5.95 in. **Grips:** Rubber. **Sights:** Adjustable rear, fixed front. **Features:** DAO. Available in blued or stainless finish. Five Star (moon) clips included.
Price: Blued $459.00
Price: Stainless $489.00

TAURUS MODEL 45-410 JUDGE

Calibers: 2.5-in. .410/.45 LC, 3-in. .410/.45 LC. **Barrels:** 3 in., 6.5 in. (blued finish). **Weights:** 35.2 oz., 22.4 oz. **Length:** 7.5 in. **Grips:** Ribber rubber. **Sights:** Fiber Optic. **Features:** DA/SA. Matte stainless and ultra-lite stainless finish. Introduced in 2007. Imported from Brazil by Taurus International.
Price: From $589.00

TAURUS JUDGE PUBLIC DEFENDER POLYMER

Caliber: .45 Colt/.410 (2.5 in.). **Capacity:** 5-round cylinder. **Barrel:** 2.5-in. **Weight:** 27 oz. **Features:** SA/DA revolver with 5-round cylinder; polymer frame; Ribber rubber-feel grips; fiber-optic front sight; adjustable rear sight; blued or stainless cylinder; shrouded hammer with cocking spur; blued finish.
Price: From $509.00

TAURUS RAGING JUDGE MAGNUM

Calibers: .454 Casull, .45 Colt, 2.5-in. and 3-in. .410. **Barrels:** 3 or 6 in. **Features:** SA/DA revolver with fixed sights with fiber-optic front; blued or stainless steel finish; vent rib for scope mounting (6-in. only); cushioned Raging Bull grips.
Price: $1,089.00

TAURUS MODEL 627 TRACKER

Caliber: .357 Magnum. **Capacity:** 7-round cylinder. **Barrels:** 4 or 6.5 in. **Weights:** 28.8, 41 oz. **Grips:** Rubber. **Sights:** Fixed front, adjustable rear. **Features:** Double-action. Stainless steel, Shadow Gray or Total Titanium; vent rib (steel models only); integral key-lock action. Imported by Taurus International.
Price: From $709.00

TAURUS MODEL 444 ULTRA-LIGHT

Caliber: .44 Magnum. **Capacity:** 5-round cylinder. **Barrels:** 2.5 or 4 in. **Weight:** 28.3 oz. **Grips:** Cushioned inset rubber. **Sights:** Fixed red-fiber optic front, adjustable rear. **Features:** UltraLite titanium blue finish, titanium/alloy frame built on Raging Bull design. Smooth trigger shoe, 1.760-in. wide, 6.280-in. tall. Barrel rate of twist 1:16, 6 grooves. Introduced 2005. Imported by Taurus International.
Price: $792.00

TAURUS MODEL 444/454 RAGING BULL SERIES

Calibers: .44 Magnum, .454 Casull. **Barrels:** 2.25 in., 5 in., 6.5 in., 8.375 in. **Weight:** 53–63 oz. **Length:** 12 in. overall (6.5 in. barrel). **Grips:** Soft black rubber. **Sights:** Patridge front, adjustable rear. **Features:** DA, ventilated rib, integral key-lock. Most models have ported barrels. Introduced 1997. Imported by Taurus International.
Price: 444 .... $753.00
Price: 454 .... $1,109.

TAURUS MODEL 605 PLY

Caliber: .357 Magnum. **Capacity:** 5-round cylinder. **Barrel:** 2 in. **Weight:** 20 oz. **Grips:** Rubber. **Sights:** Fixed. **Features:** Polymer frame steel cylinder. Blued or stainless. Introduced 1995. Imported by Taurus International.
Price: Blued **$460.00**
Price: Stainless **$507.00**

TAURUS MODEL 650 CIA

Calibers: .357 Magnum/.38 Special +P only. **Capacity:** 5-round cylinder. **Barrel:** 2 in. **Weight:** 24.5 oz. **Grips:** Rubber. **Sights:** Ramp front, square notch rear. **Features:** DAO, blued finish, integral key-lock, internal hammer. Introduced 2001. From Taurus International.
Price: From **$539.00**

TAURUS MODEL 905

Caliber: 9mm. **Capacity:** 5-round cylinder. **Barrel:** 2 in. **Features:** Small-frame revolver with rubber boot grips, fixed sights, choice of exposed or concealed hammer. Blued or stainless finish.
Price: Blued **$509.00**
Price: Stainless **$559.00**

TAURUS MODEL 692

Calibers: .38 Special/.357 Magnum or 9mm. **Capacity:** 7-round cylinder. **Barrels:** 3 or 6.5 in, ported. **Sights:** Adjustable rear, fixed front. **Grip:** "Ribber" textured. **Finish:** Matte blued or stainless. **Features:** Caliber can be changed with a swap of the cylinders which are non-fluted.
Price: **$659.00**

AMERICAN DERRINGER MODEL 1
Calibers: All popular handgun calibers plus .45 Colt/.410 Shotshell. **Capacity:** 2, (.45-70 model is single shot). **Barrel:** 3 in. **Overall length:** 4.82 in. **Weight:** 15 oz. **Features:** Manually operated hammer-block safety automatically disengages when hammer is cocked. Texas Commemorative has brass frame and is available in .38 Special, .44-40. or .45 Colt.
Price: .... $635.00–$735.00
Price: Texas Commemorative $835.00

AMERICAN DERRINGER MODEL 8
Calibers: .45 Colt/.410 shotshell. **Capacity:** 2. **Barrel:** 8 in. **Weight:** 24 oz.
Price: $915.00
Price: High polish finish $1,070.00

AMERICAN DERRINGER DA38
Calibers: .38 Special, .357 Magnum, 9mm Luger. **Barrel:** 3.3 in. **Weight:** 14.5 oz. **Features:** DA operation with hammer-block thumb safety. Barrel, receiver and all internal parts are made from stainless steel.
Price: .... $690.00–$740.00

BOND ARMS TEXAS DEFENDER DERRINGER
Calibers: Available in more than 10 calibers, from .22 LR to .45 LC/.410 shotshells. **Barrel:** 3 in. **Weight:** 20 oz. **Length:** 5 in. **Grips:** Rosewood. **Sights:** Blade front, fixed rear. **Features:** Interchangeable barrels, stainless steel firing pins, cross-bolt safety, automatic extractor for rimmed calibers. Stainless steel construction, brushed finish. Right or left hand.
Price: $493.00
Price: Interchangeable barrels, .22 LR thru .45 LC, 3 in. $139.00
Price: Interchangeable barrels, .45 LC, 3.5 in. ....$159.00–$189.00

BOND ARMS RANGER II
Caliber: .45 LC/.410 shotshells or .357 Magnum/.38 Special. **Barrel:** 4.25 in. **Weight:** 23.5 oz. **Length:** 6.25 in. **Features:** This model has a trigger guard. Intr. 2011. From Bond Arms.
Price: $673.00

BOND ARMS CENTURY 2000 DEFENDER
Calibers: .45 LC/.410 shotshells. or .357 Magnum/.38 Special. **Barrel:** 3.5 in. **Weight:** 21 oz. **Length:** 5.5 in. **Features:** Similar to Defender series.
Price: $517.00

BOND ARMS COWBOY DEFENDER
Calibers: From .22 LR to .45 LC/.410 shotshells. **Barrel:** 3 in. **Weight:** 19 oz. **Length:** 5.5 in. **Features:** Similar to Defender series. No trigger guard.
Price: $493.00

BOND ARMS SNAKE SLAYER
Calibers: .45 LC/.410 shotshell (2.5 in. or 3 in.). **Barrel:** 3.5 in. **Weight:** 21 oz. **Length:** 5.5 in. **Grips:** Extended rosewood. **Sights:** Blade front, fixed rear. **Features:** Single-action; interchangeable barrels; stainless steel firing pin. Introduced 2005.
Price: $568.00

BOND ARMS SNAKE SLAYER IV
Calibers: .45 LC/.410 shotshell (2.5 in. or 3 in.). **Barrel:** 4.25 in. **Weight:** 22 oz. **Length:** 6.25 in. **Grips:** Extended rosewood. **Sights:** Blade front, fixed rear. **Features:** Single-action; interchangeable barrels; stainless steel firing pin. Introduced 2006.
Price: $613.00

COBRA BIG-BORE DERRINGERS
Calibers: .22 WMR, .32 H&R Mag., .38 Special, 9mm Para., .380 ACP. **Barrel:** 2.75 in. **Weight:** 14 oz. **Length:** 4.65 in. overall. **Grips:** Textured black or white synthetic or laminated rosewood. **Sights:** Blade front, fixed notch rear. **Features:** Alloy frame, steel-lined barrels, steel breechblock. Plunger-type safety with integral hammer block. Black, chrome or satin finish. Introduced 2002. Made in USA by Cobra Enterprises of Utah, Inc.
Price: $187.00

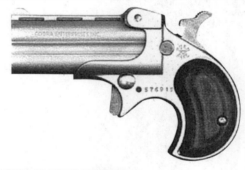

COBRA STANDARD SERIES DERRINGERS
Calibers: .22 LR, .22 WMR, .25 ACP, .32 ACP. **Barrel:** 2.4 in. **Weight:** 9.5 oz. **Length:** 4 in. overall. **Grips:** Laminated wood or pearl. **Sights:** Blade front, fixed notch rear. **Features:** Choice of black powder coat, satin nickel or chrome finish. Introduced 2002. Made in USA by Cobra Enterprises of Utah, Inc.
Price: $169.00

COBRA LONG-BORE DERRINGERS
Calibers: .22 WMR, .38 Special, 9mm. **Barrel:** 3.5 in. **Weight:** 16 oz. **Length:** 5.4 in. overall. **Grips:** Black or white synthetic or rosewood. **Sights:** Fixed. **Features:** Chrome, satin nickel, or black Teflon finish. Introduced 2002. Made in USA by Cobra Enterprises of Utah, Inc.
Price: $187.00

Prices given are believed to be accurate at time of publication however, many factors affect retail pricing so exact prices are not possible.

COBRA TITAN .45 LC/.410 DERRINGER
Calibers: .45 LC, .410 or 9mm, 2-round capacity. **Barrel:** 3.5 in. **Weight:** 16.4 oz. **Grip:** Rosewood. **Features:** Standard finishes include: satin stainless, black stainless and brushed stainless. Made in USA by Cobra Enterprises of Utah, Inc.
Price: $399.00

DOUBLETAP DERRINGER
Calibers: .45 Colt or 9mm **Barrel:** 3 in. **Weight:** 12 oz. **Length:** 5.5 in. **Sights:** Adjustable. **Features:** Over/under, two-barrel design. Rounds are fired individually with two separate trigger pulls. Tip-up design, aluminum frame.
Price: $499.00

HEIZER PS1 POCKET SHOTGUN
Calibers: .45 Colt or .410 shotshell. Single-shot. **Barrel:** Tip-up, 3.25 in. **Weight:** 22 oz. **Length:** 5.6 in. **Width:** .742 in **Height:** 3.81 in. **Features:** Available in several finishes. Standard model is matte stainless or black. Also offered in Hedy Jane series for the women in pink or in two-tone combinations of stainless and pink, blue, green, purple. Includes interchangeable AR .223 barrel. Made in the USA by Heizer Industries.
Price: $499.00

HEIZER POCKET AR
Caliber: .223 Rem./5.56 NATO. Single shot. **Barrel:** 3.75 in., ported or non-ported. **Length:** 6.375 in. **Weight:** 23 oz. **Features:** Similar to PS1 pocket shotgun but chambered for .223/5.56 rifle cartridge.
Price: $339.00

HEIZER PAK1
Caliber: 7.2x39. Similar to Pocket AR but chambered for 7.62x39mm. Single shot. **Barrel:** 3.75 in., ported or unported. **Length:** 6.375 in. **Weight:** 23 oz.
Price: $339.00

ALEXANDER ARMS AR SERIES

Calibers: .17 HMR, 5.56 NATO, 6.5 Grendel, .300 AAC, .338 Lapua Mag., .50 Beowulf. This manufacturer produces a wide range of AR-15 type rifles and carbines. **Barrels:** 16, 18, 20 or 24 in. Models are available for consumer, law enforcement and military markets. Depending on the specific model, features include forged flattop receiver with Picatinny rail, button-rifled stainless steel barrels, composite free-floating handguard, A2 flash hider, M4 collapsible stock, gas piston operating system.
Price: .17 HMR $1,210.00
Price: 5.56 NATO......................................$1,349.00
Price: 6.5 Grendel ....$1,540.00–$1,750.00
Price: .300 AAC..$1,349.00
Price: .50 Beowulf.....................$1,375.00–$1,750.00

ALEXANDER ARMS ULFBERHT

Caliber: .338 Lapua Mag. Custom-designed adjustable gas-piston operating system. **Barrel:** 27.5-in. chrome moly with three-prong flash hider. **Stock:** Magpul PRS. **Length:** 41.25 in. (folded), 50 in. (extended stock). **Weight:** 19.8 lbs.
Price: $5,800.00

M-15 LIGHT TACTICAL CARBINE

Calibers: .223 Rem., 6.8 SPC, 7.62x39mm. **Capacity:** 30-round magazine. **Barrel:** 16 in. heavy chrome lined; 1:7 in. twist, flash suppressor. **Weight:** 6 lbs. **Length:** 36 in. overall. **Stock:** Green or black composition. **Sights:** Standard A2. **Features:** Forged flattop receiver with Picatinny rail, 10-in. aluminum KeyMod handguard, anodize aluminum supper/lower receiver, flip-up sights. Introduced in 2016.
Price: $999.00

ARMALITE AR-10 PRC 260

Caliber: .260 Rem. **Barrel:** 20-in. ceramic coated stainless steel threaded with Surgeon/AWC PSR muzzle brake flash suppressor. **Weight:** 11.5 lbs. **Features:** Magpul PSR stock with adjustable comb and length of pull, 15-in. aluminum free-floating quadrail, forward assist, Timney trigger, ambidextrous safety and charging handle. Introduced in 2017.
Price: From...$3,560.00

ARMALITE AR-10(T)

Caliber: .308 Win. **Capacity:** 10-round magazine. **Barrel:** 24 in. target-weight Rock 5R custom. **Weight:** 10.4 lbs. **Length:** 43.5 in. overall. **Stock:** Green or black composition; N.M. fiberglass handguard tube. **Sights:** Detachable handle, front sight, or scope mount available. Comes with international-style flattop receiver with Picatinny rail. **Features:** National Match two-stage trigger. Forged upper receiver. Receivers hard-coat anodized. Introduced 1995. Made in USA by Armalite, Inc.
Price: Black $1,700.00
Price: AR-10, .338 Federal $1,800.00

ARMALITE AR-10 3-GUN COMPETITION RIFLE

Calibers: 7.62x1mm/.308 Win. **Capacity:** 25-round magazine. **Barrel:** 18-in. stainless steel. **Weight:** 8.9 lbs. **Features:** MBA-1 buttstock with adjustable comb and length of pull, 15-in. free-floating 3-Gun handguard, Raptor charging handle, Timney trigger, ambidextrous safety.
Price: $2,199.00

ARMALITE M15 A4 CARBINE 6.8 & 7.62X39

Calibers: 6.8 Rem., 7.62x39. **Barrel:** 16 in. chrome-lined with flash suppressor. **Weight:** 7 lbs. **Length:** 26.6 in. **Features:** Front and rear picatinny rails for mounting optics, two-stage tactical trigger, anodized aluminum/phosphate finish.
Price: $1,107.00

EAGLE-15 VERSATILE SPORTING RIFLE (VSR)

Caliber: .223 Rem/5.56x45 NATO (.223 Wylde chamber). **Capacity:** 30-shot Magpul PMAG. **Barrel:** 16-in. chrome moly with flash suppressor. **Stock:** 6-position collapsible with free-float rail system, rubberized grip. **Weight:** 6.6 lbs. **Features:** Carbine length gas system, 15-in. handguard with Key Mod attachments, forged lower and flat-top upper, Picatinny rail.
Price: $800.00

ARSENAL, INC. SLR-107F

Caliber: 7.62x39mm. **Barrel:** 16.25 in. **Weight:** 7.3 lbs. **Stock:** Left-side folding polymer stock. **Sights:** Adjustable rear. **Features:** Stamped receiver, 24mm flash hider, bayonet lug, accessory lug, stainless steel heat shield, two-stage trigger. Introduced 2008. Made in USA by Arsenal, Inc.
Price: SLR-107FR, includes scope rail $1,099.00

ARSENAL, INC. SLR-107CR

Caliber: 7.62x39mm. **Barrel:** 16.25 in. **Weight:** 6.9 lbs. **Stock:** Left-side folding polymer stock. **Sights:** Adjustable rear. **Features:** Stamped receiver, front sight block/gas block combination, 500-meter rear sight, cleaning rod, stainless steel heat shield, scope rail, and removable muzzle attachment. Introduced 2007. Made in USA by Arsenal, Inc.
Price: SLR-107CR $1,119.00

ARSENAL, INC. SLR-106CR

Caliber: 5.56 NATO. **Barrel:** 16.25 in. Steyr chrome-lined barrel, 1:7 twist rate. **Weight:** 6.9 lbs. **Stock:** Black polymer folding stock with cutout for scope rail. Stainless steel heat shield handguard. **Sights:** 500-meter rear sight and rear sight block calibrated for 5.56 NATO. Warsaw Pact scope rail. **Features:** Uses Arsenal, Bulgaria, Mil-Spec receiver, two-stage trigger, hammer and disconnector. Polymer magazines in 5- and 10-round capacity in black and green, with Arsenal logo. Others are 30-round black waffles, 20- and 30-round versions in clear/smoke waffle, featuring the "10" in a double-circle logo of Arsenal, Bulgaria. Ships with 5-round magazine, sling, cleaning kit in a tube, 16 in. cleaning rod, oil bottle. Introduced 2007. Made in USA by Arsenal, Inc.
Price: SLR-106CR...$1,200.00

AUTO-ORDNANCE 1927A-1 THOMPSON

Caliber: .45 ACP. **Barrel:** 16.5 in. **Weight:** 13 lbs. **Length:** About 41 in. overall (Deluxe). **Stock:** Walnut stock and vertical fore-end. **Sights:** Blade front, open rear adjustable for windage. **Features:** Recreation of Thompson Model 1927. Semi-auto only. Deluxe model has finned barrel, adjustable rear sight and compensator; Standard model has plain barrel and military sight. Available with 100-round drum or 30-round stick magazine. Made in USA by Auto-Ordnance Corp., a division of Kahr Arms.
Price: Deluxe w/stick magazine $1,544.00
Price: Deluxe w/drum magazine.....................................$2,061.00
Price: Lightweight model w/stick mag $1,325.00

Prices given are believed to be accurate at time of publication however, many factors affect retail pricing so exact prices are not possible.

AUTO-ORDNANCE 1927 A-1 COMMANDO

Similar to the 1927 A-1 except has Parkerized finish, black-finish wood butt, pistol grip, horizontal fore-end. Comes with black nylon sling. Introduced 1998. Made in USA by Auto-Ordnance Corp., a division of Kahr Arms.
Price: T1-C...**$1,393.00**

AUTO ORDNANCE M1 CARBINE

Caliber: .30 Carbine (15-shot magazine). **Barrel:** 18 in. **Weight:** 5.4 to 5.8 lbs. **Length:** 36.5 in. **Stock:** Wood or polymer. **Sights:** Blade front, flip-style rear. **Features:** A faithful recreation of the military carbine.
Price: **$899.00**
Price: Folding stock..**$989.00**

BARRETT MODEL 82A-1 SEMI-AUTOMATIC

Calibers: .416 Barret, 50 BMG. **Capacity:** 10-shot detachable box magazine. **Barrel:** 29 in. **Weight:** 28.5 lbs. **Length:** 57 in. overall. **Stock:** Composition with energy-absorbing recoil pad. **Sights:** Scope optional. **Features:** Semiautomatic, recoil operated with recoiling barrel. Three-lug locking bolt; muzzle brake. Adjustable bipod. Introduced 1985. Made in USA by Barrett Firearms.
Price: From..**$9,119.00**

BARRETT M107A1

Caliber: 50 BMG. **Capacity:** 10-round detachable magazine. **Barrels:** 20 or 29 in. **Sights:** 27-in. optics rail with flip-up iron sights. **Weight:** 30.9 lbs. **Finish:** Flat Dark Earth. **Features:** Four-port cylindrical muzzle brake. Quick-detachable Barrett QDL Suppressor. Adjustable bipod and monopod.
Price: **$12,281.00**

BARRETT MODEL REC7 GEN II

Calibers: 5.56 (.223), 6.8 Rem. SPC. **Capacity:** 30-round magazine. **Barrel:** 16 in. **Sights:** ARMS rear, folding front. **Weight:** 28.7 lbs. **Features:** AR-style configuration with standard 17-4 stainless piston system, two-position forward venting gas plug, chrome-lined gas block, A2 flash hider, 6-position MOE stock.
Price: **$2,759.00**

BERETTA ARX 100

Caliber: 5.56 NATO. **Capacity:** 30-round. Accepts AR magazines. **Barrel:** 16 in. with flash suppressor and quick changeability. **Features:** Ambidextrous controls, Picatinny quad rail system.
Price: **$1,600.00**

BERETTA CX4 STORM CARBINE Calibers: 9mm, 40 S&W, .45 ACP. **Barrel:** 16.6 in. **Stock:** Black synthetic with thumbhole. **Sights:** Ghost ring. **Features:** Blowback single action, ambidextrous controls, Picatinny quad rail system. Reintroduced in 2017.
Price: **$800.00**

BROWNING BAR MK 3 DBM

Caliber: .308 Win. **Capacity:** 10-round detachable magazine. **Barrel:** 18 in. **Stock:** Black composite. Other features similar to standard BAR MK III.
Price: **$1,470.00**

BUSHMASTER ACR

Calibers: 5.56mm, 6.5mm, 6.8mm. **Capacity:** 30-round polymer magazine. **Barrels:** All three calibers are available with 10.5 in., 14.5 in., 16.5 in. and 18 in. barrels. **Weights:** 14.5 in. bbl. 7 lbs. **Lengths:** 14.5 in. bbl. with stock folded: 25.75 in. with stock deployed (mid) 32.625 in., 10.5 in. bbl. with stock folded: 21.312 in., with stock deployed (mid): 27.875 in., with stock deployed and extended: 31.75 in., Folding Stock Length of Pull — 3 in. **Stock:** Fixed high-impact composite A-frame stock with rubber butt pad and sling mounts. **Features:** Cold hammer-forged barrels with Melonite coating for extreme long life. A2 birdcage-type hider to control muzzle flash and adjustable, two-position, gas piston-driven system for firing suppressed or unsuppressed, supported by hardened internal bearing rails. The Adaptive Combat Rifle (ACR) features a tool-less, quick-change barrel system available in 10.5 in., 14.5 in. and 16.5 in. and in multiple calibers. Multi-caliber bolt carrier assembly quickly and easily changes from .223/5.56mm NATO to 6.8mm Rem SPC (spec II chamber). Free-floating MIL-STD 1913 monolithic top rail for optic mounting. Fully ambidextrous controls including magazine release, bolt catch and release, fire selector and nonreciprocating charging handle. High-impact composite handguard with heat shield; accepts rail inserts. High-impact composite lower receiver with textured magazine well and modular grip storage. Fire Control: Semi and full auto two-stage standard AR capable of accepting drop-in upgrade. Magazine: Optimized for MagPul PMAG Accepts standard NATO/M-16 magazines.
Price: Basic Folder Configuration **$2,149.00**
Price: ACR Enhanced...**$2,249.00**

BUSHMASTER A2/A3 TARGET

Calibers: 5.56 NATO, .223 Rem. **Capacity:** 30-round magazine. **Barrels:** 20 in., 24 in. **Weight:** 8.43 lbs. (A2); 8.78 lbs. (A3). **Length:** 39.5 in. overall (20 in. barrel). **Stock:** Black composition; A2 type. **Sights:** Adjustable post front, adjustable aperture rear. **Features:** Patterned after Colt M-16A2. Chrome-lined barrel with manganese phosphate exterior. Available in stainless barrel. Made in USA by Bushmaster Firearms Co.
Price: A2 ....**$969.00**
Price: A3 with carrying handle **$999.00**

BUSHMASTER HEAVY-BARRELED CARBINE

Caliber: 5.56/.223. **Barrel:** 16 in. **Weights:** 6.93–7.28 lbs. **Length:** 32.5 in. overall. **Features:** AR-style carbine with chrome-lined heavy profile vanadium steel barrel, fixed or removable carry handle, six-position telestock.
Price: **$895.00**
Price: A3 with removable handle **$1,420.00**

BUSHMASTER 450 RIFLE AND CARBINE

Caliber: .450 Bushmaster. **Capacity:** 5-round magazine. **Barrels:** 20 in. (rifle), 16 in. (carbine). **Weights:** 8.3 lbs. (rifle), 8.1 lbs. (carbine). **Length:** 39.5 in. overall (rifle), 35.25 in. overall (carbine). **Features:** AR-style with chrome-lined chrome-moly barrel, synthetic stock, Izzy muzzle brake.
Price: Carbine **$1,285.00**
Price: Rifle...**$1,300.00**

BUSHMASTER TARGET

Caliber: 5.56/.223. **Capacity:** 30-round magazine. **Barrels:** 20 or 24 in. heavy or standard. **Weights:** 8.43–9.29 lbs. **Lengths:** 39.5 or 43.5 **Features:** Semiauto AR-style with chrome-lined or stainless steel 1:9 in. twist barrel, fixed or removable carry handle, manganese phosphate finish.
Price: ....**$969.00–$1,000.00**

Prices given are believed to be accurate at time of publication however, many factors affect retail pricing so exact prices are not possible.

Tactical GunDigest ⊕ **339**

BUSHMASTER M4A3 TYPE CARBINE

Caliber: 5.56/.223. **Capacity:** 30-round magazine. **Barrel:** 16 in. **Weights:** 6.22–6.7 lbs. **Lengths:** 31–32.5 in. overall. **Features:** AR-style carbine with chrome-moly vanadium steel barrel, Izzy-type flash hider, six-position telestock, various sight options, standard or multi-rail handguard, fixed or removable carry handle.
Price: $1,100.00

BUSHMASTER QUICK RESPONSE CARBINE

Caliber: 5.56/223. **Capacity:** 10-round magazine. **Barrel:** 16 in. chrome moly superlight contour with Melonite finish. **Features:** Mini red-dot detachable sight, 6-position collapsible stock, A2-type flash hider. Introduced in 2016.
Price: $769.00

CENTURY INTERNATIONAL AES-10 HI-CAP

Caliber: 7.62x39mm. **Capacity:** 30-shot magazine. **Barrel:** 23.2 in. **Weight:** NA. **Length:** 41.5 in. overall. **Stock:** Wood grip, fore-end. **Sights:** Fixed notch rear, windage-adjustable post front. **Features:** RPK-style, accepts standard double-stack AK-type mags. Side-mounted scope mount, integral carry handle, bipod. Imported by Century Arms Int'l.
Price: AES-10, From $450.00

CENTURY INTERNATIONAL GP WASR-10 HI-CAP

Caliber: 7.62x39mm. **Capacity:** 30-round magazine. **Barrel:** 16.25 in. 1:10 right-hand twist. **Weight:** 7.2 lbs. **Length:** 34.25 in. overall. **Stock:** Wood laminate or composite, grip, fore-end. **Sights:** Fixed notch rear, windage-adjustable post front. **Features:** Two 30-rd. detachable box magazines, cleaning kit, bayonet. Version of AKM rifle; U.S. parts added for BATFE compliance. Threaded muzzle, folding stock, bayonet lug, compensator, Dragunov stock available. Made in Romania by Cugir Arsenal. Imported by Century Arms Int'l.
Price: GP WASR-10, From $450.00

CENTURY INTERNATIONAL M70AB2 SPORTER

Caliber: 7.62x39mm. **Capacity:** 30-shot magazine. **Barrel:** 16.25 in. **Weight:** 7.5 lbs. **Length:** 34.25 in. overall. **Stocks:** Metal grip, wood fore-end. **Sights:** Fixed notch rear, windage-adjustable post front. **Features:** Two 30-rd. double-stack magazine, cleaning kit, compensator, bayonet lug and bayonet. Paratrooper-style Kalashnikov with under-folding stock. Imported by Century Arms Int'l.
Price: M70AB2, From..$480.00

CMMG MK SERIES

Calibers: 5.56 NATO, .308 Win., 7.62x39, .300 BLK. This company manufactures a wide range of AR and AK style rifles and carbines. Many AR/AK options offered. Listed are several variations of CMMG's many models. Made in the USA.

Price: MK4 LEM .223..$995.00
Price: MK3 .308 ....$1,595.00
Price: MK47 AKS8 7.62x39 (shown).....................$1,650.00
Price: MK4 RCE .300 BLK $1,500.00

CMMG MKW ANVIL

Caliber: .458 SOCOM. **Barrel:** 16.1 in. CMMG SV Muzzle Brake. **Weight:** 7.5 lbs. **Stock:** M4 with A2 pistol grip, 6 position mil-spec receiver extension. Introduced in 2017.
Price: From..$1,850.00

CMMG Mk4 DTR2

Caliber: .224 Valkyrie. **Capacity:** 10-round magazine (6.8 magazine). **Barrel:** 24 in. threaded. CMMG SV Muzzle Brake. **Weight:** 9.2 lbs. **Stock:** Magpul PRS with MOE Pistol grip4 with A2 pistol grip. **Features:** Model is engineered to deliver on this new cartridge's promise of long-range accuracy and high-energy performance.
Price: From..$1,699.95

COLT LE6920

Caliber: 5.56 NATO. **Barrel:** 16.1-in. chrome lined. **Sights:** Adjustable. Based on military M4. **Features:** Magpul MOE handguard, carbine stock, pistol grip, vertical grip. Direct gas/locking bolt operating system.
Price: From..$849.00–$1,099.00

COLT LE6940

Caliber: 5.56 NATO. Similar to LE1920 with Magpul MBUS backup sight, folding front, four accessory rails. One-piece monolithic upper receiver has continuous Mil-Spec rail from rear of upper to the front sight. Direct gas (LE6940) or articulating link piston (LE6940P) system.
Price: LE6940 ....$1,399.00

COLT L36960-CCU

Caliber: 5.56 NATO. **Capacity:** 30-round magazine. **Barrel:** 16-in. **Stock:** Magpul MOE SL with pistol grip. **Weight:** 6.7 lbs. **Features:** Combat Unit Carbine with 30-shot magazine. Aluminum receiver with black finish, mid-length gas system, optics ready.
Price: $1,299.00

COLT EXPANSE M4

Caliber: 5.56 NATO. **Capacity:** 30 rounds. **Barrel:** 16.1 in. **Sights:** Adjustable front post. Comes optics ready. **Weight:** 6.4 lbs. Flattop Picatinny rail. **Stock:** Adjustable M4 with A2-style grip. Economy priced AR. Introduced in 2016.
Price: $799.00

COLT MARC 901 MONOLITHIC

Caliber: .308. **Capacity:** 20 rounds. **Barrels:** 16.1 or 18 in. heavy fully floated with bayonet lug, flash hider. **Stock:** Adjustable VLTOR. **Sights:** Mil-spec flip up. **Weight:** 9.4 pounds. **Features:** One-piece flattop upper receiver with Picatinny rail, ambidextrous controls, matte black finish. Carbine model has muzzle brake, retractable Bravo stock, full-length Picatinny rail. Tubular handguard with 3 rails.
Price: $1,999.00
Price: Carbine $1,399.00

DANIEL DEFENSE AR SERIES

Caliber: 5.56 NATO/.223. **Capacity:** 20-round Magpul PMAG magazine. **Barrels:** 16 or 18 in.es. Flash suppressor. **Weight:** 7.4 lbs. **Lengths:** 34.75–37.85 in. overall. **Stock:** Glass-filled polymer with Soft Touch overmolding. Pistol grip. **Sights:** None. **Features:** Lower receiver is Mil-Spec with enhanced and flared magazine well, QD swivel attachment point. Upper receiver has M4 feed ramps. Lower and upper CNC machined of 7075-T6 aluminum, hard coat anodized. Shown is MK12, one of many AR variants offered by Daniel Defense. Made in the USA
Price: From..$1,599.00
Price: DD5VI 7.62/.308..$3.044.00

Prices given are believed to be accurate at time of publication however, many factors affect retail pricing so exact prices are not possible.

DPMS VARMINT SERIES
Calibers: .204 Ruger, .223. **Barrels:** 16 in., 20 in. or 24 in. bull or fluted profile. **Weights:** 7.75–11.75 lbs. **Lengths:** 34.5–42.25 in. overall. **Stock:** Black Zytel composite. **Sights:** None. **Features:** Flattop receiver with Picatinny top rail; hardcoat anodized receiver; aluminum free-float tube handguard; many options. From DPMS Panther Arms.
Price: .... **$939.00–$1,229.00**

DPMS PRAIRIE PANTHER
Calibers: 5.56 NATO or 6.8 SPC. **Barrels:** 20-in. 416 stainless fluted heavy 1:8 in. barrel. **Features:** Phosphate steel bolt; free-floated carbon fiber handguard; flattop upper with Picatinny rail; aluminum lower; two 30-round magazines; skeletonized Zytel stock; Choice of matte black or one of several camo finishes.
Price: .... **$1,269.00–$1,289.00**

DPMS MK12
Caliber: .308 Win./7.62 NATO. **Barrel:** 18 in. **Weight:** 8.5 lbs. **Sights:** Midwest Industry flip-up. **Features:** 4-rail free floating handguard, flash hider, extruded 7029 T6 A3 Flattop receiver.
Price: **$1,759.00**

DPMS 3G2
Calibers: .223/5.56, 6.5 Creedmoor. **Barrel:** 16 in. **Weight:** 7.1 lbs. **Stock:** Magpul STR with Hogue rubber pistol grip. **Sights:** Magpul Gen 2 BUS. **Features:** Miculek Compensator, two-stage fire control. M111 Modular handguard allows placement of sights on top rail or 45-degree angle.
Price: From.................................... **$1,129.00–$1,239.00**

DPMS LITE HUNTER
Calibers: .243, .260 Rem., .308, .338 Federal. **Barrel:** 20 in. stainless.

Weight: 8 pounds. **Stock:** Standard A2. **Features:** Two-stage match trigger. Hogue pistol grip. Optics ready top rail.
Price: **$1,499.00**

DPMS .300 AAC BLACKOUT
Caliber: .300 AAC Blackout. **Barrel:** 16-in. heavy 4150 chrome-lined. **Weight:** 7 pounds. **Stock:** Adjustable 6-position.
Price: **$1,199.00**

DPMS ORACLE
Calibers: .223/5.56 or .308/7.62. **Barrel:** 16 in. **Weights:** 6.2 (.223), 8.3 (308). Standard AR-15 fire control with A3 flattop receiver. **Finish:** Matte black or A-TACS camo.
Price: .223 ATACS... **$739, $849**
Price: .308 ATACS.. **$1,099, $1,189**

DPMS GII SERIES
Caliber: .308 Win./7.62 NATO. **Barrels:** 16, 18 in. **Weight:** From 7.25 lbs. Features: promoted as the lightest .308 AR available. Features include new extractor and ejector systems, and improved steel feed ramp. New bolt geometry provides better lock-up and strength. Offered in several configurations.
Price: AP4 (shown)... **$1,499.00**
Price: Recon **$1,759.00**
Price: SASS **$2,379.00**
Price: Hunter **$1,699.00**
Price: Bull **$1,759.00**
Price: MOE **$1,599.00**

DSA SA58 STANDARD
Caliber: .308 Win. **Barrel:** 21 in. bipod cut w/threaded flash hider. **Weight:** 8.75 lbs. **Length:** 43 in. **Stock:** Synthetic, X-Series or optional folding para stock. **Sights:** Elevation-adjustable post front, windage-adjustable rear peep. **Features:** Fully adjustable short gas system, high-grade steel or 416 stainless upper receiver. Made in USA by DSA, Inc.
Price: From.. **$1,700.00**

DSA SA58 CARBINE
Caliber: .308 Win. **Barrel:** 16.25 in. bipod cut w/threaded flash hider. **Features:** Carbine variation of FAL-style rifle. Other features identical to SA58 Standard model. Made in USA by DSA, Inc.
Price: **$1,700.00**

Prices given are believed to be accurate at time of publication however, many factors affect retail pricing so exact prices are not possible.

Tactical *GunDigest*® ⊕ **341**

DSA SA58 TACTICAL CARBINE
Caliber: .308 Win. **Barrel:** 16.25 in. fluted with A2 flash hider. **Weight:** 8.25 lbs. **Length:** 36.5 in. **Stock:** Synthetic, X-Series or optional folding para stock. **Sights:** Elevation-adjustable post front, windage-adjustable match rear peep. **Features:** Shortened fully adjustable short gas system, high-grade steel or 416 stainless upper receiver. Made in USA by DSA, Inc.
Price: **$1,975.00**

DSA SA58 MEDIUM CONTOUR
Caliber: .308 Win. **Barrel:** 21 in. w/threaded flash hider. **Weight:** 9.75 lbs. **Length:** 43 in. **Stock:** Synthetic military grade. **Sights:** Elevation-adjustable post front, windage-adjustable match rear peep. **Features:** Gas-operated semiauto with fully adjustable gas system, high-grade steel receiver. Made in USA by DSA, Inc.
Price: **$1,700.00**

DSA ZM4 AR SERIES
Caliber: .223/5.56 NATO. **Weight:** 9 pounds. **Features:** Standard Flattop rifle features include 20-in., chrome moly heavy barrel with A2 flash hider. Mil-Spec forged lower receiver, forged flattop or A2 upper. Fixed A2 stock. Carbine variations are also available with 16-in. barrels and many options.
Price: Standard Flat-Top **$820.00**
Price: MRC Multi-Role Carbine **$1,275.00**
Price: Mid Length Carbine **$834.00**
Price: Flat-Top with rail **$850.00**

EXCEL ARMS MR-22
Caliber: .22 WMR. **Capacity:** 9-shot magazine. **Barrel:** 18 in. fluted stainless steel bull barrel. **Weight:** 8 lbs. **Length:** 32.5 in. overall. **Grips:** Textured black polymer. **Sights:** Fully adjustable target sights. **Features:** Made from 17-4 stainless steel, aluminum shroud w/Weaver rail, manual safety, firing-pin block, last-round bolt-hold-open feature. Four packages with various equipment available. American made, lifetime warranty. Comes with one 9-round stainless steel magazine and a California-approved cable lock. Introduced 2006. Made in USA by Excel Arms.
Price: MR-22 .22 WMR **$538.00**

EXCEL ARMS X-SERIES
Caliber: .22 LR, 5.7x28mm (10 or 25-round); .30 Carbine (10 or 20-round magazine). 9mm (10 or 17 rounds). **Barrel:** 18 in. **Weight:** 6.25 lbs. **Length:** 34 to 38 in. **Features:** Available with or without adjustable iron sights. Blow-back action (5.57x28) or delayed blow-back (.30 Carbine).
Price: .22 LR **$504.00**
Price: 5.7x28 or 9mm .... **$795.00–$916.00**

FN15 SERIES
Caliber: 5.56x45. **Capacity:** 20 or 30 rounds. **Barrels:** 16 in., 18 in., 20 in. **Features:** AR-style rifle/carbine series with most standard features and options.
Price: Tactical II (also in .300 BLK) **$1,599.00**
Price: Standard rifle **$1,149.00**
Price: Sporting **$1,749.00**
Price: DMR II **$1,999.00**
Price: Carbine **$1,149.00**
Price: Competition **$2,240.00**

Price: Military Collector **$1,749.00**

FN 15 TACTICAL CARBINE FDA P-LOK
Caliber: 5.56x45mm. **Capacity:** 30-shot PMAG. **Barrel:** 16-in. free-floating and chrome-lined with FN 3-prong flash hider. **Stock:** B5 Systems buttstock and grip. **Weight:** 7.2 lbs. **Finish:** Flat Dark Earth. **Features:** P-LOK handguard, M-LOK accessory mounting system, hard anodized aluminum flat-top receiver with Picatinny rail, forward assist.
Price: **$1,499.00**

FNH FNAR COMPETITION
Caliber: .308 Win. **Capacity:** 10-shot magazine. **Barrel:** 20 in. fluted. **Weight:** 8.9 lbs. **Length:** 41.25 in. overall. **Sights:** None furnished. Optical rail atop receiver, three accessory rails on fore-end. **Stock:** Adjustable for comb height, length of pull, cast-on and cast-off. Blue/gray laminate. Based on BAR design.
Price: **$1,767.00**

FNH SCAR 16S Caliber: 5.56mm/.223. **Capacities:** 10 or 30 rounds. **Barrel:** 16.25 in. **Weight:** 7.25 lbs. **Lengths:** 27.5–37.5 in. (extended stock). **Stock:** Telescoping, side-folding pistol grip. A2 style pistol grip. **Sights:** Adjustable folding front and rear. **Features:** Hard anodized aluminum receiver with four accessory rails. Ambidextrous safety and mag release. Charging handle can be mounted on right or left side. Semi-auto version of newest service rifle of U.S. Special Forces.
Price: **$3,299.00**

FNH SCAR 17S Caliber: 7.62x51 NATO/.308. **Capacities:** 10 or 30 rounds. **Barrel:** 16.25 in. **Weight:** 8 lbs. **Lengths:** 28.5–38.5 in. (extended stock). **Features:** Other features the same as SCAR 16S.
Price: **$3,499.00**

FRANKLIN ARMORY 3 GR-L Caliber: 5.56mm/.223. **Capacities:** 10 or 30 rounds. **Barrel:** 18 in. fluted with threaded muzzle crown. **Weight:** 7.25 lbs. **Stock:** Magpul PRS. Adjustable comb and length of pull. **Features:** Hard anodized Desert Smoke upper receiver with full-length Picatinny rail. One of many AR type rifles and carbines offered by this manufacturer. Made in the USA.
Price: **$2,310.00**

Prices given are believed to be accurate at time of publication however, many factors affect retail pricing so exact prices are not possible.

HECKLER & KOCH MODEL MR556A1

Caliber: .223 Remington/5.56 NATO. **Capacity:** 10+1. **Barrel:** 16.5 in. **Weight:** 8.9 lbs. **Lengths:** 33.9–37.68 in. **Stock:** Black synthetic adjustable. **Features:** Uses the gas piston system found on the HK 416 and G26, which does not introduce propellant gases and carbon fouling into the rifle's interior.
Price: $3,295.00

HECKLER & KOCH MODEL MR762A1

Caliber: Similar to Model MR556A1 except chambered for 7.62x51mm/.308 Win. cartridge. **Weight:** 10 lbs. w/empty magazine. **Lengths:** 36–39.5 in. **Features:** Variety of optional sights are available. Stock has five adjustable positions.
Price: $3,995.00

HIGH STANDARD HSA-15

Calibers: .223 Remington/5.56 NATO or .300 AAC Blackout. **Capacity:** 30-round magazine. **Barrels:** A2 style with 16 or 20 in. **Features:** Fixed or collapsible stock, adjustable sights. Series of AR-style models offered in most variations with popular options. Made by High Standard Manufacturing Co.
Price: .... $785.00–$1,250.00

HI-POINT CARBINE SERIES

Calibers: .380 ACP, 9mm Para. .40 S&W, 10mm, (10-round magazine); .45 ACP (9-round). **Barrels:** 16.5 in. (17.5 in. for .40 S&W and .45). **Weight:** 4.5–7 lbs. **Length:** 31.5 in. overall. **Stock:** Black polymer, camouflage. **Sights:** Protected post front, aperture rear. Integral scope mount. **Features:** Grip-mounted magazine release. Black or chrome finish. Sling swivels. Available with laser or red-dot sights, RGB 4X scope, forward grip. Introduced 1996. Made in USA by MKS Supply, Inc.
Price: .380 ACP, From $315.00
Price: 9mm (995TS), From $315.00
Price: .40 S&W (4095TS), From $315.00
Price: .45 ACP (4595TS), From $319.00
Price: 10mm (1095TS), From $389.00

INLAND M1 1945 CARBINE

Caliber: .30 Carbine. **Capacity:** 15 rounds. **Barrel:** 18 in. **Weight:** 5 lbs. 3 oz. **Features:** A faithful reproduction of the last model that Inland manufactured in 1945, featuring a type 3 bayonet lug/barrel band, adjustable rear sight, push button safety, and walnut stock. Scout Model has 16.5-in. barrel, flash hider, synthetic stock with accessory rail. Made in the USA.
Price: $1,299.00

Price: Scout Model $1,449.00

JP ENTERPRISES LRP-07

Calibers: .308 Win, .260 Rem., 6.5 Creedmoor, .338 Federal. **Barrels:** 16–22 in., polished stainless with compensator. **Buttstock:** A2, ACE ARFX, Tactical Tactical Intent Carbine, Magpul MOE. **Grip:** Hogue Pistol Grip. **Features:** Machined upper and lower receivers with left-side charging system. MKIII Hand Guard. Adjustable gas system.
Price: From..$3,299.00

JP ENTERPRISES JP-15

Calibers: .223, .204 Ruger, 6.5 Grendel, .300 Blackout, .22 LR. **Barrels:** 18 or 24-in. **Buttstock:** Synthetic modified thumbhole or laminate thumbhole. **Grip:** Hogue Pistol grip. Basic AR-type general-purpose rifle with numerous options.
Price: From..$1,999.00

KALASHNIKOV USA

Caliber: 7.62x39mm. **Capacity:** 30-round magazine. AK-47 series made in the USA in several variants and styles. **Barrel:** 16.25 in. **Weight:** 7.52 lbs.
Price: US132S Synthetic stock $799.00
Price: US132W Wood carbine $836.00

KEL-TEC RFB

Caliber: 7.62 NATO/.308. 20-round FAL-type magazine. **Barrel:** 18 in. with threaded muzzle, A2-style flash hider. **Weight:** 8 lbs. **Features:** A bullpup short-stroke gas piston operated carbine with ambidextrous controls, reversible operating handle, Mil-Spec Picatinny rail.
Price: $1,927.00

KEL-TEC SU-16 SERIES

Caliber: 5.56 NATO/.223. **Capacity:** 10-round magazine. **Barrels:** 16 or 18.5 in. **Weights:** 4.5–5 lbs. **Features:** Offering in several rifle and carbine variations.
Price: From..............................$682.00–$900.00

LARUE TACTICAL OBR

Calibers: 5.56 NATO/.223, 7.62 NATO/.308 Win. **Barrels:** 16.1 in., 18 in. or 20 in. **Weights:** 7.5–9.25 lbs. **Features:** Manufacturer of several models of AR-style rifles and carbines. Optimized Battle Rifle (OBR) series is made in both NATO calibers. Many AR-type options available. Made in the USA
Price: OBR 5.56 ....$2,245.00
Price: OBR 7.62..$3,370.00

LEWIS MACHINE & TOOL (LMT)

Calibers: 5.56 NATO/.223, 7.62 NATO/.308 Win. **Barrels:** 16.1 in., 18 in. or 20 in. **Weights:** 7.5–9.25 lbs. **Features:** Manufacturer of a wide range of AR-style carbines with many options. SOPMOD stock, gas piston operating system, monolithic rail platform, tactical sights. Made in the USA by Lewis Machine & Tool.
Price: Standard 16 ....$1,649.00
Price: Comp 16, flattop receiver.....................$1,685.00
Price: CQB Series from....................................$2,399.00
Price: Sharpshooter Weapons System $6,499.00

Prices given are believed to be accurate at time of publication however, many factors affect retail pricing so exact prices are not possible.

Tactical GunDigest 343

MOSSBERG MMR SERIES
Caliber: 5.56 NATO. **Capacity:** 10 or 30 rounds. GIO system. **Barrel:** 16 or 18 in. with A2-style muzzle brake. **Features:** Picatinny rail, black synthetic stock, free-floating stainless barrel. Offered in several variants. Pro and Optics Ready have JM Pro match trigger. Optics Ready has 6-position stock with FLEX pad, Magpul MOE grip and trigger guard. Introduced in 2016.
Price: MMR Carbine..$938.00
Price: MMR Tactical Optics Ready..........................$1,253.00
Price: MMR Pro...$1,393.00

REMINGTON LE R4 OPERATOR NEW MEXICO
Caliber: .223. **Capacity:** 30-round magazine. **Barrel:** 16 in. with twist rate of 1:7 for heavier, longer bullets. **Weight:** 6.5 lbs. **Length:** 33.25–36.25 in. **Stock:** Magpul SL. **Sights:** Troy Industries front and rear folding battle sights. **Features:** AR-style with direct impingement gas operation. Carbine length system with mil-spec forged receiver, single-stage mil-spec trigger. Designed for a LE agency in New Mexico. Introduced in 2016 by Remington Law Enforcement Division.
Price: $1,299.00

ROCK RIVER ARMS LAR SERIES
Calibers: .223/5.56, .308/7.62, 6.8 SPC, .458 SOCOM, 9mm and .40 S&W. **Features:** These AR-15 type rifles and carbines are available with a very wide range of options. Virtually any AR configuration is offered including tactical, hunting and competition models. Some models are available in left-hand versions.
Price: ....$1,035.00–$1,845.00

RUGER AR-556
Caliber: 5.56 NATO. **Capacity:** 30-round magazine. **Features:** Basic AR M4-style Modern Sporting Rifle with direct impingement operation, forged aluminum upper and lower receivers, and cold hammer-forged chrome-moly steel barrel with M4 feed ramp cuts. Other features include Ruger Rapid Deploy folding rear sight, milled F-height gas block with post front sight, telescoping 6-position stock and one 30-round Magpul magazine. Introduced in 2015. MPR (Multi Purpose Rifle) model has 18-in. barrel with muzzle brake, flat-top upper, 15-in. free-floating handguard with Magpul M-LOK accessory slots, Magpul MOE SL collapsible buttstock and MOE grip.
Price: $799.00
Price: MPR...$899.00

LES BAER CUSTOM ULTIMATE AR 223
Caliber: .223. **Barrels:** 18 in., 20 in., 22 in., 24 in. **Weights:** 7.75–9.75 lbs. **Length:** NA. **Stock:** Black synthetic. **Sights:** None furnished; Picatinny-style flattop rail for scope mounting. **Features:** Forged receiver; Ultra single-stage trigger (Jewell two-stage trigger optional); titanium firing pin; Versa-Pod bipod; chromed National Match carrier; stainless steel, hand-lapped and cryo-treated barrel; guaranteed to shoot .5 or .75 MOA, depending on model. Made in USA by Les Baer Custom Inc.
Price: Super Varmint Model ....$2,640.00–$2870.00
Price: Super Match Model ....$2,740.00–$2960.00
Price: M4 Flattop model $2,790.00
Price: IPSC Action Model $2,890.00
Price: LBC-AR (.264 LBC-AR) $2,640.00

LES BAER ULTIMATE MATCH/SNIPER
Caliber: .308 Win. **Barrels:** 18 or 20 in. **Features:** Magpul stock, Enforcer muzzle brake.
Price: $3,940.00
Price: Ultimate Monolith SWAT Model $4,390.00

LR 300S
Caliber: 5.56 NATO. **Capacity:** 30-shot magazine. **Barrel:** 16.5 in.; 1:9 in. twist. **Weights:** 7.4–7.8 lbs. **Length:** NA. **Stock:** Folding. **Sights:** YHM flip front and rear. **Features:** Flattop receive, full-length top Picatinny rail. Phantom flash hider, multi sling mount points, field strips with no tools. Made in USA from Z-M Weapons.
Price: AXL, AXLT $2,139.00
Price: NXL $2,208.00

LWRC INTERNATIONAL M6 SERIES
Calibers: 5.56 NATO, .224 Valkyrie, .6.5 Creedmoor, 6.8 SPC, 7.62x51mm, .300 BLK. **Capacity:** 30-shot magazine. **Features:** This company makes a complete line of AR-15 type rifles operated by a short-stroke, gas piston system. A wide variety of stock, sight and finishes are available. Colors include black, Flat Dark Earth, Olive Drab Green, Patriot Brown.
Price: M6A2 ....$2,217.00
Price: M6-SPR (Special Purpose Rifle) $2,479.00
Price: REPR (Shown)...$5,139.00
Price: SIX8 A5 6.8 SPC...................................$2,600.00–$2,750.00
Price: IC-DI 224 Valkyrie $1,995.00

RUGER PC CARBINE
Caliber: 9mm. **Capacity:** 17 rounds. Interchangeable magazine wells for Ruger and Glock magazines. **Barrel:** 16.12-in. threaded and fluted. **Stock:** Glass-filled nylon synthetic. **Sights:** Adjustable ghost-ring rear, protected-blade front. **Weight:** 6.8 lbs. **Features:** Reversible magazine release and charging handle. Dead-blow action reduces felt recoil. Receiver has integrated Picatinny rail.
Price: $649.00

Prices given are believed to be accurate at time of publication however, many factors affect retail pricing so exact prices are not possible.

RUGER SR-556/SR-762

Calibers: 5.56 NATO or 7.62 NATO/.308. (SR-762 model). **Features:** AR-style semi-auto rifle with two-stage piston; quad rail handguard; Troy Industries sights; black synthetic fixed or telescoping buttstock; 16.12-in. 1:9 in. twist steel barrel with birdcage; 10- or 30-round detachable box magazine; black matte finish overall. SR-556 has takedown feature.
Price: SR-556 ....**$2,199.00**
Price: SR-762 ....**$2,349.00**

RUGER MINI-14 RANCH RIFLE

Calibers: .223 Rem., .300 Blackout (Tactical Rifle). **Capacity:** 5-shot or 20-shot detachable box magazine. **Barrel:** 18.5 in. Rifling twist 1:9 in. **Weights:** 6.75–7 lbs. **Length:** 37.25 in. overall. **Stocks:** American hardwood, steel reinforced, or synthetic. **Sights:** Protected blade front, fully adjustable Ghost Ring rear. **Features:** Fixed piston gas-operated, positive primary extraction. New buffer system, redesigned ejector system. Ruger S100RM scope rings included on Ranch Rifle. Heavier barrels added in 2008, 20-round magazine added in 2009.
Price: Mini-14/5, Ranch Rifle, blued, wood stock **$999.00**
Price: K-Mini-14/5, Ranch Rifle, stainless, scope rings **$1,069.00**
Price: Mini-14 Target Rifle: laminated thumbhole stock, heavy crowned 22 in. stainless steel barrel, other refinements **$1,259.00**
Price: Mini-14 ATI Stock: Tactical version of Mini-14 but with six-position collapsible stock or folding stock, grooved pistol grip. Multiple Picatinny optics/accessory rails **$1,089.00**
Price: Mini-14 Tactical Rifle: Similar to Mini-14 but with 16.12 in. barrel with flash hider, black synthetic stock, adjustable sights **$1,019.00**

RUGER MINI THIRTY

Caliber: Similar to the Mini-14 rifle except modified to chamber the 7.62x39 Russian service round. **Weight:** 6.75 lbs. **Barrel:** Has 6-groove barrel with 1:10 in. twist. **Features:** Ruger Integral Scope Mount bases and protected blade front, fully adjustable Ghost Ring rear. Detachable 5-shot staggered box magazine. 20-round magazines available. Stainless or matte black alloy w/synthetic stock. Introduced 1987.
Price: Matte black finish **$1,069.00**
Price: Stainless **$1,089.00**
Price: Stainless w/20-round mag **$1,139.00**

SAVAGE MSR 15/MSR 10

Calibers: AR-style series chambered in 5.56 NATO (Patrol and Recon), 6.5 Creedmoor or .308 Win. (MSR 10 Hunter and Long Range). **Barrels:** 16.1 in. (Patrol and Recon), 16 or 18 in. (Hunter), 20 or 22 in. (Long Range). Wylde chamber on Patrol and Recon models. Hunter and Long Range models have muzzle brake.
Price: Patrol **$869.00**
Price: Recon (shown) **$994.00**
Price: MSR 10 Long Range **$2,284.00**
Price: MSR 10 Hunter..**$1,481.00**

SIG-SAUER MCX

Calibers: 5.56 NATO, 7.62x39mm or .300 Blackout. **Features:** AR-style rifle. Modular system allows switching between calibers with conversion kit. Features include a 16 in. barrel, aluminum KeyMod handguards, ambi controls and charging handle, choice of side-folding or telescoping stock, auto-regulating gas system to all transition between subsonic and supersonic loads.
Price: **$2,131.00**
Price: With conversion kit **$2,188.00**

SIG 516 PATROL

Caliber: 5.56 NATO. **Features:** AR-style rifle with included 30-round magazine, 16-in. chrome-lined barrel with muzzle brake; free-floating, aluminum quad Picatinny rail, Magpul MOE adjustable stock, black anodized or Flat Dark Earth finish, various configurations available.
Price: From..**$1,888.00**

SIG-SAUER SIG716 TACTICAL PATROL

Caliber: 7.62 NATO/.308 Win. **Features:** AR-10 type rifle. Gas-piston operation with 3-round-position (4-position optional) gas valve; 16-, 18- or 20-in. chrome-lined barrel with threaded muzzle and nitride finish; free-floating aluminum quad rail fore-end with four M1913 Picatinny rails; telescoping buttstock; lower receiver is machined from a 7075-T6 Aircraft grade aluminum forging; upper receiver, machined from 7075-T6 aircraft grade aluminum with integral M1913 Picatinny rail. DMR has free-floating barrel, two-stage match-grade trigger, short-stroke pushrod operating system.
Price: **$2,385.00**
Price: Designated Marksman (DMR) **$3,108.00**

SMITH & WESSON M&P15

Caliber: 5.56mm NATO/.223. **Capacity:** 30-shot steel magazine. **Barrel:** 16 in., 1:9 in. twist. **Weight:** 6.74 lbs., w/o magazine. **Lengths:** 32–35 in. overall. **Stock:** Black synthetic. **Sights:** Adjustable post front sight, adjustable dual aperture rear sight. **Features:** 6-position telescopic stock, thermo-set M4 handguard. 14.75 in. sight radius. 7-lbs. (approx.) trigger pull. 7075 T6 aluminum upper, 4140 steel barrel. Chromed barrel bore, gas key, bolt carrier. Hard-coat black-anodized receiver and barrel finish. OR (Optics Ready) model has no sights. TS model has Magpul stock and folding sights. Made in USA by Smith & Wesson.

Price: Sport Model...$739.00
Price: OR Model..$1,069.00
Price: TS model $1,569.00

SMITH & WESSON M&P15-300
Calibers: .300 Whisper/.300 AAC Blackout. **Features:** Other specifications the same of 5.56 models.
Price: $1,119.00

SMITH & WESSON MODEL M&P15 VTAC
Caliber: .223 Remington/5.56 NATO. **Capacity:** 30-round magazine. **Barrel:** 16 in. **Weight:** 6.5 lbs. **Length:** 35 in. extended, 32 in. collapsed, overall. **Features:** Six-position CAR stock. Surefire flash-hider and G2 light with VTAC light mount; VTAC/JP handguard; JP single-stage match trigger and speed hammer; three adjustable Picatinny rails; VTAC padded two-point adjustable sling.
Price: $1,949.00

SMITH & WESSON M&P15PC CAMO
Caliber: 223 Rem/5.56 NATO, A2 configuration. **Capacity:** 10-round magazine. **Barrel:** 20 in. stainless with 1:8 in. twist. **Weight:** 8.2 lbs. **Length:** 38.5 in. overall. **Features:** AR-style, no sights but integral front and rear optics rails. Two-stage trigger, aluminum lower. Finished in Realtree Advantage Max-1 camo.
Price: $1,589.00

SMITH & WESSON M&P10
Caliber: .308 Win. **Capacity:** 10 rounds. **Barrel:** 18 in. **Weight:** 7.7 pounds. **Features:** 6-position CAR stock, black hard anodized finish. Camo finish hunting model available w/5-round magazine.
Price: $1,619.00
Price: (Camo)..$1,729.00

SPRINGFIELD ARMORY M1A
Caliber: 7.62mm NATO (.308). **Capacities:** 5- or 10-shot box magazine. **Barrel:** 25.062 in. with flash suppressor, 22 in. without suppressor. **Weight:** 9.75 lbs. **Length:** 44.25 in. overall. **Stock:** American walnut with walnut-colored heat-resistant fiberglass handguard. Matching walnut handguard available. Also available with fiberglass stock. **Sights:** Military, square blade front, full click-adjustable aperture rear. **Features:** Commercial equivalent of the U.S. M-14 service rifle with no provision for automatic firing. From Springfield Armory.
Price: SOCOM 16...$1,987.00
Price: Scout Squad, From $1,850.00
Price: Standard M1A, From $1,685.00
Price: Loaded Standard, From $1,847.00
Price: National Match, From $2,434.00
Price: Super Match (heavy premium barrel) about $2,965.00
Price: Tactical, From ....$3,619.00–$4,046.00

SPRINGFIELD ARMORY M1A SUPER MATCH
Caliber: .308 Win. **Barrel:** 22 in., heavy Douglas Premium. **Weight:** About 11 lbs. **Length:** 44.31 in. overall. **Stock:** Heavy walnut competition stock with longer pistol grip, contoured area behind the rear sight, thicker butt and fore-end, glass bedded. **Sights:** National Match front and rear. **Features:** Has figure-eight-style operating rod guide. Introduced 1987. From Springfield Armory.
Price: Approx $2,956.00

SPRINGFIELD ARMORY M1A/M-21 TACTICAL MODEL
Similar to M1A Super Match except special sniper stock with adjustable cheekpiece and rubber recoil pad. Weighs 11.6 lbs. From Springfield Armory.

Price: $3,619.00

SPRINGFIELD ARMORY SAINT
Caliber: 5.56 NATO. **Capacity:** 30-round magazine. **Barrel:** 16 in., 1:8 twist. **Weight:** 6 lbs., 11 oz. **Sights:** AR2-style fixed post front, flip-up aperture rear. **Features:** Mid-length gas system, BCM 6-position stock, Mod 3 grip PMT KeyMod handguard 7075 T6 aluminum receivers. Springfield Armory's first entry into AR category. Introduced 2016.
Price: $899.00

STAG ARMS AR-STYLE SERIES
Calibers: 5.56 NATO/.223, 6.8 SPC, 9mm Parabellum. Ten. **Capacities:** 20- or 30-shot magazine. **Features:** This manufacturer offers more than 25 AR-style rifles or carbines with many optional features including barrel length and configurations, stocks, sights, rail systems and both direct impingement and gas piston operating systems. Left-hand models are available on some products. Listed is a sampling of Stag Arms models.
Price: Model 1 ....$949.00
Price: Model 2T Carbine (Tactical) $1,130.00
Price: Model 3 Carbine $895.00
Price: Model 3G Rifle $1,459.00
Price: Model 5 Carbine (6.8) $1,045.00
Price: Stag 7 Hunter (6.8) $1,055.00
Price: Model 9 (9mm) $990.00

STI SPORTING COMPETITION
Caliber: 5.56 NATO. **Features:** AR-style semi-auto rifle with 16-in. 410 stainless 1:8 in. twist barrel; mid-length gas system; Nordic Tactical Compensator and JP Trigger group; custom STI Valkyrie handguard and gas block; flattop design with picatinny rail; anodized finish with black Teflon coating. Also available in Tactical configuration.
Price: $1,455.00

STONER SR-15 MOD2
Caliber: .223. **Capacity:** 30-round magazine. **Barrel:** 18 in. **Weight:** 7.6 lbs. **Length:** 38 in. overall. **Stock:** Mag-Pul MOE. **Sights:** Post front, fully adjustable rear (300-meter sight). **Features:** URX-4 upper receiver; two-stage trigger, 30-round magazine. Black finish. Made in USA by Knight's Mfg.
Price: $2,700.00

STONER SR-25 ACC
Caliber: 7.62 NATO. **Capacities:** 10- or 20-shot steel magazine. **Barrel:** 16 in. with flash hider. **Weight:** 8.5 lbs. **Features:** Shortened, non-slip handguard; drop-in two-stage match trigger, removable carrying handle, ambidextrous controls, matte black finish. Made in USA by Knight's Mfg. Co.
Price: $5,300.00

WILSON COMBAT TACTICAL
Caliber: 5.56mm NATO. **Capacity:** Accepts all M-16/AR-15 Style Magazines, includes one 20-round magazine. **Barrel:** 16.25 in., 1:9 in. twist, match-grade fluted. **Weight:** 6.9 lbs. **Length:** 36.25 in. overall. **Stock:** Fixed or collapsible. **Features:** Free-float ventilated aluminum quad-rail handguard, Mil-Spec Parkerized barrel and steel components, anodized receiver, precision CNC-machined upper and lower receivers, 7075 T6 aluminum forgings. Single-stage JP Trigger/ Hammer Group, Wilson Combat Tactical muzzle brake, nylon tactical rifle case. M-4T version has flat-top receiver for mounting optics, OD green furniture, 16.25 in. match-grade M-4 style barrel. SS-15 Super Sniper Tactical Rifle has 1-in-8 twist, heavy 20 in. match-grade fluted stainless steel barrel. Made in USA by Wilson Combat.
Price: ....$2,225.00–$2,450.00

ARMALITE AR-30A1

Calibers: .300 Win. Mag., .338 Lapua. **Capacity:** 5 rounds. **Barrels:** 24 in. (.300 Win.), 26 in. (.338 Lapua), competition grade. **Weight:** 12.8 lbs. **Length:** 46 in. **Stock:** Standard fixed. **Sights:** None. Accessory top rail included. **Features:** Bolt-action rifle. Muzzle brake, ambidextrous magazine release, large ejection port makes single loading easy, V-block patented bedding system, bolt-mounted safety locks firing pin. Target versions have adjustable stock. AR-31 is in .308 Win., accepts AR-10 double-stack magazines, has adjustable pistol grip stock.

Price: **$3,460.00**
Price: AR-31...**$3,460.00**

ARMALITE AR-50A1

Caliber: .50 BMG, .416 Barrett. **Capacity:** Bolt-action single-shot. **Barrel:** 30 in. with muzzle brake. National Match model (shown) has 33-in. fluted barrel. **Weight:** 34.1 lbs. **Stock:** Three-section. Extruded fore-end, machined vertical grip, forged and machined buttstock that is vertically adjustable. National Match model (.50 BMG only) has V-block patented bedding system, Armalite Skid System to ensure straight-back recoil.

Price: **$3,359.00**
Price: National Match **$4,230.00**

BARRETT MODEL 95

Caliber: 50 BMG. **Capacity:** 5-round magazine. **Barrel:** 29 in. **Weight:** 23.5 lbs. **Length:** 45 in. overall. **Stock:** Energy-absorbing recoil pad. **Sights:** Scope optional. **Features:** Bolt-action, bullpup design. Disassembles without tools; extendable bipod legs; match-grade barrel; muzzle brake. Introduced 1995. Made in USA by Barrett Firearms Mfg., Inc.

Price: From...**$6,670.00**

BARRETT MODEL 98B Caliber: .338 Lapua Magnum. **Capacity:** 10-round magazine. **Barrel:** 26 in. fluted or 20 in. **Weight:** 13.5 lbs. **Length:** 49.8 in. **Features:** Comes with two magazines, bipod, monopod, side accessory rail, hard case. Fieldcraft model chambered in .260 Rem., 6.5 Creedmoor, 7mm Rem., .308Win., .300 Win Mag. Tactical Model in .308, .300 Win Mag., .338 Lapua. Fieldcraft Lightweight Hunting Rifle in .22-250, .243, 6.5 Creedmoor, .25-06, 6.5x55 Swede, .270 Win., 7mm-08, .308, .30-06.

Price: From..**$4,850.00**
Price: Fieldcraft Model, From................................**$3,750.00**
Price: Fieldcraft Lightweight Hunting Rifle **$1,799.00**
Price: Tactical Model, From...................................**$4,419.00**

BARRETT MODEL 99 SINGLE SHOT

Calibers: .50 BMG., .416 Barrett. **Barrel:** 33 in. **Weight:** 25 lbs. **Length:** 50.4 in. overall. **Stock:** Anodized aluminum with energy-absorbing recoil pad. **Sights:** None furnished; integral M1913 scope rail. **Features:** Bolt action; detachable bipod; match-grade barrel with high-efficiency muzzle brake. Introduced 1999. Made in USA by Barrett Firearms.

Price: From...**$3,999.00–$4,199.00**

BARRETT MRAD

Calibers: .260 Rem., 6.5 Creedmoor, .308 Win., .300 Win. Mag., .338 Lapua Magnum. **Capacity:** 10-round magazine. **Barrels:** 20 in., 24 in. or 26 in. fluted or heavy. **Features:** User-interchangeable barrel system, folding stock, adjustable cheekpiece, 5-position length of pull adjustment button, match-grade trigger, 22-in. optics rail.

Price: ....**$5,850.00–$6,000.00**

BERGARA B-14 SERIES

Calibers: 6.5 Creedmoor, .270 Win., 7mm Rem. Mag., .308 Win., .30-06, .300 Win. Mag. **Barrels:** 22 or 24 in. **Weight:** 7 lbs. **Features:** Synthetic with Soft touch finish, recoil pad, swivel studs, adjustable trigger, choice of detachable mag or hinged floorplate. Made in Spain.

Price: **$825.00**
Price: Walnut Stock..**$945.00**
Price: Premier Series, From.......................................**$2,190.00**
Price: Hunting and Match Rifle (HMR), From..................**$1,150.00**

BERGARA BCR SERIES Calibers: Most popular calibers from .222 Rem. to .300 Win. Mag **Barrels:** 18, 22, 24 or 26 in. Various options available.

Price: BCR23 Sport Hunter from **$3,950.00**
Price: BCR24 Varmint Hunter from **$4,100.00**
Price: BCR25 Long Range Hunter from **$4,350.00**
Price: BCR27 Competition from **$4,950.00**

BLASER R93 LONG RANGE SPORTER 2

Caliber: .308 Win. **Capacity:** 10-round magazine. **Barrel:** 24 in. **Weight:** 10.4 lbs. **Length:** 44 in. overall. **Stock:** Aluminum with synthetic lining. **Sights:** None furnished; accepts detachable scope mount. **Features:** Straight-pull bolt action with adjustable trigger; fully adjustable stock; quick takedown; corrosion resistant finish. Introduced 1998. Imported from Germany by Blaser USA.

Price: **$4,400.00**

BROWNING X-BOLT HELL'S CANYON

Calibers: .243 Win., 26 Nosler, 6.5 Creedmoor, .270 Win., .270 WSM, 7mm-08 Rem., 7mm Rem. Mag., .308 Win., .30-06, .300 Win. Mag., .300 WSM. **Barrels:** 22–26-in. fluted and free-floating with muzzle brake or thread protector. **Stock:** A-TACS AU Camo composite with checkered grip panels. **Features:** Detachable rotary magazine, adjustable trigger, Cerakote Burnt Bronze finish on receiver and barrel.

Price: ....**$1,200.00–$1,270.00**

Prices given are believed to be accurate at time of publication however, many factors affect retail pricing so exact prices are not possible.

Tactical GunDigest® ✛ **347**

BROWNING X-BOLT PRO SERIES
Calibers: 6mm Creedmoor, 6.5 Creedmoor, 26 Nosler, 28 Nosler, .270 Win., 7mm Rem. Mag., .308 Win., .30-06., .300 Win. Mag. Detachable rotary magazine. **Barrels:** 22–26 in. Stainless steel, fluted with threaded/removable muzzle brake. **Weights:** 6–7.5 lbs. **Finish:** Cerakote Burnt Bronze. **Stock:** Second generation carbon fiber with palm swell, textured gripping surfaces. Adjustable trigger, top tang safety, sling swivel studs. Long Range has heavy sporter-contour barrel, proprietary lapping process.
Price: X-Bolt Pro...**$2,070.00–$2,130.00**
Price: X-Bolt Pro Long Range ....**$2,100.00–$2,180.00**

BUSHMASTER BA50 BOLT-ACTION
Caliber: .50 Browning BMG. **Capacity:** 10-round magazine. **Barrels:** 30 in. (rifle), 22 in. (carbine). **Weight:** 30 lbs. (rifle), 27 lbs. (carbine). **Length:** 58 in. overall (rifle), 50 in. overall (carbine). **Features:** Free-floated Lothar Walther barrel with muzzle brake, Magpul PRS adjustable stock.
Price: **$5,657.00**

CHEYTAC M-200
Caliber: .408 CheyTac. **Capacity:** 7-round magazine. **Barrel:** 30 in. **Length:** 55 in. stock extended. **Weight:** 27 lbs. (steel barrel); 24 lbs. (carbon-fiber barrel). **Stock:** Retractable. **Sights:** None, scope rail provided. **Features:** CNC-machined receiver, attachable Picatinny rail M-1913, detachable barrel, integral bipod, 3.5-lb. trigger pull, muzzle brake. Made in USA by CheyTac, LLC.
Price: From... **$11,700.00**

COOPER FIREARMS OF MONTANA
This company manufacturers bolt-action rifles in a variety of styles and in almost any factory or wildcat caliber. Features of the major model sub-category/styles are listed below. Several other styles and options are available. Classic: Available in all models. AA Claro walnut stock with 4-panel hand checkering, hand-rubbed oil-finished wood, Pachmayr pad, steel grip cap and standard sling swivel studs. Barrel is chrome-moly premium match grade Wilson Arms. All metal work has matte finish. Custom Classic: Available in all models. AAA Claro walnut stock with shadow-line beaded cheek-piece, African ebony tip, Western fleur wrap-around hand checkering, hand-rubbed oil-finished wood, Pachmayr pad, steel grip cap and standard sling swivel studs. Barrel is chrome-moly premium match grade Wilson Arms. All metal work has high gloss finish. Western Classic: Available in all models. AAA+ Claro walnut stock. Selected metal work is highlighted with case coloring. Other features same as Custom Classic. Mannlicher: Available in all models. Same features as Western Classic with full-length stock having multi-point wrap-around hand checkering. Varminter: Available in Models 21, 22, 38, 52, 54 and 57-M. Same features as Classic except heavy barrel and stock with wide fore-end, hand-checkered grip.

COOPER MODEL 21
Calibers: Virtually any factory or wildcat chambering in the .223 Rem. family is available including: .17 Rem., .19-223, Tactical 20, .204 Ruger, .222 Rem., .222 Rem. Mag., .223 Rem, .223 Rem AI, 6x45, 6x47. Single shot. **Barrels:** 22–24 in. for Classic configurations, 24–26 in. for Varminter configurations. **Weights:** 6.5–8.0 lbs., depending on type. **Stock:** AA-AAA select claro walnut, 20 LPI checkering. **Sights:** None furnished. **Features:** Three front locking-lug, bolt-action, single-shot. Action: 7.75 in. long, Sako extractor. Button ejector. Fully adjustable single-stage trigger. Options include wood upgrades, case-color metalwork, barrel fluting, custom LOP, and many others.
Price: Varminter... **$2,295.00**

COOPER MODEL 22
Calibers: Virtually any factory or wildcat chambering in the mid-size cartridge length including: .22-250 Rem., .22-250 Rem. AI, .25-06 Rem., .25-06 Rem. AI, .243 Win., .243 Win. AI, .220 Swift, .250/3000 AI, .257 Roberts, .257 Roberts AI, 7mm-08 Rem., 6mm Rem., .260 Rem., 6x284, 6.5x284, .22 BR, 6mm BR, .308 Win. Single shot. **Barrels:** 24 in. or 26 in. stainless match in Classic configurations. 24 in. or 26 in. in Varminter configurations. **Weight:** 7.5–8.0 lbs. depending on type. **Stock:** AA-AAA select claro walnut, 20 LPI checkering. **Sights:** None furnished. **Features:** Three front locking-lug bolt-action single shot. Action: 8.25 in. long, Sako-style extractor. Button ejector. Fully adjustable single-stage trigger. Options include wood upgrades, case-color metalwork, barrel fluting, custom LOP, and many others.
Price: Varminter... **$2,225.00**

COOPER MODEL 38
Calibers: .22 Hornet family of cartridges including the .17 Squirrel, .17 He Bee, .17 Ackley Hornet, .17 Mach IV, .19 Calhoon, .20 VarTarg, .221 Fireball, .22 Hornet, .22 K-Hornet, .22 Squirrel, .218 Bee, .218 Mashburn Bee. Single shot. **Barrels:** 22 in. or 24 in. in Classic configurations, 24 in. or 26 in. in Varminter configurations. **Weights:** 6.5–8.0 lbs. depending on type. **Stock:** AA-AAA select claro walnut, 20 LPI checkering. **Sights:** None furnished. **Features:** Three front locking-lug bolt-action single shot. Action: 7 in. long, Sako-style extractor. Button ejector. Fully adjustable single-stage trigger. Options include wood upgrades, case-color metalwork, barrel fluting, custom LOP, and many others.
Price: Varminter... **$2,225.00**

CZ 550 VARMINT
Similar to CZ 550 American Classic. **Calibers:** .308 Win. and .22-250. **Stock:** Kevlar, laminated. **Length:** 46.7 in. **Barrel:** 25.6 in. **Weight:** 9.1 lbs. Imported from the Czech Republic by CZ-USA.
Price: **$865.00**
Price: Kevlar **$1,037.00**
Price: Laminated **$966.00**

CZ 550 MAGNUM H.E.T.
High Energy Tactical model similar to CZ 550 American Classic. **Caliber:** .338 Lapua. **Length:** 52 in. **Barrel:** 28 in. **Weight:** 14 lbs. **Features:** Adjustable sights, satin blued barrel. Imported from the Czech Republic by CZ-USA.
Price: **$3,929.00**

DAKOTA MODEL 97
Calibers: .22-250, .375 Dakota Mag. **Barrels:** 22 in., 24 in. **Weight:** 6.1–6.5 lbs. **Length:** 43 in. overall. **Stock:** Fiberglass. **Sights:** Optional. **Features:** Matte blue finish, black stock. Right-hand action only. Introduced 1998. Made in USA by Dakota Arms, Inc.
Price: Varminter... **$4,820.00**

FRANCHI MOMENTUM
Calibers: .243 Win., 6.5 Creedmoor, .270 Win., .308 Win., .30-06, .300 Win. Mag. **Barrels:** 22 or 24 in. **Weights:** 6.5–7.5 lbs. **Stock:** Black synthetic with checkered gripping surface, recessed sling swivel studs, TSA recoil pad. **Sights:** None. **Features:** Available with Burris Fullfield II 3-9X40mm scope.
Price: Varminter...**$609.00**
Price: With Burris 3-9X scope..**$729.00**

GA PRECISION CRUSADER
Calibers: .308 Win., Custom Calibers. **Capacity:** 10+1. **Barrels:** 23 in. **Weight:** 11.5 lbs. **Stock:** McMillan A-5. **Sights:** None. **Features:** GA Precision SA Templar action, completely trued. Solid 4320 CM one piece bolt, turned from a solid piece of billet. Left-side bolt release. Bartlein stainless 5R barrel, 1:11.25 twist (contour 1.200 x 3 st .920 muzzle). Timney trigger tuned to a crisp 2.5 lbs. McMillan A5 stock in molded Gap camo, Decelerator butt pad One front stud and 4 QD flush cups, (bottom and left side). Badger Ordnance M5 Detachable Mag System: 5- and 10-round magazines available. Solid one-piece 20 MOA base attached with 8-40 Tapered head grade 8 T-15 hardware. Precision ground over-sized recoil lug double-pinned to receiver. Badger Ordnance 30mm or 34mm rings, Customer's choice of height. Over-sized tactical bolt knob installed. Rifle finished in matte CeraKote, Color - Mil Spec OD. Pillar bedded with 7075 T-6 pillars then skimmed in Marine Tex. T.A.B Gear Sling included in O.D. Green.
Price: **$4,118.00**

GA PRECISION GLADIUS
Calibers: .308 Win., Custom Calibers. **Capacity:** 10+1. **Barrels:** 18 in. w/ Surefire brake. **Weight:** 10 lbs. **Stock:** Manners T-2A. **Sights:** None. **Features:** Nicknamed "Short Sword" by SnipersHide.com founder Frank Galli. Rem 700 SA RH, completely trued. Badger Ordnance tactical knob installed. GAP Left-side bolt release. Bartlein stainless 5R barrel, 1-10 twist GAP #6 contour, 1.250 in. for 3.500 in., finishes at .900 in. on 26-in. barrel blank. Timney trigger tuned to a crisp 2.5 lbs. Manners T-2A stock in Multicam hydrographic camouflage. Adjustable KMW Loggerhead cheek. One front stud and 4 QD flush cups, (bottom and left side). Badger Ordnance M5 Detachable Mag System: 5- and 10- round magazines. Solid one-piece Badger 20 MOA base. Precision ground oversized recoil lug. Badger Ordnance 30 or 34mm scope rings, Customer's choice of height. Rifle finished in CeraKote, Matte Black. Pillar bedded with 7075 T-6 pillars then skimmed in Marine Tex. T.A.B Gear Sling included in O.D. Green. 1/2 MOA guarantee with match grade ammo.
Price: **$4,100.00**

GA PRECISION U.S. ARMY M-24
Calibers: .308 Win./7.62 NATO, .300 Win. Mag. **Capacity:** 3+1. **Barrel:** 24 in. **Stock:** H-S Precision M24. **Sights:** None. **Features:** Remington 700 long action, trued up with lugs lapped. Chambered in .308 Win./7.62 Nato Match or .300 Win. Mag. (A191). Action drilled and tapped for target sights. Correct M-24/PRT REM trigger. Surface ground recoil lug to spec. Spec one piece M-24 steel scope base. 24 in. 1-11.25 twist, 5R, stainless steel barrel 1.200 for 3 in. Straight taper to .920. Barrel drilled and tapped for front site base. Black HS Precision M-24 stock, adjustable LOP. 3 Studs. M-24 steel triggerguard. Remington trigger tuned to 2.5 lbs. Matte Black Cerakote finish. 1/2 MOA Guarantee with match grade ammunition.
Price: **$3,920.00**

GA PRECISION USMC M40A5
Calibers: .308 Win./7.62 NATO **Capacity:** 5+1. **Barrel:** 25 in. **Stock:** McMillan A4. **Sights:** None. **Features:** Remington 700 Short Action, trued up with lugs lapped. Chambered in .308 Win./7.62 NATO Match. Action slotted to USMC M40A3 specs. Correct Remington Precision Rifle Trigger - Custom shop. Heavy ground recoil lug to spec. USMC 30 MOA lugged base. USMC Spec. 1-12 twist, 6 groove, Stainless Schneider barrel 1.200 for 4-in. straight taper, contoured to .749 in. for adapter. Surefire Comp/Suppressor Adapter model MB762SSAL/RE. McMillan A4 Stock, Sniper Fill, Adjustable Saddle Cheek, Spacer System LOP adjustment, O.D. Green molded-in color. 1 Stud,

6 flush cups. PGW PVS-22 Night Vision Mount. TIS Slip Cuff Contract Sling, coyote brown with correct swivels. 7075 alloy pillar bedded in Marinetex. Badger Ordnance M5 DBM triggerguard with one 5-rd. magazine. Badger Ordnance steel rings, USMC Spec. 34mm. Remington trigger tuned to 2.5 lbs. Matte black finish. 1/2 MOA Guarantee with match grade ammunition.
Price: **$4,990.00**

H&H PRECISION TEAM BUILD
Calibers: Popular long-range and custom calibers. **Capacity:** 10+1. **Barrels:** 16–24 in. **Weights:** 11+ lbs. **Stock:** Orias Chassis. Also Available with optional MDT Chassis. **Sights:** None. **Features:** The Orias Chassis is made from 7075-T651 Billet Aluminum making it stronger and lighter than other chassis on the market. No bedding is required due to a self-adjusting recoil lug locking system with front accessory rail. 20 MOA Mil Spec integral scope rail (Available in 0, 10, 20, 30 MOA). Barrel Contour – Medium Palma Fluted (Available in Heavy Palma, MTU, Varmint, Sendero). Barrel Length - 24 in. (Optional Barrel Lengths 16-28 in.) Overall Length – 43 in. using a standard 24-in. barrel. Coatings available. Trigger – Calvin Elite Adjustable 10 oz.–2.5 lbs. Muzzle Brake – Flat 3 Port/Anti-Muzzle Rise Port On Top. Muzzle Threads – 5/8 X 24 TPI (Fits Most Standard Suppressors & Muzzle Brakes).
Price: **$4,189.00**

H&H PRECISION RANGER
Calibers: Popular long-range and custom calibers. **Capacity:** 10+1. **Barrels:** 16–28 in. **Weights:** 11+ lbs. **Stock:** Orias Chassis. **Sights:** None. **Features:** Available in standard Ranger and Heavy Tactical configurations. Receiver – H&H Heavy Tactical. 20 MOA Mil Spec integral scope rail (Available in 0, 10, 20, 30 MOA). Barrel contour – medium palma fluted (available in heavy Palma, MTU, varmint, Sendero). Standard barrel length - 24 in. Overall length – 43 in. Coatings include Cerakote tiger stripe green/grey (other options available). Calvin Elite adjustable trigger 12 oz.–2.5 lbs. Muzzle Brake is flat 3 port/anti-muzzle rise port on top. Muzzle threads are 5/8X24 TPI (fits most standard suppressors & muzzle brakes).
Price: **$4,189.00**

H&H PRECISION ALPINE

Calibers: Popular long-range and custom calibers. **Capacity:** 10+1. **Barrels:** 16–28 in. **Weights:** 9+ lbs. **Stock:** Orias Chassis. **Sights:** None. **Features:** Similar to Team Build and Ranger models, only with Sendero contour barrel, and lighter overall weight.
Price: $4,189.00

H&H PRECISION SAND TIGER SERIES

Calibers: Popular long-range and custom calibers. **Capacity:** 10+1. **Barrels:** 16–28 in. **Weights:** 9+ lbs. **Stock:** Orias Chassis. **Sights:** None. **Features:** Similar to the lighter weight Alpine models, the ST-3 "Sand Tiger" is a popular choice for competitive shooters and comes with a ¼ MOA precision accuracy guarantee. Available in M-Lok and Key-Mod configurations the ST-3 accommodates a large variety of accessories.
Price: $4,189.00

H&H PRECISION TITANIUM TI-3 SERIES

Calibers: Popular long-range and custom calibers. **Capacity:** 10+1. **Barrels:** 16–28 in. **Weights:** 11+ lbs. **Stock:** Orias Chassis. **Sights:** None. **Features:** Similar to Team Build and Ranger models, only the TI-3 Series comes with the cerakoted "titanium" chassis and "graphite black" barreled action. The color combination is popular due to the contrast in colors bringing out a lot of definition. The TI-3 comes with a ¼ MOA precision accuracy guarantee. Available in Mlok and Key-Mod configurations, the TI-3 accommodates a large variety of accessories. TI-3 comes with the quick-disconnect night vision rail, which requires no tools to mount night vision or thermal adapters.
Price: $4,189.00

HOWA GRS

Calibers: .223 Rem, .22-250, .243 Win, 6mm Creedmoor, 6.5 Creedmoor, .308 Win. **Capacity:** 10+1. **Barrels:** 20, 24 or 26 in. **Weights:** 10.5–12.5 lbs. **Stock:** Black synthetic. **Sights:** None. **Features:** Howa 1500 heavy barreled action set in a GRS Berserk stock. Pillar bedded 15% fiberglass-reinforced Durethan. Optimized stock contour for use of rear bags. Rubberized grip and forend for better friction in wet conditions. Flush cup sling mounts and push button sling loops. Forend sling mount for mounting bipods.

Push button adjustment for comb height and length of pull. Distributed by Legacy Sports International.
Price: Varies by caliber/barrel length.......................... $1,199.00–$1,249.00

HOWA HCR

Calibers: .308 Win, .243 Win, 6mm Creedmoor, 6.5 Creedmoor, .300 Win. Mag. **Capacity:** 10+1. **Barrels:** 20, 24 and 26 in. **Weights:** 10.5–12.5 lbs. **Stock:** Black, flat dark earth, or camo synthetic. **Sights:** None. **Features:** 6061-T6 aluminum chassis made by Accurate-Mag w/ free-float M-LOK forend. LUTH-AR MBA-3 buttstock mounted on a 6-position buffer tube. Adjustable length-of-pull and comb. ERGO grip. 10-round, AI-style, Accurate-Mag detachable, teflon-coated, all-steel magazine. Available in threaded barrel options. Distributed by Legacy Sports International.
Price: Varies by caliber/barrel length........................... $1,149.00–$1,659.00

HOWA KRG BRAVO

Calibers: 6mm Creedmoor, 6.5mm Creedmoor, .308 Win. **Capacity:** 10+1. **Barrels:** 20, 24 or 26 in. **Weights:** 9.9–10.2 lbs. **Stock:** KRG stock. Black or flat dark earth synthetic. **Sights:** None. **Features:** KRG Bravo chassis, full-length aluminum center section for a rigid precision bedding surface. Lightweight precision rifle. Adjustable length of pull from 12.5–15.0 in. Adjustable comb height. 10-round AICS compatible magazine. Built-in butthook for rear bag use. Grip storage compartment. MLOK compatible forend. Distributed by Legacy Sports International.
Price: Varies by caliber/barrel length........................... $1,279.00–$1,339.00

H-S PRECISION PRO-SERIES 2000

Calibers: 30 different chamberings including virtually all popular calibers. Made in hunting, tactical and competition styles with many options. **Barrels:** 20 in., 22 in., 24 in. or 26 in. depending on model and caliber. Hunting models include the Pro-Hunter Rifle (PHR) designed for magnum calibers with built-in recoil reducer and heavier barrel; Pro-Hunter Lightweight (PHL) with slim, fluted barrel; Pro-Hunter Sporter (SPR) and Pro-Hunter Varmint (VAR). Takedown, Competition and Tactical variations are available. **Stock:** H-S Precision synthetic stock in many styles and colors with full-length bedding block chassis system. Made in USA
Price: PHR... $3,795.00
Price: PHL... $3,895.00
Price: SPR... $3,495.00
Price: SPL Sporter $3,595.00
Price: VAR... $3,595.00
Price: PTD Hunter Takedown.. $3,595.00
Price: STR Short Tactical $3,895.00
Price: HTR Heavy Tactical $3,895.00
Price: Competition... $3,895.00

Prices given are believed to be accurate at time of publication however, many factors affect retail pricing so exact prices are not possible.

KIMBER MODEL 8400 PATROL TACTICAL

Calibers: .308 Win., .300 Win. Mag. **Capacity:** 5. **Barrel:** 24 in. **Weight:** 8.5 lbs. **Length:** 43.25 in. **Stock:** Reinforced carbon fiber. **Sights:** None; drilled and tapped for bases. **Features:** Mauser claw extractor, two-position wing safety, action bedded on aluminum pillars and fiberglass, free-floated barrel, match-grade adjustable trigger set at 3-3.5 lbs., matte finish. Front swivel stud only for bipod. Stainless steel bull barrel, 24 in. heavy sporter barrel wih 1:12 twist. Made in USA by Kimber Mfg. Inc.
Price: Patrol Tactical **$2,447.00**

KIMBER MODEL 84M

Calibers: .22-250 Rem., .204 Ruger, .223 Rem., .243 Win., .257 Roberts., .260 Rem., 7mm-08 Rem., .308 Win. **Capacity:** 5. **Barrels:** 22 in., 24 in., 26 in. **Weight:** 5 lbs., 10 oz.–10 lbs. **Lengths:** 41–45 in. **Stock:** Claro walnut, checkered with steel grip cap; synthetic or gray laminate. **Sights:** None; drilled and tapped for bases. **Features:** Mauser claw extractor, three-position wing safety, action bedded on aluminum pillars, free-floated barrel, match-grade trigger set at 4 lbs., matte blue finish. Includes cable lock. Introduced 2001. Montana (2008) has synthetic stock, Pachmayr Decelerator recoil pad, stainless steel 22-in. sporter barrel. Adirondack has Kevlar white/black Optifade Forest camo stock, 18-in. barrel with threaded muzzle, weighs less than 5 lbs. Made in USA by Kimber Mfg. Inc.
Price: Varmint **$1,291.00**

KIMBER ADVANCED TACTICAL SOC/SRC II

Calibers: 6.5 Creedmoor, .308 Win. SRC chambered only in .308. **Capacity:** 5-round magazine. **Barrel:** 22-in. (SOC) stainless steel, (18 in. (SRC) with threaded muzzle. **Stock:** Side-folding aluminum with adjustable comb. **Features:** Stainless steel action, matte black or Flat Dark Earth finish. 3-position Model 70-type safety.
Price: **$2,449.00**

MOSSBERG MVP SERIES

Caliber: .223/5.56 NATO. **Capacity:** 10-round AR-style magazines. **Barrels:** 16.25-in. medium bull, 20-in. fluted sporter. **Weight:** 6.5–7 lbs. **Stock:** Classic black textured polymer. **Sights:** Adjustable folding rear, adjustable blade front. **Features:** Available with factory mounted 3-9x32 scope, (4-16x50 on Varmint model). FLEX model has 20-in. fluted sporter barrel, FLEX AR-style 6-position adjustable stock. Varmint model has laminated stock, 24-in. barrel. Thunder Ranch model has 18-in. bull barrel, OD Green synthetic stock.
Price: Patrol Model...**$732.00**
Price: Patrol Model w/scope **$863.00**
Price: FLEX Model **$764.00**
Price: FLEX Model w/scope **$897.00**
Price: Thunder Ranch Model......................................**$755.00**
Price: Predator Model...**$732.00**
Price: Predator Model w/scope.................................**$872.00**
Price: Varmint Model..**$753.00**
Price: Varmint Model w/scope..................................**$912.00**
Price: Long Range Rifle (LR) **$974.00**

MOSSBERG PATRIOT

Calibers: .22-250, .243 Win., .25-06, .270 Win., 7mm-08, .7mm Rem., .308 Win., .30-06, .300 Win. Mag., .38 Win. Mag., .375 Ruger. **Capacities:** 4- or 5-round magazine. **Barrels:** 22-in. sporter or fluted. **Stock:** Walnut, laminate, camo or synthetic black. **Weights:** 7.5–8 lbs. **Finish:** Matte blued. **Sights:** Adjustable or none. Some models available with 3-9x40 scope. Other features include patented Lightning Bolt Action Trigger adjustable from 2 to 7 pounds, spiral-fluted bolt. Not all variants available in all calibers. Introduced in 2015.
Price: Walnut stock..**$438.00**
Price: Walnut with premium Vortex Crossfire scope **$649.00**
Price: Synthetic stock **$396.00**
Price: Synthetic stock with standard scope **$436.00**
Price: Laminate stock w/iron sights **$584.00**
Price: Deer THUG w/Mossy Oak Infinity Camo stock **$500.00**
Price: Bantam, From **$396.00**

MOSSBERG PATRIOT NIGHT TRAIN

Calibers: .308 Win. or .300 Win. Mag. **Features:** Tactical model with Silencerco Saker Muzzle brake, 6-24x50 scope with tactical turrets, green synthetic stock with Neoprene comb-raising kit. **Weight:** 9 lbs.
Price: Night Train with 6-24x50 scope **$811.00**

REMINGTON MODEL 700 SPS

Calibers: .22-250 Rem., 6.8 Rem SPC, .223 Rem., .243 Win., .270 Win., .270 WSM, 7mm-08 Rem., 7mm Rem. Mag., 7mm Rem. Ultra Mag., .30-06, .308 Win., .300 WSM, .300 Win. Mag., .300 Rem. Ultra Mag. **Barrels:** 20 in., 24 in. or 26 in. carbon steel. **Weights:** 7–7.6 lbs. **Lengths:** 39.6–46.5 in. overall. **Stock:** Black synthetic, sling swivel studs, SuperCell recoil pad. Woodtech model has walnut decorated synthetic stock with overmolded grip patterns. Camo stock available. **Sights:** None. **Barrel:** Bead-blasted 416 stainless steel. **Features:** Introduced 2005. SPS Stainless replaces Model 700 BDL Stainless Synthetic. Plated internal fire control component. SPS DM features detachable box magazine. SPS Varmint includes X-Mark Pro trigger, 26-in. heavy contour barrel, vented beavertail fore-end, dual front sling swivel studs. Made in U.S. by Remington Arms Co., Inc.
Price: From .... **$724.00–$838.00**

REMINGTON 700 SPS TACTICAL

Calibers: .223 .300 AAC Blackout and .308 Win. **Features:** 20-in. heavy-contour tactical-style barrel; dual-point pillar bedding; black synthetic stock with Hogue overmoldings; semi-beavertail fore-end; X-Mark Pro adjustable trigger system; satin black oxide metal finish; hinged floorplate magazine; SuperCell recoil pad.
Price: From .... **$788.00–$842.00**

REMINGTON 700 VTR A-TACS CAMO

Calibers: .223 and .308 Win. **Features:** ATACS camo finish overall; triangular contour 22-in. barrel has an integral muzzle brake; black overmold grips; 1:9 in. twist (.223 caliber), or 1:12 in. (.308) twist.
Price: $930.00

REMINGTON MODEL 700 VLS

Calibers: .204 Ruger, .223 Rem., .22-250 Rem., .243 Win., .308 Win. **Barrel:** 26-in. heavy contour barrel (0.820-in. muzzle O.D.), concave target-style barrel crown. **Weight:** 9.4 lbs. **Length:** 45.75 in. overall. **Stock:** Brown laminated stock, satin finish, with beavertail fore-end, grip cap, rubber buttpad. **Sights:** None. **Features:** Introduced 1995. Made in U.S. by Remington Arms Co., Inc.
Price: $1,056.00

REMINGTON MODEL 700 SENDERO SF II

Calibers: .25-06 Rem., .264 Win. Mag., 7mm Rem. Mag., 7mm Rem. Ultra Mag., .300 Win. Mag., .300 Rem. Ultra Mag. **Barrel:** Satin stainless 26-in. heavy contour fluted. **Weight:** 8.5 lbs. **Length:** 45.75 in. overall. **Stock:** Black composite reinforced with aramid fibers, beavertail fore-end, palm swell. **Sights:** None. **Features:** Aluminum bedding block. Drilled and tapped for scope mounts, hinged floorplate magazines. Introduced 1996. Made in U.S. by Remington Arms Co., Inc.
Price: $1,500.00

REMINGTON MODEL 700 VTR SERIES

Calibers: .204 Ruger, .22-250, .223 Rem., .243 Win., .308 Win. **Barrel:** 22-in. triangular counterbored with integrated muzzle brake. **Weight:** 7.5 lbs. **Length:** 41.625 in. overall. **Features:** Olive drab overmolded or Digital Tiger TSP Desert Camo stock with vented semi-beavertail fore-end, tactical-style dual swivel mounts for bipod, matte blue on exposed metal surfaces.
Price: From .... $825.00–$980.00

REMINGTON MODEL 700 VARMINT SF

Calibers: .22-250, .223, .220 Swift, .308 Win. **Barrel:** 26-in. stainless steel fluted. **Weight:** 8.5 lbs. **Length:** 45.75 in. **Features:** Synthetic stock with ventilated forend, stainless steel/trigger guard/floorplate, dual tactical swivels for bipod attachment.
Price: $991.00

REMINGTON MODEL 700 XCR TACTICAL

Calibers: .308 Win., .300 Win. Mag., 338 Lapua Mag. Detachable box magazine. **Barrel:** 26-in. varmint contour, fluted and free floating. **Features:** Tactical, long-range precision rifle with Bell & Carlson Tactical stock in OD Green, full-length aluminum bedding, adjustable X-Mark Pro trigger. Muzzle brake on .338 Lapua model.
Price: $1,540.00

REMINGTON 40-XB TACTICAL

Caliber: .308 Win. **Features:** Stainless steel bolt with Teflon coating; hinged floorplate; adjustable trigger; 27.25-in. tri-fluted 1:14 in. twist barrel; H-S Precision Pro Series tactical stock, black color with dark green spiderweb; two front swivel studs; one rear swivel stud; vertical pistol grip. From the Remington Custom Shop.
Price: $2,995.00

REMINGTON 40-XB RANGEMASTER

Calibers: Almost any caliber from .22 BR Rem. to .300 Rem. Ultra Mag. Single-shot or repeater. **Features:** Stainless steel bolt with Teflon coating; hinged floorplate; adjustable trigger; 27.25-in. tri-fluted 1:14 in. twist barrel; walnut stock. From the Remington Custom Shop.
Price: $2,595.00

REMINGTON 40-XS TACTICAL SERIES

Caliber: .338 Lapua Magnum. **Features:** 416 stainless steel Model 40-X 24-in. 1:12 in. twist barreled action; black polymer coating; McMillan A3 series stock with adjustable length of pull and adjustable comb; adjustable trigger and Sunny Hill heavy-duty, all-steel trigger guard; Tactical Weapons System has Harris bi-pod with quick adjust swivel lock, Leupold Mark IV 3.5-10x40 long range M1 scope with Mil-Dot reticle, Badger Ordnance all-steel Picatinny scope rail and rings, military hard case, Turner AWS tactical sling. From the Remington Custom Shop.
Price: .308 Win. $4,400.00
Price: .338 Lapua $4,950.00
Price: Tactical Weapons System, From $7,731.00

RUGER PRECISION RIFLE

Calibers: 6mm Creedmoor, 6.5 Creedmoor, .308 Win. **Capacity:** 10-round magazine. **Barrel:** Medium contour, 20 in. (.308), 24 in. (6.5). **Stock:** Folding with adjustable length of pull and comb height. Soft rubber buttplate, sling attachment points, Picatinny bottom rail. **Weight:** 9.7–11 lbs. **Features:** Three lug one-piece CNC-machined bolt with oversized handle, dual cocking cams; multi-magazine interface works with Magpul, DPMS, SR-25, M110, AICS and some M14 magazines; CNC-machined 4140 chrome-moly steel upper; Ruger Marksman adjustable trigger with wrench stored in bolt shroud; comes with two 10-round Magpul magazines. Introduced in 2016.
Price: $1,599.00
Price: With muzzle brake.. $1,799.00

RUGER GUNSITE SCOUT RIFLE

Caliber: .308 Win. **Capacity:** 10-round magazine. **Barrel:** 16.5 in. **Weight:** 7 lbs. **Length:** 38–39.5 in. **Stock:** Black laminate. **Sights:** Front post sight and rear adjustable. **Features:** Gunsite Scout Rifle is a credible rendition of Col. Jeff Cooper's "fighting carbine" scout rifle. The Ruger Gunsite Scout Rifle is a platform in the Ruger M77 family. While the Scout Rifle has M77 features such as controlled round feed and integral scope mounts (scope rings included), the 10-round detachable box magazine is the first clue this isn't your grandfather's Ruger rifle. The Ruger Gunsite Scout Rifle has a 16.5-in.

medium contour, cold hammer-forged, alloy steel barrel with a Mini-14 protected nonglare post front sight and receiver mounted, adjustable ghost ring rear sight for out-of-the-box usability. A forward-mounted Picatinny rail offers options in mounting an assortment of optics, including scout scopes available from Burris and Leupold, for "both eyes open" sighting and super-fast target acquisition.

Price: **$1,139.00**
Price: (stainless) **$1,199.00**

RUGER HAWKEYE

Calibers: .204 Ruger, .223 Rem., .243 Win., .270 Win., 6.5 Creedmoor, 7mm/08, 7mm Rem. Mag., .308 Win., .30-06, .300 Win. Mag., .338 Win. Mag., .375 Ruger, .416 Ruger. **Capacities:** 4-round magazine, except 3-round magazine for magnums; 5-round magazine for .204 Ruger and .223 Rem. **Barrels:** 22 in., 24 in. **Weight:** 6.75–8.25 lbs. **Length:** 42–44.4 in. overall. **Stock:** American walnut, laminate or synthetic. FTW has camo stock, muzzle brake. Long Range Target has adjustable target stock, heavy barrel. **Sights:** None furnished. Receiver has Ruger integral scope mount base, Ruger 1 in. rings. **Features:** Includes Ruger LC6 trigger, new red rubber recoil pad, Mauser-type controlled feeding, claw extractor, 3-position safety, hammer-forged steel barrels, Ruger scope rings. Walnut stocks have wrap-around cut checkering on the forearm, and more rounded contours on stock and top of pistol grips. Matte stainless all-weather version features synthetic stock. Hawkeye African chambered in .375 Ruger, .416 Ruger and has 23-in. blued barrel, checkered walnut stock, windage-adjustable shallow V-notch rear sight, white bead front sight. Introduced 2007.

Price: VT Varmint Target **$1,139.00**
Price: Long Range Target **$1,279.00**

SAKO TRG-22 TACTICAL RIFLE

Calibers: 6.5 Creedmoor, .308 Winchester (TRG-22). For TRG-22A1 add .260 Rem. TRG-42 only available in .300 Win. Mag., or .338 Lapua. **Features:** Target-grade Cr-Mo or stainless barrels with muzzle brake; three locking lugs; 60-degree bolt throw; adjustable two-stage target trigger; adjustable or folding synthetic stock; receiver-mounted integral 17mm axial optics rails with recoil stop-slots; tactical scope mount for modern three-turret tactical scopes (30 and 34 mm tube diameter); optional bipod. 22A1 has folding stock with two-hinge design, M-LOK fore-end, full aluminum middle chassis.

Price: TRG-22 .... **$3,495.00**
Price: TRG-22A1 .... **$6,725.00**
Price: TRG-42 .... **$4,550.00**

SAVAGE MODEL 25 VARMINTER

Calibers: .17 Hornet, .22 Hornet, .222 Rem., .204 Ruger, .223 Rem. **Capacity:** 4-round magazine. **Barrel:** 24-in. medium-contour fluted barrel with recessed target crown, free-floating sleeved barrel, dual pillar bedding. **Weight:** 8.25 lbs. **Length:** 43.75 in. overall. **Stock:** Brown laminate with beavertail-style fore-end. Thumbhole stock available. **Sights:** Weaver-style bases installed. **Features:** Diameter-specific action built around the .223 Rem. bolt head dimension. Three locking lugs, 60-degree bolt lift, AccuTrigger adjustable from 2.5–3.25 lbs. Walking Varminter has black synthetic or camo stock, 22-in. barrel. **Weight:** 7.15 lbs. **Length:** 41.75 in. Introduced 2008. Made in USA by Savage Arms, Inc.

Price: From .... **$774.00–$824.00**
Price: Walking Varminter .... **$619.00–$671.00**

SAVAGE MODEL 12 VARMINT/TARGET SERIES

Calibers: .204 Ruger, .223 Rem., .22-250 Rem. **Capacity:** 4-shot magazine. **Barrel:** 26 in. stainless barreled action, heavy fluted, free-floating and button-rifled barrel. **Weight:** 10 lbs. **Length:** 46.25 in. overall. **Stock:** Dual pillar bedded, low profile, black synthetic or laminated stock with extra-wide beavertail fore-end. **Sights:** None furnished; drilled and tapped for scope mounting. **Features:** Recessed target-style muzzle. AccuTrigger, oversized bolt handle, detachable box magazine, swivel studs. Model 112BVSS has heavy target-style prone laminated stock with high comb, Wundhammer palm swell, internal box magazine. Model 12VLP DBM has black synthetic stock, detachable

magazine, and additional chamberings in .243, .308 Win., .300 Win. Mag. Model 12FV has blued receiver. Model 12BTCSS has brown laminate vented thumbhole stock. Made in USA by Savage Arms, Inc.

Price: 12 FCV **$780.00**
Price: 12 BVSS **$1,146.00**
Price: 12 Varminter Low Profile (VLP) **$1,181.00**
Price: 12 Long Range Precision **$1,288.00**
Price: 12 BTCSS Thumbhole stock **$1,293.00**
Price: 12 Long Range Precision Varminter **$1,554.00**
Price: 12 F Class **$1,648.00**
Price: 12 Palma **$2,147.00**

SAVAGE MODEL 10 GRS

Calibers: 6.5 Creedmoor, .308 Win. **Stock:** Synthetic with adjustable comb, vertical pistol grip. **Sights:** None. Picatinny rail atop receiver. **Features:** Designed primarily for Law Enforcement. Detachable box magazine.
Price: **$1,450.00**

SAVAGE MODEL 10FP/110FP LAW ENFORCEMENT SERIES

Calibers: .223 Rem., .308 Win. (Model 10), 4-round magazine; .25-06 Rem., .300 Win. Mag., (Model 110), 3- or 4-round magazine. **Barrel:** 24 in.; matte blued free-floated heavy barrel and action. **Weight:** 6.5–6.75 lbs. **Length:** 41.75–43.75 in. overall (Model 10); 42.5–44.5 in. overall (Model 110). **Stock:** Black graphite/fiberglass composition, pillar-bedded, positive checkering. **Sights:** None furnished. Receiver drilled and tapped for scope mounting. **Features:** Black matte finish on all metal parts. Double swivel studs on the fore-end for sling and/or bipod mount. Right- or left-hand. Model 110FP introduced 1990. Model 10FP introduced 1998. Model 10FCP HS has HS Precision black synthetic tactical stock with molded alloy bedding system, Leupold 3.5-10x40 black matte scope with Mil Dot reticle, Farrell Picatinny Rail Base, flip-open lens covers, 1.25-in. sling with QD swivels, Harris bipod, Storm heavy-duty case. Made in USA by Savage Arms, Inc.

Price: Model 10FCP McMillan, McMillan fiberglass tactical stock.. **$1,591.00**
Price: Model 10FCP-HS HS Precision, HS Precision tactical stock ... **$1,315.00**
Price: Model 10FCP **$925.00**
Price: Model 10FLCP, left-hand model, standard stock
    or Accu-Stock **$975.00**
Price: Model 10FCP SR **$785.00**
Price: Model 10 Precision Carbine **$952.00**

SAVAGE 110 BA STEALTH

Calibers: .300 win, Mag., or .338 Lapua Mag. **Capacities:** Detachable 5- or 6-round box magazine. **Barrel:** 24 in. with threaded muzzle. **Stock:** Fab Defense GLR Shock buttstock, M-LOK fore-end. **Weight:** 11.125 lbs. **Features:** Adjustable AccuTrigger, Picatinny rail. Stealth Evolution has fluted heavy barrel, 10-round magazine, adjustable length of pull stock, Flat Dark Earth finish.

Price: Stealth **$1,484.00**
Price: Stealth, .338 Lapua **$1,624.00**
Price: Evolution **$1,999.00**
Price: Evolution, .338 Lapua **$2,149.00**

SAVAGE MODEL 110 TACTICAL

Caliber: .308 Win. **Capacity:** 10-round magazine. **Barrels:** 20 or 24 in. threaded and fluted heavy contour. **Weight:** 8.65 lbs. **Stock:** AccuStock with soft grip surfaces, AccuFit system. **Features:** Top Picatinny rail, right- or left-hand operation.

Price: **$784.00**
Price: Tactical Desert (6mm, 6.5 Creedmoor, FDE finish **$769.00**

SAVAGE MODEL 12 PRECISION TARGET SERIES BENCHREST

Calibers: .308 Win., 6.5x284 Norma, 6mm Norma BR. **Barrel:** 29-in. ultra-heavy. **Weight:** 12.75 lbs. **Length:** 50 in. overall. **Stock:** Gray laminate. **Features:** New Left-Load, Right-Eject target action, Target AccuTrigger adjustable from approx. 6 oz. to 2.5 lbs. oversized bolt handle, stainless extra-heavy free-floating and button-rifled barrel.
Price: **$1,629.00**

SAVAGE MODEL 12 PRECISION TARGET PALMA

Similar to Model 12 Benchrest but in .308 Win. only, 30-in. barrel, multi-adjustable stock, weighs 13.3 lbs.
Price: **$2,147.00**

SAVAGE MODEL 12 F CLASS TARGET RIFLE

Similar to Model 12 Benchrest but chambered in 6 Norma BR, 30-in. barrel, weighs 13.3 lbs.
Price: **$1,648.00**

SAVAGE MODEL 12 F/TR TARGET RIFLE

Similar to Model 12 Benchrest but in .308 Win. only, 30-in. barrel, weighs 12.65 lbs.
Price: **$1,538.00**

SAVAGE MODEL 112 MAGNUM TARGET

Caliber: .338 Lapua Magnum. Single shot. **Barrel:** 26-in. heavy with muzzle brake. **Stock:** Wood laminate. **Features:** AccuTrigger, matte black finish, oversized bolt handle, pillar bedding.
Price: **$1,177.00**

STEYR SCOUT

Calibers: .223, .243, 7mm-08, .308 Win. **Capacity:** 5- or 10-shot magazine. **Barrel:** 19 in. fluted. **Weight:** 6.5 lbs. **Length:** NA. **Stock:** Gray Zytel. **Sights:** Pop-up front and rear. **Features:** Luggage case, scout sling, two stock spacers, two magazines. Introduced 1998. Imported from Austria by Steyr Arms, Inc.
Price: **$1,725.00**

STEYR SSG08

Calibers: .243 Win., 7.62x51 NATO (.308Win), 7.62x63B (.300 Win Mag)., .338 Lapua Mag. **Capacity:** 10-round magazine. **Barrels:** 20, 23.6 or 25.6 in. **Stock:** Dural aluminum folding stock black with .280 mm long UIT-rail and various Picatinny rails. **Sights:** Front post sight and rear adjustable. **Features:** High-grade aluminum folding stock, adjustable cheekpiece and buttplate with height marking, and an ergonomical exchangeable pistol grip. Versa-Pod, muzzle brake, Picatinny rail, UIT rail on stock and various Picatinny rails on fore-end, and a 10-round HC-magazine. SBS rotary bolt

action with four frontal locking lugs, arranged in pairs. Cold-hammer-forged barrels are available in standard or compact lengths.
Price: **$5,899.00**

TIKKA T3X SERIES

Calibers: Virtually any popular chambering including .204 Ruger .222 Rem., .223 Rem., .243 Win., .25-06, 6.5x55 SE, .260 Rem., .270 Win., .260 WSM, 7mm-08, 7mm Rem. Mag., .308 Win., .30-06, .300 Win. Mag., .300 WSM. **Barrels:** 20, 22.4, 24.3 in. **Stock:** Checkered walnut, laminate or modular synthetic with interchangeable pistol grips. Newly designed recoil pad. **Features:** Offered in a variety of different models with many options. Left-hand models available. One minute-of-angle accuracy guaranteed. Introduced in 2016. Made in Finland by Sako. Imported by Beretta USA.
Price: Hunter from **$875.00**
Price: Lite from (shown) **$725.00**
Price: Varmint from **$950.00**
Price: Laminate stainless.. **$1,050.00**
Price: Forest... **$1,000.00**
Price: Tac A1 (shown).. **$1,899.00**
Price: Compact Tactical Rifle, From.................................. **$1,150.00**

WEATHERBY VANGUARD II SERIES

Calibers: .240, .257, and .300 Wby Mag. **Barrel:** 24 in. matte black. **Weights:** 7.5–8.75 lbs. **Lengths:** 44–46.75 in. overall. **Stock:** Raised comb, Monte Carlo, injection-molded composite stock. **Sights:** None furnished. **Features:** One-piece forged, fluted bolt body with three gas ports, forged and machined receiver, adjustable trigger, factory accuracy guarantee. Vanguard Stainless has 410-Series stainless steel barrel and action, bead blasted matte metal finish. Vanguard Deluxe has raised comb, semi-fancy-grade Monte Carlo walnut stock with maplewood spacers, rosewood fore-end and grip cap, polished action with high-gloss blued metalwork. Vanguard Synthetic Package includes Vanguard Synthetic rifle with Bushnell Banner 3-9x40 scope mounted and boresighted, Leupold Rifleman rings and bases, Uncle Mikes nylon sling, and Plano PRO-MAX injection-molded case. Sporter has Monte Carlo walnut stock with satin urethane finish, fineline diamond point checkering, contrasting rosewood fore-end tip, matte-blued metalwork. Sporter SS metalwork is 410 Series bead-blasted stainless steel. Vanguard Youth/Compact has 20 in. No. 1 contour barrel, short action, scaled-down nonreflective matte black hardwood stock with 12.5-in. length of pull, and full-size, injection-molded composite stock. Chambered for .223 Rem., .22-250 Rem., .243 Win., 7mm-08 Rem., .308 Win. Weighs 6.75 lbs.; OAL 38.9 in. Sub-MOA Matte and Sub-MOA Stainless models have pillar-bedded Fiberguard composite stock (Aramid, graphite unidirectional fibers and fiberglass) with 24-in. barreled action; matte black metalwork, Pachmayr Decelerator recoil pad. Sub-MOA Stainless metalwork is 410 Series bead-blasted stainless steel. Sub-MOA Varmint guaranteed to shoot 3-shot group of .99 in. or less when used with specified Weatherby factory or premium (non-Weatherby calibers) ammunition. Hand-laminated, tan Monte Carlo composite stock with black spiderwebbing; CNC-machined aluminum bedding block, 22 in. No. 3 contour barrel, recessed target crown. Varmint Special has tan injection-molded Monte Carlo composite stock, pebble grain finish, black spiderwebbing. 22 in. No. 3 contour barrel (.740-in. muzzle dia.), bead blasted matte black finish, recessed target crown. Back Country has two-stage trigger, pillar-bedded Bell & Carlson stock, 24-in. fluted barrel, three-position safety. WBY-X Series comes with choice of several contemporary camo finishes (Bonz, Black Reaper, Kryptek, Hog Reaper, Whitetail Bonz, Blaze, GH2 "Girls Hunt Too") and is primarily targeted to younger shooters. Made in USA.
Price: Vanguard Varmint Special....................................... **$849.00**
Price: H-Bar (tactical series) from .... **$1,149.00–$1,449.00**

ARMALITE AR-50
Caliber: .50 BMG **Barrel:** 31 in. **Weight:** 33.2 lbs. **Length:** 59.5 in. **Stock:** Synthetic. **Sights:** None furnished. **Features:** A single-shot bolt-action rifle designed for long-range shooting. Available in left-hand model. Made in USA by Armalite.
Price: $3,359.00

REMINGTON 40-XB RANGEMASTER TARGET
Calibers: 15 calibers from .22 BR Remington to .300 Win. Mag. **Barrel:** 27.25 in. **Weight:** 11.25 lbs. **Length:** 47 in. overall. **Stock:** American walnut, laminated thumbhole or Kevlar with high comb and beavertail fore-end stop. Rubber nonslip buttplate. **Sights:** None. Scope blocks installed. **Features:** Adjustable trigger. Stainless barrel and action. Receiver drilled and tapped for sights. Model 40-XB Tactical (2008) chambered in .308 Win., comes with guarantee of 0.75-in. maximum 5-shot groups at 100 yards. **Weight:** 10.25 lbs. Includes Teflon-coated stainless button-rifled barrel, 1:14 in. twist, 27.25-in. long, three longitudinal flutes. Bolt-action repeater, adjustable 40-X trigger and precision machined aluminum bedding block. Stock is H-S Precision Pro Series synthetic tactical stock, black with green web finish, vertical pistol grip. From Remington Custom Shop.
Price: 40-XB KS, aramid fiber stock, single shot $2,863.00
Price: 40-XB KS, aramid fiber stock, repeater $3,014.00
Price: 40-XB Tactical .308 Win. $2,992.00

REMINGTON 40-XBBR KS
Calibers: Five calibers from .22 BR to .308 Win. **Barrel:** 20 in. (light varmint class), 24 in. (heavy varmint class). **Weight:** 7.25 lbs. (light varmint class); 12 lbs. (heavy varmint class). **Length:** 38 in. (20-in. bbl.), 42 in. (24-in. bbl.). **Stock:** Aramid fiber. **Sights:** None. Supplied with scope blocks. **Features:** Unblued benchrest with stainless steel barrel, trigger adjustable from 1.5 lbs. to 3.5 lbs. Special 2-oz. trigger extra cost. Scope and mounts extra. From Remington Custom Shop.
Price: Single shot $3,950.00

REMINGTON 40-XC KS TARGET
Caliber: 7.62 NATO. **Capacity:** 5-shot. **Barrel:** 24 in., stainless steel. **Weight:** 11 lbs. without sights. **Length:** 43.5 in. overall. **Stock:** Aramid fiber. **Sights:** None furnished. **Features:** Designed to meet the needs of competitive shooters. Stainless steel barrel and action. From Remington Custom Shop.
Price: $3,067.00

SAKO TRG-22 BOLT-ACTION
Calibers: .308 Win., 10-shot magazine, .338 Lapua. **Capacity:** 5-round magazine. **Barrel:** 26 in. **Weight:** 10.25 lbs. **Length:** 45.25 in. overall. **Stock:** Reinforced polyurethane with fully adjustable cheekpiece and buttplate. **Sights:** None furnished. Optional quick-detachable, one-piece scope mount base, 1 in. or 30mm rings. **Features:** Resistance-free bolt, free-floating heavy stainless barrel, 60-degree bolt lift. Two-stage trigger is adjustable for length, pull, horizontal or vertical pitch. TRG-42 has similar features but has long action and is chambered for .338 Lapua. Imported from Finland by Beretta USA.
Price: TRG-22 .... $3,495.00
Price: TRG-22 with folding stock $6,075.00
Price: TRG-42 .... $4,445.00
Price: TRG-42 with folding stock $7,095.00

Prices given are believed to be accurate at time of publication however, many factors affect retail pricing so exact prices are not possible.

Tactical GunDigest® ⊕ **355**

BENELLI M2 TACTICAL

Gauge: 12 ga., 2 3/4 in., 3 in. **Capacity:** 5-round magazine. **Barrel:** 18.5 in. IC, M, F choke tubes. **Weight:** 6.7 lbs. **Length:** 39.75 in. overall. **Stock:** Black polymer. **Sights:** Rifle type ghost ring system, tritium night sights optional. **Features:** Semi-auto inertia recoil action. Cross-bolt safety; bolt release button; matte-finish metal. Introduced 1993. Imported from Italy by Benelli USA.

Price: From..$1,239.00–$1,359.00

BENELLI M3 TACTICAL

Gauge: 12 ga., 3 in. **Barrel:** 20 in. **Stock:** Black synthetic w/pistol grip. **Sights:** Ghost ring rear, ramp front. Convertible dual-action operation (semi-auto or pump).

Price: $1,599.00

BENELLI M4 TACTICAL

Gauge: 12 ga., 3 in. **Barrel:** 18.5 in. **Weight:** 7.8 lbs. **Length:** 40 in. overall. **Stock:** Synthetic. **Sights:** Ghost Ring rear, fixed blade front. **Features:** Auto-regulating gas-operated (ARGO) action, choke tube, Picatinny rail, standard and collapsible stocks available, optional LE tactical gun case. Introduced 2006. Imported from Italy by Benelli USA.

Price: From..$1,999.00

IAC MODEL 97T TRENCH GUN

Gauge: 12 ga., 2 3/4 in. **Barrel:** 20 in. with cylinder choke. **Stock:** Hand rubbed American walnut. **Features:** Replica of Winchester Model 1897 Trench Gun. Metal handguard, bayonet lug. Imported from China by Interstate Arms Corp.

Price: $465.00

KEL-TEC KSG BULL-PUP TWIN-TUBE

Gauge: 12 ga. **Capacity:** 13+1. **Barrel:** 18.5 in. **Overall Length:** 26.1 in. **Weight:** 8.5 lbs. (loaded). **Features:** Pump-action shotgun with two magazine tubes. The shotgun bears a resemblance to the South African designed Neostead pump-action gun. The operator is able to move a switch located near the top of the grip to select the right or left tube, or move the switch to the center to eject a shell without chambering another round. Optional accessories include a factory installed Picatinny rail with flip-up sights and a pistol grip. KSG-25 has 30-in. barrel and 20-round capacity magazine tubes.

Price: $990.00
Price: KSG-25 ....$1400.00

MOSSBERG MODEL 500 SPECIAL PURPOSE

Gauges: 12 ga., 20 ga., .410, 3 in. **Barrels:** 18.5 in., 20 in. (Cyl.). **Weight:** 7 lbs. **Stock:** Walnut-finished hardwood or black synthetic. **Sights:** Metal bead front. **Features:** Slide-action operation. Available in 6- or 8-round models. Top-mounted safety, double action slide bars, swivel studs, rubber recoil pad. Blue, Parkerized, Marinecote finishes. Mossberg Cablelock included. The HS410 Home Security model chambered for .410 with 3 in. chamber; has pistol grip fore-end, thick recoil pad, muzzle brake and has special spreader choke on the 18.5-in. barrel. Overall length is 37.5 in. Blued finish; synthetic field stock. Mossberg Cablelock and video included. Mariner model has Marinecote metal finish to resist rust and corrosion. Synthetic field stock; pistol grip kit included. 500 Tactical 6-shot has black synthetic tactical stock. Introduced 1990.

Price: 500 Mariner...$636.00
Price: HS410 Home Security.......................................$477.00
Price: Home Security 20 ga. $631.00
Price: FLEX Tactical ....$583.00–$630.00
Price: 500 Chainsaw pistol grip only; removable top handle $547.00
Price: JIC (Just In Case)..$500.00
Price: Thunder Ranch $514.00

MOSSBERG MODEL 500 SUPER BANTAM PUMP

Same as the Model 500 Sporting Pump except 12 or 20 ga., 22-in. vent rib Accu-Choke barrel with choke tube set; has 1 in. shorter stock, reduced length from pistol grip to trigger, reduced fore-end reach. Introduced 1992.
Price: $419.00
Price: Combo with extra slug barrel, camo finish $549.00

MOSSBERG 510 MINI BANTAM

Gauges: 20 ga., .410 bore, 3 in. **Barrel:** 18.5 in. vent-rib. **Weight:** 5 lbs. **Length:** 34.75 in. **Stock:** Synthetic with optional Mossy Oak Break-Up Infinity, Muddy Girl pink/black camo. **Features:** Available in either 20 ga. or .410 bore, the Mini features an 18.5-in. vent-rib barrel with dual bead sights. Parents don't have to worry about their young shooter growing out of this gun too quick, the adjustable classic stock can be adjusted from 10.5 to 11.5-in. length of pull so the Mini can grow with your youngster.

Price: From ....$419.00–$466.00

Prices given are believed to be accurate at time of publication however, many factors affect retail pricing so exact prices are not possible.

MOSSBERG MODEL 590 SPECIAL PURPOSE

Gauges: 12 ga., 20 ga., .410 3 in. **Capacity:** 9-round magazine. **Barrel:** 20 in. (Cyl.). **Weight:** 7.25 lbs. **Stock:** Synthetic field or Speedfeed. **Sights:** Metal bead front or Ghost Ring. **Features:** Slide action. Top-mounted safety, double slide action bars. Comes with heat shield, bayonet lug, swivel studs, rubber recoil pad. Blue, Parkerized or Marinecote finish. Shockwave has 14-inch heavy walled barrel, Raptor pistol grip, wrapped fore-end and is fully BATFE compliant. Magpul model has Magpul SGA stock with adjustable comb and length of pull. Mossberg Cablelock included. From Mossberg.

Price: From...$559.00
Price: Flex Tactical $672.00
Price: Tactical Tri-Rail Adjustable $879.00
Price: Mariner $756.00
Price: Shockwave $455.00
Price: MagPul 9-shot $836.00

MOSSBERG 930 SPECIAL PURPOSE SERIES

Gauge: 12 ga., 3 in. **Barrel:** 28 in. flat ventilated rib. **Weight:** 7.3 lbs. **Length:** 49 in.. **Stock:** Composite stock with close radius pistol grip; Speed Lock forearm; textured gripping surfaces; shim adjustable for length of pull, cast and drop; Mossy Oak Bottomland camo finish; Dura-Touch Armor Coating. **Features:** 930 Special Purpose shotguns feature a self-regulating gas system that vents excess gas to aid in recoil reduction and eliminate stress on critical components.

Price: Tactical 5-Round..$714.00
Price: Home Security $662.00
Price: Standard Stock..$787.00
Price: Pistol Grip 8-Round $883.00
Price: 5-Round Combo w/extra 18.5-in. barrel $679.00

REMINGTON MODEL 870 PUMP AND MODEL 1100 AUTOLOADER TACTICAL SHOTGUNS

Gauges: 870: 12 ga., 2 3/4 or 3 in.; 1100: 2 3/4 in. **Barrels:** 18 in., 20 in., 22 in. (Cyl or IC). **Weight:** 7.5–7.75 lbs. **Length:** 38.5–42.5 in. overall. **Stock:** Black synthetic, synthetic Speedfeed IV full pistol-grip stock, or Knoxx Industries SpecOps stock w/recoil-absorbing spring-loaded cam and adjustable length of pull (12 in. to 16 in., 870 only). **Sights:** Front post w/dot only on 870; rib and front dot on 1100. **Features:** R3 recoil pads, LimbSaver technology to reduce felt recoil, 2-, 3- or 4-round extensions based on barrel length; matte-olive-drab barrels and receivers. Model 1100 Tactical is available with Speedfeed IV pistol grip stock or standard black synthetic stock and fore-end. Speedfeed IV model has an 18-in. barrel with two-shot extension. Standard synthetic-stocked version is equipped with 22-in. barrel and four-round extension. Introduced 2006. From Remington Arms Co.

Price: 870 Express Tactical Knoxx 20 ga. $555.00
Price: 870 Express Magpul $898.00
Price: 870 Special Purpose Marine (nickel)......................$841.00
Price: 1100 TAC-4 ....$1,015.00

REMINGTON 870 EXPRESS TACTICAL A-TACS CAMO

Gauge: 12 ga., 2 3/4 and 3 in. **Features:** Pump-action shotgun. Full A-TACS digitized camo; 18.5-in. barrel; extended ported Tactical RemChoke;

SpeedFeed IV pistol-grip stock with SuperCell recoil pad; fully adjustable XS Ghost Ring Sight rail with removable white bead front sight; 7-round capacity with factory-installed 2-shot extension; drilled and tapped receiver; sling swivel stud.

Price: $720.00

REMINGTON 870 DM SERIES

Gauge: 12 ga. (2 3/4 in. and 3 in. interchangeably). **Capacity:** Detachable 6-round magazine. **Barrel:** 18.5-in. cylinder bore. **Stock:** Hardwood or black synthetic with textured gripping surfaces. Tac-14 DM model features short pistol grip buttstock and 14-inch barrel.

Price: $559.00

REMINGTON MODEL 870 EXPRESS TACTICAL

Similar to Model 870 but in 12 ga. only (2 3/4 in. and 3 in. interchangeably) with 18.5-in. barrel, Tactical RemChoke extended/ported choke tube, black synthetic buttstock and fore-end, extended magazine tube, gray powder coat finish overall. 38.5 in. overall length. Weighs 7.5 lbs.

Price: $601.00
Price: Model 870 TAC Desert Recon; desert camo stock
        and sand-toned metal surfaces $692.00
Price: Tactical Magpul $898.00

REMINGTON 887 NITRO MAG TACTICAL

Gauge: 12 ga., 2 3/4 to 3 1/2 in. **Features:** Pump-action shotgun,18.5-in. barrel with ported, extended tactical RemChoke; 2-shot magazine extension; barrel clamp with integral Picatinny rails; ArmorLokt coating; synthetic stock and fore-end with specially contour grip panels.

Price: $534.00

TRISTAR COBRA

Gauge: 12 ga., 3 in. **Barrel:** 28 in. **Weight:** 6.7 lbs. Three Beretta-style choke tubes (IC, M, F). **Length:** NA. **Stock:** Matte black synthetic stock and forearm. **Sights:** Vent rib with matted sight plane. **Features:** Five-year warranty. Cobra Tactical Pump Shotgun magazine holds 7, return spring in forearm, 20-in. barrel, Cylinder choke. Introduced 2008. Imported by Tristar Sporting Arms Ltd.

Price: Tactical...$319.00–$429.00

TRISTAR TEC12 AUTO/PUMP

Gauge: 12 ga. 3 in. **Barrel:** 20-in. ported barrel with fixed cylinder choke. Capable of operating in pump-action or semi-auto model with the turn of a dial. **Stock:** Pistol-grip synthetic with matte black finish. **Weight:** 7.4 lbs. **Sights:** Ghost-ring rear, raised bridge fiber-optic front. Picatinny rail.

Price: $689.00

Prices given are believed to be accurate at time of publication however, many factors affect retail pricing so exact prices are not possible.

Tactical GunDigest® ⟡ **357**

RETICLE DIRECTORY
BY MANUFACTURER

BURRIS
burrisoptics.com

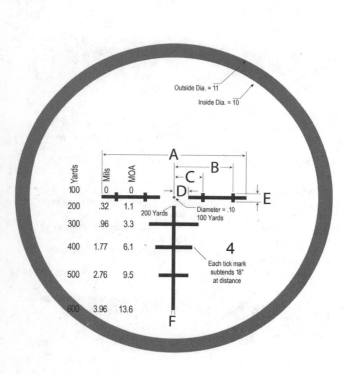

Yards	Mils	MOA
100	0	0
200	.32	1.1
300	.96	3.3
400	1.77	6.1
500	2.76	9.5
600	3.96	13.6

Outside Dia. = 11
Inside Dia. = 10
Diameter = .10
200 Yards
100 Yards
Each tick mark subtends 18" at distance

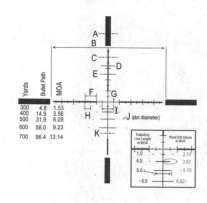

Yards	Bullet Path	MOA
300	4.8	1.53
400	14.9	3.56
500	31.9	6.09
600	58.0	9.23
700	96.4	13.14

(dot diameter)

Trajectory Line Length in MOA	Wind Drift Values in MOA
1.0	2.74
4.0	3.87
5.0	5.15
6.0	6.62

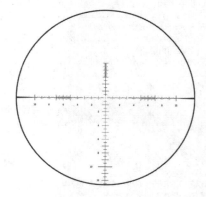

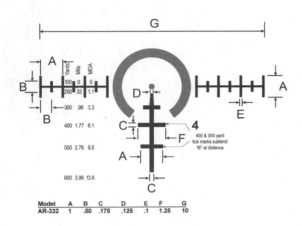

Model	A	B	C	D	E	F	G
AR-332	1	.50	.175	.125	.1	1.25	10

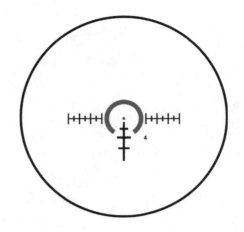

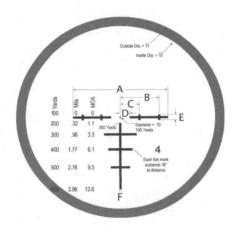

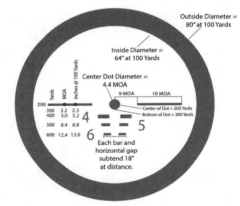

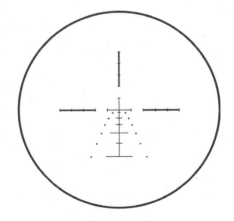

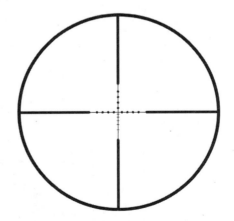

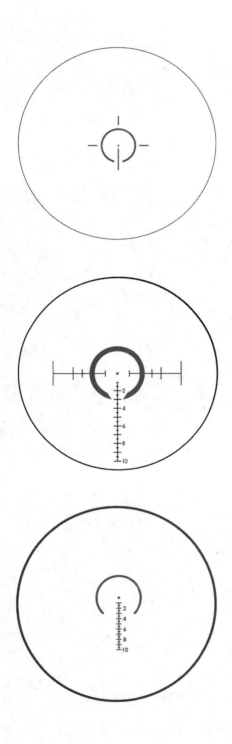

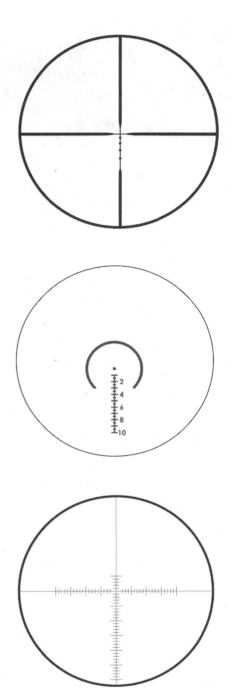

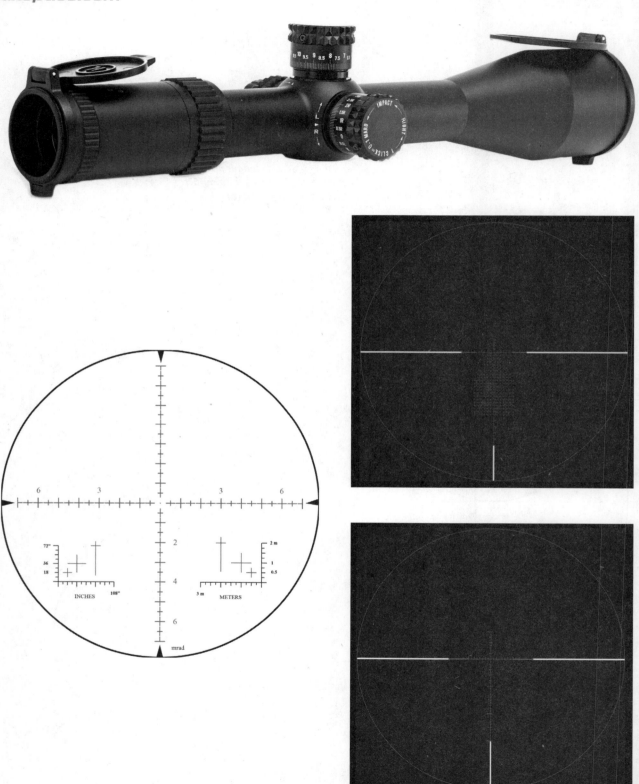

HORUSVISION
horusvision.com

Horus Vision no longer produces scopes, but its reticles are used in the optics of many major manufacturers, including Burris, Bushnell, Kahles, Nightforce and several others.

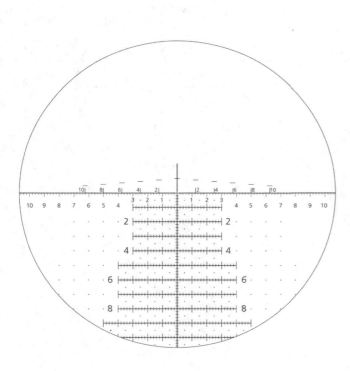

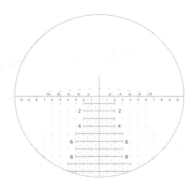

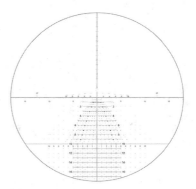

KAHLES

kahles.at/us/

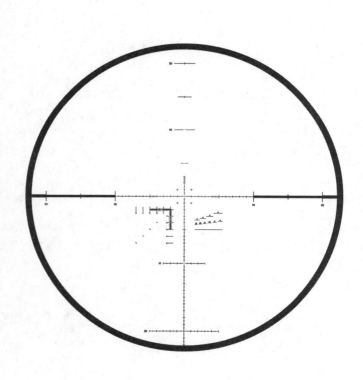

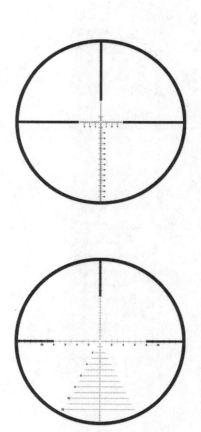

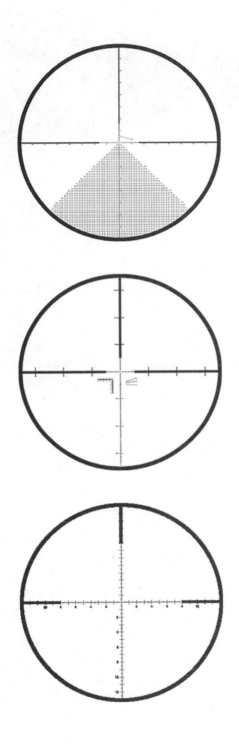

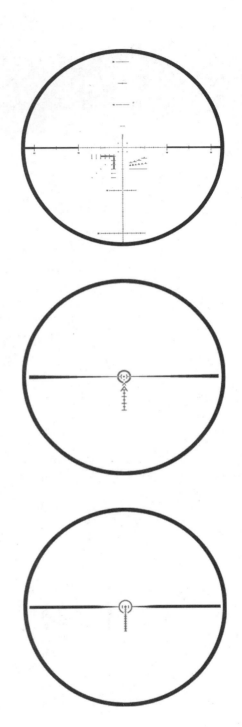

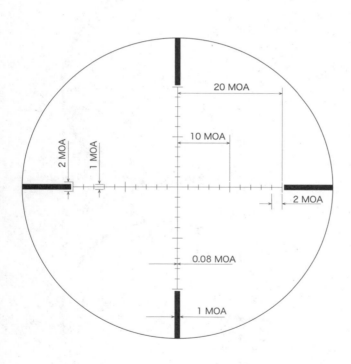

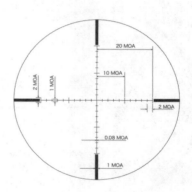

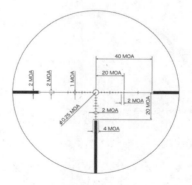

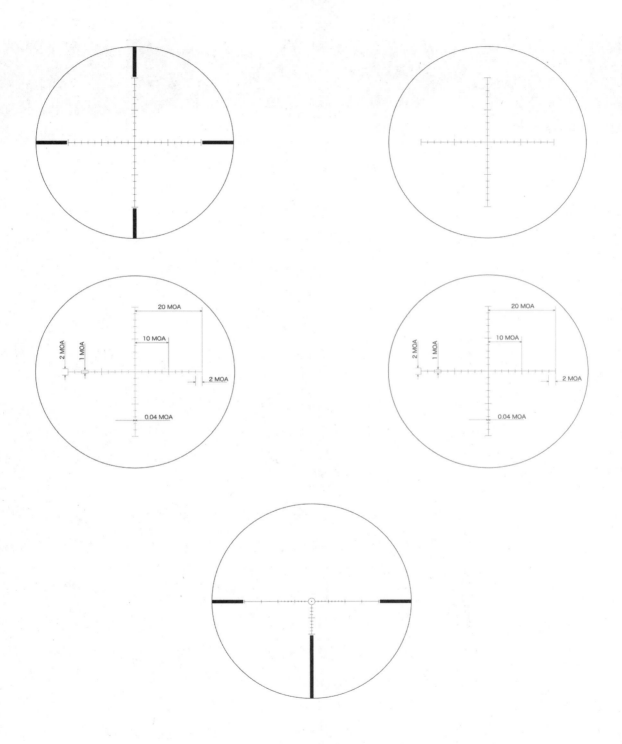

NIGHT FORCE
nightforceoptics.com

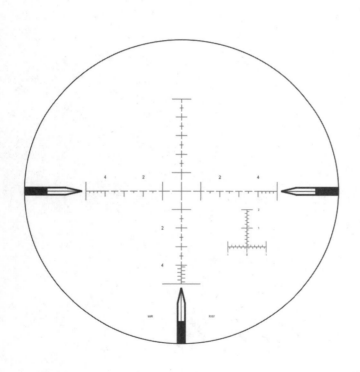

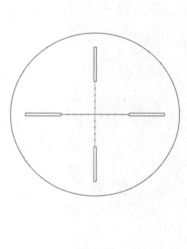

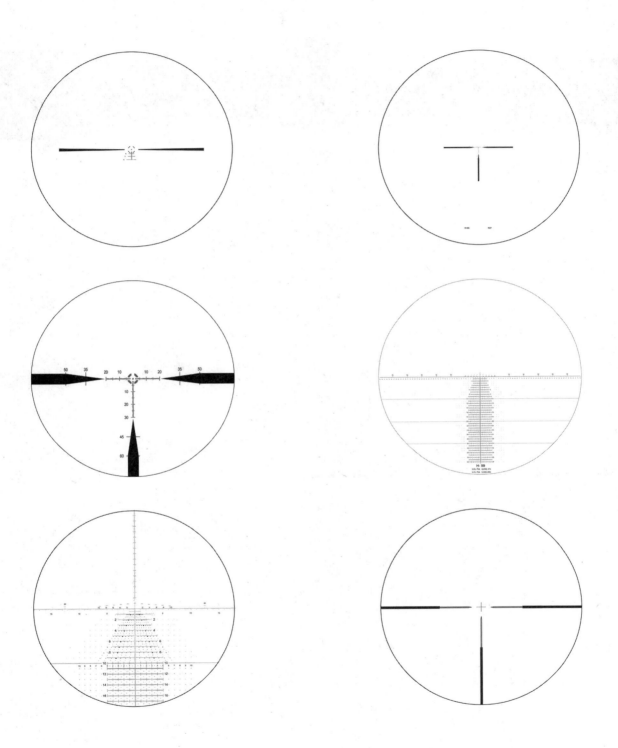

SCHMIDT & BENDER

schmidtundbender.de/en/

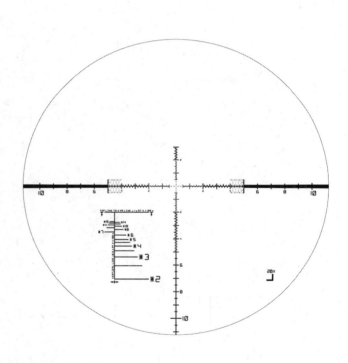

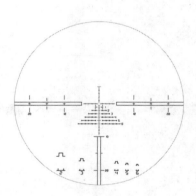

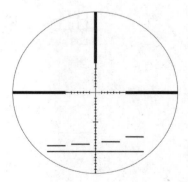

SIG
sigsauer.com

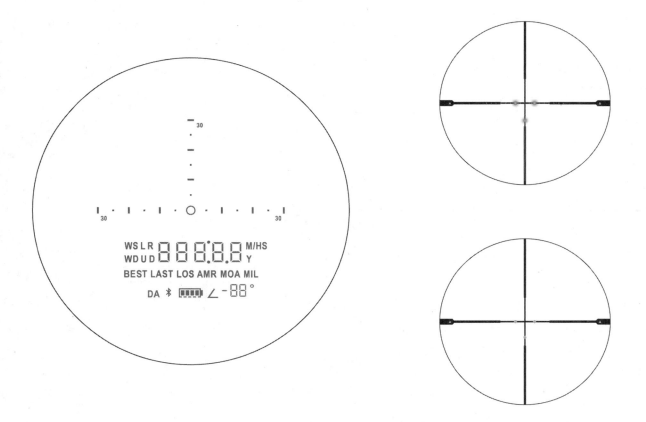

STEINER
steiner-optics.com

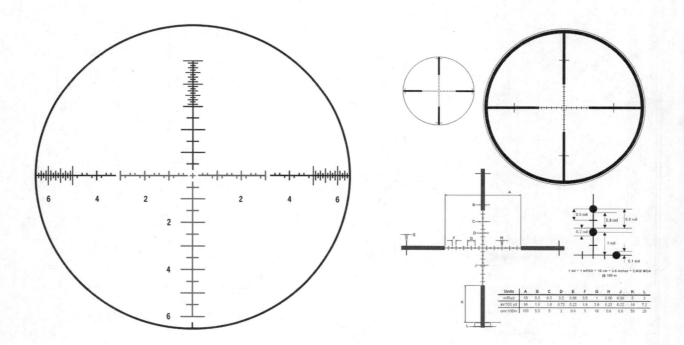

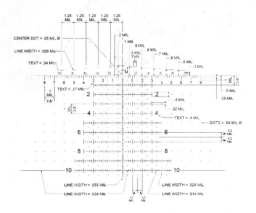

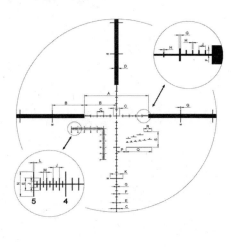

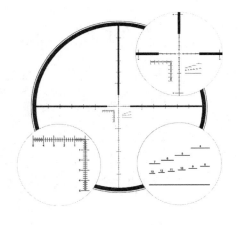

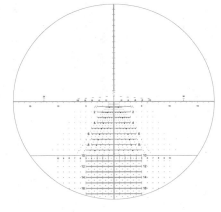

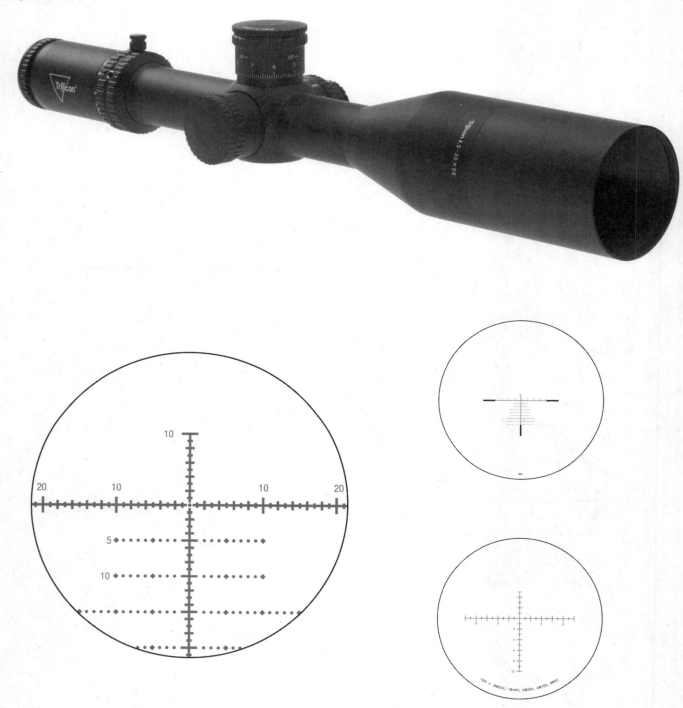

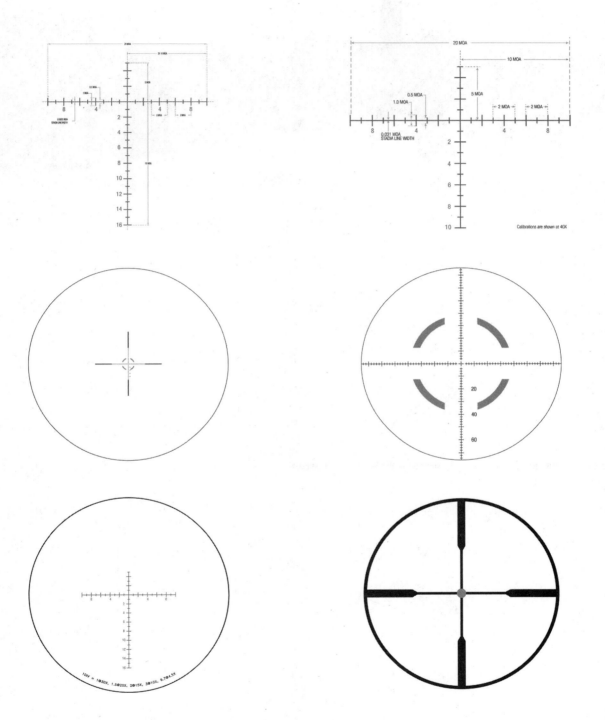

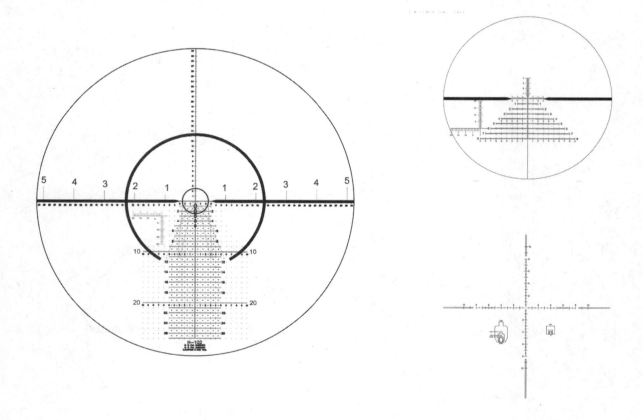

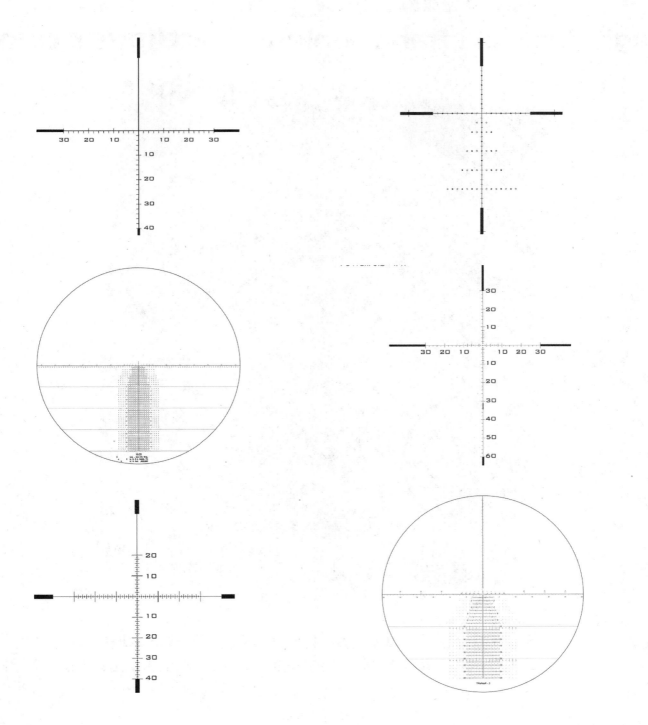

To see more reticles,
download your FREE
digital reticle handbook at gundigest.com.

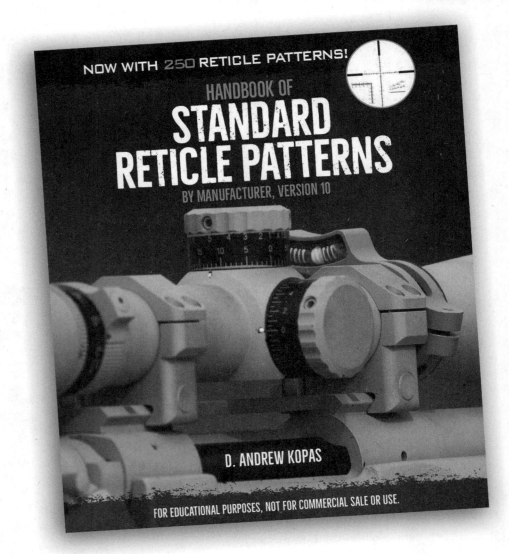

This handy 126-page reference contains diagrams of tactical reticles from all the major optics manufacturers.

Visit gundigest.com/reticlebook

THE Tactical Gun Digest
WEB DIRECTORY

AMMUNITION AND COMPONENTS

2 Monkey Trading **www.2monkey.com**

2nd Amendment Ammunition **www.secondammo.com**

Accurate Reloading Powders **www.accuratepowder.com**

Advanced Tactical **www.advancedtactical.com**

Aguila Ammunition **www.aguilaammo.com**

Alexander Arms **www.alexanderarms.com**

Alliant Powder **www.alliantpowder.com**

American Derringer Co. **www.amderringer.com**

American Eagle **www.federalpremium.com**

American Pioneer Powder **www.americanpioneerpowder.com**

American Specialty Ammunition **www.americanspecialityammo.com**

Ammo Depot **www.ammodepot.com**

Ammo Importers **www.ammoimporters.com**

Ammo-Up **www.ammoupusa.com**

Applied Ballistics Munitions **www.buyabmammo.com**

Arizona Ammunition, Inc. **www.arizonaammunition.net**

Armscor **www.us.armscor.com**

ASYM Precision Ammunition **www.asymammo.com**

Atesci **www.atesci.com**

Australian Munitions **www.australian-munitions.com**

B&T (USA) **www.bt-ag.ch**

Ballistic Products Inc. **www.ballisticproducts.com**

Barnes Bullets **www.barnesbullets.com**

Baschieri & Pellagri **www.baschieri-pellagri.com**

Berger Bullets, Ltd. **www.bergerbullets.com**

Berry's Mfg., Inc. **www.berrysmfg.com**

Big Bore Express **www.powerbeltbullets.com**

Black Hills Ammunition, Inc. **www.black-hills.com**

BlackHorn209 **www.blackhorn209.com**

Brenneke of America Ltd. **www.brennekeusa.com**

Browning **www.browning.com**

Buffalo Arms **www.buffaloarms.com**

Buffalo Bore Ammunition **www.buffalobore.com**

Buffalo Cartridge Co. **www.buffalocartridge.com**

Calhoon, James, Bullets **www.jamescalhoon.com**

Cartuchos Saga **www.saga.es**

Cast Performance Bullet **www.grizzlycartridge.com**

CCI **www.cci-ammunition.com**

Century International Arms **www.centuryarms.com**

Cheaper Than Dirt **www.cheaperthandirt.com**

Cheddite France **www.cheddite.com**

Claybuster Wads **www.claybusterwads.com**

Combined Tactical Systems **www.combinedsystems.com**

Cor-Bon/Glaser **www.corbon.com**

Creedmoor Sports **www.creedmoorsports.com**

Custom Cartridge **www.customcartridge.com**

Cutting Edge Bullets **www.cuttingedgebullets.com**

Dakota Arms **www.dakotaarms.com**

DDupleks, Ltd. **www.ddupleks.com**

Dead Nuts Manufacturing **www.deadnutsmfg.us**

Defense Technology Corp. **www.defense-technology.com**

Denver Bullets **www.denverbullets.com**

Desperado Cowboy Bullets **www.cowboybullets.com**

Dillon Precision **www.dillonprecision.com**

Double Tap Ammunition **www.doubletapammo.net**

Down Range Mfg. **www.downrangemfg.com**

Dynamic Research Technologies **www.drtammo.com**

E. Arthur Brown Co. **www.wabco.com**

EcoSlug **www.eco-slug.com**

Eley Ammunition **www.eley.co.uk**

Environ-Metal **www.hevishot.com**

Estate Cartridge **www.estatecartridge.com**

Federal Cartridge Co. **www.federalpremium.com**

Fiocchi of America **www.fiocchiusa.com**

G2 Research **www.g2rammo.com**

Gamebore Cartridge **www.gamebore.com**

GaugeMate **www.gaugemate.com**

Glaser Safety Slug, Inc. **www.corbon.com**

GOEX Inc. **www.goexpowder.com**

Graf & Sons **www.grafs.com**

Grizzly Cartridge Co. **www.grizzlycartridge.com**

Haendler & Natermann **www.hn-sport.de**

Hawk Bullets **www.hawkbullets.com**

Herter's Ammunition **www.cabelas.com**

Hevi.Shot **www.hevishot.com**

High Precision Down Range **www.hprammo.com**

Hodgdon Powder **www.hodgdon.com**

Hornady **www.hornady.com**

HSM Ammunition **www.thehuntingshack.com**

Huntington Reloading Products **www.huntingtons.com**

IMR Smokeless Powders **www.imrpowder.com**

International Cartridge Corp **www.iccammo.com**

J&G Sales **www.jgsales.com**

James Calhoon **www.jamescalhoon.com**

Kent Cartridge America **www.kentgamebore.com**

Knight Bullets **www.benchrest.com/knight/**

Lapua **www.lapua.com**

Lawrence Brand Shot **www.lawrencebrandshot.com**

Lazzeroni Arms **www.lazzeroni.com**

Leadheads Bullets **www.proshootpro.com**

Lehigh Defense **www.lehighdefense.com**

Lightfield Ammunition Corp **www.litfld.com**

Lyman **www.lymanproducts.com**

Magnum Muzzleloading Products **www.mmpsabots.com**

Magnus Bullets **www.magnusbullets.com**

MagSafe Ammo **www.magsafeonline.com**

Magtech **www.magtechammunition.com**

Meister Bullets **www.meisterbullets.com**

Midway USA **www.midwayusa.com**

Mitchell's Mausers **www.mauser.org**

National Bullet Co. **www.nationalbullet.com**

Navy Arms **www.navyarms.com**

Nobel Sport **www.nobelsportammo.com**

Norma **www.norma.cc**

North Fork Technologies **www.northforkbullets.com**

Nosler Bullets, Inc. **www.nosler.com**

Old Western Scrounger **www.ows-ammo.com**

Pattern Control **www.patterncontrol.com**

PCP Ammunition **www.pcpammo.com**

Piney Mountain Ammunition

www.pineymountainammunitionco.com

PMC **www.pmcammo.com**

PolyCase Ammunition **www.polycaseammo.com**

Polywad **www.polywad.com**

PowerBelt Bullets **www.powerbeltbullets.com**

PPU Ammunition **www.prvipartizan.com**

PR Bullets **www.prbullet.com**

Precision Delta **www.precisiondelta.com**

Precision Reloading **www.precisionreloading.com**

Pro Load Ammunition **www.proload.com**

Prvi Partizan Ammunition **www.prvipartizan.com**

Rainier Ballistics **www.rainierballistics.com**

Ram Shot Powder **www.ramshot.com**

Rare Ammunition **www.rareammo.com**

Reloading Specialties Inc. **www.reloadingspecialtiesinc.com**

Remington **www.remington.com**

Rio Ammunition **www.rioammo.com**

Rocky Mountain Cartridge **www.rockymountaincartride.com**

Sauvestre Ammunition **www.centuryarms.com**

SBR Ammunition **www.sbrammunition.com**

Schuetzen Powder **www.schuetzenpowder.com**

Sellier & Bellot **www.sellier-bellot.cz**

Shilen **www.shilen.com**

Sierra **www.sierrabullets.com**

SIG Sauer **www.sigammo.com**

Silver State Armory **www.ssarmory.com**

Simunition **www.simunition.com**

SinterFire, Inc. **www.sinterfire.com**

Spectra Shot **www.spectrashot.com**

Speer Ammunition **www.speer-ammo.com**

Speer Bullets **www.speer-bullets.com**

Sporting Supplies Int'l Inc. **www.wolfammo.com**

Starline **www.starlinebrass.com**

Stealth Gunpowder **www.stealthgunpowder.com**

Swift Bullets Co. **www.swiftbullets.com**

Tannerite **www.tannerite.com**

Tascosa Cartridge Co. **www.tascosacartridge.com**

Ted Nugent Ammunition **www.americantactical.us**

Ten-X Ammunition **www.tenxammo.com**

Top Brass **www.topbrass-inc.com**

TulAmmo **www.tulammousa.com**

Velocity Tactics **www.velocitytactics.com**

Vihtavuori **www.vihtavuori.com**

Weatherby **www.weatherby.com**

Western Powders Inc. **www.westernpowders.com**

Widener's Reloading & Shooters Supply **www.wideners.com**

Winchester Ammunition **www.winchester.com**

Windjammer Tournament Wads **www.windjammer-wads.com**

Wolf Ammunition **www.wolfammo.com**

Woodleigh Bullets **www.woodleighbullets.com.au**

Xtreme Bullets **www.xtremebullets.com**

Zanders Sporting Goods **www.gzanders.com**

CASES, SAFES, GUN LOCKS AND CABINETS

Ace Case Co. **www.acecase.com**

AG English Sales Co. **www.agenglish.com**

Dee Zee **www.deezee.com**

American Security Products **www.amsecusa.com**

Americase **www.americase.com**

Assault Systems **www.elitesurvival.com**

Avery Outdoors, Inc. **www.averyoutdoors.com**

Birchwood Casey **www.birchwoodcasey.com**

Bore-Stores **www.borestores.com**

Boyt Harness Co. **www.boytharness.com**

Gardall Safes **www.gardall.com**

Campbell Industrial Supply **www.gun-racks.com**

Cannon Safe Co. **www.cannonsafe.com**

Fort Knox Safes **www.ftknox.com**

Franzen Security Products **www.securecase.com**

Goldenrod Dehumidifiers **www.goldenroddehumidifiers.com**

Gunlocker Phoenix USA Inc. **www.gunlocker.com**

Gun Storage Solutions **www.storemoreguns.com**

GunVault **www.gunvault.com**

Hakuba USA Inc. **www.hakubausa.com**

Heritage Safe Co. **www.heritagesafe.com**

Homak Safes **www.homak.com**

Hunter Company **www.huntercompany.com**

Liberty Safe & Security **www.libertysafe.com**

Morton Enterprises **www.uniquecases.com**

New Innovative Products **www.starlightcases.com**

Pelican Products **www.pelican.com**

Phoenix USA Inc. **www.gunlocker.com**

Plano Molding Co. **www.planomolding.com**

Plasticase, Inc. **www.nanuk.com**

Rhino Safe **www.rhinosafe.com**

Rotary Gun Racks **www.gun-racks.com**

Sack-Ups **www.sackups.com**

Safe Tech, Inc. **www.safrgun.com**

Securecase **www.securecase.com**

Sentry Safe **www.sentrysafe.com**

Shot Lock Corp. **www.shotlock.com**

SKB Cases **www.skbcases.com**

Smart Lock Technology Inc. **www.smartlock.com**

Snap Safe **www.snapsafe.com**

Sportsmans Steel Safe Co. **www.sportsmansteelsafes.com**

Stack-On Safes **www.stackon.com**

Starlight Cases **www.starlightcases.com**

Strong Case **www.strongcasebytnb.com**

Technoframes **www.technoframes.com**

Titan Gun Safes **www.titangunsafes.com**

Tracker Safe **www.trackersafe.com**

T.Z. Case Int'l **www.tzcase.com**

U.S. Explosive Storage **www.usexplosivestorage.com**

Vanguard World **www.vanguardworld.com**

Versatile Rack Co. **www.versatilegunrack.com**

V-Line Industries **www.vlineind.com**

Winchester Safes **www.winchestersafes.com**

Ziegel Engineering **www.ziegeleng.com**

CHOKE DEVICES, RECOIL REDUCERS, SUPPRESSORS AND ACCURACY DEVICES

ACT Tactical **www.blackwidowshooters.com**

Advanced Armament Corp. **www.advanced-armament.com**

Alpha Dog Silencers **www.alphadogsilencers.com**

100 Straight Products **www.100straight.com**

Briley Mfg. **www.briley.com**

Carlson's **www.choketube.com**

Colonial Arms **www.colonialarms.com**

Comp-N-Choke **www.comp-n-choke.com**

Elite Iron **www.eliteiron.net**

Gemtech **www.gem-tech.com**

Great Lakes Tactical **www.gltactical.com**

KDF, Inc. **www.kdfguns.com**

Kick's Industries **www.kicks-ind.com**

LimbSaver **www.limbsaver.com**

Lyman Products **www.lymanproducts.com**

Mag-Na-Port Int'l Inc. **www.magnaport.com**

Metro Gun **www.metrogun.com**

Operators Suppressor Systems **www.osssuppressors.com**

Patternmaster Chokes **www.patternmaster.com**

Poly-Choke **www.polychoke.com**

SilencerCo **www.silencerco.com**

Silencer Shop **www.silencershop.com**

Sims Vibration Laboratory **www.limbsaver.com**

SRT Arms **www.srtarms.com**

SureFire **www.surefire.com**

Teague Precision Chokes **www.teaguechokes.com**

Truglo **www.truglo.com**

Trulock Tool **www.trulockchokes.com**

Vais Arms, Inc. **www.muzzlebrakes.com**

CHRONOGRAPHS AND BALLISTIC SOFTWARE

Barnes Ballistic Program **www.barnesbullets.com**

Ballisticard Systems **www.ballisticards.com**

Competition Electronics **www.competitionelectronics.com**

Competitive Edge Dynamics **www.cedhk.com**

Hodgdon Shotshell Program **www.hodgdon.com**

Lee Shooter Program **www.leeprecision.com**

NECO **www.neconos.com**

Oehler Research Inc. **www.oehler-research.com**

PACT **www.pact.com**

ProChrony **www.competitionelectronics.com**

Quickload **www.neconos.com**

RCBS Load **www.rcbs.com**

Shooting Chrony **www.shootingchrony.com**

Sierra Infinity Ballistics Program **www.sierrabullets.com**

Winchester Ballistics Calculator **www.winchester.com**

CLEANING PRODUCTS

Accupro **www.accupro.com**

Ballistol USA **www.ballistol.com**

Birchwood Casey **www.birchwoodcasey.com**

Bore Tech **www.boretech.com**

Break-Free, Inc. **www.break-free.com**

Bruno Shooters Supply **www.brunoshooters.com**

Butch's Bore Shine **www.butchsboreshine.com**

C.J. Weapons Accessories **www.cjweapons.com**

Clenzoil **www.clenzoil.com**

Corrosion Technologies **www.corrosionx.com**

Dewey Mfg. **www.deweyrods.com**

DuraCoat **www.lauerweaponry.com**

Emby Enterprises **www.alltemptacticallube.com**

Extreme Gun Care **www.extremeguncare.com**

G96 **www.g96.com**

Gun Butter **www.gunbutter.com**

Gun Cleaners **www.guncleaners.com**

Gunslick Gun Care **www.gunslick.com**

Gunzilla **www.topduckproducts.com**

Hoppes **www.hoppes.com**

Hydrosorbent Products **www.dehumidify.com**

Inhibitor VCI Products **www.theinhibitor.com**

Jag Brush **www.jagbrush.com**

KG Industries **www.kgcoatings.com**

L&R Ultrasonics **www.ultrasonics.com**

Lyman **www.lymanproducts.com**

Mil-Comm Products **www.mil-comm.com**

Montana X-Treme **www.montanaxtreme.com**

MPT Industries **www.mptindustries.com**

Mpro7 Gun Care **www.mp7.com**

Old West Snake Oil **www.oldwestsnakeoil.com**

Otis Technology, Inc. **www.otisgun.com**

Outers **www.outers-guncare.com**

Prolix Lubricant **www.prolixlubricant.com**

ProShot Products **www.proshotproducts.com**

ProTec Lubricants **www.proteclubricants.com**
Rigel Products **www.rigelproducts.com**
Sagebrush Products **www.sagebrushproducts.com**
Sentry Solutions Ltd. **www.sentrysolutions.com**
Shooters Choice Gun Care **www.shooters-choice.com**
Slip 2000 **www.slip2000.com**
Southern Bloomer Mfg. **www.southernbloomer.com**
Stony Point Products **www.unclemikes.com**
Top Duck Products, LLC **www.topduckproducts.com**
Triangle Patch **www.trianglepatch.com**
Wipe-Out **www.sharpshootr.com**
World's Fastest Gun Bore Cleaner **www.michaels-oregon.com**

FIREARM AUCTION SITES

Alderfer Auction **www.alderferauction.com**
Amoskeag Auction Co. **www.amoskeagauction.com**
Antique Guns **www.antiqueguns.com**
Auction Arms **www.auctionarms.com**
Batterman's Auctions **www.battermans.com**
Bonhams & Butterfields **www.bonhams.com/usarms**
Cowan's **www.cowans.com**
Fontaine's Auction Gallery **www.fontainesauction.net**
Guns America **www.gunsamerica.com**
Gun Broker **www.gunbroker.com**
Guns International **www.gunsinternational.com**
Heritage Auction Galleries **www.ha.com**
James D. Julia, Inc. **www.jamesdjulia.com**
Little John's Auction Service **www.littlejohnsauctionservice.net**
Lock, Stock & Barrel Investments **www.lsbauctions.com**
Morphy Auctions **www.morphyauctions.com**
Poulin Auction Co. **www.poulinantiques.com**
Rock Island Auction Co. **www.rockislandauction.com**
Wallis & Wallis **www.wallisandwallis.org**

FIREARM MANUFACTURERS AND IMPORTERS

Accu-Tek **www.accu-tekfirearms.com**
Accuracy Int'l North America **www.accuracyinternational.com**
Adcor Defense **www.adcorindustries.com**
AGP Arms In. **www.agparms.com**

AIM **www.aimsurplus.com**
AirForce Airguns **www.airforceairguns.com**
Air Gun Inc. **www.airrifle-china.com**
Air Ordnance/Tippmann Armory **www.tippmannarmory.com**
Airguns of Arizona **www.airgunsofarizona.com**
Alexander Arms **www.alexanderarms.com**
America Remembers **www.americaremembers.com**
American Classic **www.americanclassic1911.com**
American Derringer Corp. **www.amderringer.com**
American Spirit Arms **www.americanspirtarms.com**
American Tactical Imports **www.americantactical.us**
American Classic **www.eagleimportsinc.com**
American Western Arms **www.awaguns.com**
Angstadt Arms **www.angstadtarms.com**
Anschutz **www.anschutz-sporters.com**
AR-7 Industries **www.ar-7.com**
Ares Defense Systems **www.aresdefense.com**
Armalite **www.armalite.com**
Armi Sport **www.armisport.com**
Armscor Precision Internationl **www.armscor.com**
Armscorp USA Inc. **www.armscorpusa.com**
Arrieta **www.arrietashotguns.com**
Arsenal Inc. **www.arsenalinc.com**
Atlanta Cutlery Corp. **www.atlantacutlery.com**
Atlas Gun Works **www.atlas-gunworks.com**
ATA Arms **www.ataarms.com**
Auto-Ordnance Corp. **www.tommygun.com**
AYA **www.aya-fineguns.com**
B&T (USA) **www.bt-ag.ch**
Ballard Rifles **www.ballardrifles.com**
Barrett Firearms Mfg. **www.barrettrifles.com**
Bat Machine Co. **www.batmachine.com**
Battle Arms Development **www.battlearmsdevelopment.com**
Beeman Precision Airguns **www.beeman.com**
Benelli USA Corp. **www.benelliusa.com**
Benjamin Sheridan **www.crosman.com**
Beretta U.S.A. **www.berettausa.com**
Bergara Rifles **www.bergararifles.com**
Bernardelli **www.bernardelli.com**
Bersa **www.bersa.com**

Bighorn Arms **www.bighornarms.com**

Big Horn Armory **www.bighornarmory.com**

Blaser Jagdwaffen Gmbh **www.blaser.de**

Bleiker **www.bleiker.ch**

Bond Arms **www.bondarms.com**

Borden Rifles, Inc. **www.bordenrifles.com**

Boss & Co. **www.bossguns.co.uk**

Bowen Classic Arms **www.bowenclassicarms.com**

Breda **www.bredafucili.com**

Briley Mfg. **www.briley.com**

BRNO Arms **www.cz-usa.com**

Brown, E. Arthur **www.eabco.com**

Brown, Ed Products **www.edbrown.com**

Brown, McKay **www.mckaybrown.com**

Browning **www.browning.com**

BRP Corp. **www.brpguns.com**

BUL Ltd. **www.bultransmark.com**

Bushmaster Firearms **www.bushmaster.com**

BWE Firearms **www.bwefirearms.com**

Cabot Guns **www.cabotguns.com**

Caesar Guerini USA **www.gueriniusa.com**

Calico **www.calicoweaponsystems.com**

Caracal **www.caracal-usa.com**

Carolina Arms Group **www.carolinaarmsgroup.com**

Caspian Arms, Ltd. **www.caspianarmsltd.com**

CDNN Sports **www.cdnnsports.com**

Century Arms **www.centuryarms.com**

Champlin Firearms **www.champlinarms.com**

Charles Daly **www.charlesdaly.com**

Charter Arms **www.charterfirearms.com**

CheyTac USA **www.cheytac.com**

Chiappa Firearms **www.chiappafirearms.com**

Christensen Arms **www.christensenarms.com**

Cimarron Firearms Co. **www.cimarron-firearms.com**

CK Arms/Freedom Gunworks **www.ckarms.com**

Clark Custom Guns **www.clarkcustomguns.com**

CMMG **www.cmmginc.com**

Cobalt Kinetics **www.cobaltarms.com**

Cobra Enterprises **www.cobrapistols.net**

Cogswell & Harrison **www.cogswellandharrison.com**

Collector's Armory, Ltd. **www.collectorsarmory.com**

Colt's Mfg Co. **www.colt.com**

Comanche **www.eagleimportsinc.com**

Connecticut Shotgun Mfg. Co. **www.connecticutshotgun.com**

Connecticut Valley Arms **www.cva.com**

Coonan, Inc. **www.coonaninc.com**

Cooper Firearms **www.cooperfirearms.com**

Core Rifle Systems **www.core15.com**

Corner Shot **www.cornershot.com**

CPA Rifles **www.singleshotrifles.com**

Crickett Rifles **www.crickett.com**

Crosman **www.crosman.com**

CVA **www.cva.com**

Cylinder & Slide Shop **www.cylinder-slide.com**

Czechp Int'l **www.czechpoint-usa.com**

CZ USA **www.cz-usa.com**

Daisy Mfg Co. **www.daisy.com**

Daniel Defense **www.danieldefense.com**

Dan Wesson **www.danwessonfirearms.com**

Dakota Arms Inc. **www.dakotaarms.com**

Desert Eagle **www.magnumresearch.com**

Detonics USA **www.detonicsdefense.com**

Devil Dog Arms **www.devildogarms.com**

Diamondback **www.diamondbackamerica.com**

Diana **www.diana-airguns.de**

Dixie Gun Works **www.dixiegunworks.com**

Double D Armory **www.ddarmory.com**

DoubleStar **www.star15.com**

Downsizer Corp. **www.downsizer.com**

DPMS, Inc. **www.dpmsinc.com**

DSA Inc. **www.dsarms.com**

Dumoulin **www.dumoulin-herstal.com**

EAA Corp. **www.eaacorp.com**

Eagle Imports, Inc. **www.eagleimportsinc.com**

Ed Brown Products **www.edbrown.com**

EMF Co. **www.emf-company.com**

Empty Shell **www.emptyshell.com**

E.R. Shaw **www.ershawbarrels.com**

European American Armory Corp. **www.eaacorp.com**

Evans, William **www.williamevans.com**

Excel Arms **www.excelarms.com**

Fabarm **www.fabarm.com**

Fausti USA **www.faustiusa.com**

FightLite Industries **www.fightlite.com**

Flint River Armory **www.flintriverarmory.com**

Flodman Guns **www.flodman.com**

FMK **www.fmkfirearms.com**

FN Herstal **www.fnherstal.com**

FN America **www.fnamerica.com**

FNH USA **www.fnhusa.com**

Franchi **www.franchiusa.com**

Franklin Armory **www.franklinarmory.com**

Freedom Arms **www.freedomarms.com**

Freedom Group, Inc. **www.freedom-group.com**

Galazan **www.connecticutshotgun.com**

Gambo Renato **www.renatogamba.it**

Gamo **www.gamo.com**

GA Precision **www.gaprecision.net**

Gary Reeder Custom Guns **www.reedercustomguns.com**

German Sport Guns **www.german-sport-guns.com**

Gibbs Rifle Company **www.gibbsrifle.com**

Glock **www.glock.com**

Griffin & Howe **www.griffinhowe.com**

Gunbroker.com **www.gunbroker.com**

Guncrafter Industries **www.guncrafterindustries.com**

Gun Room Co. **www.onlylongrange.com**

Hammerli **www.carl-walther.com**

Hardened Arms **www.hardenedarms.com**

Hatsan Arms Co. **www.hatsan.com.tr**

Heckler and Koch **www.hk-usa.com**

Heizer Defense **www.heizerdefense.com**

Henry Repeating Arms Co. **www.henryrepeating.com**

Heritage Mfg. **www.heritagemfg.com**

High Standard Mfg. **www.highstandard.com**

Hi-Point Firearms **www.hi-pointfirearms.com**

Holland & Holland **www.hollandandholland.com**

Honor Defense **www.honordefense.com**

Horizon Firearms **www.horizonfirearms.com**

Howa **www.howausa.com**

H&R 1871 Firearms **www.hr1871.com**

H-S Precision **www.hsprecision.com**

Hunters Lodge Corp. **www.hunterslodge.com**

Hudson Manufacturing **www.hudsonmfg.com**

Inland Arms **www.inland-mfg.com**

International Military Antiques, Inc. **www.ima-usa.com**

Inter Ordnance **www.interordnance.com**

ISSC, LLC **www.issc-austria.com**

Ithaca Gun Co. **www.ithacagun.com**

Iver Johnson Arms **www.iverjohnsonarms.com**

IWI US Inc. **www.iwi.us**

Izhevsky Mekhanichesky Zavod **www.baikalinc.ru**

James River Armory **www.jamesriverarmory.com**

Jarrett Rifles, Inc. **www.jarrettrifles.com**

Jesse James Firearms **www.jjfu.com**

J&G Sales, Ltd. **www.jgsales.com**

Johannsen Express Rifle **www.johannsen-jagd.de**

JP Enterprises, Inc. **www.jprifles.com**

Kahr Arms/Auto-Ordnance **www.kahr.com**

Kalashnikov USA **www.kalashnikov-usa.com**

KDF, Inc. **www.kdfguns.com**

KE Arms **www.kearms.com**

Keystone Sporting Arms **www.keystonesportingarmsllc.com**

Kifaru **www.kifaru.net**

Kimber **www.kimberamerica.com**

Kingston Armory **www.kingstonarmory.com**

Knight's Armament Co. **www.knightarmco.com**

Knight Rifles **www.knightrifles.com**

Kolar **www.kolararms.com**

Korth **www.korthwaffen.de**

Krebs Custom Guns **www.krebscustom.com**

Kriss **www.kriss-usa.com**

Krieghoff Int'l **www.krieghoff.com**

KY Imports, Inc. **www.kyimports.com**

K-VAR **www.k-var.com**

Larue **www.laruetactical.com**

Layke Tactical **www.layketactical.com**

Lazzeroni Arms Co. **www.lazzeroni.com**

Legacy Sports International **www.legacysports.com**

Legendary Arms Works **www.legendaryarmsworks.com**

Les Baer Custom, Inc. **www.lesbaer.com**

Lewis Machine & Tool Co. **www.lewismachine.net**

Linebaugh Custom Sixguns **www.customsixguns.com**

Lionheart **www.lionheartindustries.com**

Ljutic **www.ljuticgun.com**

Llama **www.eagleimportsinc.com**

LMT Defense **www.lmtdefense.com**

Lyman **www.lymanproducts.com**

LWRC Int'l **www.lwrci.com**

MAC **www.eagleimportsinc.com**

Magnum Research **www.magnumresearch.com**

Majestic Arms **www.majesticarms.com**

Marksman Products **www.marksman.com**

Marlin **www.marlinfirearms.com**

MasterPiece Arms **www.masterpiecearms.com**

Mauser **www.mauser.com**

McMillan Firearms **www.mcmillanfirearms.com**

Meacham Rifles **www.meachamrifles.com**

Merkel USA **www-die-jagd.de**

Milkor USA **www.milkorusainc.com**

Miltech **www.miltecharms.com**

MOA Maximum **www.moaguns.com**

MOA Precision **www.moaprecision.com**

Modern Weapon Systems **www.modernweaponsystems.com**

Montana Rifle Co. **www.montanarifleco.com**

Mossberg **www.mossberg.com**

Navy Arms **www.navyarms.com**

New England Arms Corp. **www.newenglandarms.com**

New England Custom Gun **www.newenglandcustomgun.com**

New Ultra Light Arms **www.newultralight.com**

Nighthawk Custom **www.nighthawkcustom.com**

North American Arms **www.northamericanarms.com**

Nosler **www.nosler.com**

O.F. Mossberg & Sons **www.mossberg.com**

Ohio Ordnance Works **www.ohioordnanceworks.com**

Olympic Arms **www.olyarms.com**

Osprey Defense **www.gaspiston.com**

Panther Arms **www.dpmsinc.com**

Pedersoli Davide & Co. **www.davide-pedersoli.com**

Perazzi **www.perazzi.com**

Pietta **www.pietta.it**

Piotti **www.piotti.com/en**

Pistol Dynamics **www.pistoldynamics.com**

PKP Knife-Pistol **www.sanjuanenterprise.com**

Pointer Shotguns **www.legacysports.com/catalog/pointer**

Power Custom **www.powercustom.com**

Precision Small Arm Inc. **www.precisionsmallarms.com**

Primary Weapons Systems **www.primaryweapons.com**

Proof Research **www.proofresearch.com**

PTR 91,Inc. **www.ptr91.com**

Purdey & Sons **www.purdey.com**

Pyramyd Air **www.pyramydair.com**

Quarter Minute Magnums **www.quarterminutemagnums.com**

Remington **www.remington.com**

Republic Forge **www.republicforge.com**

Rifles, Inc. **www.riflesinc.com**

Rigby **www.johnrigbyandco.com**

Ritter & Stark **www.ritterstark.com**

Riverman Gun Works **www.rivermangunworks.com**

Rizzini USA **www.rizziniusa.com**

RM Equipment, Inc. **www.40mm.com**

Robar Companies, Inc. **www.robarguns.com**

Roberts Defense **www.robertsdefense.com**

Robinson Armament Co. **www.robarm.com**

Rock Island Armory **www.armscor.com**

Rock River Arms, Inc. **www.rockriverarms.com**

Rossi Arms **www.rossiusa.com**

RUAG Ammotec **www.ruag.com**

Ruger **www.ruger.com**

Safety Harbor Firearms **www.safetyharborfirearms.com**

Sarco **www.sarcoinc.com**

Sarsilmaz Silah San **www.sarsilmaz.com**

Sauer & Sohn **www.sauer.de**

Savage Arms Inc. **www.savagearms.com**

Scattergun Technologies Inc. **www.wilsoncombat.com**

SCCY Firearms **www.sccy.com**

Schmeisser Gmbh **www.schmeisser-germany.de**

SD Tactical Arms **www.sdtacticalarms.com**

Searcy Enterprises **www.searcyent.com**

Seecamp **www.seecamp.com**

Shaw **www.ershawbarrels.com**

Shilen Rifles **www.shilen.com**

Shiloh Rifle Mfg. **www.shilohrifle.com**

Sig Sauer, Inc. **www.sigsauer.com**

Simpson Ltd. **www.simpsonltd.com**

SKB Shotguns **www.skbshotguns.com**

Smith & Wesson **www.smith-wesson.com**

Southeast Arms, Inc. **www.southeastarms.net**

Sovereign Shotguns **www.barrettrifles.com**

Springfield Armory **www.springfield-armory.com**

SPS **www.eagleimportsinc.com**

SSK Industries **www.sskindustries.com**

Stag Arms **www.stagarms.com**

Stevens **www.savagearms.com**

Steyr Arms, Inc. **www.steyrarms.com**

STI International **www.stiguns.com**

Stoeger Industries **www.stoegerindustries.com**

Strayer-Voigt Inc. **www.sviguns.com**

Sturm, Ruger & Company **www.ruger.com**

Surgeon Rifles **www.surgeonrifles.com**

Tactical Solutions **www.tacticalsol.com**

Tar-Hunt Slug Guns, Inc. **www.tarhunt.com**

Taser Int'l **www.taser.com**

Taurus **www.taurususa.com**

Tempco Mfg. Co. **www.tempcomfg.com**

Thompson/Center Arms **www.tcarms.com**

Tikka **www.tikka.fi**

Time Precision **www.benchrest.com/timeprecision**

TNW, Inc. **www.tnwfirearms.com**

Traditions **www.traditionsfirearms.com**

Tristar Sporting Arms **www.tristarsportingarms.com**

Turnbull Mfg. Co. **www.turnbullmfg.com**

Uberti **www.ubertireplicas.com**

Ultra Light Arms **www.newultralight.com**

Umarex **www.umarex.com**

U.S. Armament Corp. **www.usarmamentcorp.com**

Uselton Arms, Inc. **www.useltonarmsinc.com**

Valkyrie Arms **www.valkyriearms.com**

Vektor Arms **www.vektorarms.com**

Verney-Carron **www.verney-carron.com**

Volquartsen Custom Ltd. **www.volquartsen.com**

Warrior **www.warrior.co**

Walther USA **www.waltherarms.com**

Weapon Depot **www.weapondepot.com**

Weatherby **www.weatherby.com**

Webley and Scott Ltd. **www.webley.co.uk**

Westley Richards **www.westleyrichards.com**

Wild West Guns **www.wildwestguns.com**

William Larkin Moore & Co. **www.williamlarkinmoore.com**

Wilson Combat **www.wilsoncombat.com**

Winchester Rifles and Shotguns **www.winchesterguns.com**

GUN PARTS, BARRELS, AFTERMARKET ACCESSORIES

300 Below **www.300below.com**

Accuracy International of North America
www.accuracyinternational.us

Accuracy Speaks, Inc. **www.accuracyspeaks.com**

Accuracy Systems **www.accuracysystemsinc.com**

Accurate Airguns **www.accurateairguns.com**

Advantage Arms **www.advantagearms.com**

AG Composites **www.agcomposites.com**

Aim Surplus **www.aimsurplus.com**

American Spirit Arms Corp. **www.americanspiritarms.com**

Amhurst-Depot **www.amherst-depot.com**

Apex Gun Parts **www.apexgunparts.com**

Armaspec **www.armaspec.com**

Armatac Industries **www.armatac.com**

Arthur Brown Co. **www.eabco.com**

Asia Sourcing Corp. **www.asiasourcing.com**

Barnes Precision Machine **www.barnesprecision.com**

Bar-Sto Precision Machine **www.barsto.com**

Bellm TC's **www.bellmtcs.com**

Belt Mountain Enterprises **www.beltmountain.com**

Bergara Barrels **www.bergarabarrels.com**

Beyer Barrels **www.beyerbarrels.com**

Bighorn Arms **www.bighornarms.com**

Bill Wiseman & Co. **www.wisemanballistics.com**

Bluegrass Gun Works **www.rocksolidind.com**

Bravo Company USA **www.bravocompanyusa.com**

Briley **www.briley.com**

Brownells **www.brownells.com**

B-Square **www.b-square.com**

Buffer Tech **www.buffer-tech.com**

Bullberry Barrel Works **www.bullberry.com**

Bulldog Barrels **www.bulldogbarrels.com**

Bullet Central **www.bulletcentral.com**

Bushmaster Firearms/Quality Parts **www.bushmaster.com**

Butler Creek Corp **www.butlercreek.com**

Cape Outfitters Inc. **www.capeoutfitters.com**

Cavalry Arms **www.cavalryarms.com**

Caspian Arms Ltd. **www.caspianarms.com**

CDNN Sports **www.cdnnsports.com**

Cheaper Than Dirt **www.cheaperthandirt.com**

Chesnut Ridge **www.chestnutridge.com/**

Choate Machine & Tool Co. **www.riflestock.com**

Christie's Products **www.1022cental.com**

CJ Weapons Accessories **www.cjweapons.com**

Colonial Arms **www.colonialarms.com**

Comp-N-Choke **www.comp-n-choke.com**

Criterion Barrels **www.criterionbarrels.com**

Custom Gun Rails **www.customgunrails.com**

Cylinder & Slide Shop **www.cylinder-slide.com**

Dave Manson Precision Reamers **www.mansonreamers.com**

DC Machine **www.dcmachine.net**

Digi-Twist **www.fmtcorp.com**

Dixie Gun Works **www.dixiegun.com**

DPMS **www.dpmsinc.com**

D.S. Arms **www.dsarms.com**

E. Arthur Brown Co. **www.eabco.com**

Ed Brown Products **www.edbrown.com**

EFK/Fire Dragon **www.efkfiredragon.com**

E.R. Shaw **www.ershawbarrels.com**

FJ Fedderson Rifle Barrels **www.gunbarrels.net**

FTF Industries **www.ftfindustries.com**

Fulton Armory **www.fulton-armory.com**

Galazan **www.connecticutshotgun.com**

Gemtech **www.gem-tech.com**

Gentry, David **www.gentrycustom.com**

GG&G **www.gggaz.com**

Great Lakes Tactical **www.gltactical.com**

Green Mountain Rifle Barrels **www.gmriflebarrel.com**

Gun Parts Corp. **www.gunpartscorp.com**

Guntec USA **www.guntecusa.com**

Harris Engineering **www.harrisbipods.com**

Hart Rifle Barrels **www.hartbarrels.com**

Hastings Barrels **www.hastingsbarrels.com**

Heinie Specialty Products **www.heinie.com**

High Performance Firearms/Hiperfire **www.hiperfire.com**

HKS Products **www.hksspeedloaders.com**

Holland Shooters Supply **www.hollandguns.com**

H-S Precision **www.hsprecision.com**

100 Straight Products **www.100straight.c**

I.M.A. **www.ima-usa.com**

Jarvis, Inc. **www.jarvis-custom.com**

J&T Distributing **www.jtdistributing.com**

JP Enterprises **www.jprifles.com**

Keng's Firearms Specialties **www.versapod.com**

KG Industries **www.kgcoatings.com**

Kick Eez **www.kickeezproducts.com**

Kidd Triggers **www.coolguyguns.com**

KM Tactical **www.kmtactical.net**

Knoxx Industries **www.impactguns.com**

Krieger Barrels **www.kriegerbarrels.com**

K-VAR Corp. **www.k-var.com**

LaRue Tactical **www.laruetactical.com**

Les Baer Custom, Inc. **www.lesbaer.com**

Lilja Barrels **www.riflebarrels.com**

Lone Wolf Dist. **www.lonewolfdist.com**

Lothar Walther Precision Tools **www.lothar-walther.de**

M&A Parts, Inc. **www.mapartsinc.com**

Magna-Matic Defense **www.magna-matic-defense.com**

Magpul Industries Corp. **www.magpul.com**

Majestic Arms **www.majesticarms.com**

MEC-GAR USA **www.mec-gar.com**

Mech Tech Systems **www.mechtechsys.com**

Mesa Tactical **www.mesatactical.com**

Midway USA **www.midwayusa.com**

Model 1 Sales **www.model1sales.com**

New England Custom Gun Service

www.newenglandcustomgun.com

NIC Industries **www.nicindustries.com**

North Mfg. Co. **www.rifle-barrels.com**

Numrich Gun Parts Corp. **www.e-gunparts.com**

Osprey Defense LLC **www.gaspiston.com**

Pac-Nor Barrels **www.pac-nor.com**

Power Custom, Inc. **www.powercustom.com**

Precision Reflex **www.pri-mounts.com**

Promag Industries **www.promagindustries.com**

RCI-XRAIL **www.xrailbyrci.com**

Red Star Arms **www.redstararms.com**

River Bank Armory **www.riverbankarmory.com**

Riverman Gun Works **www.rivermangunworks.com**

Rock Creek Barrels **www.rockcreekbarrels.com**

Royal Arms Int'l **www.royalarms.com**

R.W. Hart **www.rwhart.com**

Sage Control Ordnance **www.sageinternationalltd.com**

Sarco Inc. **www.sarcoinc.com**

Scattergun Technologies Inc. **www.wilsoncombat.com**

Schuemann Barrels **www.schuemann.com**

Score High Gunsmithing **www.scorehi.com**

Shaw Barrels **www.ershawbarrels.com**

Shilen **www.shilen.com**

SilencerCo **www.silencerco.com**

Sims Vibration Laboratory **www.limbsaver.com**

Slide Fire **www.slidefire.com**

Smith & Alexander Inc. **www.smithandalexander.com**

Sprinco USA **www.sprinco.com**

Springfield Sporters, Inc. **www.ssporters.com**

STI Int'l **www.stiguns.com**

S&S Firearms **www.ssfirearms.com**

SSK Industries **www.sskindustries.com**

Sun Devil Mfg. **www.sundevilmfg.com**

Sunny Hill Enterprises **www.sunny-hill.com**

Tac Star **www.lymanproducts.com**

Tactical Innovations **www.tacticalinc.com**

Tactical Solutions **www.tacticalsol.com**

Tapco **www.tapco.com**

Triple K Manufacturing Co. Inc. **www.triplek.com**

Ultimak **www.ultimak.com**

Verney-Carron SA **www.verney-carron.com**

Vintage Ordnance **www.vintageordnance.com**

Vltor Weapon Systems **www.vltor.com**

Volquartsen Custom Ltd. **www.volquartsen.com**

W.C. Wolff Co. **www.gunsprings.com**

Weigand Combat Handguns **www.jackweigand.com**

Western Gun Parts **www.westerngunparts.com**

Wilson Arms **www.wilsonarms.com**

Wilson Combat **www.wilsoncombat.com**

XLR Industries **www.xlrindustries.com**

GUNSMITHING SUPPLIES AND INSTRUCTION

4-D Products **www.4-dproducts.com**

American Gunsmithing Institute
www.americangunsmith.com

Baron Technology **www.baronengraving.com**

Battenfeld Technologies **www.btibrands.com**

Bellm TC's **www.bellmtcs.com**

Blue Ridge Machinery & Tools
www.blueridgemachinery.com

Brownells, Inc. **www.brownells.com**

B-Square Co. **www.b-square.com**

Cerakote Firearm Coatings **www.ncindustries.com**

Clymer Mfg. Co. **www.clymertool.com**

Dem-Bart **www.dembartco.com**

Doug Turnbull Restoration **www.turnbullrestoration.com**

Du-Lite Corp. **www.dulite.com**

DuraCoat Firearm Finishes **www.lauerweaponry.com**

Dvorak Instruments **www.dvorakinstruments.com**

Gradiant Lens Corp. **www.gradientlens.com**

Grizzly Industrial **www.grizzly.com**

Gunline Tools **www.gunline.com**

Harbor Freight **www.harborfreight.com**

JGS Precision Tool Mfg. LLC **www.jgstools.com**

Mag-Na-Port International **www.magnaport.com**

Manson Precision Reamers **www.mansonreamers.com**

Midway USA **www.midwayusa.com**

Murray State College **www.mscok.edu**

New England Custom Gun Service
www.newenglandcustomgun.com

Olympus America Inc. **www.olympus.com**

Pacific Tool & Gauge **www.pacifictoolandgauge.com**

Penn Foster Career School **www.pennfoster.edu**

Pennsylvania Gunsmith School **www.pagunsmith.edu**

Piedmont Community College **www.piedmontcc.edu**

Precision Metalsmiths, Inc.

   www.precisionmetalsmiths.com

Sonoran Desert Institute **www.sdi.edu**

Trinidad State Junior College **www.trinidadstate.edu**

HANDGUN GRIPS

Ajax Custom Grips, Inc. **www.ajaxgrips.com**

Altamont Co. **www.altamontco.com**

Aluma Grips **www.alumagrips.com**

Barami Corp. **www.hipgrip.com**

Crimson Trace Corp. **www.crimsontrace.com**

Decal Grip **www.decalgrip.com**

Eagle Grips **www.eaglegrips.com**

Falcon Industries **www.ergogrips.net**

Handgun Grips **www.handgungrips.com**

Herrett's Stocks **www.herrettstocks.com**

Hogue Grips **www.hogueinc.com**

Kirk Ratajesak **www.kgratajesak.com**

N.C. Ordnance **www.gungrip.com**

Nill-Grips USA **www.nill-grips.com**

Pachmayr **www.pachmayr.com**

Pearce Grips **www.pearcegrip.com**

Rio Grande Custom Grips **www.riograndecustomgrips.com**

Talon Grips **www.talongrips.com**

Uncle Mike's **www.unclemikes.com**

HOLSTERS AND LEATHER PRODUCTS

Active Pro Gear **www.activeprogear.com**

Akah **www.akah.de**

Aker Leather Products **www.akerleather.com**

Alessi Distributor R&F Inc. **www.alessigunholsters.com**

Alien Gear Holsters **www.aliengearholsters.com**

Armor Holdings **www.holsters.com**

Bagmaster **www.bagmaster.com**

Barranti Leather **www.barrantileather.com**

Bianchi International **www.safariland.com/our-brands/bianchi**

Black Dog Machine **www.blackdogmachinellc.net**

Blackhawk Outdoors **www.blackhawk.com**

Blackhills Leather **www.blackhillsleather.com**

Boyt Harness Co. **www.boytharness.com**

Bravo Concealment **www.bravoconcealment.com**

Brigade Gun Leather **www.brigadegunleather.com**

Clipdraw **www.clipdraw.com**

Comp-Tac Victory Gear **www.comp-tac.com**

Concealed Carrie **www.concealedcarrie.com**

Concealment Shop Inc. **www.theconcealmentshop.com**

Coronado Leather Co. **www.coronadoleather.com**

Creedmoor Sports, Inc. **www.creedmoorsports.com**

Cross Breed Holsters **www.crossbreedholsters.com**

Deep Conceal **www.deepconceal.com**

Defense Security Products **www.thunderwear.com**

DeSantis Holster **www.desantisholster.com**

Dillon Precision **www.dillonprecision.com**

Don Hume Leathergoods, Inc. **www.donhume.com**

DSG Holsters **www.dssgarms.com**

Duty Smith **www.dutysmith.com**

Elite Survival **www.elitesurvival.com**

El Paso Saddlery **www.epsaddlery.com**

Fobus USA **www.fobusholster.com**

Frontier Gun Leather **www.frontiergunleather.com**

Galco **www.usgalco.com**

Gilmore's Sports Concepts **www.gilmoresports.com**

Gould & Goodrich **www.gouldusa.com**

High Noon Holsters **www.highnoonholsters.com**

Holsters.com **www.holsters.com**

Houston Gun Holsters **www.houstongunholsters.com**

Hunter Co. **www.huntercompany.com**

JBP/Master's Holsters **www.jbpholsters.com**

KJ Leather **www.kbarjleather.com**

KNJ **www.knjmfg.com**

Kramer Leather **www.kramerleather.com**

K-Rounds Holsters **www.krounds.com**

Mernickle Holsters **www.mernickleholsters.com**

Milt Sparks Leather **www.miltsparks.com**

Mitch Rosen Extraordinary Gunleather **www.mitchrosen.com**

N82 Tactical **www.n82tactical.com**

Pacific Canvas & Leather Co. **www.pacificcanvasandleather.com**

Pager Pal **www.pagerpal.com**

Phalanx Corp. **www.smartholster.com**

Purdy Gear **www.purdygear.com**

Safariland Ltd. Inc. **www.safariland.com**

Shooting Systems Group Inc. **www.shootingsystems.com**

Simply Rugged Holsters **www.simplyrugged.com**

Snagmag Magazine Holster **www.snagmag.com**

Sneaky Pete Holsters **www.sneakypete.com**

Skyline Tool Works **www.clipdraw.com**

Stellar Rigs **www.stellarrigs.com**

Talon Holsters **www.talonholsters.com**

Tex Shoemaker & Sons **www.texshoemaker.com**

The Outdoor Connection **www.outdoorconnection.com**

Tuff Products **www.tuffproducts.com**

Triple K Manufacturing Co. **www.triplek.com**

Urban Carry Holsters **www.urbancarryholsters.com**

Wilson Combat **www.wilsoncombat.com**

Wright Leatherworks **www.wrightleatherworks.com**

MISCELLANEOUS SHOOTING PRODUCTS

ADCO Sales **www.adcosales.com**

American Body Armor **www.americanbodyarmor.com**

AMI Defense w**ww.amidefense.com**

Ammo-Up **www.ammoupusa.com**

Battenfeld Technologies **www.btibrands.com**

Beartooth **www.beartoothproducts.com**

Burnham Brothers **www.burnhambrothers.com**

Collectors Armory **www.collectorsarmory.com**

Dead Ringer Hunting **www.deadringerhunting.com**

Deben Group Industries Inc. **www.deben.com**

E.A.R., Inc. **www.earinc.com**

ESP **www.espamerica.com**

Global Gun Safety **www.globalgunsafety.com**

GunSkins **www.gunskins.com**

Gunstands **www.gunstands.com**

Howard Leight Hearing Protectors **www.howardleight.com**

Hunters Specialities **www.hunterspec.com**

Johnny Stewart Wildlife Calls **www.hunterspec.com**

Joseph Chiarello Gun Insurance **www.guninsurance.com**

Mec-Gar USA **www.mec-gar.com**

Merit Corporation **www.meritcorporation.com**

Michaels of Oregon Co. **www.michaels-oregon.com**

Midway USA **www.midwayusa.com**

MT2, LLC **www.mt2.com**

MTM Case-Gard **www.mtmcase-gard.com**

Natchez Shooters Supplies **www.natchezss.com**

Oakley, Inc. **www.usstandardissue.com**

Plano Molding **www.planomolding.com**

Practical Air Rifle Training Systems **www.smallarms.com**

Pro-Ears **www.pro-ears.com**

Quantico Tactical **www.quanticotactical.com**

Santa Cruz Gunlocks **www.santacruzgunlocks.com**

Sergeants Gun Cleaner **www.sergeantsguncleaner.com**

Second Chance Body Armor Inc. **www.secondchance.com**

SilencerCo **www.silencerco.com**

Smart Lock Technologies **www.smartlock.com**

SportEAR **www.sportear.com**

Surefire **www.surefire.com**

Taser Int'l **www.taser.com**

Walker's Game Ear Inc. **www.walkersgameear.com**

MUZZLELOADING FIREARMS AND PRODUCTS

American Pioneer Powder **www.americanpioneerpowder.com**

Armi Sport **www.armisport.com**

Barnes Bullets **www.barnesbullets.com**

Black Powder Products **www.bpiguns.com**

Buckeye Barrels **www.buckeyebarrels.com**

Cabin Creek Muzzleloading **www.cabincreek.net**

CVA **www.cva.com**

Caywood Gunmakers **www.caywoodguns.com**

Davide Perdsoli & Co. **www.davide-pedersoli.com**

Dixie Gun Works, Inc. **www.dixiegun.com**

Goex Black Powder **www.goexpowder.com**

Green Mountain Rifle Barrel Co. **www.gmriflebarrel.com**

Gunstocks Plus **www.gunstocksplus.com**

Gun Works **www.thegunworks.com**

Honorable Company of Horners **www.hornguild.org**

Hornady **www.hornady.com**

Jedediah Starr Trading Co. **www.jedediah-starr.com**

Jim Chambers Flintlocks **www.flintlocks.com**

Knight Rifles **www.knightrifles.com**

Knob Mountain **www.knobmountainmuzzleloading.com**

The Leatherman **www.blackpowderbags.com**

Log Cabin Shop **www.logcabinshop.com**

L&R Lock Co. **www.lr-rpl.com**

Lyman **www.lymanproducts.com**

Muzzleload Magnum Products **www.mmpsabots.com**

Navy Arms **www.navyarms.com**

Nosler, Inc. **www.nosler.com**

Palmetto Arms **www.palmetto.it**

Parker Productions **www.parkerproductionsinc.com**

Pecatonica River **www.longrifles-pr.com**

Pietta **www.pietta.it**

Powerbelt Bullets **www.powerbeltbullets.com**

Precision Rifle Dead Center Bullets **www.prbullet.com**

R.E. Davis Co. **www.redaviscompany.com**

Rightnour Mfg. Co. Inc. **www.rmcsports.com**

Savage Arms, Inc. **www.savagearms.com**

Schuetzen Powder **www.schuetzenpowder.com**

TDC **www.tdcmfg.com**

Tennessee Valley Muzzleloading

  www.tennesseevalleymuzzleloading.com

Thompson Center Arms **www.tcarms.com**

Tiger Hunt Stocks **www.gunstockwood.com**

Track of the Wolf **www.trackofthewolf.com**

Traditions Performance Muzzleloading **www.traditionsfirearms.com**

Turnbull Restoration & Mfg. **www.turnbullmfg.com**

Vernon C. Davis & Co. **www.stonewallcreekoutfitters.com**

PUBLICATIONS, VIDEOS AND CDs

Arms and Military Press **www.skennerton.com**

A&J Arms Booksellers **www.ajarmsbooksellers.com**

American Cop **www.americancopmagazine.com**

American Gunsmithing Institute **www.americangunsmith.com**

American Handgunner **www.americanhandgunner.com**

American Hunter **www.nrapublications.org**

American Pioneer Video **www.americanpioneervideo.com**

American Rifleman **www.nrapublications.org**

Athlon Outdoors **www.athlonoptics.com**

Backwoodsman **www.backwoodsmanmag.com**

BLADE Magazine **www.blademag.com**

Blue Book Publications **www.bluebookinc.com**

Combat Handguns **www.combathandguns.com**

Concealed Carry **www.uscca.us**

Cornell Publications **www.cornellpubs.com**

Deer & Deer Hunting **www.deeranddeerhunting.com**

Field & Stream **www.fieldandstream.com**

Firearms News **www.firearmsnews.com**

FMG Publications **www.fmgpubs.com**

Fouling Shot **www.castbulletassoc.org**

Fur-Fish-Game **www.furfishgame.com**

George Shumway Publisher **www.shumwaypublisher.com**

Grays Sporting Journal **www.grayssportingjournal.com**

Gun Digest, The Magazine **www.gundigest.com**

Gun Digest Books **www.gundigeststore.com**

Gun Dog **www.gundogmag.com**

Gun Mag **www.thegunmag.com**

Gun Tests **www.gun-tests.com**

Gun Video **www.gunvideo.com**

Gun World **www.gunworld.com**

Guns & Ammo **www.gunsandammo.com**

GUNS Magazine **www.gunsmagazine.com**

Guns of the Old West **www.gunsoftheoldwest.com**

Handloader **www.riflemagazine.com**

Handguns **www.handguns.com**

Hendon Publishing Co. **www.hendonpub.com**

Heritage Gun Books **www.gunbooks.com**

Krause Publications **www.krause.com**

Law and Order **www.hendonpub.com**

Man at Arms **www.manatarmsbooks.com**

Muzzle Blasts **www.nmlra.org**

Muzzleloader **www.muzzleloadermag.com**

North American Whitetail **www.northamericanwhitetail.com**

On-Target Productions **www.ontargetdvds.com**

Outdoor Channel **www.outdoorchannel.com**

Outdoor Life **www.outdoorlife.com**

Petersen's Hunting **www.petersenshunting.com**

Police and Security News **www.policeandsecuritynews.com**

Police Magazine **www.policemag.com**

Primitive Arts Video **www.primitiveartsvideo.com**

Pursuit Channel **www.pursuitchannel.com**

Recoil Gun Magazine **www.recoilweb.com**

Rifle Magazine **www.riflemagazine.com**

Rifle Shooter Magazine **www.rifleshootermag.com**

Safari Press Inc. **www.safaripress.com**

Shoot! Magazine **www.shootmagazine.com**

Shooting Illustrated **www.nrapublications.org**

Shooting Industry **www.shootingindustry.com**

Shooting Times Magazine **www.shootingtimes.com**

Shooting Sports Retailer **www.shootingsportsretailer.com**

Shooting Sports USA **www.nrapublications.org**

Shop Deer Hunting **www.shopdeerhunting.com**

Shotgun Report **www.shotgunreport.com**

Shotgun Sports Magazine **www.shotgunsportsmagazine.com**

Single Shot Exchange **www.singleshotexchange.com**

Single Shot Rifle Journal **www.assra.com**

Skyhorse Publishing **www.skyhorsepublishing.com**

Small Arms Review **www.smallarmsreview.com**

Sporting Classics **www.sportingclassics.com**

Sports Afield **www.sportsafield.com**

Sportsman Channel **www.thesportsmanchannel.com**

Sportsmen on Film **www.sportsmenonfilm.com**

Standard Catalog of Firearms **www.gundigeststore.com**

Successful Hunter **www.riflemagazine.com**

SWAT Magazine **www.swatmag.com**

Trapper & Predator Caller **www.trapperpredatorcaller.com**

Turkey & Turkey Hunting **www.turkeyandturkeyhunting.com**

Varmint Hunter **www.varminthunter.com**

VSP Publications **www.gunbooks.com**

Wildfowl **www.wildfowlmag.com**

RELOADING TOOLS

21st Century Shooting **www.xxicsi.com**

Ballisti-Cast Mfg. **www.ballisti-cast.com**

Battenfeld Technologies **www.btibrands.com**

Black Hills Shooters Supply **www.bhshooters.com**

Bruno Shooters Supply **www.brunoshooters.com**

Buffalo Arms **www.buffaloarms.com**

CabineTree **www.castingstuff.com**

Camdex, Inc. **www.camdexloader.com**

CH/4D Custom Die **www.ch4d.com**

Corbin Mfg & Supply Co. **www.corbins.com**

Dillon Precision **www.dillonprecision.com**

Forster Precision Products **www.forsterproducts.com**

Gracey Trimmer **www.matchprep.com**

Harrell's Precision **www.harrellsprec.com**

Hornady **www.hornady.com**

Hunter's Supply, Inc. **wwwhunters-supply.com**

Huntington Reloading Products **www.huntingtons.com**

J & J Products Co. **www.jandjproducts.com**

Lead Bullet Technology **www.lbtmoulds.com**

Lee Precision, Inc. **www.leeprecision.com**

L.E. Wilson **www.lewilson.com**

Little Crow Gun Works **www.littlecrowgunworks.com**

Littleton Shotmaker **www.littletonshotmaker.com**

Load Data **www.loaddata.com**

Lyman **www.lymanproducts.com**

Mayville Engineering Co. (MEC) **www.mecreloaders.com**

Midway USA **www.midwayusa.com**

Montana Bullet Works **www.montanabulletworks.com**

NECO **www.neconos.com**

NEI **www.neihandtools.com**

Neil Jones Custom Products **www.neiljones.com**

New Lachaussee SA **www.lachaussee.com**

Ponsness/Warren **www.reloaders.com**

Precision Reloading **www.precisionreloading.com**

Quinetics Corp. **www.quineticscorp.com**

RCBS **www.rcbs.com**

Redding Reloading Equipment **www.redding-reloading.com**

Sinclair Int'l Inc. **www.sinclairintl.com**

Stealth Gunpowder **www.stealthgunpowder.com**

Stoney Point Products Inc. **www.stoneypoint.com**

Vickerman Seating Die **www.castingstuff.com**

RESTS— BENCH, PORTABLE, ATTACHABLE

Accu-Shot **www.accu-shot.com**

Battenfeld Technologies **www.btibrands.com**

Bench Master **www.bench-master.com**

B-Square **www.b-square.com**

Center Mass, Inc. **www.centermassinc.com**

Desert Mountain Mfg. **www.benchmasterusa.com**

DOA Tactical **www.doatactical.com**

Harris Engineering Inc. **www.harrisbipods**

KFS Industries **www.versapod.com**

Level-Lok **www.levellok.com**

Midway **www.midwayusa.com**

Rotary Gun Racks **www.gun-racks.com**

R.W. Hart **www.rwhart.com**

Sinclair Intl, Inc. **www.sinclairintl.com**

Shooting Bench USA **www.shootingbenchusa.com**

Stoney Point Products **www.stoneypoint.com**

Target Shooting **www.targetshooting.com**

SCOPES, SIGHTS, MOUNTS AND ACCESSORIES

Accumount **www.accumounts.com**

Accusight **www.accusight.com**

Advantage Tactical Sight **www.advantagetactical.com**

Aimpoint **www.aimpoint.com**

Aim Shot, Inc. **www.aimshot.com**

Aimtech Mount Systems **www.aimtech-mounts.com**

Alaska Arms, LLC **https://alaskaarmsllc.com**

Alpen Outdoor Corp. **www.alpenoutdoor.com**

American Technologies Network, Corp. **www.atncorp.com**

AmeriGlo, LLC **www.ameriglo.net**

ArmaLaser **www.armalaser.com**

Amerigun USA **www.amerigunusa.com**

Armament Technology, Inc. **www.armament.com**

ARMS **www.armsmounts.com**

Athlon Optics **www.athlonoptics.com**

ATN **www.atncorp.com**

Badger Ordnance **www.badgerordnance.com**

Barrett **www.barrettrifles.com**

Beamshot-Quarton **www.beamshot.com**

BKL Technologies, Inc. **www.bkltech.com**

BSA Optics **www.bsaoptics.com**

B-Square **www.b-square.com**

Burris **www.burrisoptics.com**

Bushnell Performance Optics **www.bushnell.com**

Carl Zeiss Optical Inc. **www.zeiss.com**

CenterPoint Precision Optics **www.centerpointoptics.com**

Centurion Arms **www.centurionarms.com**

C-More Systems **www.cmore.com**

Conetrol Scope Mounts **www.conetrol.com**

Crimson Trace Corp. **www.crimsontrace.com**

D&L Sports **www.disports.com**

DuraSight Scope Mounting Systems **www.durasight.com**

EasyHit, Inc. **www.easyhit.com**

EAW **www.eaw.de**

Elcan Optical Technologies **www.elcan. com**

Electro-Optics Technologies **www.eotech.com**

Elusive Technologies **www.elusivetechnologies.com**

EoTech **www.eotechinc.com**

Eurooptik Ltd. **www.eurooptik.com**

Field Sport Inc. **www.fieldsportinc.com**

GG&G **www.gggaz.com**

Gilmore Sports **www.gilmoresports.com**

Gradient Lens Corp. **www.gradientlens.com**

Guangzhou Bosma Corp. **www.bosmaoptics.com**

Hahn Precision **www.hahn-precision.com**

Hi-Lux Optics **www.hi-luxoptics.com**

HIVIZ **www.hivizsights.com**

Horus Vision **www.horusvision.com**

Huskemaw Optics **www.huskemawoptics.com**

Insight **www.insighttechnology.com**

Ironsighter Co. **www.ironsighter.com**

Kahles **www.kahlesusa.com**

KenSight **www.kensight.com**

Knight's Armament **www.knightarmco.com**

Konus **www.konus.com**

LaRue Tactical **www.laruetactical.com**

Lasergrips **www.crimsontrace.com**

LaserLyte **www.laserlytesights.com**

LaserMax Inc. **www.lasermax.com**

Laser Products **www.surefire.com**

Leapers, Inc. **www.leapers.com**

Leatherwood **www.hi-luxoptics.com**

Leica Camera Inc. **www.leica-camera.com**

Leupold **www.leupold.com**

Lewis Machine and Tool **www.lmtdefense.com**

Lewis Machine & Tool **www.lewismachine.net**

LightForce/NightForce USA **www.nightforceoptics.com**

LUCID LLC **www.mylucidgear.com**

Lyman **www.lymanproducts.com**

Lynx **www.b-square.com**

Matech **www.matech.net**

Marble's Gunsights **www.marblearms.com**

Meopta **www.meopta.com**

Meprolight **www.meprolight.com**

Mini-Scout-Mount **www.amegaranges.com**

Minox USA **www.minox.com**

Montana Vintage Arms **www.montanavintagearms.com**

Mounting Solutions Plus **www.mountsplus.com**

NAIT **www.nait.com**

Newcon International Ltd. **www.newcon-optik.com**

NG2 Defense **www.ng2defense.com**

Night Force Optics **www.nightforceoptics.com**

Night Ops Tactical **www.nightopstactical.com**

Night Optics USA, Inc. **www.nightoptics.com**

Night Owl Optics **www.nightowloptics.com**

Nikon Inc. **www.nikonhunting.com**

Nitehog **www.nitehog.com**

Nite Site LLC **www.darkwidowgear.com**

North American Integrated Technologies **www.nait.com**

Novak Sights **www.novaksights.com**

O.K. Weber, Inc. **www.okweber.com**

Optolyth-Optic **www.optolyth.de**

Precision Reflex **www.pri-mounts.com**

Pride Fowler, Inc. **www.rapidreticle.com**

Redfield **www.redfield.com**

Schmidt & Bender **www.schmidtundbender.de**

Scopecoat **www.scopecoat.com**

Scopelevel **www.scopelevel.com**

SIG Sauer **www.sigsauer.com**

Sightmark **www.sightmark.com**

Simmons **www.simmonsoptics.com**

S&K **www.scopemounts.com**

Springfield Armory **www.springfield-armory.com**

Steiner Optik **www.steiner-optics.com**

Sun Optics USA **www.sunopticsusa.com**

Sure-Fire **www.surefire.com**

SWATSCOPE **www.swatscope.com**

Talley Mfg. Co. **www.talleyrings.com**

Steve Earle Scope Blocks **www.steveearleproducts.com**

Swarovski Optik **www.swarovskioptik.com**

Tacomhq **www.tacomhq.com**

Tasco **www.tasco.com**

Tech Sights **www.tech-sights.com**

Trijicon Inc. **www.trijicon.com**

Trinity Force **www.trinityforce.com**

Troy Industries **www.troyind.com**

Truglo Inc. **www.truglo.com**

Ultimak **www.ultimak.com**

UltraDot **www.ultradotusa.com**

U.S. Night Vision **www.usnightvision.com**

U.S. Optics Technologies Inc. **www.usoptics.com**

Valdada-IOR Optics **www.valdada.com**

Viridian Green Laser Sights **www.viridiangreenlaser.com**

Vortex Optics **www.vortexoptics.com**

Warne **www.warnescopemounts.com**

Weaver Scopes **www.weaveroptics.com**

Wilcox Industries Corp **www.wilcoxind.com**

Williams Gun Sight Co. **www.williamsgunsight.com**

Wilson Combat **www.wilsoncombat.com**

XS Sight Systems **www.xssights.com**

Zeiss **www.zeiss.com**

SHOOTING ORGANIZATIONS, SCHOOLS AND MUSEUMS

Accuracy 1st, Inc. **www.accuracy1st.com**

Amateur Trapshooting Assoc. **www.shootata.com**

American Custom Gunmakers Guild **www.acgg.org**

American Gunsmithing Institute **www.americangunsmith.com**

American Pistolsmiths Guild **www.americanpistol.com**
American Single Shot Rifle Assoc. **www.assra.com**
American Snipers **www.americansnipers.org**
Assoc. of Firearm & Tool Mark Examiners **www.afte.org**
Autry National Center of the American West **www.theautry.org**
BATFE **www.atf.gov**
Boone and Crockett Club **www.boone-crockett.org**
Browning Collectors Association **www.browningcollectors.com**
Buffalo Bill Center of the West **www.centerofthewest.org**
Buckmasters, Ltd. **www.buckmasters.com**
Cast Bullet Assoc. **www.castbulletassoc.org**
Citizens Committee for the Right to Keep & Bear Arms
    www. ccrkba.org
Civilian Marksmanship Program **www.odcmp.com**
Colorado School of Trades **www.schooloftrades.edu**
Contemporary Longrifle Assoc. **www.longrifle.com**
Colt Collectors Assoc. **www.coltcollectors.com**
Cylinder & Slide Pistolsmithing Schools **www.cylinder-slide. com**
Ducks Unlimited **www.ducks.org**
4-H Shooting Sports Program **www.4-hshootingsports.org**
Fifty Caliber Shooters Assoc. **www.fcsa.org**
Firearms Coalition **www.nealknox.com**
Fox Collectors Association **www.foxcollectors.com**
Front Sight Firearms Training Institute **www.frontsight.com**
Garand Collectors Assoc. **www.thegca.org**
German Gun Collectors Assoc. **www.germanguns.com**
Gibbs Military Collectors Club **www.gibbsrifle.com**
Gun Clubs **www.associatedgunclubs.org**
Gun Owners Action League **www.goal.org**
Gun Owners of America **www.gunowners.org**
Gun Trade Asssoc. Ltd. **www.gtaltd.co.uk**
Gunsite Training Center, Inc. **www.gunsite.com**
Hunting and Shooting Sports Heritage Fund **www.hsshf.org**
I.C.E. Training **www.icetraining.us**
International Ammunition Assoc. **www.cartridgecollectors.org**
IWA **www.iwa.info**
International Defensive Pistol Assoc. **www.idpa.com**
International Handgun Metallic Silhouette Assoc. **www.ihmsa.org**
International Hunter Education Assoc. **www.ihea.com**
International Single Shot Assoc. **www.issa-schuetzen.org**
Ithaca Owners **www.ithacaowners.com**

Jews for the Preservation of Firearms Ownership **www.jpfo.org**
L.C. Smith Collectors Assoc. **www.lcsmith.org**
Lefever Arms Collectors Assoc. **www.lefevercollectors.com**
Mannlicher Collectors Assoc. **www.mannlicher.org**
Marlin Firearms Collectors Assoc. **www.marlin-collectors.com**
Mule Deer Foundation **www.muledeer.org**
Muzzle Loaders Assoc. of Great Britain **www.mlagb.com**
National 4-H Shooting Sports **www.4-hshootingsports.org**
National Association of Sporting Goods Wholesalers
    www.nasgw.org
National Benchrest Shooters Assoc. **www.nbrsa.com**
National Defense Industrial Assoc. **www.ndia.org**
National Cowboy & Western Heritage Museum
    www.nationalcowboymuseum.org
National Firearms Museum **www.nramuseum.org**
National Mossberg Collectors Assoc.
    www.mossbergcollectors.org
National Muzzle Loading Rifle Assoc. **www.nmlra.org**
National Rifle Association **www.nra.org**
National Rifle Association ILA **www.nraila.org**
National Shooting Sports Foundation **www.nssf.org**
National Tactical Officers Assoc. **www.ntoa.org**
National Wild Turkey Federation **www.nwtf.com**
NICS/FBI **www.fbi.gov**
North American Hunting Club **www.huntingclub.com**
Order of Edwardian Gunners (Vintagers) **www.vintagers.org**
Outdoor Industry Foundation
    www.outdoorindustryfoundation.org
Parker Gun Collectors Assoc. **www.parkerguns.org**
Pennsylvania Gunsmith School **www.pagunsmith.com**
Pheasants Forever **www.pheasantsforever.org**
Piedmont Community College **www.piedmontcc.edu**
Quail & Upland Wildlife Federation **www.quwf.net**
Quail Forever **www.quailforever.org**
Remington Society of America **www.remingtonsociety.com**
Right To Keep and Bear Arms **www.rkba.org**
Rocky Mountain Elk Foundation **www.rmef.org**
Ruffed Grouse Society **www.ruffedgrousesociety.org**
Ruger Collectors Assoc. **www.rugercollectorsassociation.com**
Ruger Owners & Collectors Society **www.rugersociety.com**
SAAMI **www.saami.org**

Safari Club International **www.scifirstforhunters.org**

Sako Collectors Club **www.sakocollectors.com**

Scholastic Clay Target Program

   www.sssfonline.org/scholasti-clay-target-program

Scholastic Shooting Sports Foundation **www.sssfonline.org**

Second Amendment Foundation **www.saf.org**

Shooting for Women Alliance

   www.shootingforwomenalliance. com

Sig Sauer Academy **www.sigsauer.com**

Single Action Shooting Society **www.sassnet.com**

Smith & Wesson Collectors Assoc. **www.theswca.org**

L.C. Smith Collectors Assoc. **www.lcsmith.org**

Steel Challenge Pistol Tournament **www.steelchallenge.com**

Students for Second Amendment **www.sf2a.org**

Sturgis Economic Development Corp.

   www.sturgisdevelopment.com

Suarez Training **www.warriortalk.com**

Tactical Defense Institute **www.tdiohio.com**

Tactical Life **www.tactical-life.com**

Thompson/Center Assoc.

   www.thompsoncenterassociation.org

Thunder Ranch **www.thunderranchinc.com**

Trapshooters Homepage **www.trapshooters.com**

Trinidad State Junior College **www.trinidadstate.edu**

United Sportsmen's Youth Foundation **www.usyf.com**

Universal Shooting Academy

   www.universalshootingacademy.com

U.S. Concealed Carry Association **www.uscca.us**

U.S. Fish and Wildlife Service **www.fws.gov**

U.S. Practical Shooting Assoc. **www.uspsa.org**

U.S. Sportsmen's Alliance **www.ussportsmen.org**

USA Shooting **www.usashooting.com**

Weatherby Collectors Assoc. **www.weatherbycollectors.com**

Wild Sheep Foundation **www.wildsheepfoundation.org**

Winchester Arms Collectors Assoc.

   www.winchestercollector.com

STOCKS, GRIPS, FORE-ENDS

10/22 Fun Gun **www.1022fungun.com**

Advanced Technology **www.atigunstocks.com**

AG Composites **www.agcomposites.com**

Battenfeld Technologies **www.btibrands.com**

Bell & Carlson, Inc. **www.bellandcarlson.com**

Butler Creek Corp **www.butlercreek.com**

Cadex **www.vikingtactics.com**

Calico Hardwoods, Inc. **www.calicohardwoods.com**

Choate Machine **www.riflestock.com**

Command Arms **www.commandarms.com**

C-More Systems **www.cmore.com**

D&L Sports **www.dlsports.com**

E. Arthur Brown Co. **www.eabco.com**

Fajen **www.battenfeldtechnologies.com**

Grip Pod **www.grippod.com**

Gun Stock Blanks **www.gunstockblanks.com**

Herrett's Stocks **www.herrettstocks.com**

High Tech Specialties **www.hightech-specialties.com**

Hogue Grips **www.getgrip.com**

Knight's Mfg. Co. **wwwknightarmco.com**

Knoxx Industries **www.blackhawk.com**

KZ Tactical **www.kleyzion.com**

LaRue Tactical **www.laruetactical.com**

Lewis Machine & Tool **www.lewismachine.net**

Magpul **www.magpul.com**

Manners Composite Stocks **www.mannersstocks.com**

McMillan Fiberglass Stocks **www.mcmfamily.com**

Phoenix Technology/Kicklite **www.kicklitestocks.com**

Precision Gun Works **www.precisiongunstocks.com**

Ram-Line **www.outers-guncare.com**

Richards Microfit Stocks **www.rifle-stocks.com**

Rimrock Rifle Stock **www.bordenrifles.com**

Royal Arms Gunstocks **www.royalarmsgunstocks.com**

Speedfeed **www.safariland.com**

Tango Down **www.tangodown.com**

TAPCO **www.tapco.com**

Slide Fire **www.slidefire.com**

Stocky's **www.stockysstocks.com**

Surefire **www.surefire.com**

Tiger-Hunt Curly Maple Gunstocks **www.gunstockwood.com**

UTG Pro **www.leapers.com**

Wenig Custom Gunstocks Inc. **www.wenig.com**

Wilcox Industries **www.wilcoxind.com**

Yankee Hill **www.yhm.net**

TARGETS AND RANGE EQUIPMENT

Action Target Co. **www.actiontarget.com**

Advanced Training Systems **www.atsusa.biz**

Alco Target **www.alcotarget.com**

Arntzen Targets **www.arntzentargets.com**

Birchwood Casey **www.birchwoodcasey.com**

Caswell Meggitt Defense Systems **www.mds-caswell.com**

Champion Traps & Targets **www.championtarget.com**

Custom Metal Products **www.custommetalprod.com**

Laser Shot **www.lasershot.com**

MGM Targets **www.mgmtargets.com**

MTM Products **www.mtmcase-gard.com**

National Muzzleloading Rifle Assoc. **www.nmlra.org**

National Target Co. **www.nationaltarget.com**

Newbold Target Systems **www.newboldtargets.com**

Paragon Tactical **www.paragontactical.com**

PJL Targets **www.pjltargets.com**

Savage Range Systems **www.savagerangesystems.com**

ShatterBlast Targets **www.daisy.com**

Super Trap Bullet Containment Systems **www.supertrap.com**

Thompson Target Technology **www.thompsontarget.com**

Thundershot Exploding Targets **www.gryphonenergetics.com**

Unique Tek **www.uniquetek.com**

Visible Impact Targets **www.crosman.com**

White Flyer **www.whiteflyer.com**

TRIGGERS

American Trigger Corp. **www.americantrigger.com**

Brownells **www.brownells.com**

Geissele Automatics **https://geissele.com**

Huber Concepts **www.huberconcepts.com**

Jard, Inc. **www.jardinc.com**

Kidd Triggers **www.coolguyguns.com**

Shilen **www.shilen.com**

Spec-Tech Industries, Inc. **www.spec-tech-industries.com**

Timney Triggers **www.timneytriggers.com**

Williams Trigger Specialties **www.williamstriggers.com**

MAJOR SHOOTING WEBSITES AND LINKS

24 Hour Campfire **www.24hourcampfire.com**

Accurate Shooter **www.6mmbr.com**

Alphabetic Index of Links **www.gunsgunsguns.com**

Ammo Guide **www.ammoguide.com**

Auction Arms **www.auctionarms.com**

Benchrest Central **www.benchrest.com**

Big Game Hunt **www.biggamehunt.net**

Bullseye Pistol **www.bullseyepistol.com**

Firearms History **www.researchpress.co.uk**

Glock Talk **www.glocktalk.com**

Gun Broker Auctions **www.gunbroker.com**

Gun Blast **www.gunblast.com**

Gun Boards **www.gunboards.com**

Gun Digest **www. gundigest.com**

Gun Digest Gun Values **https://gunvalues.gundigest.com**

Guns & Ammo Forum **www.gunsandammo.com**

GunsAmerica **www.gunsamerica.com**

Gun Shop Finder **www.gunshopfinder.com**

Guns and Hunting **www.gunsandhunting.com**

Hunt and Shoot (NSSF) **www.huntandshoot.org**

Keep and Bear Arms **www.keepandbeararms.com**

Leverguns **www.leverguns.com**

Load Swap **www.loadswap.com**

Long Range Hunting **www.longrangehunting.com**

Real Guns **www.realguns.com**

Ruger Forum **www.rugerforum.com**

Savage Shooters **www.savageshooters.com**

Shooters Forum **www.shootersforum.com**

Shotgun Sports Resource Guide **www.shotgunsports.com**

Shotgun World **www.shotgunworld.com**

Sniper's Hide **www.snipershide.com**

Sportsman's Web **www.sportsmansweb.com**

Tactical-Life **www.tactical-life.com**

The Gun Room **www.doublegun.com**

Wing Shooting USA **www.wingshootingusa.org**